War, Genocide and Cultural Memory

War, Genocide and Cultural Memory

The Waffen-SS, 1933 to Today

Claus Bundgård Christensen,
Niels Bo Poulsen and Peter Scharff Smith

ANTHEM PRESS

Anthem Press
An imprint of Wimbledon Publishing Company
www.anthempress.com

This edition first published in UK and USA 2023
by ANTHEM PRESS
75–76 Blackfriars Road, London SE1 8HA, UK
or PO Box 9779, London SW19 7ZG, UK
and
244 Madison Ave #116, New York, NY 10016, USA

First published in the UK and USA by Anthem Press in 2023

British Library Cataloguing-in-Publication Data
A catalogue record for this book is available from the British Library.

Library of Congress Cataloging-in-Publication Data
A catalog record for this book has been requested.

ISBN-13: 978-1-83999-002-1 (Pbk)
ISBN-10: 183-9-99002-3 (Pbk)

Cover credit: Image of Waffen-SS soldiers from the Danish National Museum.

This title is also available as an e-book.

CONTENTS

ABOUT THE AUTHORS

Claus Bundgård Christensen is Associate Professor of History at Roskilde University, Denmark. He has written extensively about the Waffen-SS, WWII, First World War, Black Market 1939–1950, Danish Fascism, Transnational Dimensions of Nordic Right-Wing Extremism and The Holocaust. He is the author and co-author of several praised books. For *Danskere på vestfronten 1914–1918* he received the Danish Award History Book of the Year 2009 and The Svend Henningsen Award 2009. Claus has published in English, French, Danish, Norwegian, Dutch and German on, for example, veteran culture and the First World War, crime in wartime, as well as on the Nazi war of extermination. He is the editor and co-editor of several publications. In 2018, he received a grant from The Augustinus Foundation to the project *Wilfred and his Danish Boys 1932–1947*. This project is at study of Wilfred Petersen and his organization who invented a Nordic form of Nazism in the interwar period. His latest book is *Følg Wilfred! Radikalisering, revolution og nazistisk subkultur (Follow Wilfred! Radicalization, revolution and Nazi subculture)*, Gyldendal 2022.

Niels Bo Poulsen is Director of the Institute for Strategy and War Studies at the Royal Danish Defence College, Copenhagen (since 2008). Prior to that he worked for 10 years in the Danish Ministry of Foreign Affairs. Niels Bo Poulsen is MA in History and East European Studies from Roskilde and Copenhagen Universities (1996) and holds a PhD from Copenhagen University (2005). The topic of his dissertation was the Soviet Investigation of Nazi War Crimes during and after the Second World War. Niels Bo Poulsen is author of a substantial number of books and articles on the two world wars, contemporary Russian military affairs, and war veterans. His works have been published in Danish, Dutch, English, German, Norwegian, Russian, Swedish and Ukrainian. Currently Niels Bo Poulsen is heading a project on the Danish armed forces' international missions since 1990. He is also editor of the section on military history of the *Springer Handbook of Military Sciences* and editor-in-chief of the peer reviewed journal *Fra krig og fred* (From war and peace) published by the Danish branch of the International Commission of Military History.

Peter Scharff Smith is Professor in the Sociology of Law at the University in Oslo, Norway. He has studied history and social science, holds a PhD from the University of Copenhagen and has also done research at the University of Cambridge and at the Danish Institute for Human Rights. Peter has written extensively about the Waffen-SS and the war of extermination at the Eastern front, and has also conducted numerous large-scale studies on prisons, punishment, and human rights internationally and in the Nordic countries. He has furthermore worked with practical prison and human rights reform projects together with NGO's and criminal justice agencies in different European countries. Peter has published books and articles in English, Danish, Norwegian, Dutch, and German on, for example, prison history, the children of prisoners, solitary confinement in prisons, as well as on the history of the Waffen-SS and the Nazi war of extermination at the Eastern Front. He is the author or co-author of nine monographs and co-editor of several edited collections. His latest books in English are Jules Lobel and Peter Scharff Smith (eds.): Solitary Confinement: Effects, Practices, and Pathways towards Reform Oxford University Press 2020, and Rachel Condry and Peter Scharff Smith (eds.): Prisons, Punishment, and the Family: Towards a New Sociology of Punishment? Oxford University Press 2018.

FOREWORD

The work behind this book began more than 25 years ago when we, the authors, were young history students at Roskilde University in Denmark. During our studies we came across the fact that thousands of Danes (how many was unknown at the time) had joined the Waffen-SS and chosen to fight for Hitler during the second world war. Yet no one had examined the history of these men whose actions so obviously ran counter to the many stories of resistance fighters and the rescue of the Danish Jews that we had been brought up with. In contrast, the academic, and indeed the national, interest in those who had chosen the wrong side was almost non-existing. This caught our common interest to a great degree and we chose to study this phenomenon.

Starting out as students we spend four very exiting years interviewing former SS-soldiers, and digging through archives in Germany, the Czech Republic, Russia, Sweden and Denmark in an attempt to locate the Danish volunteers in the vast machinery of the Third Reich. It was sometimes like looking for a needle in a haystack and with little money in our student pockets we spend many nights at youth hostels around Europe while researching huge amounts of Nazi records in different archives during the day. Remembering those days together now, when finishing this book, makes us smile as we think back on the immense amounts of time and energy that we were able to dedicate to our academic endeavours in that early phase of our lives. In 1998, we published a book on the Danish volunteers in the Waffen-SS for the first time documenting, among other things, how these Danes had committed war crimes and in various ways contributed to the Nazi war of extermination.

We also realised from the start that the Waffen-SS was an organization that could tell us something unique about human behaviour and the power of ideology and hence we continued our research. We kept finding new material about the SS-men from a wide range of sources including not only official archives but also private collectors who, for example, had diaries and letters written by soldiers at the front. In 2008, we decided that the time had come to apply for funding for a full-scale study of the entire Waffen-SS. We obtained a generous grant from the Danish Research Council and thanks to this we could now expand our ambitions. The following five years we visited archives in numerous countries on three different continents and located and studied hundreds of thousands of SS- and Nazi documents that had survived the war. In 2015, we published a book in Danish on the history of the Waffen-SS, which later came out also in Dutch and Norwegian. In 2019, we decided to write up a new and updated history of the Waffen-SS – the book you are now reading. It draws on all our previous research and especially our book manuscript from 2015, which has been restructured and to a significant extent re-written, and further benefitted from the incorporation of new literature and new sources.

It is completely impossible to thank all the people and organizations who have helped us throughout all our years doing this research. There are simply too many to name. This includes, for example, all the helpful staff in the countless archives we have visited and it includes the many colleagues, in the Nordic countries as well as internationally, who we have had the great pleasure to discuss the subject with. Also, many thanks to the private collectors who have supplied us with useful material, and the institutions which have housed us during different parts of our research careers. The latter includes The Royal Danish Defense College, Roskilde University, The Danish Institute for Human Rights, and The University in Oslo. We would also very much like to thank Dr Kjeld Galster for translating our 2015 book manuscript into English. Furthermore, a big thanks to the team at Anthem press which has helped us out with this book. Finally, the biggest thanks of all goes to our families for their continued support and especially for being their wonderful selves!

Chapter One

INTRODUCTION

One of the most astonishing paradoxes in modern military history is the fact that, during the Second World War, the extreme racist SS organisation engendered an army, which was possibly the most multi-ethnic and transnational army that the twentieth century ever witnessed. This was brought about by the establishment of a military branch of the SS, the Waffen-SS. During its existence, it expanded from a modest bodyguard at Hitler's disposal to a mass army through whose ranks passed more than a million men. Until the outbreak of war, the SS maintained high standards as to personnel, who were all volunteers. Not only did they have to meet tough physical and racial demands; by joining, they also entered a Nazi order of warriors demanding absolute faith in Hitler, unconditional subordination and profound ideological dedication as the pillars of their martial calling.

The head of the SS, the *Reichsführer-SS* Heinrich Himmler, envisaged an élite force of devoted Nazis, who would alternate between active duty in the field and other kinds of SS activities. They were not only to be soldiers but also role models leading a life as wholly dedicated SS men. They were to let their identity as members of the 'order' permeate all their doings including choice of spouse, reproduction, interior decoration of their homes, and celebration of red-letter days. Himmler hoped to create an elite of committed Nazis, welded together in a loyal brotherhood and hardened through war into merciless individuals, who would pitilessly annihilate the Third Reich's real and alleged enemies; be they hostile troops, Jews, mentally ill or any other so-called sub-humans.

While, until the outbreak of war, this order remained relatively homogeneous, the situation changed markedly during the war. Now, the SS began to moderate the demands on race and physical capability, introduced conscription and started to recruit from all over Europe. With these changes, the SS got new recruits, for example, from Norway, who were often as ideologically zealous as were the original German members. However, men who merely wished to avoid forced labour or were pressured into signing up also joined the ranks – individuals, who might not have heard of the SS before, now saw themselves in the uniform of this organisation. Additionally, there were hundreds of thousands of recruits from ethnic groups, whom the SS would never have admitted before the war.

This diverse crowd of soldiers was employed on almost all European fronts in all kinds of warfare and atrocities. The soldiers were extensively engaged in the Holocaust and brutal counter-insurgency operations against civilians. They served in the Balkans, they fought against the Allied armies in Italy, they struggled on the western front in 1940 as well as after D-day and they confronted the Red Army in the east. They alternated between combat tasks, guarding concentration camps and murdering innocent civilians. The Waffen-SS soldiers gained a reputation for being elite, but in reality, this was far from always the case. A number of SS units became very powerful formations during certain periods of the war, but often the military performance of the Waffen-SS was mediocre and sometimes even lousy.

Regardless of how the individual soldier or his unit performed, there was no doubt about the organisation's leadership or the Waffen-SS' *raison d'être* on the battlefield. The soldiers of the Waffen-SS embodied Himmler's attempt to create a Nazi order of warriors. They were the Nazis' European soldiers fighting for the Third Reich's dominance of the remainder of Europe, and this included genocide of immense proportions.

This book will study the Waffen-SS from four different perspectives: First, the Waffen-SS will be described from the perspective of the SS leadership and with the point of departure in the organisation's long-term planning and policies. However, if we want to thoroughly understand the history of the Waffen-SS, we must look beyond Himmler's and the SS leadership's endeavours to implement their ideals.

Therefore, the top-down perspective will be complemented by the experience of individual soldiers. Using, for example, letters, diaries, SS court cases and original reports from the frontline, we will look at the extent to which the leadership's plans were actually implemented and how the personnel understood their role and experienced life in the uniform. It is particularly interesting to follow the attempt to create, within the Waffen-SS, a culture thoroughly permeated by ideology. Did the soldiers become fanatical Nazis, who unconditionally adopted the SS' *Weltanschauung*, and, if not, what sort of conflict arose between ideology, external stimuli (such as the reality of life at the front and in the occupied territories) and the outlook of the individual soldiers? Not ending the book with the Nazi defeat in 1945, but including the post-war history of the Waffen-SS veterans, helps us understand the reach and long-term impact of Nazi ideology.

The book's third track deals with the interaction between, on the one hand, the more than 30 ethnic and religious groups serving with the Waffen-SS and, on the other, the SS organisation's leadership, aim and values. Therefore, the means utilised by the SS to embrace the diversity and to solve problems thus arising will be scrutinised and analysed.

Finally, the book's fourth track will delve into the proportions and character of the crimes committed by the Waffen-SS. These will be studied in the context of the military use of the Waffen-SS and the ongoing massive ideological conditioning of the soldiers. In the SS' mental universe, killing women and children in cold blood was as self-evident a part of the trade as was combating regular enemy formations with tactical skill.

It has been our ambition with this book to write a new, comprehensive history of the military branch of the SS. We have attempted to do this by exploiting all the existing literature on the matter and utilising significant amounts of new source material which has enabled us to shed light on a wide range of Waffen-SS' activities previously neglected. The lacuna in existing research, which this work will venture to cover, comprises, for example, the use of the SS' internal judiciary as a means of ideological control, the collaboration between the many non-German nationalities within the Waffen-SS, the countless crimes committed by Waffen-SS soldiers and the veterans' fate after the war.

Literature and sources: from fascination and apology to scholarly exploration

Browsing a large international bookshop or surfing the internet, one soon becomes aware of an extensive list of publications on the Waffen-SS. However, the vast majority of such works is about uniforms and equipment, epic land battles or the experiences of individual soldiers. In other words, they are mostly concerned with military technology or specific accounts of military history. Moreover, a vast portion of this literature is tainted by the authors' fascination of the Waffen-SS, and much of it has been written by old veterans or others sympathetic to their cause. In such works, the Waffen-SS is dealt with as a purely military phenomenon detached from Nazism, Holocaust and the SS per se. Such an apologetic approach, however, does not mirror reality. The Waffen-SS was, throughout its existence, a part of the general SS, many of its soldiers remained convinced Nazis to the end, and the officers and non-commissioned officers (NCOs), who controlled the men and directed their actions and behaviour, were selected on the basis of their ideological disposition. Moreover, almost all Waffen-SS formations were involved in Nazi crimes, which is largely ignored or merely superficially dealt with by the apologetic literature.

Scholarly literature – based on comprehensive archival studies – on the Waffen-SS is still relatively scant, albeit that, over recent years, a considerable development has taken place. While this has brought about a number of specialised volumes, works aiming at large-scale synthesis have been few and far between. Over the last 50 years, only four such works have appeared and they are very diverse. In 1966, the American historian George Stein published what has now become a reference work on the topic. In this, he placed particular emphasis on creating a general overview of what the Waffen-SS actually was as well as on refuting the SS veterans' attempts at disconnecting the Waffen-SS from Nazism and the crimes of the Third Reich. In 1982, the German historian Bernd Wegener published his doctoral dissertation in which he scrutinised primarily the training, structure and ideology of the Waffen-SS, and in particular studied the officer corps' background and sociopolitical characteristics. The military perspective and the organisation's transnational character, however, did not receive similar attention. In 2007, the French historian Jean Luc Leleu published a far-reaching study on the Waffen-SS as a military phenomenon. His analysis especially brings new insight into the military aspects of Waffen-SS and its deployment on the western front in 1940 and 1944–45. The most recent attemt at synthesising the history of the Waffen-SS is offered by Klaus-Jürgen Bremm who argues that the Waffen-SS had very limited fighting qualities.

Recent decades have furthermore seen the publication of literature characterised by giving attention to individual Waffen-SS formations and specific aspects of the history of the organisation as a whole. Moreover, there has been a considerable growth in the number of works dealing with other branches of the SS, thus throwing light on the interaction among its various institutions and elements. Therefore, today's Waffen-SS researchers have at their disposal, for example, a wide range of biographical material on key personalities. Also, the ideology of the SS has undergone serious examination. Additionally, several anthologies and monographs provide an insight into the history and the crimes of individual divisions and other units, and a number of non-German nationalities' service with the Waffen-SS has been studied. Equally importantly, apart from works concerning the examination of the SS and its crimes, an extensive literature has sprung up focusing on the Third Reich's regular armed forces – especially the army – and their part in the Nazi war of extermination on the eastern front, thereby allowing comparison between the practices of the Waffen-SS and the army.

Importantly, this book has benefitted from the existence of a large body of archival material, much of which has been only modestly examined earlier, or not at all. The present study describes the Waffen-SS on the basis of material found in more than 20 archives in 16 different countries, namely Austria, the Czech Republic, Denmark, France, Germany, Israel, the Netherlands, Norway, the Russian Federation, Switzerland, Serbia, Slovenia, South Africa, Sweden, the United Kingdom and the United States. This comprises a wide-ranging selection of material such as records from the SS, contemporary Allied documents, letters from soldiers, diaries and memoirs. Other major groups of material are derived from the investigations into war crimes, from intelligence services and other organisations with a vested interest in the SS soldiers' post-war networks and veteran societies. Such material makes it possible to study the Waffen-SS not merely as a hierarchical organisation but as a living organisation made up of human beings. Thanks to all the new archival material, we can expand our study beyond the view from Berlin and the archives of the central SS administration, and now also focus on the lower echelons of the Waffen-SS, life at the front, training of personnel, corporate culture and the mentality within the units, as well as activities among the veterans after the war.

The history of the Waffen-SS: before, during and after the war

This book comprises five parts. The first part deals with the organisational and military history of the Waffen-SS from 1920 to 1945. It initially covers the organisation's development up to and including the first war years of 1939 and 1940, when Waffen-SS formations – still relatively few in numbers – were first employed in battle. During these years, the foundations were laid for the military branch of the SS, and so was the political and judicial footing of the SS organisation. Thus, this period in the history of the Waffen-SS is delineated by, on the one hand, the organisational and ideological establishment of Nazism and the SS, and, on the other, two limited employments on active service of the newly established, armed SS formations. By 1940, a small number of divisions had been raised taking part in the German campaign in the west. However, the military prowess left much to be desired, particularly in Poland, but in western Europe in 1940, too. But the SS soldiers seemed to prove reliable and efficient in another area. In the 1930s, not least during the campaign in Poland, SS troops showed remarkable willingness to act with brutality against their own as well as against the enemies of Nazism. Nonetheless, these atrocities were modest compared with those to come. Following that, another phase of the Waffen-SS took place during the years 1941–43. After the German onslaught against the Soviet Union in the summer of 1941, the Waffen-SS was employed in severe combat on the eastern front. Dying willingly for Nazism, the formations fighting there during these years were, to a large extent, living up to Himmler's ideals of political soldiers. The SS soldiers thus engaged became an important component in the Third Reich's plans for extermination and forced relocation of millions of civilians, and the soldiers were instrumental in the Holocaust and the Nazis'monstrous crimes in general. At the same time, the Waffen-SS developed from being merely a handful of formations to an army with army corps and a two-digit number of divisions, some of which were among the best-equipped and hard-fighting German formations. However, the losses were enormous and defeats increased in numbers. During the last two war years, 1943–45, the Waffen-SS developed into a mass army as the SS under Himmler became the most powerful organisation in the Third Reich. This was a period characterised by the huge clashes on the eastern front as well as the western Allies' opening of the second front in the west. Moreover, Hitler launched his last big offensives in the Ardennes and in Hungary both of which saw the Waffen-SS in a key role though unable to turn the fortune of war in Germany's favour. The rather strong formations still remaining, which were employed in these operations, as well as a number of somewhat weaker SS divisions had one thing in common, the atrocities against prisoners-of-war and civilians continued, but now, as war weariness had set in, the terror was increasingly directed also against German civilians and fellow soldiers.

In order to understand how all this happened, and not least how and why the SS soldiers took a very active part in the extreme violence unleashed by the regime, we need to focus on the role of Nazism within the Waffen-SS. Thus, the second part of the book focuses on two interconnected issues: the ideological conditioning of the Waffen-SS and the internal judicial and penal system developed by the organisation. The political soldier was moulded through systematical indoctrination. The aim was, on the one hand, to leave the soldiers with a positive vision of a Nazi future, and, on the other, to produce a well-defined image of the enemy and a reason for his annihilation. This part will also gauge the reception of the propaganda by the Waffen-SS personnel. As not everyone could, or wished to, live up to the Nazi *Weltanschauung*, the SS used punishment as yet another means of persuasion. The SS had its own judiciary and produced an extraordinary ideological legal culture. Consequently, those who challenged the ideological vision might be in for extraordinarily severe sanctions. This system, too, will be dealt with in this part of the book.

The huge expansion of the Waffen-SS, which began in earnest in 1941 and gathered momentum in the following years, brought thousands of Europeans from north, south, east and west into the organisation. These men represented a variety of nations and religions, and their presence was a challenge to the foundation of the Waffen-SS. The third part of the book focuses on this theme: the development of the Waffen-SS from a German army to a transnational and multi-ethnic one. In the beginning, the new recruits were partly ethnic Germans from beyond the German borders – so-called *Volksdeutsche* – and partly Germanic volunteers from 'racially kindred' countries in the north and west. But from 1943 onwards, large groups of foreign nations – so-called *Fremdvölker* – men who, from the Nazi point of view, were not of Nordic-Germanic ethnicity, entered into the ranks of the Waffen-SS.[1] At the same time, a number of men were conscripted against their will. Thus, the enormous increase in personnel strength, which the Waffen-SS experienced during the war, was to a large extent brought about through enlistment of soldiers, who did not live up to the original notion that the SS should be a racial brotherhood of volunteers.

From the beginning to the end, the Waffen-SS took part in the regime's countless atrocities in and outside Germany, and in the fourth part of the book, we address this dimension of the organisation thoroughly. We describe the many ways in which the Waffen-SS participated in the war of extermination and the Holocaust and we seek to understand how this came about. The war crimes committed by the soldiers indicate the role that ideology played among the soldiers but may also be seen as one of more mechanisms, which contributed to integrating the men into the SS by strengthening solidarity and the will to fight to the last man.

Following the defeat in 1945, a new era of the Waffen-SS' history commences, which is the subject of this book's fifth and last part. Upon the deaths of Hitler and Himmler, the Waffen-SS ceased to exist, but thousands of its members survived and their fate will be investigated. We shall look into their prisoner-of-war time, their prosecution and their flight or re-integration in their native countries. The SS veterans' post-war lives can shed some light on the degree to which the SS still had a mental hold on its former employees. Moreover, we shall investigate the reasons why and how the Waffen-SS still fascinates the public to such a remarkable degree as is obviously the case today.

---

1. The notion *Fremdvölker* is markedly racist and was employed by the Germans to describe a range of ethnic groups from southern and eastern Europe, whom the Nazis recruited for the Waffen-SS without recognising them as racially equal with the Germans and other Germanic peoples. As will be set out later in this book, the Germans used to designate as 'Germanic' those being closest related to the Germans and of the purest racial stock in Nazi terms. Throughout the book, these notions will be used in italics without quotation marks.

Part I

THE ORGANISATIONAL AND MILITARY HISTORY OF THE WAFFEN-SS

Three Phases in the History of the Waffen-SS

The organisational and military history of the Waffen-SS is short, frantic and violent beyond comprehension. It began in the early 1920s and ended abruptly in 1945 with the fall of the Third Reich. Despite its brevity in time, the development of the Waffen-SS was also characterised by a mixture of organic development and considerable fragmentation caused by events and ad hoc decisions. This history can nevertheless be viewed as a number of phases which will each be treated separately in the three following chapters. The first of these, Chapter 2, covers the period beginning with the foundational pre-war development of the SS and the first war-years in 1939 and 1940, where the Waffen-SS formations were still relatively insignificant and few in numbers. During these years, the foundations were laid for the military branch of the SS, and the political and judicial footing of the SS organisation was established. This period in the history of the Waffen-SS is delineated by, on the one hand, the organisational and ideological establishment of Nazism and the SS, and, on the other, two limited employments of active service for the newly established, armed SS formations.

Chapter 3 will treat the second phase in the organisational and military history of the Waffen-SS which stretches from 1941 to 1943 and begins in earnest with the German onslaught against the Soviet Union in the summer of 1941. The campaign in the east had the short-term consequence that Himmler's sphere of authority increased considerably, and the power, influence and size of the SS and Waffen-SS grew in tandem. The prolonged war against the Soviet Union eroded Hitler's faith in the steadfastness of his army commanders and conversely made the Waffen-SS look like the model Nazi soldiers of the future. However, it was also during the war against the Soviet Union that the military SS drastically changed its ethnic composition and began to field more, and more insufficiently trained, officers and men. Finally, the invasion marked a new nadir of German behaviour in the occupied territories and it contributed to radicalising Nazi treatment of prisoners-of-war and civilians even further. Now, the war of extermination entered its decisive phase moving quickly towards the Nazis' attempt at total physical annihilation of Europe's Jews. Although the war dragged on, it did not necessarily appear lost. Therefore, the SS leadership acted, in particular in 1941–1942, as if the war would eventually bring victory and huge gains of territory eastwards. Thus, during this period, the dynamics inside the SS were not only about mobilising personnel and resources for the fight against Germany's increasingly powerful opponents. It was just as much about planning the future Greater German Empire.

In many ways, the Allied invasion in June 1944 and the attempted assassination of Hitler in July the same year can be seen as the beginning of the last chapter of the Waffen-SS' war history – Chapter 4 in this book. By 1944, Waffen-SS could field more than 500,000 men and, even in the last year of the war, some of its divisions were very powerful formations. With seven armoured divisions, a number of corps commands and, finally, armies, Waffen-SS had become a regular army of great importance in a number of the hot spots of the war. In the wake of the failed attempt on Hitler's life, the SS increased its influence in the Third Reich and, as Himmler assumed command of the reserve army, the internal balance of power had undeniably swung from the *Wehrmacht* to the SS.

Between December 1944 and March 1945, Hitler launched his last big offensives in the Ardennes and in Hungary both of which saw the Waffen-SS in a key role, though unable to turn the fortune of war in Germany's favour. In the process, the SS demonstrated its inability to create a war-winning military force out of its supplies of man power and arms.

Over the last war year, Waffen-SS' record of atrocities continued to expand. This happened at all fronts, though to varying extent from bloody suppression of uprisings in Warsaw and Slovakia, through massacres on civilians in France and Italy, to killings of prisoners-of-war and murders during the 'death marches' of the end phase of Holocaust. In the very last months of the war, Waffen-SS units also used terror against German civilians to prevent defeatism and surrender.

Although, in 1945, the SS and the Waffen-SS was dissolved by the allies, Waffen-SS survivors carried their experiences with them into captivity and into their subsequent lives. Thus, at the end of the war, the last word on the Waffen-SS had been neither spoken nor written. When, on 1–2 May, the last shot rang out in streets of Berlin, another war – the battle for the history of the Waffen-SS – commenced. But before we get that far we will have to go back to the early 1920s – to a Germany haunted by the loss of the Great War and to a cultural and economic landscape that proved fertile ground for Nazism and an emerging SS organisation.

Chapter Two

FROM HITLER'S BODYGUARD
TO THE WAFFEN-SS

After the defeat in the First World War, Germany was marred by considerable polarisation and by the presence and activities of para-military organisations. Economic chaos and extensive poverty together with street fights, political assassinations and coup-d'état attempts characterised life in the Weimar Republic of 1918. Shortly after the foundation in 1920 of the *Nationalsozialistische Deutsche Arbeiterpartei* (NSDAP) Hitler became leader. It was one of the political parties, which employed violence in its political struggle most determinedly. In the beginning, the NSDAP engaged various para-military organisations to protect their own meetings and harass those of other parties. However, gradually the party developed its own body of Nazi street bullies, the SA. Perhaps the most important sub-division of this organisation was the *Stoßtrupp Adolf Hitler*. At the same time, Hitler had a small number of men for his personal protection – the *Stabswache* (staff close protection team).[1] The *Stoßtrupp* and the *Stabswache* would guard the party meetings and bully gate crashers, and the roots of the *Schutzstaffel* can be traced back to these units. Like the general SA and other Nazi organisations, these entities were dissolved in the wake of the Beer Hall Putsch in November 1923.

After Hitler's release from prison in the spring of 1925, his bodyguard was re-formed under Julius Schreck. This Munich-based team of merely eight men was soon to be re-designated the *Schutzstaffel*, and Schreck would become the first in a succession of SS leaders. Although, generally, the Nazis were very inspired by the inter-war para-military organisations, using the word *Staffel* was original. The word originated with the German army which used it to designate minor mounted, motorised or flying detachments. In September 1925, Hitler ordered Schreck to raise, and assume command of, a network of similar detachments all over Germany. Each *Staffel* should consist of ten men selected among the most trustworthy local party members. These were raised in a number of German cities, and in 1926 there were 26 such SS units in Germany.[2]

Schreck was a devoted Nazi, but his organisational and political skills were mediocre and the newly formed SS units were weak. Thus, as early as 1926, Hitler dismissed him from his post. The new boss was the founder of *Stoßtrupp Adolf Hitler*, Joseph Berchtold, who soon replaced his title as *Oberleiter* (senior leader) *der SS* by *Reichsführer-SS*. Berchtold

---

1. Robert Lewis Koehl, *The Black Corps: The Structure and Power Struggles of the Nazi SS* (University of Wisconsin Press, 1983), pp 11–15.
2. Ibid., pp 21ff. Bastian Hein, *Elite für Volk und Führer?: die Allgemeine SS und ihre Mitglieder 1925–1945* (2012, Oldenburg Verlag) pp 40ff.

was considerably more activist than Schreck. During the year of 1926, he managed to expand the organisation to about 1,000 men in 75 local detachments and he raised considerable funds from supporting members. As a recognition he was given custody of the so-called *Blutfahne* (blood colour), the Nazi prime vestige of the 1923 coup-d'état attempt.[3] After the 1926 re-subordination under the SA, Berchtold relinquished command to Erhard Heiden. However, as Heiden's laissez-faire leadership resulted in a dramatic loss of members, there were voices within the party suggesting to disband the SS. In 1929, Heiden retired from the leadership, and left the post to his second-in-command.

This, the 28-year-old agricultural graduate Heinrich Himmler, came from a substantial, Bavarian Bourgeois family, and he was ambitious, clever and hard-working.[4] Himmler initiated a process extricating the SS from the constraints of the SA, and under his leadership the SS started to expand.[5] The *Schutzstaffel* was no longer a mere protection unit, it also ran an expanding intelligence service.[6] Moreover, the SS started to detach itself from the shadows of the SA.[7] While in the late summer of 1930, the SA in Berlin rebelled against the local NSDAP leadership under Joseph Goebbels, the Berlin SS sided with Goebbels – and thus with Hitler.[8] The SS maintained this role as a kind of party police the following years partly because too much street violence could lead to the party being banned, thus forfeiting its chances to win elections. One of the means employed to protect the party's legality was body searching SA members for weapons prior to larger gatherings. A practice which did not produce cordial feelings between the two organisations.[9]

However, the SS mentality did not differ too much from the street brawl culture of the SA.[10] On the contrary, in a political climate of increasing brutalisation, which – from late 1929 onwards – went hand in hand with economic crisis, mass unemployment and social gloom, the SS appeared even more activist and violent than the SA.[11] Young Dieter may serve as an example of SS' street viciousness.[12] Born into a craftsman's family in Greifswald on the Baltic, as a 15-year-old in 1927 he joined the SA and the NSDAP. In 1931, this physically fit young man – he was a keen boxer – transferred

3. Hans Buchheim, Martin Broszat, Hans Adolf Jacobsen and Helmut Krausnick, *Anatomie des SS-Staates*, 6. Aufl. (DTV Deutscher Taschenbuch, 1994), p 31.
4. Hein (2012), p 40, note 10.
5. Concerning Himmler's personality and actions as head of the SS, see Peter Longerich, *Heinrich Himmler* (Siedler, 2008). See also Hein (2012), p 47.
6. Robert Gerwarth, *Hitler's Hangman: The Life of Heydrich* (Yale University Press, 2011), p 111.
7. Koehl (1983), p 34.
8. Peter Longerich, *Geschichte der SA* (Verlag C.H. Beck, 2003), pp 103ff.
9. Koehl (1983), p 47.
10. Hein (2012), p 54 and p 56ff. See also Koehl (1983), p 48, note 37 for a somewhat different view.
11. Concerning the Nazis' way to power see, inter alia, Martin Broszat, *Die Machtergreifung: Der Aufstieg der NSDAP u. d. Zerstörung d. Weimarer Republik* (Dt. Taschenbuch-Verl), 1984, and Richard Evans, *The Coming of the Third Reich* (Penguin Press, 2004).
12. Dieter is a pseudonym. Due to the rules and regulations in particular archives and in connection with particular archival groups, pseudonyms will be used on occasion throughout the book.

from the SA to SS. Before as well as after the transfer he was a dedicated participant in the struggle against those who the Nazis perceived as their enemies, and – according to his own testimony – before 1933 he had already joined more than 40 clashes. Dieter was known for his ruthless behaviour during these brawls, which earned him the *nom-de-guerre* of Putsch Dieter (coup-d'état Dieter), and, in 1931, in a clash with communists he suffered a broken skull, which left him unconscious for several days. Later, together with fellow Nazis he beat up five communists as revenge. This assault was so violent that he was subsequently sentenced to three months' imprisonment. In the summer of 1932, having participated in an *SS-Rollkommando* – a motorised patrol – hunting communists in Greifswald and surroundings he had to go underground. After the Nazi *Machtergreifung* in early 1933, like many other SA and SS men Dieter was enlisted as an auxiliary policeman. However, on 2 July, after an extended birthday celebration, he assaulted a communist fishing from a river bank. Having been severely beaten up, the communist was hauled into the river where he drowned. Dieter had to go underground once more and remain so until the case was hushed up. Later, he got involved in even more violence and was temporarily degraded from *Sturmführer* (lieutenant) to *Sturmmann* (private).[13] Moreover, after the so-called Röhm coup he experienced a brief stint as a concentration camp detainee, and in 1936 he was sentenced to 12 months' imprisonment for a brawl with an SA *Standartenführer* (colonel).[14] Nonetheless, Dieter remained with the SS becoming, in 1942, a soldier of the Waffen-SS. In this capacity – and as a war criminal in the final phase of the war – we shall re-join him later in this book.

In October 1929, the Wall Street Crash put an end to a number of comparatively peaceful years. To the Weimar Republic the subsequent mixture of economic plight, street violence and frustrations turned out to be a toxic cocktail. On 30 January, President Hindenburg appointed Hitler *Reichskanzler*. Four weeks later, the *Reichstag* (parliament) burned down, which the Nazi construed as a prelude to a communist coup-d'état. However, already before this incident huge numbers of SA and SS men had been employed as auxiliary policemen. Prior to the general elections on 5 March, the Nazis assaulted the communists and, similarly, they employed violence, press censorship and prohibition of speech to intimidate various other political groups.[15] After the elections, the Nazis tightened their grip on power in spite of having won only a modest majority of the seats. This was facilitated primarily through taking control over the security police in the various provinces. In March 1933, Himmler was appointed *Polizeipräsident* (police commissioner) in Munich and, in April, chief of the Bavarian political police. Little more than a year hence, he controlled the political police in most parts of Germany.[16]

---

13. For a German-English translation of the SS rank system, see appendix p. XXX -.
14 Sentence No 428 in H.I. Sagel-Grande, H.H. Fuchs, C.F. Rüter and Fritz Bauer, *Justiz und NS-Verbrechen: Sammlung deutscher Strafurteile wegen nationalsozialistischer Tötungsverbrechen, 1945–1966*, vol. XIII (University Press Amsterdam, 1975), pp 584–614.
15. Koehl (1983), pp 65ff.
16. Buchheim, Hans, et al., *Anatomie des SS Staates* (Fischer Taschenbuch Verlag, 1994), pp 35ff.; George H. Stein, *The Waffen SS: Hitler's Elite Guard at War, 1939–1945* (Cornell University Press, 1984), p 2.

Hitler's ascent to power helped create a sense of elite status among the SS men and during fall 1933, the SS headquarters noted that lately, there had been an increasing number of cases where SS members, due to their membership in the SS, came into conflict with the authorities by insisting on rights they were not entitled to or by 'behaving in a manner likely to damage the reputation of the SS'.[17] Just one among several indicators that the SS increasingly developed a corporate spirit, where members saw themselves as being part of a separate and elevated Nazi caste.

This was also the case in neighbouring Austria, whereto the SA and the SS had expanded in the previous years (the SA since 1929 and the SS since 1930). Here a significant SA and SS infrastructure was established prior to the failed Nazi coup in summer 1934. Especially the 89. SS-Standarte in Vienna, consisting mainly of police men and former soldiers, was a highly militarized entity, and during the badly organized coup, this unit acted as a military spearhead. Several hundred men from its ranks were issued weapons and were assigned with seizing important buildings, such as the prime minister's office, the post office, etc. After the failed putsch, thousands of SA and SS men fled to Germany.[18] Some of these Austrian Nazi refuges became concentration camp guards, while others were given additional military training by the SS, which by then had operated military units for more than a year.

In spring 1933, a novel branch of the SS, later to become the biggest, appeared on the horizon. This was the armed branch – subsequently to become known as the Waffen-SS. A possible date on its birth certificate might be 17 March 1933 because, on this day, Hitler ordered the revitalisation of the *Stabswache*.[19] Josef (Sepp) Dietrich, a Nazi veteran, was tasked with raising a 20-man bodyguard, whose primary duty would be the protection of the *Führerhauptquartier* (Hitler's headquarters) as well as Hitler's life. Although Hitler was *Reichskanzler*, the Nazis, so far, wielded only superficial control of society and feared plots.[20] Thus, Hitler wished his life guards to be commanded by one of his old cronies right back from the early days of forming the NSDAP.

In 1892, Dietrich was born into a poor Bavarian farmhand family and after school he got work in the hotel line of business. Throughout the Great War, he served in the Bavarian army as a gunner and with a tank unit. In the early inter-war years, Dietrich was active in the Bavarian Freikorps Oberland, which played a key role

---

17. BAB, NS 7/2, *SS Hauptamt, Gruppenbefehl Nr. 4*, 6 October 1933.
18. Christiane Rothländer, *Die Anfänge der Wiener SS* (Böhlau Verlag, 2012), especially pp 26f, 405ff, 444ff, 577ff. Rothländer (2012), pp 516ff., and Valdis O. Lumans, 'Recruiting Volksdeutsche for the Waffen-SS: From Skimming the Cream to Scraping the Dregs' in Sanders Marble (ed), *Scraping the Barrel: The Military Use of Substandard Manpower, 1860–1960* (Fordham University Press, 2012), p 203.
19. James J. Weingartner, 'Sepp Dietrich, Heinrich Himmler, and the Leibstandarte SS Adolf Hitler, 1933–1938' in *Central European History*, vol. 1, No. 3, 1968, pp 264–84. See also YH, O.68, 565, *Lebenslauf des SS-Oberst-Gruppenführer und Panzer-Generalobersten der Waffen-SS Sepp Dietrich*, s.a.
20. Stein (1984), p 3.

in Hitler's hapless coup-d'état in Munich in November 1923.[21] In May 1928, he joined the SS, made quick progress and became part of the leading circle.[22] Due to his close relationship with Hitler, the Berlin *Stabswache* was directly subordinated to Dietrich, and for that reason there was little power to be wielded by SS boss Himmler and his men. In November 1933, having briefly been designated *Sonderkommando Berlin*, the unit once more changed its name. This time to the well-known and abiding *SS-Leibstandarte* (Life Regiment) *Adolf Hitler*.

Dietrich's men did not only perform security tasks related directly to Hitler's, they also participated in suppressing 'enemies' of the regime. In March 1935, for example, led by the Gestapo (Secret State Police) 20 men of the *Leibstandarte* were detailed for an action against Berlin's gay society. Following interrogation at Berlin's police headquarters, the detainees, who had been withheld during a number of raids, were sent

Figure 2.1 *SS-Leibstandarte* (Life Regiment) Adolf Hitler holds a parade in Berlin during the interwar years (Frihedsmusset)

---

21. Hagen Schulze, *Freikorps und Republik, 1918–1920* (Harald Boldt Verlag, 1969). See also Charles Messenger, *Hitler's Gladiator: The Life and Times of Oberstgruppenführer and Panzergeneraloberst der Waffen-SS Sepp Dietrich* (Brassey's Defence Publishers, 1988).
22. Andreas Schulz and Günter Wegmann, *Die Generale der Waffen-SS und der Polizei: [1933–1945]: Die militärischen Werdegänge der Generale, sowie der Ärzte, Veterinäre, Intendanten, Richter und Ministerialbeamten im Generalsrang*, vol. 1 (Biblio-Verl., 2003), pp 237ff.; Christoper Clark, 'Josef, "Sepp" Dietrich' in Ronald Smelserand Enrico Syring (eds.), *Die SS: Elite unter dem Totenkopf; 30 Lebensläufe* (Schöningh, 2003), pp 119ff.

to Concentration Camp Columbia Haus.[23] A concentration camp where *Leibstandarte* members were frequently detailed for guard duty until 1935 where the *SS-Wachtruppe Oranienburg-Colombia* took over.[24] The participation in such undertakings was aided by establishing a telephone line directly between the staff of the *Leibstandarte* and the Gestapo headquarters in Berlin.[25]

The *Leibstandarte* was accommodated in one of Germany's most modern and well-equipped barracks in the Berlin Lichterfelde neighbourhood, in the former *Preussische Hauptkadettenanstalt* (Main Prussian Military Academy) where some of the Second Reich's best officers had been trained. The increasing number of men (ca. 600 in the summer of 1933) were issued with light infantry weapons and were trained in the military training areas outside Berlin. The 9th Prussian Infantry Regiment – one of the army's élite units – was among their partners. Initially, the relations among Dietrich, his officers and those of the army were excellent, because the army did not see the small band of lightly armed SS soldiers as a threat.[26]

The *Leibstandarte* was not the only SS unit, whose training and equipment was supported by the police or the army. After the *Machtergreifung*, SS men were employed in several places around the country in an auxiliary police capacity and, later that year, they would form battalion sized so-called political stand-by units (*politische Bereitschaften*). They were equipped with small arms and were deployed to intimidate and terrorise the regime's opponents.[27] Apart from easy access to weapons, the status as auxiliary police also allowed funding by the national police. Similarly, the *Leibstandarte* was funded by the state.[28]

At midnight on 9 November 1933, however, it was made obvious that neither the *Leibstandarte* nor the stand-by units were ordinary security detachments. That night, in commemoration of their failed Beer Hall coup-d'état 10 years before, the Nazis staged a grand ceremony at the Feldherrnhalle in Munich. The whole *Leibstandarte* together with representatives of all other SS units were formed up in the darkness before Hitler. They were there to swear an oath of allegiance to him until death in his capacity of self-styled *Führer* (leader) of the German people.[29]

Some six months later, on 30 June 1934, SS units seized SA facilities all over Germany, allegedly in order to suppress a rebellion led by Ernst Röhm, chief of the SA.

23. BAMA, RS4/1620, Report, 11 March 1935.
24. Geoffrey P. Megargee (eds.), *Encyclopedia of Camps and Ghettos, 1933–1945*, vol. 1, Pt. A. (Indiana University Press, 2009), pp 59ff.; James J. Weingartner, *Hitler's Guard; the Story of the Leibstandarte SS Adolf Hitler, 1933–1945* (Southern Illinois University Press, 1974), p 19; Kurt Schilde, *Vom Columbia-Haus zum Schulenburgring: Dokumentation mit Lebensgeschichten von Opfern des Widerstandes und der Verfolgung von 1933 bis 1945 aus dem Bezirk Tempelhof* (Hentrich, 1987), pp 41ff.
25. Weingartner (1974), p 10.
26. Weingartner (1968). See also Bernd Wegner, *Hitlers politische Soldaten: Die Waffen-SS 1933–1945: Leitbild, Struktur und Funktion einer nationalsozialistischen Elite* (Ferdinand Schöningh, 1990), pp 89ff.; Paul Hausser, *Soldaten wie andere auch: Der Weg der Waffen-SS* (Munin Verl., 1966), p 12.
27. Koehl (1983), p 80; Wegner (1990), pp 81ff.
28. Ibid.
29. Stein (1984), p 5.

In reality, however, the SS was used by Hitler to decapitate, the increasingly unruly SA by apprehension or murder of individuals figuring on 'black lists' issued prior to the operation.[30] Apparently Dietrich personally oversaw the execution of six high-ranking SA men, while *Leibstandarte* men left in the Lichterfelde barracks in Berlin over several days murdered close to 150 detainees who had been brought to the compound.[31] Similarly, the murder of the main character, Röhm, was perpetrated by men of the SS, that is the chief of concentration camps, Theodor Eicke, assisted by his adjutant Michael Lippert. Both of these were later to assume command of Waffen-SS divisions.[32] About 200 persons from all over Germany fell victims to the purge. Merely half of them were SA members, and in several places SS men used the opportunity to settle old grudges arresting, beating up or killing personal adversaries.[33] Obviously, the SS was well pleased with being used as an interior force tasked with suppressing treacherous parts of the Nazi movement. Not only did the *Leibstandarte* keep Röhm's horse as a trophy in their stables in Lichterfelde, but also the officers openly boasted to have participated in the Night of the Long Knives and confessed to wishing to have killed even more.[34] Although these killings were not a topic for general conversation, they engendered the feeling that the SS was above the Nazi movement in general, not least because in Himmler's words 'the SS had proven to be capable of confronting the comrades who had failed, standing them against the wall and shooting them'.[35] The reward was soon to come. On 20 July 1934, the SS was officially made an independent party organisation at a par with the SA, which had now been considerably weakened. In the long run, 'the Röhm affair' had huge implications for Himmler's ability to build an SS empire, and – by creating the Waffen-SS – to challenge the German army. Beginning from this point, and lasting almost until the end of the war, Himmler was viewed by Hitler as faithful, ideologically devoted and capable – thus a man who could be trusted with big enterprises without threatening the Führer's authority.

The Nazi Elite

The killings committed by SS men in wake of the 'Röhm coup' reflected a more general trend: The SS men saw themselves as an order of particularly exquisite national socialists, who were bound to lead the transformation of German nation into a Nazi community.[36] Through deliberate racial selection of new members and vetting

---

30. Hein (2012), pp 87ff.
31. Weingartner (1968), p 277.
32. Longerich (2003), pp 206ff.
33. Hein (2012), p 88.
34. Weingartner (1968), p 277. BAMA, N756/65a, Report from a *BDM-Gruppenführerin* for Rubach, *Bannführer 231 Opladen* concerning conversation with officer of the LAH, 22 July 1935.
35. BAB, NS19/4010, *Rede des Reichsführers SS bei der SS-Gruppenführertagung in Posen am 4. Oktober 1943*. BAMA, N756/65a, Report from a *BDM-Gruppenführerin* concerning conversation with officer of the LAH, 22 July 1935. Weingartner (1968), p 277.
36. Eckart Conze, 'Adel unter dem Totenkopf. Die Idee eines Neuadels in den Gesellschaftsvorstellungen der SS' in Eckart Conze and Monika Wienfort (eds.), *Adel und Moderne: Deutschland im europäischen Vergleich im 19. und 20. Jahrhundert* (Böhlau, 2004).

of the men's spouses it was endeavoured to avoid racial degeneration of SS.[37] For this reason there were a number of racial and physical demands to be fulfilled before entry, a height of 170 cm being among them. Moreover, a family tree back to at least the year 1800 was required in order to make sure that there would be no Jews, insane or otherwise 'inferior' persons among the ancestors.[38] On top of these internal measures, the 'Order' image was carefully groomed to facilitate esprit-de-corps and to impress the surrounding world.[39]

With a view to forming the SS men, there was a strong emphasis on sports and other physical activities, which were elements in the SS leadership' perception of body and race.[40] Also, the spirit of the SS man was to be nurtured; substantial ideological schooling was part and parcel of membership in the SS. Himmler hoped that even the everyday life of the order's members eventually would take place in a universe permeated by SS artefacts, which included kitchen utensils and furniture produced by his black order and marketed at favourable prices.[41]

In the 1930s, a number of SS characteristics found their permanent appearances. There were, for example, the lightning-like SS *Siegrune* (victory rune), and the skull which adorned the peaked and forage caps. The use of runes were to become widespread in the SS, as for instance on soldiers' graves or in divisional badges.[42] The well-cut black uniform, which was used as full dress and service dress was introduced in the early 1930s. It conveyed the élite impression, which the SS so desired and, at the same time, set the personnel apart from the SA's brown and the army's grey.[43]

Realizing that the scattered armed SS units were assuming a permanent character, rather than merely being a transitional remedy during the consolidation of Nazi power, the Army High Command was keen on getting the SS' military role defined and delineated. On 24 September 1934, the War Office issued an order fixing the size of the SS, which was then termed the *Verfügungstruppe* (militarised troops), at three regiments and a signals battalion. At the same time, it was ordered that apart from the *Leibstandarte*, so far the units should not be organised as regiments, but be kept as battalions. The responsibility for the military training of the SS troops would rest with the army. Moreover, it was stated that in war-time the armed SS would be placed at the army's disposal. In that case the SS would be allowed to draft and arm 25,000 extra personnel, who – under the designation of police reinforcements – would assist

---

37. Wegner (1990). Hein (2012).

38. Hein (2012), pp 113ff.

39. Ibid., p 102. Jochen Lehnhardt, Die Waffen-SS. Geburt einer Legende (Ferdinand Schöningh, 2017).

40. Berno Bahro, *Der SS-Sport: Organisation, Funktion, Bedeutung* (Ferdinand Schöningh, 2013), p 61.

41. Longerich (2008), pp 269f.

42. In October 1940 the Y-shaped so-called death rune was introduced for use on tombstones for fallen SS soldiers. *Verordnungsblatt der Waffen-SS*, no. 10, 10 October 1940, pt. 209.

43. Lehnhardt (2017), pp 123–28.

Figure 2.2 Heinrich Himmler (Frihedsmuseet)

the army safeguarding the internal security. Although the order imposed constraints on the size and role of military SS, it also legitimised the existence of an armed SS separate from the *Reichswehr*, and granted the SS troops the same formal rights as army soldiers. It was implied that, in the long run, the armed SS units would be fused into a fully equipped division and the SS was also authorised to run military academies, the so-called *SS-Junkerschulen*.[44]

Notwithstanding the military organisation of armed SS units, they were so far seen exclusively as an instrument to be used for internal purposes, such as riots or attempts of coups-d'état.[45] However, apparently Himmler, from early on, harboured the ambition that the armed SS ought to develop into a Nazi elite and a military élite formation,

---

44. Wegner (1990), pp 86ff., and BAMA, RH2/1158a, *Der Chef der Heeresleitung T.A.Nr. 5367/34* of 15 October 1934 and, attached, *Erlass betr. SS-Verfügungstruppen* of. 24 September 1934. For a survey of the dislocation of the *Verfügungstruppe* units at the time, see BAMA, RH2/1158a, *Der Chef der Heeresleitung T.A.Nr. 5530/34*, 18 December 1934.

45. BAB, NS19/3582, Replica of letter from Hitler to *Reichswehrminister* Blomberg and Himmler, 2 February 1935. Ibid: Undated *Aktennotiz 230/15* concerning conversation Himmler's with Hitler 18 October 1935.

which by its sheer presence spread the Nazi values to the conservative army.[46] Hence, War Secretary Blomberg's September order did not create a lasting peace between the army leadership and the SS, and the following years were characterized by tensions and conflicts between the two.[47]

Six months later, Hitler re-introduced conscription. The armed forces, which, from then onwards, were designated *Wehrmacht*, were to be built by huge re-armaments. The *Verfügungstruppe*, too, were influenced by these changes. As of 22 May 1935, Hitler declared that, henceforth, service with the *Verfügungstruppe* would qualify as national service.[48] Initially, however, there would be no expansion of the SS troops. On the contrary, the army, which was about to swell to 38 divisions, went out of its way to prohibit the fusion of the scattered SS *Verfügungstruppe* battalions into a division.[49]

Step by step, however, Himmler built up his armed forces. Shortly, after the order of 1934, he managed to raise a reconnaissance unit as well as one of engineers – an obvious hint that the ambition to set up an entire SS division was far from shelved.[50] Additionally, the SS wished to find out how it would be possible to provide highly professional training for the military units without being dependent on the army. In November 1936, therefore, an inspectorate for the *Verfügungstruppe* was set up under Lieutenant General Paul Hausser.[51] Already before the war, this experienced officer had served in the Prussian army and since then in the *Reichswehr*. In 1934, he had joined the SS becoming commandant of the Junkerschule in Braunsweig. Now Hauser was able to take control over organisation, training and employment of SS troops, and, for all practical purposes, his office was now the SS' military operational staff and remained so until its abolition in 1940.[52] Like Sepp Dietrich, Hausser would become of great importance to the history of the SS. In 1936, the SS *Verfügungstruppe* battalions were combined to form regiments, which the SS designated *Standarten*. While *Standarte Deutschland* set up with headquarters in Munich under Felix Steiner, *Standarte Germania* was placed in Hamburg with Karl Maria Demelhuber as its commander. In 1938, after the annexation of Austria, the *Standarte Der Führer* was added under Georg Keppler in Vienna. Because the *Leibstandarte* was of regimental strength, the SS now had four

46. Stein (1984), pp 15ff.
47. Walter Warlimont, *Im Hauptquartier der deutschen Wehrmacht 39–45* (Bernard & Graefe Verlag, 1978), p 189.
48. BAB, NS19/3582, Letter from *Reichsinnenminister* Frick to Himmler, *SS-Führerschule in Braunschweig und Tölz,* 16 January 1936.
49. Stein (1984), p 8.
50. BAB, NS19/3582, Letter from Hitler to *Reichswehrminister* Blomberg and *Reichsführer-SS* Himmler, 2 February 1935. BAMA, RH2/1158a, Letter from Blomberg to Himmler et al., 8 December 1934. See also Wegner (1990), p 92.
51. The following is based on ibid., p 97ff.
52. Enrico Syring, 'Paul Hausser. "Türöffner" und Kommandeur "seiner" Waffen-SS' in Smelser and Syring (2003), pp 190ff., and Hausser (1966), pp 19ff.

regiments at its disposal. The *Verfügungstruppe* had grown from about 5,000 men in 1935 to more than 14,000 officers and men by the end of 1938.[53]

Among the above-mentioned commanders, Steiner, proved to be the most influential in turning the armed SS in to a warfighting force. Retiring from the army at a more modest level than Hauser (he was a major), but, unlike the 'Hindenburg-Conservative' Hausser, Steiner turned out to be more inclined towards Nazism and much more innovative. He worked tirelessly on reshaping army training along the lines of his experiences from the Great War.[54] After joining the *Verfügungstruppe* in 1935, Steiner was appointed as commanding officer of a battalion and, later, of the *Standarte Deutschland*. Training his troops, he emphasised exploiting the experiences made by the trench warfare *Stoßtruppen* (stormtroops) that, in the last part of the First World War, became an élite arm of the German infantry. A close and positive relationship amongst the men and their superiors was encouraged in lieu of drill, hierarchies and rigid discipline. Soldiers were to be trained to co-operate within small teams, display initiative, and build up physical prowess that would match the requirements in the field rather than what might look nice on the parade ground. In the spring of 1939, having made a deep impression on Hitler during an exercise demonstrating masked advance through the terrain, Steiner became Himmler's 'military darling.'[55] Yet, Steiner's influence should not be overestimated – during the 1930s, the Steiner school was but one out of several competing approaches to the *Verfügungstruppe*, although it spread throughout significant parts of the Waffen-SS during the war.[56]

From 1936 onwards, officers were gazetted to the various units fresh out of the SS' own military academies in Bad Tölz in Bavaria and Braunsweig in Saxony.[57] These academies allowed the SS to form their own ideologically schooled cadres of political officers, who could command military units as well as be employed as leaders in the organisation per se.[58] The first class of officer cadets graduated in April 1935. They were attached to various parts of the organisation including the security service, SD, the so-called *Totenkopfverbände* in the concentration camps, and various central offices of the SS administration.[59]

---

53. Numbers in Wegner (1990), p 104, Table 3. Additionally, there were the following important support units: *Nachrichtensturmbann* in Unna, *Pionersturmbann* in Dresden, *Sanitätsabteilung VT* and *Artilleriestandarte*as of the summer of 1939. B136/5147, *Die Organisatorische Entwicklung der bewaffneten SS-Verbände zwischen 1933 und 1945 und deren Verhältnis zur Wehrmacht*, 31 March 1954.

54. Mark P. Gingerich, 'Felix Steiner. Himmlers "ausgesprochenes Lieblingskind"' in Smelser and Syring (2003), p 435.

55. Gingerich (2003). See also Andreas Schulz and Günter Wegmann, *Die Generale der Waffen-SS und der Polizei: [1933–1945]: die militärischen Werdegange der Generale, sowie der Ärzte, Veterinäre, Intendanten, Richter und Ministerialbeamten im Generalsrang*, vol. 5, V (Biblio-Verl., 2011), p 461.

56. Wegner (1990), p 177.

57. Bernhard Kiekenap, *SS-Junkerschule: SA und SS in Braunschweig* (Appelhans, 2008), pp 115ff.; Jay Hatheway, *In Perfect Formation: SS Ideology and the SS-Junkerschule-Tölz* (Schiffer Pub., 1999), pp 78ff.

58. *RGVA, 1372/5/45*, Himmler order, 4 November 1937.

59. Koehl (1983), p 137.

The introduction of the *Verfügungstruppe* and the *Junkerschulen* were not the only innovations happening within the SS in autumn 1934 and early 1935. During that period a number of organisational changes saw the light of day.[60] It was desirable to be able to distinguish between those who performed salaried work as, for example, soldiers in *Verfügungstruppe*, concentration camp guards, or SD men from those who were not active in the same fashion. To comprise the latter, the *Allgemeine-SS* was introduced in 1934.[61] On the same note, the administrative service was professionalised when Himmler employed 42-year-old Oswald Pohl, an admin officer of the German Navy. During the war, he would become the overall leader of the administration of the concentration camps and of the network of commercial facilities, which was being developed simultaneously. For these reasons, Pohl was also to play a key role in the raising of the Waffen-SS. Much of the military equipment and the economic resources, which were needed to run the forces, were provided through his services.[62]

The formation of the armed SS gathered additional momentum from the Blomberg-Fritsch incident in January and February 1938. The dismissal of the Secretary for War, Blomberg, as well as the Army Commander, Werner Thomas Ludwig Freiherr von Fritsch allowed the Nazis to tighten control of the German armed forces as Hitler installed himself on top of the new tri-service *Oberkommando der Wehrmacht* (OKW or armed forces supreme command). This weakening of the army made it difficult for it to oppose Himmler's ambitions, and, on 17 August 1938, Hitler ordered that the *Verfügungstruppe*, the *Totenkopfverbände* and their filler units were to be organised as military organisations, which, in peacetime, would be under Himmler's – not the army's – command. Weapons and equipment were to be provided by the *Wehrmacht*. Concerning the *Verfügungstruppe* it was stated that these were units subordinated to the party and at Hitler's disposal. In case of mobilisation, the *Verfügungstruppe* might either come under the *OKH* (*Oberkommando des Heeres* or Army High Command) or be given domestic political tasks under Himmler.[63]

Streamlining and Fusion with the Police

The possibility of using the *Verfügungstruppe* for suppressing a possible uprising against the Nazis in Germany went hand in glove with Himmler's notion of taking over responsibility for internal security.[64] As early as 1933–1934 Himmler had control of the majority of German security police, and with a *Führer* order in 1936 he was appointed the first incumbent of the office of leader of all German police forces. The long-term

---

60. René Rohrkamp, 'Weltanschaulich gefestigte Kämpfer': *Die Soldaten der Waffen-SS 1933–1945: Organisation – Personal – Sozialstrukturen* (Schöningh, 2010); Wegener (1990); Koehl (1983).
61. Hein (2012), p 91.
62. Longerich (2008), p 179; Michael Allen, 'Oswald Pohl – Chef der SS-Wirtschaftsunternehmen' in Smelser and Syring (2003), pp 394ff.
63. Wegner (1990), pp 112ff.
64. BAB, NS19/4012, *Rede des Reichsführers-SS, Reichsinnenminister Himmler auf der Tagung der RPA-Leiter am 28. Januar 1944.*

goal was to make the police and the SS the collective Nazi state protection force against ideologically defined enemies.[65]

In 1937, in order to ease the control of the growing organisation and to strengthen the process of fusion of SS and police, Himmler set up a new kind of post. From now on, in every SS-*Oberabschnitt* (a territorial division) there would be a *Höhere SS- und Polizeiführer* (HSSPF or higher police and SS leader), who would be overall responsible for all police and SS matters in his area.[66] Subsequently, such posts were established in most of occupied Europe, and throughout the war, the incumbents would co-operate a lot with the Waffen-SS. In some cases, the HSSPFs would lead military operations performed by SS troops or employing them in 'security tasks.'[67]

In subsequent years, an ever-increasing integration of SS and police took place, and in 1941, Himmler declared that the SS rested on three pillars; viz. *Allgemeine SS*, *Waffen-SS* and the police.[68] The fusion of the SS and the police materialised in the creation of a unified security agency – the *Reichssicherheitshauptamt*– in Berlin (1939) as well as in extensive use of police forces in SS' killing activities at the eastern front. Also, two Waffen-SS divisions manned primarily by policemen were eventually set up.

Until 1938, the three *Verfügungstruppe*regiments, Germania, Deutschland and Der Führer, each had its own regional recruiting base. The *Leibstandarte*, however, recruited from all over Germany.[69] Nonetheless, the early recruitment was lousily organised and there was widespread rivalry about recruits with other parts of the SS.[70] As of the summer 1938 therefore, the recruiting process was streamlined. The first step was the appointment of the zealous Gottlob Berger as head of the *SS-Ergänzungsamt* (SS recruiting office), who would be responsible for the recruiting effort.[71] The following year, Berger introduced a structure similar to that of the army. A recruiting office with salaried personnel was established in every *SS-Oberabschnitt* (geographically equivalent to an army *Wehrkreis*or military district). Here, the actual recruiting was performed, applicants were examined and those not meeting the SS standards were rejected.[72] Throughout the war, Berger would play a decisive role in the development of the Waffen-SS. Born in 1896, like many of his contemporaries he had the First World War and Freikorps experience as a reserve officer. In the aftermath of the war

---

65. Ruth Bettina Birn, *Die höheren SS- und Polizeiführer: Himmlers Vertreter im Reich und in den besetzten Gebieten* (Droste Verlag, 1986), pp 8ff.; Michael Wildt, *Generation des Unbedingten: das Führungskorps des Reichssicherheitshauptamtes* (Hamburger Edition, 2002), pp 209ff.

66. Birn (1986), pp 6ff.

67. Birn (1986). Passim.

68. Buchheim et al. (1994), p 102.

69. BAB, NS19/370, Chief of SS-Hauptamt to all SS-Oberabschnitte and others, *Einstellung in die SS-Verfügungstruppe*, 4 September 1936.

70. BAB, NS19/218, *Einrichtung eines SS-Ergänzungsamtes*, 20 April 1938. See also Mark Philip Gingerich, *Toward a Brotherhood of Arms: Waffen-SS Recruitment of Germanic Volunteers, 1940–1945* (Ph.D. dissertation), University of Wisconsin-Madison, 1991, pp 43ff.; Hein (2012), p 261.

71. BAB, NS19/218, *Einrichtung eines SS-Ergänzungsamtes*, 20 April 1938.

72. Gingerich (1991), pp 45ff.

he was a PT teacher, and in 1930 he entered the SA. In 1936, he swapped PT for a salaried job with a provincial SS unit and, two years hence, he moved to Berlin. Thereafter, Berger became a real high-flyer entering Himmler's innermost circle and making it as far as head of the *SS-Hauptamt* and also becoming a responsible for the suppression of an uprising in Slovakia in fall 1944.[73]

Gearing Up for Campaign in Poland

The armed SS formations became integrated in Germany's territorial expansion already from the spring 1938 annexation of Austria – where Leibstandarte Adolf Hitler spearheaded the troops entering the country. The next Nazi aggression – that against Czechoslovakia in fall 1938 – also involved SS troops, and illustrates how the armed formations of the SS were useful in waging what we would now call 'hybrid warfare'. Apart from the Austrians enrolled into the German SS after the failed 1934 coup, there were at this stage only few *Volksdeutsche* in the *Verfügungstruppe*. Recruiting foreigners was generally fraught with diplomatic difficulties, because a large portion of the early *Volksdeutsche* recruits were either deserters from the armies of their home countries or had been forced into exile due to Nazi activities.[74] The Czechoslovak Sudetenland was one of the areas whence the SS received such recruits.[75] Shortly before the German occupation in October 1938, the relations between the SS and the *Sudetendeutsche* (Volksdeutsche in the Sudetenland) developed further.[76] In September, the *Sudetendeutsche Freikorps* (SFK) was formed as a part of Hitler's plans for the attack. This corps consisted of Czech citizens with a German inclination, they were secretly armed by the Third Reich and was reinforced by personnel from the *SS-Totenkopfstandarte*.[77] The aim was to stir internal trouble and harass border posts in order to keep the Czechoslovak authorities under pressure and boost the *Sudetendeutsche*'s desire to be joined with Germany. The SFK grew within a very brief period and had, by October, swelled to 34,000 men in 41 battalions. The corps was controlled by the OKH, though with some involvement by the *Volksdeutsche Mittelstelle* (VOMI, i.e. the German Racial Assistance Office), which had been created by Himmler in 1937. On 30 September – the day when, according to the Munich Agreement, the Sudetenland was to be ceded to Germany – Hitler ordered that the corps be subordinated to Himmler. All three

73. Gerhard Rempel, 'Gottlob Berger. "Ein Schwabengeneral der Tat"' in Smelser and Syring (2003), pp 45–60. See also Schulz and Wegman (2003), bd. 1, pp 85–93.

74. Lumans in *Marble* (2012), pp 202ff.

75 Lumans in ibid., p 204.

76. The following is based on Martin Broszat, 'Das Sudetendeutsche Freikorps', *Vierteljahrshefte für Zeitgeschichte, Jahrgang 9, Heft 1*, 1961, pp 30f., and Werner Röhr, 'Der "Fall Grün" und das Sudetendeutsche Freikorps' in Hans Henning Hahn (ed.), *Hundert Jahre sudetendeutsche Geschichte: eine völkische Bewegung in drei Staaten* (Lang, 2007), pp 241ff.

77. Gerhard Engel, *At the Heart of the Reich. The Secret Diary of Hitler's Army Adjutant* (Greenhill Books, 2005), pp 53ff.

SS-Standarten took part in the deployment into the Sudetenland, and *Standarte Germania* immediately began terrorising the Czech population.[78]

In spring 1939, Hitler signed the initial order for *Fall Weiß*, the attack on Poland. On 1 September, German troops unleashed what became six bloody war years in Europe. At the outbreak of war, the true Nazi potential for violence was let loose in earnest. For Himmler and the SS this meant that they could start putting the regime's and the organisation's radical ideology into practice. New tasks – such as Germanisation of large tracts of Poland and extradition of Jews and Poles from these areas – went hand in hand with setting up an occupation administration where police and SS troops played key roles. The campaign, and subsequent occupation, greatly brutalised the SS troops who committed a number of atrocities on their way through the country.[79]

In the spring of 1939, the armed SS was merely a small crowd of men staffing two strands in the organisation. The first strand was the *Totenkopfverbände*, while the second comprised the *Leibstandarte* and the *Verfügungstruppe*. During the winter 1938–1939, these were mobilised and in March 1939 they included four fully motorised regiments. When Germany – in obvious violation of the Munich Agreement – occupied the remainder of Czechoslovakia, this part of the SS was employed within the framework of some of the army's armoured divisions.[80]

It was Himmler's ambition to organise his troops in divisions and – as a long-term goal – in corps. The opportunity arose when, in the summer of 1939, Hitler attended *Regiment Deutschland*'s exercise at Münsterlager. As usual, in the Waffen-SS, the exercise was executed with live ammunition – including artillery barrages – and Hitler was so impressed that, a few weeks later, he ordered the formation of an *SS-Verfügungsdivision*. This would require that the army provided the equipment necessary for forming an artillery regiment. Although this happened so quickly that the regiment was ready for the invasion of Poland, it delayed, until the end of fighting, the full implementation of the plans for forming the division.[81] For this reason, the *Verfügungstruppe* regiments were sent piecemeal into combat in Poland.

During the process leading up to the invasion of Poland on 1 September 1939, the SS did in no way keep to the sidelines. Since May 1939, the SD and the Gestapo had prepared to make arrests of Germanophobe elements in Poland and, in July, the formation of *Einsatzgruppen* (task forces) began. Their tasks would be the elimination of those hostile to the Reich operating in the hinterland of advancing German troops.[82]

78. Hans Umbreit, *Deutsche Militärverwaltungen 1938/39: d. militär. Besetzung d. Tschechoslowakei u. Polens* (Deutsche VerlagsAnstalt), 1977, p 40, note 143. Helmuth Groscurth (ed.), *Tagebücher eines Abwehroffiziers: 1938–1940 Helmut Krausnick und Harald C. Deutsch* (Deutsche Verlagsanstalt), 1970, p 541.

79. Michael Wildt, *An Uncompromising Generation: The Nazi Leadership of the Reich Security Main Office* (University of Wisconsin Press, 2009), p 218.

80. Stein (1984), pp 21ff.

81. Ibid, pp 25ff.

82. Dorothee Weitbrecht, 'Ermächtigung zur Vernichtung. Die Einsatzgruppen in Polen im Herbst 1939', in KlausMichael Mallmannand Bogdan Musial (eds.), *Genesis des Genozids: Polen 1939–1941* (Wissenschaftliche Buchgesellschaft, 2004), p 58. Wildt (2009), pp 218ff.

Moreover, the SD was to insert agents provocateurs. Heydrich's security policemen were to stage a number of mock border violation incidents vindicating the Nazi attacks. Last there was a wish to let the *Verfügungstruppe* and *Leibstandarte* units prove their military value and legitimise the SS 'order' through front service.[83]

The Waffen-SS in the Polish Campaign

In spite of an almost equal force ratio, the German attackers profited from a number of decisive advantages. While Germany fielded 15 armoured or motorised divisions with 3,600 armoured cars and tanks, Poland had only one armoured brigade and all together 750 armoured vehicles. About 2,000 German aircraft and pilots, several of whom had been trained in the Spanish Civil War, faced merely 900 Polish aeroplanes of a somewhat dated construction and inferior quality.[84]

Among the German troops, standing ready for the attack was an assortment of SS units: *Leibstandarte* and the SS engineer battalion formed an independent combat group, but also *Regiment Germania* was deployed as was *Regiment Deutschland*, together with the *SS-Aufklärungssturmbann* (reconnaissance squadron) and the recently formed SS artillery regiment, the latter was part of the army's *Panzerdivision Kempf*.[85] Finally, in June 1939, a part of *4th SS-Totenkopfstandarte* was smuggled from Berlin to Gdansk (Danzig). Dressed as tourists, the 4,000 soldiers should beef up the city's armed home guard, the *SS-Heimwehr Danzig*.[86]

Many of the norms for the army's use of SS troops, which would last to the end of the war, were established during the Polish campaign of 1939. SS units and formations were subordinated to divisions, corps, armies or army groups as integral parts of the established chain of command. The actual combat tasks and movements on the battlefield were assigned by the formations with which they served – at this stage typically division or corps. However, the control was loose enough to allow considerable internal autonomy and to enable the troops to combine conventional fighting with committing ideologically motivated crimes.

When the German attack commenced, the *Heimwehr* engaged in the fighting for Danzig and supported the attack on the Polish fort Westerplatte, which controlled the entry into the city's harbour.[87] As the fighting died out the SS men made brutal arrests

83. Longerich (2008), pp 439ff.
84. *Das Deutsche Reich und Der Zweite Weltkrieg*, vol. 2, pp 110ff.; Richard J. Evans, *The Third Reich at War: How the Nazis Led Germany from Conquest to Disaster* (Penguin, 2009), p 3.
85. *Das Deutsche Reich und Der Zweite Weltkrieg*, vol. 2, p 103.; Heinz Höhne, *Der Orden unter dem Totenkopf: die Geschichte der SS* (Weltbild-Verlag, 1995), p 419.; Stein (1984), p 28.; Otto Weidinger, *Das Reich I, 1934–1939* (J.J. Fedorowicz Publishing, 1990), pp 94ff.; Weingartner (1974), pp 32ff.
86. Rolf Michaelis, *SS-Heimwehr Danzig in Poland, 1939* (Schiffer Military History, 2008).
87. On *Heimwehr Danzig's* fighting see VAP, N, 2. SS-Pz. Div. 'T', box 8, *Bericht über den Einsatz der SS-Heimwehr vom 31.8.1939 bis 21.9.1939*. See also Martin Cüppers, '"[...] auf eine so saubere und anständige SS-mäßige Art": die Waffen-SS in Polen 1939–1941' in Mallmann and Musial (2004), p 92.

of Jews and Poles and vandalised many Jewish flats.[88] Furthermore, in the basement of the school, which *Heimwehr Danzig* had made its headquarters, an interim concentration camp was set up. Here, 3–400 Jews and Poles were detained, whom the SS had rounded up around the city. Under the direction of Max Pauli, later to become commandant of the concentration camp Neuengamme, the prisoners were subjected to humiliation and torture, and some were murdered.[89]

For many of the SS men the initial fighting was far from painless. On 4 September, following severe clashes at the Warta River, the *Leibstandarte* – the only motorised SS unit – spearheaded XIII Army Corps and succeeded in crossing this important waterway. Having crossed also with all its other formations, the corps advanced quickly towards the industrial city Lutzhoping to envelop a group of Polish divisions around Poznńa. The following days, though, the *Leibstandarte* progressed only at a modest pace. Its vehicles had troubles with crossing watercourses, on which many bridges had been demolished and, frequently, when they moved off the roads they got stuck in the sandy terrain. Moreover, fears of Polish flanking attacks made commanders hesitant about advancing. Paradoxically, the motorised – and in their own imagination daring – *Leibstandarte* soldiers actually blocked the roads to the infantry advancing on foot behind them. To add insult to injury, the *Leibstandarte* was encircled by Polish troops and had to be relieved by attacks by the units behind them.[90]

Elsewhere the situation was not much better. Already on the first day of the campaign, problems arose as units of the *Panzerdivision Kempf* engaged in a frontal attack against a well-fortified border defence position at Mława. After several attacks had caused severe casualties the SS troops were able to move forward in earnest when the Poles abandoned the Mława position on the third day.[91] After this, the attack gathered momentum as *Panzerdivision Kempf* spearheaded the advance towards the fortified city Modlin, northwest of Warsaw where they were joined by the *Leibstandarte*. During the days of 14–19 September, the *Leibstandarte* managed to seal off the eastern approach, thus contributing to the capture of 105,000 prisoners-of-war. Of these, no less the 20,000 were taken by the *Leibstandarte* and the 4th *Panzerdivision*.[92] Then, the *Leibstandarte* joined the siege troops around Modlin. Also, *Standarte Deutschland* was employed against one of the forts sustaining very heavy casualties in the process.[93]

The successful co-operation between motorised and armoured units and formations as well as a forceful and efficient air force led to a quick defeat of Poland.

---

88. Schenk (1995), pp 71ff.
89. Ibid., p 80. See also BB, E27, 1000/721, Archiv nr. 9928, Bd. 4, D110, *Deserteurbericht*, 11 May 1943, p 9.
90. Weingartner (1974), pp 33ff.
91. Otto Weidinger, 'Abschied von einem Soldaten – und von einem Freunde', *Der Freiwillige*, Vol. 12, No. 6, 1964, p 16.
92. Weingartner (1974), p 36. See also Hans Reinhardt, 'Die 4. Pz.-Div. Vor Warschau und an der Bzura vom 9.-20.9.1939', *Der Freiwillige*, Vol. 6, No. 10, 1958, pp 7–11.
93. Ibid.

However, the German army's successes obscure the fact that there were flaws as well. Equipment, which did not live up to the requirements, inadequate intelligence and reconnaissance, and shortcomings in the troops' training and experience.[94] Moreover, in the army's view, the SS' battle performance in Poland left much to be desired. The *Leibstandarte* was under operational control by XIII Army Corps, who was harsh in its criticism of the regiment's performance during the first week of the campaign. The advance had been too slow and orders had not been properly executed. The army corps concluded that 'the *SS-Leibstandarte Adolf Hitler* has not accomplished the tasks ordered by corps', and went on to state that 'the troops' underperformance was not due to the quality of the personnel, but caused by the lack of training of officers and NCOs'.[95] The *Panzerdivision Kempf* was also in for censure. After a week of fighting, the Third Army considered extricating the formation from the battle due to inadequacies in training and organisation, disband it and reduce the attached SS units, which they would then recommend that the Army Group might use as operational reserves.[96]

The German losses during the Polish campaign were limited. There had been 15,000 dead and missing and 30,000 wounded as opposed to 200,000 Polish casualties. According to a later count, the Waffen-SS lost 372 killed, of whom 123 were from the *Leibstandarte*, 300 wounded and three missing.[97] To a regimental size unit this was a considerable loss, and the SS left the battlefield with a reputation for taking large casualties due to incompetence.[98] A veteran of this campaign remembered it primarily because of the high casualty rate and the many road accidents – issues which come down to poor leadership and flawed training.[99]

Prelude to the War of Extermination

The onslaught on Poland was the beginning of the suppression of the country and the eradication of its Jews. As early as during the first few days of the campaign, the German army committed widespread atrocities. Therefore, with a view to the subsequent attack

94. *Das Deutsche Reich und Der Zweite Weltkrieg*, vol. 2, pp 134ff.
95. Helmuth Groscurt, *Tagebücher eines Abwehroffiziers 1938–1940* (Deutsche Verlags-Anstalt, 1970), pp 367ff., appendix 1. BAMA, RH 24-13/ 20, Kurzer Erfahrungsbericht und Zustandebericht Korpskommando XIII, 7 October 1939.
96. Hans Umbreit, *Deutsche Militärverwaltungen 1938/39: d. militär. Besetzung d. Tschechoslowakei u. Polens* (Deutsche Verlags-Anstalt, 1977), p 163. According to an internal SS memo, nonetheless, Steiner, who commanded one of the SS units under *Division Kempf* was praised for the conduct of his command during battle. BAB, SSO, 153B, SS Personalhauptamt *Aktenvermerk*, 6 September 1940.
97. BAB, NS19/2109, Letter of 31 August 1942 from Dr. Korherr to Himmler, *Die Kriegsverluste der SS nach dem Stand der statistischen Erfassung vom 15. Juli 1942*. Messenger (1988), p 75.
98. Höhne (1995), p 419; Messenger (1988), pp 75ff.
99. BB, E27, 1000/721, *Archiv nr. 9928, Bd.4, SS 103, Deserteurbericht*, 3 February 1943. See also in same archival package D110, *Deserteurbericht*, 11 May 1943, p 19.

on the Soviet Union the Polish campaign has been termed the 'Prelude to the War of Extermination.'[100] There was a wide variety of reasons for the many outrages during that campaign. The Nazis saw the Poles as primitive sub-humans, who had been suppressing the country's ethnic German group for years. Such negative stereotypes were boosted by the soldiers' first experiences in Poland and pervasive rumours of Polish maltreatment of local *Volksdeutsche*. Moreover, they feared the Polish franc tireurs and their allegedly dodgy combat techniques. Finally, owing to the soldiers' inexperience, without really knowing what was happening, they frequently clashed with each other. Moreover, as was true of the army as well, the SS units had difficulties spotting the muzzle flashes, when the enemy attacked from well-concealed positions.[101] This led to faulty assumptions of being attacked by irregular forces and snipers entailing wild and un-coordinated fire – occasionally against own troops.[102]

The SS shared these impressions with the army, but because of their ideological indoctrination they were likely more inclined to interpret the behaviour by the Poles as expressions of racial character traits.[103] Despite the German army's injustices in Poland a number of acts committed by Waffen-SS units still stood out. While, at numerous occasions, the army shot hostages out of hand or torched houses and villages, its archives do not reveal instructions as detailed as the orders of the *Leibstandarte* concerning the combat against franc tireurs. According to the latter, in areas where there was reason to believe that civilians took up arms against the Germans, all males capable of bearing arms were to be shot.[104] The unit's behaviour during the first days of battle bears witness to the fact that this contingency order was indeed carried out in practise. During its advance, the *Leibstandarte* shot several civilians in the villages Bolesławiec and Wieruszów while, at the same time, burning large parts of these to the ground. On 3–4 September, together with the Wehrmacht's *Infanterieregiment 95*, the unit moved into the town Złoczew encountering no opposition. As in so many other places, the soldiers saw a franc tireur behind every lamppost and reacted so violently that *Infanterieregiment 95* received orders from division to stop immediately 'that meaningless slaughter on – mostly non-existent – franc tireurs'. The order also forbade 'the torching of farms and villages whence allegedly fire is opened'. To underline that division saw no threat from franc tireurs the onward march was to be accomplished with unloaded weapons and without hand grenades tucked into the soldiers' belts. However, before this order could be implemented, the *Leibstandarte* and the infantry regiment had already killed 200 civilians during their ravaging in Złoczew.[105]

---

100. Jochen Böhler, *Auftakt zum Vernichtungskrieg: die Wehrmacht in Polen 1939*, 2. Aufl. (Fischer Taschenbuch Verlag, 2006). See also Alexander B. Rossino, *Hitler Strikes Poland* (University Press of Kansas, 2003).

101. Böhler (2006), pp 68, 80, 113, and 155.

102. VAP, N, 1. SS-PZ.DIV. LAH nr. 5, SS-Ustuf. Hansen 12/LAH, the 9th day of war. Weingartner (1974), p 33, and Messenger (1988), p 74. See also *Das Deutsche Reich und Der Zweite Weltkrieg*, vol. 2, p 133; Böhler (2006), pp 154ff.

103. As an example, see VAP, N, 1. SS-PZ.DIV. LAH nr. 5, SS-Ustuf. Hansen 12/LAH, concerning the 1st, 4th, 7th, 9th and 10th–11th day of war.

104. Böhler (2006), p 152.

105. Ibid., p 224.

During the subsequent weeks' fighting, the *Leibstandarte*'s brutality did in no way abate. In the night 18/19 September, a gruesome event took place in the village of Błonie. Here, the *Obermusikmeister* (bandmaster) of the *Leibstandarte*'s band, Müller-John, had about 50 Jewish civilians shot. This was subsequently prosecuted by the Wehrmacht's judicial proceedings officer, but the charge was dropped, after Sepp Dietrich personally contacted Hitler.[106] Another *Leibstandarte* officer later to become widely known, Kurt Meyer, was eventually charged with shooting several Jews in connection with the seizure of Modlin.[107] Also, the SS units with *Panzerdivision Kempf* made their presence felt. From East Prussia southwards this division blasted a trail of pogroms, burnt synagogues and committed other injustices culminating in the shooting of 50 Jewish forced labourers repairing a bridge near the town Krasnosielc.[108] Besides beating and killing, SS soldiers from *Panzerdivision Kempf* herded a group of Jews into the synagogue and started soaking it with kerosene. Only just before ignition they were stopped by an army officer.[109]

The SS personnel's readiness to solve non-military political tasks without orders was noticed by the army. General Ewald von Kleist, who had the *Standarte Germania* under his authority, had to be explicit in prohibiting all kinds of policing activity. Similarly restraining orders were given to a crowd of SS engineers who had assumed police responsibility within the general's area of operations.[110]

Hitler's aim with the occupation of Poland was radical, racial reorganisation as well as German colonisation and exploitation of the country, and the most important agents in achieving this objective were other SS units namely the *Einsatzgruppen*. Two weeks prior to the campaign, their leaders received their instructions from Heydrich's right-hand man, the lawyer Werner Best. The Polish intelligentsia and upper class were pointed out as the anchors of expected future resistance against German occupation, and it was indicated that mass executions might be an efficacious measure.[111] Already in the first days of the campaign, this turned out to be the case. On 3 September, the Polish army abandoned the city Bydgoscz. The following day – that is, before the arrival of the German army on the fifth – a Polish militia clashed with the city's *Volksdeutsche*. Apparently, this stimulated the SD's *Einsatzkommando 2* arriving in the afternoon of the fifth, because over the following days more than a hundred Polish civilians were executed by that unit.[112]

It was not only the *SD Einsatzgruppen* that took part in this type of action. The *Totenkopf-standarten Oberbayern, Brandenburg* and *Thüringen* were all employed in an *Einsatzgruppe* capacity in the areas of Poland within the Eighth and Tenth Armies' theatres of operation.[113]

---

106. Ibid., pp 224ff.
107. Peter Lieb, *Konventioneller Krieg oder NS-Weltanschauungskrieg? Kriegführung und Partisanenbekämpfung in Frankreich 1943/44* (Oldenburg, 2007), p 159.
108. Böhler (2006), pp 227ff. See also Stein (1984), p 271.
109. Rossino (2003), pp 105ff.
110. Umbreit (1977), p 163.
111. Weitbrecht in Mallmann and Musial (2004), pp 58ff.
112. Wildt (2009), pp 225ff.; Gerwarth (2011), pp 142ff.
113. Totenkopf Standarten remained 'Totenkopf Standarten' until February 1941, when they were re-designated SS-Infanterieregimenter. Martin Cüppers, *Wegbereiter der Shoa. Die Waffen-SS, der KommandostabReichsführer-SS und die Judenvernichtung 1939–1945* (Primus, 2011), p 27.

Among these three, the misdeeds of the *Brandenburg Standarte* is the best-known. On 13 September, it advanced into Poland, and its activities included arson, terror and execution of the leading Jews in the city Włocławek. Moreover, in Bydgoscz 800 persons were arrested and shot on account of to their alleged resistance potential.[114] As the army had difficulties understanding the need to incarcerate all Włocławek's Jews in the local prison, which could hardly accommodate the city's 10,000 Jews, the adjutant of the *Standarte Brandenburg* replied that this would not be a problem as they were to be shot, anyway.[115] Later in war the men committing these crimes would become Waffen-SS soldiers, as the Totenkopfstandarte were used to form additional regiments.

Given that such acts were in accordance with the Nazi war aims, it is, therefore, not surprising that, on 4 October after the termination of the campaign, Hitler declared a general amnesty, so that the perpetrators of the crimes thus committed did not have to face trial.[116] Shortly after, on 17 October, a decisive step was taken concerning the future employment of the SS. On this day, Hitler ordained that from then onwards the SS and the police would be subject to an independent administration of justice (*SS- und Polizeigerichtsbarkeit*). Hence, from this time onwards the SS and the police might commit injustices without fearing punishment, as long as these were of an ideological nature.[117]

Poland – a Laboratory of Race Politics

Neither the army's dissatisfaction concerning the underperformance of the SS, nor its protests concerning injustices, made any impression on Hitler. On the contrary, at a visit on 19 September he decided to raise two more divisions in addition to the *Verfügungsdivision*. These two divisions were to be formed by personnel from the *Totenkopf* units and the uniformed police force and named accordingly, that is the *Polizei Division* viz. *Totenkopf Division*.[118] The large number of men received from the *Totenkopf Standarten*, the *Allgemeine-SS* and the police meant that many soldiers in these three division were relatively old. In 1940, 42 percent of the soldiers (including those of the *Totenkopf Standarten*) were 28 years or more. In the *Division Totenkopf* alone, this was true of 62 percent of the ranks.[119] Simultaneously, these SS units, which had fought with *Panzerdivision Kempf*, were moved to Plzeň in the Protectorate

---

114. Ibid., pp 39ff.
115. Umbreit (1977), p 163.
116. Weitbrecht in Mallmann and Musial (2004), p 65.
117. Concerning this, see later chapter on the administration of justice in the Waffen-SS. See also Wegner (1990), pp 319ff.
118. Gerhard Engel, *At the Heart of the Reich: The Secret Diary of Hitler's Army Adjutant* (Greenhill Books, 2005), p 75. Friedrich Husemann, *Die guten Glaubens waren. Band 1: Geschichte der SS-PolizeiDivision (4. SS-Polizei-Panzer-GrenadierDivision) 1939–1942* (Munin Verlag, 1971), pp 17ff.; Sydnor (1990), pp 41ff.
119. Rohrkamp (2010), p 323.

WAR, GENOCIDE AND CULTURAL MEMORY

Bohemia-Moravia to form the *SS-Verfügungsdivision*, which would later be named *Das Reich*.[120] The *Leibstandarte*, too, moved west to the Koblenz area.[121]

The fact that many SS units were withdrawn, however, did not mean that Himmler had lost interest in Poland. On the contrary, during the war, Poland would become the country with the heaviest concentration of police and SS authorities, and Himmler built his strongest power bases there.[122] Newly raised *Totenkopf* unit were located across the country and organised as a network of cavalry units under the aegis of the first *SS-Totenkopf-Reiterstandarte* under Hermann Fegelein who was, later, to marry Eva Braun's sister Margarete, thus becoming Hitler's brother-in-law.[123] Born in 1906, Fegelein, after an unsuccessful career in the Bavarian police, joined the SS in 1930 where he quickly rose in rank within the SS cavalry. In 1935, he became co-founder of an SS riding academy in Munich. In 1939, he was promoted *Obersturmbannführer* in Waffen-SS, and Himmler made him commanding officer of the first *SS-Totenkopf-Reiterstandarte*. Fegelein was to become heavily involved in the Holocaust, and he later commanded the SS cavalry in a number of murder actions in the Soviet Union. In the last days of the war, he was with Hitler in the Führer's war rooms in Berlin, but tried to go underground a few days before the city fell. His attempt miscarried and he was apprehended by the SS. On 28 or 29 April 1945, he was shot for desertion in the garden of the Reich Chancellery.[124]

In the same time, an extensive SS infrastructure in Poland materialised. It comprised concentration and extermination camps, rehousing facilities for *Volksdeutsche*, and barracks for the SS soldiers. Mostly, these installations were placed close to each other. This was true, in particular, for the Lublin area. Another important locale was the training area Dębica that, over the war years, was to become one of the most important Waffen-SS training grounds. The soldiers there took part in clearing the ghettoes, in deportations to the extermination camp Bełżec, as well as in the exploitation of forced labourers in the training area.[125] Other important duty stations lay in or near Warsaw, where *Totenkopf Standarte 8*, *SS-Reiterstandarte 1* and the *Totenkopf Division*'s filler personnel battalion as well as the SS cavalry training unit were stationed for shorter or longer periods.[126]

120. Otto Weidinger, *Division Das Reich: der Weg der 2. SS-Panzer-Division 'Das Reich': die Geschichte der Stammdivision der Waffen-SS. 1943–1945*, vol. 5 (Munin, 1982), pp 277ff.
121. Messenger (1988), pp 76ff.
122. Martin Broszat, *Nationalsozialistische Polenpolitik 1939–1945* (Fischer-Bücherei, 1965), p 60.
123. Volker Riess, 'Hermann Fegelein – Parveneu ohne Skrupel' in Smelser and Syring (2003), pp 160ff.
124. Ibid.
125. http://www.lexikon-der-wehrmacht.de/Karte/TruppenubungsplatzeSS/Truppenubungs platzeSSDebica-R.htm. Accessed on 29 September 201. Cüppers (2011), pp 288ff.
126. Stephan Lehnstaedt, *Okkupation im Osten: Besatzeralltag in Warschau und Minsk 1939–1944* (Oldenburg Wissenschaftsverlag, 2010), pp 42ff.; Wilson (2000), p 150; Andrzej Wirth (ed.), *The Stroop Report: The Jewish Quarter of Warsaw Is No More!* transl. by Sybil Milton (Pantheon Books, 1979).

Many police units and commanders, who had learned their trade through killings and deportations in Poland, would also act as perpetrators in the Soviet Union. The SS' participation in the campaign and the subsequent occupation of Poland has been aptly described as a kind of 'laboratory of race politics'. In many ways this would form a template for the further development of the war of extermination and for Holocaust. Moreover, in this respect the Polish campaign greatly influenced the participating SS units' perception of the limits of violence – or rather their absence.[127]

In September 1940, addressing officers of the *Leibstandarte* Himmler illustrated how the crimes in Poland had become an important point of reference to the SS and the Waffen-SS. He praised his organisation for having had the necessary 'robustness' to do the deeds that had been 'needed' in Poland. This included completing the forced relocation of thousands of Poles in 40 degrees (Celcius) below zero and killing thousands of members of the country's leading tier.[128]

The Waffen-SS becomes an Official Designation

On 19 July 1940, in an address to the *Reichstag* Hitler used – for the first time officially – the term 'Waffen-SS'.[129] However, internal SS documents reveal that the term was employed as early as the late autumn of 1939, and from November onwards it became everyday language within the SS administration.[130] Shortly after, Berger informed Himmler that he had had a three-and-a-half-hour long meeting with the OKW and, in spite of considerable difficulties, had achieved their confirmation of the term 'Waffen-SS.'[131] Berger was now well under way with having the term officially acknowledged as a corporate designation of all armed components of the SS. This was opportune for reasons of status and due to the advantages it provided when collaborating with external institutions.[132] In April 1941, Himmler officially ordered that all armed elements of the SS be united under the name 'Waffen-SS,' which entailed that the terms *SS-Verfügungstruppe* and *SS-Totenkopfverbände* were abolished.[133]

As mentioned earlier, in September 1939 Hitler had decided to raise the *Verfügungsdivision* and two additional Waffen-SS divisions. In October, the formation of these three divisions was officially approved, as was the enlargement of the *Leibstandarte* to a reinforced and fully motorised regiment.[134] In early 1940, the three divisions were officially formed. While the *SS-Verfügungsdivision* (which, at the end of 1940, was re-named *Das Reich*) was formed by amalgamating the three regiments *Deutschland*, *Germania* and

127. Mallmann in Mallmann and Musial (2004), p 82.; Cüppers in ibid., p 104; Lieb (2007), pp 15ff.
128. Longerich (2008), p 481.
129. Stein (1984), p 90.
130. Wegener (1990), p 127. See also Sydnor (1990), p 45.
131. BAB, NS19/1863, Letter from Berger to Himmler of 16 December 1939.
132. Stein (1984), p 39.
133. BAB, NS33/271, SS Führungshauptamt, *Zusammensetzung der Waffen-SS*, 22 April 1941.
134. See Sydnor (1990), p 45, and Stein (1984), p 32.

Der Führer, the *Division Totenkopf* and the *SS-Polizei-Division*, which had been raised in autumn and winter 1939, were primarily filled by policemen and personnel from the *Totenkopf Standarten*.[135] However, some personnel came from other SS institutions. Thus, the *Division Totenkopf* welcomed men from *Allgemeine-SS*, *Ordnungspolizei* and other units of the *Verfügungstruppe*.[136] The large number of men received from the *Totenkopf Standarten*, the *Allgemeine-SS* and the police meant that many soldiers in these three division were relatively old. In 1940, 42 percent of the soldiers (including those of the *Totenkopf Standarten*) were 28 years or more. In the *Division Totenkopf* alone, this was true of 62 percent of the ranks.[137]

On 15 August 1940, yet another element, the *Führungshauptamt* (Operational Headquarters-SS), was added contributing to the ongoing militarisation of the SS. Himmler wished to use this as his 'command post for the military direction of the Waffen-SS' and for commanding and training the *Allgemeine-SS*. [138] Moreover, the inspectorate for the concentration camps was made a sub-division of this office. Himmler took upon himself the superior leadership, but appointed *Brigadeführer* (major general) Hans Jüttner as his chief of staff.[139] Jüttner would become one of the key organisers of the Waffen-SS. He had fought as a volunteer in the First World War, in 1931 he had joined the SA, and in 1935 he had become a member of the armed SS. Because of his talents and experience he advanced quickly and already one year later he was gazetted to the staff of the *Verfügungstruppe* in Berlin under Paul Hausser.[140] One of Jüttner's first decisions as the chief of staff at *Führungshauptamt* was to subordinate the *Totenkopf Standarte*'s filler units under the Waffen-SS, strengthening his, and ultimately Himmler's, control of these units. The filler units used to be under Theodor Eicke's command, but henceforth Jüttner would be the one responsible for their formation, equipment and training.[141]

Recruitment under Stress

The establishment of new SS divisions put considerable pressure on the recruitment system, and in 1940, systematic recruitment of non-German Germanic volunteers commenced while, at the same time, the Waffen-SS increased its enlistment of *Volksdeutsche*. However, still the focus of attention was on recruits from within the German borders.[142]

135. Stein (1984), p 32.
136. Sydnor (1990), p 46. On recruitment of personnel for the *Division Totenkopf*, see also Rohrkamp (2010), p 323.
137. Rohrkamp (2010), p 323.
138. RGVA, 1372/5/22, RFSS order of 18 August 1940 on establishing the *Führungshauptamt* as well as other material concerning this case.
139. Ibid. See also Cüppers (2011), p 90.
140. Jan Erik Schulte, 'Hans Jüttner. Der Mann im Hintergrund der Waffen-SS' in Smelser and Syring (2003), pp 276ff.
141. Se Sydnor (1990), p 133.
142. See, inter alia, BAB, NS19/1863, Letter from Berger to Himmler, *Werbung Volksdeutscher und Männer germanischer Blutes,*17 June 1940. See also Stein (1984), pp 46ff.

The whole issue of recruitment in Germany comprised a potential for conflict with the *Wehrmacht*. Germany conscripted recruits and was at war, so the Waffen-SS could not just circumvent the three services and enlist any one they fancied. National servicemen were shared according to an agreed basis for distribution with 66 percent army, 25 percent air force and 9 percent navy. Since the Waffen-SS was not part of this equation, filling up its new divisions would indeed be a very distant prospect (with the exception of the *Verfügungsdivision* that was made up of already existing regiments).[143] However, with impressive administrative dexterity the SS got around this difficulty by transferring large numbers of men directly from the *Totenkopf Standarten* to *Division Totenkopf* and the police division. As these men were already in the SS, they were under Himmler's command and at his disposal. This meant that, within the existing set of rules, which were already approved by Hitler, the SS could recruit for the *Totenkopf Standarten* without worrying about the *Wehrmacht*. Moreover, employment with these units exempted the men from service with the armed forces of the *Wehrmacht*. In this way, the Waffen-SS actually circumvented the *Wehrmacht*'s monopoly as well as the agreements on recruitment.[144]

One possible source for recruitment was the SA. Himmler had ordered that, in January 1940, the SA would have to place personnel from all over Germany at the Waffen-SS' disposal. However, this failed to produce the desired result.[145] What appeared during 1940 was instead the contours of increasing reliance on more or less forced enrolment. In May 1940, Berger admitted that, here and there in Bavaria, there had been incidents of 'more or less compulsory' drafting of conscripts and that methods had been applied, which he categorised as 'unbecoming' for the SS.[146] One such case concerned 57 workers at the dockyard in Danzig, all of them members of the SS, who had been asked to fill in a form concerning 'voluntary obligation' to report for service with the Waffen-SS. A letter sent personally to two SS men, reminded them of their obligation as members of the SS to 'unqualified obedience.' Further, they were told that everyone suffering a hero's death died for the German people and that this was 'a nobler blessing than what any church could offer.' Therefore, the letter writer, *Oberscharführer* Wilhelm Oswald, took for granted that the recipients 'would obey and report for duty [...] with their forms filled in and two photos' – and if they did not, they would be punished.[147] Not surprisingly, the *Wehrmacht*'s local recruiting office was not pleased since, as a matter of principle, they had all potential servicemen at their disposal. There were many such incidents bearing witness to the fact that SS employees acted creatively using various ruses and tricks to bypass the rules agreed with the *Wehrmacht*.[148]

---

143. Stein (1984), pp 34ff.
144. Ibid., pp 23, 38ff. and 102ff.
145. BAB, NS19/1863, Letter of 16 January 1940 from Berger to Himmler, *Musterungen in der SA*.
146. BAB, NS19/1863, Letter of 4 May 1940 from Berger to the chief of staff of *SS-Oberabschnitt Süd*, *SS-Brigadeführer* Jaegy. See also Cüppers (2011), p 86.
147. BAMA, RH14/44. Letter of 27 May 1940, *An die SS-Bewerber Hentschel u. Schalau*.
148. For more examples see BAMA, RH14/44.

On the Attack

On 10 May, the German invasion of France and the Benelux countries began. Army Group B attacked the Netherlands and northern Belgium, while Army Group A advanced into Luxembourg and southern Belgium towards France. Two Waffen-SS formations were foreseen to play a role in the initial offensive – the *Leibstandarte* and the *Verfügungsdivision*. Both were under operational control of Army Group B and participated in the attack on the Netherlands.[149] During the first phase, the police division was reserve behind Army Group C, but was later to follow in the wake of General Heinz Guderian's armoured group under Army Group A.[150] To Eicke's chagrin, *Division Totenkopf* was part of the OKH reserve and therefore not participating in the first attack wave. But thanks to the rapid advance of the German troops, in order to join General Hermann Hoth's fifth *Panzerkorps* under Army Group A, this division was set in motion through the southern Netherlands and Belgium less than a week later.[151]

On 10 May in the morning, surprising a group of Dutch frontier guards the *Leibstandarte* advanced into the Netherlands. Opposition was slack and, within a matter of 48 hours, the formation's motorbike company – under the command of the later commander of *Division Hitlerjugend*, Kurt Meyer – had advanced more than 100 km into the country.[152] On 14 May, *Leibstandarte* moved into Rotterdam, which, by then, had been reduced by aerial bombardment and, therefore, offered only limited resistance. On the way to Rotterdam the *Leibstandarte* was involved in heavy fighting during the assault on the Grebbe defensive line north-west of Utrecht along with the *Regiment der Führer* of the *Verfügungsdivision*.[153] For three days, 11–13 May, the well-entrenched Dutch soldiers fought fiercely against the German attackers.[154] During the fight, the commanding officer of one of the battalions, the former concentration camp commandant Hilmar Wäckerle, tried to break through the lines advancing behind a human shield of Dutch prisoners-of-war. As this miscarried, the men attempted anew this time by dressing in Dutch uniforms.[155]

On 13 May, the Germans unleashed a violent air attack on Sedan followed by the crossing of the river Meuse. While as early as the evening of the same day three Germans bridgeheads had been established around the city, French resistance

149. Weingartner (1974), p 39; Otto Weidinger, *Kameraden bis zum Ende: der Weg des SS-Panzergrenadier-Regiments 4 »DF« 19391945: Die Geschichte einer deutsch-österreichischen Kampfgemeinschaft* (Plesse-Verlag, 1962), p 37; James Lucas, *Das Reich: The Military Role of the 2nd SS Division* (Cassell, 2006), p 37; Stein (1984), p 61.
150. Stein (1984), p 61; Kurt-Gerhard Klietmann, *Die Waffen-SS: Eine Dokumentatio* (Der Freiwillige, 1965), p 123; Husemann (1971), vol. 1, pp 25ff.
151. Sydnor (1990), pp 86 and 91.
152. Weingartner (1974), p 39.
153. Gerbet (1995), p 124.
154. Klietmann (1965), p 89; Weidinger (1962), pp 29ff.
155. Gerard Tewwisscha van Scheltinga, *Trouw zonder eer. Het gewelddadige leven van eenSS-officier* (Aspekt, 2008), p 272.

in the area collapsed.[156] On 15 May in the morning, merely five days after the launch of the initial attack – the French prime minister, M Paul Reynaud, telephoned his British colleague, Winston Churchill, to tell him that, 'We have been defeated [...] The front is broken near Sedan; they are pouring through in great numbers with tanks and armoured cars.'[157] His prophesy turned out correct. Four days later, the first German troops reached Abbeville on the coast of the Channel, and the Franco-British forces in Belgium were cut off from their French hinterland.

Over the following days, the Allies launched a desperate counter-attack south to re-establish contact. The *Leibstandarte* and the *Totenkopf* were moved to the area around Arras to check the Allied operation. For close to two weeks, the two divisions were involved in a sequence of engagements with French and British troops supported by armour.[158] On 19 May, as the *Totenkopf* was under way, it got its baptism of fire in a number of villages in close combat with Franco-Moroccan soldiers followed up by tank attacks.[159] On 22 May, the *Leibstandarte* sensed the aftermath of the failed Allied counter-attack, as weak French forces attacked near Valenciennes.[160] On 24 May, the OKH ordered a temporary halt to the advance on Dunkirk. On the same day, the *Leibstandarte* had taken up positions on the Aa Canal and, ignoring the order, soldiers from the division crossed the canal and took the village Watten as well as the hills behind it.[161] A few days later, the *Leibstandarte* launched an attack from Watten against Wormhoudt, 20 km south of Dunkirk. In the afternoon of the 28th, after a day's hard combat Leibstandarte-soldiers took the town, where they committed one of the western campaign's gravest German war crimes by murdering between 80 and 100 British prisoners-of-war.[162]

With respect to the scope of crimes against prisoners-of-war and civilians the campaign in the west differed a lot from the onslaught on Poland the previous year. In France, the Netherlands and Belgium the overall numbers were now considerably lower. The reason was, primarily, that the Nazis perceived their opponents as members of a nobler race than the citizens of Poland. Nonetheless, there are examples of atrocities, such as the massacre at Wormhoudt and the atrocities committed by both the army and the Waffen-SS against black soldiers in service with French colonial units. Comparatively, the Waffen-SS committed more crimes against civilians and prisoners-of-war than the army, and especially the *Totenkopf* earned themselves a bad record.[163]

---

156. Frieser (2012), pp 173ff.; Jackson (2004), pp 44ff.
157. Jackson (2004), p 9.
158. Sydnor (1990), pp 91ff.; Weingartner (1974), p 42.
159. Sydnor (1990), p 93.
160. Weingartner (1974), p 42.
161. Ibid., pp 42ff.
162. Cecilie Damgaard Carlsen and Henry Lias Büchmann Nielsen, *Waffen-SS på Vestfronten. Et studium af massakrerne på allierede krigsfanger 1940 og 1944* (RUC, unpublished thesis, 2012), pp 58ff. In IfZG, NO-605 there are some German Photostats, which are, however, blemished by bad quality.
163. Johannes Hürter, *Hitlers Heerführer: die deutschen Oberbefehlshaberim Krieg gegen die Sowjetunion 1941/42* (Oldenburg, 2007), p 188; Lieb (2007), p 19, Raffael Scheck, *Hitler's African Victims: The German Army Massacres of Black French Soldiers in 1940* (Cambridge University Press, 2006).

Out of an estimated 600 civilians and prisoners killed during the campaign, this division accounted for 260.[164] At more occasions, the *Division Totenkopf* shot black or Arabic French colonial soldiers. On 19 June, for instance its soldiers refused to take prisoners and shot all 30 Moroccans involved in the clash.[165] The *Totenkopf* soldiers also were responsible for the most well-known crime during the western campaign. On 27 May, at Le Paradis they massacred almost 100 men of the Royal Norfolk Regiment who had barricaded themselves in a farm, where they kept the Waffen-SS at bay until they ran out of ammunition.[166]

Since the German army was not superior in terms of modern equipment its quick victory in the west came unexpectedly to all. What made the success was – apart from the tactical employment of substantial air forces – the ability and the determination to concentrate large forces in what the Germans saw as the decisive sector; the Ardennes and the Sedan area.

While the Waffen-SS played an insignificant role in the overall victory, its formations performed better in the west than during the Polish campaign. It was a mixed record, however, the combat power of the *Regiment der Führer*, for instance, was criticised by the army.[167] Conversely, in the autumn of the same year, the *Regiment Deutschland*, also of the *Verfügungsdivision*, was praised for its contribution to the fights. Not least, this applied to Felix Steiner – later to become commander of *Division Wiking* – who was awarded the Knight's Cross.[168] After the campaign in the west, six Waffen-SS soldiers received Knight's Crosses – among them notably the commanding officer of the *Leibstandarte*, Sepp Dietrich.[169] This did, however, not translate into public acclaim. In Hitler's October 1939 victory address he failed to mention the role of SS units in the Polish campaign, and the Waffen-SS only occupied a minor place in Hitler's speech in the Reichstag on 19 July 1940 – on par with signal and logistics units.[170]

Among the indicators of a mediocre military performance was that the casualty rates had been huge. After merely eighteen days' contact with the enemy, and of

---

164. Lieb (2007), p 19, note 22. Because of uncertainty, numbers of killed black French soldiers do not figure. While Lieb having scrutinised the sources estimates that 'die Opferzahl mehrere Hundert betrug, vielleicht sogar auch im Tausenderbereich lag' (ibid., p 18), Scheck believes – with a point of departure in non-corroborated testimonies that the number would lie between 1,500 and 3,000. According to him various army divisions committed such killings (see table 1, pp 54ff. in Scheck (2006). On the numbers mentioned, see Raffael Scheck, '"They Are Just Savages": German Massacres of Black Soldiers from the French Army in 1940', *The Journal of Modern History*, Vol. 77, No. 2, June 2005, p 325,
165. Sydnor (1990), p 117.
166. NAKEW, WO308/734 *Le Paradis, War Crimes Interrogation Unit*, 1946. See also ibid., pp 104ff.
167. BAB, NS19/3501.
168. BAB, SS0 153B, SS-Personalhauptamt, *RK Vorschlag, No. 166*, no date.
169. Stein (1984), pp 90ff.
170. Lehnhardt (2017), p 204.

these only seven days of intensive combat, the *Totenkopf* had lost 1,152 men which was a little more than 10 percent of the formation's effective combat strength. It was particularly serious that 300 officers had been killed or wounded, and this forced Himmler to find filler personnel at the *Junkerschule* in Bad Tölz – officer cadets who had not yet finished their training.[171] Also other Waffen-SS formations had had many casualties among their officers. It was worst in the *Verfügungsdivision*, which had had 2,020 casualties as early as the beginning of June.[172] After the French capitulation, it was therefore a top priority of Himmler's to get new recruits and to further expand the Waffen-SS.

Recruitment and Expansion after the Victory in the West

On 30 June 1940, the SS numbered 316,000 men of which the Waffen-SS counted 105,000; active as well as reservists.[173] In seven years, the military branch of the SS had grown from small bands of men with light arms to a regular military force. Still, the Waffen-SS' handful of divisions paled beside the army's far more than one hundred.[174]

After the conquest of adjacent Germanic states to the north and west, the opportunity arose to recruit more systematically in neighbouring countries. The effort to draft manpower outside Germany's borders was, however, less about getting additional hands, and more about extending the influence of the SS to the newly conquered states. Between 1940 and December 1940, the SS set up recruitment offices in Copenhagen, Oslo and The Hague.[175] These offices were meant to provide personnel to *Standarte Nordland* in Vienna and *Standarte Westland* in Munich – two new regiments to be manned by volunteers from Scandinavia vis. the Benelux countries.[176] The same year, a Waffen-SS introductory course was set up in Sennheim in order to train and ideologically indoctrinate such recruits. In December 1940, Steiner was appointed commander of a newly raised division, the 5th *SS Division Germania* (shortly after renamed *Wiking*), comprising the regiments

---

171. Sydnor (1990), pp 119 and 112.

172. Stein (1984), pp 73 and 81.

173. BAB, NS48/1/2, *Statistisches Jahrbuch der Schutzstaffel der NSDAP 1940. Entwurf.* This number does not seem to agree with the 124,199 men mentioned earlier as being present prior to the attack on France, the Netherlands and Belgium. See Rohrkamp (2010), pp 321ff. This discrepancy might be explained by different ways of counting the personnel depending on whom were considered Waffen-SS. The aggregate losses during the campaign in the west counted less than 20,000.

174. Julian Jackson, *France: The Dark Years, 1940–1944* (Oxford University Press, 2003), p 33.

175. Terje Emberland and Matthew Kott, *Himmlers Norge: Nordmenn i det storgermanske prosjekt* (Aschehoug., 2012.), p 199.

176. BAB, NS19/132. Letter of 7 June 1940 from Himmler to von Brauchitsch.

Germania, Westland and *Nordland*.[177] Waffen-SS recruitment was also supplemented by additional campaigns among the ethnic German minorities east and south of Germany; and in Romania in particular the SS achieved success in generating more manpower.[178] Nonetheless, these new efforts did not achieve remarkable results in 1940, and failed to live up to Himmler's ambition.[179]

---

177. Peter Strassner, *Europäische Freiwillige: die Geschichte der 5. SS-Panzerdivision Wiking*, 2. verb. Aufl. (Munin Verlag, 1968), p 22. Moreover, in the first documents the *Wiking* is referred to as the 'Nordic Division'. BAB, NS19/3506, *Führungshauptamt, Aufstellung einer leichten Nachrichten Kolonne f. nord. Division*, 12.11.1940.

178. BAB, NS19/1863, Letter of 17 June 1940 from Berger to Himmler, *Werbung Volksdeutscher und Männer germanischer Blutes*.

179. Jean-Luc Leleu, *La Waffen-SS: Soldats politiques en guerre* (Librairie Académique Perrin, 2007), chapter 3. See also BAB, NS48/1/2, *Statistisches Jahrbuch der Schutzstaffel der NSDAP 1940. Entwurf.* Rohrkamp (2010), pp 321ff.

Chapter Three

WAR OF EXTERMINATION

On 2 July 1941 – some two weeks after the Nazi attack on the Soviet Union – one of division *Wiking's* Dutch volunteers drew a y-shaped death rune in his diary. Next to the rune he wrote the name of his regiment's commanding officer *Standartenführer* Hilmar Wäckerle. An SS veteran and former commandant of the concentration camp Dachau, Wäckerle had found his death on the very same day hit by a bullet – possibly from a sniper. The remainder of that day's diary note ran 'No 1 Company spend their time off shooting Jews, who have been involved in "partisan activity"'.[1] This sentence hinted at a bloody extermination of Jews, which had been initiated by *Wiking* soldiers and local Ukrainian extremists. Two of the major characteristics of the invasion, which *Division Wiking* was now a part of, is in a way condensed in this brief diary note. Like the German formations generally, the SS divisions were to suffer immense casualties – even among high-ranking officers like Wäckerle. Moreover, the campaign engendered a further radicalisation of the German policy towards Jews and other groups of civilians, and the Nazi occupation regime in the East, and soldiers of the *Waffen-SS* would become important pawns in this process.

Dating back to fall 1940, Hitlers intention to attack the Soviet Union materialised in December 1940 as *Weisung Nr. 21* (Instruction No 21) *Fall Barbarossa*.[2] Through the attack Germany wished to achieve liberty of action in the area from the Baltic Sea to the Urals and wanted to facilitate a massive 'ethnic reorganisation', which would eventually cost millions of Soviet citizens their lives. These plans were obvious from the succession of orders and directives conceived by the top-level German civil and military authorities prior to the attack. On 13 March 1941, the *OKW* disseminated the *Richtlinien auf Sondergebieten zur Weisung nr. 21* (guidelines concerning certain areas covered by Instruction No 21). Himmler's SS and police units thus assumed an independent role moving with the military vanguard in order to 'pacify' the areas conquered by the army. In other words, they were meant to commit systematic atrocities on a grand scale.[3] Shortly afterwards, the *OKH* distributed a document describing and controlling the role of the *SD*'s (the SS intelligence service) *Sonderkommandos* in the area of operation. *Sonderkommandos* were sub-units of the four *Einsatzgruppen*, A, B, C and D, and were to

---

1. NIOD, 244/991, diary of M.R., 2 July 1941.
2. *Weisung nr. 21*, reprint in Walther Hubatsch (Ed.), *Hitlers Weisungen für die Kriegführung 1939–1945: Dokumente des Oberkommandos der Wehrmacht* (Dorfler im Nebel-Verl.,2000), p 84ff.
3. *OKW, Richtlinien auf Sondergebieten zur Weisung Nr. 21*, 13 March 1941, reprinted as document No. 1 in Buchheim et al. (1994), pp 478–481.

operate in the areas of responsibility of Army Groups North, Centre and South, as well as in the Crimea and in the Caucasus.[4] The collaboration between the killing units and the army generally ran smoothly culminating in the enormous massacre at Babiy Yar. Here, the army command and the *Sonderkommando 4 a* collaborated efficiently, registering, collecting and killing the town's Jewish population. During three days from 29 September 1941 onwards, the SS men attached to the *Sonderkommando* killed about 33,000 Jews with the army's full approval and support.[5]

Two more directives had direct effect on the troops' combat behaviour. The so-called *Gerichtsbarkeitserlass* (ordinance on administration of justice) disseminated in May of the same year, cancelled the obligation to prosecute crimes perpetrated by soldiers against the civilian population in the Soviet Union.[6] The reason given was that the troops must be able to 'defend themselves without mercy against any threat by the hostile population' and without fear that they might be prosecuted. Therefore, this ordinance comprised a catalogue of measures which could legally be applied when confronted with opposition by the locals. Civilians taking up arms should be shot out of hand as if 'trying to escape arrest'. Officers from commanding officers upwards might implement collective punitive action such as the torching of villages, whence the troops had been ambushed. One passage was emblematic of the whole spirit of this ordinance, and of the upcoming battles as a whole, namely that all suspects were to be brought before an officer right away. Then, without any legal proceedings, he would decide, if the suspect should be shot or let go.[7]

In June, furthermore, the *OKW* issued the so-called *Kommissarbefehl* (Commissar Order) according to which all Red Army political commissars should be killed upon seizure. In case that these were not identified until later, as for instance upon arrival in a prisoner-of-war camp, they were to be handed over to the *Sonderkommandos*, who would then undertake the killing.[8] The *Kommissarbefehl* and the *Gerichtsbarkeitserlass* were not the only violations of international law with regard to prisoners of war. The living

---

4. Draft OKH Order concerning *SD's Sonderkommandos* in the area of operation, 26 March 1941, reprinted as document No. 2 in ibid., pp 482–483. Final OKH Order: *Regelung des Einsatzes der Sicherheitspolizei und des SD im Verbande des Heeres, 28.4.1941*, reprinted as document No. 3, ibid., pp 483–485.
5. Bernd Boll and Hans Safrian, 'Auf dem Weg nach Stalingrad. Die 6. Armee' in Hannes Heer and Klaus Naumann, *Vernichtungskrieg: Verbrechen der Wehrmacht 1941–1944* (Zweitausendeins, 1995), pp 260–296. For the Wehrmacht's role in Holocaust in Belarus, see Waitman Wade Beorn, *Marching into Darkness: The Wehrmacht and the Holocaust in Belarus* (Harvard University Press, 2014), p 64ff.
6. About the Einsatzgruppen's tasks as they were described before Barbarossa, see Angrick (2003), p 104ff. About the systematic murder of the Soviet Jews, see, interalia, Helmut Krausnick, *Hitlers Einsatzgruppen: die Truppe des Weltanschauungskrieges 1938–1942*, Durchges. Ausg. (Fischer-Taschenbuch-Verl., 1998).
7. *Richtlinien für die Behandlung politischer Kommissare*, 6 June 1941. Reprinted as document No. 12 in Ibid., pp 500–503. See also document No. 13 in ibid., p 503.
8. *Erlass über die Ausübung der Kriegsgerichtsbarkeit im Gebiet 'Barbarossa' und über besondere Maßnahmen der Truppe*, 13 May 1941. Reprinted as document No. 8 in Buchheim et al. (1994), pp 493–498.

conditions in prisoner-of-war camps along with numerous executions of prisoners entailed that a staggering 3.3 million out of 5 million Soviet soldiers died in German custody during the war.[9]

While the *Kommissarbefehl* as well as the *Gerichtsbarkeitserlass* were internal, secret documents, which the common soldier should not know in detail, the general outline of these were communicated to the troops right down to the lowest level through the *Richtlinienfür das Verhalten der Truppe in Russland* (Guide Lines for the Conduct of the Troops in Russia), which were read aloud to the troops immediately before the attack was launched. The initial lines went: 'Bolshevism is the mortal enemy of the National Socialist German people. This subversive ideology and its supporters are the objective of Germany's struggle. This fight requires ruthless and energetic action against Bolshevist smear campaigners, saboteurs, *franc-tireurs*, and Jews as well as complete neutralisation of any kind of active or passive resistance.'[10] The Soviet soldiers were characterised as persons of whom all sort of dirty tricks were to be expected. Allegedly, this was true specifically of the Red Army's Asian soldiery, who were described as 'inscrutable, unpredictable, treacherous and insensitive'.[11]

Over the following years, the above-mentioned orders as well as the succession of declarations conceived at lower levels were to shape warfare on the Eastern Front. German front soldiers committed countless war crimes, and in the hinterland the SS and the police – assisted by the armed forces and German civil authorities – perpetrated systematic extermination of Soviet Jews and mass murder of Romani, communist activists and the mentally ill. Moreover, counter insurgency operations – in particular in Belarus – frequently developed into massacres of the civilian population.[12]

---

9. Alfred Streim, *Die Behandlung sowjetischer Kriegsgefangener im 'Fall Barbarossa' eine Dokumentation unter Berücksichtigung der Unterlagen deutscher Strafverfolgungsbehörden und der Materialien der Zentralen Stelle der Landesjustizverwaltungen zur Aufklärung von NS-Verbrechen* (Müller, Juristischer Verlag, 1981), and Christian Streit, *Keine Kameraden: die Wehrmacht und die sowjetischen Kriegsgefangenen 1941–1945* (Dt. Verlagsanst., 1978).
10. AOK 17, 4.6.1941. Richtlinien für das Verhaltender Truppe in Russland. Reprinted as document No. 11 in Buchheim et al. (1994), pp 499–500, here p 499.
11. Ibid p 499.
12. See, interalia, relevant chapters in Horst Boog, Jürgen Forster and Joachim Hoffmann, *Der Angriffaufdie Sowjetunion* (Fischer Taschenbuchverlag, 1991): Jürgen Forster, 'Das Unternehmen "Barbarossa" als Eroberungs- und Vernichtungskrieg' (s.479–541), Jurgen Forster, 'Die Sicherung des "Lebensraumes"' (pp 1202–1288) and Rolf-Dieter Muller, 'Das Scheitern der wirtschaftlichen "Blitzkriegstrategie"' (in particular pp 1168–1201). Over the last decade, a number of studies have revealed regional differences. Christian Gerlach, *Kalkulierte Morde: die deutsche Wirtschafts- und Vernichtungspolitik in Weißrusland 1941 bis 1944* (Hamburger Edition, 1999); Seppo Myllyniemi, *Die Neuordnung der Baltischen Länder, 1941–1944: nationalsozialistischen Inhalt der deutschen Besatzungspolitik* (SuomenHistoriallinenSeura, 1973); Karel C. Berkhoff, *Harvest of Despair: Life and Death in Ukraine under Nazi Rule* (Belknap Press of Harvard University Press, 2004). On the parts of the Leningrad Region under German occupation, see Johannes Due Enstad, *Soviet Citizens under German Occupation. Life, Death and Power in Northwest Russia 1941–1944*, Ph.D. dissertation, University of Oslo, 2013.

Balkan Interlude

On 27 March 1941, while preparations for Barbarossa was ongoing the pro-German Yugoslav government fell in a *coup d'état*. While on the same day, Hitler ordered attacks against Yugoslavia and Greece, Himmler discussed the situation at a meeting with Heydrich and the head of his secretariat, Karl Wolff.[13] The day after, he ordered his only available motorised division, *Das Reich*, to be deployed from France to Romania, whence it was to join the attack.[14] On 6 April, the actual invasion was launched including violent air assaults on the capital, Belgrade, which cost at least 1,500 human lives.[15]

Even before the final decision was taken to attack Yugoslavia, the German armed forces' leadership had initiated planning for Operation Marita, an assault on Greece. Therefore, from February 1941 onwards Axis forces, including the *Leibstandarte* (now a brigade), were being deployed to Bulgaria and Romania, which were allied with Germany. The two attacks were now combined and especially the *Leibstandarte* participated in heavy fighting when entering Greece. Even before the last Allied troops left mainland Greece on 30 April, the *Leibstandarte* had crossed the Patras Bay to Peloponnesus and reached, together with 5[th]Armoured Division, the extreme south of Greece.[16] *Das Reich* employment in the Balkan campaign was not extensive and the divisions total number of casualties in Yugoslavia amounted to a mere 30 killed plus an unknown number of wounded and missing.[17] Shortly after the conquest of Belgrade on 17 April, Yugoslavia capitulated. The next day, 18 April, in revenge for an ambush on an SS man, the *Das Reich Division* executed 36 Serbs.[18] This event in its own way demonstrated the beginning of an immensely brutal occupation regime, which would, over the next four years, cost around a million human lives, and with the Waffen-SS very much involved in the atrocities.

Lowering the Recruitment Standards

While *Leibstandarte* and *Das Reich* fought in the Balkans, the preparations for Barbarossa went ahead in the central SS offices in Berlin. In the days around 9 April, Himmler appointed three out of four future HSSPFs (*Höher SS Polizeiführer*) for the Soviet

---

13. Witte et al. (1999), p 140.
14. Stein (1984), p 28. While the Leibstandarte was already deployed to Bulgaria with a view to taking part in the attack on Greece, the Totenkopf Division was at the disposal of Operation Attila, the codename for a possible German invasion of Vichy-France. Sydnor (1990), p 161, note 16.
15. Detlef Vogel, 'Der deutsche Überfall auf Jugoslawien und Griechenland', in Schreiber et al. (1984), p 458.
16. Weingartner (1974), p 52ff. Detlef Vogel in Schreiber et al. (1984), p 481.
17. This has been calculated on the basis of SS records showing that the losses during the Balkan campaign had been 105 killed. To get to Das Reich's losses one must deduct those of the Leibstandarte, totalling 72 killed. BAB, NS19/2109, Letter of 31 August 1942 from Dr. Korherr to Himmler, *Die Kriegsverluste der SS nach dem Stand der statistischen Erfassung vom 15. Juli 1942.*
18. Shepherd (2012) p 87.

Union. Shortly afterwards, he achieved the army's approbation that not only would SS police chiefs be active in the hinterland, they could also receive reinforcement from the SS, and the police who could act without army supervision.[19] As a supplement to the *SD*'s *Sonderkommandos*, Himmler set up a number of new SS units, among which were the two motorised brigades, the first and the second SS Infantry Brigades. Moreover, in September 1941, the two existing cavalry regiments had been joined in the *SS-Kavallerie-Brigade* under the command of Hermann Fegelein.[20]

The month of May saw renewed large-scale recruiting efforts in Germany as well as in occupied Northern Europe. Like the year before, pressure and threats were employed in order to ascertain sufficient numbers.[21] In early April 1941, the *Standarte Nordwest* was also raised for Dutch and Flemish volunteers. Men recruited for this unit did not have to live up to the general physical SS standards and were therefore not eligible as members of the SS Order.[22] After the Soviet Union had been attacked, it was decided to raise a new kind of units, national legions, for Germanic volunteers. During summer 1941, this led to setting up the Legion Norway, Free Corps Denmark, and a Dutch and a Flemish legion. In relation to the self-perception of the SS, it was even more

Figure 3.1 Personnel from the *SS Polizei Division* on horseback in Russia in the late summer of 1941 (Frihedsmuseet)

---

19. According to Himmler's service diary, on 8 April 1941 he had a meeting on Barbarossa with the head of ORPO, Daluege. And on 9 April 1941 he met the head of *SS-Hauptamt Verwaltung und Wirtschaft*, Otto Pohl, on the same topic. Witte (1999), p 146ff. Concerning the appointment of HSSPFs, see ibid. and Cuppers (2011), p 63ff.
20. Cüppers (2011), p 28, 70ff.
21. BAB, NS19/3518, Letter of 16 June 1941 from Berger to Dr Brandt, *Beschwerde OKW uber Mai-Aktion*; Stein (1984), p 151ff.
22. Stein (1984), p 150.

remarkable that, also in the first half of 1941, a Finnish volunteer unit was raised. The formation at the end of June of *SS-Freiwilligen Bataillon Nordost* (SS Volunteer Battalion North-East), whose ca 750 soldiers were attached to *Division Wiking*, signalled that future SS soldiers might not necessarily have to be of Nordic-Germanic race. Although there were Swedes among those recruited, in the Nazi perspective the Finnish majority was racially inferior.[23] In fact, the SS' notion of race anlog with its recruitment policy was undergoing a gradual re-definition and development, which, over the years to come, would fundamentally change the composition of the *Waffen-SS*.

As a supplement to the existing divisions, and with a view to being deployed to the northern-most front, a new SS formation, the *SS Kampfgruppe Nord* (SS Battle Group North), was raised – soon to be re-designated *SS Division Nord*. Its units were moved via north Norway to northern Finland where they were to cross the border into the Soviet Union.[24] In early June, additional SS units moved into staging areas on the Soviet border. While *Totenkopf* was now in East Prussia, *Das Reich* and *Wiking* were in Lublin, and the *Leibstandarte* was in the Prague area.[25] Moreover, also the two SS infantry brigades and the cavalry regiments were being concentrated in the *Gouvernement-Général*. The *SS Polizei Division*, did not leave France until the attack was set in motion. Nevertheless, almost all available major SS formations were standing ready for the attack.

23. BAB, NS19/539, contains a number of key documents concerning the emergence of this battalion, its training and 1941–1943. See also BAB, NS19/3518, SS-Führungshauptamt Order of 19 June 1941, *Afstellung des SS-Freiwilligen Btl. Nordost*. It appears that, in the spring of 1941, Gottlob Berger probed the flexibility of the racial criteria, which is used to be rather rigid. This becomes obvious as, in April, he suggested to Himmler – in vain though – that 700 Ukrainians be enlisted although merely 10 per cent of these were 'racially acceptable'. Ibid., p 152ff. That these criteria were under pressure can be seen from the contrast between Berger's assurance to Himmler in the spring of 1940 that enlistment in Finland would focus on the Finnish Swedes, begin on the Aaland Isles and avoid 'Mongols'. BAB, NS19/1711, Letter of 29 August 1940 from Berger to Himmler. See also George H. Stein og H. Peter Krosby, 'Das finnische Freiwilligen-Bataillon der Waffen-SS', *Vierteljahrshefte für Zeitgeschichte*, vol. 14, no 4, 1966, pp 413–453.
24. Stein (1984), p 107ff. The two *Totenkopf Standarten* were renamed on this occasion *SS-Infanterieregiment* 6 and 7. On 22 June 1941, Division Nord's total strength was 10,018. BAB, NS19/1520, *SS-Führungshauptamt, Starken und Verluste der SS-Divisionen*, 24 March 1942. See also ibid., p 20, note 3 for almost equal but slightly smaller numbers for the strengths of the SS-divisions at the end of June 1941. The difference is hardly due to combat casualties in between, but rather reflect the uncertainty which characterised many SS reports on strength and casualties. See also Franz Schreiber, *Kampf unter dem Nordlicht: deutsch-finnische Waffenbrüderschaft am Polarkreis; die Geschichte der 6. SS-Gebirgs-Division Nord* (Munin Verlag, 1969), p 34ff.
25. Sydnor (1990), p 155. By the end of June 1941, the Division was at 17,265 men: BAB, NS19/1520, *SS-Führungshauptamt, Starken und Verluste der SS-Divisionen*, 24 March 1942; Stein (1984), p 120, note 3. Das Reich was at 19,026 and Wiking 19,377 men. Although officially the *Leibstandarte* was a division, at 11,535 men it was somewhat below the authorised divisional establishment, as was Division Nord as well: BAB, NS19/1520, *SS-Führungshauptamt, Starken und Verluste der SS-Divisionen*, 24 March 1942. Stein (1984), p 120, note 3.

Figure 3.2 A soldier from the *Totenkopf* division in difficult terrain on the Eastern Front (Frihedsmuseet)

Genocide in the East

With 3.6 million soldiers, 3,600 tanks and 2.700 aircraft Operation Barbarossa was not only to become the largest attack in military history, but also the most atrocious war of extermination and colonisation the world had seen. Bearing in mind how willingly the German armed forces' complied with the orders to eliminate Jews and how openly the Nazi leadership's stated that it wished to eradicate Jewish Bolshevism, it comes as no surprise that the SS troops acted with scaring efficiency, considerable local initiative and often enthusiasm when they committed atrocities and killed civilians. Notably, the *Waffen-SS* units under the *Kommandostab Reichsführer-SS* and the *HSSPFs'* police units became prime movers in radicalising the ongoing activities.

On 10 July, after the swift early advance of the German units, Himmler ordered *HSSPF* Bach-Zelewski to formally take charge of the two SS brigades, the cavalry regiments as well as some police battalions. They were all to be employed in 'security operations' in the occupied territories in the east.[26] Initially, the focus was on the Pripyat Marshes. This vast area of swamps and brushwood, with almost no roads, lay in Poland, Belarus and Ukraine. Initially, the army had enveloped the marshes and now feared that the remaining

---

26. Cüppers (2011), p 125ff.

Soviet units might ambush the Germans in their flank. Thus, the army was grateful for Himmler's offer to send considerable SS forces into the swamps.[27]

In August 1941, the cavalry regiments and the second SS Brigade commenced their operations in Pripyat. Right from the outset, these developed into outright killing sprees against the areas large Jewish population group. In many respects this became a turning point where the German atrocities on the Eastern Front transitioned into systematic exterminations of Jews. As early as 7 August, Bach-Zelewski wired Berlin that together the two cavalry regiments units had killed 7,819 people.[28] Merely a week later, Fegelein's *SS-Kavalerie-Regiment 2* reported 14,000 'looters' killed – looters being a euphemism for Jews of both sexes and any age.[29]

In the late summer, other killer units on the Eastern Front began murdering women and children. The unique characteristic of the conduct of the SS mounted units was that they aspired to systematically exterminate all Jews in the areas they passed through. Thus, for example, the *SS-Kavallerie-Regiment 1* commanded by Gustav Lombard reported the 'de-Judaification' of an area of 4,000 km².[30] Having concluded operations in the Pripyat area, the cavalry moved on eastwards through Belarus. This did not lessen the extent of the killings. In early September, the mounted SS units murdered 7,000 Jews in Babruysk.[31]

Division Wiking's Bloody Road through Ukraine

Also, other *Waffen-SS* divisions were deeply involved in the killing of the Soviet Jews from the first days of the invasion. Amongst the front-line units, *Division Wiking* seems to have been the most active contributor to the Holocaust on the Eastern Front in 1941. From 1 July 1941, when this formation passed the big city of Lviv and until sometime into the autumn, its troops participated in numerous killings of members of the Jewish population in Galicia and further into Ukraine.

Soviet security forces had perpetrated a considerable number of massacres on political and other prisoners in Lviv and various other places during the days before the Germans arrived. The total number of those executed in the western parts of the Soviet Union was, according to the NKVD, approximately 10,000 – an estimate which is certainly much too low.[32] In Lviv alone, at least 12,000 prisoners seems to

27. Ibid., p 132ff.
28. NAKEW, HW 16/6, Report on the tapping of German police and SS radio-telegraphy from 3 July to 14 August 1941.
29. VAP, N, RFSS KDOS, bx No. 24, *SS-Kavallerie-Regiment 2, Bericht über den Einsatz Pripjetsümpfe*, 12 August 1941.
30. Cüppers (2011), p 177.
31. Martin Dean, *Encyclopaedia of Camps and Ghettos, 1933–1945* (Ed.) Geoffrey P Megargee, vol. 2 Pt. B. (Indiana Univ. Press, 2012), p 1650.
32. Alexander Kokurin, 'Evacuation of the Convicts from the Prisons of the Latvian SSR People's Commissariat of the Interior 1941' in Andris Caune (Ed.), *Latvia in World War II* (Latvijas vestures institutaapgads, 2000), p 301. This number includes 400 prisoners, who were shot in Lithuania. The reports on prisoners killed are not complete with details from all the prisons and camps in the western part of the USSR, which were ordered to be evacuated.

have been killed.[33] Such events, which, in many places, the soldiers experienced at close quarters, were interpreted through the SS soldiers' ideological filter; just as it had been the case in Poland the previous year. In the eyes of many an SS soldier this was the manifestation of Jewish Bolshevism, which they had heard so much about at school and during training.[34] Already on 28 June, the day when *Wiking* marched into the Soviet Union a Dutch SS soldier noted in his diary that at Kholm he had seen the first corpses of 'genuine Jews' and that they 'had got what they deserved'.[35]

The ideological demonization of the enemy showed its explosive potential as the news of German casualties began to arrive. Thus, for instance, when, on 2 July 1941, the commanding officer of the *Westland* regiment, Hilmar Wäckerle, was killed, his death was attributed to an ambush by a 'Jewish partisan'. For this reason, a village close by was torched and Galicia's Jewish population was made free prey to the soldiers of the division.[36] Even the same day, *Westland* men went 'partisan shooting.' They simply rounded up and killed whomever might be identified as a Jew by dress or by speaking Yiddish. According to one eye witness, a soldier of the division's bakery company, Jews caught in nearby Zloczow were forced to run the gauntlet while soldiers beat them with rifle butts and stabbed them with bayonets. Thereupon they were shot. The same evening, the division informed that Wäckerle had been killed by a Jewish sniper, and that *Wiking* soldiers were now free to shoot any Jew en route during their advance.[37]

On 3 July 1941, a massacre of between 600 and 830 Jews took place in Zborob. According to an *Einsatzgruppe* report this was an action performed by the *Waffen-SS* in retaliation for Soviet atrocities.[38] Apparently, *Division Wiking* was behind this.[39] On the day after, the 4th of July, soldiers of the same formation struck again, this time in the town Tarnopil. Here, 10 German

---

33. Jan Gross, *Revolution from Abroad* (Princetown University Press, 2002), p 179–181. A somewhat lower number is found in Bogdan Musial, *'Konterrevolutionäre Elemente sind zu erschießen'. Die Brutalisierung des deutschsowjetischen Krieges im Sommer 1941* (Propyläen, 2000), p 98ff.

34. For the testimony by a soldier of Division Wiking on the killings of Jews in Galizia and the prior anti-Jewish teaching of his unit, see YV, O.53, 137, affidavit by H.O.O. in Nuremberg 24 [?] July 1947 (Nuremberg document 4434), p 9.

35. NIOD, 244/991, Diary by M.R., entry of 28 June 1941.

36. See later in this book for discussions of different versions of the death of Wäckerle.

37. YV, O.53, 137, affidavit by H.O.O. in Nuremberg 24 [?] July 1947 (Nuremberg document 4434), p 9. Concerning Westland soldiers' Jew hunt, see NIOD, 244/991, diary by M.R., entry of 2 July 1941. This is thoroughly described in Terwisscha van Scheltinga (2008), p 349ff.

38. The highest number appears from Soviet investigation; the lowest from the reports by the Einsatzgruppen. Martin Dean, Encyclopaedia of Camps and Ghettos, 1933–1945: Ghettos in German-Occupied East Europe, Mel Hecker (Ed.), vol. 2. Pt. A. (Indiana University Press, 2012), p 849. Ereignismeldung UdSSR Nr. 19, 11.7.1941, reprinted in Klaus-Michael Mallmann, Andrej Angrick, Jürgen Matthaus og Martin Cüppers, *Die 'Ereignismeldungen UdSSR' 1941* (Wissenschaftliche Buchgesellschaft, 2011), p 104.

39. On the same day, IV Korps reported that units of Division Wiking wew blocking the roads between Lviv and Zolochiv. Moreover, 'Einzelne Angehörige der Div. gehen inzwischen auf

soldiers were found dead in the town's prison and an extensive pogrom was launched by *Einsatzkommando 4b*. Using arson and hand grenades *Wiking* soldiers destroyed Jewish homes.[40] The town's synagogue was razed as well. A Dutch volunteer commented, 'What a beautiful sight it was to see the Chief Rabbi dangling from the tower of his synagogue and subsequently torch it'.[41] Thousands of Jews were killed in this pogrom by the combined efforts of Ukrainian partisans, German soldiers and SS men. It is uncertain how many of the killings should be attributed to *Wiking* soldiers but, alone in one action, men of the division murdered 80 Jews after they had been forced to clean the town's slaughter house.[42] Moreover, in late July and early August 1941 *Wiking* men appear to have been involved in killings in the cities of Hrymajliv, Husiatyn, Tarashcha, Talnoye, Berdichev, Zhitomir, Smila and Dneprodzerzhinsk.[43] Most of these actions were perpetrated by reserve, baker, butcher, workshop and engineer sub-units, which had nothing to do in the front lines.[44]

Himmler paid several visits to his SS formations on the Eastern Front, and he also visited western Ukraine at, approximately, the time when *Division Wiking*

Juden jagen'. HLC, Private archive Terje Emberland, Box 1, copy of report of 3 July 1941, at 10.30 a.m. to the chief of the general staff of IV Korps. A testimony by a German prisoner-of-war in Soviet custody given in 1947 concerning Regiment Westland's liquidation of 500 persons appears to concern the same incident. RGVA, 451/P, 5/151.

40. Mallmann et. al. (2011), p 133; Dean (2012), p 837. On the 10 German soldiers, who are also mentioned in the above Ereignismeldung, see BAMA, RW 2/148, Letter of 7 July 1941 from *Art. Kommandeur 129 Stadtkommandant Tarnopol to Wehrmachtsauskunftstelle für Kriegsgräber und Kriegerverluste*.

41. NIOD, 244/1254, diary W., P.A.G. In a nearby town, too, Wiking soldiers torched the synagogue. YV, O.53, 137, affidavit by H.O.O. in Nuremberg 24 [?] July 1947 (Nuremberg document 4434), p 11.

42. YV, O.53, 137, affidavit by H.O.O. in Nuremberg 24 [?] July 1947 (Nuremberg document 4434), p 11.

43. Concerning Hrymajliv, Husiatyn and Tajnoje see Emberland and Kott (2012), p 241ff. and 246. Concerning Zhytomyr see YV, O.53, 137, affidavit by H.O.O. in Nuremberg 24 [?] July 1947 (Nuremberg document 4434), p 12. Where at least 70 killed Jews in this town are mentioned. On Smela see Martin Dean, *Encyclopedia of Camps and Ghettos, 1933–1945*, vol. 2, Part. B, s.1603. On Tarashcha see ibid., vol. 2 Pt. B., s.1606. On Zhytomyr and Berdychiv see ibid., vol. 2 Pt. B., s.1518. Both accusations are based on testimony by SS-Rottenführer Hans Isenmann given during prosecution in Kyiv, January 1946. About 20 July, Wiking's main force's axis of advance ran through Taraschka, but the material browsed does not indicate its presence in Berdychiv. This testimony was also used by Emberland and Kott (2012), p 242. Concerning Kamyanske (formerly Dniprodzerzhynsk) seeTestimony by Fr. Schuler, Regiment Westland reprinted in Hannes Heer, *'Stets zu Erschiessen sind Frauen, die in der Rote nArmee dienen', Geständnisse deutscher Kriegsgefangenen über ihren Einsatz an derOstfront* (Hamburger Edition, 1995), p 19.

44. For the possible involvement of soldiers of Wiking's filler battalion were involved in murdering 90 Jewish children in the town of Bila Tserkva. Emberland and Kott (2012), p 245. Cf. Boll and Safrian in Heer and Naumann (1995), p 278.

was marching through. On 25 July, he sent his wife, Margarete, a letter with some touristic snapshots of – among other places – Lviv, Dubno, Rovno and Lutsk. Himmler did not relate to his wife what his men were actually doing there, but he noted in his letter that there was quite a lot of work to be done and that it proceeded well. Moreover, he added that he 'slept tight and well' during the night.[45]

The SS Divisions in the Northern Sector of the Front

While *Wiking* fought and murdered in Ukraine, the remaining SS formations were employed in other sectors of the front. The *Totenkopf* and police divisions were subordinated to Army Group North moving along the northern axis of attack with Leningrad as their eventual objective. During their tour of duty as occupation force in France, the police division had been rejuvenated as almost 10,000 older policemen had been substituted by younger men.[46] As opposed to all other SS divisions the police division still had not been motorised, but remained horse-drawn. Being a part of the army group reserve it played a relatively modest role in the early days of fast advance. Conversely, *Division Totenkopf* was a part of General Hoepner's *Panzergruppe 4* (4th Armoured Group) and was to perform the important task of being the army group's motorised and armoured spearhead. At the end of June, it was moved up front and became engaged in severe fighting at the Stalin Line, the Soviet fortifications along the 1939 border.[47]

The division then moved on north-eastwards to the area south of Lake Ilmen. Here, at the end of September, along with other German formations the division was hit by an extensive Soviet counter offensive and, in early November, it ground to a complete halt. *Totenkopf* and various other formations of the 16th Army dug in along a line from the southern bank of Lake Ilmen to Lake Seliger west of the city Demyansk.[48] The following months' combat entailed that, in February 1942 the *Totenkopf Division* and German forces in the area were encircled in the Demyansk Pocket. Not until April 1942, did the 95,000 troops there regain contact with the German main line.[49]

In August 1941, the police division saw active combat for the first time. This was during the operations against the last Soviet defensive line before Leningrad, a line which ran along the Luga River, and was defended by numerous Soviet tanks.[50] In mid-September 1941, the division managed to reach the Leningrad suburbs taking Pushkin on the outskirts some 15 km from thee big city. Simultaneously, it was realised that the 18th Army, to which the police division was subordinated, was too weak to take Leningrad.

45. Katrin Himmler and Michael Wildt, *Himmler privat: Briefe eines Massenmörders* (Piper, 2014), p 242.
46. Husemann (1971), vol. 1, p 36.
47. Ibid., Sydnor (1990), p 93ff.
48. Sydnor (1990), p 200ff.
49. Ibid. Chapter 7.
50. BAB, NS19/3648, Letter of 12 August 1941 from divisional commander Krüger to Himmler. On the fighting in the Luga line, see also Husemann (1971), vol. 1, p 48ff., p 78.

Therefore, the army took to the defensive, and the police division had to spend the rest of 1941 in the Pushkin area as part of the investment force outside Leningrad.[51]

Further north, the primary mission of *Division Nord* and the independent *SS Infanterieregiment 9* was to reach the important port of Murmansk, and to cut the railroad line between that city and Kirov to the south.[52] However, *Division Nord* had a bad start. The troops were poorly trained, the going was heavy, and the Soviet fortifications extensive. Shortly, after launching its initial assault on the Salla Hills in Lapland this formation suffered a disastrous defeat. The division's frontal attack on the well-fortified Soviet positions, as well as the subsequent struggle, entailed a loss of up to 600 men. News of the defeat – including tales of flight and defeatism among the inadequately trained and somewhat elderly soldiers – soon reached Berlin. Neither quick allocation of replacement personnel nor the closest scrutiny of the division by top-level SS authorities helped boost morale or efficiency.[53] In mid-August, following the nervous breakdown of *Sturmbannfuhrer* (Major) Marks an army lieutenant colonel had to take over command of *SS-Infanterieregiment 6*. In a subsequent report he described the whole division as a weak formation, which in spite of reasonable morale would be able to attack only under favourable circumstances.[54]

The Central and the Southern Parts of the Front

Army Group Centre's mission was to advance along the central axis via Minsk and Smolensk towards Moscow. The *Das Reich Division* was in this army group and, initially, it advanced smoothly with fewer casualties than the year before during the campaign in the West.[55] However, the following month the fighting intensified. From the end of July onwards, the division as well as other German forces in the Smolensk-Yelnya area suffered powerful Soviet counterattacks. *Das Reich* casualties increased

51. Husemann (1971), vol. 1, p 111ff.
52. Neither unit has been scholarly researched. For a description by one of the unit's veterans see Schreiber (1969). For fighting in the Murmansk region see Earl F. Ziemkeog Magna E. Bauer, *Moscow to Stalingrad: Decision in the East* (Military Heritage Press, 1988), p 220ff.
53. Schreiber (1969), p 58: 16 officers killed or missing, 245 other ranks killed and 307 wounded. In a speech shortly after the battle Himmler mentioned a slightly higher number (13 killed and 12 wounded officers, 200 other ranks killed and 400 wounded). BAB, NS19/4008, *Der Reichsführer SS zu den Führern der Ersatzmannschaften für die Kampfgruppe Nord am Sonntag, in Stettin, 13.7.1941*. The division's casualty survey until 24 July gives a somewhat lower estimate. Of the division's total personnel strength of 10,668, until 24 July 1941 there were 15 officers and 122 other ranks killed as well as 12 officers and 331 other ranks wounded. This discrepancy might be due to the fact that, subsequently, quite a few slightly wounded returned to their units. BAMA, RS3-6/7, SS Division Nord, 24.7.41. On the fights see also BAB, NS19/3499, Travel report on Wolfff's visit to Norway. Oslo, 20 July 1941.
54. BAMA, RS3-6/7, Colonel lieutenant Münch, *Gefechtsbericht*, 21 August 1941
55. BAMA, RH24-46/7, KTB Das Reich, p 143. From 26 June to 27 July 1941 it sustained 55 killed and wounded officers as well as 1,322 killed, wounded, and missing NCOs and men. The previous year this division had sustained more than 2,000 casualties.

rapidly and doubled in comparison with the previous month.[56] Moreover, the fighting now was characterised by repeated Soviet tank attacks.[57] In August, while the battle of Smolensk was still raging, *Das Reich* was subordinated to *XXIV Panzerkorps* (24th Armoured Corps) and dispatched south to the Romny area east of Kiev. Operations there were part of a major encirclement manoeuvre aimed at investing the Soviet south-west front near Kiev.[58] On 16 September, the German forces arriving from the north linked up with *Panzergruppe 1*, which was advancing from south-west. Thus, one of the war's largest encirclements so far was now brought to a close. Of the 650,000 prisoners allegedly taken by German troops during the battle of Kiev, *Das Reich's* share amounted to 17,000.[59]

Like *Division Wiking*, the *Leibstandarte* was under Army Group South. Its route planned for an advance through Ukraine, and its mission was to take Kiev and Kharkov and eventually the Caucasus with its rich oilfields. On 1 July 1941, the *Leibstandarte* was employed. First, it was engaged in clashes at Lutsk, where the unit was tasked with holding a bridgehead on the river Styr against extensive Soviet counterattacks; then the division was moved towards south-east to Rovno. Already on 9 July, it reached Zhitomir 100 km west of Kiev.[60] Shortly afterwards, the *Leibstandarte* as well as *Division Wiking* were moved on to Uman, 150 km south of Kiev, where these two formations contributed considerably to the encirclement of 100,000 Soviet troops.[61] Moreover, the *Leibstandarte* had taken the city of Archangel and the important heights surrounding it, and the general-officer-commanding *XXXXVIII Armeekorps* (48th Corps), General Werner Kempf, subsequently described its conduct during the battle as exemplary.[62] Early September, the *Leibstandarte* came under the 11th Army, whose objective was the Crimea. This was to mark the beginning of a stage when the division frequently had to split up and fight in front sectors lying wide apart.[63]

Gearing up for New Operations

On 2 October 1941, Army Group Centre launched Operation Taifun, which aimed at investing and taking Moscow before the winter would put an end to major operations. Although the SS divisions had invaded the Soviet Union on full establishment strength

---

56. Over the period 28 July to 22 August 1941 there were 99 officers and 2,408 other ranks killed, wounded or missing. BAMA, RH24-46/7, KTB Das Reich, p 143
57. John Erickson, *The Road to Stalingrad* (Weidenfeld, 1993), p 181ff.
58. Hausser (1966), p 108. Ernst Klink, 'Die Operationsführung' in Boog et al. (1991), p 595ff.
59. BAB, NS19/3501, *Gefangene und Beute vom Beginn Einsatz Ost bis 14.10.1941*, 20 December 1941.
60. BAB, NS19/2854, *Tagesmeldungen der SS-Divisionen*, 6 July 1941; Weingartner (1974), p 59ff.
61. Ziemke and Bauer (1988), p 32. See combat reports from Leibstandarte concerning this battle in VAP, N, 1. SS-PZ.DIV. LAH, package 1 and BAMA, RS3-1/24.
62. BAMA, RS3-1/24, Letter of 8 August 1941 from Gen.Kdo. XXXXVIII A.K. (mot)/general officer commanding.
63. BB, Archiv nr. 9928, Bd. 5, *Deserteurbericht 17.8.1943* nr. 160. On the combat see Christensen et al. (1998), p 103ff. Daily casualties sustained by divisions employed in the bridgehead are estimated at 300 all ranks. Klink in Boog et al. (1991), p 600.

of both personnel and equipment, when launching Operation Taifun they were as run-down as the army's formations. Seen through the division's own eyes, *Das Reich*'s vehicle situation was 'disastrous' and this was further aggravated by its participation in offensive operations from 6 October onwards.[64] First, it had to fight in the Yelnya position and, after its breakthrough there, the division positioned itself right up front along the important main road to Moscow. Over the following days Soviet forces counterattacked from the north and the east and even, occasionally, from the west.[65] After this, further clashes followed on-route to the next Soviet defence line at Mozhaysk. The advance was severely hampered by adverse weather conditions; the autumnal rain alternated with snow and frost causing utterly soggy ground. At this moment, the second Armoured Army reported that its motorised formations moved at a mere one kilometre an hour and, noticeably, only when they had no contact with enemy forces.[66] Interrupted by severe fighting, during which the division experienced the full weight of the Soviet rocket launchers and the effective T-34 tanks, they moved on towards the area near Istra north of Moscow.[67]

On 20 October, shortly after the divisional commander, Hausser, had been severely wounded, his ADC, *Hauptsturmführer* (Captain) Kröger wrote to *Führungshauptamt* (Operational Headquarters-SS) in Berlin that 'now this formation is about to be exhausted as to officers, men and vehicles'.[68] The accumulated casualties were at 8,000, of whom 1,500 had died.[69] The casualty rate – 42 per cent of the troops that *Das Reich* had first deployed on the Eastern Front – was high, but not exceptional. At the same time, *Division Totenkopf* had lost 47 per cent of its original personnel.[70] *Division Wiking* had been luckier having lost only 20 per cent of the troops employed.[71]

In spite of the rapidly mounting losses, which were definitely true for army formations as well, the German leadership banked on further results in 1941. Apart from the execution of Operation Taifun, Rostov-na-Donu on the southern front would have to be taken. This large industrial city close to the Don River's estuary on the Sea of Azov was the key to the Caucasus. There was no longer any illusion of winning the war before the winter would manifest itself for real, but it was assumed that the Soviet Union's offensive power was eventually exhausted. Thus, the *Führungshauptamt* planned – obviously with Himmler's full acquiescence – pulling out some divisions from the Eastern

---

64. BAB, NS19/3501, Report of 10 October 1941 from Das Reich to Führungshauptamt, *Bericht SS-Division Reich*.
65. Ibid.
66. Klink in Boog et al. (1991), p 663.
67. IfZG, ED 373/1, Hugo Landgraf's diary, 14 October 1941. See also Michael K. Jones, *Tilbagetoget: Hitlers første nederlag*, translated by Ole Steen Hansen, Gyldendal, 2011, p 76.
68. BAB, NS19/3501, Letter of 20 October 1941 from Hauptsturmführer Kröger to SS-Führungshauptamt, *Bericht SS-Division 'Reich' über den Einsatz ab 10.10.41*.
69. BAB, NS19/3501, Report of 24 October 1941 from Das Reich to Führungshauptamt, *Personelle Verluste der SS-Division Reich*. One month hence the aggregate casualties had risen to 900 persons more. BAB, NS19/3165, Survey of Das Reich's casualties, 22 June–28 November 1941.
70. Casualty numbers of individual divisions can be seen in BAB, NS19/2854, *Tagesmeldungen der SS-Divisionen, Verlustmeldungen*, 17 November 1941.
71. Christensen et al. (1998), p 107.

Front during the winter in order to facilitate their re-organisation.[72] Optimism was not limited to the offices in Berlin. Army Group Centre observed with equanimity how new Soviet troops were positioned in front of Moscow. It was told that 'the forces with which the Red Army now confronts us are insufficient for launching a major offensive'.[73] This turned out to be a grave miscalculation of the Soviet resources, and the last months of 1941 would see the first major withdrawal of Third Reich troops.

Approximate location of major Waffen-SS units, July 1941

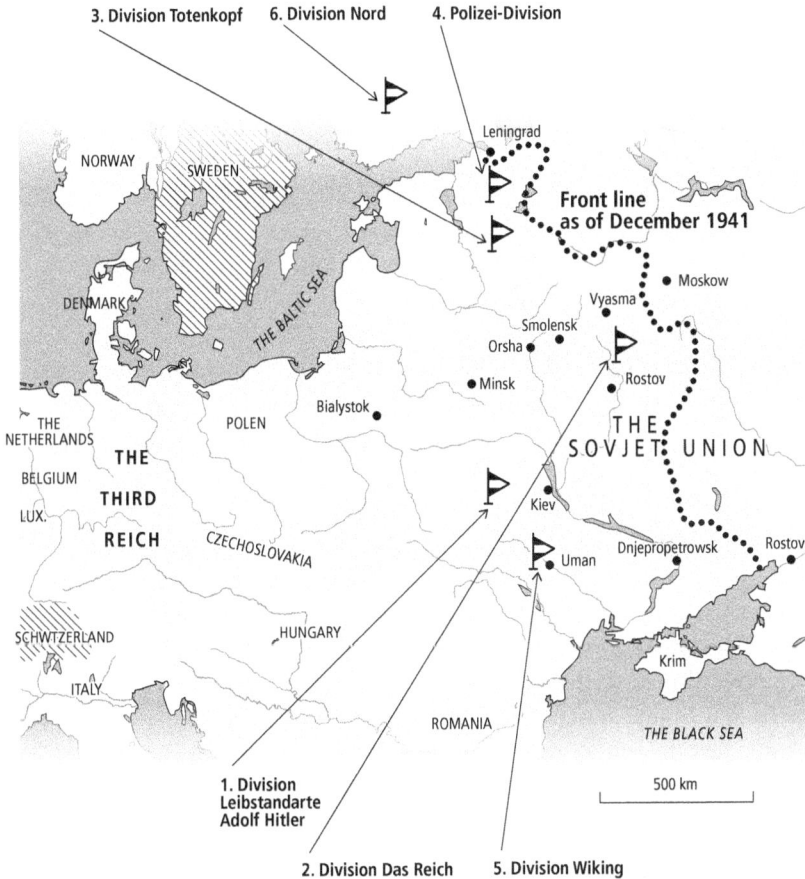

72. BAB, NS19/3499, Letter of 13 November 1941 from SS-Führungshauptamt to Himmler. In the margin of a meeting in The Führer's HQ on 5 November Himmler noted the theme 'Neuorganisation i.d. Waffen-SS' on a memo just before lunch with Hitler, see Witte et al. (1999), 5.11.1941, p 254. There is reason to believe that this triggered the letter of 13 November from Führungshauptamt. That letter was probably discussed in a telephone conversation between Himmler and Jüttner on the same day at 5.55 pm. According to Himmler's official diary they discussed the possible deployment of 4. SS-Infantry division to the front, withdrawal of 9. and 11. SS. Regiments, conversion of the Battle Group North and the motorisation of the police division, see ibid., 13.11.1941, p 259. On the conversion plans see also Hubatsch (2000), Weisung Nr. 37 den 10.10.1941, p 162 and *Durchführungsbestimmungen Nr. 1 zur Weisung Nr. 37*, 7 November 1941, p 166.
73. Jones (2011), p 153.

From Offensive to Defensive

As early as 20 October, the *Leibstandarte,* together with the army's 13th and 14th Armoured Divisions, were ordered to attack out of the coal rich Donetsk region against Rostov-na-Donu. Heavy rain ruined the roads causing significant logistic difficulties, which caused considerable delays to the advance.[74] Two days hence, severe hostile counterattacks materialised, and corps headquarters had to temporarily cancel the offensive operations.[75] During the following days, rain alternated with severe cold – on 14 November, for instance, minus 20 degrees Celsius was measured in *Wiking*'s area– and the potent Soviet counterattacks continued. On 17 November, nonetheless a new march order for Rostov was issued and, in spite of occasional pitched clashes, on 20 November troops from the *Leibstandarte* and 14th Armoured Division managed to break through into the city.[76] After about a day's street fighting the city was in German hands and, on top of that, the city's most important bridge across the Don was undamaged.[77] However, the rejoicing was short-lived. On 28 November, a major Soviet attack was launched against the German forces in the Rostov area. Reckoning the opposition to amount to about 21 Soviet divisions, third Armoured Corps was unable to hold its ground. Thus, a few days after their capture of the city the Germans had to leave it again.[78] The retreat, which occasionally looked rather like flight, ended as new positions were taken up along the Mius River running north from Taganrog on the Sea of Azov.

A few days after this limited, but important, Soviet success, the Red Army launched a major offensive near Moscow.[79] On 6 December, following a night with temperatures down to minus 38 degrees Celsius, three Soviet army groups – fronts in Soviet terminology – attacked the German forces outside Moscow. *Division Das Reich* was among the formations hit by this counteroffensive. The division and its neighbouring formations had run out of steam about 35 km outside the city where they faced hastily prepared but valiantly defended positions and minefields.[80] Although Hitler had ordered his troops to hold their ground, the massive Soviet onslaught left them no choice but to retreat, more or less to where Operation Taifun's line of departure had been.[81]

Moreover, further to the south the struggle now assumed a purely defensive character. After the withdrawal from Rostov the divisions *Leibstandarte* and *Wiking* were to spend almost seven months on the defensive along the Mius River. Already

---

74. Christensen et al. (1998), p 107.
75. BAMA, RS3-1/24, Bericht über den Einsatz der LSSAH vom 19.10.–26.10.41, 27 October 1941.
76. Christensen et al. (1998), p 107ff.
77. Weingartner (1974), p 65; Erickson (1993), p 265.
78. Ziemkeand Bauer (1988), p 55.
79. For Soviet and German views respectively on the offensive see Erickson (1993), p 267ff. and Ziemke and Bauer (1988), p 69ff.
80. Ziemke and Bauer (1988), p 53 and 65ff.
81. Kommandostab-Reichsführer-SS, Kriegstagebuch Nr.1, entry of 13 December1941, reprinted in Fritz Baade, *Unsere Ehre heißt Treue; Kriegstagebuch des Kommandostabes Reichsführer SS, Tätigkeitsberichte der 1. und 2. SS-Inf.-Brigade, der 1. SS-Kav.- Brigade und von Sonderkommandos der SS* (Europa Verlag, 1965), p 83.

prior to taking up positions along the Mius, these formations were severely run-down. According to a report sent by the second-in-command of the *Leibstandarte*'s *Kriegsberichter Zug* (war reporter platoon) shortly after the retreat from the Mius, the previous eight days had been the most difficult and shattering ones for the formation. It was the first time that the *Leibstandarte* had to yield on the field of battle. The number of vehicles was now down to 15% of the park of the early stages of Barbarossa. Moreover, as winter equipment still had not arrived the men walked bare-footed in their boots in 20 degrees below zero.[82]

Hitler paid one of his rare visits to the front immediately after the retreat from Rostov, and the *Leibstandarte* was the formation he chose to see.[83] This visit coincided with a rapidly escalating crisis in confidence between Hitler and the military leadership. On 1 December, Hitler had dismissed the commander of Army Group South, Gerd von Rundstedt. Rundstedt had refused to overrule the order, given at a lower level of command, to withdraw from Rostov. On 2 December, as the retreat towards the Mius continued, Hitler travelled on to Army Group South. Accompanied by the new army group commander, Walter von Reichenau, they flew to Mariupol, where they met the general-officer-commanding *Panzergruppe 1*, Ewald von Kleist, as well as Sepp Dietrich. Hitler's choice to see exactly the *Leibstandarte* was probably because he expected that Dietrich, his old Nazi brother-in-arms, would tell him the truth about the retreat from Rostov without too many pessimistic undertones on the impossibility of winning the war. And he was not disappointed. A contemporary observer from the SS claimed that 'Dietrich could tell Hitler a lot of things, which he did not know.' According to Dietrich the *Leibstandarte* was not to blame for the withdrawal. Rather the failure lay with other authorities, whom, rightly, the Führer had made responsible.[84] Here, probably, the newly sacked Rundstedt was on his mind. In Dietrich's version the retreat from Rostov was a military necessity, but also characterised by panicking army formations and staunch SS units.[85] Thus, it was claimed that the rear guard, consisting of the 35 men of the *Leibstandarte*'s *Kriegsberichter Zug*, had made an exemplary withdrawal with 200,000 Soviet troops on their heels.[86]

Apparently, the division's soldiers were pleased with the unexpected *Führer* visit. One Norwegian SS raw recruit was among the reinforcements hastily flown in on the day

---

82. BAB, NS19/2440, Covering letter of 10 December 1941 from Günther d'Alquem to Himmler's personal secretariat. Report of 5 December 1941 from acting platoon commander, the war record platoon of the Leibstandarte, attached. BAB, NS19/3494, Letter of 5 December 1941 from Himmler to Dietrich.
83. Weingartner (1974), p 67ff.; Ziemke and Bauer (1988), p 55ff.
84. BAB, NS19/2440, Covering letter of 10 December 1941 from Günther d' Alquem to Himmler's personal secretariat. Report of 5 December 1941 from acting platoon commander, the war record platoon of the Leibstandarte, attached.
85. Weingartner (1974), p 67.
86. BAB, NS19/2440, Covering letter of 10 December 1941 from Günther d' Alquem to Himmler's personal secretariat. Report of 5 December 1941 from acting platoon commander, the war record platoon of the Leibstandarte, attached.

of the visit. On the military airfield, where they landed, the soldiers suddenly saw a motorcade, and in one of the smart cars sat Hitler.

> As he saw the company he stopped and stepped out of the car. He appeared a little pale, but spirited, good-humoured and very calm. '*Heil Männer*' was his challenge, and the company responded '*Heil Hitler*' [...] Then Hitler said a few words, asked some of the boys a few things, and then he boarded his plane and flew on [...] I must admit that this was a pleasant and extraordinary surprise for us that I almost cannot describe. The Führer himself had called on us in far-away Russia.[87]

The winter position on the Mius was a strong one and the changing weather was a helpful partner in its defence. Thus, over the following months, the *Wiking* and the *Leibstandarte* withstood a number of major Soviet attacks sustaining only limited casualties themselves.[88]

Consequences of Operation Barbarossa

In many ways the period between the late summer of 1941 and the beginning of 1942 is a milestone in the military history of the war. Not only was it an indication that the blitzkrieg strategy was eventually rendered useless when faced with an opponent with resources, space and, not least, the political will to fight to the end irrespective of the losses incurred. Moreover, the losses of vital equipment – and, even worse, of experienced officers and men – were immense. At the end of the day, Hitler's confidence in the General Staff and senior officers deteriorated because of the problems on the Eastern Front. In Hitler's eyes it was formations like the *Leibstandarte*, *Das Reich* and *Totenkopf* that stabilised the front when in the winter of 1941, the Red Army attacked, because they were characterised by ideological zeal and the spirit of self-sacrifice rather than military professionalism. This contributed greatly to carving out a place for the Waffen-SS in Hitler's mind, and for the first – but certainly not last – time he underscored the military proves of the armed SS in his public addresses.[89] Logically, the thread was picked up by the SS, and in December 1941 Berger claimed that the Waffen-SS during the first six months of the campaign 'had demonstrated itself to be the backbone of the army'.[90]

---

87. HLC, Sigurd Sørlie's private archive, P1-Andreas B. Nilsson, letter of 5 December 1941. See also RK, 1353 Rigspolitichefen, Politiets Efterretningstjeneste, 1945–1950, copy of Knud Nordentoft's diary, entry of 7 December 1941.
88. BAMA, RS3-1/24, *Bericht über die Kampfhandlungen der LSSAH i.d. Zeit vom 25.12.41–18.1.1942. Ic den 18.1.1942*. No Wiking war diary exists concerning this period. However, the Leibstandarte war diary gives the impression of changing weather with temperatures between extreme cold and thaw, numerous rebuffs of Soviet attacks and limited casualties. BAMA, RS3-1/30, *Kriegstagebuch nr. 5, 16.12.1941–16.7.1942*. Secondary literature on Wiking, who occupied an adjacent sector of the Mius position, seems to confirm this. See the diary notes by the SS officer Ranzau Engelhardt in *RK, 6926, Privatarkiv, Dagbogsoptegnelser*.
89. Lehnhardt (2017), p 206f.
90. BAB, NS19/3565, Berger to Himmler, *Besprechung OKW*, 8.12.1941.

Thus, the turn of year saw Himmler provided with a much improved opportunity for expanding the military branch of the SS. The first reward was due as early as at the end of January 1942 when Hitler ordered reinforcement of the *Leibstandarte* by one tank battalion. Notably, this battalion boasted the state-of-the-art *Panzerkampfwagen IV* (Mark IV tank) armed with a 75 mm anti-tank gun with armour piercing ammunition.[91]

1942: From Blitzkrieg to War of Attrition

On 1 January 1942, a Danish Nazi with close ties to the Waffen-SS noted in his diary that 'it is incredible how the Russians can keep on fighting'.[92] All over Europe Nazi followers had hoped for a quick defeat of the Soviet Union. While this expectation now faded, a new enemy was added as, in the wake of the Japanese attack on 7 December 1941 on the American naval base Pearl Harbor, Germany had declared war on the United States. However, this development did not necessarily diminish the soldiery's confidence in Nazism and the Führer. A Flemish SS soldier wrote home that he and his colleagues had suffered immensely 'during the dreadful Russian winter', but what was needed now was ideological spirit: 'One is 100 percent National Socialist or not at all' he declared.[93] This was the perception higher up as well. In early 1942, the Nazi leadership was convinced that victory would eventually ensue, though the road might be somewhat longer than expected the year before. What would turn the tide would be a more determined and radical commitment.

It followed from this perspective, that there was still good reason to plan for the post-war future. Himmler initiated a number of projects with a view to creation of a Greater Germany reaching from the Canal Coast to the Urals and uniting all Germanic peoples. This vast area would have to be cleared of Jews and other enemies of the Reich. It should be populated by German soldier-farmers, who would rule over serfs of Polish, Russian and other Slavonic descent.[94] In close connexion with the mass killings and deportations Himmler therefore launched a number of resettlement and Germanisation projects in the East.

Great Plans for the Future

Until the spring thaw, which caused the fighting to abate, the Waffen-SS had suffered a huge number of casualties. However, this did not prevent its expansion. In May 1942, the SS got Hitler's approval of a substantial growth. The organisation was now allowed to operate seven peacetime divisions (as opposed to four the year before), as well as running three *Junkerschulen* (two the previous year) and five NCO training centres (two

91. Weingartner (1974), p 68ff.
92. RK, 1353, *Rigspolitichefen, Politiets Efterretningstjeneste 1945–1950*, Copy of Knud Nordentoft's diary.
93. BAB, NS19/351, *Auszüge aus Briefen aus Flandern*.
94. Longerich (2008), p 271ff.

the previous year). The permitted peacetime strength of the Waffen-SS was more than doubled to 147,414 from a level of 73,409 in 1941.[95] Therefore, even in the unlikely event of a sudden end to the war, Himmler would have a huge military might at his disposal, which might be barracked and employed in occupied countries and areas foreseen to be colonised and Germanised.

In April, orders were issued for the seventh division to be raised under a former Romanian general – the *Volksdeutche* SS officer – Arthur Phleps.[96] The division was designated *SS-Freiwilligen-Gebirgs-Division Prinz Eugen*. It differed from other Waffen-SS divisions by being manned primarily by *Volksdeutsche* – mostly from Yugoslavia.[97] Another novelty was the Cavalry Division which came about by reinforcing Fegelein's run down cavalry brigade.[98] Moreover, from spring into the late autumn and early winter 1942, in the large training area Debica an Estonian legion would be formed.[99] In December 1942, Hitler approved the formation of two more divisions named *Hohenstaufen* and *Frundsberg*. Another important development within the Waffen-SS was increased motorisation and allocation of tanks. In January and February, *Leibstandarte* and *Division Das Reich* received tank battalions, as did *Totenkopf* and *Wiking* in April and May.[100]

Offensive Operations in the Caucasus

In the summer, a new German operation was launched in the east. This offensive, called *Blau*, was set in motion in June 1942. It employed exclusively forces of Army Group South. The aim was the oilfields in and around the Caucasus, but Hitler hoped to also envelop and annihilate huge Soviet forces thus depriving the enemy of his last reserves. Moreover, the objectives included some generously yielding agricultural areas. The combination of these three elements would – it was assumed – lead to the final collapse of the Soviet war economy. Additionally, the plan was to facilitate further operations into the Middle East.[101] On 28 June, the German forces attacked east of Kursk and, within the first 24 hours, the armoured formations covered 50 km.

---

95.   BAB, NS19/3514, Letter of 11 May 1942 from Pohl to Himmler.
96.   Schulz and Zinke (2008), pp 508–513.
97.   BAB, NS19/3519, *SS-Führungshauptamt betr. Aufstellung der Freiwilligen Gebirgsdivision, 1.4.1942*. Thomas Casagrande, *Die volksdeutsche SS-Division 'Prinz Eugen': Die Banater Schwaben und die nationalsozialistischen Kriegsverbrechen* (Campus-Verl., 2003), p 183ff.
98.   Wilson (2000), p 157ff.BAMA, RS3-8/6, SS-Kav., 17.8.1942.
99.   Prit Buttar, *Between Giants: The Battle for the Baltics in World War II* (Osprey Publishing, 2013), p 139.
100. Weingartner (1974), p 69. Stein (1984), p 202. The dates mentioned in Stein do not always tally with other available sources. For example, already in April 1942 one armoured unit was ordered transferred from *Das Reich* to *Wiking*, BAB, NS19/2571, *Führungshauptamt* order of 18 April 1942. An armoured unit for *Das Reich* was formed as per order of February 1942, and one more in April. BAB, NS19/2571, order of 11 February 1942.
101. Wegner in Horst Boog et al. (1990), *Das Deutsche Reich und der zweite Weltkrieg*, vol. 6, p 761ff.

The strategically important city Voronezh was quickly taken, and fourth Armoured Army, one out of the two employed in this operation, continued towards the lower part of River Don. By mid-July, the German formations had covered more than 600 km in less than three weeks, but contrary to expectations no major Soviet forces had been enveloped and defeated.[102]

On 21 July, *Division Wiking* joined the offensive by being assigned with attacking the important industrial city Rostov-na-Donu (Rostov on Don) in the wake of 13th Armoured Infantry Division. As early as two days later, Rostov was in German hands. By the 31st, *Division Wiking* had taken close to 8,000 prisoners, while only slight casualties were sustained.[103]

Now, Hitler had Army Group South split into two formations, each with its on onward axis of attack. Army Group A, including *Division Wiking*, was to advance along the Black Sea coast, seize the Caucasian oilfields, and proceed as far as Baku – more than 1,000 km from Rostov. At the same time, Army Group B was to take Stalingrad employing a relatively small contingent of the entire forces. Thanks to the new Soviet tactics of avoiding encirclement by withdrawing, *Division Wiking* sped forward and, as early as the evening of 3 August, it established a bridgehead on the River Kuban north of the Caucasus mountain range. The day after, the bridgehead came under heavy Soviet attack, but *Wiking* repelled the onslaught employing the newly arrived tanks and – in their own estimation – annihilated an enemy battalion.[104] On 10 August, the first Caucasian oilfields near the city Maikop were seized, and for *Wiking* a period characterised by 'security and counter insurgency operations' began.[105]

In mid-September, *Wiking* was dispatched 400 km further east to link up with the first Armoured Army, whose forces – under dogged enemy resistance – tried to take the two only decent roads through the Caucasus range to Georgia and the oilfields near the Chechen main city, Grozny.[106] On 6 October, after fierce clashes with the enemy *Wiking* seized the town Malgobek, but north-west of Grozny the offensive ground to a halt. During the following days the formations in the area became subject to vigorous counter attacks. The Soviet infantry and tank units had significant artillery and air supports and aerial or mortar bombardment caused considerable losses.[107] In late December, the division was relieved and withdrawn from central Caucasus – thoroughly run down.[108]

102. Robert M. Citino, *Death of the Wehrmacht. The German Campaigns of 1942* (University Press of Kansas, 2007), p 176; Anders Frankson and NiklasZetterling, *Slaget om Kursk: historiens største panserslag*, trans. Lars Rosenkvist (Aschehoug, 2003), p 49ff. On *Wiking*'s activity in *Blau*, see Strassner (1968), p 124ff.

103. BAB, NS19/2317, Gefechtsbericht vom 17.7.–5.8. 1942. See also Christensen et al. (1998), p 112ff.

104. BAB, NS19/2317, Gefechtsberichtvom 17.7.–5.8. 1942.

105. BAB, SSO, personal file concerning Riedweg, Franz, letter of 2 September 1942 from Riedweg to Berger, see also Strassner (1968), p 147ff.

106. Citino (2007), p 239ff.

107. Ziemke and Bauer (1988), p 379. RK, Personal archive 6926, R. Engelhardt, 'Krigsoplevelser'.

108. Christensen et al. (1998), p 120.

On the Defensive

In 1942, the southern front was the only place in the Soviet Union where the Third Reich conducted offensive operations. Thus, apart from minor offensive initiatives, German forces spent the year on the defensive, and sustained considerable losses despite generally unsuccesful Soviet attacks.

Until April, two army corps – including *Division Totenkopf* – were completely encircled in the above-mentioned Demyansk pocket and had to be replenished by means of an air bridge.[109] On 21 April, after hard combat a German rescuing formation supported by a breakout operation by the encircled *Totenkopf* units succeeded in opening a narrow route between the pocket and the German main line of resistance.[110] However, this did not solve the problems for the hard-pressed German forces around Demyansk. The battle in the area continued, and during the summer the corridor into the pocket was subjected to vigorous Soviet attacks.[111]

While, at the outset of the campaign in Russia, the *Totenkopf* division was at a strength of 17,265 men, by 20 March 1942 it had sustained 12,625 casualties, of which about half had been incurred since January of the same year.[112] In May 1942, in spite of having received filler personnel, the division was down to a mere 6,700 men who would remain engaged in intensive fighting over the summer of 1942.[113] Although the Danish SS unit *Frikorps Denmark* was airlifted in to the area in early May, the deployment of this small formation yielded little relief, as it soon suffered heavy casualties.[114] In a letter of early August, the deputy divisional commander, *Oberführer* Max Simon, wrote to his superior, Theodor Eicke, that the condition of the *Totenkopf* was appalling. He described the soldiers as 'poor souls' who had lived for months on end in sheer filth where trench feet, dysentery, fever and nephritis were the order of the day.[115] Now, this made Eicke warn Hans Jüttner, director of the *Führungshauptamt*, that if the Totenkopf was not relieved before three weeks it would cease to exist as a division.[116] It was not until mid-October, when German operations had expanded the corridor into the pocket sufficiently to prevent enemy artillery interfering that the surviving *Totenkopf* soldiers were ordered to leave.[117]

---

109. Christensen et al. (1998), p 144. See also Franz Josef Merkl, General Simon: *Lebensgeschichten eines SS-Führer: Erkundungen zu Gewalt und Karriere, Kriminalität und Justiz, Legenden und öffentlichen Auseinandersetzungen* (Wissner, 2010), p 201ff.
110. Jones (2011), p 287ff.
111. BAMA, RH20-16, Armeebefehl Nr. 34, 6.6.1942 and BAMA RH 20-16/111, Abgehende Befehle, 14/4–16/6 1942, Armeebefehl Nr. 34. See also Jones (2011), 290.
112. Sydnor (1990), p 222.
113. Ibid., p 225ff.
114. Christensen et al. (1998), p 144ff.
115. RK, DAN, T175, col. 108, p 2631921, Div.Gef.st., 2 August 1942. BAMA, RS3/3-19, *Gesundheit der Truppen*, 1 August 1942 and Ibid.*Gesundheit der Truppen*, 12 August 1942.
116. RK, DAN, T175, col. 108, p 2631918, From Eicke to Jüttner, 5 August 1942.
117. Sydnor (1990), p 251; Wegner in Horst Boog et al. (1990), *Das Deutsche Reich und der zweite Weltkrieg*, vol. 6, p 901ff.

The Leningrad front, too, remained unchanged compared with the manoeuvre warfare in the south. Over the year, several Waffen-SS formations served here, including the police division and the legions Norway, Flanders and the Netherlands.[118] One can get an impression of the fighting in this sector by taking a closer look at Legion Norway which in February 1942, 800-man strong, was employed at the Leningrad front and subordinated to Battle Group Jeckeln. In his previous job as *HSSPF Ostland*, the battle group commander, Friedrich Jeckeln, had during the preceding moths carried the direct responsibility for the mass murder of thousands of Jewish men, women and children.[119] Formed on 17 February 1942, Battle Group Jeckeln included parts of the police division, Legion Norway, *V Bataillon/Leibstandarte*, some independent police battalions and other minor units as well as Estonian *Schutzmannschaft* battalions.[120] This pooling of minor units was a reaction to the huge losses suffered by the police and other divisions that had besieged Leningrad since the autumn of 1941.

Upon arrival at the front, Legion Norway was allocated a relatively calm part of the battle group's 15 km sector, which ran north-west from the town Pushkin south of Leningrad towards the Gulf of Finland. Thus, apart from countering minor Soviet attacks and answering sporadic artillery fire, the legion was not really employed until mid-April. On 16 April, a combat patrol under the officer commanding the legion's fourth company, Ragnar Berg, was stuck in a minefield. In the ensuing fight, this patrol as well as a reinforcing squad were neutralised suffering six killed and a number of wounded. The Germans also – falsely – believed *Unterscharführer* Kjell Jöntvedt killed and abandoned in no-man's land. He did, actually, survive but was captured by the Soviets and gave testimony of conditions in the Legion.[121] Over the following months, scattered fighting and patrolling in no-man's land as well as behind enemy lines had all the attributes of traditional trench warfare.[122] When, at the end of May, the legion moved to a new position it had already suffered 50 dead and, of course, a number of wounded. These were serious losses considering the size of the Legion. Throughout the rest of the year, when the legion was employed in successive positions in the Leningrad theatre of military operations, casualties remained at five to ten killed every month.[123]

---

118. Husemann (1971); Klietmann (1965); Christensen et al., *Historisk Tidsskrift* 100, nr. 2, 2000, p 423, https://tidsskrift.dk/index.php/historisktidsskrift/article/ view/50282. Moreover, the second SS Brigade fought at the Volkhov front about 100 km east and south-east of Leningrad. Klietmann (1965), p 314ff.

119. Richard Breitman 'Friedrich Jeckeln' in Smelserog Syring (2003), p 271ff.

120. BAMA, RS4/34, *Kampfgruppe Jeckeln (stab) KTB nr. 1, 4.3.1942–13.8.1942*. Note that the battle group was formed on 1 February 1942 which, however, does not tally with the staff's was diary, cf. Emberland and Kott (2012), p 271. The Legion's employment at the Leningrad front has been described in detail, but uncritically by Arneberg (2004). For a briefer, but far better founded, account see Emberland and Kott (2012), p 271ff.

121. BAMA, RS4/34, *Kampfgruppe Jeckeln (stab) KTB Nr. 1*, 16 April 1942; Emberland and Kott (2012), p 277.

122. BAMA, RS4/34, *Kampfgruppe Jeckeln (stab) KTB Nr. 1*.

123. The count is from a survey of the legion's losses in Arneberg (2004), p 231ff.

On 20 July, a particularly violent Soviet attack hit the legion as well as adjacent Estonian *Schutzmannschaft* units. It was not until after very costly combat and reinforcement by the second SS Brigade that the frontline was re-established.[124] Casualties during the trench warfare throughout the remainder of 1942 were primarily due to snipers and artillery. In a letter of late October, a Norwegian soldier laconically noted that 'the Soviet shells give their regards to us rather frequently.' In the same letter he described his daily routine in the dugout, where the combat against rats and lice characterised life.[125] The combination of a static frontline, constant peril and continuous losses restricted the opportunities for rest and recuperation behind the lines; and the filthy living conditions corrupted the legion's morale. Shortly, after the fighting on 16 April, *Unterscharführer* Kjell Jøntvedt gave his interrogators a detailed account of the conditions with the Norwegian legion. Apart from giving information about the personnel strength, the leading officers' names and the unit's dislocation, he told about troop morale and discipline, which he characterised as good, and the soldiers' food, which he found abundant. Moreover, he assumed that most soldiers rejoiced that the 'dreadful Russian winter' was over, and he predicted that the time had come when the war might be crowned by German victory.[126]

It must have come as an unpleasant revelation to the legionnaires that the summer did not bring the expected victory but renewed fighting and that the Soviet Union showed no signs of exhaustion. At the onset of autumn, the time at the front had worn the Norwegians down as most of them had been continuously employed since February. In a letter a Norwegian volunteer complained about his boss: 'only the major goes to Norway.'[127] This complaint was not the only one and, what was worse, the situation was characterised by a number of desertions.[128] In September, another Norwegian volunteer wrote to his wife that if he had to stay in this place for another winter he would try to kill himself.[129]

Waffen-SS in the killing Fields of Belarus

During the course of 1942, extermination camps like Auschwitz, Sobibor and Treblinka acquired a central role in the genocide, which the Germans had launched in 1941. Moreover, the suppression of partisan activity, for which Himmler carried the main responsibility, became a well-orchestrated part of the Holocaust. Some of

124. BAMA, RS4/34, *Kampfgruppe Jeckeln (stab) KTB Nr. 1*, 20.7.1942; Emberland and Kott (2012), p 277.
125. HLC, Sigurd Sørlie's personal archive: P29-Gard Holtskog. Letter of 11 October 1942.
126. Протокол опроса военнопленного 'Норвежского добровольческого легиона' Ентведта Киель (Interrogation Report concerning POW Jøntvedt, Kjell of the 'Norwegian Voluntary Legion'). The NKVD's first division with 42nd Soviet Army, 16 April 1942. From the FSB archive, St. Petersburg, available at URL http://ru.wikisource.
127. Christensen et al., *Historisk Tidsskrift*, vol. 100, no. 2, 2000, p 443.
128. Ibid., p 439ff.
129. Ibid., p 443.

the worst crimes were perpetrated in the Soviet Union and, primarily, in Belarus. Nowhere else were the combination of counter insurgency, systematic massacres and Holocaust as obvious as here. From the early days of the campaign in the east, when there was no organised Soviet resistance movement, suppression of partisans was used as a vindication for killing civilian Jews under the pretext given by Himmler already in July 1941 that all Soviet Jews were to be regarded as partisans.[130] Very little time elapsed until this perception spread from the SS to the army. Thus, in the autumn 1941 at an army counter insurgency course it was stated that 'where the partisan is you will find a Jew; and where the Jew is you will find a partisan'.[131]

The instruction concerning counter insurgency, which had been disseminated before the attack on the Soviet Union, included a wide range of collective punitive measures such as execution without trial, torching of villages, and killing of villagers. These measures were copiously applied by the army as well as the Waffen-SS. The brutality becomes evident through the fact that while, until March 1942, 63,257 so-called partisans had been killed in action or executed, only 638 Germans had lost their lives in fighting partisans on the eastern front and 1,355 had been wounded.[132]

Not only did the partisans' activity increase over the first six months of 1942, the huge German losses and the Red Army's actions made it difficult to detach sufficient units for counter insurgency operations in the hinterland. This state of affairs was the background for Himmler's and a number of minor Waffen-SS units' tasks in counter insurgency in the summer of 1942. At this time, a compilation of orders by Hitler made Himmler responsible for what was henceforth called 'suppression of gangs', and a specific job as *Chef der Bandenkampfverbände* was set up with HSSPF Bach-Zelewski as incumbent.[133]

The centre of attention was Belarus where the SS had a number of units, among which was *SS-Sonderkommando Dirlewanger* with roots in a unit of poachers with criminal records, whose formation Hitler had sanctioned in 1940. Its commander, *Oberführer* Oskar Dirlewanger, had close ties with Berger. Dirlewanger had fought in the First World War, and he was subsequently active in various Freikorps. Moreover, he fought with the German Condor Legion in the Spanish Civil War.[134] He applied for membership of the SS but was refused, primarily because of a sentence for intercourse with an underage. In the summer 1940, however, thanks to Berger's interference Dirlewanger was exonerated, joined the Waffen-SS, and was appointed commander of

---

130. Peter Longerich, *Der ungeschriebene Befehl. Hitler und der Weg zur 'Endlösung'* (PiperVerlag, 2001), p 102.

131. Jurgen Forster, *Die Sicherung des 'Lebensraumes'* in Boog, et al. (1991), p 1240.

132. Hannes Heer, *Die Logik des Vernichtungskrieges. Wehrmacht und Partisanenkampf* in Heer and Naumann (1995), p 109.

133. BAB, NS 19/1671, Weisung Nr. 46 and other documents. BAMA, RH 19-II/153. See also Koehl (1983), p 203ff., Longerich (2008), p 646ff.; Philip W. Blood, *Hitler's Bandit Hunters: The SS and the Nazi Occupation of Europe* (Potomac Books, 2006), p 63ff. Cuppers (2011), p 256ff.

134. YV, Recordgr. O.68, F.Nr, 569, Oskar Dirlewanger, *Abschrift der politischen Beurteilung des Dr. Oskar Dirlewangerdurch SD-Oberabschnitt Süd-West, Stuttgart* 14 May 1938.

the eponymous unit, which initially counted only 70 men.[135] It was subordinated to *SS-und Polizeiführer* Odilo Globocnik and employed in the Lublin area of the Gouvernement Générale tasked with police and counter insurgency missions.[136]

Sonderkommando Dirlewanger was employed in counter insurgency operations, first in Poland, then in Belarus. These were conducted with a cruelty that made it notorious as one of the worst killer formations of the Second World War.[137] This, however, caused occasional troubles for Dirlewanger as well as for his protector, Gottlob Berger. In January 1942, following a series of complaints by HSSPF Friedrich-Wilhelm Krüger, the *Sonderkommando* was deployed from Poland to Belarus. It had been involved in serious and widespread black-marketing and bribery that characterised the Gouvernement Générale, and Dirlewanger, personally, was accused of intercourse with one or more Jewesses. Moreover, he was accused of having used unorthodox execution methods – having had a Lublin medical doctor poisoning 57 Jews – but, seen from an SS perspective, this might have been a minor offence.[138]

A letter of summer 1942 illustrated Dirlewanger's methods in Poland. In this Krüger asked Berger for immediate reinforcements because of the increased partisan activity that had sprung up since Dirlewanger left the area. Berger answered stating that the increase in partisan activity had only justified the *Sonderkommando*'s proverb, 'rather shoot two Poles too many, than one too few'. Thus, Berger asked Himmler for permission to raise one more unit ad modem Dirlewanger. This, however, never happened.[139]

The move to Belarus, where the formation worked from 1942 to 44, did not soften up its methods. Here, it took part in 27 major and a few minor partisan suppression operations. The reports on the formation's operations in Belarus mentioned huge losses among the opponents, who were generally characterised as bandits, suspects or Jews, while own casualties were slight. The reason for this was that, mostly, these actions were executions or deportations of civilians.[140] In June 1942, the *Sonderkommando* together with *Einsatzkommando 8* conducted, for example, an action between Babruysk and Mogilev killing 1,741. The reality was that this was a massacre on villagers and Jews hiding in the woods, which becomes obvious from the poor exploit of merely seven small arms and absolutely no losses on the German side.[141] Increasingly, the methods employed

135. Christian Ingrao, *The SS Dirlewanger Brigade: The History of the Black Hunters* (Skyhorse Pub., 2011); Hans-Peter Klausch, *Antifaschisten in SS-Uniform: Schicksal und Widerstand der deutschen politischen KZ-Häftlinge, Zuchthaus- und Wehrmachtstrafgefangenen in der SS-Sonderformation Dirlewanger.* (Edition Temmen, 1993); French L. MacLean, *The Cruel Hunters: SS-Sonderkommando Dirlewanger, Hitler's Most Notorious Anti-Partisan Unit* (Schiffer Pub., 1998).
136. Ingrao (2011), p 10.
137. For a survey of *Sonderkommando Dirlewanger*'s atrocities at the eastern front, see MacLean (1998); Ingrao (2011).
138. Ingrao (2011), p 14ff and 107ff. See also BAMA RS3/36/11b, Letter of 22 January 1942 from Dirlewanger to Berger.
139. NS19/1671, Letter of 17 June 1942 to Himmler from Berger.
140. Ingrao (2011), pp 16, 18 and 22.
141. Gerlach (1999), p 899.

in suppressing the partisans and their assumed civilian helpers developed into turning areas with intense resistance activity into 'dead zones', which meant that all civilian inhabitants were either murdered or sent to Germany as slave labourers, while livestock, crops and furniture were confiscated, and all property razed to the ground.

Along with *Sonderkommando Dirlewanger*, the first SS Infantry Brigade was an important player in these atrocities. In August and September 1942, for example, the first SS Infantry Brigade and some police and *Schutzmannschaft* battalions carried out Operation *Sumpffieber* in which 10,063 persons were killed out of which more than 8,000 were Jews.[142]

In July 1944, *Sonderkommando Dirlewanger* was re-deployed to Poland. In the late summer of 1944, it took part in the suppression of the Polish Home Army's rebellion in Warsaw, and during the months of August and September it executed ca. 30,000 Polish civilians there.[143] In February 1945, it was re-designated *36. Waffen-Grenadier-Division der SS*, and fought as such at the eastern front until, in April, it was encircled by the Red Army south of Berlin. Dirlewanger's end was brutal. In May 1945, having been imprisoned by the French, he was apparently beat to death by his Polish guards.[144]

1943 – The Waffen-SS Diversifies

In many respects, 1943 was a turning point in the war as well as a crucial year for the Waffen-SS. For Germany the year began in the worst conceivable way with the 6th Army's complete annihilation at Stalingrad. Since no SS units had fought in that battle, the defeat did not have any immediate consequence for the Waffen-SS. However, this fact contributed to the mutual distrust between the upper echelons of the army and the SS. Martin Bormann, Hitler's influential secretary and leader of the party secretariat, wrote to Himmler attaching a letter from General Hermann Reinecke. The general lamented that, with the army, there was a strong aversion to the Waffen-SS. He stressed bitterly that the Waffen-SS was only ordered up front when the laurels of victory were to be reaped, and he asked with indignation why none of its formations had been employed at Stalingrad.[145] On his part, Himmler contributed to the acrimony by claiming that the Waffen-SS had no share in temporary setbacks at the fronts. This was an attitude shared by many SS officers. Had the Waffen-SS been present, the Stalingrad disaster would never have happened, so they claimed.[146]

In spite of huge losses at the eastern front the military branch of the SS kept growing. The formation of two more divisions, approved by Hitler in December 1942, was bound to begin. To man these formations, the SS had to conscript personnel, and thousands

---

142. Ibid., p 703.
143. Ingrao (2011), p 39.
144. Ibid., p 179; Knut Stang, 'Dr. OskarDirlewanger' in Klaus-Michael Mallmann and Gerhard Paul, *Karrieren der Gewalt: nationalsozialistische Täterbiographien*, 2, durchges. Aufl., Sonderausg (Primus, 2011), p 73.
145. BAB, NS19/2968, Letter of 19 May 1943 from Bormann to Himmler.
146. Leleu (2007), p 537.

of young Germans in labour camps under *Reichsarbeitsdienst* (State Labour Service) were contacted and forced or lured into the SS uniform.[147] While the first of these was called *9. SS-Panzer-Grenadier-Division Hohenstaufen*, the other was named *10. SS-Panzer-Grenadier-Division Karl der Große* (Charlemagne) which was soon changed to *Frundsberg*.[148] Towards the end of the year, the formation of *17. SS-Panzer-Grenadier-Division Götz von Berlichingen* was also initiated. Like *Hohenstaufen* and *Frundsberg* – it was largely filled up with German conscripts and *Volksdeutsche*.[149] The *12. SS-Panzer-Grenadier-Division Hitlerjugend* was also formed in 1943 as an, in many ways, natural result of the close cooperation between *Hitlerjugend* and the Waffen-SS. The result was a division with a remarkable youthful and ideologically committed rank-and-file. In October, Himmler – like Hitler and Göring – also had a division named after him. The *16. SS-Panzer-Grenadier-Division Reichsführer-SS*.[150] Like this division also the *11. SS-Freiwilligen-Panzer-Grenadier-Division Nordland which* had been raised earlier in the year was composed of Romanian *Volksdeutsche* plus personnel from the disbanded legions. New ethnic groups, so-called *Fremdvölker*, were also introduced into the Waffen-SS during 1943 – in units such as the *13. Waffen-Gebirgs-Division-SS Handschar*, the*14. SS-Freiwilligen-Grenadier-Division (Galizia Nr. 1)* andthe*15. Waffen-Grenadier-Division der SS (*Latvian *Nr. 1)*.[151] In addition to the numerous divisions, 1943 saw the formation of a number of SS corps.

The Fight for Kharkiv

One of the events which contributed to the development of the Waffen-SS was the successful recapture of Kharkiv in eastern Ukraine in spring 1943.[152] In January, Soviet forces had vanquished the German sixth army at Stalingrad and, as a part of a new offensive against the now severely shaken German forces at the south-eastern front, this city – an important traffic hub and the fourth largest in the Soviet Union – was Stalin's first objective. The Germans rushed reinforcement to the area and, in February, the newly formed SS armoured corps arrived at the front, and Paul Hausser assumed command over the defence of the Kharkiv sector.[153] Initially, while the corps was composed of the divisions *Das Reich* and *Leibstandarte*, *Division Totenkopf* was on its way to the eastern front to join the corps.[154]

---

147. BAB, NS19/3943, Letter of 30 December 1942 on the formation of new SS-divisions. See also Wilhelm Tieke, *Im Feuersturm letzter Kriegsjahre: II. SS-Panzerkorps mit 9. und 10. SS-Division 'Hohenstaufen' und 'Frundsberg'*, 2. verbesserte Aufl. (MuninVerlag, 1978), p 16ff.

148. BAMA, RS3-10, *SS-Panzer-Grenadier-Division-Karl der Große, Unterlagen für eine Belehrung über Karl der Große*, 5 March 1943.

149. Tieke (1978), p 13ff.

150. Merkl (2010), p 253ff.

151. BAB, NS19/3504; BAB, NS19/3523; BAB, NS19/1785; SU, Hoover Archives, *15. Waffen-SS 15 Grenadier Division* Box 9; BAMA, N756/170a, '*Aufstellung der SS-Freiw. Division ,Galizien'*, Führungshauptamt, 30 July 1943.

152. Erickson (1996), p 47.

153. BAMA, RS2-2/4, *KTB Nr.4, 9.1.1943–26.3.1943*, 9 February1943.

154. BAMA, RS2-2/4, *KTB Nr.3, 1.11.1942–8.1.1943* and *KTB Nr.4, 9.1.1943–26.3.1943*.

The corps' mission was to hold Kharkiv at any cost and, the first days of battle went well. On 4 February, Soviet forces reached River Donets east of Kharkiv, but the *Leibstandarte*, which sat in good defensive positions on the western bank, managed to block their immediate crossing. However, there were places at the flanks where the Germans failed to stop the attackers and on, 10 February, Soviet units had crossed in enough place and in sufficient numbers to threaten encirclement of the city. On the 15th, they approached the city from several directions.[155] In the entry for 15 February, in the corps' war diary the critical development is described hour by hour. Hausser ordered his units to break clean, but a little later Hitler ordered that the city must be held regardless of costs. While, according to the war diary the order was received at 16.30 (4.30 p.m.), preparations for abandoning the city had been going on since 12.50. As withdrawal was already proceeding it made no sense to abide by Hitler's order and, though the order was repeated at 18.42 (6.42 p.m.), the corps still did not comply.[156]

Hausser's withdrawal from Kharkiv failed to disenamor Hitler with the Waffen-SS as the retreat soon was transformed in to a counter-attack. Despite getting stuck in the mud towards Poltava, Division Totenkopf arrived in time to participate a pincer movement aiming at recapturing the lost city, planned by Erich von Mannstein, commander of Army Group South. While General Hermann Hoth's fourth armoured army would attack north from forming up positions south-east of Kharkiv, the Waffen-SS corps was to advance in a south-easterly direction from Poltava. If successful, the attack would result in the occupation of Kharkiv and, en route, the Soviet sixth army could be destroyed.[157]

The Red Army had advanced so quickly that adequate force protection and combat readiness were compromised. Thus, in the morning of 20 February, when the German counter-attack set in the Soviet troops were caught on the wrong foot. The Russian sixth army's reaction was to continue west, whereby the German forces were allowed to tie a noose around them. Over the next days, the armoured corps wreaked massive havoc among the Soviet formations while seizing or destroying lots of equipment. Many Soviet tanks ran out of petrol and were abandoned by their fleeing crews. In about a week's fight, the armoured corps and Hoth's armoured army annihilated the bulk of two Soviet armies. In total, the German side claimed to have destroyed or seized 615 tanks, 400 howitzers and other pieces of artillery and 600 anti-tank guns as well as captured 9,000 prisoners.[158]

While, over the next few weeks, the Germans pushed the Red Army further back, the SS armoured corps swung east round Kharkiv to cut off any Soviet attempts at escaping towards the Donets.[159] On 5 March, together with Hoth's armoured army, the corps advanced towards Kharkiv city. On the ninth, the SS troops were

---

155. Erickson (1996), p 47.
156. BAMA, RS2-2/4, *KTB Nr.4, 9.1.1943–26.3.1943*, 15 February 1943.
157. Sydnor (1990), p 267ff.
158. Ibid., p 268ff. See also Weingartner (1974), p 75.
159. Erickson (1996), p 51ff.

Figure 3.3 Soldiers from Legion Norway take the oath of allegiance in the winter of 1942 in Russia (Frihedsmuseet)

on the westerns outskirts. The divisions *Das Reich* and *Totenkopf* had been ordered to circumvent the city and head for the Donets river, but contrary to Hoth's instructions, Hausser ordered a large number of troops to attack the city centre, which led to bloody street fighting and huge losses. Nonetheless, the bulk of *Totenkopf* continued around the city enveloping the Soviet forces.[160] On 15 March, German radio informed that Kharkiv had been taken by Waffen-SS formations. Despite the losses associated with the fighting in the city Hitler was ecstatic singing the praise of his favourite, Dietrich – claiming he was a great strategist.[161]

The Tank Battle at Kursk

Hausser's and his armoured corps' next major operation would be the battle at Kursk. Taking place in the first half of July, it unfolded on the boundary between Army Groups South and Centre. Since the autumn 1941, the city Kursk had been in German hands but it had been re-taken by the Red Army in February 1943. During spring, Hitler and his generals planned a new eastward bound offensive nicknamed *Zitadelle*. At Kursk the Soviet positions formed a bulge towards the west, and it was this that would be the target of a German pincer movement. The aim was to regain the initiative at the eastern front, disengage German forces by shortening the front line considerably, as well as wear down the Soviet personnel reserves and take prisoners who might be

160. Sydnor (1990), p 278ff.; Weingartner (1974), p 76.
161. Clark in Smelser and Syring (2003), p 125.

used as forced labourers in Germany.[162] More than once, Hitler postponed the attack, primarily to wait for the arrival of new Panther tanks. Consequently, by the end of the planning and forming up period a huge armoured force was concentrated and the battle has gone into history as the biggest tank battle ever.[163]

The three Waffen-SS divisions *Leibstandarte*, *Das Reich* and *Totenkopf* were again parts of Hausser's formation, which was now designated second SS Armoured Corps. *Division Wiking* constituted part of the operational reserve.[164]

In the early hours of 5 July, when *Zitadelle* was launched, two enormous armies were facing each other. The German force numbered 777,000 troops and 2,451 tanks and self-propelled guns as well as 7,500 artillery pieces and mortars. Moreover, the attack was to be supported by 1,830 aircraft. The Soviet defenders fielded 1,336,000 men 3,489 tanks and self-propelled guns as well as 22,000 artillery pieces and mortars under two fronts. The air support force had 3,500 aircraft at its disposal. Unlike the Germans, the Soviet forces kept a huge strategic reserve formed up within reasonable distance behind the front. This, the Steppe Front, numbered 573,000 troops, 1,639 tanks as well as 9,200 artillery pieces and mortars.[165]

However, the Germans were confident that their formations' superior operational efficiency and the quality of their equipment would prevail.[166] Three new types of armour, viz. the heavily armoured tank destroyer *Elefant* equipped with an 88 mm gun capable of penetrating all enemy armour at considerable distance as well as the two new tank models *Panther* and *Tiger I* were employed. A number of these new weapon systems went to the Waffen-SS divisions.[167]

What characterised the first few days of the Kursk battle were massive clashes of troops and tanks with substantial casualties sustained by the German side; and even worse as far as the Soviets were concerned. On the southern axis of attack some German formations – among these the second SS armoured corps – advanced considerably during the first few days; although heavy rain slowed down the movements, even that of tracked vehicles, and hampered logistic sustenance.[168] On 8 July, *Division Das Reich* reported that 100 enemy tanks were believed to have been neutralised until then. However, the opposition was tough. The Germans were repeatedly counter-attacked by tank formations up to 140 strong.[169] Moreover, the Soviet field fortifications were well-consolidated with anti-tank weapons, mine fields and various other obstacles.

162. Töppel in Schulte et al. (2014), p 317.
163. Stephen G. Fritz, *Ostkrieg: Hitler's War of Extermination in the East* (University Press of Kentucky, 2011), p 338ff.; Frankson and Zetterling (2003); Zentner and Bedürftig (1993), p 327.
164. Erickson (1996), p 105.
165. Frankson and Zetterling (2003), p 144. Erickson's number are at a slight variance. For example, 2,700 tanks and self-propelled guns on the German side. See Erickson (1996), p 97.
166. Frankson and Zetterling (2003), p 146.
167 David M. Glantz and Jonathan M. House, *The Battle of Kursk* (University Press of Kansas, 1999), p 17ff.
168. BAMA, RS2-2/4, KTB Nr.4, 9.1.1943–26.3.1943. See 5.7.1943 onwards.
169. BAMA, RS2-2/4, KTB Nr.4, 9.1.1943–26.3.1943. See 5.7.1943 onwards. On *Das Reich* during the first days of the Kursk battle, see also Lucas (2006), p 106ff.

On the first day of battle, in spite of these the armoured corps penetrated eight kilometres into the enemy defences and inflicted severe damage. Nonetheless, the corps sustained casualties too and, on the first day alone, it lost 1,000 troops of which 100 killed while 27 tanks and self-propelled guns were damaged or destroyed.[170]

By the 10th, *Totenkopf* had managed to establish a bridgehead on the far side of the river Psel – the last natural obstacle before Kursk.[171] Then, on the 12th, the Red Army counter-attacked in earnest. On this day, the 270 German tanks and self-propelled guns faced 850 Soviet ones, and this massive array stopped the Waffen-SS' advance. Although the German troops managed to hold their positions until, on the 14th, the Soviet counter-attack was called off, the losses of equipment were substantial. *Division Totenkopf* alone lost half of its tanks and other vehicles.[172]

Already on 13 July, Hitler called off the offensive. Apart from considerable losses and limited results, the reason was the development in the western theatre of war. On 10 July, British and US troops had landed in Sicily, and Hitler decided to transfer the second SS armoured corps HQ and the *Leibstandarte* to Italy.[173] Moreover, the Red Army had launched an offensive at Oryol thus menacing the German northern axis of attack at Kursk.[174]

While the total German losses at Kursk were 56,000 men, of whom 10–11,000 had been killed; Soviet casualties numbered 177,000 with 40,000 estimated fatalities – losses inflicted in little more than one week's intensive combat.[175] Nonetheless, the Battle of Kursk was a defeat of the German east army, which would never again be able to mount such an offensive.

Partisan War in Yugoslavia

One of the bloodiest chapters in the Waffen-SS history was written in the Balkans where several of its field units, including *Prinz Eugen* and *Nordland* took part in a brutal occupation regime and suppressions of partisans. When, in 1941, the multi-ethnic Yugoslavia was occupied by the Axis powers, the Serbs were almost alone in offering resistance. The Croats had been promised independence and, generally, they welcomed the invaders.[176] In the country there were many *Volksdeutsche* as well as the Muslim Bosniacs, and both these groups became targets for Waffen-SS recruitment.[177]

---

170. Frankson and Zetterling (2003), p 149.
171. Sydnor (1990), p 285.
172. Ibid., p 286ff.
173. BAMA, RS2-2/4, KTB Nr.4, 9.1.1943–26.3.1943. See 3.8., 9.8. and 13.8.1943; Fritz (2011), p 350ff.; Sydnor (1990), p 292.
174. Glantz and House (1999), p 197ff.
175. On Red Army losses see ibid., p 274ff., on German losses see Frankson and Zetterling (2003), p 204. Nothing indicates that Waffen-SS' casualty rate was any higher than that of the *Wehrmacht*. See Töppel in Schulte et al. (2014), p 327.
176. Casagrande (2003), p 155.
177. Ibid., p 160.

Over the following years, a variety of anti-German resistance groups sprang up with Josip Broz's (Tito's) communist partisans as the most important. They competed with the more conservative Serb *Chetniks*, and the Axis occupation heralded a conflict that was as much a civil war as one of resistance.[178]

Partisan activity began in earnest in the wake of the German onslaught on the Soviet Union in June 1941.[179] From the very beginning, the Germans retaliated draconically – in particular in the Serbian parts of the country – not least against the Jewish community.[180] On 2 October 1941, in retaliation of a partisan ambush on a lorry column 2,000 Jews were shot; and on 12 October such killings were systematised.[181] On that day, it was ordered that, for every German killed, 100 prisoners or hostages were to be shot and, for every wounded German, 50 would have to pay with their lives.[182] Up until November, 8,000 Jewish men were shot – officially as retaliation for Germans killed or wounded. These men's relatives were interned and later, during spring 1942, killed in mobile gas chambers.[183]

Mass executions and massacres as reprisals for partisan activities became a praxis that spread beyond the group of Jews. In June 1942, for instance, Himmler ordered the *HPSSF Alpeland* to conduct a four weeks long action in the northernmost part of the occupied Yugoslav area in order to stop all partisan activity there. The action was to be conducted in a ruthless manner, and all communities supporting the partisans were to be annihilated. This entailed execution of all men of a so-called 'guilty' family, or even kin, and concentration camp for the women.[184]

In October 1942, *Prinz Eugen* was employed in suppression of partisans in Serbia, but was moved to Croatia in December where, seen with SS eyes, it distinguished itself fighting partisans by ruthlessly repressing the civilian population.[185] On 12 July 1943, for example, the division massacred 40 men, women and children who had gathered in a mosque in the Bosnian town Košutica.[186] The division perpetrated several similar actions, and murdered more civilians than other German units in the area.[187] Having co-operated with Croatian troops in several actions, *Prinz Eugen* spent September and October 1943 disarming Italian forces on the Adriatic coast, which like earlier in the war

---

178. Charles D. Melson, 'German Counterinsurgency in the Balkans: The Prinz Eugen Division Example, 1942–1944', *The Journal of Slavic Military Studies*, vol. 20, No. 4, 2007, p 707ff.
179. Casagrande (2003), p 168.
180. Walter Manoschek, *'Gehst mit Juden erschiessen?'. Die Vernichtung der Juden in Serbien* in Heer and Naumann (1995), p 42.
181. Casagrande (2003), p 172.
182. Casagrande (2003), p 170.
183. Longerich (2008), p 563.
184. Longerich (2008), p 646.
185. Cf. Casagrande (2003), p 229, 236 and 244ff.
186. BAB, NS19/1434, *Einsatzkommando 2* to *Einsatzgruppe E in Agram, 15.4 43. Aktennotiz über die Besprechung des Reichsführers-SS mit SS-Obergruppenführer Phleps am 28.7.43.* See also Casagrande (2003), p 259.
187. Ibid., p 260.

included executing prisoners and civilians.[188] *Division Prinz Eugen* was also involved in tough fighting against partisan units for example near Split in September. The opponents had artillery at their disposal at was estimated to be 'superior'.[189] The fighting cost *Prinz Eugen* 753 men of whom 82 killed and 85 missing, while the rest were wounded. Enemy casualties were summed up to 1,200 dead.[190]

The mounting resistance in Yugoslavia and the vacuum created by Italy's collapse, forced the SS to rush raw troops to the area in late summer 1943. In August 1943, the newly formed *III. Germanische SS-Panzer-Korps* was ordered to deploy to Croatia with its two core units SS-*Panzergrenadier-Division Nordland* and SS-*Panzergrenadier-Brigade Nederland*. The corps and its units had only been under formation since May 1943 and Gottlob Berger warned in vain Himmler that 'Eighty percent of the men are not only lacking any sort of weapons training; even more dangerously, they are without any weapons'.[191] The soldiers were nevertheless engaged in skirmishes with partisans, and they also killed civilians and burned villages.[192] A former Danish soldier from *Nordland* told about one such action where 'the inhabitants were all shot and what remained was burned'.[193] A Norwegian SS soldier stated in his memoires that 'when villages were suspected of having supported the enemy, they were looted completely, the houses were torched, and the inhabitants were glad if they got out alive'.[194]

The Waffen-SS Women

Originally, the Waffen-SS was a 'men only' organisation. However, women did play a role in the military part of the SS, especially after 1943. As early as 1929, Himmler had declared that the SS should not remain a traditional men's and soldiers' organisation, but ought, over time, to develop into an order for both sexes joined in a so-called *SS-Sippengemeinschaft* (union of kinship). Through admission of the best men and women, the SS was to develop into the New Germany's racial élite.

---

188. BAMA, RH24-15/16, *Anlagen z. Ktb., XV Gebirgsarmeekorps*, concerning *Prinz Eugen*. See under 27.–28.9.43. Manachem She, *Die Ermordung italienischer Kriegsgefangener, September–November 1943* in Heer and Naumann (1995), p 193.

189. BAMA, RH24-15/9, *XV Gebirgsarmeekorps, Ktb. Band II, 23.8.43–31.10.43*, 14 September 1943.

190. Ibid., 2 October 1943.

191. Jens Westemeier, *Hans Robert Jauss. Jugend, Krieg und Internierung* (Konstanz University Press, 2016), p 97.

192. HLC, Sigurd Sørlies personal archive, P22 – Knut Baardseth, Diary 6 September, 7. September, 14 September, 15–18 October, 2 November and 9 November 1943. Christensen et al. (1998), p 202ff.; Egil Ulateig, *Dagbok fra ein rotnorsk nazist* (Oslo, 1987), pp 166f.; Sigurd Sørlie, *Solkors eller hakekors. Nordmenn i Waffen-SS 1941–1945*. PhD dissertation (Institutt for arkeologi, konservering og historie, Universitetet i Oslo. 2014), p 362ff.; Westemeier (2016), p 97 ff.

193. Christensen et al. (1998), p 204ff.

194. Bjorn Lindstad, *Den frivillige. En frontkjemper forteller sin historie* (Kagge Forlag, 2010), p 95.

However, this was not to be understood as a blueprint for female influence in either politics or war.[195] On the contrary, the Third Reich's view was that women should be wives and mothers playing no role in public life. Women's tasks concerned the family sphere; a point of view that did not change at all during the war. Unlike what happened in other warring great powers, Germany never systematically mobilised the women. Nonetheless, gradually they took over military functions in the hinterland and joined organisations supporting the war effort.[196] During the Second World War, nearly 500,000 women were employed by the armed forces as so-called *Wehrmachthelferinnen*. Moreover, women of various other organisations also contributed to the war effort. They worked on fortifications, the performed air raid warning, and served as nurses in field hospitals.[197]

The wartime shortage of personnel meant that more and more women would fill posts with the SS, though never to the same extent as with the *Wehrmacht* or the Medical Service. While the *Wehrmacht* had had women attached long before the war, the SS did not start systematic recruitment until 1943.[198] However, new ground had been broken the year before when Ernst Sachs, the director of the *Ferndmeldewesen der SS* (SS Signals Corps), raised a women's auxiliary signals and radio service. Their training facility was the brand new establishment, the *Reichsschule für SS-Helferinnen* in Oberehnheim. The influx of women at this time had to do with the general expansion of the Waffen-SS. The arrival of the women helped free men from administrative work and helped make up for the chronic personnel shortage. Ca. 3,000 women became *SS-Helferinnen*, but these were not the only women in the SS. While about 8,000 women were employed by the SS as civilians, other 4,000 performed duties as *Aufseherinnen* (attendants) in concentration camps.[199] All these groups were termed as *SS Gefolge* (SS entourage). The designation subjected the women to SS jurisdiction.[200]

195. Gudrun Schwarz, *Eine Frau an seiner Seite: Ehefrauen in der, 'SS-Sippengemeinschaft'* (Aufbau Taschenbuch Verlag, 2000), p 18ff.

196. Wolffram Wette, *Militarismus in Deutschland: Geschichte einer kriegerischen Kultur* (Primus, 2008), p 186ff.; Claudia Koonz, *Mothers in the Fatherland: Women, the Family, and Nazi Politics* (St. Martin's Press, 1986), p 177ff.

197. Jutta Mühlenberg, *Das SS-Helferinnenkorps: Ausbildung, Einsatz und Entnazifizierung der weiblichen Angehörigen der Waffen-SS 1942–1949* (Hamburger Edition, 2010), p 13.

198. Before that year there were female civilian employees. Primarily, they worked in offices etc. See BAMA, N756/251, *Der Reichsführer-SS, Rihtlinien für die Betreuung der im Bericht der SS und Polizei eingesetzten deutschen Frauen, insbesonders in den Gebieten ausserhalb der Reichgrenze*, 31 November 1942.

199. Mühlenberg (2010), p 14.

200. On *SS-Gefolge*, see Claus Bundgaard Christensen, 'Kvinderne fra Lublin. Bevogtningspersonalet i Majdanek', *Historisk Tidsskrift* vol. 106, nr. 2, 2013, p 564 ff.

Chapter Four

FALL AND OBLITERATION

In September 1944, the SS' statistical office compiled a comprehensive survey of personnel. Despite casualties the overall number was still ca. 800,000 men, of whom 200,000 were attached to the *Allgemeine SS*, whereas the Waffen-SS with 594,443 constituted the vast majority of the organization. This number included a considerable group of personnel serving in the concentration camps.[1]

At this stage, the Waffen-SS was twice as large as in 1942 and had reached its numerical culmination point. Himmler could now boast seven armoured divisions and a number of corps commands, several of which would be employed in 1944's hot spots. The increased strength of the Waffen-SS mirrored the relative influence of the SS vis-a-vis other key institutions in The Third Reich. On 22 July 1944, the attempted assassination of Hitler further strengthened Himmler's already strong position in the Nazi hierarchy. On the same day, Hitler handed over command of the reserve army from the *Wehrmacht* to his *Reichsführer-SS* who thereby took charge of 1.9 million men.[2] Thus, Himmler had made incursions deep into army territory, now being responsible for weaponry, prisoner-of-war camps and not least recruiting, training and allocation of personnel.

The year 1944 also saw the first SS generals appointed to army command. In July, Paul Hausser was appointed commander of the seventh army, and in August, Sepp Dietrich assumed command of the fifth armoured army – both of these were stationed in Normandy. These appointments were parts of a general trend with the armed forces elevating a new élite of Nazis into the top-tiers of the military hierarchy, frequently despite their limited experience with the conduct of major operations.[3] This drift led to a de-professionalisation of the supreme military leadership culminating in the late autumn, when Himmler assumed personal command of the *Heeresgruppe Oberrhein* (Army Group Upper Rhine).[4]

---

1. BAB, NS19/1471, *Statistisch-Wissenschaftliches Institut des Reichsführers-SS*, 19 September 1944. See also BAB, NS19/1474, *Statistisch-Wissenschaftliches Institut des Reichsführers-SS*, 23 May 1944.
2. Jürgen Förster, *Die Wehrmacht im NS-Staat: eine strukturgeschichtliche Analyse*, durchgesehene Auflage (Oldenburg, 2009, p 131ff.; Longerich (2008), p 716ff.; Ian Kershaw, *The End: Hitler's Germany, 1944–1945* (Allen Lane, 2011), p 35ff.
3. Peter Lieb (2007), p 96.
4. Detlef Vogel, 'Deutsche und alliierte Kriegsführungim Westen', in *Das Deutsche Reich in der Defensive, Das deutsche Reich und der Zweite Weltkrieg*, Vol. 7 (Deutsche Verlags-Anstalt, 2001), p 617.

New Envelopments at the Eastern Front

During the first months, a mini-Stalingrad seemed to develop in the snow-clad landscapes of the southern part of the eastern front. After Kursk in the autumn 1943, Army Group South had to withdraw across the Dnieper. The plan was to consolidate the front there, but before the Germans were able to dig in the so-called Panther position, the Red Army had established several bridgeheads on the western bank interspersed among the Germans. In late January 1944, the Russians broke out of the bridgeheads enveloping 55,000 German troops, including *Division Wiking* and a recently established unit – *SS-Sturmbrigade Wallonien* – in the Cherkasy pocket 75 km south of Kiev.[5] Several weeks of tough fighting followed, during which the Germans hoped for salvage from outside. Hitler ordered that the 'fortress on the Dnieper' must not be abandoned. However, the attempts to open a corridor to the enveloped troops was hampered by mud caused by the thaw, shortage of fuel and flawed co-ordination. Among the relieving forces was a part of the *Leibstandarte*, which, at the beginning of the operation, had about 100 tanks and tank destroyers at its disposal. However, as early as 15 February they reported that because of extremely deep mire only three tanks and one tank destroyer were left moving. All of these were busily engaged recovering tanks and soft skinned vehicles.[6] For these reasons and because of Soviet opposition the attack ran out of steam at about 10 km from the beleaguered troops. On 16 February, it appeared that the Soviet line between the pocket and the bulk of the relief forces was rather thin, and the commander of Army Group South, Erich von Mannstein, ordered the encircled troops to attempt a breakout the same evening.[7] *Wiking* was to spearhead one of the three groups of forces tasked with performing the operation.[8] The distance to be covered would imply severe fighting with Soviet troops as well as crossing the icy river Gniloy Tikich. The division's attempts to lay a bridge did not succeed and instead the troops were ferried or swam across. Many perished during the endeavour. However, despite the physical and mental hardships the enveloped troops got out of the pocket in considerable numbers. The main part of the *SS-Sturmbrigade Wallonien*, a little less than 2,000 men fought their way out and so did 8,000 of Wiking's 11,500.[9] While all heavy weapons and a large number of wounded soldiers had to be left in the pocket, around 36,000 got out.[10]

---

5.   Zetterling and Frankson (2006), p 272ff. and Frieser in *Die Ostfront 1943/44. Der Krieg im Osten und an den Nebenfronten, Das deutsche Reich und der Zweite Weltkrieg*, Vol. 8 (München: Deutsche Verlags-Anstalt, 2007), pp 394–419; Erickson (1996), p 176ff. On Wiking, see also Strassner (1968), p 231ff. Nikolaus v. Vormann, *Tscherkassy* (Scharnhorst Buchkameradschaft, 1954), p 79ff.

6.   Zetterling and Frankson (2006), p 318. Frieser in *Die Ostfront 1943/44. Der Krieg im Osten und an den Nebenfronten, Das deutsche Reich und der Zweite Weltkrieg*, Vol. 8 (München: Deutsche Verlags-Anstalt, 2007), p 403.

7.   Frieser in *Die Ostfront 1943/44. Der Krieg im Osten und an den Nebenfronten, Das deutsche Reich und der Zweite Weltkrieg*, Vol. 8 (München: Deutsche Verlags-Anstalt, 2007), p 408.

8.   Zetterling and Frankson (2006), p 272ff.

9.   Ibid., p 319.

10. Frieser in *Die Ostfront 1943/44. Der Krieg im Osten und an den Nebenfronten, Das deutsche Reich und der Zweite Weltkrieg*, Vol. 8 (München: Deutsche Verlags-Anstalt, 2007), p 416.

After a brief period of rest and recuperation, *Division Wiking* was employed in relieving a German force that had been cut off at the town Kovel in north-western Ukraine. Kovel was an important junction in the south-western part of the hardly passable Pripyat swamps. At this stage, this area was a last ditch stand to prohibit the second Belarus Front advancing deep into Poland, whereby the German eastern front would be split in a northern and a southern part. Hitler's reaction to this menace was ordering the town held to the last man standing and employing the second battalion of *Division Wiking*' stank regiment. This battalion had received the new Panther tanks and was spearheading the relief force together with *Regiment Germania*'s third battalion, which was at full establishment strength. The soldiers who had just about got out of the Cherkasy pocket were less than enthusiastic. In mid-March, a company commander of *Wiking*'s *Regiment Westland* wrote to his parents,

> After the tough fighting in the pocket we were, despite everything, deprived of our leave, which had been promised by the top-level. Instead, we are now again being employed in the most difficult kind of operations. This is indeed disgraceful; this way even the most dedicated idealism will vanish.[11]

Other Waffen-SS formations, too, were heavily engaged at the eastern front. At the end of March, the whole first armoured army, ca. 220,000 troops, were encircled by first and second Ukrainian Front forces. This happened near the city Kamianets-Podilskyi close to the border with Romania, and everything indicated that the army would be annihilated. In that case, the German southern front would collapse and the road into the Balkans would be open to Soviet forces. However, Erich von Mannstein managed to persuade Hitler that the army might fight its way through towards north-west, while at the same time the second SS armoured corps was employed in a supporting attack. At his disposal Hausser, the corps commander, had the two Waffen-SS divisions *Hohenstaufen* and *Frundsberg*. These were dispatched by forced transport from France and, on 5 April, the attack on the pocket – which had in the meantime moved 100 km west – was launched. Over the first 24 hours, *Hohenstaufen* and *Frundsberg* advanced about 50 km linking up with the armoured army's advance parties the next morning. Not only did this save most of the soldiers and the army's heavy equipment, it also allowed the army to reinforce and stabilise the tottering southern front on the Romanian border.[12]

The tactical successes, however, came at a price. *Leibstandarte*, which had fought at Cherkasy and then ended up among the beleaguered formations of first armoured army, was by then almost completely run down and had to be re-formed in France.[13] It had been planned to redeploy Hausser's armoured corps to western Europe, but the situation did not allow it to be extricated from the threadbare eastern frontline.

---

11. Fritz Hahl' *Mit 'Westland' im Osten. Ein Leben zwischen 1922 und 1945* (Munin Verlag, 2000), p 135.
12. The above is based on Frieser in Frieserand Schmider (2007), pp 432–447; Erickson (1993), p 183ff.; Dtöber (1976) vol. 1, p 35ff. See also Stein (1984), p 218.
13. Weingartner (1974), p 92ff.

Instead *Hohenstaufen* was employed in a vain attempt to relieve the threatened city Ternopil (Tarnopol), which Hitler had ordered to be held at any cost. Not only did this city fall before *Hohenstaufen* and other formations could relieve it, the 48th corps, which was tasked with co-ordinating the attack, expressed dissatisfaction with the Waffen-SS officers' capabilities.[14] Also the corps' other division *Frundsberg* got deeply entangled in fighting, and during the period 5–20 April, alone it sustained 2,000 casualties.[15] When the Allied landings in Normandy were launched two months later, Hitler came to regret bitterly that the corps remained at the eastern front, and it was in all haste moved from east to west to contribute to the fighting there.[16]

Defensive Operations in the Wake of Operation Bagration

Almost simultaneously with the D-Day landings, SS troops at the eastern front were engaged anew, when, in June–July 1944, Army Group Centre collapsed. On 22 June, the German frontline in Belarus this was hit by a major Soviet offensive named Operation Bagration. A mere five weeks hence, the Russians had imposed on the Germans the loss of a quarter of a million men, pushed the enemy 600 km west and the connexion between Army Group North and Army Group Centre had been severed.[17]

Now, *Divisions Totenkopf* and *Wiking* became involved in an attempt to stabilize the front. In May and June, after more than a year's continuous fight at the eastern front, *Totenkopf* received a brief rest and recuperation period in Romania. In July, the division, which had, in the meantime, received Panther tanks, was again sent up the lines. Field Marshal Walter Model, the commander of Army Group Centre, ordered the division to Hrodna (Grodno) in today's Belarus. Before the city was a huge gap in the front, and the fall of Grodno would open the way to East Prussia as well as towards south-west, that is into central Poland and Warsaw. Although fighting an opposition many times its own strength, *Totenkopf* managed to keep the Red Army at bay for 11 days. On 18 July, Model allowed the division to break clean and withdraw to the Polish capital.[18]

However, this was only a brief respite for the German defence of Poland. On 13 July, while Operation Bagration was still on, a new Soviet offensive was launched against Lviv (Lemberg, Lvov) in the south-eastern corner of Poland. Moreover, a few days later another large-scale attack commenced from the eastern parts of the country. From late July to mid-August, *Totenkopf* and *Wiking* became crucial pawns in the defensive struggle against strong enemy forces east of Warsaw.[19] Here, they were subordinated to the newly formed fourth SS armoured corps. The German formations, including the two Waffen-SS

14. BAMA, RH24-48/151, *Erfahrungsbericht des XXXXVIII Panser Korps über den Entsatz-Angriff auf Tarnopol vom 11.4.–17.4.44, Gen.KDo.XXXXVIII.Pz.Korps*, 22 April 1944.
15. BAMA, N756/159c, *10. SS-Panzer-Division 'Frundsberg', Verlustmeldung*, 24 April 1944.
16. Frieser in Frieser and Schmider (2007), p 447.
17. Karl-Heinz Frieser, 'Der Zusammenbruch der Heeresgruppe Mitte im Sommer 1944' in Frieser and Schmider (2007), pp 526–603.
18. Sydnor (1990), p 302ff.
19. Frieser and Schmider (2007), pp 583f.

divisions, succeeded in stabilising the front so well that this part held until January 1945. At the same time, a mixed force of SS and army units under Bach-Zelewski had ample opportunity to bloodily defeat the Polish Home Army's uprising in Warsaw.[20]

The Narvafront

Further north, around the Estonian town of Narva the SS played a significant role, too.[21] Since the autumn 1942, the front near Leningrad, where the 18th German army was, had been rather static. This was a low-priority area characterised by the absence of large-scale operations. It had been diluted of German troops for some time, but, in December 1943, the 18th Army received a welcome reinforcement in the shape of Felix Steiner's *III. Germanisches Panzerkorps* including *Division Nordland* and *Brigade Nederland*. They were immediately employed around a Soviet bridgehead west of Leningrad – the Oranienbaum pocket.[22]

On 14 January 1944, the peaceful conditions in this sector came to an end. As an element in a major, well-concerted offensive, large Soviet formations attacked across a 400-km sector. In the Germanic armoured corps' sector, the attack was supported by a protracted artillery barrage from heavy batteries at Kronstadt naval base and Soviet battleships and cruisers anchored close by. Nonetheless, the initial phase of the offensive was a disappointment to the Russians. Steiner employed parts of *Division Nordland* in successive counter-attacks – according to Soviet sources, up to 30 on one day – and it was not until after three days' struggle and committing the Soviet reserves that the front began to quiver.[23] Soon after, the rather scarce German troops of the pretty weak 18th army had to retreat west. Not until early February 1944, the front was stabilized along the Estonian border.[24] Until then, the combat had inflicted rather heavy losses on the formations of the SS corps. For example, up until 1 February, *Nordland's* losses amounted to 350 killed, 1,251 wounded and 412 missing (of whom, however, some later re-joined their units).[25]

It was of huge military, political and economic importance that the Germans had succeeded in halting their retreat at river Narva on the Estonian border. Here, the terrain along the Narva provided one of the best defensive opportunities in as much as the huge lake Peipus protected the southern flank and the Gulf of Finland the northern one. Thus, the attackers could not outflank the defenders. Steiner's armoured corps

---

20. On the Warsaw uprising and the crimes perpetrated see Norman Davies, *Rising' 44. The Battle for Warsaw* (Penguin Books, 2005). See also the chapter on Waffen-SS crimes.
21. Toomas Hiio, 'Combat in Estonia in 1944' in Hiio (2006); Christensen et al. (1998), p 216ff.; Wilhelm Tieke, *Tragödie um die Treue*, (Munin-Verlag, 1971).
22. Christensen et al. (1998).
23. Vladimir Besjanov, *Desjat Stalinskikh udarov* (Ast, 2005), p 52; Tieke (1971), p 27ff.
24. Apart from the Waffen-SS formations just mentioned, a police division battle group (primarily composed of its artillery regiment and three infantry battalions) of ca. 500 troops were also involved in these clashes. Friedrich Husemann, *Die guten Glaubens waren. Band 2 :Geschichte der SS-Polizei-Division (4. SS-Polizei-Panzer-Grenadier-Division) 1943–1945* (Munin Verlag, 1973).
25. BAMA, N.756/164b, *Zustandsbericht der 11. SS-PZ GrenDiv Nordland /175, Nr. 2, 1.1.–31.1.1944.*

commanding the newly formed Estonian 20th SS division, Division Nordland and Brigade Nederland was responsible for defending the area around the town of Narva – the centrepiece of the German defence.

Even before German troops had taken up their positions along the river, Soviet forces launched new attacks and established bridgeheads north and south of the town of Narva. While the northern bridgehead was easily annihilated, the southern one remained on Soviet hands. In the following days and weeks, this would become a focal point in the struggle for Narva. The fighting cost the defenders dearly, and, at the end of February, the general-officer-commanding Nordland, Fritz von Scholz, described his formation as deeply impressed by the heavy losses and fit for defensive operations, only. If Scholz's report is to be trusted, there was nothing wrong with the soldiers' combat zeal; it was the losses of officers and NCOs which prohibited offensive activity.[26]

The spring thaw and huge Soviet casualties meant that, from mid-April, the fight grew positional characterised by artillery barrages and minor Soviet attempts of gaining tactical advantages. This went on until, on 24 July, a new Soviet major offensive was launched where after the Germanic armoured corps began its pre-planned retreat to new positions on a ridge 20 km further west – the Tannenberg position. One of Brigade Nederland's two regiments was annihilated during the retreat, but all other units arrived safely in the new position. At this moment, the defenders were reinforced by two more SS formations, viz. *Kampfgruppe Rehmann* of *Division Langemarck* and *Sturmbrigade Wallonien*.[27] With these reinforcements the Narva front became a virtual Waffen-SS front, which provided German propaganda with a golden opportunity to highlight this sector as the successful, united European people's 'defence against Bolshevism'. In August 1944, 25 Estonian infantry battalions were assembled at the Narva front together with 24 staffed by German, Scandinavian, Dutch, Flemish and Wallonian soldiers.[28] From the end of July onwards, a violent battle raged in the Tannenberg position until, in mid-September, German forces abandoned Estonia.

Opening of the Second Front – Fights in the West

On 6 June 1944, Fritz Knöchlein, commanding officer of *Nordland*'s *Regiment 23 Norge*, issued a proclamation for his men. The regiment was fighting at Narva and the personnel was briefed on the Allied landings in Normandy the same day. According to Knöchlein, the war had now reached a decisive stage. He prophesied that the 'throng of barbarians of the Asian steppes' would join the Anglo-American onslaught and fall upon Europe with renewed energy, because 'the Jew in Moscow is one and the same as the Jew in London and New York'.[29] In May 1944, a company commander of *Division Totenkopf*,

26. BAMA, N.756/164/b, *Zustandsbericht der 11 SS-PZ Gren.Div.Nordland, 1.2.–29.2.1944*. BAMA, RS2-3/2, *Generalkommando III. (germ.) SS-Panzerkorps, Tätigkeitsbericht, 31.3.1933*, p 11. Tieke (1971), p 54ff.; Hiio (2006), pp 1047–1055.
27. Tieke (1971), p 63ff. Hiio (2006), pp 1047–1060.
28. Hiio (2006), p 1057.
29. HLC, Private archive Terje Emberland, 'Dagsbefaling til 23. SS-Panzergrenadierregiment Norge den 6.6.1944' reprinted in *Feltposten*, Nr. 6, June 1944, p 2.

Knöchlein had been responsible for the Le Paradis massacre on British prisoner, and the Waffen-SS units employed against the Allies in Normandy would commit similar atrocities in the time to come.

As the Allied armada approached the French coast, the German Commander-in-Chief West, *Generalfeldmarschall* (Field Marshal) Gerd von Rundstedt, had rallied 1.5 million troops under his aegis.[30] Most of these were *bodenständige* (territorial) infantry divisions with no means of transportation. Also, the personnel's quality, weaponry and motivation left much to be desired. Thus, the crucial elements of the German defence were the armoured divisions, which von Rundstedt either had under his command already or was allotted during the battle. Characteristically, no less than five out of eleven armoured divisions were of the Waffen-SS.[31] These were *Leibstandarte, Das Reich, Hohenstaufen, Frundsberg* and *Hitlerjugend*. Additionally, there were the mechanised divisions *Götz von Berlichingen* and two heavy tank battalions, *Schwere SS-Panzerabteilung 101* and *102*. These were subordinate to the two SS corps employed in Normandy, *I.* and *II. SS Panzerkorps*.[32] Of the aggregate forces under C-in-C West, 110,000 were Waffen-SS men, and the SS divisions had more and younger personnel as well as better weaponry than that of similar army units.[33] The allocation of the powerful Panther tank may serve as illustration. While in early July, 51 per cent of the Waffen-SS tank fleet were Panthers, in the army armoured divisions only 26 per cent were of that make. As to the even more powerful Tiger tank, the SS had 80 per cent of those employed in Normandy at their disposal.[34] Conversely, the beyond competition, strongest German tank formation in Normandy prior to the Allied invasion was not of the Waffen-SS, but the army's *Panzer-Lehr-Division*.[35]

Hitlerjugend was the first SS division to get ground contact with the invading forces. As, during the early hours of 6 June, it became obvious that the invasion was in progress, the German high command wished to crush the Allied beachheads before the attackers could consolidate their positions. *Hitlerjugend* was released at 2.30 p.m. and deployed towards Caen – a march which was fraught with difficulties because of the Allied local air supremacy. It was not only the Hitlerjugend soldiers who had to be constantly on the look-out for enemy air attacks. The Allied command of the airspace over Normandy was so overwhelming that the 12,000 sorties on D-Day were met by only 319 German fighters and, on this day none of the Allied aeroplanes was shot down by German aircraft.[36] The air strikes delayed the German movements significantly and several formations did not arrive in time for the co-ordinated attack on the Anglo-Canadian forces planned to be launched on 7 June. Nonetheless, as early as during the afternoon of 6 June, parts of the *Hitlerjugend* division managed to engage British and Canadian

---

30. Horst Boog, *Das Deutsche Reich und der Zweite Weltkrieg*, Vol. 7 (Dt. Verl.-Anst., 2001), p 419ff.
31. Lieb (2007), p 101.
32. Niklas Zetterling, *Normandy 1944: German Military Organization, Combat Power and Organizational Effectiveness* (J.J. Fedorowicz Publishing, 2000), p 177ff.
33. Lieb (2007), p 113.
34. Numbers are from ibid., p 112.
35. John A. English, *Surrender Invites Death. Fighting the SS in Normandy* (Stackpole Books, 2011).
36. Keegan (1994), p 143.

invasion troops. In this early phase, they turned out to be an opponent to be reckoned with. According to its own statements, which must be taken with a pinch of salt though, the division's armoured regiment destroyed scores of Allied tanks.[37] However, the dogged Waffen-SS resistance made it clear that Bernard Montgomery's Allied forces would make no immediate conquest of Caen.

During these fights, *Division Hitlerjugend*'s strength was quickly diluted.[38] On one of the early days, a soldier wrote laconically in his notebook: 'Tommy does have a lot of artillery'.[39] This turned out to be a very precise observation, and, on the 11th and 18th, the division was subjected to heavy artillery bombardment.[40] On 18 June, the division's aggregate number of losses was 6,164 killed, wounded and missing. This was a casualty rate much higher than any other SS formation in Normandy.[41] The superior force facing the Germans wore on the morale. A British report on prisoners-of-war (POWs) concerning the period 16–22 June established that the morale among *Division Hitlerjugend* POWs had sagged somewhat due to huge losses, and that the Allied superiority in personnel and equipment 'continued to make an impression'.[42] A Leibstandarte soldier, whose unit relieved one from the *Hitlerjugend* defending Caen, described in his memoirs the shocking meeting with the very young German soldiers 'standing in front of us like human wrecks, haggard, filthy and staring blankly ahead.[43] Moreover, in addition to the ongoing struggle, the shortage of filler personnel was felt by the soldiers. Up until July, *Hitlerjugend* and *Leibstandarte* had received 1,000 replacements for 7,500 losses.[44]

There were other SS troops fighting in the Caen area. On 12 June, the British attacked the village Villers-Bocage south-west of Caen. Here occurred one of the best-known episodes in the Waffen-SS' war history. A Tiger Tank commanded by *Obersturmführer* Michael Wittmann of the *Schwere SS-Panzerabteilung 101* took on a British Cromwell tank squadron. During the ensuing fight, Wittmann's tank alone neutralised the entire British column, a deed which secured him hero status in the fascination literature on the Waffen-SS.[45] However, the rejoicing was short-lived. In August, during

37. Szamveber (2012), p 40.
38. VAP, 12. SS-PZ.DIV HJ, box Nr. 1, *Kriegstagebuch Nr. 1 des SS-Pz.Gren.Rgt. 26, 6.6.1944–20.7.1944, Gefechts- und Verflegungsstarken*. From 6 to 22 June the regiment's strength dropped from 53 officers, 252 NCOs and 2,080 soldiers to 34 officers, 145 NCOs and 1,254 soldiers.
39. BAMA, B.438, 12.6.1944.
40. VAP, N.12. *SS-Pz.Div.HJ, box 1, Gefechtsbericht der Panzer Aufklärungs Abteilung 12* [undated, probably ca. 12 June 1944]. Ibid, box 2, KTB nr. 3 *12. SS-panzer-Div. Hitlerjugend, II./SS-Panzer-Rgt.12, 6.6.–30.8.1944*, Entry on 18 June.
41. BAMA, RH21-5/50, *Anlage 133 zu KTB, PzGr. West. An Obkdo. H.Gr.B*, undated [maybe 20 July 1944].
42. NAKEW, WO208/3634, Report on German morale from interrogation of PW passing through Kempton Park Camp. 16–22 July 1944.
43. Jörn Roes, *Freiwillig in den Krieg. Auf den Spuren einer verlohrenen Jugend* (Edition q, 2005), p 145.
44. However, possibly the lightly wounded remained with their unit and would, after their convalescence, come back in a fighting capacity. BAMA, RH21-5/50, *Anlage 133 zu KTB, PzGr. West. An Obkdo. H.Gr.B*, undated [possibly 20 July 1944]
45. Thus, on visits to the churchyard in Normandy where Wittmann is buried, these authors have noticed that there are almost always fresh flowers on his tomb.

the continued battle Wittmann and his tank crew were killed. At that stage, according to SS counting Wittmann had eliminated 138 tanks and 132 anti-tank guns.[46]

On 26 June, reinforcement from the eastern front approached the combat zone in Normandy. Among these was the second SS armoured corps comprising the divisions *Hohenstaufen* and *Frundsberg*. On that same day, a *Hitlerjugend* soldier named Fritz Boem wrote a letter declaring that where the Waffen-SS stood no enemy would pass and that 'the name Hitlerjugend was a designation one could be proud of wearing on one's sleeve'.[47] However, the Allies were well aware of the forthcoming reinforcements, and exactly the 26th was the day when British and Canadian forces launched Operation Epsom with the aim of taking Caen before the second SS arrived.[48] Epsom was preceded by massive bombardment. Naval gunfire and a creeping barrage hit the *Hitlerjugend* with stunning result. The casualties – including Boem who fell during the day – increased alarmingly. However, despite the long-range artillery's effect small pockets of Waffen-SS soldiers carried on even after the main battle line's collapse. In the evening the *Hitlerjugend*, supported by the 21st armoured division, succeeded in halting the advance, thus gaining a respite allowing the second SS armoured corps to move into position and counter-attack. At that moment, the British had lost 50 tanks, but the *Hitlerjugend Division*, too, was badly mauled and other Waffen-SS units suffered heavy losses as well.[49] For example, in the first day of the counter-attack, *Frundsberg* lost 38 tanks and on 2 July the division reported that it had lost 571 men to Allied artillery fire over 36 hours. Since 29 June, *Hohenstaufen* had lost 800–900 wounded and 300 killed. The units of this division had been under continuous bombardment for 10–12 hours, and in one regimental sector 6–8,000 ground bursts had been counted within 3½ hours.[50]

Although the Waffen-SS' counter-offensive of 29–30 June succeeded in halting Operation Epsom, on the longer term it had been a vain effort. In the evening of 7 July, a massive British aerial bombardment heralded a renewed onslaught on Caen. *Hitlerjugend* started pulling out of the north-western part of the city leaving a rear-guard, which, on the following day, fought relentlessly against Allied troops. Eventually, the Allied seized Caen, though a month later than originally planned. In spite of the efforts at Caen there was no reason for the Germans to celebrate. German troops had not managed to engage the enemy on the beaches and, as Meyer, the commander of *Hitlerjugend*, had confidently predicted 'throw the small fish back into the water'.

In the German propaganda the Waffen-SS forces in Normandy was portrayed as combat decisive.[51] The occurrences in the context of Operation Epsom were, in many

---

46. On Wittmans as a person, see his personnel file in BAB, SSO 003C, including Himmler's proposal of 20 June 1944 on awarding him the Knight's Cross with swords and oak leaves. Will Fey, *Armor Battles of the Waffen-SS* (Stackpole Books, 2003), p 101; Beevor (2012), p 191ff.

47. SU, Lerner Collection, Box No. 2, Document report 20 July 1944.

48. Luther (1987), p 210ff.;Beevor (2012), p 228ff.;Szamveber (2012), p 102ff., Meyer (2005), p 410ff. and VAP, N.12. *SS-Pz.Div.HJ, KTB Nr. 3, 12. SS-Panzer-Div. Hitlerjugend II./ SS-Panzer-gt.12.*

49. During the first day of Epsom, allegedly, the division lost 700 men. Luther (1987), p 214.

50. BAMA, N756/157/b, *Hohenstaufen, Lagebericht 29.6–2.7.1944.*

51. Lehnhardt (2014), p 474.

respects, characteristic of the efforts done by army and SS armour during the struggle in Normandy. Although their local counter-attacks and defensive operations incurred nasty losses on the Allies, they were rarely in a position to launch major concerted multi-divisional counter-strikes supported by own artillery and aircraft.[52]

The Murder Division

Division Hitlerjugend became well known on the Allied side not only for its military opposition on the battlefield. In 1944, a court of inquiry under the Supreme Headquarters Allied Expeditionary Forces (SHAEF) filed a report on *Division Hitlerjugend*'s atrocities against POWs taken subsequent to the landings in Normandy. This detailed account stated that 'the 12th SS armoured division (Hitlerjugend) displayed a behaviour which was constantly characterised by brutality and ruthlessness'. The background for this assessment was that, during the weeks after the landings, the *Hitlerjugend* soldiers had murdered 156 Canadians and a number of British soldiers – thereby earning themselves the nickname 'Division Mord' (Murder Division) among other German troops.[53]

The killings of Allied POWs already began during the first clashes.[54] On 7 July, there were intense fights near the village Authier between soldiers of the Canadian North Nova Scotia Highlanders and *Hitlerjugend*'s 25th mechanised infantry regiment's third battalion commanded by *Obersturmbannführer* Karl-Heinz Milius. Before surrendering themselves, the Canadians had inflicted a loss of 28 killed on the young SS soldiers.[55] Several of the Canadians were then subjected to threats and jeers. J.M. MacDonald, one of the prisoners, recalled that several Germans were foaming with anger. Such reactions were by no means unusual in the heat of battle. However, shortly afterwards the situation developed. Having surrendered, Lorne Brown, who was wounded, was ordered to stand up and, while he tried to stand, an SS soldier knocked him to the ground, pressed him down under his boot and, eventually, killed him with his bayonet. It is likely that the murder of Brown was spontaneous, committed in wrath because of the Canadians' opposition shortly before, and hence not the consequence of an order, but this killing triggered a chain reaction of unprovoked violence against the Canadians. A squad of eight prisoners were ordered to take their helmets of, whereupon fire was opened against them. All in all, 37 Canadians were murdered by soldiers of Milius' unit in separate incidents on the first day of fighting.[56]

---

52. Vogel (2001), 'Deutsche und alliierte Kriegsführung im Westen', p 548.
53. NAKEW, WO309/2244, Supplementary Report of the Supreme Headquarters, Allied Expeditionary Force Court of Inquiry. Shooting of Allied Prisoners of War by 12 SS Panzer Division (Hitler-Jugend) Normandy, France 7–21 June 1944; Lieb (2007), p 160.
54. The most important examination of atrocities perpetrated in the summer 1944 by the Hitlerjugend is Howard Margolian, *Conduct Unbecoming: The Story of the Murder of Canadian Prisoners of War in Normandy* (2000). See also NAKEW, WO309/2244, Supplementary Report of the Supreme Headquarters, Allied Expeditionary Force Court of Inquiry. Shooting of Allied Prisoners of War by 12 SS Panzer Division (Hitler-Jugend) Normandy, France 7–21 June 1944.
55. Ibid., p 58.
56. Ibid. chapter 5.

On 7 and 8 June, additional murders were committed near the Premonstratensian monastery Abbaye d'Ardenne (Ardenne Abbey).[57] Here lay the HQ of *Hitlerjugend*'s 25th mechanised infantry regiment (*25. Panzer-Grenadier-Regiment*), and under Kurt Meyer's command, following interrogation, 11 Allied prisoners were executed in the monastery's small garden. Ensuing forensic examination established that out of the eleven prisoners six were killed by blows to their heads, the rest by being shot through the skull. The day after, this fate befell seven more Canadian prisoners brought to the abbey by a German officer. A German eye witness, who had also been present at the previous incident, stated that Kurt Meyer was annoyed with this officer openly declaring that in the future no prisoners were to be taken. Then he left the garden and, after a brief interrogation, the officer, whom Meyer had had an argument with, had the seven prisoners shot.[58] Until 11 June, when *Hitlerjugend*'s killings of prisoners abated, one in seven Canadian fatalities in the beachhead was not due to combat, but to murder after capture.[59]

There is much indicating that the willingness to commit crimes was pervasive with the *Hitlerjugend* officers. Of 156 killings of prisoners perpetrated under the authority of officers, individuals at the level of commanding officer or higher were responsible for 120 of these.[60] The majority of the officers in *Hitlerjugend* had been transferred from *Leibstandarte*. They had been employed at the eastern front where many had acquired the brutal and murderous practise that they were now continuing in Normandy.[61] For example Kurt Meyer, in his earlier capacity with the *Leibstandarte* had ordered a village near Kharkiv massacred in retaliation for an ambush by local partisans.[62] One of the worst perpetrators was the commanding officer of *SS-Panzer-Grenadier-Regiment 26*, Wilhelm Mohnke, who was later to take command of the *Leibstandarte*.[63] He was also a seasoned killer: In 1940, during the fights in France he had been responsible for the massacre at Wormhoudt where more than 80 British prisoners were shot.[64]

It has been suggested that officers consciously used the killing of prisoners for the purpose of building up team spirit.[65] However, there were other factors involved in brutalising the men, such as their youth and level of indoctrination brought about

---

57. Ibid. p. 70.
58. Ibid., p 82ff.
59. English (2011), p 63.
60. Margolian (2000), p 103.
61. Lieb (2007) as well as Margolian (2000) emphasise the importance of the culture of brutalisation acquired at the eastern front. The connection of the eastern front and the methods used in Normandy were scrutinised by Allied authorities as early as 1944. See interrogation of Meyer in NAKEW, WO309/2244, Supplementary Report of the Supreme Headquarters, Allied Expeditionary Force Court of Inquiry. Shooting of Allied Prisoners of War by 12 SS Panzer Division (Hitler-Jugend) Normandy, France 7–21 June 1944.
62. NAKEW, WO208/4364, G.R.G.G. Report No. 230, 5.12.1944.
63. Margolian (2000), p 90ff.
64. Ian Sayer and Douglas Botting, *Hitler's last General. The case against Wilhelm Mohnke* (Bantam Press, 1989), p 86ff.
65. Lieb (2007), p 163.

by 11 years of child and youth life in the Third Reich. Moreover, apparently it came as a surprise to the soldiers that, contrary to the propaganda narrative, the British and the Canadians did not break by first encounter with the enemy but fought audaciously and efficiently.[66]

Operation Market Garden

After almost eigth weeks of fighting, the German resistance along the Allied beachhead eventually crumbled, and by late August 100.000 German troops were enveloped in the Falaise Pocket in Normandy. The Germans were lucky to have the second SS armoured corps immediately east of the pocket. This corps succeeded in opening a narrow corridor to the beleaguered troops. However, the open terrain in combination with excellent flying weather made the Germans easy targets for the Allied airmen. The withdrawal developed into chaotic flight, in which almost all equipment had to be abandoned, and at termination of the Falaise Pocket the Allied results were 10,000 killed Germans, 50,000 POWs and scores of enemy equipment captured or destroyed.[67]

Of the 35–40,000 troops succeeding in extracting themselves from the Falaise Pocket there were quite a few of the Waffen-SS.[68] But their divisions were severely reduced and their units had been badly mauled and splintered during the break-out operation, and their heavy equipment was left useless on the field of battle. On 22 August, in its war diary the fifth armoured army made a status of the escaped parties of the Waffen-SS formations:

> *No 10 SS armoured division: weak infantry units, strength so far unknown, no tanks, no artillery. No 12 SS armoured division: 300 men, ten tanks, no artillery. No 1 SS armoured division: no information so far. No 2 SS armoured division: 450 men, fifteen tanks, six [gun] barrels. No 9 SS armoured division: 460 men, 20-25 tanks, 20 [gun] barrels.*[69]

Now, the Germans were disorganised and weakened, and the Waffen-SS formations were in need of a respite for re-formation.[70] The situation, therefore, indicated a quick conclusion of the war – probably before the end of the year – and, over the following weeks, the Allies advanced rapidly. On 24 August, Paris was taken and, on 4 September, the frontline ran from Antwerp in the north to Aachen to the north-east. Thereafter, the advance was hampered by a number of factors: German forces were transferred to the area from other fronts. Moreover, most of the military staffs had managed to

---

66. Margolian (2000).
67. Vogel (2001), p 561.
68. Ibid.
69. Rolf Michaelis, *Die 10. SS-Panzer-Division 'Frundsberg'* (Michaelis-Verlag, 2004), p 69ff.
70. Between July and September, the *Leibstandarte* had lost more than 5,000 men and so much equipment that their official divisional history categorised the formation as 'shattered'. Rudolf Lehmann and Ralf Tiemann, *Die Leibstandarte*, VI/1(Munin Verlag, 1986). The aggregate losses with *Das Reich* are not known, but as early as 10 July it had sustained 1,200 casualties. Zetterling (2000), p 318ff. The losses with the *Frundsberg* and the *Hohenstaufes* tab were probably 5,000 each over the summer 1944. Ibid., p 335ff. Accumulated losses with *Götz von Berlichingen* are assumed to be ca. 8,000 men. Ibid., p 368.

extract themselves out of the Falaise Pocket, thus providing continued leadership of the troops. At the same time, since it had not been possible to open the large French ports on the Atlantic and Chanel coasts, the Allies had difficulties supplying their front formations – forcing them to prioritise.

On this background, Montgomery, the commander of the 21st Army Group, approved the plans for Operation Market Garden.[71] The mission was to seize and secure the bridges into the Netherlands across the Meuse, Waal and Rhine.[72] Thence, a thrust was to be made into the industrial heartland of Germany – the Ruhr – thus cutting off the *Wehrmacht* forces in the Netherlands. If everything went according to plan, the war might be over by Christmas.

On 17 September, the airborne phase, called 'Market', saw 20,000 British and American troops dropped over Eindhoven, Veghel, Groesbeck, Nijmegen and Arnhem. Subsequently, air landed troops were to follow swelling the total number to about 35,000 and making 'Market' the largest air transport operation in history. Later, that day the ground phase, 'Garden', was launched as XXX British Corps started their 95-km advance from Belgium towards the Rhine. Its mission was to provide connection of the bridges taken by the airborne troops.

It is a widespread, but incorrect, assumption that the Allies knew nothing of the presence of second SS armoured corps' armoured divisions *Hohenstaufen* and *Frundsberg*. Ultra-information had warned SHAEF that the *Frundsberg* was near Arnhem and that *Hohenstaufen* was also present in the area.[73] Both divisions were being re-organised after the fights in France, and lacked vital parts of their men and equipment.[74] Nonetheless, the Waffen-SS formations did contribute decisively to the failure of Market Garden. The Allies had underestimated the Germans' flexibility, fighting power, and co-ordination skill – all of which allowed the Waffen-SS to counter-attack almost immediately. Receiving the initial reports on enemy air drops, General Wilhelm Bittrich, general-officer-commanding second SS armoured corps, ordered the *Hohenstaufen* to seize the crucial Rhine bridge at Arnhem, while dispatching the *Frundsberg* towards Nijmegen (Nimwegen) to take control of the bridges across the Waal. At Arnhem, several days of persistent fight ensued over the possession of the bridge, and additional Waffen-SS units were engaged, including the recently raised Dutch volunteer unit *SS-Brigade Landsturm Nederland*, whose soldiers, however, deserted to the allies in considerable numbers.[75]

---

71. Vogel (2001), p 563ff.; Russell F. Weigley, 'Normandy to Faialse. A Critique of Allied Planning in 1944' in *Historical Perspectives of the Operational Art* (Center of Military History. United States Army, 2005), pp 393–414.

72. Robert J. Kershaw, *It Never Snows in September: The German View of Market-Garden and the Battle of Arnhem, September 1944* (Ian Allan Pub., 2008); Lloyd Clark, *Arnhem: Jumping the Rhine, 1944 and 1945: The Greatest Airborne Battle in History* (Headline Review, 2008); Boog (2001), p 606ff.

73. Boog (2001), p 608.

74. Wilhelm Tieke, *Im Feuersturm letzter Kriegsjahre: II. SS-Panzerkorps mit 9. Und 10. SS-Division 'Hohenstaufen' und 'Frundsberg'* (Munin-Verlag, 1975), p 313.

75. Ibid., p 317. Letter of 31 October 1944 from Rauter to Herff, reprinted as document No. 597 in N.K.C.A. 'T Veld, *De SS en Nederland. Documenten uit SS-Archieven 1935–1945*, vol. 2 (Martinus Nijhoff, 1976), p 1425.

The plan for Market Garden rested on the assumption of quick seizure of all the bridges and the creation of a continuous, connecting 'forward line own troops'. But the Waffen-SS' counter-attacks in combination with the slow progress of the ground troops on the Eindhoven-Nijmegen road – nicknamed Hell's Highway by the Americans – proved deadly for the British paras tasked with taking the Arnhem bridge. On the 25th, they had to give up the northern bank of the Rhine.

Only about 2,000 troopers of the British first Airborne Division managed to get back to own main forces. The remainder were either killed or wounded or had to surrender to *Hohenstaufen*. Although the second SS armoured corps was scattered and depleted, the fights demonstrated that, even at this stage, parts of the Waffen-SS were still opponents to be reckoned with. The British and American casualties were not disastrous, but the defeat gave the Germans a sorely needed breathing space. As for the Allies, all hope of concluding the war by the end of the year was now lost.

Wacht am Rhein – the Last Offensive in the West

At Christmas 1944, the Germans launched their last big offensive operation in the west – *Wacht am Rhein* (Watch on the Rhine) – also known as the Battle of the Bulge. In every respect this was a hazardous enterprise with very limited chance of success.[76] As in France, a large proportion of the troops engaged were of the Waffen-SS. Operation *Wacht am Rhein* was to be carried out by Army Group B including the newly formed sixth SS armoured army, the fifth armoured army and the seventh army – 13 *Volksgrenadier* (infantry) divisions and five armoured divisions; 200,000 men, 600 armoured vehicles and 1,600 pieces of artillery. The plan called for attack across a front of 170 km from Monschau to Echternach in the Ardennes. The objectives were the seizure of the vital Allied supply harbour at Antwerp and the cut off of Allied forces in Flanders and the Netherlands.

The leading part that was to be played by Dietrich's armoured SS army signified the military importance of the Waffen-SS in this late phase of the war. This army combined, primarily, the re-organised SS armoured divisions that had fought against the Allies in France. The *Hohenstaufen* soldiers were being conditioned for the upcoming operations through lectures entitled, for example, 'Judaism as the leader of plutocracy and Bolshevism'.[77] In addition to pep talks, the Waffen-SS formations were allotted a large number of tanks and tank destroyers and more or less brought up to full size.[78]

---

76. Boog (2001), p 619ff.; John S.D. Eisenhower, *The Bitter Woods: The Dramatic Story, Told at All Echelons; from Supreme Command to Squad Leader; of the Crisis That Shook the Western Coalition: Hitler's Surprise Ardennes Offensive* (Putnam, 1969), p 105ff.
77. BAMA, RS3, 9/7, *Ausbildungsrichtlinien für die Auffrischung der 9. SS-Pz.Nachr.Abt.Hohenstaufen*, 17 September, 1944.
78. BAMA, N.756/158/a, *Auffrischung der Panzerverbände der Waffen-SS im Westen, 22.9.1944*. See also ibid, *Auffrischung der Panzerverbände der Waffen-SS im Westen, 18. October 1944*. In October 1944, the *Schwerer SS-Panzerabteilung 501* received, for example, 42 King Tiger tanks, while Das Reich got 36 Panther tanks.

However, the quality and training of the filler personnel was often lacking. Many came were middle-aged men in their forties and fifties from the German minorities in Central Europe and the Balkans, and their fighting spirit waned along with the increasing prospects of defeat.[79] Even the training of those described as 'reasonably good human material', which was the case of, for example, the very young *Hitlerjugend* recruits, left much to be desired. On 7 November, one *Hitlerjugend* battalion was declared ready for defensive operations, though 400 of its recruits had not fired a single shot.[80] Even worse, although the units and sub-units were now on full establishment strength, the lack of officers and NCOs hampered command.[81]

Together with *Volksgrenadier* divisions and *Fallschirmjäger* (paras), the divisions of the second SS armoured corps were to attack the Americans without consideration for their own flanks and advance towards the Meuse at Liège. Then, the armoured divisions were to continue towards Antwerp, while the remainder should build a defensive front facing north. The key unit in this phase of the operation was a battlegroup combined by units of the *Leibstandarte* and the *Schwere SS-Panzerabteilung 501*, which was equipped with King Tigers (Tiger II).[82] The battlegroup was commanded by *Obersturmbannführer* Joachim 'Jochen' Peiper and therefore carried his name. Peiper had previously worked as Himmler's ADC and as an SS officer he combined ideological fanaticism, war criminal behaviour and limited military skills.[83]

On 16 December, the first day of the offensive, *Kampfgruppe Peiper* was to advance to the Meuse and cross it. However, the initial phase was not particularly successful. Several units were halted by American resistance and several of the bridges had been demolished. In the end, Peiper ordered his battlegroup to cross the frontline through a minefield. This manœuvre proved remarkably successful, and his unit faced almost no opposition en route to their first objective, the village Honfeld. There, new challenges arose in the form of mountain roads of limited passability, and the battle group swung towards the village Büllingen.

Like most German units, Peiper's battle group had started with very little fuel and he hoped to be able to refuel from American dumps at Büllingen. The American troops there were actually successfully defeated and the vehicles were refuelled. Thence, *Kampfgruppe Peiper* continued west. On 18/19 December, though, due to supply problems as well as determined American resistance the battle group got stuck near the village La Gleize. At that moment, the unit was more than 30 km short of the Meuse – the offensive's first major objective. Shortly afterwards, Peiper's soldiers were cut off from own troops by an American counter-attack and, on the 23rd, they

---

79. Weingartner (1974), p 119.
80. BAMA, B438/84, *Tätigkeitsbericht des II./Btl.Rgt.26 12. SS-Pz.Div. 'H.J.' vom 3.9.44.5.12.44*, entry 7.11.1944.
81. Jens Westemeier, *Himmler's Krieger. Joachim Peiper und die Waffen-SS in Krieg und Nachkriegszeit*, 1. Edition (Schöningh, 2014).
82. Jens Westemeier, *Joachim Peiper: A Biography of Himmler's SS Commander* (Schiffer Military History, 2007), p 106ff. SS also Westemeier (2014).
83. Westemeier (2014).

were ordered to retrace their steps to behind the German lines. About 800 men, including Peiper himself, succeeded in doing so, but all heavy weapons had to be abandoned on the battlefield.

Before the withdrawal, this unit had committed one of the most notorious war crimes perpetrated on the western front during the Second World War. On 17 December, 80 American POWs were shot in a field near a crossroads at the small town Malmédy. The primary perpetrator was *Sturmbannführer* Werner Poetschke, who was at the crossroads due to engine trouble on his Panther tank. Due to the delay caused by the technical difficulties as well as the general haste of the operation, Poetschke was stressed and aggressive. Moreover, his composure suffered from the effects of a dressing-down, which, shortly before, Peiper had dealt him in front of his men. At Malmédy 100 American prisoners were kept guarded in a field. Because of the bad roads on the axis of advance, Poetschke did not wish to leave a unit of engineers guarding the POWs. More than once, he had ordered the Americans – in English – to act as drivers on the captured vehicles, but they had ignored this pretending not to understand. Thus, when his tank was ready, he ordered the prisoners to be shot, while he himself moved on. While only a few prisoners managed to escape, fire was opened from a machinegun mounted on a halftrack vehicle. The wounded were shot in the back of their heads. Subsequent forensic examination showed traces of fouling in the heads of 40 of the victims.[84]

This crime was characteristic of the battle group's conduct during the offensive and Peiper had himself declared that one would have to do as in Russia shooting all possible prisoners. The killings of the Americans were followed by the murder of around 250 Belgian civilians and resistance fighters in retaliation of alleged – real or imagined – partisan ambushes.[85]

At this stage, the offensive was grinding to a halt due to determined American resistance and Allied relief attacks. On 3 January 1945, although the objectives had not been taken and Antwerp had not even been threatened, the OKW called off the offensive ordering the troops to fall back.[86]

Counter-insurgency and Violence against Civilians in the West

The Waffen-SS' employment in counter-insurgency at the eastern front had all the characteristics of a genocide and, to a significant extent, the same is true of the German army's efforts in that regard. However, being transferred to the western theatre of war, generally, the army behaved with a higher degree of restraint, while the Waffen-SS units had a more difficult time abandoning their usual routine, as events during the Ardennes offensive illustrates. Also, a number of incidents in France and Italy bear testimony to this.

---

84. James J. Weingartner, *Crossroads of Death: The Story of the Malmédy Massacre and Trial* (University of California Press, 1979); Westemeier (2014), pp 331–356.
85. Westemeier (2014), p 349.
86. Stein (1984). Boog (2001), p 631.

The *Division Das Reich* was responsible for the worst of all these atrocities. In June 1944, this was perpetrated in the small town Oradour-sur-Glane in the south-west of France where 642 civilian inhabitants were massacred.[87]

At the time of the invasion, *la Résistance*'s actions meant that large areas were actually more or less under partisan control.[88] On occasions, Communist partisans succeeded in taking control of several towns and, in some of these cases, collaborators and Germans POWs were killed. This climate of increasing German fear and frustration was the backdrop for *Das Reich's* start of operations. On 5 June, *SS-Brigadeführer* Heinz Lammerding, the division's head, suggested to his boss, *General der Panzertruppe* Walter Krüger, that in order to cut the partisans off from their recruiting basis it might be useful to transport 5,000 men from the area Aurillac-Cahors-Brive. Moreover, he proposed to hang three partisans for every wounded German soldier and 10 for every killed.[89] After the Allied landing, Lammerding's proposals were partially implemented, and during the days to follow a virtual bloodbath took place culminating in the massacres of Tulle and Oradour-sur-Glane.[90]

On 7 June, the Communist *Résistance, Francs-Tireurs et Partisans* (FTP), succeeded in taking most of the town Tulle that lay on *Das Reich*'s northbound axis of advance.[91] About 140 German soldiers lost their lives during the partisans' attack. Most of them perished fighting, but some were shot after capture. On the 8th, units of *Das Reich* arrived, and being vastly superior to the tired and ill-equipped FTP fighters, they took Tulle almost without fighting. Most of the partisans had retreated to the mountains, but *Das Reich* then apprehended 3,000 local men who were herded into the village's arms factory. Allegedly some mutilated German bodies were found and possibly because of this, Lammerding decided to retaliate. The SS personnel then hung 99 persons from the lamp post and balconies of Tulle.

On 10 June I Battalion, *SS-Panzergrenadier-Regiment 4 'Der Führer'*, a unit subordinated *Das Reich*, moved to the area of Oradour-sur-Glane. This minuscule town comprised 250 properties and 330 inhabitants, though due to the influx of refugees, this number swelled to about 650. Strangely, so far this town had not seen very many Germans and, until the arrival of *Das Reich*, the inhabitants had been spared the privations of war. Adolf Diekmann, commanding officer of the battalion was in an agitated mood, as he had been informed that French partisans had caught his close friend, the commanding officer of the III Battalion, Helmuth Kämpfe.[92] All available evidence, however, indicates that there were no partisans in Oradour-sur-Glane.[93]

---

87. Peter Lieb, 'Repercussions of Eastern Front Experiences on Anti-Partisan Warfare in France 1943–1944', *Journal of Strategic Studies* 31, No. 5, 2008, pp 797-823, and Lieb (2007), p 131ff.
88. Jean-Jacques Fouchae, *Massacre at Oradour: France, 1944. Coming to Grips with Terror*, (Northern Illinois University Press), 2005, p 42ff.; Sarah Bennett Farmer, *Martyred Village: Commemorating the 1944 Massacre at Oradour-Sur-Glane* (University of California Press, 1999).
89. Lieb (2008), p 818.
90. BAMA, RS4/1293, Lammerding, no date, 1944. However, the order is of June.
91. Fouchae (2005), p 102ff. and Max Hastings, *Das Reich: The March of the 2nd Panzer Division Through France, June 1944*, (Pan, 2009), p 131ff.
92. The is some confusion concerning this man's name. It was indeed Adolf Diekmann and not, as intimated by Hastings, (2009) Otto Dickmann.
93. Fouchae (2005), p 96ff., Hastings (2009) p 185, and Lieb, *Journal of Strategic Studies* 31, No. 5, 2008, s.368ff.

On 11 June about 2.15 pm, on two halftracks and eight lorries Diekmann and one of his companies arrived in Oradour-sur-Glane. Thereupon, the inhabitants were ordered to assemble in the central town square, Camp de Foire. Those thus gathered were divided into two groups, viz. one of men, another of women and children. Subsequently, the men were led forth in crowds of 40–50 each and locked up in barns and garages guarded by SS men. At about 3.30 pm the soldiers opened up against the buildings where the men were incarcerated and the edifices were then torched. Only few survived. Women and children were dragooned into the church and, having killed the men, the soldiers set fire to this building as well. Apart from a few lucky ones, those trying to escape were gunned down or killed by hand grenades from the soldiers investing the church.

After the war, the apologetic Waffen-SS friendly literature tried to diminish and explain away the atrocities at Oradour and Tulle, but these were far from the only crimes committed by *Das Reich* personnel during this phase of the war.[94] Between 10 and 11 June, while a battalion of *Regiment Deutschland* killed 107 civilians including women and children, *Der Führer* executed 67 men in Argenton-sur-Creuse as part of the counter-insurgency activity.[95] Of 7,900 'bandits' killed in France between the day of invasion and the end of June, 4,000 of these had fallen victim to *Das Reich* soldiers' killing sprees.[96] Today, it is impossible to say how many were actually members of the *Maquis* resistance but, as in Oradour, many died in acts of retaliation where no one distinguished between partisans and casual, unarmed civilians.[97]

In Italy, too, several SS divisions were employed in actions against partisans and civilians. The most notorious of these was the *Division Reichsführer-SS*. August to October 1944, this division perpetrated a number of atrocities that cost more than 2,000 persons their lives. That meant that within a limited time-frame this formation would be responsible for the deaths of about 20 per cent of the 10,000 civilians falling prey to German punitive actions in Italy.[98]

Also, another SS division operated in Mediterranean theatre; the recently formed *24. Waffen-Gebirgs-(Karstjäger) Division der SS*.[99] It was employed against partisans in the Alpine regions between Italy and Slovenia. From the very few surviving combat reports it appears that this SS-unit rarely took any prisoners and carried out several massacres.[100] In its most well-known massacre, on 30 April 1944, 263 villagers perished when the division attacked the village Lipa.[101]

---

94. NAKEW, WO208/3624, Consolidated report on interrogation of four PW of SS pzgrenregt 'Der Führer' Kempton Park Camp 7 July 1944.
95. Lieb (2008), p 819.
96. Ibid.
97. Lieb (2007).
98. Carlo Gentile, '*Politische Soldaten;' Die 16. SS-Panzer-Grenadier-Division "Reichsführer-SS" in Italien 1944'*, *Quellen und Forschungen aus italienischen Archiven und Bibliotheken*, Vol 81, 2001), p 534.
99. BAMA, N756/189/a, Hans Brandt, 30.6.1944. See also Vopersal (1975).
100. Megargee (2009), p 659. On prisoners see BAMA, N756/189/a, Erwin Röslen, 1975.
101. Peter Engelbrecht, 'Die Massaker der Pottensteiner SS-Karstwehr 1943–1944 in Slowenien'. Gerhard Jochem and Georg Seiderer (eds.), *Entrechtung, Vertreibung, Mord: NS-Unrecht in Slowenien und seine Spuren in Bayern 1941–1945* (Metropol, 2005), p 228ff.

Waffen-SS barracks, schools, etc.

1945: End Game

In 1944–1945, within the army and the Waffen-SS 300 divisions were extant.[102] This might give the impression of considerable fighting power, but appearances are deceptive. Compared with earlier stages personnel as well as equipment were depleted.[103] Because of the shortage of fuel and ammunition many *Waffen-SS* and *Wehrmacht* units had no heavy weapons at their disposal and had to cope with ordinary small arms. Now and then, however, these were in short supply too.[104] This was a stark contrast to the Red Army's huge numbers of tanks and artillery; and the western Allies, notably the Americans, were even more lavishly supplied – in particular with fuel and ammunition. Moreover, the RAF and the USAAF had assumed almost complete air supremacy in the west.

In mid-February 1945, before the big Allied offensives commenced across the Rhine and the Oder, there were Waffen-SS divisions in nearly all frontal sectors of the rapidly shrinking Third Reich.[105] The total tally of divisions would soon after reach 38, and the Waffen-SS now manned posts as army group commanders. Moreover, they had one army command, 12 corps commands and numerous HQs of minor formations.[106] In early 1945, when counted by personnel, tanks and artillery still many divisions were quite powerful. In a way, filling up battered divisions had become easier as the frontline shrank, and in his capacity as commander of the reserve army Himmler had got access to replacement personnel. However, the filler personnel falling in over the last months of the war were neither voluntary nor particularly well-trained and often made up of elderly men and boys down to the age of 16 years.[107] At the beginning of 1945, the SS even considered to draft all remaining Hitlerjugend boys born in 1929, that is, those who would turn 16 over the year. This would have allowed the formation of 10 more SS divisions.[108]

Early in the year, Himmler ordered the gaps in *Division Hitlerjugend* be filled by boys of precisely that class. According to Himmler, these very young persons were to receive

---

102. Andreas Kunz, 'Die Wehrmacht 1944/45', in Jörg Echternkamp and Rolf-Dieter Müller, Das Deutsche Reich und der Zweite Weltkrieg, Vol. 10/2, (Dt. Verl.-Anst., 2008), p 18ff., and Andreas Kunz, *Wehrmacht und Niederlage: die bewaffnete Macht in der Endphase der nationalsozialistischen Herrschaft 1944 bis 1945*, 2. Aufl., (Oldenburg Wissenschaftsverlag, 2007) and John Zimmermann, 'Die deutsche militärische Kriegführung im Westen 1944/45' in Horst Boogand Rolf-Dieter Müller, *Das Deutsche Reich und der Zweite Weltkrieg*, Vol. 10/1, (Dt.Verl.-Anst., 2008).
103. Kunz (2008), p 19.
104. Kunz (2008), p 21.
105. BAMA, NS33/12, *Verbände und fechtende Sonder-Truppen d. Waffen-SS, Stand 18.2.1945*.
106. On 28 January 1945, Paul Hausser was appointed commander of Army Group G – a post he filled until 3 April 1945. Schulz and Wegmann (2005), p 86. During the period 30 November 1944–23 January 1945, Himmler commanded Army Group Oberrhein and 24 January–20 March 1945 Army Group Vistula. Ibid., p 258ff.
107. BAB, B438/359, *Die 35.SS-Polizei-Infanterie-Division, 1982*. Pierik (2001), p 256.
108. BAB, SS0 83B, *Personalakten Fritz Schmedes, Betr. Ergebnisse der Besprechung mit SS-Obersturmbannführer Grothmann am 16.2.1945 in der Feldkommandostelle, Berlin, 17.2.1945*.

first rate nourishment, but this was definitely not what 16-year-old Günter Lucks experienced when he, in March 1945, entered one of the division's battle groups.[109] Nor did the equipment status impress Günter. Due to shortages, the young recruits were dressed in a combination of Italian and German uniforms and 'there weren't even steel helmets to all the blokes'. The vehicle park in this, previously powerful division, was not much better. 'We had no tanks and we weren't even motorised'.[110]

A couple of examples shows how rapidly fighting power could erode. In January 1945, Army Group South characterised divisions *Totenkopf* and *Wiking* as having the fighting power classification I – the top-level of a continuum. For example, *Totenkopf* was 80 per cent motorised.[111] After offensive employment in Hungary under fourth SS Armoured Corps, however, the division had not very much armour left. On 13 February, a survey showed that, now, the formation had only nine *Panzerkampfwagen IV*, seven Panther tanks, seven tank destroyers *Jagdpanzer IV* and 17 pieces of self-propelled artillery, and that the degree of motorisation had dropped considerably.[112] A similar drop can be observed in *Das Reich:* On 28 March, the fighting power classification was only III. One reason for that was limited flexibility – motorisation was down to 60 per cent.[113]

Although its combat power was declining rapidly the Waffen-SS was to play a significant role in the death throes of the Third Reich, and it was key to the leadership's hopes to save Nazism. Thus, generally in the Waffen-SS units staffed by Germans and Germanic volunteers the morale was higher than in most *Wehrmacht* formations. According to Allied intelligence summaries, the Waffen-SS personnel captured during the Battle of the Bulge, which continued into January 1945, were of remarkably 'high morale – some even fanatically determined to accomplish their tasks'. The only others displaying similar zeal were the paratroopers who had been employed in the same offensive.[114] A week later another report told that among German forces in the Ardennes sector – in particular the hastily formed *Volksgrenadier* divisions – combat fervour and morale were yielding. Conversely, the Waffen-SS continued to fight as undauntedly and fanatically 'as they used to do'.[115]

After being liberated in January 1945, an American major, who had been captured during the Battle of the Bulge, told about a longish conversation he had with Peiper concerning the chances of a German victory. This talk provides examples of

109. YV, O.68, F.Nr. 625, *Betr. Ergebnisse der Besprechung mit SS-Obersturmbannführer Grothmann am 16.2.1945 in der Feld-Kommandostelle,Berlin*, 17.2.1945.
110. Günter Lucks, *Ich war Hitlers letztes Aufgebot: meine Erlebnisse als SS-Kindersoldat*, Harald Stutte (ed.) (Rowohlt Taschenbuch, 2010), p 60ff.
111. BAMA, N/756/183/a, *Wochenmeldung Stand vom. 6 Januar 1945*.
112. BAMA, RS2.4/1, *Stärke- und Verlustmeldung vom 13 Februar 1945*.
113. Weidinger (1982), p 481. BAMA, RH2/1465, Stand. 1.1.–1.3.1945.
114. NAKEW, WO219/4713, Weekly Intelligence Summary for Psychological Warfare 14, 2 January 1945. See also NAKEW, WO219/4713, Weekly Intelligence Summary for Psychological Warfare 12, 16 December 1944.
115. NAKEW, WO219/4713, Weekly Intelligence Summary for Psychological Warfare 15, 9 January 1945.

the arguments used by Peiper when trying to convince his men of the benefits of fighting on. Peiper claimed that a new reserve army had been formed – complete with men and tanks – that a new submarine campaign had sunk large tonnages in the English Channel, and that the Luftwaffe would soon employ new aircraft types that, although few in numbers, would be superior to the Allies' aeroplanes and secure the German advance.[116] Peiper was not the only one building such castles in the air. In *Division Das Reich* similar rumours flourished during the start of the offensive.[117] It is easy to imagine that, if such hopes are let down, morale will make a substantial dip. For example, two weeks after the end of war, in a bugged conversation with a fellow prisoner, Karl Wolff, formerly the highest-ranking SS civil servant in Italy and one of Himmler's confidants, stated that, having spoken with friends serving in the *Leibstandarte* during the Ardennes offensive, he had lost all hope of a German victory.[118]

Nonetheless, evidently, in parts of the Waffen-SS the combat morale did not break down. On 26 March, the third army made an evaluation of its subordinate formations, and *Division Nordland* got a positive comment. At this late stage, *Nordland* 'had demonstrated an excellent fighting spirit' and, after receiving filler personnel it might be employed in offensive operations once more. Thus, this division stuck out as much better than the other formations under this army, be they army or late-formed Waffen-SS divisions.[119] Such a zeal at this late moment may have had several causes. One being that propaganda had focused on the disastrous consequences of defeat.[120] An example can be seen in *Division Götz von Berlichingen's* field newspaper *Die Eiserne Faust*. The issue of 3 March tells that Germany would fight it out to the end, because defeat would entail either death or life-long forced labour in Siberia.[121] An almost simultaneous flyer for the troops of the third Germanic armoured corps told that the enemy intended to extinguish 'our very existence'.[122]

It contributed to galvanising the fighting spirit that many soldiers believed they were fighting for their own survival. Much more than their Wehrmacht colleagues, the soldiers of the Waffen-SS had a reason to fear for their lives in case they surrendered – a fear that the officers and NCOs kindled systematically among the raw recruits.[123] Having participated in atrocities, many soldiers had enough blood on their hands to fear what might happen if they were captured. On top of the fear of being shot while

---

116. NAKEW, WO219/4713, Weekly Intelligence Summary for Psychological Warfare 15, 9 January 1945. On these conversations see also Weingartner (1979).

117. Leleu (2007).

118. NAKEW, WO208/4517, Bug report CSDIC/CMF/X 169, of 26 May 1945.

119. These were *25. Panzerdivision, 9. Panzerjägerdivision, 5. Jägerdivision, 23. SS-division, 27. SS-division* and *28. SS-division*. BAMA, N756/164/b, AOK 3, 26.3.1945: 'Ausgezeichneten Kampfgeist'.

120. For a discussion based on the *army*, see Bartov (1992), p 106ff.

121. BAMA, RS3-17/29, *Die Eiserne Faust* 11. III-45.

122. BAMA, RS3/5, *III SS Pz.Korps, 20.3.1945*. For a third example see, SU, 15. *Waffen-SS Grenadier Division, Box 14, Betr. Formierung der Kampfgruppe Russmanis, 7.2.1945*.

123. NAKEW, WO209/2244, Exhibit No. 6, Record of the Evidence of Grenadier George Mertens, 10 March 1945, p 2.

surrendering, many non-German volunteers from the occupied European states dreaded what might happen coming home. They might be imprisoned or even sentenced to death for having fought for the enemy. An American intelligence report of 1945 tells that *Division Landsturm Nederland*, though not particularly powerful, fought courageously because the personnel were 'outcasts' who had committed treason. According to this report, 'they could prolong their existence only as long as they kept fighting'.[124]

The Last SS Divisions

Until the very last days, Waffen-SS kept raising divisions, but these were so merely on paper. This goes for the *29. Waffen-Grenadier-Division der SS (italienische Nr. 1)*, which, as of spring 1945, was designated 'division'. This was an already existing unit being upgraded, and the same happened to *Landsturm Nederland* in February when it became the *34. SS-Grenadier-Division Landsturm Nederland*. However, it remained a brigade size unit. Likewise, with the French unit being elevated to *33. Waffen-Grenadier-Division der SS Charlemagne*.[125]

While the new Italian division was employed in northern Italy, on 30 January the *32. SS-Freiwilligen-Grenadier-Division* was flung into battle against the Red Army. Late-January, this division had been formed in some hurry and key personnel brought together from the *Junkerschule* in Lauenburg and the training establishment Kurmark. To a large extent, the soldiers were individuals on their way back from leave to their parent units further east and soldiers from disbanded units.[126] Shortly after formation, the division was employed in the defensive line along the Oder.[127] Already on 28 February, the division had registered 2,159 casualties and it was almost wiped out in the final fights along the Oder.[128]

Another new division similarly employed at the Oder front was the *35. SS- und Polizei-Grenadier-Division*, which had been formed at the end of March. While the officer corps was made up mainly of officer cadets from the *Junkerschule* in Brunswick, the NCOs and soldiers came from uniformed police and police reserve transferred from the police academy in Weimar and from two *Volkssturm* battalions.[129] In mid-April, it was employed in the defence of the town Guben on the river Neiße and subsequently, in the Battle of Halbe south-east of Berlin the division was completely annihilated by the Red Army.[130]

124. BAMA, N756/202/b, *34. SS Gren. Div. Landsturm Nederland, 1945*.
125. 'De SS en Nederland. Documenten Uit SS-archieven 1935–1945' (1976), Vol.1, p 384 and Wilhelm Tieke, *Das Ende zwischen Oder und Elbe: der Kampf um Berlin 1945* (Motorbuch,1994), p 35ff.
126. NAKEW, HW 1/3651, CX/MSS/R.523 (A), 19.4.1945.
127. Tieke (1994), p 34ff.
128. Ibid.
129. BAMA, N756/203, *Polizei-Waffenschule in Hellerau, 24.3.1945* and Bernhard HeinrichLankenau, *Polizei im Einsatz während des Krieges 1939–1945 in Rheinland-Westfalen* (Hauschild, 1957), p 215ff.
130. BAMA, B438/359, *Die 35. SS-Polizei-Infanterie-Division, 1945* and Lankenau (1957).

On 26 February, with a basis in Bratislava (Preßburg) the penultimate Waffen-SS division –*Lützow* – was raised. This formation, too, was to comprise a disparate selection of personnel. There were soldiers of the remnants of the 8th and 22nd cavalry divisions, which had perished during the battle of Budapest, and a contingent of *Volksdeutsche* form Hungary. The formation was finalised on 10 April, but at that moment the division had no heavy weapons whatsoever. *Lützow* was then employed north of Vienna, then it retreated west and, eventually, it surrendered to the Americans.[131]

The very last Waffen-SS division was named *38. SS-Grenadier-Division Nibelungen*. It was tasked with halting the American advance in the front sector between Mannheim and Karlsruhe.[132] The division was raised in March, and personnel, training and equipment testify to the desperation characterising the military leadership at this stage. In January, the *Nibelungen* had got the project designation *38. SS-Division Junkerschule Tölz*, because that was where the majority of its personnel was found.[133] Additionally, the division was filled up with 16- to 17-year-olds, some even younger.[134] Most of them came from the National Socialist élite schools, the *Adolf-Hitler-Schulen*, which lay spread across the Third Reich. Boys of these institutions were now gathered at the *Adolf-Hitler-Schule* Sonthofen near Bad Tölz. Later, one of these boys described how the headmaster, *Obergebietsführer* Kurt Petter, had held a 'rousing speech' whose focal point was, 'we are all going to join the Waffen-SS'.[135] In March, when the formation began in the Black Forest area, the novices were given a piece of paper that they were to sign thus acknowledging that their entry in the Waffen-SS happened voluntarily. It is obvious that these boys were under a considerable social pressure from their instructors as well as their fellow officer cadets. A 16-year-old, Hardy Krüger – a German and later on internationally acclaimed actor – was among those enrolled in this division. In 2006, in an interview with the German newspaper *Bild Zeitung* he claimed that his was an unmitigated compulsory enlistment, and that he personally had felt abhorrence carrying the SS runes on his uniform.[136] However, one should not underrate the importance of the fact that most of the youngsters came from

---

131. BAMA, N756/199/b, *SS-Führungshauptamt, 26.2.1945* and *Notizen nach Führervortrag, 26.3.1945.* See also Klietmann (1965), p 303.

132. NAKEW, HW 1/3651, CX/MSS/T504/7, 28 March 1945.

133. BAMA, N756/210/a, *SS-Führungshauptamt 21.1.1945.* However, the designation *Nibelungen* was used concurrently. See BAMA, M262/A26, *Hoeh. SS-U. Pol. Frh. BoemenMaehren, 6.1.1945.*

134. BAMA, N756/210/a, *38. SS-Grenadier-Division 'Nibelungen'. Aufstellung und Einsatz der jüngsten Division der Waffen-SS.* Documentation by Wolfgang Vopersal (1984) and Klaus Schneider, *Spuren der Nibelungen 1945: die Kämpfe bei Bad Abbach und die Rettung von Regensburg: eine Dokumentation über Soldaten der 38. Grenadier-Division 'Nibelungen' der Waffen-SS* (K. Vowinckel-Verlag, 1999), p 15.

135. Ibid., s.16. BAMA, N756/210/a, 38. SS-Grenadier-Division 'Nibelungen'. Aufstellung und Einsatz der jüngsten Division derWaffen-SS. Documentationby Wolfgang Vopersal (1984). 'Wir sollen alle zur Waffen-SS'.

136. http://www.bild.de/news/aktuell/news/grass-hardy-krueger-737574.bild.html, accessed on 20 February 2014.

dedicated Nazi homes, and that through the *Adolf-Hitler-Schulen* they were ideologically brainwashed. Dieter Sprockhoff, another of the young soldiers, remembered how 'most of us entered this vocation with the highest degree of enthusiasm'.[137] The middle-aged men of the customs department and the *RAD*, who also trickled into the *Nibelungen*, were presumably less naïve and less enthusiastic.[138]

On 21 April, the division was committed against American forces that had crossed the Danube in the area near Bad Abbach, ca. 10 km from Regensburg, and, until 27 April, *Nibelungen* fought alongside other Waffen-SS and *Wehrmacht* formations. On about 24 April, the *Wehrmacht* soldier Richard Müller and eight others left of his company met 200 *Nibelungen* soldiers of one of its two infantry regiments, and what struck him was the age of them: 'at nineteen, I appeared a grown-up, seasoned soldier'.[139] Over the following hours, together with Müller and his lot, the boy soldiers tried to stem the tide of advancing Americans near a small village in the Bad Abbach area. Mostly, from cover among the houses the soldiers fought launching their man held anti-tank weapons against enemy vehicles. Several American tanks were hit, and the attackers were successfully repelled. However, what in the eyes of the young and inexperienced soldiers might have looked like victory, was merely a lull until the enemy had re-grouped and called in artillery support. The day after, a new American attack brushed away the Germans.[140] Over the following days, the division withdrew further towards the Alps on the Austrian border. On 8 May, in the town Reitim Winkl the youngest of the Waffen-SS divisions surrendered to the US Army.

The Battle for Budapest

As new Waffen-SS divisions were formed, others perished. Two of these were *8. SS-Kavallerie division Florian Geyer* and *22. Freiwilligen-Kavallerie division der SS*, which ended up being enveloped and annihilated by the Red Army in Budapest. While the *Florian Geyer* was an old Waffen-SS division dating back from 1942, the 22nd division, was not formed until spring 1944.[141] Early 1945, Army Group South estimated this division's combat value as belonging to category III, the bottom but one class. This was, primarily, due to the personnel's ethnic composition of low-motivated *Volksdeutsche*.[142]

---

137. Schneider (1999), p 17ff.
138. BAMA, N756/210/a, 38. SS-Grenadier-Division 'Nibelungen'. *Aufstellung und Einsatz der jüngsten Division der Waffen-SS.*Documentation by Wolfgang Vopersal (1984).
139. BAMA, N756/210/a, *Bericht Richard Müller, August 1983, 'Mit meinen fast 19 Jahren kam ich mir erwachsen und altgedient vor'.*
140. BAMA, N756/210/a, *Bericht Richard Müller, August 1983.*
141. BAMA, N756/190/a, Order by Jüttner, SS-Führungshauptamt, *Aufstellung einer SS-Freiw. Gren.Div. in Ungarn,* 29 April 1944.This division was frequently designated Maria Theresia, but this was an unofficial title, which was not used by the Waffen-SS.
142. BAMA, N/756, 183/a, *Anlage zu Obkdo.D.Hr.Gr.Sud, Nr.//45, 18.1.1945.*

Since 1939, Hungary had been allied with Germany and thus acquired additional territories from adjacent countries. After the Stalingrad disaster, Hungary tried to quit this association that had been very costly to the country. In March 1944, this led to German occupation which paved the way for the SS into Hungary. Over the following months the Holocaust there reached its apex as, until July, around 437,000 Hungarian Jews were dispatched to concentration camps.[143] By the end of October, the Red Army and its Romanian allies were preparing to attack the Hungarian capital, Budapest.[144] Second only to Romania, Hungary was the German war machinery's most important oil provider. Moreover, the possession of Budapest was a precondition for keeping Vienna on German hands, wherefore, in the winter and early spring 1945, Hitler launched several counter-offensives in Hungary and on 1 December, he declared the city a fortress to be held to the last man.

On 24 December, Budapest was encircled by Red Army troops. Hitler ordered the 79,000 German and Hungarian defenders to fight from house to house. In addition to 13,000 men, 75 guns and 41 tanks from the German army, the defence force consisted of 8,000 men of *Florian Geyer* and 11,500 of the 22nd cavalry division. Together these two had 67 guns and 46 tanks. Moreover, there were minor SS and police units as well as 38,000 Hungarian soldiers, policemen and militia.[145]

While some of the Second World War's fiercest clashes followed inside the city, the German army command planned a counter-offensive.[146] General Gille, commanding the sixth SS armoured corps, was appointed leader of this operation.[147] On Christmas eve 1944, Hitler ordered that Gille's corps be transferred from Poland to Hungary. His task force for this *Operation Konrad* would include his own relatively strong divisions *Totenkopf* and *Wiking* as well as two army infantry divisions; all in all, about 60,000 troops and 200 tanks.

On 1 January 1945, the offensive was launched, albeit under the rather constraining conditions of not having fully deployed the task force units. Both *Wiking* and *Totenkopf* were soon checked by the Red Army. Between 1 and 7 January, Gille's troops sustained losses amounting to 3,500 men and 39 tanks and self-propelled artillery pieces.[148] Nonetheless, the attack was carried on under Luftwaffe support, and, on 12 January, *Wiking*'s advance parties stood only 17 km from the Hungarian capital. At that stage, the corps had finally lost momentum and, on the same day, Gille ordered retreat. On the 18th, after re-grouping, a renewed operation was set in motion from the area between the lake Balaton and the city, and on 24 January, *Totenkopf* were some 30 km from Budapest. Only three days later, however, the Red Army launched a counter-offensive. The Red Army's

---

143. Longerich (2008).
144. Ibid., p 874ff.
145. Krisztián Ungváry, *Battle for Budapest: One Hundred Days in World War II* (I.B.Tauris, 2003), p 322ff.
146. BAMA, RS2-9/1, Photocopy of KTB 1 January–16 February 1945.
147. Sydnor (1990), p 308ff., Ungváry (2003), p 162ff.; Erickson (1996), p 432ff.
148. Ungváry (2003), p 163. These numbers include supporting army units and two Hungarian Waffen-SS battalions. *Totenkopf, Wiking* and 4th corps' corps troops apparently lost 2,938 men. Strassner, (1968), p 328.

superiority was overwhelming and, over February, the armoured corps had to abandon all the areas that had been seized since the beginning of the renewed offensive.[149]

Meanwhile, the defenders of Budapest were running out of munitions and supplies. Despite Hitler's order to the contrary, SS-Obergruppenführer Karl Pfeffer-Wildenbruch, the commandant in Budapest, had repeatedly applied for permission to break out of the city. On the night 11–12 February, his troops attempted a break-out with a view to fighting their way back to the German main forces. This succeeded on a strictly limited scale only. While Pfeffer-Wildenbruch was taken prisoner, Joachim Rumohr, commander of *Florian Geyer*, and August Zehender, commanding the 22nd cavalry division, apparently both committed suicides – as did many other Waffen-SS men.[150] Over the following days it materialised that, of those fleeing the city, only few had managed to reach the German lines. Of 27,000 taking part in the evasion attempt, only 700 were successful.[151]

Supressing 'Defatism'

In the final phase of the war, the SS' terror measures were increasingly turned against the Germans themselves. In his capacity as home secretary, Himmler repeatedly warned that he who might fail his 'national duty' would lose his life, and among the draconic measures was the so-called flag order stating that in buildings where the white flag was hoisted, all males would be shot.[152]

In March 1945, the last commanding officer of *Regiment 24 Danmark*, Per Sørensen, wrote, 'It is hardly any surprise that the war has developed badly of late – if they demobbed the entire SS it would be over tomorrow'.[153] To many civilians, the Waffen-SS formations, which fought longer and more assiduously that most army units, were symbols of the fanatical and pointless death throes brought on by the regime.[154] The pejorative designation *Kriegsverlänger* (war prolonger) was often whispered to bystanders or shouted from a safe distance, when SS soldiers were seen marching past.[155] It was, however, a risky business to demonstrate defeatism in the presence of the Waffen-SS. An example of terror against civilians can be seen with the 13th SS army corps under *Gruppenführer* Max Simon.[156] As in 1945, fighting moved onto German ground, the army corps' tribunal became a much-feared institution amongst the Bavarians. In April and May, this summary court passed numerous death sentences. In the town Brettheim three

---

149. Ungváry (2003), p 168ff.
150. Ibid., pp 62 and 184.
151. BAMA, RS2-9/1, Photocopy of KTB 1 January–16 February 1945.
152. Kunz in Echternkamp and Müller (2008), p 16 and Zimmermann in Boog and Müller (2008), p 368ff.
153. Christensen et al. (1998), p 240.
154. Sven Keller, 'Elite am Ende. Die Waffen-SS in der letzten Phase des Krieges 1945' in Schulte et al. (2014), pp 354–376.
155. Christensen et al. (1998), p 239.BAMA, N756/2107a, *38. SS-Grenadier-Division 'Nibelungen'. Aufstellung und Einsatz der jüngsten Division der Waffen-SS.* Documentation by Wolfgang Vopersal (1984).
156. Merkl (2010).

men were hanged for having disarmed a group of Hitlerjugend boys, who had been detailed to face the Americans. As the local party chairman *Ortsgruppenleiter* Lenhard Wolfmeyer asked for mercy for the doomed men, Simon replied, 'that would suit you gentlemen. When everything went well for us, you shouted *Heil Hitler*, and now you stab us in the back. Such characters are hanged'.[157] It was not only civilians who were murdered. In numerous cases Waffen-SS personnel and soldiers of the *Wehrmacht* were hanged for desertion after a summery trial.[158]

The civilian population was also targeted by the underground *Werwolf* (werewolf) organisation.[159] This stay-behind network had been established in order to combat Allied invaders and was subordinated to the higher SS and police leaders of the various German regions. There were possibly 5–6,000 members, but the regional activities were disparate and the enthusiasm of the members varied. Operations included sabotage, arson, murder of German civil servants, assaults of women who had been seen in the company of Allied soldiers and killing of burgomasters who had collaborated with the Americans. Waffen-SS personnel, primarily NCOs and junior officers, were employed as werewolves, which led to tensions between the two organisations because of the shortage of personnel at the fronts.[160]

The Waffen-SS and the End Phase of Holocaust

The last months of the war were characterised by a final wave of atrocities against concentration camp prisoners.[161] As camps in the near-front area were vacated, the prisoners were forced to march on foot to camps in central and southern Germany. During these 'death marches' large parties of exhausted prisoners perished. Not only did many die from hunger, diseases and exposure, also massacres on smaller or larger groups meant death to many a detainee.[162]

The perpetrators were a mixed group of people, whose identities are not always easily established. There were representatives of various parts of the *Wehrmacht*, the SS, *Gestapo*, *Volkssturm* and Hitlerjugend as well as ordinary civilians who had been issued with weapons and drafted for the occasion by local authorities. In a number of cases, the Waffen-SS assumed the leadership. In March 1945, for example, *Das Reich* officer Wilhelm Mohr was involved in the killing of 30 Jews in the minor Austrian town Jennersdorf where, in 1944, a small camp had been set up to imprison Hungarian Jews.

---

157. Ibid., p 341.
158. See, For example, the case of two young anti-aircraft gun assistants. Ibid., p 357.
159. Alexander Perry Biddiscombe, *Werwolf!: The History of the National Socialist Guerrilla Movement, 1944–1946* (University of Toronto Press, 1998).
160. For an example, see ibid., p 32.
161. On the last phase in the camps see Jon Bridgman and Richard H. Jones, *The End of the Holocaust: The Liberation of the Camps* (Areopagitica Press, 1990), and Daniel Blatman, *The Death Marches: The Final Phase of Nazi Genocide*, translated by Chaya Galai (Belknap Press of Harvard University Press, 2011), Dan Stone, *The liberation of the camps. The end of the Holocaust and its aftermath* (Yale University Aess, 2015).
162. Blatman (2011).

In February, Mohr had taken over command of two Waffen-SS companies comprising Bosniaks and Croatian *Volksdeutsche*. On arrival in that town they were ordered to kill sick prisoners, who were not to participate in the upcoming 'evacuation' to Graz.[163] Another example of Waffen-SS participation in massacres is the shooting of 20 Jews, who had tried to escape from a column marching out of Graz on 4 April. They were killed in a gorge in the mountainous terrain.[164]

There is a case – rich on details – concerning a maintenance company of *Division Das Reich*. In April 1945, in Austria this company killed a small group of Jews, and since a lot of witnesses testified after the war, it has been possible to scrutinise the minutiae. Close to the company's workshop sentries apprehended 10 Jews, who claimed to have been released from a camp in Hungary shortly beforehand. Nonetheless, the officer commanding, *Hauptsturmführer* Paul Anton Reiter, decided that they were to be killed. The prisoners were goaded into a wood where they were forced to dig their own graves. En route, they were beaten and forced to double so – as their tormentors put it – they might 'keep warm in their graves'. After these maltreatments and humiliations, they were ordered to lie down on their stomachs in the grave whereupon they were killed, shot through their heads. Shortly afterwards, a Russian prisoner was killed in the same way. Either out of curiosity or because they had been among the guards, many of the company's soldiers saw the executions. Police investigations in the 1960s made it clear that even those, who had seen nothing, were well-informed of what had happened. Despite the evidence against him, Reiter denied everything. However, in 1967, the *Landesgericht* (high court) in Munich sentenced him to imprisonment for life.[165]

The Battle for Berlin

When on 16 April 1945, the Red Army launched its assault on Berlin, the majority of the most powerful Waffen-SS divisions were in Hungary or at other fronts. The Soviet attackers made a disappointing start sustaining huge casualties at the Seelower Höhen east of the city. However, after this initial set-back the progress was significant and within days Berlin was threatened with being enveloped both from the north and the south. Hitler, who remained in the capital, relied on the Waffen-SS to conduct a relieving attack from the north-west by the eleventh army under Felix Steiner. On 22 April, it was clear that Steiner's attack was nothing but castles in the air. Hitler went into hysterics, removed Steiner from his post, and decided to stay in Berlin to the end.[166]

Now, Hitler felt betrayed even by the Waffen-SS, but had he ventured out of his bunker, he would have beheld that exactly these troops were still fighting. The core of Berlin's modest defensive array was made up of Waffen-SS troops and, to a large

163. Ibid., p 227ff.
164. Ibid., p 228ff.
165. BL, B162/5011. There is a detailed description of the course of events in the interrogation protocol concerning the former *Rottenführer* Schneider, Munich 12 July 1965.
166. Stein (1984), p 242.

extent, these were foreigners.[167] The Waffen-SS personnel protecting Hitler in his last hide-out were largely of *Division Nordland* reinforced by a group of the French *Division Charlemagne* and a battalion of the 15th Latvian division.[168] Among the German SS soldiers were Himmler's *Begleitbataillon RFSS* and the special *Leibstandarte* battalion guarding the *Führer* HQ and the government quarter.[169] These units were parts of *Kampfgruppe Mohnke*, whose commander had killed British POWs in 1940 and murdered Canadians in 1944. He was now *Brigadeführer* and responsible for the protection of Berlin's governmental structures.

In March 1945, after a failed attempt – *Unternehmen Sonnenwende* – to defeat Soviet forces in Pomerania, *Division Nordland* had been withdrawn for rest and recuperation to a place somewhat west of the Oder.[170] When the Soviet offensive started, the division formed the reserve for Theodor Busse's ninth army that was tasked with checking the attack in the Oder line. However, the division was not to be committed in the river valley but closer to Berlin. On 17 April, *Division Nordland* took up positions at Strausberg halfway between the capital and the increasingly wobbly front on the Oder. In the following clashes, elements of the division fell back towards north-west but large parts were pushed back towards the city-centre.[171] In the capital many small, local engagements were fought, by the now depleted unit. *Divisions Nordland*'s last commander, *Brigadeführer* Gustav Krukenberg, has since characterised the division's regiments as being of battalion size.[172] Another snag was the lack of fuel and tanks. In most places the defence was conducted using small arms and shoulder-launched anti-tank weapons. Ten King Tigers belonging to SS-*Panzer-Abteilung 503* were employed in the suburbs and, there alone, according to their own testimony, they neutralised 64 Russian tanks.[173]

Near the district city hall of Neukölln the French Waffen-SS soldiers put up a staunch resistance and, though they sustained huge casualties, on 2 May, when the city gave up fighting they still held the crossroads of Wilhelmstraße-Prinz Albrecht Straße, where some of the most important Nazi institutions and ministries lay.[174] According to Krukenberg, within 24 hours, one Frenchman alone killed six Soviet T-34 tanks by means of *Panzerfäuste*.[175]

Between 30 April and 2 May, most of the Waffen-SS soldiers in Berlin attempted breaking out in order to reach the American lines on the Elbe, but there were other results of the desperation of defeat. Some sought death in frenzied attacks, and others actually committed suicide.[176]

---

167. For an SS-perspective see Tieke (1971), p 205.
168. Carrard (2010), p 55ff.
169. Stein (1984), p 242.
170. Christensen et al. (1998), p 238ff.
171. Tieke (1971), p 205.
172. BAMA, B438/359, Gustav Krukenberg, *Kampftage in Berlin 24.4.–2.5.1945*, 1964.
173. BAMA, B438/355, *Die Schwere SS-Panzer-Abteilung 503 im Fronteinsatz, IX 1952.*
174. Ibid.
175. BAMA, B438/359, *Gustav Krukenberg, Kampftage in Berlin 24.4.–2.5.1945*, 1964.
176. Antony Beevor, *Berlin: The Downfall 1945* (Penguin Books, 2002), p 388ff. Christian Goeschel, *Selbstmord im dritten Reich*, transl. Klaus Binder (Suhrkamp, 2011), p 230ff.

Part II

IDEOLOGY, DISCIPLINE AND PUNISHMENT IN THE WAFFEN-SS

Chapter Five

IDEOLOGICAL TRAINING IN THE WAFFEN-SS

In January 1941, the *Deutsche Zeitung in Norwegen* featured an article about the Waffen-SS. The men in the black uniforms were described as 'a new kind of German soldiers', who were not only warriors but also 'bearers of the revolution':

> Over the daily challenges he sees the greatness of the political programme that, under German leadership, will shape the new Europe. His thoughts fortified by the SS tuition, he sees the Nordic spirit come alive and, like a modern Viking, he pushes on towards the Greater Germanic future.[1]

In other words, the soldiers were expected not only to fight with weapons in hand – they were tasked with a broader and more wide-ranging mission: Through ideological training, they were to be moulded into SS champions of Nazism throughout Europe.

From the early days of the Waffen-SS the ideological teaching was comprehensive and zealous, and in some ways the ambitions only seemed to grow as the war progressed. An instructive example can be found as late as seven weeks before the end of the war. On 19 March 1945, *Division Hitlerjugend*'s *Feldersatz Bataillon* (replacement battalion) received a 40-pages instruction describing in considerable detail the future ideological training.[2] The core message of the planned teachings was that the Jews had caused the adversities of the previous years. The war could however still be won, because providence had sent Hitler to Germany and since all Germans devoted themselves unconditionally to victory, the Third Reich would prevail.[3] Indeed, as we shall see in the following, the detailed and elaborate ideological instructions and training manuals were not a peace time phenomenon, nor a mere sideshow, but on the contrary a central SS objective.

Ideology and the Waffen-SS

From the early thirties, the SS spent considerable resources on creating and nurturing an ideological worldview among its members. Disseminating Nazi norms and values, not only served as a way of demonstrating that the SS was the elite of National

---

1. *Deutsche Zeitung in Norwegen*, No. 21, 25 January 1941, p 3.
2. VAP, 12. SS-PZ.DIV HJ, No. 4, file 40.
3. Ibid.

Socialism, it was also an important remedy in amalgamating the SS and the police and in making sure that the different parts of the SS did not grow apart.[4] Not only did the SS idealize martial and military values, but also war in itself because, according to the SS, it served to eradicate the weak and the inferior and it exposed true leadership. Nowhere was this combination of racial wetting, ideological training and warrior ethos applied more intensively than in the Waffen-SS, where the intention was to create an army of political soldiers.

By drafting what was believed to be racially superior men and by infusing them with a solid dose of Nazi *Weltanschauung*, the military branch of the SS was supposed to demonstrate superior fighting qualities compared to the armies of the Kaiser and the Weimar Republic, commanded as they were by officers of noble pedigree and with a narrow-minded, conservative outlook. The world-view that was to imbue the SS soldiers' thoughts and behaviour took its point of departure in the general Nazi ideology but also encompassed specific SS traits. This included a strong focus on implementing the racial doctrine of Nazism, as well the SS notion of being an order of warriors and the vanguard of the Nazi movement.[5] Racial theory, anti-Semitism, agrarian romanticism, glorification of German history, masculinity and elitism were fused in the SS. From this mixture grew a belief of being the bearers of a special racial character, attitude and life style.[6] Practice should prevail over theory – as explained by one of Himmler's chief ideologists, Walther Darré, the SS men did not need to possess a deep 'knowledge of the National Socialism' ideology as long as they 'lived it'.[7]

However, although the SS was conceptualized as a whole, the various branches developed along different tracks. Furthermore, the official dogma and Himmler's ideas and plans were partly disparate to the huge multi-ethnical expansion of the Waffen-SS and they would be further challenged by realities at the frontline. For that reason, their application in the field was multi-facetted and, as we shall see, the outcome was sometimes inconsistent and paradoxical.[8]

Nonetheless, a number of concepts remained central to the SS' understanding of the Nazi doctrine: race, anti-Semitism, *Blut und Boden* (the people and its native soil), nationalism, anti-liberalism, authoritarianism, the *Führerprinzip*, the chivalrous ideal, loyalty and the death cult. These terms and values may for analytical purposes be grouped into three main categories: (1) The concept of race as the foundation of

---

4. Hans-Christian Harten, *Himmlers Lehrer. Die Weltanschauliche Schulung in der SS 1933–1945* (Ferdinand Schöningh, 2014).
5. Concerning the SS' and Himmler's development of Nazi ideology, see Jürgen Matthäus *'Die "Judenfrage" als Schulungsthema von SS und Polizei'* in Jürgen Matthäus, Konrad Kwiet, Jürgen Förster, Richard Breitman and Udo Rennert, *Ausbildungsziel Judenmord? 'Weltanschauliche Erziehung' von SS, Polizei und Waffen-SS im Rahmen der 'Endlösung'* (Fischer Taschenbuch Verlag, 2003), p 37.
6. Buchheim et al. (1994), p 232. Buchheim arguably underestimates the importance of the SS' ideological teaching. For a brief discussion of this, see Emberland and Kott (2012), p 43.
7. Cüppers (2011), p 98.
8. Matthäus et al. (2003), p 15ff.

Nazi belief; (2) The *Führerprinzip* – loyalty to Hitler and the spirit of self-sacrifice; (3) The perception of SS as an élite order. While the notion of race and the *Führerprinzip* were elements of Nazi ideology throughout the Third Reich; the conception of being an order was much more singular to the SS. However, all three elements fused in a special way in the black order and are essential to understanding the mentality of the SS.[9]

Racial Ideology and the SS

A specific SS mentality and ideology started to manifest itself within the Nazi movement around 1931. Himmler phrased these thoughts, but in the initial phase he was inspired especially by Darré, who had been the main contributor to the NSDAP's agricultural policy and who had authored a number of Nazi pamphlets.[10]

Darré was of the school that was characterised by a high degree of fascination with Scandinavia and, who believed that the population there had the purest Nordic-Germanic blood. Moreover, he saw agriculture as the natural occupation for Germans and other Germanic peoples – in contrast to modern urban life which he thought corrupted the race.[11] To a large extent, Himmler adopted this rural romanticism and he imagined that the concept might be implemented by strengthening the farmer communities in Germany and by establishing Germanic agricultural colonies in the occupied territories of Eastern Europe right up to the Urals.[12]

In 1931, Himmler appointed Darré chief of the newly established *SS Rasse- und Siedlungshauptamt* (RuSHA, main race and settlement office). This new SS office should contribute to bringing the Germans back to the farmlands but it should also set up racial criteria for admission to the SS.[13] In June 1931, Himmler promulgated rules for, for example, height and age of future applicants. Himmler, personally, scrutinised applications from prospective SS men and placed particular emphasis on the attached photos. A few years hence he explained the method used for this visual race screening. By looking at the photos one should single out what might be alien to the race: 'Were there traces of foreign blood, did the applicant have exceptionally high cheekbones?' If so,

9. Concerning the SS' and Waffen-SS' ideology, see inter alia Matthäus et al. (2003); Longerich (2008); Wegner (1990), as well as Jorunn Sem Fure and TerjeEmberland (eds.), *Jakten på Germania: fra norden svermeri til SS-arkeologi* (Humanist Forlag, 2009). A recent in-depth study of the source material is Harten (2014). See also Florian Wolf-Roskosch, *Ideologie der Waffen-SS. Ideologische Mobilmachung der Waffen-SS 1942–45* (Diserta Verlag, 2014).
10. Harten (2014), p 17ff. See also Hatheway (1999), p 22, and Robert Wistrich and Hermann Weiss, *Wer war wer im Dritten Reich: ein biographisches Lexikon; Anhänger, Mitläufer, Gegner aus Politik, Wirtschaft, Militär, Kunst und Wissenschaft*, translatedby Joachim Rehork (Fischer-Taschenbuch-Verl., 1993), p 59.
11. Harten (2014), p 17ff. See also Stefan Arvidsson 'Germania' in Fure and Emberland (2009), p 22 and IfZG, ZS 77-1.
12. Heather Pringle 'Fra forfedrenes rom til "Ahnenerbe"' in Fure and Emberland (2009), p 117. See also Emberland and Kott (2012), p 182.
13. Longerich (2008), p 126, Wistrich and Weiss (1993), p 59. Koehl (1983), p 51.

Himmler claimed, one might immediately reject the applicant for looking like a Slav or a Mongol.[14] Since character and appearance were inherited traits, the individual SS man's heritage was of decisive importance to his suitability. Not only did the men have to show a pedigree without Jewish forbears, they also had to ascertain that their offspring would be racially sound. At the turn of the year 1931–1932, an engagement and wedding edict was issued making the SS men's choice of wife an SS matter aimed at improvement of the Nordic-Germanic race.[15]

During the years 1932–1933, the intake into the SS increased considerably and new physical and race-related conditions were introduced and a new system of regional race experts – so-called race rapporteurs – was inaugurated.[16] During subsequent years, the issue was regularly revisited to make sure that nobody would enter the SS without the proper lineage. How the racial guidelines were implemented at the local level is illustrated by an internal memo from the *Leibstandarte Adolf Hitler* in December 1935 in which it was ordered to:

> initiate immediate provision of information warranting Aryan descend of all SS candidates. The data must reach back at least to the year 1800. Applicants who already have an approved genealogical table [...] will submit it instantly to the personnel branch. Since the obtainment of an SS number depends rigorously on proof of Aryan lineage the documentation must be requisitioned as quickly as possible.[17]

Since the internal SS court was tasked with prosecuting those who violated the rules, it was obvious that the admission and marital regulations were more than mere formalities. In July 1935, for instance, steps were taken to punish those who had violated the demand for prior approval of engagements and marriages.[18] Apparently, a significant number of SS-men had married without approval, and, later that month, it was emphasised that, in future, such an action would have 'dire consequences'.[19] This, however, failed to solve the problem – a prominent case in point was Waffen-SS General Herbert Otto Gille who never submitted the required Aryan certificate.[20]

14. Longerich (2008), p 124ff. Excerpts from a 1937 speech by Himmler, where he told about his previous inspections of SS applications. Peter Longerich, *Heinrich Himmler: Europas bøddel* (Broe, 2009), p 125.
15. BAB, NS7/3, *Sammlung von Erlassen des Hauptamtes SS-Gericht 1940–41*, p 9ff. See aslo Hein (2012), p 99ff.
16. Koehl (1983), p 83.
17. BAMA, RS4/1564, *Standartenbefehl No. 150*, 7 December1935.
18. BAB, NS7/2, *Sammlung von Erlassen des Hauptamtes SS-Gericht 1933–39*, pp 23f. Letter from th eChef der SS-Hauptamtes SS-Gruppenführer Heissmeyer, *Genehmigung zur Verlobung und Heirat of 3 July 1935*.
19. BAB, NS7/2, *Sammlung von Erlassen des Hauptamtes SS-Gericht 1933–39*, p 25, letter of 19 July 1935.Without any detriment to his career the Waffen-SS General Herbert Otto Gille never submitted the required Aryan certificate.
20. Schulz and Wegmann (2003), p 374.

The notion of a superior Nordic-Germanic race was central to Nazism and Hans F.K. Günther was instrumental in defining the meaning of this. In 1930, Günther had been appointed professor of racial science at the university of Jena. Over the following years, he achieved semi-official status as the Nazis' key expert on racial theory. His book *Rassenkunde des deutschen Volkes* (the German people's racial science) from 1922 appeared in 16 editions and became the Nazi reference work on the issue. In his work Günther described six main races, which he defined with point of departure in alleged physical and mental traits. This materialised as a racial psychology, according to which a number of mental and spiritual capacities characterised the nature of the individual race. The dolichocephalic, blond and tall Nordic race Günther saw as the embodiment of diligence, heroism, willpower, courteousness and leadership qualities.[21]

Gradually a kind of SS quality continuum developed. On top was the so-called Nordic-Germanic race. The term Germanic was never precisely delineated by the Nazis, but it was based, for example, on Günther's notion of race and a miscellany of historical, geographical and linguistic arguments.[22] As with large parts of the preceding *völkische* ('ethnic') movement, the underlying logic was an alleged connexion between the physical environment inhabited by various past human societies and their racial characteristics. The various people of the Nordic-Germanic race had obtained their particularly fortunate qualities from the tough living conditions prevalent in their primeval home in northern Scandinavia. For the same reason, Himmler believed that, apart from northern Europe, the most favourable habitat for the Germanic man would be the conquered eastern territories where climate and other conditions were like those at home. Conversely, in SS eyes, history had proved that the Germanic tribes that had migrated south in times bygone had been corrupted by the sun, the different surroundings and the influence of alien races.[23]

Which nations belonged to a given race was not clearly defined because nation was not the only criterion for race. As a German or a Swede, one might be of low racial value if, among one's forebears, there was a large proportion of alien blood. For this reason, the SS used the term *Ordensfähig* or *SS-fähig* as a quality mark for those who, racially, lived up to the criteria for membership of the SS Order. Implicitly, this meant that there were also a group of Germanics, who did not meet the requirements – such as many *Volksdeutsche* recruited outside Germany. Apart from the obvious variations of racial purity, it was possible that in ethnic groups, which from linguistic and cultural points of view were not racially Germanic, there might be a certain extent of Germanic blood. Thus, in a publication from 1944 the Slav Croats were described as an 'ancient

---

21. Terje Emberland 'Viking og odelsbonde' in Fure and Emberland (2009), p 129ff. See also Hans F.K. Günther, *Rassenkunde des deutschen Volkes*, 9th edition(J .F .Lehmanns Verlag, 1926).
22. Gingerich (1991), p 38ff.
23. BAB, NS19/4009, *Rede des Reichsführers-SS am 23.11.1942 – SS-Junkerschule Tölz*, p 7ff.

Figure 5.1 Himmler visits Norwegian volunteers (Frihedsmuseet)

people of warriors and seafarers with Gothic hearts and Slavonic tongues, whose Nordic-Dinaric racial heritage is still active'.[24] Also at this stage, the Ukrainians were described as a people with particularly strong Nordic and Dinaric race features.[25] Considering this flexibility, it is hardly surprising that, during the war, the Germanic group was successively augmented to comprise soldiers from an increasing number of countries, which, presumably, was due to a wish to include more and more ethnic groups in the SS.[26]

One should bear this opportunistic adaptability in mind when nations were classified as to their suitability to be included in the Nordic Germanic race. When in spring 1944, *Hauptamt*'s chief, Gottlob Berger, as well as Hans Jüttner, directing the *Führungsamt*, produced a survey of the principal groups of Germanic volunteers, it contained not only Reich Germans and *Volksdeutsche* but also a wide variety of North- and West-European nationalities.[27]

---

24. Ruth Bettina Birn, 'Die SS – Ideologie und Herrschaftsausübung: zur Frage der Inkorporierung von "Fremdvölkischen"' in Jan Erik Schulte (ed.), *Die SS, Himmler und die Wewelsburg, Schriftenreihe des Kreismuseums Wewelsburg* 7 (Schöningh, 2009), p 65. Another – and slightly less pompous – example of the high percentage of Germanic blood with the Croats, see VAB, MNO.FNRD, Boks 6, 42/1Gen.Kdo. V. SS-Geb.Korps, Abt. VI – Fu./Kl., *BefehlfürpolitischeSchulung*, 12 May 1944.
25. YV, M53, 274, Division Galizien, *An alle deutschen Führer der Division*, Section VI, 1 February 1944.
26. Kenneth W. Estes, *A European Anabasis Western European Volunteers in the German Army and SS, 1940–1945* (Columbia University Press, 2008), Chapter 4.
27. BAB, NS33/31, *Rede des SS-Obergruppenführer Jüttner auf der SS-Führer-Tagung in Prag am 13. April 1944*, pp 9–11; BAB, NS19/3987, Undated speech by Gottlob Berger 1944 (perhaps at the *VI Tagung auf der Plassenburg vom 28.2. bis 5.3.1944*).

Right after the Germanic race came the Dinaric. It comprised Balkan and South-European nations, and was distinctly separate from the 'lower races'. These encompassed Slavs, Asians, blacks and other non-Europeans. At the extreme bottom of the ladder were the Jews, who were perceived as the virtual opposite of everything that the SS esteemed.[28] Anti-Semitism was not only a main thread in the SS' racial ideology, it appeared in considerable detail in instructions to the rank and file. According to SS ideologues – and in full harmony with the Nazis' general perception of the world – the machinations of the Jews explanied almost everything that Germany was against.

Based on its racist foundation, Nazism developed an extremely ruthless and brutal praxis. The concept of 'sub-humans' (*untermenschen*) dehumanised of large segments of the world's inhabitants. As Bernd Wegner noted in his pathbreaking study of the Waffen-SS, morally speaking, the SS' ideology was entirely devoid of humanistic boundaries. Unlike many contemporary, competing ideologies it had no built-in humane or moral curb.[29] This was the ultimate realisation of what Harald Welzer has termed 'National Socialist morale', according to which it was considered 'good and useful' to help solve the 'Jewish question', and to do this in such a radical manner that future historians would never have seen but only heard of Jews.[30] The SS created a total dehumanisation of its racially defined opponents and made their subjugation or annihilation the SS man's duty. In a world, which was characterised by an eternal struggle among the races, there was no room for compassion.[31]

Führer Cult, Spirit of Self-sacrifice and Obedience

In 1935, the young and ambitious architect, Albert Speer, accompanied Hitler on a drive to Nuremberg. The trip was unofficial and conducted with discretion, but the rumour that Hitler was underway spread along the route. The roads soon filled with 'euphoric citizens' and during a lunch break at an inn 'thousands of people gathered calling for Hitler'.[32] The *Führer* cult, like the notion of race, was a central element in Nazism and the Third Reich. In the SS it was linked with the expectation that the SS man would be willing to pay the ultimate price and with the idea that the entire national willpower had been concentrated in one man, thus making the Führer's will law. This materialised at several levels. As an organisation, the SS found its role in 1934 by stabbing the SA in the back, thus serving Hitler uncompromisingly. As early as the previous year, the oath of allegiance to Hitler had been introduced after which members of the SS vowed him unconditional obedience.[33] Additionally, the *SS-Leibsstandarte* served as Hitler's life guard and, right until the end of the war – and even beyond his death – the Waffen-SS

---

28. Günther (1926); Cüppers (2011), pp 102 and 107.
29. Wegner (1990), p 47.
30. Welzer (2006), p. 48.
31. Hatheway (1999), p 38. For an illustrative example of how this played out in a Waffen-SS division see BAMA, RS2-2/14, *Ic. Sonderbefehl* 2.5.1943.
32. Albert Speer, *Erinnerungen* (Propyläen-Verlag; Ullstein, 1969), pp 77ff.
33. Hatheway (1999), p 29.

sang his praise. As can be seen from the Waffen-SS soldiers' correspondence, belief in Hitler also was crucial in maintaining the fighting spirit. Even during the extensive withdrawals on the eastern front, many were convinced that, soon, the Führer would save them by means of some wonder weapon or otherwise turn the fortune of war.[34]

The Führer worship and the unconditional compliance with the wishes of Hitler and his appointed leaders – in the case of the SS, Himmler – was true of Nazism generally. However, with the SS men this entailed that they saw themselves and their organisation in particular as embodying the loyalty and obedience to their supreme commander.[35] That is why they embraced the motto, 'Meine Ehre heißt Treue' – my honour means loyalty.

The SS as an Order

Not only was the SS to unite racially pure men, who would make any sacrifice for their *Führer*, but, at the same time, Himmler wanted to create an order-like organisation which would bond the members together through the use of symbols, ceremonies and rituals. In many respects, the outcome was a cult where work, private life and organisation were welded together allowing the SS men to see themselves as members of a brotherhood. While racial ideology and the *Führer* cult were common to the all the Nazi organisations of the Third Reich, the 'order' and the élite self-perception provided the SS with a distinct outlook.

Various factors contributed to the view of the SS as an order, viz. the uniforms, the symbols, the militaristic discipline, the creation of an independent SS-jurisdiction, the elitist self-perception, the peculiar ceremonies, the cultivation of a distinct code of honour, and the creation of a specific Germanic understanding of history. Moreover, the organisation assumed eugenic control of the SS men's private lives through its procedures for vetting their spouses and controlling their reproduction. All in all, Himmler wished the SS to be an order of lineage and 'a closely-knit community whose members allowed its Weltanschauung to dominate their lives completely'.[36] The elitist pretentions of the SS were also cultivated though a romanticised ideal of chivalry presupposing that the members acted with 'decency' in all aspects of life. This demand included elements like generosity, honesty, magnanimity, loyalty and fellowship. Himmler thought that these characteristics were especially affiliated with the Germanic race.[37] A supporting element was a host of ceremonies in which artefacts and rituals, allegedly derived from the history of the Nordic-Germanic ancestors, were used.[38]

Considering the totalitarian attitude to the lives of its members, it is hardly surprising that the SS had a strained relationship with the major religions, and in particular, the Catholic faith was an object for Nazi scorn. First and foremost,

---

34. Christensen et al. (1998), p 426.
35. Buchheim et al. (1994), p 215ff.
36. Longerich (2008), p 267.
37. Speech by Himmler in 1935, here quoted from *SS Germansk Budstikke*, no. 5, 1942, p 218.
38. Longerich (2008), p 289.

the problem was the split loyalty generated by religious affiliation; not least in relation to an authority figure such as the pope. Among the Christian canons that Himmler found above all annoying, were the sexual morale and the notion of peace and mercy. The former collided with his ideas on eugenics aimed at breeding an Aryan élite and ascertaining its proliferation – if need be though pre- or extra-marital liaisons. The latter, similarly, was conflicting with the SS' willingness to unrestrained use of force against the SS-appointed enemies of the Third Reich.[39] Within the SS as well as the Waffen-SS this led to determined efforts to persuade the members to leave the established churches.

Teaching *Weltanschauung* to the SS-men

A series of surviving regimental orders from the *Leibstandarte* allows insight into how the SS handled ideological training during the years following the *Machtergreifung*. The main issues in these orders were organisational and practical matters but Nazi ideology nevertheless clearly characterized the daily life in the prestigious Berlin-Lichterfelde barracks. In one of these orders, a six-days-course on genetics and eugenics was announced, in which participation was compulsory for all medical doctors of the unit.[40] In the same order, one fourth of all announced issues had a clearly ideological leaning, and it was, for example, emphasised that all commanders had to take part in lectures concerning race and Weltanschauung.[41] On 11 September 1934, for instance, Professor Schwartz-Bostunitsch lectured on 'Soviet Russia and Judaism', and all officers from platoon commander upwards had to attend.[42] One item was entitled 'Jewish shopkeepers'. It was complained that SS soldiers had bought ready-made garb in a shop at Kurfürstendamm whose owner was Jewish.[43] This problem was also addressed in earlier as well as later orders and clearly had the attention of the central leadership.[44] On 5 November 1934, Himmler issued an order forbidding and criminalising purchases in Jewish shops, and he stated that such activity would be an insult against the foundations of National Socialism.[45]

In 1938, the teaching of Weltanschauung was re-organised and the responsibility was transferred from the RuSHA to the *Hauptamt*. The reason was a disagreement between the head of RuSHA, Darré, and Himmler, which, eventually, led to the dismissal of the former.[46] From now on, the head teachers were appointed by Himmler personally.[47] In September 1940, another crucial change took place making the commanding officer responsible for all military and ideological teaching of his company. It was stressed

---

39. Ibid., p 252.
40. BAMA, RS4/1564, *Standartenbefehl No. 412 D*, 4 December 1934, pt. 1.
41. Ibid, pts. 6 and 8.
42. BAMA, RS4/1564, *Standartenbefehl No. 1112 D*.
43. BAMA, RS4/1564, *Standartenbefehl No. 612 D*.
44. Ibid. *1412 D*.
45. BAB, NS7/2, *Sammlung von Erlassen des Hauptamtes SS-Gericht 1933-39*, p 8.
46. Harten (2014), p 20; Emberland and Kott (2012), p 182; Longerich (2008), p 429.
47. Forster 2003, in Matthäus (2003), p 94.

that 'the Weltanschauung teaching is no less important than military training and
the two must be fused to form a concluded entity. The aim of this is the creation
of the political soldier of the Waffen-SS'.[48] At the same time, WE leaders (*Führer für
Weltanschauliche Erziehung* or Leaders of Weltanschauung teaching) replaced the former
head teachers. By means of providing relevant educational material and leading
the ideological teaching, the WE leaders were to assist the company commanders
in their work creating political soldiers.[49] The directive stated that the personnel should
be briefed on day-to-day politics on a regular basis and that an ideological lecture
should be given at least once a week. It was underscored that the socio-political lectures
should not stand alone; the *Weltanschauung* teaching should be present 'always and
everywhere'.[50]

In an effort to ensure such an absolute ideological environment a variety of media and
communication, such as films, were employed. For example, in a directive concerning
the practical execution of political schooling from May 1943, a host of activities and
devices were described, such as Film Wagen (mobile film shows) and Kraft durchFreude
personnel (entertainers), foundation of sport clubs, use of radio sets, loud-speaker cars,
selection of reading material for the men, organization of celebrations and feasts as well
as of leisure-time activities.[51]

Studying practice, it becomes clear that already prior to this directive, the means
used to politicize the troops were extensive. In September 1940, for instance, Himmler
announced that, during the upcoming winter, all the SS and police would watch
the anti-Semitic propaganda film *Jud Süß (the* Jew Suss).[52] Slides was another type of
media frequently used. In July 1942, an artillery training and filler regiment in Munich
noted the availability of around 40 different series of slides on, for example, the Thirty
Years War, Judaism, free masonry and bolshevism. Moreover, there were eugenics
series concerning the mixture of races, fertility and *Rassenkunde von Günther*.[53] The SS
took the lead also in the field of music as, in January 1942, Jüttner ordered all units
to cleanse their musical repertoire of undesirable Jewish influence. For this purpose,
he recommended that units utilized the *Lexicon der Juden in der Musik* (encyclopaedia on
Jews in Music) published in 1941. A list of undesirable composers, hits, marches and
other music was attached.[54]

48. VAP, *SS-Artillerie Ausbildungs- und Ersatz Regiment*, K 17, file 24.
49. Wegner (1990), p 189.
50. VAP, *SS-Artillerie Ausbildungs- und Ersatz Regiment*, K 17, file 24.
51. VAP, *SS-Artilleri Ausbildungs- und Ersatz Regiment*, K 17, file 24, directive on putting RFSS
order of 24 February 1943 (on the WE) into practice, 13 May 1943.
52. RGVA, 1372/5/7, Himmler's instruction, Tgb. Nr. 35/142/40, 30 September 1940.
53. VAP, *SS-ArtillerieAusbildungs- und Ersatz Regiment*, K 17, file 24, Letter from SS-Art. Ausb.u.Ers.
Rgt, Munich of 31 July 1942.
54. YV, M36, 20.2, *SS-Standortverwaltung Bruhn*, SS-Fuhrungshauptamt, 20 January1942.

Rituals and Social Evenings

Another important element in the ideological repertoire which suited the nature of the SS-order was the many rituals that were practiced in semi-religious fashion. The *Morgenfeiern* (morning celebrations), for example, could be conducted either as huge official revels, or locally arranged socio-political events in the units. A poster gives us an example of how such an event was held at the *Schiller Theater* in Berlin on 20 June 1943. Two state actors performed accompanied by *Führungshauptamt*'s own staff band and a *Hitlerjugend* choir. A fanfare initiated the performance followed by a homage to the fallen, whereupon selected excerpts from Hitler's speeches were read. Then, the *Morgenfeier* went on with, for example, the first movement of Schumann's Fourth Symphony, reading from *Mein Kampf*, music by Bach and recitations of Fichte.[55] As an instruction made clear, this was also the basic model for the small-scale events taking place with the units.[56] This instruction carried an ambience of death glorification, for example by highlighting and promulgating stories of soldiers who confronted death heroically while fighting for the Nazi cause. Singing *Das Heltenlied der Gruppe Förster* (the heroic song about the Section Förster), a song about a section which fought until death, is one example.[57] The instructing booklet *Feier und Freizeit* (celebration and leisure-time) offered a note of caution, that such arrangements should not transgress into a 'celebratory psychosis' (*Feirgestaltungspsykose*), in which every available media and material was employed.[58] Nonetheless, the basic model of deliberately mixing different activities remained the template. On 19 September 1943, for example, the SS artillery training regiment held a morning celebration with music, speeches, songs and recitals from Clausewitz and Hitler.[59]

Occasions for ideological celebratory ceremonies included National Socialist red-letter days like the *Machtergreifung* on 30 January, Hitler's birthday 20 April, and the Beer Hall Putsch on 9 November.[60] Other typical – and more SS specific – celebrations included the celebration of summer and winter solstice, as well as the Yule Tide with SS candles especially made for the occasion.[61] At a winter solstice celebration in 1942 the speaker explained that since time immemorial Teutons had celebrated solstice. In semi-religious phrases he carried on that the fighters at the front 'were in harmony

---

55. VAP, *SS-Artillerie Ausbildungs- und Ersatz Regiment*, K 17, file26. *VI – Unterlagen zu verschiedenen Feiern*.
56. Ibid, Two suggestions for 'Morgenfeier der SS'. 11 pages, no author and date are mentioned.
57. Ibid.
58. VAP, *SS-Artillerie Ausbildungs- und Ersatz Regiment*, K 17, file 26, *VI– Unterlagen zu verschiedenen Feiern*. The booklet was published by *Abteilung Feiergestaltung – Reichsführung SS*. Date of publishing is unknown, but it is assumed to be before the war.
59. VAP, *SS-Artillerie Ausbildungs- und Ersatz Regiment*, K 17, file26, *VI – Unterlagen zu verschiedenen Feiern, Morgenfeier der 9./SS.A.A.u.E.R am 19 September 1943*.
60. BAMA, RS2/2/3, KTB No.3, 1.11.1942–8.1.1943, 9.11.1942.
61. Longerich (2008), p 289.

with the spirit of the winter solstice', and would lay down their lives for victory, their *Führer* and their people.[62] Also, the fallen soldiers could be used to galvanize the men ideologically by means of commemoration ceremonies (*Totenfeier*) of fallen SS soldiers – for example at a burial site.[63]

From the Class Room to the Front

The gradual influx of not so willing soldiers in combination with increasing ethnic diversification of the SS presented the organization with considerable ideological challenges. It responded partly by modifying certain ideological aspects, and partly by competementalizing it, so that different groups received tailored messages. This normally happened in their own language, and not only by means of instructions in the classroom or when receiving the order of the day, but also through a host of SS pamflets and other publications.[64]

However, the fact that the SS put a considerable effort into molding its soldiers' worldview, does not nessearily mean that the result corresponded to the objective. What happened when the political aims met with reality at the frontline? On the one hand, ideology was to lay the normative and intellectual foundation allowing mass killing to be perceived as good, self-sacrificing, chivalrous Nazi deeds. On the other, there were circumstances and acts at the front and among the men that did not really fit into the Nazi universe. At the same time, the Waffen-SS developed into an increasingly multi-ethnical organization, which in no way lived up to the original vision of a Germanic racial community. There was a long way from Himmler's desk to life with the units, and it was in no way given that all plans and instructions were put into practice. The following chapter will illustrate what actually happened when the SS Weltanschauung was turned into a living instrument.

---

62. VAP, *SS-Artillerie Ausbildungs- und Ersatz Regiment, K 17, file 26, VI – Unterlagen zu verschiedenen Feiern, Rede zur Sonnwendfeier am 21.1942.*
63. BAMA, RS3/10, *Ehrenfriedhöfe 1943.*
64. See for example the material in BAB, NS 31/449.

Chapter Six

SEXUALITY, RACE AND RELIGION: IDEOLOGY IN PRACTISE

The ideological SS universe helps us better understand the actions of the SS men, including the way they rationalized their war crimes and atrocities – a theme we will return to in a later chapter on Waffen-SS atrocities. The question of how ideology influenced and shaped practice at the front is, however, broader and even more complex as we shall see in the following.

Racial Differentiation at the Front

Moving eastwards, the soldiers of the Third Reich faced various ethnic groups which caused countless ideologically motivated reactions among the Waffen-SS men. In October 1941, for example, a Norwegian soldier in the Wiking division informed in a letter that he had lately been guarding POWs, most of whom were Ukrainians. Among these, he found that there was "much strangeness to behold" and continued:

> Here were the most peculiar, diverse and ugly characters I have ever met. Occasionally one would encounter a fair-skinned Germanic type (maybe a descendant of a Norwegian Viking?). Otherwise, mainly small, black, unassuming men. Especially those representing the Asiatic Mongol type were a hideous lot.[1]

A report from the second SS Cavalry Regiment August 1941 on the massacre in the Pripet Marshes also made a point of distinguishing different groups from each other. Here, the Ukrainians made a relatively good impression: 'although they were small, they all were of a harmonious figure and build and had a clear look'.[2] As was the case in the Pripet Marshes, such race evaluations could have drastic consequences for the locals. An order from Himmler's personal command staff stated that areas populated by *völkisch* Germans or Ukrainians, where they did not like the Poles and the Russians, were to be protected. Conversely, where the population was friendly towards the Poles or were 'racially and humanly inferior' everyone under suspicion of supporting partisans should be shot and their villages torched.[3] Thus, in this and similar cases a racial distinction

---

1. HLC, Sigurd Soerlie's private archive. P1-Andreas B. Nilsson, Letter of 19 October 1941.
2. VAP, RFSS KDOS, No. 24, comprehensive report on the massacre in the Pripet Marshes 13 August 1941. See reportfromthe 2nd SS Cavalry Regt p 460.
3. VAP, RFSS KDOS nr. 24, *Kommandobefehl, Richtlinien fur die Durchkämmung und Durchstreifung von Sumpfgebieten durch Reitereinheiten*, 28 July1941.

was made between the so-called sub-humans and those who might not be *Volksdeutsche* or Germanic, but were deemed racially acceptable to a degree where their lives were preserved.

Naturally, racial differentiation also applied to the SS internally. In the summer of 1943, for instance, general Steiner instructed his armoured corps to place emphasis on racial and physical appearance when selecting officer material.[4] However, the racial quality control went beyond the mere selection of officers and men; it also determined whom the individual member might marry and have children with. Here, the ideological aims and norms for the sexual activity and reproduction of the SS men were clear, although it could be difficult to enforce all aspects of the ideological policy especially during wartime.

Marriage and Germanic Children

As already stated, becoming eligible for the SS required a race certificate and an ancestry reaching far back; and to ensure racially pure wives, marriages were to be vetted. But to what degree were these policies practised? No doubt, this was near to Himmler's heart, and, in the first six months of 1937, 308 men were dismissed from the SS because of breach of the engagement and marriage regulations. In June 1937, however, Himmler decided to suspend punishment for contravention of these rules, and in 1940 he declared that there would be no final decisions taken in such matters until the end of the war.[5] Moreover, during the war, the procedure concerning engagements was simplified.[6] It is likely that the reasons for these changes were of a pragmatic nature. In the end, probably, Himmler would not wish to dismiss too many young men, and the mounting casualties at the front made it indispensable that the men married in order to reproduce the race. Himmler stressed the latter argument in as much as he wished to 'restrict the formalities' to 'considerably improve the inclination to marry' taking in his stride 'the mistakes' that would inevitably be made during the war.[7]

Despite increased pragmatism, ideology still influenced marital policy for the rank and file very significantly. In 1941, Himmler ruled that, before approval of women chosen as future soldiers' wives, the shape of their legs should be considered. He also made various other limitations in the members' freedom of action in this field.[8] In 1940, a prospective couple was ordered to settle in Germany to facilitate serious 'Germanisation' of the Czech bride-to-be. In 1942, Himmler undertook to consider approval of marriage between an SS man and the Polish mother of his three children if the latter would accept to 'submit to a Germanisation programme'.[9]

---

4. BAMA, RS2/3-5. Letter from *Gen.Kdo III (germ) SS-Panzerkorps, Richtlinien für die Auswahl des germanischen Führernachwuches*, 25 May 1943. See also Letter from *Gen.Kdo III (germ) SS-Panzerkorps, Aufbau und Erziehung der germanischen SS-Truppen*, 30 May 1943.
5. Longerich (2008), p 369.
6. Ibid., p 339ff.
7. Ibid., p 340.
8. Longerich (2008), p 340ff.
9. Ibid., p 341.

In September 1942, as an element of his activist marriage policy Himmler wrote to his corps, divisional and regional commanders that he had noticed that many refused their men's wishes to marry on account of their youth (22–23 years). Himmler found this wrong and declared that if one was old enough to die, he would also be old enough to marry. It was, above all, important that the young SS men reproduced before they died which Himmler implored everyone to understand.[10]

Indeed, the SS men were expected to father a good many children and, in 1936, Himmler fixed the number at four.[11] The 1939 outbreak of war increased the SS' ambitions on behalf of its members. In October 1939, in an order Himmler championed the idea that the SS men might have extramarital relations with German women to make sure they did not die on the field of battle without having produced any offspring.[12] Over and over again, Himmler returned to this theme. In the autumn of 1942, Himmler asked Jüttner to find out whether it was possible that married officers, NCOs and men of the divisions Das Reich and Leibstandarte temporarily stationed in France might get their wives out and live with them in hired cottages or hotels for a fortnight or so.[13] A year later, another scheme – inspired by an article in one of the navy's magazines – was implemented. There in 1942 a medical doctor had recommended that childless men tried to harmonise their leaves with their wives' periods so that they would be at home whenever the chance of conception was optimum.[14] In July that year, the SS had the article published in 50,000 copies with a view to letting it circulate among SS and police units at the front.[15] Shortly afterwards, it was directed that all Waffen-SS units stationed in Germany were to make sure that the wives might visit their husbands for five or six days in order to facilitate the production of 'Aryan' children.[16] Apparently, this was a very welcome measure, and the Waffen-SS commander-in-chief in Hungary enlarged its sphere of operation to include Hungary.[17] During the months November 1943 to June 1944 alone, the SS reimbursed wives' travel and accommodation expenses of 111,600 Reich mark. This equalled 1,000 spouses' visits in seven months.[18]

10. VAP, *SS ärtzliche Akademie Graz*, K2, file 5. RFSS, *Heiratsgenehmigung für Angehörige der Waffen-SS*, 30 September 1942. See also VAP, letter in SS-Rekr. Depot 'Dep'. K.2.
11. Hein (2012), p 101.
12. Longerich (2008), p 476ff. This ordinance received some attention, which is underscored by the fact that, during interrogation in February 1943, it was repeated by an SS deserter with considerable precision. BB, E27, 1000/721, Archivenr. 9928,Bd.4, SS 103, *Deserteurbericht* 3 February 1943, p 23.
13. BAB, NS19/2769, Letter from Himmler to Jüttner, 27 October 1942.
14. BAB, NS19/3594, Hans Sievers, 'Mahnung und Verpflichtung', ... *gegen Engeland*, nr. 200, 10 December 1942.
15. BAB, NS19/3594, Hauptamt to Persönlicher Stab Reichsführer-SS, *Sonderdruck Mahnung und Verpflichtung*, 21 July 1943.
16. BAB, NS19/3594, Reichsführer-SS, *Planmäßiger Urlaub*, 25 August 1943.
17. BAB, NS19/3594, Telex from Himmler to Befehlshaber der Waffen-SS in Ungarn, 13 July 1944. Himmler ordered instead that applications for an eight days' sojourn for the wife could be forwarded to his personal staff so that he might decide on an ad hoc basis.
18. BAB, NS19/3594, *Zusammenstellung der von November 1943 bis Juni 1944 gezahlten Betrage für planmäßigen Urlaub*, 30 June 1944. That about 1,000 wives travelled has been calculated on

The Prohibition of Sexual Intercourse with Other Races

The long-term aim behind the SS leadership's ideological and eugenic ambition to control the personnel's engagements and marriages was to prevent 'racial contamination'. This was from a Nazi point of view an acute challenge in the Balkans, the Soviet Union and the rest of eastern Europe, where the inhabitants were generally considered sub-humans. In April 1939, after the inclusion of the Slav Czechs in Germany, a prohibition of having sex with women of 'other races' was therefore instituted.[19] Violations of this ban were to be prosecuted and the minimum penalty was eviction from the SS.[20]

As a consequence of the campaign in Poland, a number of cases of SS men's intercourse with Polish women were discussed at the highest levels. The SS court of justice was unsure how to handle these occurrences. On 12 December 1940, the head of *Hauptamt SS-Gericht* (main office of the SS court of justice), Paul Scharfe, requested a clarification of Himmler's attitude to the issue of sexual relations with Polish women.[21] The answer intimated that Himmler had discussed the matter with Hitler, and the result was that incidents of this kind were to be prosecuted.[22]

Nonetheless, there was still some uncertainty as to the interpretation of the ban on intercourse with women of other races and to which soldiers it might apply. In September 1941, the commander of *Standarte Nordwest* wrote to *Gericht des Kommando-Stabes RF-SS* asking whether Dutch and Flemish volunteers were also to be prosecuted in such cases. Lately, there had been more incidents of intercourse between Polish women and personnel of his unit, and he requested a basic clarification of the issue.[23] On 25 October, Himmler's personal SS judge, Horst Bender – entitled *Der SS-Richter beim Reichsführer-SS und Chef der Deutschen Polizei*– answered that the prohibition did indeed apply to Germanic volunteers as well, and thus to *Standarte Nordwest*. However, Himmler had decided that in cases of a first-time violation the sanction should be disciplinary, only.[24] Uncertainty also existed as to which ethnic groups were comprised – that is, which women. On 13 October 1941, second SS Brigade approached Himmler's command staff for guidance in a case concerning intercourse with a Russian woman. The Brigade wished to ascertain that the ban did not only cover Czech and Polish women, but Russian as well.[25]

---

the basis of an average cost of 120 Reich mark per trip (cf. a survey of the costs of ten such visits in SS-Oberabschnitt Nordost, *Besuch der SS-Angehörigen durch ihre Ehefrauen*, 13 May 1944. For previous travels see examples in package BAB, NS19/3594.

19. See, inter alia, BAB, NS7/265, sundry letters with reference to this ban of 19 April 1939, and Longerich (2008), p 502.
20. Volker Koop, *Dem Führer ein Kind schenken; die SS-Organisation Lebensborn* (Bohlau, 2007), p 184.
21. BAB, NS7/265, Various letters on *Geschlectsverkehr mit Polinnen*, pp 1–5.
22. Ibid.
23. BAB, NS7/265, *Geschlectsverkehr mit Frauen anderrassiger Bevölkerung 1940–1941*, p 7, letter from an SS-Oberführer and commander of the SS-Freiwilligen-Standarte 'Nordwest', to Gericht des Kommando-Stabes RF-SS, 23 September 1941.
24. BAB, NS7/265, SS-Richter beim RF-SS tocommander Standarte Nordwest, 25 October 1941. See also BAB, NS7/4, Hauptamt SS-Gericht, *ZehnterSammelerlass*, 15 January 1942, p 18.
25. BAB, NS7/265, p 10, Telegram from 2nd SS-Brigade to Kdo Stab RF-SS, 13 October 1941.

No doubt, the ban on intercourse with women of alien races was a key issue to Himmler. On 24 October, he wrote to Justice Horst Bender expressing the wish to be informed of 'every single case of SS men's association with female Russians, Ukrainians etc'.[26] As soon as the following day, Bender forwarded this wish to *Hauptamt SS-Gericht*. In the letter the designation 'Russian, Ukrainian woman' was struck out, and a racial precision was added in handwriting: 'Females in the occupied areas, who are not *Volksdeutsche*'.[27] The following month, this order was approved and expanded. It was now made clear that Himmler demanded an investigation of all known cases of sexual intercourse between SS men and non-*Volksdeutsche* women in the occupied areas of Russia. Himmler wanted to have these cases submitted to him, so that he might personally make the decision in every single case. In order to be able to evaluate the racial aspects he wished, in every case, to receive photos of the culprit as well as of the woman.[28]

As early as the winter 1941, it appeared that, although the central authorities desired to display diligence and meticulousness in this ideologically very delicate matter, realities at the front were not easily controlled.[29] Initial reports on contraventions from Waffen-SS units confirmed that in this particular area there was a schism between ideological theory and realities at the front. For example, after an inspection tour to SS hospitals and convalescence homes in the area of *HSSPF Ukraine/Russland Süd*, the head physician of the SS, Professor, Dr Karl Gebhardt, informed his boss and old friend, Himmler, that the main activity there was treatment of skin and venereal diseases.[30]

Transgressions in this field had mostly been met with only disciplinary sanctions but in the summer of 1942, Himmler ordered that the ban on intercourse with women of other races was to be emphasised and that such offences must always be punished as cases of insubordination (i.e. as a criminal case). Moreover, Himmler wished to have all cases submitted for his personal decision.[31] However, a vast number of cases kept rolling into the SS courts.[32] In May 1943, the problems reached a level where a meeting of SS judges was convened with a view to considering 'intercourse with women of another race'.[33] The resulting memo left little doubt

26. BAB, NS7/265, p 17, Letter from Himmler to SS-Richter Bender, 24 October 1941.
27. BAB, NS7/265, p 18, Bender to Hauptamt SS-Gericht 25 October 1941. It was no rare event that SS men under suspicion defended themselves with having believed that the woman was actually *volksdeutsch*. On this, see Maren Roger, *Kriegsbeziehungen. Intimität, Gewalt und Prostitution im besetzten Polen 1939 bis 1945* (S. Fischer, 2015), pp 141f.
28. BAB, NS7/265, p 23, *Geschlechtsverkehr von Angehörigen der SS und Polizei mit einer andersrassigen Bevölkerung*, 12 November 1941.
29. BAB, NS7/3, *Sammlung von Erlassen des Hauptamtes SS-Gericht 1940–1941*, p 109. Letter on *Geschlechtsverkehr von Angehörigen der SS und Polizei mit andersrassigen Frauen*, 9 December 1941.
30. Ibid., p 449.
31. VAP, N.1, SS-Pz-Div. LAH, box 4, Circular from SS-Führungshauptamt, 10 July 1942, *Geschlechtsverkehr von Angehörigen der SS und Polizei mit Frauen einer andersrassigen Bevölkerung*.
32. See for instance letters in VAP, SS-Rekr. Depot 'Dep'. K.2 og K.3.
33. BAB, NS7/13, *Richtertagung in München am 7.5.1943 – Bericht und Vermerke zu diversen Besprechungspunkten, Vermerk*, 13 May 1943 (pp 7–9).

about the realities at the front. For example, 'in the Leibstandarte intercourse with women of another race happens over and over again. This is a result of having many women collaborators of another race working in supply and similar units. In many places this has developed into a kind of concubine-like relations'.[34] According to the memo, the commanding officer had told his men that this ban simply did not apply, and that 'it had been conceived by people who had merely a theoretical understanding of things'.[35] Division Das Reich experienced a similar situation and had decided not to prosecute breaches of the ban at all. The police division, too, was pragmatic, and the court in Kiev informed that 50 per cent of the SS and police personnel violated the prohibition. The court in Kraków (Krakau) opined, that in the Gouvernement Générale, Himmler's order was impracticable. Standartenführer Dr Günther Reineke declared that the order was only paperwork and would have to be cancelled, which Gruppenführer Franz Breithaupt then would discuss with Himmler at first opportunity.[36] Having gathered this evidence, the SS judges suggested that, as far as this actual matter was concerned, the ideological aims would have to yield to realities at the front. Himmler, however, did not want to give up and, as a compromise, he introduced some relaxation of the rules. On 8 September 1943, he wrote to the chief of police and security that he was positive as to abrogation of the ban concerning Estonians and Latvians, but that it would have to survive in the case of Lithuanians because of their racial inferiority.[37]

The intercourse problem worried the leadership not only because of fear of 'racial pollution', but also because emotional involvement might lead to sympathies for a population that was to be oppressed. These liaisons were not only a matter of sexual satisfaction; they might endanger the SS' ideals on how and with whom to engage. This was underscored in a notice in the *Verordnungsblatt der Waffen-SS* (Waffen-SS orders) that informed of SS men who had regular correspondence with *fremdvölkischen Arbeiterinnen* (female workers of a foreign ethnicity), whom they had met at the front, and there had been more than one occurrence where marriage had been promised.[38]

Religious Worship

The strained relationship with Christianity was one field where the SS was in open opposition to the society at large, and the SS was well aware of this.[39] Internally, the negative attitude towards Christianity was clear, but externally a smoother approach to church policy was chosen. This was clearly a tactical and pragmatic more than an ideological choice. Hence, in September 1935, Himmler banned some songs containing verses offensive to the Church. This concerned songs like the *Judenraus, Pabst*

---

34. Ibid.
35. Ibid., see also Röger (2015), p 216.
36. Ibid.
37. BAB, NS19/382, *Politische und militarische Entwicklung in Estland und Letland.*
38. *Verordnungsblatt der Waffen-SS*, vol. 3, no. 22, 15 November 1942, item 406, p 97.
39. Höhne (1995), p 417ff.; Rohrkamp (2010), p 225ff.

hinaus (Jews vanish, Pope get lost).[40] At the same time, Himmler forbade the writing, dissemination and singing of songs of a tactless or unsavoury nature referring to ecclesiastical proceedings or day-to-day affairs. Breach of this decree would entail expulsion from the SS. This matter was believed to be serious enough to have it repeated on a monthly basis to all members.[41] This, however, was a tactical measure, and, a few years hence, Himmler declared that a final clash with the Church was imminent.[42] As of November 1937, SS men were prohibited from appearing in their SS uniforms in church – even at weddings.[43] In 1939, as the police division was formed and the army suggested that army chaplains be attached, Himmler flatly refused declaring that with that division the only roles for clerics would be as drivers.[44] The church struggle went both ways, and it happened that officers were excommunicated from the RC Church – events that were closely watched by the SS.[45]

Sixty-eight per cent of the entire SS officer corps registered as *gottgläubig*, that is credulous, though without membership of any religious community. Apparently, this percentage was highest in Himmler's inner circle and with the central SS authorities.[46] This might indicate career considerations or institutional pressure rather that personal conviction. Incidents of desecration of crucifixes, clashes with clerics and other varieties of blasphemous behaviour, however, suggest that, even on the lowest rungs of the ladder, anti-clerical elements were at large.[47] It appears, that quite frequently, there were local incidents of a more far-reaching nature than was appreciated in Berlin. Notably, this became prevalent as, from 1942 onwards, the SS turned to forced enlistment.[48] In 1943, a South-German Catholic was involuntarily enlisted in the Waffen-SS. From his time in barracks he remembered how the officers' anti-clerical feelings were let loose. The raw recruits were told by their company commander that he would personally shoot those who might soil the SS uniform by wearing it in church.[49] Similarly, a Dutch

---

40. About this song, see Robert A. Pois, *National Socialism and the Religion of Nature* (Croom Helm, 1986), p 46.

41. RGVA, 1372/3/38, ZK Tgb.Nr. Ch. 608/35, *Liedverbote*, 20 September 1935.

42. Longerich (2008), p 280.

43. Verordnungsblatt der Waffen-SS, vol. 3, no.15, 1 August 1942, ref. 268, *Teilnahme SS Angehöriger an kirchlichen Handlungen*.

44. Engel and Kotze, (2005), p 82.

45. BAB, NS19/1204, Letter from Frick to Wolff, 3 May 1939. BAB, NS19/1552, Letter from Berger to Himmler betr. Leon Degrelle, 21 December 1943.

46. Birn (1986), p 358.

47. For examples from the Leibstandarte before the war, see Weingartner (1974), p 28. See also BAB, NS19/2855: Prosecution concerning five incidents of sacrilege terminated 24 July 1941.

48. For a number of cases see BAB, NS19/2242, notably one from the Archiepiscopal See in Freiburg to the OKW, *Waffen-SS und Kirchenaustritt*, 25 November 1942; Ibid.: Letter from Bormann to Himmler, 22 March 1943 and a circular from the NSDAP's party secretariat of 26 April 1943. See also BAB, NS33/31, *Rede des SS-Obergruppenführer Jüttner auf der SS-Führer-Tagung in Prag am 13 April 1944*, p 6ff.

49. Alois Janzer, *Als in Deutschland die Blutfahnen wehten: unfreiwillig bei der Waffen-SS ; Erinnerungen 1943–1948* (Lauber, 2010).

officer cadet at the *Junkerschule* in Bad Tölz told how parts of the tutorial staff taunted Christianity and spoke ill about the numerous crucifixes adoring the school's environs.[50] The church issue was ambiguous also in the relations with the national legions. While, on the one hand, it was tolerated that some of these incorporated army chaplains, on the other, they were soon to be got rid of.[51] German as well as foreign SS soldiers were actively foiled in their wishes to attend church when off parade.[52]

Nonetheless, little by little various forms of institutionalised religion found its way into the Waffen-SS. Most obvious was the rights, which Himmler, bestowed upon the Muslim soldiers in the fields of food and religious practise. But Christianity also sneaked into the organisation. This was not only the case with the Ukrainian division, in which there were army chaplains, but also in other places. In a letter from the front at Narva, a Dutch volunteer wrote that the Rumanian *Volksdeutsche* in this place had brought their own chaplain – which he, who was himself of a practicing Catholic family, perceived with great sympathy.[53]

In October 1943, the Junkerschule in Bad Tölz decided that Sunday training should be arranged with a view to allowing Wallonian officer cadets to attend service in the nearby churches.[54] In July 1944, Himmler underscored that Flemish volunteers should be given the opportunity to attend church on Sundays.[55] It seems natural to see some connexion between these concessions and the abating fortune of war, apparently helping to allow increasing pragmatism.

The Impact of Ideology

In September 1944, a WE leader in Prague complained that not all his colleagues imbued their soldiers sufficiently with the National Socialist ideas. In his view, the trouble was that many had a superficial relationship with ideology and merely exploited political phrases without really believing what they professed: 'They have at their disposal a certain vocabulary, which – with sufficient boldness – may be used for a cursorily convenient ideological teaching [...] However, our Weltanschauung is no harlot, but a noble lady who must be worshipped and wooed'.[56] Thus, the WE leader focussed on whether Nazism had actually been thoroughly internalised by the SS men or it had merely remained a surface phenomenon, which one might address pragmatically and opportunistically.

---

50. NIOD, 249-0761A., SS Junkerschule Tölz, 29 October 1948.
51. This happened in Legions Norway and Flanders. See chapter on Germanic volunteers.
52. BAB, NS19/2373, Letter from Rauter to Himmler, 10 June 1943.
53. NIOD, Coll. Doc. II, 758 A, 12, SS-Vrijwilligers, copy of letter from BJVAB to his parents, 25 June 1944.
54. Letter from Lehrgruppe B, Junkerschule Bad Tölz, *Sonntagsdienst der Junker*, 21 October 1943, copied in R. Schulze-Kossens,*Militärischer Führernachwuchs der Waffen-SS. Die Junkerschulen* (Munin Verlag, 1982), p 179.
55. BAB, NS19/1666, Letter from Himmler to Hauptamt, Führungshauptamt and HSSPF Jungclaus in Brussels, 27 July 1944.
56. VAPSS-Artillerie Ausbildungs- und Ersatz Regiment, K 17, file 25, *Abt. VI – Presseübersichten 'Wochenbriefe'*, 7 September 1944.

There were huge differences among the SS units that were formed during the war – not least as far as their personnel composition, their ideological zeal and their motivation were concerned. There is little doubt that a majority of the soldiers in the early divisions and those who volunteered without pressure were generally ideologically motivated. Although the officers and NCOs were the primary trendsetters, there are many signs that the organisation's spirit and culture had a much broader foundation.[57] Ca. 75 per cent of all Reich German Waffen-SS soldiers were members of one or more National Socialist organisations. In comparison, only 34 per cent of the *Wehrmacht* soldier upheld similar memberships. Moreover, almost three in four of the Waffen-SS men who were members of such organisation were born between 1922 and 1928.[58] In other words, they were very young and characterised by growing up in Nazi Germany.[59] Having spent most of their formative years in the Third Reich, they were likely easily influenced by Waffen-SS' ideological teaching.

In 1944, *Hauptamt* found it necessary to remind leaders that the teaching material was to remain with the units. Apparently, there was a tendency among the teachers 'to see these pamphlets as their personal possession to be taken along when transferred to new duty stations, where after new instructors had to ask for new sets of teaching aids'.[60] The star of SS publications, the *Leithefte*, was particularly popular and preferred literature. In *Hauptamt*'s archive, numerous letters from officers and men sing their praise asking for more copies or earlier issues.[61] In many diaries and letters from Waffen-SS soldiers there is positive mentioning of the ideological teaching and, as we can see from the *Leithefte* example, the soldiery wished to supplement it by private study. A Norwegian volunteer, who had been wounded and hospitalised in Germany in 1942, even devoured the Nazi Philosopher Alfred Rosenberg's *Mythos des 20. Jahrhundert* (Myth of the twentieth Century), though he found it 'heavy going with lots of foreign words'.[62] Some soldiers of Division Das Reich got hold of the Nazi publication *Gott und Volk*; and soon a reading circle materialised. Evenings on end, they took turns reading aloud and followed up with heated discussions on the content.[63]

The image of the Red Army's soldiers as not only brutal creatures, but racially disposed for cruelty shows that the SS ideology was indeed internalised. A Norwegian SS man regarded the Russian prisoners as 'unalloyed Mongols' who were 'vile to look at'. He dreaded 'what might happen to fair haired Nordic women if ever Scandinavia were to be occupied by such characters'.[64] This demonization of the foe

---

57. Stein (1984), p 125.
58. Rohrkamp (2010), p 69.
59. Ibid., p 74.
60. *Verordnungsblatt der Waffen-SS*, vol. 5, no. 19, 1 October 1944, ref. 614.
61. BAB, NS31/75, Letter to Hauptamt from Gerhard Krause, 23 April 1942. Package includes a number of letters of a similar kind from officers as well as private soldiers.
62. HLC, Sigurd Soerlie's archive: P1-Andreas B. Nilsson, undated letter.
63. Helmut Günther, *Hot Motors, Cold Feet. A Memoir of Service with the Motorcycle Battalion of SS-Division 'Reich' 1940–1941* (J.J. Fedorowicz Publishing, 2004).
64. Ben Esper, Tjerkassy. *En norsk ambulansekjorers oplevelser på Østfronten 1943–1944* (Forlaget Zac, 1981), p 15.

help provoke violence – even against one's own fellow soldiers. There are examples of SS men shooting their wounded comrades rather than leaving them behind.[65]

There were, of course, nuances in soldiers' attitude to the ideological messages. This materialises in a conversation in the autumn of 1944 with Standartenführer Hans Linger, former commander of the Division Götz von Berlichingen and a captain of the German army, who were both prisoners of war in the Great Britain. According to Linger, ideological tuition at the *Junkerschulen* was neither comprehensive nor thorough, and he was himself deeply disappointed. Linger also felt that political teaching did not take up much time with the units – he avowed that the WE leaders were typical professor characters whom no soldier really respected. In one, particularly serious case, the WE leader was a civilian from a major newspaper. Linger found his writings of such poor standard that they were useful only for 'wiping one's arse'. This annoyed him, because the modern army needed decent political training and Linger believed that much was to be learned from the Soviet commissar system in that regard.[66]

The impact of the ideological teaching was challenged by other problems as well. A Dutch recruit at Sennheim confessed that, considering the 'Babylonian linguistic confusion', he was not surprised that a few fell asleep during theoretical lectures.[67] The presence, after 1941, of many nationalities also meant that there were cultural differences among the various groups. The ideology was a given to many SS men having grown up in Germany as well as to some non-German North and West-European volunteers with connexion to Nazi circles in their home countries. Conversely, to many East-Europeans, who might have been involuntarily enlisted, as well as being at a lower rung on the 'racial ladder', might have found it difficult to identify themselves fully with the Nazi Weltanschauung.

During their training, the Waffen-SS soldiers became deeply involved in a comprehensive ideological project, and as the war progressed the Nazi Weltanschauung was increasingly enforced. One of the last surviving Waffen-SS documents show how the ideology was upheld to the last. On 2 May 1945, the Waffen-SS commander-in-chief in Bohemia-Moravia wrote in his order of the day: 'Our Führer died heroically in his struggle for the capital of the Reich. The Führer lives on. The Weltanschauung that he created cannot and will not fall. The struggle continues'.[68] As we shall see later in this book, quite a few SS soldiers held on to such beliefs even after the war.

---

65. Ibid, s.41, see also Karl-Heinz Frieser, who denies that the Germans shot their wounded in the Korsun-Cherkassy Pocket – 'Die Rückzugsoperationen der Heeresgruppe Süd in der Ukraine' in Karl-Heinz Friser and Klaus Schmider, *Die Ostfront 1943/44. Der Krieg im Osten und an den Nebenfronten*, Das deutsche Reich und der Zweite Weltkrieg, Vol. 8 (Deutsche Verlags-Anstalt, 2007), s.339–492, p 415. For more examples that the SS shot the wounded and on wounded soldiers' suicide see Bundgard Christensen et al. (1998), p 325ff.
66. NAKEW, WO208/4140, SRM 1216, SS-Standartenführer Linger's (17 SS PZ div.) conversation with a captain.
67. NIOD Coll. Doc. II, 750A SS-Vrijwilligers, exerpt from letter of 15 April 1943 from KPV to an acquaintance in the Netherlands.
68. VAP, SS-ärtzliche Akademie Graz, K2, file5, Feldeinheit 'Klein',*Tagesbefehl nr. 10*, 2 May 1945. Same message can be found in Feld-Ersatz-Einheit 'Schweigert', 4 May 45.

Chapter Seven

PUNISHMENT AND DISCIPLINE IN THE WAFFEN-SS: LAW AND LEGAL PRACTICE IN THE RACIAL STATE

On the 18th of January 1942, Himmler's private judge wrote to the central SS office responsible for the management of the SS courts. This judge – whose official title was 'SS-Richter beim RFSS' – functioned as a sort of liaison-officer between Himmler and his bureaucracy in matters concerning the SS courts and the SS legal code. This particular letter was a reminder to the SS-bureaucrats that Himmler personally demanded to see all applications for pardon in cases concerning the death penalty within the SS-court system. As in previous correspondence it was stressed that Himmler required that these applications contained detailed CV's and descriptions concerning the parents and the family including actual photographs of the parents.[1]

Himmler's priorities in these cases had nothing to with concern for the welfare of the next of kin of the SS men who had been sentenced to death. On the contrary, the letter reveals two other central phenomena when it comes to punishment and discipline in the Waffen-SS: on the one hand, the ever-present importance of ideology in the formulation and practice of SS law, and on the other hand Himmler's minute interest in every possible detail in that regard. Simply put the Reichsführer-SS wanted to racially screen and evaluate his SS-men down to extraordinary detail and the SS court system and the SS legal code provided ample opportunity to do just that. For the men involved this could be a matter of life and death. Having a racially strong family (in Himmler's eyes) might provide a pardon for an SS soldier with a death sentence hanging over his head. In that way, the head of the SS organisation believed, he could save the Germanic blood he thought so precious for the future of the Third Reich.

The Third Reich: A Dual State or a Racial State?

One of the earliest academic attempts to explain the legal developments during the Third Reich was Ernst Fraenkel's impressive work 'The Dual State' published already in 1941. Here, Fraenkel produced an 'ethnography of Nazi law' and managed

---

1. BAB, NS7, 53, *Gnadenbefugnisse in Sachen des Obersten SS-und Polizeigerichts,* letter from *Der SS-Richter beim RFSS* to *Hauptamt SS-Gericht, Vorbereitung der Entscheidung des RF-SS über Gnadengesuche bei Todesstrafen,* 18 January 1942.

to smuggle his manuscript out of Germany to get it published in the USA.[2] In his book, Fraenkel identified two different spheres of official authority in Nazi Germany, one that he called the 'normative state' and another, which he termed the 'prerogative state'. The normative state consisted of the traditional German legal order, including the Nazification of the existing legal system, while the prerogative state was where institutions such as the SS wielded arbitrary power.[3] According to Fraenkel, the latter state required courts to handle political questions not from a legal point of view but from a political point of view and furthermore waged 'perpetual warfare against all those dictates of conscience not in harmony with its teachings'.[4] The normative state, on the other hand, was made up by the traditional formal (and rational) German law and had the traditional courts as its 'guardians'.[5] Nevertheless, Fraenkel saw the two forms of state as complementing each other.[6] They formed a whole although the prerogative state could always overrule the power of the normative state. Still, the normative state could to a limited extent protect citizens, for example when 'humane judges' in ordinary courts chose to give individuals a prison sentence in order to keep them out of concentration camps and hence avoid the power of the prerogative state.[7]

There is no doubt that Fraenkel's analytical distinction captures some very interesting aspects of law and terror during the Reich, and not least how old and new institutions were intertwined in the Nazi dictatorship. Furthermore, the dual state theory also explain why the Nazi state couldn't do entirely without the old legal order. In that sense, the normative state – the ordinary courts, for example, as well as laws and bureaucratic traditions pre-dating the Nazi era – actually supported the continued existence of the prerogative state and thereby the Third Reich.[8] Fraenkel's theory however risks downplaying some of the ways in which the normative and the prerogative state came to resemble each other during the Third Reich. Both these spheres of the state operated on a basis of formal law and often shared a tendency to interpret law in an ideological manner. In that sense they not only existed in a 'state of tension'[9] – they also to some degree mirrored each other.

2. Jens Meierhenrich 'An Ethnography of Nazi Law: The Intellectual Foundations of Ernst Fraenkel's Theory of dictatorship' in Ernst Fraenkel *The Dual State. A Contribution to the Theory of Dictatorship* (Oxford University Press 2017).

3. Ernst Fraenkel *The Dual State. A Contribution to the Theory of Dictatorship* (Oxford University Press 2017). See also *Alan* E. Steinweis and Robert D. Rachlin 'Introduction. The Law in Nazi Germany and the Holocaust', Steinweis and Rachlin (eds.) *The Law in Nazi Germany. Ideology, Opportunism, and the Perversion of Justice* (berghahn 2015), p 2.

4. Fraenkel 2017, pp 50 and 54.

5. Ernst Fraenkel *The Dual State. A Contribution to the Theory of Dictatorship* (The Lawbook Exchange Ltd.), 2010, p 73.

6. Fraenkel (2010), p 71.

7. Meierhenrich (2017), p xxxvi.

8. Jens Meierhenrich *The remnants of the Rechtsstaat. An Ethnography of Nazi Law* (Oxford University Press, 2018), p 248. See also Fraenkel (2010), p 71. According to Werner Best, this supportive role of the normative state was the sole Raison d'être for the normative state, Fraenkel (2010), p 62.

9. Meierhenrich (2017), p lxx.

As courts in the normative state declared time and time again, Hitler's words were law and under his reign the state had absolute power.[10] Furthermore, the prerogative state did not simply operate 'by arbitrary measures', as sometimes argued by Fraenkel.[11] As we shall see, there was a certain degree of formality and reliability also in SS law and thereby a rational and formalized side, as well as an ideological and irrational side, to the SS machinery of extermination. In the words of Michael Wildt this type of Nazi institution was to some extent characterised by 'laborious administrative procedures' as any old bureaucracy, but through its well-defined ideological and political purpose it nevertheless became a very dynamic institution, which within the context of the SS and the Third Reich produced an unlimited, radical ideology.[12]

SS Law in the Racial State

As will be described in this chapter, the SS, an institution lying at the very centre of the prerogative state, created and interpreted law in a manner which in many ways did not differ significantly from what took place in ordinary German courts.[13] To capture this aspect of governing in the SS and the Third Reich it perhaps makes more sense to describe the Nazi dictatorship not only as a dual state but also as a 'Racial State' as others have done before.[14] In this 'Racial state' ideology and race were often the primary policy considerations regardless of whether we look at the SS, the Gestapo or institutions operating primarily within the framework of the normative state. As we shall see in this chapter, the SS courts and SS judges were engaged in interpreting and producing general rules, law and legal standards where ideology and race played a central role. In doing so they often laid bare the obvious political motives and guidelines of the regime as in the case against Max Täubner where the court specifically stated that the 'Jews must be exterminated; there is no loss in any of the killed Jews'.[15] This, however, was not simply a legal system of arbitrary power, although it had nothing to do with a 'rechtsstaat' and the Rule of Law. It was an ideological legal system based on a mixture of Nazi laws and ideological interpretations of old laws deriving from the normative German state.[16] And the way

---

10. Fraenkel (2010), pp 3ff.
11. Ibid, p 153.
12. Wildt (2009), p 436; Wildt (2005).
13. When Meierhenrich states that the prerogative state only produced substantively irrational law which was arbitrary and did not rely on general rules it is not correct (as the remainder of this chapter will demonstrate). Meierhenrich (2017), p lxxx.
14. Michael Burleigh and Wolfgang Wippermann, *The Racial State. Germany 1933–1945* (Cambridge University Press, 1994). Fraenkel was of course well aware of the overarching importance of the question of race. See, for example, Fraenkel 2017, pp 108f. Indeed, one can argue that these concepts – the racial state and the dual state – do not exclude each other.
15. Dick De Mildt 'Getting Away with Murder: The Täubner Case' in Stoltzfus and Friedlander (eds.) *Nazi Crimes and the Law* (Cambridge University Press 2016), p 104.
16. An irrational formal system of law in a Weberian sense, although arguably sometimes also substantial irrational.

SS law was employed and interpreted mattered greatly for the hundreds of thousands of SS soldiers, and others who were subjected to SS jurisdiction.

SS Law from the "Mactergreifung" to the Legal Code of 1939

From the early 1930s, Himmler began developing regulations, which applied to all members of the organisation. As we shall see, these contained detailed ideological directions concerning how the SS men should behave and how they should lead their lives. Along the same lines an internal code of justice was created which called for breaches of discipline to be punished in various ways. Moreover, after the 1933 *Machtergreifung*, a set of rules was drawn up concerning disciplinary sanctions and procedures for complaints.[17] Right up to 1939, this remained an internal procedure and the heaviest sanction was expulsion from the SS. Members were still subjected to ordinary German courts in cases concerning criminal behaviour and violations of penal law and civil law. In wartime the members of the armed SS would be subjected to the *Wehrmacht*'s military justice. The SS regarded this as problematic restraints on its own power which, for example, hampered the SS' ability to influence and form its staff through the production and operation of legal ideological norms. Moreover, the existing system allowed that, in wartime, the *Wehrmacht* might interfere with what the SS saw as their internal affairs. This state of affairs caused problems in Poland in 1939.

On a number of occasions during the campaign in Poland, open conflict broke out between the *Wehrmacht* and the SS concerning the SS soldiers' behaviour. Several army formations complained about killings and atrocities against local civilians committed by SS and police personnel.[18] However, after the Polish campaign Himmler succeeded in extracting the Waffen-SS from the *Wehrmacht* jurisdiction and setting up an independent judiciary. As a result, the SS could from then on handle such cases themselves without any external involvement.

Parts of the existing research literature, suggest that the SS got its own legal system and an independent judiciary because of the atrocities committed in Poland, but this was not the case.[19] The plans had been underway for some time, and the SS' wish to establish its own jurisdiction can be traced as far back as the autumn of 1934. In the fall of 1938, Hitler supported this, and in 1939 he gave his fundamental approval.[20] In October 1939 - after the invasion and defeat of Poland had initiated the Nazi war of extermination - this resulted in the founding of a SS and police legal authority ("SS- und Polizeigericht"), which was given jurisdiction over the majority of the SS' own troops.[21]

---

17. Called *Disziplinarstraf- und Beschwerdeordnung*, Wegner (1990), p 319.
18. Christopher Theel 'Parzifal unter den Gangstern? Die SS- und Polizeigerichtsbarkeit in Polen 1939–1945' in Jan Erik Schulte, Peter Lieb og Bernd Wegner, *Die Waffen-SS. Neue Forschungen* (Verlag Ferdinand Schöningh GmbH, 2014), p 66ff.
19. Stein (1984), p 30.
20. Theel in Schulte et al. (2014), p 61ff. Longerich traces this development back to 1937 (not to 1934), Longerich (2008), p 501. See also Wegner (1990), p 321.
21. See BAB, NS7/2, p 107ff., Letter of 20 November 1939, *Verordnung übereine Sondergerichtsbarkeit*, promulgated on 17 October and in force from 30 October 1939.

To a considerable degree, the new SS and police legal system took its point of departure in the *Wehrmacht*'s existing martial law, but incorporated the norms and ideology of the SS. The result was a system that, on the one hand, carried on with many existing rules, while, on the other, based all legal decisions on the SS' ideological universe with Himmler as the chief legal executive. This way, the SS and police justice authority became a potent ideological tool of formal social control, and, at the same time, the *Wehrmacht*'s power over SS units shrank considerably.

Military Justice in the Wehrmacht

In many respects, the administration of justice within the armed forces prior to the *Machtergreifung* provided an excellent point of departure for Nazifying warfare. On the one hand, military justice was not exactly characterised by liberal or humanistic ideas, and on the other, the German army after the First World War was influenced by right wing radicalism and anti-democratic ideological notions of how Jews and Marxists had corrupted the nation from within and laid the ground for the defeat. An at the time widespread form of xenophobic thinking which obviously did not lie far from National Socialist concepts.[22]

German military justice rested on a heritage from the disciplined Prussian army and had remained relatively untouched by The Enlightenment and the otherwise extensive legal reforms of the 18th and 19th centuries.[23] Throughout the existence of the Third Reich, the military penal statute book of 1872, as well as the 1898 system of military justice, remained in force.[24] Nonetheless, upon the *Machtergreifung*, a new, overriding system of military justice was set up. It was meant to strengthen troop discipline and would provide the backdrop for ideological indoctrination of the *Wehrmacht*.[25] The year 1934, saw the introduction of an oath of allegiance to Hitler personally, and in 1935, the Führer was made supreme commander of the armed forces. Simultaneously, to strengthen the discipline and keep the *Wehrmacht* tidy, military justice was tightened, inter alia, by more frequent use of the death penalty.[26] While, during the First World War, the Imperial German army executed 48 of its soldiers, a staggering 12,000 death sentences were consummated by the Wehrmacht during the Second World War. There is much to suggest that more than half of these were ideologically motivated having little to do with military or disciplinary concerns.[27]

Until October 1939, the SS men were subject to the military judiciary of the *Wehrmacht*, a system that was partly reminiscent of the nineteenth century's draconian military discipline,

22. Manfred Messerschmidt, *Die Wehrmachtjustiz 1933–1945* (Schöningh, 2008), p 10ff.
23. Ibid., p xi and 4ff.
24. Peter Kalmbach, *Wehrmachtjustiz* (Metropol-Verlag, 2012), p 21.
25. Ibid., p 22ff.
26. See a number of articles from the journal *Zeitschrift für Wehrrecht*, quoted and explained in ibid., p 24.
27. Messerschmidt (2008), p 396 and Bartov (1992), p 95ff.

partly influenced by Hitler's whims and Nazi ideology. However, from Himmler's point of view there was still room for shoring up the ideological elements. Moreover, in his view the *Wehrmacht* legal system had one crucial weakness; it was not under his own and the SS' control.

The SS' Own Jurisdiction: Scope, Ideology and Control

On 17 October 1939, the special SS and police jurisdiction was introduced thus creating a new legal system entirely under Himmler's control. This legal code not only covered ordinary offences against civil or martial law such as murder, violence, theft, insubordination and desertion; it also specified the death penalty for homosexuality and criminalised sexual intercourse with Jews and other 'racially alien elements'. The SS and police jurisdiction fused the *Wehrmacht's* legal system – which was only marginally amended – with the hitherto internal SS code.[28] This meant that, like the *Wehrmacht's* courts martial, the SS and police judiciary might pass sentences in all civil cases committed by their personnel during their service.[29]

When judging a soldier's concrete deeds, the issue was not merely the actual phrasing of rules and legislation, but just as much how and in what way these were interpreted. In the spring of 1942, the head of the SS courts explained:

> The new type of SS judge combines ideological reliability and professionalism. In his judgement and determination, he is not restrained by formalities. Even where no SS and police penal law exists, he will find means and ways to ascertain that National Socialist ideology, SS norms, and the sound judgement of the people will be prioritized.[30]

In other words, it was not simply a matter of allowing SS courts to wield arbitrary power (the prerogative state), it was a matter of how to use and apply law ideologically in the 'Racial state'. Furthermore, Himmler frequently interfered in the SS' legal rulings, to declare his interpretation of the rules, and to rescind, change or approve the sentences.[31] This generally also led to more focus on ideology, because to Himmler the SS court was a tool for putting *Gleichschaltung* (political unity) and lifestyle conformity into practise.[32] In accordance with the SS' self-image as a Nazi spearhead and élite the long-term plan was to make the SS' legal system influence all forms of penal law in the Third Reich.[33]

28. Wegner (1990), p 320, and Longerich (2008), p 502f. See also Bianca Vieregge, *Die Gerichtsbarkeit einer 'Elite': Nationalsozialistische Rechtssprechung am Beispiel der SS- und Polizei-Gerichtsbarkeit* (Nomos, 2002), p 7ff. Non-military cases might be ruled by civil courts of justice.
29. Vieregge (2002), p 30ff.
30. BAB, NS7/4, *Sammlung von Erlassen des Hauptamtes SS-Gericht 1942 jan.-juni, Bericht über die Dienstbesprechung der dienstältesten SS-Richter in Danzig und Zoppot vom 30. April bis 2. Mai 1942.* Christopher Theel mentions this theme in Schulte et al. (2014), p 64.
31. See various court matter in BAB, NS7. See also Longerich (2008), p 502.
32. Ibid., p 462.
33. Vieregge (2002), p 17.

When in October 1939, the SS and police court system was introduced, initially it applied only to the armed SS including the *Verfügungstruppe, Totenkopf* units, *SS-Junkerschulen*, the staffs of the HSSPFs and those police units on active military service.[34] However, during the war the SS court's jurisdiction was considerably extended to include the *Allgemeine SS* and all the security police (*Kripo* and *Gestapo*). Moreover, foreigners serving with the *Schutzmannschaften*, locally formed police units in Eastern Europe, and the Polish and Ukrainian policemen controlled by the SS in the Gouvernement Générale all came under SS jurisdiction. This also included female assistants at SS and police service stations, Red Cross personnel with Waffen-SS units, as well as the para-military *Nationalsozialistisches Kraftfahrerkorps* (NSKK or Nazi corps of drivers). In some areas, even civilians were sentenced by SS and police courts, and, in April 1943, the SS assumed responsibility for the prosecution of civilians whose offences had primarily targeted the SS and the police. From September 1944 onwards, the *Wehrmacht*'s prisoners-of-war came under SS' jurisdiction. In this way, the SS' jurisdiction was extended very significantly during the war and came to include people outside of the SS.[35] In September 1944, however, a minor constraint on the authority of the SS court was introduced in the wake of the attempted assassination of Hitler on 20 July. It was decided that all political cases within the *Wehrmacht*, the SS and the police were to be prosecuted by the Nazi *Volksgerichtshof*.[36] In this chapter, we concentrate on the application of SS law with regard to SS soldiers and typically at the front and do not cover, for example, SS courts in the occupied countries in western Europe and the way in which these handed out judgments against civilians.

The SS regulation from the 1930s, which stipulated penalties for violations of the Nazi ideologically defined 'code of honour', were now integrated with the SS legal system. Punishments in this area included expulsion from the SS, imprisonment and capital punishment. It applied whenever a criminal offence involved a serious breach of NSDAP's or SS' fundamental principles.[37] Moreover, the penal regulations of martial law were to be interpreted in the light of the 'aim and philosophy' of the SS and police justice.[38] The formal legal basis was § 3 of the SS and police code stating that martial law always must be subordinated expedient application.[39] What was expedient, was to the SS primarily a matter of ideology.[40]

The term *Rassenschande* provides an example of how military justice and the SS ideology became ingrained. In Nazi legal terminology *Rassenschande* meant bringing disgrace on the German race by contamination of the blood through intercourse with a Jew.

---

34. See BAB, NS7/2, Letter of 20 November 1939. See also ibid., p 6ff. and 18ff.
35. Ibid., p 20ff., and Longerich (2008), p 501. See also Emmett, Stuart 'Strafvollzugslager der SS und Polizei. Himmler's wartime institutions for the detention of Waffen-SS and polizei criminals' (Fonthill 2017).
36. Vieregge (2002), p 32.
37. Ibid., p 8.
38. Ibid., p 9.
39. Ibid.
40. Similarly, ideology was the basis for the work at the disciplinary office at the SS court's headquarters in Berlin (the highest authority on disciplinary sanctions and directly under Himmler). BAB, NS7/8, *Organisation des SS-HauptamtesSS-Gericht 1942–44*, undated.

Since this was unknown to the *Wehrmacht*'s martial law, that system was of little use to the SS in this respect. Therefore, the SS chose to interpret 'discipline' as comprising a demand that the SS soldiers obey the Nazi *Weltanschauung*. This way, the SS courts might construe *Rassenschande* as a violation of military discipline, which was punishable, ultimately by capital punishment.[41]

The SS Court's Construction and Organisation

Even before the actual SS jurisdiction was implemented in 1939, there were internal rules and regulations governing admission, engagement, marriage etc. and determining penalties. At the time, the toughest punishment was eviction from the SS. As in October 1933, the Munich SS local leadership had received several complaints about SS men who had misbehaved and tried to corrupt local authorities, these members were warned that if they did not obey the rules in this field they would be 'ruthlessly expelled from the ranks of the SS'.[42] In September 1934, a disciplinary court was set up at Himmler's staff.[43] This office dealt with internal disciplinary matters such as the personnel's breaches on SS rules, but still it was not a regular legal authority.

On creation of the special SS jurisdiction, the SS' central administration got its own legal office, which was later upgraded to a *Hauptamt* – a main office. The *Hauptamt SS-Gericht* carried the overriding administrative responsibility for all cases of discipline, complaints and honour as well as for the SS judiciary.[44] While this field was directly under Himmler's overall responsibility, *Gruppenführer* Paul Scharfe was appointed leader and remained so until 1942. He was not trained in jurisprudence – which was not at all required – but he had many years of experience from leading posts in the SS legal system.[45] The head of the SS courts was primarily a guarantor of ideological perseverance. Indeed, Himmler was generally sceptical of lawyers, and in 1942 he simply stated that no lawyer would ever become head of the SS' legal organisation.[46] Generally, not wishing to bury himself and the organisation in issues of legal interpretation, Himmler focussed on the practical use of the SS courts.[47] In line with these thoughts, Scharfe claimed that while military training and secession from the Church were the prime criteria for future heads of the SS court's main office, legal education would be directly detrimental.[48]

---

41. Vieregge (2002), p 106ff.
42. BAB, NS7/2, *Gruppenbefehl Nr. 4*, 6 October 1933, p 1ff.
43. BAB, NS7/2, p 10, letter of 20 December 1934.
44. Vieregge (2002), p 35. See also BAB, NS7/8, *Organisation des SS-Hauptamtes SS-Gericht 1942–1944*, pp 4ff.
45. See Ibid., p 39ff.
46. Wegner (1990), p 324; Vieregge (2002), p 41.
47. BAB, NS7/36, from SS-Richter beim RF-SS to Hauptamt SS-Gericht, 30 July 1940, p 1.
48. Wegner (1990), p 324.

This aversion against the legal profession was of course an expression of the power of ideology within the SS. When passing sentences, the law was subjugated the political – i.e. Nazi ideology. At the same time, this provided Himmler with a convenient personal latitude.

The individual courts were at the bottom of the SS legal system. Typically, they were collocated with police stations in major cities and units in the field.[49] The actual locales, of course, changes throughout the war. Towards the end of 1943, there were 31 SS courts in Germany and the occupied areas including Kraków, Oslo, Copenhagen, Paris, Riga and Zagreb.[50] Additionally, there were courts at corps, divisional and similar levels within Waffen-SS units in the field.[51] Moreover, local SS courts were set up with regional designations.[52] But there were also courts at lower levels as, for instance, with independent units like the SS brigades, and so-called *Feldgerichte* (field courts-martial) were concurrently established.[53] At divisional level, typically, the general officer commanding was the proceedings officer. At the SS main offices this task lay with the *Hauptamt* heads, and the HSSPFs were in similar positions vis-à-vis all SS personnel in areas, which was not subordinated other judicial authorities.[54] Among the tasks of each judicial authority was deciding whether an offence was a disciplinary matter of an act under penal law.[55]

In 1940, a supreme SS and police court – the *Oberstes SS- und Polizei-Gericht* – was set up in Munich with a view to securing a uniform case law.[56] However, this court was primarily a co-ordinating and settling body since the real decisions were taken at an even higher level, viz. the *Reichsführer*'s supreme judge – *Der SS-Richter beimReichsführer-SS und Chef der deutschen Polizei* – or Himmler personally. This judge, *Oberführer* Horst Bender, was Himmler's deputy and he frequently made statements on legal matters on his behalf. The topmost figure in this system was Himmler himself, a function he persistently exercised. He endeavoured to rein in his legal organisation and he interfered in an astonishingly large number of individual cases. As late as August 1944, it was mentioned in a letter, that Himmler still wished to have certain criminal cases submitted for his personal decision.[57] Earlier that year, the individual SS courts had been reminded that they were to submit their capital offence rulings immediately and not, as it frequently happened, after three to four months. It was stressed that this was important because Himmler took a great interest in the monthly quota of death sentences as well as in the character of those confirmed and executed.[58]

---

49. See BAB, NS7/1, Personal- und Organisationsbefehledes Hauptamtes SS-Gericht 1940–1945. For a description of the system see also organigram in Vieregge (2002), p 255 and 251ff.

50. BAB, NS7/6, *Einsetzung von Inspektionsrichtern*, 21 December 1943.

51. Vieregge (2002), p 52.

52. BAB, NS7/1, *Personal- und Organisationsbefehle des Hauptamtes SS-Gericht 1940–1945*.

53. Ibid.

54. BAB, NS7/2, Letter of 20 November 1939, *Verordnung über eine Sondergerichtsbarkeit*, of 17 October, in force from 30 October 1939, p 107ff.

55. Wegner (1990), p 47ff.

56. Vieregge (2002), p 47ff.

57. BAB, NS7/52/6, p 17, *Entscheidungsvorbehalt des Reichsführer-SS bei Strafverfügungen*, 2 August 1944,.

58. BAB, NS7/52/7, *Vorlage von Strafakten beim RFSS bei hohen Strafen nach Rechtskraft*, 28 April 1944.

Case Law in the Waffen-SS

What was punishable in the SS? Until the autumn of 1939, the answer can be found in the internal regulations for disciplinary sanctions. In 1937, the SS had 20 fixed categories within which felonies were to be registered. These included 'infringements upon the discipline', violation of the 'engagement and marriage decree', transgressions against the 'fundamental maxims of the organisation', 'political unreliability', 'lack of honesty', 'drunk and disorderly', 'private life theft' and 'sex crimes'.[59] Breach of the organisation's *Grundsätze* – the 'fundamental maxims' – was punished as so-called honour penalties and might lead to expulsion from the SS – also after 1939.[60] According to a letter from 1935, the disciplinary sanction included 'mild' imprisonment, which might be up to a fortnight's incarceration, and 'harder' imprisonment of up to 30 days.[61] Moreover, eviction was a risk as well.[62]

Thus, even before the introduction of new penal rules in 1939, the SS used imprisonment as a sanction. Thereafter, the scope of punishments was broadened to embrace even capital punishment. In July 1940, the head of the SS court's *Hauptamt*, Paul Scharfe, issued an instruction on the SS and police courts' jurisdiction, which provided an expressive account of what was about to be established.[63] In wartime, it was explained, all offences against discipline (*Manneszucht*) or the demand for soldierly courage (*das Gebotsoldatischen Mutes*) might be punished by death, life imprisonment or indefinite incarceration if considerations for troop security so demanded. This might be the case in the events of absence without leave (AWOL), cowardice, insubordination, assaulting superiors, mutiny, looting and violations of sentry duties.[64] More than one day's AWOL was to be punished (not merely disciplinarily sanctioned), and more than three days meant a year's imprisonment at the very least. Desertion, i.e. attempted avoidance of further military service, would invariably be punished by death, life imprisonment or indefinite incarceration. Subversive activity (*Zersetzung der Wehrkraft*) as well as self-mutilation and other acts damaging the fighting power were capital offences. Looting and violations of private property were to be sanctioned severely by at least one year's imprisonment. It was also explained that desecration of the race and male prostitution, i.e. homosexuality, were severe defilements of the National Socialist *Weltanschauung* and were, therefore, to be most harshly punished. It was also mentioned that 'religious riots' might harm National Socialism and must be sanctioned as insubordination. Misdemeanours related to alcohol should be sternly punished, as 'an SS man is not drunk and disorderly'.[65]

---

59. BAB, NS7/2, Letter of 10 May 1937 from RF-SS signed by Scharfe, *Statistik über Disziplinarfälle*, p 69ff. The form was to be used all over the SS including with the SS-*Verfügungstruppe* (with the SS-*Junkerschulen*) and the SS-*Totenkopfverbände*.
60. BAB, NS7/3, Letter of 15 July 1940 from RF-SS, Hauptamt SS-Gericht, *Sondergerichtsbarkeit der SS und Polizei*.
61. BAB, NS7/2, Letter of 16 March 1935 from RF-SS (SS-Gericht Nr. 10448/35).
62. On pre-war disciplinary punishments in the SS, see also Emmett (2017).
63. BAB, NS7/3, Letter of 15 July 1940 from RF-SS, Hauptamt SS-Gericht, *Sondergerichtsbarkeit der SS und Polizei*.
64. Ibid.
65. Ibid.

However, one thing was what the leadership wished to achieve, quite another was reality at the individual courts and especially with the units at the front. From time to time, there was a marked discrepancy between rules and theory on the one hand (law in the books) and the practical realities on the other (law in action).[66] Also, and unsurprisingly given the scope and haste of the war, a certain inconsistency developed in several fields as, for instance, concerning desertion. This meant that soldiers on the ground could not always be certain which sanction might be applied for a given offence.

Regardless, compared with German law before the *Machtergreifung* the sanctions used were harsh. Many offences could be punished by death or long-term incarceration. However, similar crimes were not necessarily punished in like ways. If there was an ideological explanation of a deed, the penalty could be lenient or non-existent.[67]

There is no comprehensive statistic covering the whole war on offenses in the Waffen-SS which the courts chose to prosecute and which sentences were handed down. Thus, it is hard to specify how many soldiers were actually accused and for which offences. However, a statistic concerning the first three months of 1943 provides a snapshot of how the SS legal system was used in mid-war.[68] During this period 2,764 SS personnel and policemen were sentenced. While violations of private property (theft etc.) made up 42 per cent of these cases, disciplinary cases made 21 per cent, and 17 per cent were *Treuepflichtverletzungen*– breaches of the oath of allegiance to Hitler. All in all, these three categories combined were 80 per cent of all sentences passed. There were 345 cases of theft from the armed forces, 250 of stealing from fellow soldiers, 250 of insubordination, 135 of dereliction of sentry duties and 71 of freeing prisoners. There had been 337 sentences for AWOL, 43 cases of subversive activity and 65 desertions. Compared with figures from the last three months of 1942 this was a decline of sentences for the latter from 74 to 65 and a considerable drop in sentences for looting from 161 to 96.[69]

The statistic also reveals that while half of these sentences concerned the SS, (a total of 1,391) the remainder were on the police and other units. According to this material there were more sentences for theft and desertion among SS personnel, but the police excelled in convictions for dereliction of guard duties and insubordination. Moreover, the police had more cases of lootings and liberation of prisoners.

Out of 1.391 convictions, four were on the *Allgemeine SS*, while the rest concerned the Waffen-SS pointing to the fact that it was overwhelmingly among the troops at the front that disciplinary offences were perpetrated.[70] Out of all SS' convicts there were 194 Volksdeutsche, 74 Germanic SS volunteers and 144 Germanic legionnaires, i.e. men from the national contingents, which the SS had had formed in the summer of 1941.

---

66. See previous examples in this chapter and in the chapter on the role of ideology. See also Wegner (1990), p 330.
67. Vieregge (2002), p 145.
68. BAB, NS19/1916, *Kriminalstatistik des Hauptamtes SS Gericht für das 1. Vierteljahr 1943*.
69. Ibid.
70. It must be also taken into consideration that while, in early 1943, the *Waffen-SS* counted 200,000 men, the *Allgemeine SS* had only 60,000. Stein (1984), p 203 and Hein (2012), p 291.

Of those convicted for desertion 18 were *germanic* SS volunteers or legionnaires, i.e. close to a third of all such cases. Among the 199 AWOL sentences 54 were on SS volunteers or legionnaires – again disproportionately many.

Of the aggregate number of SS personnel, policemen and others prosecuted, 171 were acquitted, while 86 were let off. Among the sentences thus handed down were 69 of capital punishments, 192 of long-term imprisonment, 1,876 of imprisonment, four of fortress arrest, 557 of detention and 66 of fines. Of the death sentences, 16 concerned desertions (fourteen were executed), 10 were for subversion (eight were executed). Moreover, 130 men were evicted from the SS, 255 were excluded (which was slightly less dishonourable), 44 were otherwise disengaged from the SS and 23 were demoted.[71]

The fact that so many cases were about theft, breach of the oath of allegiance, and disciplinary misconduct has been seen as an indication that the SS never fully lived up to its self-perception of being a chivalrous order in which loyalty and discipline were key values.[72] It is, however, doubtful if this should be interpreted as a general dissociation between the men's behaviour and the SS' ideological self-image. First and foremost, it is likely that the SS courts investigated with particular diligence the cases concerning their high priority ideological issues. This was about petty theft from fellow soldiers, so-called *Kameradendiebstahl*, which was regarded partly as a character flaw or even as racial inferiority on the part of the thief, partly as an infringement of private property, which in Himmler's eyes was sacrilege with respect to ancient Germanic tradition.[73] Secondly, it is necessary to peer into the distribution of sentences within the organisation. This is particularly relevant in the case of the Waffen-SS, where the personnel became increasingly heterogeneous leaving room for a widespread diversity of motives for committing crimes. Moreover, the case law was uneven, and often the perpetrators race would be consequential to the harshness of the sentence.

With *Division Wiking*'s *Regiment Westland* parallel statistics for the whole of 1941 were compiled allowing 'SS crimes' to be compared with ordinary military offenses committed within the *Wehrmacht*. Here, it turned out that this regiment had fewer cases of desertion and AWOL than its army equivalent. However, as far as looting and insubordination were concerned the frequency with *Regiment Westland* was double that of the *Wehrmacht*.[74]

We have to be cautious when comparing statistics from different units and different phases of the war. Different circumstances might have influenced the number of perpetrations which were detected and brought before either an SS court or a court martial as well as how many were actually prosecuted thoroughly right up to their conclusion. On 22 January 1942, an SS court officer sent a 31-pages report to the head of the main office, Scharfe, in which he analysed the proceedings of the SS court and pointed at a number of possible errors that, in his view, had influenced the verdicts.

71. BAB, NS19/1916, *Kriminalstatistik des Hauptamtes SS Gericht für das 1. Vierteljahr 1943*.
72. Wegner (1990), p 331.
73. Vieregge (2002), pp 77ff.
74. BAB, NS7/205, *Straf- und Disziplinarstatistik des SS-Regiments 'Westland'*, undated.

This report and later conversations between Scharfe and judges in the field revealed that the court system was plagued by logistic troubles and shortage of resources, including a shortage of judges.[75]

Capital Punishment

While statistics concerning rulings by the SS courts allow only a limited overview, a comprehensive survey of death sentences passed between 1 September 1939 and 30 June 1944 does exist. Throughout this period, 1,001 persons thus condemned were executed under the SS and police courts' jurisdiction. These were 376 SS men, 138 policemen and 198 persons from auxiliary units (typically *Schutzmannschaften*), as well as 289 'other persons' – partisans and similar individuals sentenced by SS and police courts.[76] The survey also reveals that the brutality increased over the war years since the number of death sentences grew steadily. While in 1939–1940 seven death sentences were passed, the number grew to 24 in 1941, 183 in 1942, 386 in 1943 and 401 in the first six months of 1944.[77] Similarly, the Wehrmacht's death penalty practice tightened during the war. While in 1940, 559 were executed, 4,626 were sentenced in 1943, though the number dropped to 3,328 the year after.[78] Notwithstanding this brutalisation of the Wehrmacht justice, the frequency of death sentences compared with other punishments were higher within the SS than the Wehrmacht. In 1942, 1,7 per cent of all Wehrmacht sentences were death sentences as opposed to 3,6 per cent with the SS. Since the equivalent figures for 1943 were 2,4 and 2,8 respectively, a certain equalising seems to have taken place. Generally, in this respect there was a marked difference between the German and the Allied forces. Throughout the Second World War, less than 300 executions were carried out by British, French and the US authorities. Conversely, while about 30,000 Germans seem to have been sentenced to death by their own military tribunals, 12,000 were actually executed.[79]

Normally, but not always, executions were carried out by firing squads. In the late summer and autumn of 1943, the number of cases of desertions and AWOL from the SS and police units in Croatia increased drastically because – so the SS – partisans

75. BAB, NS7/318, *Aufhebung von urteilen auf Grund von Rechtsgutachten des Hauptamtes SS-Gericht. Bericht des SS-Sturmbannführers Dr. Pohl […] über Diskrepanz zwischen den für das Gericht bestehenden praktischen Gegebenheiten und theoretischer.* BAB, NS7/4, *Sammlung von Erlassen des Hauptamtes SS-Gericht 1942 Jan.-Juni, Bericht uber die Dienstbesprechung der dienstaltesten SS-Richter in Danzig und Zoppot vom 30. April bis 2. Mai 1942.*
76. Wegner (1990), p 331.
77. Ibid.
78. Messerschmidt (2008), p 163.
79. Wachsmann (2004), p 264. However, the number of death sentences was even higher with the Soviet Army. Here, officially, 157,000 were condemned during the war. Considering the force ratio of the Red Army and the Wehrmacht this means that the frequency of capital punishment was four times as high in the Russian forces. Alexander N. Yakovel, *A Century of Violence in Soviet Russia* (Yale University Press, 2002), p 174. See also Vadim J.Birstein, *Smersh. Stalin's Secret Weapon* (Biteback Publishing, 2013), p 2.

had infiltrated the units to spy and sabotage. The local SS court wished to apply especially draconic measures and applied for permission to execute by hanging, which, in November 1943, Himmler granted.[80] In the spring of 1944, Dr Barth, the head of this SS court, reported that three executions had been carried out by hanging – one in December 1943, two in January 1944. New cases had been initiated, but still the court awaited the reaction concerning the newly implemented punishment of 'first flogging, then hanging'.[81] In this way, the SS court in Croatia re-introduced a century-old tradition of public corporal punishment prior to public execution.

There was a certain leeway for reprieve, but this required Himmler's personal intervention. All petitions for mercy were to be submitted to him, and it appears that in these cases, too, the race issue played a certain role in his decision-making. In January 1942, thus, Himmler emphasised that in capital punishment cases petitions for mercy invariably had to have certificates of good conduct attached including information on the family and photographs of the parents. Only in matters of particular urgency would Himmler accept petitions without detailed information on the applicant's family.[82]

Desertions

One of the crimes that might entail capital punishment was desertion. This, however, was no given, but during the war it became increasingly common. Nonetheless, even late in the war incarceration was a possible sanction in lieu of execution. The severity of the punishment depended on various factors such as from which unit and commander the desertion happened. Moreover, the actual circumstances were of importance to the investigation of the case, as well as whether or not the judge wanted to state an example to discipline the remaining SS personnel. On top of that: the offender's race. These factors might influence the decision to accuse the individual of being AWOL instead of desertion. Basically, the punishment for desertion would be either death, life imprisonment or indeterminate imprisonment. AWOL, too, was a serious offence, which, in the case of more than 24 hours' absence, might result not only in disciplinary sanctions but criminal prosecution and long incarceration or execution.[83] Nevertheless, if the absence lasted less than one day, there was ample latitude for employing disciplinary sanction or detention of limited duration.

---

80. The number of cases of desertion and AWOL increased to 21 up until August 1943. In August and September there were 244 such cases and between 1 and 10 October 80. BAB, NS7/349, *Vollstreckung der Todesstrafe bei Verurteilungen wegen Bandenbegunstigung und Fahnenflucht mit Bandenverbindung im Bereich des Gerichts der Dienststelle Fp.47942 F (BDO Kroatien) gegenüber kroatischen Freiwilligen 1943–1944*, Letter of 5 November 1943 from Hauptamt SS-Gericht to SS-Richter beim RF-SS, Bender and letter of 4 April 1944.

81. BAB, NS7/349, 6 May 1944.

82. BAB, NS7/53, *Gnadenbefugnisse in Sachen des Obersten SS- und Polizeigerichts, 1940*. Letter of 18 January 1942 from Der SS-Richter beim RF-SS to Hauptamt SS-Gericht, *Vorbereitung der Entscheidung des RF-SS über Gnadengesuche bei Todesstrafen*.

83. BAB, NS7/3, Letter of 15 July 1940, from RF-SS, Hauptamt SS-Gericht, *Der Sondergerichtsbarkeit der SS und Polizei*, p 47ff.

Even so, there are examples that even brief absenteeism was interpreted as desertion, thus increasing the risk of a death sentence. In November 1942, this was seen in one of the Cavalry Division's regiments. Here, a 20-year old SS man, probably of *Volksdeutsch* ancestry, was punished by eight days' guard room detention for disobedience. On 18 November, this man was detailed for field fortifications work, but while the guard, who was supposed to keep an eye on him, briefly slipped away, he used the opportunity to abscond. The young soldier managed to get as far as the village Sselzo, where he found a field kitchen and got some food. However, three hours later he was arrested by a lieutenant.[84] The circumstances pointed to accusing the soldier of being AWOL for less than 24 hours. As he was already under guard room arrest, this might have been an aggravating circumstance, but since he had turned up at the field kitchen and not tried to leave the area, nothing else indicated any intention of desertion. Nonetheless, the commanding officer held a different view. He saw the incident as attempted desertion and told the SS court how he wished the prosecution to proceed.

> As this case is the first since [the regiment's] employment at the front, Regiment finds that a castigation which – apart from punishing the offender – will deter the others will be adequate. The composition of the personnel – up to 60 percent of them Volksdeutsche – raises fear that if this case is not exemplarily punished, similarly dithering men might wish also to avoid clashes with the enemy. The commanding officer believes that the sanction must be severe enough to secure that no one else might choose such escape from facing the foe.[85]

It is likely that the CO's attitude was sharpened by the characterisation of the young SS soldier stated in the case file. They ran that the accused 'did not possess any Weltanschauung attitude' and that he was 'a totally inferior subject'. He was also described as one always asking for food from other units and even having begged bread from Russian prisoners-of-war. The accused claimed that he had merely been in Sselzo to get some food and have his socks dried. Although we do not know the outcome there is much to suggest that the young man was doomed and executed for desertion.[86]

Conversely, there are examples that even in cases of prolonged absence it was chosen not to perceive this as desertion but merely as AWOL. Another SS soldier in the very same division, was found guilty of 1½ days AWOL and sentenced to 21 days of guard room detention.[87] As late as May 1944, a *Sturmmann* of Division Das Reich was sentenced to a year and two months imprisonment and eviction from the SS for having, without authorisation, prolonged his leave by two weeks and for having forged his leave pass accordingly.[88]

---

84. BAMA, RS4/1062, File 2, 3. SS kav.reg. 3, Letter of 18 November 1942.
85. Ibid., Letter of 22 November 1942.
86. Ibid., various letters.
87. Ibid., Letter of 30 July 1942.
88. BAB, NS7/143, *Divisionssonderbefehl*, 17 May 44, p 1.

In cases both interpreted and ruled as desertion, the penalties might vary considerably. In December 1943, two SS signallers of an *SS-Nachrichten-Ersatz* unit in Nuremberg were sentenced to 10 years' imprisonment and eviction from the SS for having intended to abscond and flee to Italy or Switzerland.[89] Under other circumstances, the ruling might just as well have been capital punishment.

The penal practise changed during the war, but even in the early years of conflict death sentences were not unheard of. Thus in the order of the day on 4 April 1941, *Division Totenkopf* published the execution of a soldier having defected allegedly to join the French Foreign Legion.[90] It appears from the statistics mentioned above that of the 65 rulings on desertion passed during the first six months of 1943, 16 were death sentences (and of these 14 were executed).[91] This bears witness to the fact that SS men who deserted stood a considerable risk of ending up before a firing squad and that this risk increased as the war progressed. However, there was no automatic practice in this field and, even in mid-war, the number of death sentences were only a minor proportion of the court rulings.

Although quite a few SS men were executed, a comparison with the *Wehrmacht* on the basis of the figures from 1943 shows, interestingly, that capital punishment for desertion was more frequent with the army than with the SS, though the latter had more cases of this kind. While, during the first three months of 1943, the SS court executed 25 per cent of those convicted for desertion, the army did so with 52 per cent – or a total number of 439. Seen in relation to the relative personnel strength, the SS had 33 per cent more convictions for desertion than the Wehrmacht.[92] This may be because of the multi-ethnic composition of the Waffen-SS and the increased use of compulsory enlistment, which led to many disciplinary difficulties and a lack of community feeling among the troops. Summing up, the SS case law concerning desertions was no more brutal then that of the *Wehrmacht*, rather the opposite. All in all, in comparison with the First World War the practises of the SS as well as the army show a remarkable brutalisation.

Subversion and Self-mutilation

Also, *Wehrkraftzersetzung* (subversion) was seen as a very serious crime that might, in worst case, entail capital punishment. In the first six months of 1943, 43 cases were registered equalling two thirds of the cases of desertion. Ten of these resulted in executions corresponding to 25 per cent or almost the same as for desertions. In the *Wehrmacht* that was different. Here, too, there were many cases of subversion – almost as many as those of desertions – but the number of death sentences was lower. While from April to June 1944, there were 2,131 rulings on desertion, and 1,033 were death sentences, out of 2,188 cases of *Wehrkraftzersetzung* only 341 ended up the same way. Moreover, there are indications that quite a few were never executed. Three quarterly statistics from earlier

---

89. BAMA, RS4/1587, *Abteilungs-Tagesbefehl Nr. 19*, of 8/9 December 1943.
90. VAP, N, 3.SS-Pz.Div.T. K.1, *Divisions-Tagesbefehl Nr. 33*, of 4 April 1941.
91. BAB, NS19/1916, *Kriminalstatistik des Hauptamtes SS Gericht fur das 1. Vierteljahr 1943*.
92. Messerschmidt (2008), p 138.

in the war – 1942 and 1943 – show that in these periods merely five, six and nine per cent of such sentences were effected.[93]

Frequently, subversive activity took the form of self-mutilation, which in many ways was tantamount to desertion as the aim was getting away from the front by making oneself useless. Obviously, the effect of such action was undermining the Third Reich's military might, but the death penalty was not a given. There are many examples that incarceration might also be used as a sanction. In December 1943, thus, an SS signaller was sentenced to 10 years' imprisonment and eviction from the SS for this offence.[94] That punishment was also imposed on a Norwegian legionnaire for having shot himself through one hand. He was imprisoned in the SS detainees' department of the Concentration Camp Dachau. A mere year later, *Hauptamt SS-Gericht* alleviated this sentence to service in a penal company at the front. That this mitigation came about might be on account of his young age or because his brother – also a member of the SS – had been lobbying successfully on his behalf.[95] Paradoxically, attempted suicide might also count as subversion thus causing capital punishment.[96]

Homosexuality and the SS Court

Homosexuality ran counter to National Socialist ideology and its gender stereotypes. The Nazis' – and especially the SS' – ideal was a patriarchal society where men had to live up to an old-fashioned chivalrous and martial model, while the women should bear sound, Germanic children and take care of domestic activities. Within this universe, homosexuality was seen as a threat against the soldierly male solidarity, troop discipline and society in general. It was regarded as an unhealthy practice, which unsettled the gender roles and endangered the biological proliferation of the Germanic race.

Thus, all over the Third Reich the *Machtergreifung* marked the beginning of persecution of homosexuals.[97] The SS was particularly homophobic, which did not only materialise as persecution of homosexuals but also as a worry about their possible intrusion into the ranks of the organisation. On 15 November 1941, Hitler issued a decree on 'sanitation of the SS and the police'. This stated that if an SS man commits sodomy with another man or lets himself be used for such purpose, he must be executed. This was to apply to all regardless of age.[98] Although Himmler introduced an obligation to report such cases, it is doubtful to what extent the keeping clean decree was actually followed.[99] However, there are

93. Ibid., p 200.
94. BAMA, RS4/1587, Orders of the day 1939–1944, *Abteilungs-Tagesbefehl Nr. 19*, of 8/9 December 1943.
95. HLC, Sigurd Sørlie'sprivate archive, P22 – Knut Baardseth, Diary 25 July 1943.
96. Vieregge (2002), p 136.
97. Anna Maria Sigmund, '*Das Geschlechtsleben bestimmen wir': Sexualität im Dritten Reich* (Heyne, 2009), p 179.
98. BAB, NS7/3, *Sammlung von Erlassen des Hauptamtes SS-Gericht 1940–1941*, p 108. See also BAB, NS7/5, *Zwölfter Sammelerlass*, 1 August 1942, p 33.
99. Vieregge (2002), p 119.

examples of prosecution of such cases and of dire consequences.[100] While many such cases were concluded by execution, on some occasions long prison sentences were applied.[101] In September 1944, a sergeant of *Division Nordland* was accused of homosexual activity. Allegedly he had masturbated with a comrade and on four occasions made advances to other men. The accused's superiors declared him a decent and brave soldier, who had been awarded the Iron Cross second and first classes, but he was sentenced to death and executed, nevertheless.[102] Rumours and accusations of homosexuality were therefore very serious matters for any member of the SS. Thus, a platoon commander in the Waffen-SS propaganda unit *Standarte Kurt Eggers* reported that – on the third hand – he had heard that a Danish soldier was known in Denmark to be homosexual. This platoon commander informed that he was investigating the matter, thus intimating that within the SS such matters could not be easily dismissed.[103] Obviously, this was Himmler's attitude as well. When his own nephew, who served with the Waffen-SS, became entangled in a case on homosexuality he had him executed to state an example.[104] From an SS perspective, suicide was the easier solution to its members' homosexuality. It is not easy to find out whether this was a frequent occurrence, but, in June 1941, allegedly Horst Peiper, an officer of the *Division Totenkopf*, was forced to take his own life on accusation of being homosexual. In his personal file the suicide was hushed up as death by accident.[105]

Theft from Fellow Soldiers

Basically, it will always cause problems to a military unit's cohesion if its soldiers steal from each other. With the SS this offence, too, was made a matter of ideology. A memo from 1940 stated that it was the *Reichsführer*'s wish that the 'sanctity of the right of ownership' be honoured. Breaches of this sacredness might be punished by detention, but also by the SS' honour penalties, which hinted that this was indeed one of the key ideological issues.[106] In March 1943, an SS signaller was convicted for having violated 'the foundations of the SS ethos' by participating in theft from a fellow SS man.[107]

---

100. BAB, NS7/1084, *SS- und Polizeigericht XVII Rusland-Mitte, Verschiedenes 1942–1944*.
101. Vieregge (2002), p 119ff.
102. See Christensen et al. (1998), p 321.
103. BAMA, RS4/42, Kurt Eggers, Report of 28 January 1942, *Neuafbau des 5. Zuges*.
104. Eugen Kogon, *SS – Hitlers Terrorkorps* (Roth, 1991), p 375. See also Himmler's service diary under 4 December where he mentions a meeting with his personal judge SS-Obersturmbannführer Bendner, concerning this case, p 283. Another example is that, in 1935, Himmler dismissed the head of the Hauptamt, Wittje, from his post on suspicion of homosexuality. In the following years Himmler had this accusation thoroughly examined and, eventually, had Wittje evicted from the SS. Longerich, *Heinrich Himmler. Biografie*, p 414ff.
105. Westemeier, *Joachim Peiper*, p 40.
106. BAB, NS7/3, Letter of 15 July 1940 from RF-SS, Hauptamt SS-Gericht, *der Sondergerichtsbarkeit der SS und Polizei*, pp 47ff.
107. BAMA, RS4/1062, SS.Kav.Reg.3, Letter of 29 March 1943.

The SS preferred to handle such cases seriously, but the magnitude of the phenomenon made this a delicate matter. A record from 1942 estimated theft among the personnel to amount to between 10 and 14 per cent of all crime within the SS, which made it tricky to use the harsher penalties like imprisonment, eviction or capital punishment.[108] Therefore, apparently, short or medium length detention became the norm. In the first quarter of 1943, the SS courts prosecuted 1,200 cases of theft, and while in 58 per cent of these the sentence was for up to six months, only seven per cent were punished by harsher incarceration.[109]

In August 1942, Division Das Reich reported that theft from fellow soldiers was a serious problem, which might entail dire consequences. In August, there had been four cases of theft and three suicides, and two of these seemed to have resulted from stealing and the subsequent fear of the consequences.[110] In September of that year, the same division had 24 cases prosecuted and, again, two out of three suicides were apparently motivated by fear of the punishment for the robberies thus committed.[111] Because of the inclination to suicide in lots of minor cases, Himmler allowed more lenient punishment for petty theft – not least of food – which no longer necessarily had to end a soldier's career with the SS. If the culprit had a decent service record and had not been punished previously he might be re-habilitated after conclusion of his front service.[112]

Like stealing from fellow soldiers, looting was a violation of the right of ownership and was, therefore also forbidden. However, under the euphemistic designation of commandeering it was acceptable if it was for war purposes and for the benefit of the troops.[113] It also mattered that such appropriation was from civilians, who – in particular in the occupied east territories – were practically without legal rights. The fact that theft from other soldiers was a serious crime, while seizure of civilian property in occupied areas was leniently dealt with, was in perfect harmony with the Nazi race theories. In this ideological perspective there was little need to respect any rights of ownership of, for example, Poles or Russians. Similarly, during *Division Das Reich*'s stay in Ukraine, the general officer commanding openly made a difference between stealing from *Volksdeutsche* or from Ukrainians.[114] The crux of that matter was of course that while theft from Germans was an abomination, commandeering from the locals was quite another matter. This did not mean that robbery from

---

108. Wegner (1990), p 329.
109. BAB, NS19/1916, *Kriminalstatistik des Hauptamtes SS Gericht für das 1. Vierteljahr1943*. See also ibid., p 330.
110. BAMA, RS2/2/2, KTB No.2, 2nd part, 26.7.1942-31.10.1942, 2. SS Pz. Korps, *Tätigkeitsbericht nr. 2, 1.8–31.8.1942, Ic.*
111. BAMA, RS/22/2, KTB No.2, 2nd part, 26.7.1942-31.10.1942, 2. SS Pz. Korps, *Tätigkeitsbericht nr. 3, 1.9.–30.9.1942, Ic.*
112. BAB, NS7/4, *Hauptamt SS-Gericht*, 24 January 1942.
113. BAB, NS7/3, Letter of 15 August 1940 from RF-SS, *Hauptamt SS Gericht*, p 47ff.
114. Wegner (1990), p 326.

Russians or Ukrainians was never investigated, but it had to reach a much more serious level before anything was done.[115]

Two matters were sure to cause trouble. Unrestrained looting might be harmful to German forces, because the goods might have been more reasonably distributed. Moreover, excessive robbery might be politically detrimental. The *Leibstandarte*'s stint in Italy 1943 shows an example of certain constraints being applied. As the units employed in counter insurgency operations in the larger cities of Northern Italy committed rape, robbery and looting on a large scale, division had two soldiers executed and many sentenced to long terms of imprisonment.[116] When, later, the frontline moved backwards into Germany the prosecution practice changed. From then on, robbery that was now directed against 'compatriots' was punished draconically.[117]

War Crimes and the SS Court

The Waffen-SS soldiers' war crimes, their nature, reasons and scope will be dealt with in a separate chapter later in this book. The following will merely shed light on how the SS courts – for obvious reasons – did in no way hamper the Nazi war of annihilation. With respect to SS legitimacy, the crux of the matter was whether or not any given action – as for instance the shooting of civilians – had been ordered or had been initiated without permission, in which case it could in some cases be seen as a breach of discipline.

On the one hand, the 'shootings of Jews without order and reason' (*Judenerschiesungen ohne Befehl und Befugnis*) were acts that were not necessitated by military logic. On the other, these were a logical consequence of the war of extermination, and they were easily buttressed ideologically. Therefore, Himmler's solution to this conundrum was to ask for explanations of whether or not such shootings had been ideologically motivated. Thus, the motive would determine if any prosecution was to be set in motion. If the motive had been political, the SS man would get away with impunity, but were it sexual or sadistic he would be punished.[118]

115. For an example on robbery of a Russian family see BAMA, RS4/1062, Case of 16 January 1943 against SS-Reiter N concerning looting of Russian civilians. He was accused of having taken four bottles of petrol, two bars of soap, slippers, one bracelet and two children's pullovers from a Russian household. The verdict is unknown. For another case, see BAMA, RS3/8, 48, SS-Kav.Brigade 1, 31 July 1941.
116. NAKEW, WO209/2244, PWIS(H)/LDC/299, Report on interrogation of PW KP 49359 Sturmbannführer Jacob Hanreich, 29 August 1944, p 4. BAB, NS19/2220, handwritten, undated letter for Kommando der SS-Gruppen, Mailand. On a case of large-scale looting by the Waffen-SS, see also BAMA, RH20-8/78, *Anlage 5 zu Standortkdtr, CharkowIa 25/43 g.Kdos.v.7.3.43.*
117. BAMA, RS3/15-16, 15.W-SS Division, 27 February 45: Looting was dealt with by drumhead court martial.
118. Wegner (1990), p 326. The package NS7/247 in Bundesarchiv Berlin seems particularly interesting. It tells about *Bestrafung von Judenerschießungen ohne Befehl und Befugnis.*

We find an illustration of this in the previously mentioned procedure against *Untersturmführer* Max Täubner, the commander of first SS Brigade's maintenance platoon, who between September and December 1941 personally shot about 1,000 Jews. According to the SS court, while initially the shooting had proceeded in 'an orderly manner' it later developed into serious cruelty. On this background Täubner was sentenced to 10 years' imprisonment for negligence of duty. The court stated that the killings had been necessary, but had been carried out in an undignified manner. In January 1945, though, Himmler pardoned Taübner.[119] Personal participation in murder of Jews was not in itself an SS criminal court matter, but the way it was carried out might entail disciplinary problems requiring SS court action. There was no reason to see Täubner's 1,000 killings as any breach of the SS *Grundanschauungen* (basic views), which theft from fellow SS men would certainly have been. Nor was this a matter – as for instance homosexuality – which violated SS values calling for a death sentence. On the contrary, Täubner was deemed ideologically decent and was, eventually, pardoned. As the court clearly stated: 'The defendant should not be punished for the actions against the Jews as such. The Jews must be exterminated; there is no loss in any of the killed Jews'.[120]

Imprisonment and Penal Units

Deprivation of liberty might be either simple detention or harsh detention, which were short sentences to be served under various conditions. Incarceration might also be several years of imprisonment which on some occasions might have to be served in a concentration camps. It happened, not surprisingly, that the offenders of *Division Totenkopf* served their sentences in the concentration camps, which, originally, had been subordinated to their divisional commander, Eicke.[121] However, also the shorter spells of detention might have to be served under unpleasant circumstances. *Division Totenkopf* let soldiers sentenced to harsh detention sit in solitary confinement for up to 30 days on bread and water.[122]

Delinquents of the *Wehrmacht* frequently served their sentences in ordinary prison cells, and most were put up in the Elmsland Prison known for its brutal treatment of its prisoners.[123] The SS, however, preferred to keep its convicts within their own system. This can be seen from a discussion on how to treat Norwegian SS volunteers sentenced by the SS courts. It was suggested to either let them serve their time in ordinary German prisons or in Norway, but both these proposals were dismissed in favour of the SS'

---

119. Vieregge (2002), p 140ff.
120. Dick De Mildt 'Getting Away with Murder: The Täubner Case' in Stoltzfus and Friedlander (eds.) *Nazi Crimes and the Law* (Cambridge University Press 2016), p 104.
121. On transfer of sentenced *Totenkopf* personnel, see Sydnor (1990), p 74.
122. Ibid.
123. Wachsmann (2004), p 264. See also Emmett (2017).

own penal facilities.[124] Although the SS had the concentration camps at their disposal, special detention camps and sections were set up to accommodate those serving SS sentences.[125] A special section of Concentration Camp Dachau was used as was – even more importantly – *Strafvollzugslager der SS und Polizei in Danzig-Matzkau*. While those who were sentenced to long-term imprisonment went to Dachau, the lucky ones serving merely ordinary imprisonment were sent to Danzig-Matzkau, which had been opened in the second half of 1941. Here, in 1942, there were 2,000 SS prisoners.[126] The camp also contained a separate detention section for Germanic SS volunteers.[127]

Many death and imprisonment sentences were commuted to *Bewährung*, i.e. service with penal units. Moreover, soldiers already serving a sentence of incarceration might opt for joining such units, which entailed exoneration through completion of particularly dangerous tasks. These units were well-known also in the Wehrmacht.[128] As early as 1939, Hitler had thought about using prisoners for military purposes, but it was not until 1940 at the emergence of *SS-Sonderkommando Dirlewanger* that this idea was put into practise.[129] While this unit enrolled ordinary criminals from German prisons, it also formed sub-units exclusively for members of the SS. Until the end of 1941, SS personnel was typically transferred to the *Wehrmacht* penal units, but, as in subsequent years more SS units were formed, this traffic ceased.[130]

A report from the commander of a penal unit illustrates the tasks typically allocated to these soldiers. After the war, this man was accused of having participated in the suppression of the Warsaw Uprising of 1944 and in connection with his trial he told about his stint as the commanding officer of a penal battalion. His unit had been ordered to attack a position 800 meters in front of the main line of contact, which had entailed four days of uninterrupted combat under terrible conditions including frequent close combat. Only 18 of his men survived.[131] Similar casualty rates were seen with the *Wehrmacht*, where the average life expectancy for such units was about six months before complete annihilation.[132] However, not all penal units were detailed

124. BAB, NS7/380, *Strafvollzug und Bewährungseinheiten [...] nicht deutsche SS Angehörigen und Freiwilligen.*
125. See BAB, NS7/364, *Errichtung einer Arrest- und Haftanstalt der SS und Polizei in Berlin.*
126. BAMA, N756/283/a, *Bericht über das Strafvollzugslager der SS und Polizei Danzig-Matzkau*, 1. Februar 1943.
127. BAB, NS7/380, *Strafvollzug und Bewährungseinheiten [...] nicht deutsche SS Angehörigen und Freiwilligen.*
128. See Thomas Kuhne, *Kameradschaft: die Soldaten des nationalsozialistischen Krieges und das 20. Jahrhundert* (Vandenhoeck& Ruprecht, 2006), p 126.
129. Wachsmann (2004), p 262ff.
130. BAB, NS7/378, Der Reichsführer-SS, 31 October 1941. See also BAMA, N756/283/a, SS-Hauptamt, SS-Gericht, Überstellung SS und polizeigerichtlich Verurteilter zur Bewährungseinheit 'Verlorener Haufen', 14 June 1941.
131. Sentence No. 860 in C.F. Rüter and L. Hekelaar Gombert, *Justiz und NS-Verbrechen: Sammlung deutscher Strafurteile wegen nationalsozialistischer Tötungsverbrechen, 1945–1966. Vol. XLIII* (Amsterdam University Press (AUP), Saur, 2010), 685, p 483ff., here p 488.
132. Wachsmann (2004), p 266.

to suicide missions. For example, an *Arbeitsabteilung* (labour battalion) was formed near the training area Debicia.[133] Later during the war, convicted Waffen-SS soldiers were also utilised in the military industry.[134]

The Sacred Spirit

The soldiers' discipline was not only governed by the SS judiciary and its courts. Many factors could support or undermine discipline – not least the quality and character of leadership. Another element, which most likely had a significant effect on internal discipline was termed 'the sacred spirit' among the men.

In 1941, the Danish officer, Per Sørensen, praised his company for exercising stalwart internal social control. In a letter to his parents he described how it was 'a pleasure to work with such men. The tone they use among themselves is fine and they keep an impressive internal order'. This particular description of the soldiery's discipline happened on a very bloody background. The letter was written 10 days after a crowd of soldiers from the same unit, the *Frikorps Danmark*, had assaulted an NCO. Following a minor incident at the firing range, this mugging had been encouraged by another, and slightly higher-ranking, NCO. What had probably been meant as a reprimand ended up a fatality as one of the eight attackers had fractured the victim's skull with the handle of his bayonet. Two of those involved were sentenced to three-and-a-half years' imprisonment to be served after the war.[135]

Often, the soldiers serving with the Waffen-SS called the internal discipline 'the sacred spirit'. Usually, this was put into practice by beating up the alleged culprit – i.e. employing varying degrees of violence against those not complying with the rules. This terminology was also known in the *Wehrmacht* where it was part of the traditional social culture.[136] Infractions did not need to be particularly grave to spark violent sanction. After the war, a Dutch volunteer explained how a soldier, who had stolen two bars of chocolate, 'was beaten up' until 'his head became quite triangular' because he would not admit the theft.[137]

It was not uncommon for the NCOs to be aware of what was happening among the soldiers, and now and then they might even have encouraged it. NCOs were not allowed to use physical sanctions, but they might rest assured that the soldiers would themselves mete out a fitting castigation. In the case of a Flemish soldier of *Division Das Reich* who, because of chronical pains of the chest, made an error during drill, the *Hauptsscharführer* punished the platoon collectively not making any secret of whom

133. BAB, NS7/378, Der Reichsführer-SS, 31 October 1941.
134. BAB, NS7/365, Himmler, no date 1943.BAB, NS7/365, *Arbeitseinsatz von Strafgefangenen des Strafvollzugslagers der SS und Polizei Danzig-Matzkau bei den Daimler-Benz-Werke in Berlin-Tegel*, 25.2.1943
135. Christensen et al. (1998), p 321ff.
136. Kühne (2006), p 125.
137. Bjarne Salling Pedersen and Georg Rasmussen, *I krig for fjenden – SS-frivillig Georg Rasmussens erindringer*, 2. edition (Informations Forlag, 2012), p 47.

was to blame. The following night, the man was exposed to 'the sacred spirit' during which he happened to swallow parts of his false teeth. Next night, fearing another similar treatmentt, he deserted.[138]

A *Leibstandarte* soldier from Alsace, who had been compulsorily enrolled, experienced a harsh 'sacred spirit' treatment obviously inspired by a superior. During the fighting in Normandy, one soldier tried to desert and, to make an example to the other *Volksdeutsche*, the company commander ordered his comrades to beat him to death, which duly happened.[139]

Penal Practice towards Germanic and other Non-German Waffen-SS Volunteers

There are examples that various groups of foreign soldiers in the Waffen-SS were given special consideration, but the basic rule was that all and sundry were subject to the SS judiciary and legislation. Thus, in January 1942, it was stated that 'the foreign volunteers are, without exception, subjected to German law'.[140] This fundamental issue was not up for discussion. On 2 October 1941, an SS court letter specified that as soon as a man had joined the SS he was to be instructed about this matter.[141]

Himmler was quite specific on this point, and in the rules and regulation for personnel and trainees at the prep-school at Sennheim one might see a telling example. The purpose of that school was that, upon completion of a course, the trainee would join the Waffen-SS.[142] Although on arrival and during courses, the men were still not members of the Waffen-SS, Himmler insisted that from the moment they set foot in Sennheim they were under the SS' military jurisdiction. However, he accepted that in the case of desertion ordinary detention, i.e. not long-term imprisonment, would be a reasonable sanction. His motive for this was that, as far as Weltanschauung and military life was concerned, one could not make the same demands on the Germanic volunteers as on the Germans.[143]

Nonetheless, Himmler pointed out to the judiciary that the case law issue with respect to the non-German volunteers was a delicate one. On 4 March 1941, he explained that the general situation and the foreign policy circumstances concerning the foreign volunteers demanded that special considerations be made. Himmler wished, inter alia, to see all applications for resignation, and all criminal cases against non-German SS men in order to decide whether or not he would rule personally. He also stressed the importance that all volunteers were made aware that they were under SS jurisdiction, though, at the same time, their brief stint with the organisation might ameliorate their cases.[144]

---

138. VAP, SS-*Das Reich 'DR'. Rgt. Langemarck*, box 52, prosecution of SS-Schütze JL, September–October 1942.
139. MMC, TE331, Eugène Finance.
140. BAB, NS7/4, Hauptamt SS-Gericht, *Zehnter Sammelerlass*, 15 January 1942, p 17.
141. BAB, NS7/87, Letter of 2 October 1941.
142. Christensen et al. (1998), pp 281ff.
143. BAB, NS7/87, *Strafrechtliche Behandlung von nicht-deutschen Angehörigen der SS*. Letter of 10 October 1942 from SS-Richter beim RF-SS to the head of the SS-Hauptamt, SS-Gruppenführer und Generalleutnantder Waffen-SS Berger.
144. BAB, NS7/87, Letter of 4 March 1941.

Desertions by Germanic volunteers was a matter which the SS courts tried to handle relatively leniently. In January 1942, an internal instruction explained that, in two cases, Himmler had ruled that deserters got away with only two years imprisonment followed by forced labour to the end of the war.[145] In October of the same year, repeating his view Himmler noticed that the Germanic volunteers had been only briefly with the SS and had not had the same amount of Weltanschauung and military tuition as the German soldiers of the Reich.[146]

However, Germanic volunteers could not just ignore the SS legal system with impunity. It appeared from a letter of 18 January 1942, that those deserting to their place of origin could not go free merely by handing in their resignation – they had to be prosecuted.[147] In January 1942, it was also made clear that the ban on 'intercourse with women of other races' applied for foreign soldiers, too.[148] In the same month, Himmler ordered that a group of volunteers of *Legion Niederlande* were to be instructed that desertion might entail capital punishment.[149] Nonetheless, it seems that, during the first years of the war, rather lenient sentences were passed on Germanic volunteers. Thus, in 1941 two Dutch deserters were given one and two years of imprisonment respectively.[150] The same year, Waffen-SS volunteers of Legion Norway were mildly treated for desertion and self-mutilation, and charges were made of AWOL in lieu of desertion.[151] As late as 1944, a Norwegian having committed self-mutilation was relatively leniently treated with only nine months, because, as it was explained, foreign volunteers would only be sentenced to death if a milder sentence would endanger troop discipline.[152]

Concerning cases like desertion, the court might promulgate certain guidelines for specific ethnic groups or individual nationalities. Thus, on 9 May 1942, Paul Scharfe wrote an instruction concerning Danish volunteers stating that, for political reasons, in cases of desertion and AWOL these were to be treated with greater latitude than other Germanic groups.[153] The nature of these 'political reasons' is not disclosed in the letter, but there is reason to believe that it had to do with the so-called peaceful occupation of Denmark and her co-operative government.

---

145. BAB, NS7/4, *Hauptamt SS-Gericht, Zehnter Sammelerlass*, 15 January 1942, p 18.
146. BAB, NS7/5, *Sammlung von Erlassen des Hauptamtes SS-Gericht 1942 Juli-Dez.*, Letter of 15 October 1942, Hauptamt SS-Gericht.
147. BAB, NS7/87, Letter of 18 January 1942 from SS-Richter beim RF-SS.
148. BAB, NS7/4, *Hauptamt SS-Gericht, Zehnter Sammelerlass*, 15 January 1942, p 18.
149. BAB, NS7/251, *Fahnenflucht [...] Legion Niederlande (1941–1942)*. This was about a group comprising 130 Dutch volunteers who wished to be discharged and re-patriated, which was not approved by the SS.
150. NIOD, 205, *Kommandostab RFSS, Abt. III, Tätigkeitsbericht für die Zeit von 15. 21.12.1941, 1.2.1942*.
151. Claus Bundgaard Christensen, Niels Bo Poulsen and Peter Scharff Smith, 'Legion Norge. Forskelle og ligheder med de øvrige "germanske" legioner i Waffen SS', *Historisk Tidsskrift*, *Vol. 100, No. 2*, 2000, pp 440ff.
152. RO, RAFA-3182, J.B., SS-Pz.Gren Rgt. Norway, St.L Nr. 181/44, SS- und Polizeigericht IX, *Feldurtei* l, 30 September 1944.
153. BAB, NS7/4, *Sammlung von Erlassen des Hauptamtes SS-Gericht 1942 Jan.-Juni*, Letter of 9 May 1942, *Strafverfahren gegen dänische Freiwilligen*.

There is a basic difference between the ways the North-European Germanic volunteers and those of other ethnicities were treated. In the summer 1944, for example, this became apparent from the treatment of Italian soldiers of the *Division Reichsführer-SS*. The division wished to execute 50 Italians for desertion in order to make an example to the other men, and Himmler agreed as he did in a number of similar cases.[154]

The material available does not give any hint of individual considerations, which make these trials markedly different from those against Germanic soldiers, although, in the last part of the war, the case law reveals that discipline was also tightened towards them. Nevertheless, at the same time as 50 Italians were condemned en bloc, a Norwegian, who had been on sick leave, was able to procrastinate for three months while not returning to his unit. In September 1944, after being arrested at his home he was sentenced to nine months' detention. The court argued for not ruling his absence as desertion but merely as AWOL because, after all, he had been willing 'to do his bit at the front in the European fight for freedom'. Moreover, being a Norwegian he was allegedly characterised by the same fierce soldierly norms as were the Germans.[155]

However, as the war progressed, practice was tightened for the Germanic volunteers, too. In January 1944, HSSPF Rauter wrote to Himmler concerning *Landstorm Nederland* and Guard Battalion North-West, which had experienced increasing AWOL problems. Now, he wished to act more sternly, for example, by using the death penalty.[156] Also, the earlier mentioned lenient policy vis a vis Danes in cases of desertion and AWOL, was to a certain degree revised during the late phase of the war.[157]

Another deliberation with the SS was whether the *Volksdeutsche* living outside Germany were eligible for national service on account of being 'German'. Although as early as in August 1942, Himmler had stated that they were, this did not immediately effect the case law. The various authorities held different opinions on whether it was possible to draft *Volksdeutsche* into the Waffen-SS and punish them if they did not turn up.[158] In February 1943, the *Hauptamt SS-Gericht* had to enquire at the supreme bench concerning two Croat *Volksdeutsche*, who had not reacted on being called up

---

154. BAB, NS7/98, *Strafgerichtliche Behandlung italienischer Freiwilligen*, various letters.
155. RO, RAFA-3182, Files concerning K.A.A., SS-Schütze,SS-Pz.Gren.A.u.E.Btl. 5, Ellwangen, St.L.I. 230/44, SS- und Polizeigericht IX Feldurteil, 13 October 1944.
156. BAB, NS19/3403, *Richtlinien des Reichsführers-SS zur Gewinnung niederlandischer Freiwilligen für die Waffen-SS*, Letter of 11 January 1944. Christensen et al. (1998), p 313. RK, Rigspolitiet, SS und Polizeigericht XXX Kopenhagen, 9 January 1945. RK, Rigspolitiet, SS und Polizeigericht XXX Kopenhagen, Letter of 22 March 1945 from Concentration Camp Neuengamme.
157. Christensen et al. (1998), p 313.RK, Rigspolitiet, SS und Polizeigericht XXX Kopenhagen, 9 January 1945.RK, Rigspolitiet, SS und Polizeigericht XXX Kopenhagen, Letter of 22 March 1945 from Concentration Camp Neuengamme.
158. BAB, NS7/91, Internal letter from *Hauptamt SS-Gericht*, *Überstellung ungarischer und volksdeutscher Freiwilligen zur Arbeitsabteilung der Waffen-SS bei Dienstverweigerung*, 18 November 1942.

for military service. It appeared that several German authorities had been involved and disagreed internally. The SS court was in doubt on whether to punish them and asked for Himmler's ruling on the matter.[159] His decision in this case is unknown, but a contemporary case show that eventually some kind of sentence might have been passed. In December 1942, a case of three Hungarian *Volksdeutsche*, who had refused to take the oath of allegiance, was submitted to Himmler. The *Reichsführer* decided that these three should not be sent to a concentration camp but to the forced labour camp Danzig-Matzkau, where they served one year under a somewhat more liberal regime than that of a concentration camp. The sojourn there was expected to motivate them to serve with the Waffen-SS. Thus, the aim was that the three acquired a decent German and learned to appreciate their duty to the 'real fatherland'.[160]

Ideology and Race in the SS Court System

As demonstrated in this chapter, the court system of the SS and the accompanying informal practices, such as 'the sacred spirit', proved to be an important tool in the ideological regimentation of the Waffen-SS. Not only, were offenses defined on an ideological basis, the alleged perpetrators and their motives were subject to 'racial evaluation', thereby creating a system where possible ameliorating individual circumstances were primarily taken into account in cases against soldiers of German and Germanic origin. Soldiers who the SS judged to have lesser racial value, especially *Fremdvölker*, were often judged collectively and based on an ad hoc ideologically motivated suspicion of their low reliability and cowardice, rather than on any detailed consideration of the nuances of the offense itself. Thus, the juridical system of the SS on the one hand substantially contributed to the Waffen-SS' inherent inability to fully integrate its Eastern European soldiers and to treat them on an equal footing with German and Germanic soldiers. On the other hand, SS law continuously fuelled and furthered the ideological ambitions of the Nazi 'Racial state'.

Political Soldiers?

Did the men with runes on their collars and skulls in their peaked caps become the fanatical political soldiers that Hitler and Himmler had dreamed of? Ideology was present all over training depots, barracks, field cinemas and at the front and materialised as formalized tuition, orders of the day, shows, social evenings and celebrations of feasts. Anti-Semitism was everywhere in the form of cardboard targets for bayonet practise, and in a courtroom an ideological appraisal might make all the difference between life and death. The SS legal system was the realisation of

---

159. BAB, NS7/91, *SS- und Polizeigericht VII, Ermittlungsverfahren gegen die ehemaligen SS-Angehörigen kroatischer Staatsangehörigkeit Leopold Pfeffer und Nikolaus Wittje*, 6 Februar 1943 and *Hauptamt SS-Gericht to SS-Richter beim Reichsführer-SS, Völkische Wehrdienstpflicht von Volksdeutschen ausländischer Staatsangehörigkeit*, 17 February 1943.

160. BAB, NS7/91, *Der SS-Richter beim Reichsführer SS und Chef der Deutschen Polizei*, 17 January 1942.

Himmler's and the SS leadership's vision of a set of rules and regulations based on National Socialism lending an ideological dimension even to the choice of spouse or sexual partner and fixing sanctions for non-observance.

Officers were those receiving the most thorough education in this field. Not only were they the leadership tier, but they conveyed and interpreted the ideology in an army which changed enormously during the war. In the first war years everyone, regardless of rank, was a loyal Nazi who had joined voluntarily. This segment, however, shrank and more and more recruits were drafted against their will. This meant that many a Waffen-SS man was not very different ideologically from his *Wehrmacht* fellow soldier. Moreover, the huge influx of foreigners gradually turned the Waffen-SS into a multi-ethnic organisation. Among the newcomers were the North-European volunteers, who were generally motivated by Nazism, as well as large groups of compulsorily enrolled East-Europeans who did not necessarily share the ideological zeal. Facing this vast and varied group of SS personnel, the officers played an important role in the propagation of the Nazi Weltanschauung and the SS' creed.

As the war progressed, rather than diminishing, this ideological effort increased in order to compensate for the dwindling fortune of war. Generally speaking, this development was parallel with that of the *Wehrmacht* where, from the late summer 1944, *Nationalsocialistische Führungsoffiziere* were introduced – a parallel to the SS WE Führer.

More than once, Himmler's ideological wishes and attitudes had to be flexed, amended or simply ignored in the face of reality. Thus, practical actuality in the field and the composition of the personnel would influence the ideology. This became obvious in connection with the rules for sexual relations with East-European women and at realising that not all soldiers would change their religious creed. The latter was true for both Catholics and Muslims with the Waffen-SS. The trend towards pragmatism also emerged in the legal aspect, where Germans, *Volksdeutsche*, Germanic volunteers and *Fremdvölker* were treated in different ways. The logic seems to have been that Germans irrespective of their place of birth were under obligation to fight for Germany. The Germanic volunteers got preferential treatment because they were the personification of the SS ideal of the good race. They might be regarded as idealists, although they had not had the same Nazi and militaristic upbringing as had the young of the Third Reich. Finally, it seems that sentences on South-Europeans and *Fremdvölker* were more severe than others due to the supposed racial and ideological inferiority.

Did ideology play a larger role in the SS than with the *Wehrmacht*? This clearly was the case, but only to some extent. In the Waffen-SS there were almost certainly a higher ratio of fanatical political soldiers among the officers and the volunteers. The number of former *Hitlerjugend* members and devoted Nazis was larger than in the *Wehrmacht*. In the last years of the war the ratio of voluntary Waffen-SS soldiers diminished along with the enrolment of less motivated soldiers. However, the framework personnel generally remained staunch political soldiers to the last. The worldview on which they acted and the culture they established determined, among other things, the frequency with which the Waffen-SS more often than other German forces became entangled in war crimes.

Part III

A EUROPEAN NAZI ARMY: FOREIGNERS IN THE WAFFEN-SS

From Racial Community to Multi-ethnic Army – Waffen-SS Turns European

As early as in the mid-1930s, SS began admitting non-German citizens into its ranks. These were, primarily, ethnic Germans from adjacent states, but from 1938 the organisation officially welcomed other nationalities of the 'Nordic-Germanic race.' Initially, this meant citizens from the northern and western neighbouring countries. The key notion, though, remained that the SS should be an exclusive order into which only racially pure Germans and other Germanic volunteers sharing the Nazi creed would be allowed.

In 1941-2, Waffen-SS began to adjust these conditions. *Standarte Nordwest* and various national legions introduced men into the military branch of the SS who did not live up to the order's demands for physical height, race and ideological determination. At the same time, an element of compulsion was added to the enrolment methods. This happened for example, in occupied Yugoslavia, where *Volksdeutsche* men were forced to serve with the Waffen-SS. From there, this trend spread to other countries with large ethnic German minorities that might be coerced or manipulated into joining. As mentioned previously, more or less compulsory methods had already been used to recruit personnel in Germany, but now this began on a massive scale. In the last war-years, tens of thousands of German conscripts were systematically transferred to the Waffen-SS without the slightest trace of voluntariness. Additionally, nationalities that were formerly looked down upon – on account of being of a 'lower race' – were now recruited. These included Ukrainians, Russians, Central-Asian Muslims as well as Serbs and Bosnians.

Although a certain mollification characterised the attitude to nationalities, the Waffen-SS, as well as the SS per se, remained an organisation which was controlled from Germany and by Germans. The very top was entirely German, and as a general rule, non-German commanders were to be found at no higher levels than company or, at the most, occasionally battalion. Thus, the history of the non-German citizens in the Waffen-SS must be seen in the context of an ethnically stratified organisationcharacterised by tensions among ethnic groups due to language, culture and gradings in the racial hierarchy.

According to SS propaganda, the Waffen-SS' many ethnic groups were united in their struggle against the 'godless bolshevism' and the equally corrupt 'American materialism' and fought to protect European culture and values. This is a story that can be found, even today, in many popular historical works on the military branch of the SS. However, as we shall see shortly, over the last war-years the Waffen-SS became a highly fragmented organisation. This did not mean that the only reason for recruitment was to procure sufficient cannon fodder. The SS remained an ideologically defined organisation and, as previously discussed, during the war SS-staff began to argue that Germanic racial characteristics could be found among individuals, groups or even nations, which had formerly been dismissed as racially unworthy. Within the logic of the SS this made them worthy of becoming Waffen-SS soldiers who might not equal their German and north-western European counterparts but still were to be treated with a certain degree of decency.

Through investigation of, first, the Germanic volunteers, then the *Volksdeutsche* and last the so-called *Fremdvölker* the next three chapters will describe how the SS handled the challenges arising from expansion beyond the borders of the *Reich* and the problems and solutions that ensued.

Chapter Eight

GERMANIC AND WESTERN EUROPEAN VOLUNTEERS IN THE WAFFEN-SS

From the late 1930s to 1945, between 45,000 and 50,000 Germanic volunteers entered the Waffen-SS. The largest group was 23–25,000 Dutch followed by about 10,000 Flemings. Ca. 6,000 Danes and as many Norwegians also served with the Waffen-SS.[1] In addition to these there were a limited number of British, Swiss and Swedes who volunteered.

According to Nazi racial belief, the Germans were merely one of more Germanic peoples related by blood which included Danes, Dutch, Flemings, Norwegians, Swedes and Germans as well as a number of smaller groups all originating from the Germanic tribes. These had allegedly populated Europe since, in a distant past, they immigrated, along with other Aryan peoples, from the Himalayas.[2] The Germans were believed to be the most important of those making up the Nordic, or Nordic-Germanic, race. This, again, was but one – though supposedly the most important one – of the Aryan races.[3]

Far from all Nazi leaders attached particular importance to this, allegedly, common Germanic inheritance. However, the notion of bringing all Germanic polities together under German leadership was popular with the SS. Along with more traditional cynical ponderings on empire and realpolitik this engendered the ambition of making the SS a 'Pan-Germanic' organisation. This goal was to be achieved partly through the recruitment of Germanic volunteers for the Waffen-SS.[4]

---

1. The total number enrolled is somewhat uncertain because the SS material is updated until various dates in 1944 only, and because SS' internal lists are imprecise. The number here are from Christensen et al. (1998), p 491ff.; Perry Pierik, *From Leningrad to Berlin: Dutch Volunteers in the Service of the German Waffen-SS 1941–1945: The Political and Military History of the Legion, Brigade and Division Known as 'Nederland'* (New Ed., Aspect, 2001), p 56ff.; Bruno de Wever, *Oostfronters: Vlamingen in het Vlaams Legioenen de Waffen SS* (Lannoo, 1984), p 149; Ivo de Figueiredo, 'De norske frontkjemperne–hva litteraturen sier og veien videre' *HistoriskTidsskrift*, No. 4, 2001, note 1. See also Stein (1984), p 138ff. Too high numbers can be found in the apologetic literature, for example, in Felix Steiner, *Die Freiwilligen der Waffen-SS: Idee und Opfergang* (Deutsche Verlagsgesellschaft, 1992), p 77.

2. Allan A. Lund, *Hitlers håndlangere: Heinrich Himmler og den nazistiske raceideologi* (Samleren, 2001).

3. Günther (1926), p 55ff.

4. This topic has been dealt with in detail by Emberland and Kott (2012).

European Nazism and the Germanic Volunteers

The Germanic volunteers were kindred spirits of the German Nazis like no one else among the non-German groups in the Waffen-SS in that they were almost entirely voluntarily recruited, and generally speaking wanted to fight for a National Socialist Europe modelled on the Germany of the 1930s.

Recruitment of Waffen-SS soldiers from neighbouring Germanic states was part of a deliberate strategy towards establishing and securing the SS power beyond Germany's borders. The idea was to expand the organisation through a combination of providing foreign Germanic personnel for service at the front and setting up SS branches in all the countries in question. The local SS organisations were to be the footholds for integration of new land into a Greater Germany.[5] Not military requirements, but this long-term aim was the ulterior agenda, which was clearly stated by the HSSPF in the occupied Netherlands, Hanns Albin Rauter. In September 1941, he wrote to Himmler about recruiting Dutch citizens; 'If we have these 5,000 SS men on our side I should not worry about the future of Holland'.[6] The Waffen-SS was in other words a means at the immediate disposal of the SS leadership, which was perceived as instrumental in creating Germanic solidarity. In addition, the Nazis were convinced that common battle experiences with the colours of the Waffen-SS would create a strong frontline-community and intensify identification with the SS. The combat service was seen as valuable because, apart from forming each individual's character, it was thought to produce integration across linguistic and national differences.[7]

The Germanics and SS' Long-Term Plans

On several occasions, Himmler stated how the SS and the post-war Europe dominated by Germany ought to look. Frequently, such statements were vague and inconsistent – as were those of Hitler – but they were obviously seriously meant and, over the war years, major efforts were made to implement them.[8]

Most importantly, the Greater German Reich was to comprise a larger area than the sum of the territories of the constituent countries ante bellum. Not only should the Germanic peoples unite and receive increments of blood through immigration

---

5. Wegner in *Militärgeschichtliche Mitteilungen*, No. 2, 1980, pp 101–136, here p 101ff.
6. Letter of 16 September 1941 from Rauter to Himmler, reprinted as document 79 in T'Veld (1976), vol.1, p 579.
7. Gingerich (1991), p 60.
8. On Himmler's statements about the post-war SS and the Reich see, interalia, BAB, NS19/4009, *Der Reichsführer-SS vor den Oberabschnittsführern und Hauptamtschefs im Haus der Flieger in Berlin am 9. Juni 1942.* Ibid.: *Rede des Reichsführer am 16. September 1942 in der Feldkommandostelle vor den Teilnehmern an der SS- und Polizeiführertagung, einberufen von SS-Obergruppenführer Prutzmann, HSSPF Russland Süd og Rede des Reichsführers-SS am 23.11.1942 – SS-Junkerschule Tölz.* BAB, NS19/4010, *Rede des Reichsführer-SS vor den Reichs- und Gauleitern in Posen am 6 Oktober 1943.* BAB, NS 19/1558, Himmler to Seyss-Inquart on 5 March 1942. As late as January 1945, Himmler apparently discussed with his closest collaborators about the Greater German Reich See BAB, NS19/653, Document note of 23 January 1945.

to Europe by Germans from, for example, North and South America, large tracts of the occupied territories in the east were to be colonised. According to Nazi plans, parts of Poland, Ukraine, the Baltic States and the Crimea should be populated by Germanic settlers.[9]

These ideas found their most concrete form in the planning process known as *Generalplan Ost*.[10] This was not a comprehensive design, but a sequence of scenarios for colonisation of the eastern space. Tasked by Himmler and the minister for the occupied Soviet Union, Alfred Rosenberg, various agencies conceived parts of this plan between 1940 and 1943. One of the common elements was that, depending on their alleged racial value, the populace in the east would be subjected to a combination of assimilation, subjugation and extermination. While Germans and other Germanic people should settle on the land thus available, between 30 and 50 million persons of Slavic descent were to disappear – either through expulsion or annihilation. From Himmler's point of view, it was of great importance that those resettled in the east, whether Germans, Dutch or Norwegians, would quickly realise that their true identity lay with a united Germanic people, and colonisation would therefore spearhead the creation of a Greater Germanic Reich.[11] Although *Generalplan Ost* demanded so many resources that they could be fully implemented in peacetime only, several steps were taken during the war and many of these involved the German and Germanic soldiers in the Waffen-SS.[12]

Himmler planned concentrations of *Volksdeutsche* on a grand scale in three places in Ukraine. One of these was Hegewald in the Zhytomir area, 100 km from Kiev, which had been foreseen by the *Generalplan Ost* as a future resettlement site. This part of Ukraine comprised some of the most fertile areas of the Soviet Union and there was already a high density of *Volksdeutsche*. Moreover, in October 1941, Himmler had decided to set up a field HQ at a former Soviet airbase there. During the war, these elements were possibly the primary reasons for the SS to initiate, a large-scale colonisation of the area. Together, the *Volksdeutsche* and 60 *Wehrbauer*, settled there since 1942, could farm the land. At the same time, a permanently stationed Waffen-SS training battalion as well as HQ troops could defend them against partisans. From summer 1942 to spring 1943, 10,000 Ukrainians were forced to leave, while a similar number of *Volksdeutsche* were moved in. They came from other parts of Ukraine marching, primarily, on the main road from Zhytomir and Berdychiv. In August, the SS reported this area completely 'cleansed' of Jews and Romas where after the new settlers were allocated the equipment left behind by the victims. Concentrations of this magnitude had other reasons than simple economies of scale: Himmler succeeded in persuading Hitler to approve direct SS administration

---

9.   Wegner (1990), p 299.
10. Götz Aly and Susanne Heim, *Architects of Annihilation: Auschwitz and the Logic of Destruction* (Weidenfeld & Nicolson, 2003), p 252ff.
11. BAB, NS19/4009, *Rede des Reichsführers-SS am 23.11.1942 – SS-Junkerschule Tölz*, p 16.
12. Apart from the following examples, this is true of the configuration of SS and police strongpoints, training areas and supply depots. These were of importance to military and police activities, but they were also nodal points in the colonisation process. Jan Theo Schulte, *Zwangsarbeit und Vernichtung: Das Wirtschaftsimperium der SS* (Schöningh Verlag, 2001), p 318, note 306.

of these 500 square kilometres, despite the East Ministry's basic responsibility for all of western Ukraine.[13] Although the largest area, Hegewald was not the only example that the SS was used to facilitate the Germanisation of the Soviet Union. In 1942, in the Rostov area on the Sea of Azov further to the south-east, Germanic soldiers of *Division Wiking* were employed in developing the small *Volksdeutsche* village Uspenska into a model Germanic town.[14]

The Polish area of Lublin was another zone that Himmler decided to colonise during the war, and the *SS und Polizeiführer* Odilo Globocnik was given the responsibility for this process.[15] The Germanic element would entail settling Norwegians and Dutch next to the *Volksdeutsche* already present in the area.[16] Space for Germanisation was made by elimination of Jews, mentally ill, and members of the Polish upper and middle classes as well as by driving away the Polish farmers.[17]

As early as in late 1939, the SS began deportation of Poles from the Warthegau – the western-most part of occupied Poland, while Jews were murdered on the spot or sent to ghettos or death camps in the Gouvernement Générale. While *Volksdeutsche* were resettled on the farmland – being assisted by young Nazis undergoing agricultural training – high-ranking SS men were allocated estates.[18] Thus, the widow of the fallen commander of the *Frikorps Danmark*, Christian Frederik von Schalburg, was allotted the estate Murke, and Himmler took a keen interest in the settling of the family.[19]

The trend of mixing the various Germanic groups also materialised within the officer corps. In March 1943, on formation of the Germanic armoured corps, Himmler stressed that this paved the way for German NCOs and soldiers to serve under Germanic officers. He also declared that the next *Reichsführer-SS* would not necessarily be a German. In Himmler's scheme of things, together with army, navy, air force and security police, the SS (and the Waffen-SS) of the coming Greater German Reich would be one of the institutions that all member states would have in common.[20]

---

13. Wendy Lower, 'A New Ordering of Space and Race: Nazi Colonial Dreams in Zhytomyr, Ukraine, 1941–1944'. *German Studies Review*, Vol. 25, No. 2, May, 2002, p 172.

14. Emberland and Kott (2012), p 364.

15. Aly and Heim (2003), p 275ff.

16. According to Emberland and Kott (2012), p 212ff. up to seven young Norwegians undergoing agricultural training stayed in that area in 1942. While until 1943, 120 Dutch moved in, 30 of these brought their families. Note by *Germanische Leitstelle* 12 October 1943, reprinted as document 473 in 'T Veld (1976), vol. 2, p 1231ff.

17. Aly and Heim (2003), p 277.

18. Mikkel Kirkebæk, *Beredt for Danmark: Nationalsocialistisk ungdom 1932–1945* (Høst & Søn, 2004), p 238ff.

19. Mikkel Kirkebæk, *Schalburg: en patriotisk landsforræder* (Gyldendal, 2008), p 377ff.

20. Letter of 11 December 1941 from Himmler to Rauter, reprinted as document 96 i 'T Veld (1976), vol. 1, p 612. See also Martin R. Gutmann, *Building a Nazi Europe. The SS's Germanic Volunteers* (Cambridge University Press, 2017), pp 33–38.

The National Legions

Until the launch of Operation Barbarossa, recruitment for the Waffen-SS followed the general rules laid down by the SS. These included fairly strict demands concerning physical condition and racial purity and, of course, volunteers had to share the Nazi world view. Moreover, different nationalities were mixed with Germans so that the feeling of Germanic community might flourish.

The onslaught on the Soviet Union, June 1941, changed the situation in the occupied countries. Conservative and nationalistic groups, who had previously been hostile to Germany while at the same time rejecting communism, generally welcomed the attack. German propaganda did the utmost to exploit this. At the time, the German perception of the operation was that it would be of a limited duration, and that Germany would be able to cope alone and reap the reward. When, subsequently, Germany gave its benedictions of the formation of outright national legions to be employed at the eastern front, it was a propaganda stunt aimed at passing the operation off as a European crusade against Bolshevism.[21] Eventually, these legions would fight with the Waffen-SS, but this was not a development that the SS had set in motion. It is highly likely that, when Operation Barbarossa was launched, the SS preferred recruiting of non-Germans to happen through the already existing Germanic formations.[22] However, shortly after the launch of the operation, spontaneous suggestions were made in occupied or Fascist countries to dispatch national contingents to join the fight against the 'godless Bolshevists' at the eastern front. And what was worse, in the eyes of the SS, two important competitors, the foreign ministry and the *Wehrmacht*, immediately supported the idea.

On 24 June, the Norwegian Nazi leader, Vidkun Quisling, started probing for possibilities to dispatch Norwegian soldiers to the eastern front. On the 29th, in an address on the radio, Reich Commissar Terboven announced that he had got Hitler's approval of raising a Norwegian legion, which was to be employed against Soviet forces in Finland.[23] Simultaneously, a Danish volunteer unit, the *Frikorps Danmark*, was being formed, though, initially, without the SS as a driving force. The main characters were the German envoy, Cecil von Renthe-Fink, and various Danish officers. On 23 June, these officers had approached the legation proposing to send a volunteer unit to Finland.[24] However, Finnish reactions appeared lukewarm and, over the following days, the SS and the Danish National Socialist Workers' Party (DNSAP) picked up the gauntlet. The DNSAP launched a public and comprehensive campaign to recruit for *Regiment Nordland*. At the same time, the party chief of staff, Commander Svend Kofoed Wodschow, began to look for an apt candidate for the post as the commanding officer of the planned unit – *Frikorps Danmark*. On 28 June, the Danish artillery officer Lieutenant

---

21. Jürgen Förster, '*Freiwillige für den Kreuzzug Europas gegen den Bolschewismus*' in Horst Boog et al. (1991), p 1081ff.
22. Gingerich (1991), p 171ff.
23. Emberland and Kott (2012).
24. Christensen et al. in Schulte (2014), p 200ff.

Colonel Christian Peter Kryssing, accepted. The day after, the party paper, *Fædrelandet* (the mother country), declared the *Frikorps Danmark* was now being raised.[25]

A note by Himmler indicates that, at the time, one week after the German attack on the Soviet Union, no fixed plans for raising such national units existed within the SS. The note, dotted down during a stay at the *Führer* HQ, informs that Hitler had approved Norwegian, Croat, Spanish and Italian legions. Other Germanic legion were not mentioned at all, which was due to the fact that also in the Netherlands and Flanders the legions were raised by local initiative.[26] In the Netherlands, the leader

Figure 8.1 General-officer-commanding *Division Wiking* Felix Steiner (Frihedsmuseet)

25. *Fædrelandet, 29.6.1941.* On Kryssing, see Christensen et al. (1998), p 417ff and Claus Christensen, Niels Bo Poulsen and Peter Scharff Smith, 'Kryssing og de østfrontsfrivillige', *Siden Saxo*, No. 1, 1995, pp 50–58, as well as Thomas Harder, *Kryssing. Manden, der valgte forkert* (Lindhardt og Ringhof, 2014). On the formation see also Henning Poulsen *Besættelsesmagten og de danske nazister: Det politiske forhold mellem tyske myndigheder og nazistiske kredse i Danmark 1940–43* (Gyldendal 1970), p 288ff.
26. NS19/1871, Himmler's note of 29 June 1941.

of the small Fascist party *Nationaal Front*, Arnold Meyer took the first step towards raising a national legion. On 28 June, in an article in the party newspaper he proposed the creation of unit of volunteers to fight at the eastern front. Two days later, the HSSPF Rauter informed Himmler encouraging him to support the idea. A few days into July, fortified by the *Auswärtiges Amt* in Berlin Reich Commissar Seyss-Inquart, too, had subscribed to the concept, and the headhunting for a commanding officer went ahead. Retired chief of the Dutch general staff, Hendrik Alexander Seyffardt, was chosen. The general, who at the time was 68 years of age, accepted. On 10 July, the first posters signed by Seyffardt went up in the Dutch cities calling for volunteers for a legion to fight Bolshevism. Initially, NSB, who competed with Meyer's *Nationaal Front*, was not amused. However, as Seyffardt, who was a clandestine member of the NSB, had accepted the position the party reluctantly backed the effort.[27] It was not until a week into July, that also Flanders got started. On the 8th, *Volk enStaat*, the newspaper of the Nazi *Vlaams Nationaal Verbond* (VNV), published a proclamation telling that since, eventually, Bolshevism had shown its true colours, Europe must fight united against bondage and for the preservation of Christianity. Thus, the raising of a *Vlaams Legioen* was proclaimed. All able-bodied men, regardless of party affiliation, might serve in this legion.

It was further told that the command language would be Flemish, that Flemish officers would be in charge and that a fusion with the Netherlands legion might happen.[28] What the Dutch and Flemish Nazis desired the most was a Dutch-Flemish nation, and a joined military unit might lead to this end. To the SS, however, this was a challenge because the *Standarte Nordwest*, raised in the spring, thereby lost some of its recruiting appeal. In order not to lose the grip completely, in early August, the SS agreed with the VNV on the development in Flanders.[29]

Within the Nazi leadership in Germany, apparently, there were co-ordinating difficulties as well. Not until 30 June, a meeting was called for the *Auswärtiges Amt*, *Wehrmacht*, *SS-Hauptamt* and NSDAP's foreign affairs office to discuss foreign, voluntary units for the eastern front. Here, agreement was reached on the basic rules for the formation of such units.[30] A few days later, Hitler allowed the *Wehrmacht* to recruit in Germanic countries and the SS' monopoly was about to be ruptured.[31] On 7 July, nonetheless Himmler finally succeeded in securing SS' role with respect to the national legions. At a meeting at *Auswärtiges Amt* it was decided that the SS would take responsibility for all the Germanic and the Wallonian legions. However, soon the latter was taken over by the army together with all other non-Germanic units.[32]

27. 'T Veld (1976), vol. 1, pp 334–342. See also Gingerich (1991), p 189ff.
28. Wever (1984), p 50. Gingerich wrongly dates the raising the late July and early August. (1991), p 195ff.
29. Bruno De Wever, '"Rebellen" an der Ostfront. Die flämischen Freiwilligen der Legion "Flandern" und der Waffen-SS', *Vierteljahrshefte für Zeitgeschichte* Vol. 39, No. 4, 1991, p 593.
30. Förster in Horst Boog et al. (1991), p 1083.
31. Gingerich (1991), p 173.
32. Ibid., p 175.

Although over the following years, the Wehrmacht did actually recruit in Germanic states, albeit on a limited scale, by retaining control of the legions the SS managed to preserve two recruiting approaches. While one was decidedly Nazi and elitist and aimed at attracting members to the Waffen-SS directly; the other went by the legions, was national, less elitist and upheld more modest demands for physical fitness.

Although formally, the legions were raised on a national and apolitical basis, from the outset the liaison with the local Nazi parties and the SS was both close and obvious. Thus, of ca. 60 recruiting places spread over Denmark almost all also accommodated a DSNAP party office.[33] In the Netherlands the SS had its own Regiment Westland recruiting office, which also served as that of the Dutch legion. A non-Nazi NCO of the legion complained that recruiting meetings were frequently held at hotels, whose owners were notorious NSB supporters.[34] In Norway, not only were Quisling and *Nasjonal Samling* among the founding fathers of the legion, they also contributed significant resources to the recruitment.[35] This combined with German interference worried the legion's staff. Would Norwegians really believe the unit to be apolitical when seeing its members wearing helmets displaying swastikas and SS runes and saluting with their right arms stretched out rather than in the traditional military manner?[36]

Behind the scenes, the local Nazi leaders in Denmark, Norway and the Netherlands saw the legions as useful instruments. Not only were they suitable as party armies, they might also serve as a means to restoring, under Nazi leadership, the countries' lost sovereign governance.[37] In Norway, Quisling saw the fighting at the eastern front as an opportunity to regain the army's allegedly lost honour. At the same time, the legion should become the open sesame to establishing colonies in the 'lost ancient Norwegian soil' in northern Russia.[38] The legion organisation of the early phases pointed to a future re-establishment of a Norwegian army. Bypassing the SS, a fairly large legion staff was set up in Oslo foreseen as the head of as many as seven battalions.[39] In the Netherlands, too, the NSB regarded the legion as its rightful possession. At one occasion, allegedly Mussert threatened HSSPF Rauter to withdraw the legion and use it to seize power and, subsequently, re-organise it as the nucleus of a new national army.[40]

---

33. *Fædrelandet*, 7 July 1941
34. 'T Veld (1976), vol. 1, p 342. Sytze van der Zee, *25.000 landverraders. De SS in Nederland. Nederland in de SS*, (Kruseman 1967), p 138ff.
35. In April 1942, inter alia, the party conducted a large-scale recruiting campaign. See 'Meldungen aus Norwegen Nr. 37 vom 31. März 1942', reprinted in Stein Ugelvik Larsen (ed.), *Meldungen aus Norwegen 1940–1945:die geheimen Lageberichte des Befehlshabers der Sicherheitspolizei und des SD in Norwegen*. Vol. 2 (Oldenburg, 2008), p 571.
36. HLC, private archive Terje Emberland, *Oberst Kjeldstrup, dagbogsoptegnelser*, entries on 25 June, 20 July and 20 September 1941.
37. BAB, NS19/1667, Letter of 16 September 1942 from Steiner to Berger.
38. Terje Emberland and Matthew Kott, *Himmler's Norge* (manuscript), p 244.
39. HLC, private archive Terje Emberland, *Oberst Kjeldstrup, dagbogsoptegnelser*, entries on 20 July and 12 October 1941.
40. BAB, NS19/1561, Letter of 1 February 1942 from Rauter to Himmler.

In order to achieve maximum impact, the SS used the local Nazi parties as recruiting agencies, but it was obvious that the legions might develop into purely national party guards or otherwise be used against the interests of the SS.[41] Thus, in the autumn 1941, the SS tightened the control of the legions. On 6 November 1941, Himmler issued a circular letter setting out guidelines for the formation and use of foreign units of volunteers.[42] Here, it was stated that the legions were to be national units with their own leadership and the command language should be either national or German. This was in harmony with the original German pledges made during the summer when the legions were brought into existence. However, it was now stressed that leadership, training and organisation had to follow German regulations. Moreover, the volunteers were subjected to German military law and procedures. Personnel matters, discipline, complaints and honour related issues were to be handled according to SS regulations, though with leeway for exceptions during a transitional phase and with emphasis on national peculiarities and character. On the same day, Himmler laid down rules for the relationship between the national regulars and the German permanent staff instructors detailed by the SS. It was stressed that the instructors were there to give advice, not order, and that they had no command authority.[43] These regulations were necessary because the detailing of the staffs had led to certain conflicts with the national legions' leaderships. Internal disagreement among the officers of some legions was a challenge. The reason was that the newly raised units operated outside the usual military hierarchies of the individual countries and under a command structure that was bound to cause confusion and conflicts of authority. Germans as well as local Nazi parties took part in these internal power struggles. In Norway this materialised as a clash of the commander of the legion, Colonel Finn Kjeldstrup, with the commanding officer of the only battalion, major Jørgen Bakke. If Kjeldstrup's diary is to be trusted, Bakke schemed with German-friendly elements of *Nasjonal Samling* to have the legion staff dissolved and have himself appointed supreme commander.[44] In early December 1941, he succeeded. The staff was morphed into a recruiting and welfare office, and Bakke experienced a brief stint as legion commander.[45] What Kjeldstrup wrote about two months later is characteristic of the relationship between the two men – and probably also among quite a few other Norwegian legion officers who had been drawn into this affair. He described Bakke as 'a vile, scheming liar' who was 'undisciplined and disloyal'. As to his practical abilities the comment was 'an inferior officer'.[46] A couple of months previously, Kjeldstrup had tried to have Bakke cashiered. To the SS he had accused Bakke of being a free mason, and

---

41. Letter of 24 September 1941 from Berger to Jüttner, reprinted as document 81 in 'T Veld (1976), vol. 1, p 581ff.
42. BAB, NS19/3565.
43. Ibid.
44. HLC, private archive Terje Emberland, *Oberst Kjeldstrup, dagbogsoptegnelser*, entries on 9 and 20 October and 17 December 1941 as well as 18 January 1942.
45. Ibid., A brief survey of miscellaneous issues of interest, 1 January 1942.
46. Ibid., entry on 18 January 1942.

he had demanded a police investigation into an alleged pub brawl, where Bakke was said to have been drunk and disorderly wearing uniform, hitting several guests, among whom a lady.[47] This, in combination with the Germans' dwindling confidence in his leadership qualities, might have contributed to making Bakke's stint as legion commander a short one. In mid-December, he was replaced by Major Arthur Quist, and was transferred to *Division Wiking*.[48] It is not known if the Dutch and the Flemish legions were fraught with similar disagreement. There were less national officers and, from the outset, the SS dominated the leaderships. Like Legion Norway, *Frikorps Danmark* upheld a certain autonomy and had close ties with the DNSAP, and here, too, there was a serious clash. In February 1942, therefore the *Frikorps'* commander, Kryssing, relinquished command to the fervent Nazi and anti-Semite officer of *Division Wiking*, Christian Frederik von Schalburg.[49]

While the internal disagreements among the officers was not always noticed or even relevant to the NCOs and men, everyone was aware of the German breach of the promises on which the legions had been raised. The Dutch General Seyffardt had made it a condition that the legion's commanding officer should always be a Dutch, that the legion should fight with the old orange, white and blue Dutch Princes' Colour, and that, in addition to swearing an oath of allegiance to Hitler, the legionnaires should vow to their own colour. None of this ever happened.[50] In the other legions there were similar problems. Reich Commissar Terboven's order concerning the formation of Legion Norway stated that the unit would be commanded by Norwegians and follow Norwegian regulations. However, Himmler's circular letter of November 1941 streamlined the guidelines for all four national legions ruling that command, training and formation were to follow German procedures.[51] This change was detrimental first of all to the regular officers and NCOs. All of a sudden, their professional ethos was rendered superfluous, and the German training staffs' position similarly strengthened.

About six weeks after the formation of the Norwegian legion, the Oslo-based staff was asked to send 20-30 NCOs, so far recruited, on a course at the SS' NCO school in Lauenburg. This request followed a piece of information a few weeks before that the legion was to be formed in Germany – not Norway, as originally agreed. The SS also went back on a number of other promises made by German authorities in Oslo.[52] The news about the course was the last straw that broke the camel's back, and

47. Ibid., entry on 22 October and 4 December 1941.
48. Christensen et al. (2000), p 431ff. See also Emberland and Kott (2012), p 266.
49. Christensen et al. (1998), p 130ff.
50. T Veld (1976), vol. 1, p 340.
51. VAP, Legion Norge, package 2, file 12, *Betr. Vereidung der Freiwilligen Legion 'Norwegen'*, 25 September 1941. VAP, *Legion Norge*, package 1, file7, *Aufstellung und Einsatz ausländischer Freiwilligenverbande*, 6 November 1941.
52. HLC, private archive Terje Emberland, *Oberst Kjeldstrup, dagbogsoptegnelser*, entry on 22 July and 10 August 1941. On Legion Norway's training, transfer to Germany etc., see (2014), p 195ff.

it entailed serious scrutiny by the staff in Oslo of what might be the Germans' ulterior motives. The deliberation can be traced thanks to the temporary commander, Colonel Kjeldstrup's diary. He writes about this:

> The duration of the course is ten days. However, due to changes of previous agreements my staff officers have become so suspicious [...] that they do not expect to come back to Norway. Next step would be – so they prophesied – that the remainder would be detailed the same way and employed at the front without being united in one Norwegian battle group.[53]

Kjeldstrup suggested that this called for cool consideration as the conditions in Germany were probably better than in Norway. There, the experiences gained at the eastern front was implemented in exercises and training facilities. This, though, did not encourage his subordinates. One offered the opinion that the Germans consciously aimed at letting the legion bleed white in order to drain *Nasjonal Samling* of power.[54]

The daily routines with the legions were marred by distrust and frictions between their own officers and personnel on the one side and the attached German training staffs on the other. The Norwegian legion's first impression of the German instructors was that they were incredibly young, constantly interfering taking charge regardless of the presence of Norwegian officers, and instructing in German.[55] The relationship between the Norwegian officers and the instructors was not exactly perfect. One reason might be that it was the German chief instructor who, in December 1941, had Bakke dismissed from the post as legion commander.[56] During the autumn of 1941, similarly, a vendetta went on between the German head instructor with *Frikorps Danmark* and the legions Danish commander, Kryssing. However, since neither the SS nor the many Nazis within the unit cared much about him he was replaced by von Schalburg, and the troubles ceased.[57]

In the Dutch and the Flemish legions, the German officers did not stop at offering their advice. Shortly after the formation of the Dutch legion, the designated commander, Gerhard Stroink, resigned because of the unsatisfactory collaboration with the Waffen-SS. Five more Dutch officers followed in his steps. Among the Dutch volunteers there was a dearth of officers and, consequently, Germans officers filled the gaps as company commanders as well as commanders of both legions.[58] And as, accidentally, a German officer shot a Dutch sentry, relations were not improved. As one soldier put it, 'the Germans were shouting and corrupt'.[59] However, it was in the Flemish legion that the tensions were the most obvious. Arriving in their staging area in Poland, the Flemish volunteers realised that their new commander was the German *Standartenführer* Otto Reich, who claimed

---

53. HLC, private archive Terje Emberland, *Oberst Kjeldstrup, dagbogsoptegnelser,* entry on 11 August 1941.
54. Ibid.
55. Ibid., Entry in 22 August 1941.
56. Christensen et al., *Historisk Tidsskrift* 100, nr. 2, 2000, p 428ff.
57. Christensen et al. (1998), p 132ff.
58. Stein (1984), p 154.
59. 'T Veld (1976), vol. 1, p 816, note 1.

to be unaware of the terms of their enrolment. Not least, he found it outright ridiculous that, with reference to the original agreement, they insisted that they were entitled to having an army chaplain. This snag the SS solved by refusing the clergyman permission to travel to the front.[60] Reich's view on the history of Flanders and its future very likely aggravated the already strained relations. If a contemporary report can be trusted, he told the legionnaires that their language was nothing but 'a German dialect'. Moreover, Reich instructed the men that 'the sensible thing to do' was to forget about their 'Flemish descent' and allow themselves to be 'Germanised'.[61] At the same time, the Flemish volunteers experienced scorn, spite and threats by their German company commanders. One German officer had threatened with his pistol, administered caning, and arrogantly accused the soldiers of being 'a filthy people' and 'Romas'.[62] Himmler reacted furiously when, in spring 1942, a letter from de Clerq reached his desk, but at that time the damage had already been done in this as well as in all the other legions.

On this background, it is hardly surprising that a great many men were frustrated, and that a large number of volunteers had to be repatriated.[63] During the autumn, not only did *Legion Nederland* experience many desertions, 300 out of 2,500 had to be repatriated on account of 'cowardice or homesickness' – so the Haag-based recruiting office.[64] On the other hand, the soldiers' own explanation was that they wished to return home due to the SS' abundant failures to honour their promises.[65] Apart from the repatriations requested by the soldiers, the SS also trimmed the personnel. On the one hand, officers and others who were seen as potential 'troublemakers' were transferred from the legions to ordinary Waffen-SS units.[66] On the other, soldiers with a record, who had been enrolled by mistake, were now repatriated.[67] However, these actions entailed two problems. It caused a reduction of troops and not all those repatriated would speak nicely about their experiences with the SS, which, of course, influenced further recruitment.

---

60. Jüttner order, 26 July and 24 September 1941, reprinted as document 73 and 80 respectively in ibid., pp 568 and 581.VAP, N SS-Fr. Leg. *'Nor'*, *ks. 1, Bericht über das Verhältnis des deutschen Ausbildungsstabes zur Führung der Freiw.-Legion 'Norwegen'*, 2.3.1942. A problem arose in the Norwegian legion where, initially, a chaplain was attached. In February 1942, however, he was repatriated on SS insistence. BAB, SSO 006A. *Personalakte Geelmuyden, BAB, SSO 006A. VAP, N SS-Fr. Leg. 'Nor'*, Box 1, Letter from *SS-Führungshauptamt* to the legion commander, 11 December 1941.
61. De Wever, (1991), p 596.
62. BAB, NS19/2305, Letter of 13 April 1942 from Himmler to Berger and Jüttner, and NS19/3522, letter of 17 February 1942 from de Clerq to Himmler, as well as letter of 25 March 1942 from Berger to Jüttner.
63. Apart from the Danes in Klagenfurt, mentioned previously, see also the interrogation of 11 Dutch volunteers in Sennheim in spring 1941, who had had second thoughts. NIOD Coll. Doc. II, 750A *SS-Vrijwilligers, Vernehmnungsniederschriften, Sennheim*, 14 March 1941.
64. NIOD, 205 Militair-Historisch Archiev Praag, *Befehlshaber der Waffen-SS in den Niederlanden*. Telex of 15 September 1941 from Leib to Berger, reprinted as document 77 in 'T Veld (1976), vol. 1, p 382ff.
65. Gingerich (1991), p 194.
66. Christensen et al. (2000), p 429. Christensen et al. (1998), p 136ff.
67. BAB, NS19/1557, Letter of 28 May 1942 from Lettow-Vorbeck to Berger. IfZG, NO-2099, note of 27 November 1941 by Gottlob Berger.

From Legions to Armoured Corps

With the multifarious difficulties as the backdrop, it appears understandable that the legions never reached the size that had been foreseen from the outset. Instead of regiments, merely battalion size units saw the light of day, and when, at the end of 1941, these units were successively employed at the eastern front casualties combined with repatriations and sickness exceeded the available filler personnel resources. In June 1942, for instance, the Flemish legion had shrunk from 25 officers, 78 NCOs and 1,009 men to 13, 26 and 288 respectively.[68] During its only three months' employment at Demyansk, *Frikorps Danmark* was reduced from almost 700 personnel to a little less than 225.[69] However, while the other legions remained at the front, in September and October 1942 *Frikorps Danmark* went on leave in Denmark in its entirety, which probably contributed to creating a better mood than in the other legions. While this went on, the field post censorship noticed a sharp decline of the morale among the Norwegian legionnaires, who had then spent six months continuously in the trenches at Leningrad.[70]

Figure 8.2 The Danish legion, *Frikorps Danmark*, during leave in Denmark in 1942 (Frihedsmuseet)

---

68. Estes (2008), pp 46 and 48. From January to July 1942, Legion Nederland went from a total strength of ca. 2,700 to ca. 1,200 officers, NCOs and men. See ibid., p 44.
69. Helge Klint (ed.), *Krigsdagbog 7. maj-11. august 1942* (Richard Levin, 1978), p 16.
70. Christensen et al. (2000), p 443.

In the early autumn 1942, the SS began considering the possibility of fusing all Germanic volunteers in one common organisation, instead of keeping them apart in small units of little military value and with strained relations with their national Nazi-parties.[71] The head of the office for Germanic volunteers, *Germanische Leitstelle*, Franz Riedweg, and the general-officer-commanding *Division Wiking*, Felix Steiner jointly proposed the dissolution of the national legions. At the same time, Himmler nursed the idea of incorporating them into first and second SS infantry brigades.[72] While Steiner's idea was to fuse these units in a powerful Germanic armoured corps including *Division Wiking* and several other formations of Germanic volunteers, Himmler's intention was rather to use the legionnaires in counter-insurgency operations behind the front – a plan that had taken form since autumn 1941.[73] The reason why Steiner's

Figure 8.3 The Danish legion, *Frikorps Danmark*, had intimate connections with the biggest Danish Nazi party, DNSAP. Here families and sympathizers greet Danish Waffen-SS volunteers on home leave. The photo was taken by DNSAP's propaganda unit (Frihedsmuseet)

71. NAWA, 362, ZZ-16, Box 43, Riedweg, Franz, Letter of 2 September 1942 from Riedweg to Berger. BAB, NS19/1667, Letter of 16 September 1942 from Steiner to Berger. See also Christensen et al. (1998), p 190, as well as Emberland and Kott (2012), p 427. For concrete examples see BAB, NS19/375, *Befehle: Germanische Freiwilligen Leitstelle. 1942–1944. SS-Hauptamt – Amt VI: Montatsbericht/Oktober 1942.*
72. BAB, NS19/3753, Note of 24 September 1942 for Wolff and Jüttner on behalf of Himmler. The process towards the formation of the third Germanic armoured corps has been described in depth by Wegner (1980), pp 101–136.
73. Niels Bo Poulsen, '"Germanic" SS-Soldiers and Nazi Counterinsurgency Warfare 1941–1945', *Insurgency and Counterinsurgency: Irregular Warfare from 1800 to the Present*, (Den Haag, 2001), pp 293–302.

idea prevailed was, possibly, that, from the autumn 1942, Himmler, seeing the mounting troubles at the front, found it wise to raise further formations for front service rather than employing the Germanic volunteers in less visible operations in the hinterland.

In March 1943, the order to disband the legions and join all Germanic volunteers in one corps was issued.[74] Subsequently, the legions at the front were relieved and most of them concentrated in the training area Grafenwöhr in southern Germany. Over the summer 1943, two new units were formed there viz. the *SS-Panzergrenadier-Freiwilligen-Division Nordland* and the *SS-Freiwilligen-Panzergrenadier-Brigade Nederland*, both of which were to be incorporated in the newly formed third Germanic armoured corps (*III. Germanische Panzerkorps*). The dissolution of the legions was bound to cause political trouble and, after longish deliberations, it was agreed to limit the possible damage by naming *Nordland*'s two infantry regiments '*Danmark*' and '*Norge*' and to gather personnel from the respective legions in the first Battalion of each of these. In order not to risk any 'greater Netherlands contamination', the Flemings, however, were kept completely separate from this corps.[75] Instead of that, the Flemish legion was allotted tank destroyers, anti-tank guns and a Finnish battalion thereby forming sixth *SS-Freiwilligen-Sturmbrigade-Langemarck*.[76] The demise of the legions generated widespread dissatisfaction and led to several applications for resignation, and many soldiers refused to swear the renewed oath which was required at the formal transfer to the SS.[77]

The decision to transform the legions into divisions and regiments was followed up by intensive recruiting efforts in order to fill the ranks. At the end of February 1943, the SS agreed with *Organisation Todt* (O.T.) that the Waffen-SS might recruit from its labour camps. The aim was to enrol 5-6,000 Germanic workers below the age of 40.[78] In August 1943, about 8,000 men had signed up, of whom around half would eventually join the ranks of the Waffen-SS.[79] However, these initiatives were far from enough to

74. NAWA, T175, r.59, 2574736ff. Letter of 10 February 1943 from Berger to Himmler. BAB, NS19/48, Himmlers order of 3 March 1943, *Aufstellung des germanischen Korps*.
75. BAB, NS19/159, Letter of 24 April 1943 from Reichsführer-SS to SS-Hauptamt and SS-Führungshauptamt.
76. BAB, NS19/3523, Jüttner's directive of 31 May 1943 concerning formation. By the end of the year, the brigade's strength was a couple of thousands. See BAMA, RH2/3043, *6. SS-Freiwilligen-Sturmbrigade-Langemarck*, 6 December 1943.
77. Letter of 25 March 1943 from Jüttner to Himmler, *Weiterverpflichtung germanischer Freiwilliger*. RK, Danica, package 85, Ordner 1128.BAB, NS19/1481, Mussert, 7.4.1943 and BAB,NS19/1481, *Der Reichskommissar für die Besetzten Niederländische Gebite, 9.4.1943* Christensen et al. (1998). DeWewer (1991), p 606ff.
78. Franz W. Seidler, *Die Organisation Todt: Bauen für Staat u. Wehrmacht 1938–1945* (Bernard & Graefe, 1987), p 137. On the internal decision-making in the SS, see BAB NS19/1735: Letter of 30 January 1943 from Himmler to Hauptamt and Führungshauptamt (ibid.). Letter of 4 February 1943 from Hauptamt to Himmler.
79. NAWA, T175, r.59, p 2574773, Letter of 21 August 1943 from Berger to Himmler. Of the 8,000 men recruited, 6,083 had so far been mustered, and of these 3,154 had been found fit for service with the SS. Consequently, it may be assumed that eventually some 4,000 men were enlisted.

provide the necessary personnel for the units thus foreseen, and SS therefore had to infuse 8,000 *Volksdeutsche* from Romania into the Germanic Corps.[80] In December 1943, *Division Nordland* – the corps' largest formation – included 5,900 *Volksdeutsche*, 4,100 Reich Germans, almost 1,400 Danes, ca. 800 Norwegians, 274 Dutch, 38 Swedes and 24 Flemings.[81]

On the formation of the corps, *Division Wiking*'s *Regiment Nordland* was broken and its personnel was transferred to the division of the same name. The gap left in *Wiking*'s ranks led to inclusion of Estonians into the SS' inner circle of Germanic soldiers. In the autumn of 1942, Berger had informed Himmler that the applicants for membership of the Estonian legion, which was being raised at the time, were of particularly good blood and Himmler was asked to decide whether a branch of *Germanische Leitstelle* should be set up in Tallinn.[82] In the Summer 1943, the Estonian soldiers, whom the SS found the best qualified, were transferred to *Division Wiking* and organised in a battalion designated *Narwa*.

The Germanic Officer Corps

The various Germanic nations provided very disparate numbers of officers. Relatively speaking, *Frikorps Danmark* and *Legion Norge* had the largest proportion of own officers – almost every officer post had a compatriot as its incumbent.[83] Quite a few Danish officers reported for duty with the Waffen-SS, 55 to be precise.[84] In accordance with the SS guidelines, on completion of follow-up training an SS rank similar to their national status would be conferred upon Germanic officers.[85] Regardless of previous officer training in their home countries, many Germanic officers had to undergo extra training at SS' own training centres because, in the eyes of the SS, they were not at a par with their German opposite numbers and did not know the German service rules and regulations.[86] Prospective officer material among the Germanic private soldiers was a much appreciated commodity. They could be more easily moulded into the SS worldview than those undergoing follow-up training and they

---

80. BAB, NS19/3363, Letter of 29 March 1943 from Himmler to Rauter. Paul Milata, *Zwischen Hitler, Stalin und Antonescu: Rumäniendeutsche in der Waffen-SS* (Böhlau Verlag, 2009), p 256ff.
81. BAMA, RS2-3/2, Gen Kdo. III SS Pz Korps IIa: *Tätigkeitsbericht vom 26.5.1943 bis 31.3.1944.*
82. BAB, NS19/375, *SS-Hauptamt – Amt VI: Montatsbericht/Oktober 1942.*
83. While all 24 officers with *Frikorps Danmark* were Danish citizens, only 24 of 66 officers with *Legion Nederland* were Dutch. In the Flemish legion the numbers were 14 out of 25. As of 1 January 1942, there were 40 Norwegian officers in *Legion Norge*. VAP, N SS-Fr. Leg. 'Nor', Box 1; Estes (2008), Chapter 2.
84. RK, Forsvarets arkiv, Box 90A, *Liste des Ersatzkommandos Dänemark über die Rekrutierungen dänischer Offiziere und Unteroffiziere bis 26.6.1943.*
85. VAP, *Legion Norge*, package 1, file 7, *Aufstellung und Einsatz ausländischer Freiwilligenverbände*, 6 November 1941.
86. BAB, NS19/3987, 'Auf dem Weg zum germanischen Reich'. Undated speech by Gottlob Berger [maybe at the '*VI Tagung' auf der Plassenburg vom 28.2. bis 5.3.1944*].

would become a resource in their home countries when these, after German victory, would eventually have to be Nazified.[87]

Therefore, a number of courses were run at the *Junkerschule* in Bad Tölz; both for Germanic officers and for potential cadets.[88] With due consideration for the foreigners' linguistic difficulties, allowance was made for extra time when writing exam papers.[89] In early 1944, more than 500 Germanic volunteers had passed through the courses at Bad Tölz thus creating a considerable number of Germanic subalterns.[90] The officer-to-private ratio differed considerably among the Germanic nations. While in March 1944, 19 per cent of all Danish volunteers with the Waffen-SS were officers or NCOs, with the Norwegians it was 12 per cent, and among the Dutch 10.[91] These differences may have influenced the integration of the various groups of volunteers in the Waffen-SS. As one in five Danes wore badges of rank, this provided a pool of men who could act as leaders and role models, or liaise between Danes and

Figure 8.4 Volunteers from the Netherlands depart for Germany in 1941 (Frihedsmuseet)

87. BAB, NS19/375, Hauptamt order of 24 August 1942, *Amt VI betr. Germanische Führerausbildung in Tölz.*
88. Schulze-Kossens (1982), p 55ff. And 171ff.
89. BAMA, RS5/988, *Junkerschule Braunschweig.*
90. BAB, NS19/3987, 'Auf dem Weg zum germanischen Reich'. Undated speech by Gottlob Berger [maybe at the *'VI Tagung' auf der Plassenburg vom 28.2. bis 5.3.1944*].
91. BAMA, RS2-3/2. *Tätigkeitsbericht des Korps Kommandos des III. (germ.) SS-Panzerkorps vom 31.3.1944.* See also Christensen et al. (2000), p 444.

Germans thus making things run smoothly. Not least, this was true of charismatic persons like the *Frikorps* commander, von Schalburg, and, later, the commanding officer of *Regiment Danmark* Per Sørensen, who both acquired hero status within the Danish Nazi environment.[92]

National Conflicts

The SS wanted to establish branches in the occupied countries because it was hardly to be expected that the Pan-Germanic feelings would spring forth by themselves. It was feared that the local Nazis would nurture narrow patriotic feelings or regional identities.[93] The latter possibility was obvious with regard to the Flemish and the Dutch Nazis' hopes of a union – possibly including the Boers in South Africa – a notion that the SS called the *grossdietsche* idea (The concept of a greater Netherlands). To avoid this, the SS tried to keep these volunteer groups apart.[94] As far as the Scandinavian volunteers were concerned, it was feared that these might have desires of a greater Scandinavia in the form of a defensive alliance or a federation. As explained by Erich Lorenz, the leader of the SS recruiting office in Copenhagen: 'The notion of a particular Nordic community including Finland is an idea that, though not necessarily dangerous, is an obstruction to the Pan-Germanic project'.[95]

Conversely, many Germanic volunteers perceived the SS bravado on Pan-Germanism as a blind for Germanisation. As already shown, in 1940, this attitude was pervasive among the recruits with *Regiments Nordland* and *Westland*. Moreover, in 1942, the SS enthusiastic Norwegian, Per Imerslund, observed that the national differences within *Division Wiking* were so strong that they might 'turn into hatred'. In an internal letter to the Norwegian Nazi party he also explained how German Wiking officers addressed their Germanic subordinates in problematic ways. Nonetheless, he mentioned that the crucial underlying issue was that for many '*Wiking* soldiers it was incredibly difficult to find friends among the German SS men'.[96]

92. Kirkebæk (2008). Claus Christensen, Niels Bo Poulsen and Peter Scharff Smith, 'Per Sørensen: Officer og gerningsmand' in Rasmus Mariager, *Danskere i krig, 1936–1948* (Gyldendal, 2009), pp 91–127.
93. BAB, NS19/375, *SS-Hauptamt – Amt VI: Montatsbericht/Oktober 1942*.
94. Letter from Berger to Jüttner, 16.9.1941, reprinted as document 78 in 'T Veld (1976), vol. 1, s.573.
95. Poulsen (1970), p 278. See also SD's comments on the Norwegian NS-minister Prytz's proposal of the creation of a Nordic Union in 'Sonderbericht an das RSHA vom 6. Mai 1942' reprinted in Larsen (2008), p 644. On the menace to the Greater Germanic Idea from the *grossdietsche* and the Pan-Scandinavian ideas, see also Himmler's letter to Heydrich and Wilhelm Rediess of 16 February 1942, reprinted as document 117 in 'T Veld (1976), vol. 1, p 643ff.
96. BAB, NS19/3519, Letter of 9 February 1942 from Berger to Führungshauptamt, *Freiwillige aus germanischen Ländern*, Annex 4: *Bericht eines norwegischen Kriegsfreiwilligen*, undated (possibly early 1942).

German sentiments concerning the smaller Germanic nations were reciprocated. Among Danish, Norwegian and Swedish volunteers the notion of coming from the ancient Nordic home of the Germanic race was widespread. This fact in combination with the Viking legacy made many see themselves as superior to the Germans. Norwegians juxtaposed German strictness with a more laid-back Norwegian attitude. Returning legionnaires entertained their families with 'grotesque examples [...] of German discipline contrasted by the sound Norwegian common sense'.[97] Swedish SS soldiers regarded the Nazi regimentation of their German brothers-in-arms as so extreme that they would walk right into a wall without a wink, if they were so ordered to; and they boasted that the SS would never succeed in breaking the Viking brood's thirst of independence.[98] However, it was not only with respect to the Germans that there were tensions and prejudices. Some Norwegian volunteers held the opinion that 'a considerable part of the Netherlands Waffen-SS soldiers were criminals' who had escaped a prison sentence on the condition of atoning their sins at the front.[99] It appears from memoirs and letters from Scandinavian volunteers that many were very dissatisfied with having to serve with Romanian *Volksdeutsche* in the Germanic armoured corps. One volunteer, who had been a pig breeder in Denmark, opined that, when eating, the Romanians sounded worse than 'sows', and that they were 'weird'.[100] From the front at Narva, a Norwegian NCO wrote to his family that, although there were many good fellows among the *Volksdeutsche*, the majority of them got on his nerves lacking 'Nordic spirit and willpower'. Thus, he wrote them off as 'completely devoid of Nordic attitude'.[101]

Himmler keenly followed the Germanic volunteers' wellbeing and intervened to protect them against perceived injustices; especially those springing from German officers' overbearing attitude. Despite threats of punishment, he never fully succeeded in eradicating national prejudices and tensions between the Germans and the Germanic minorities. As late as in April 1944, Berger lamented, in a somewhat polemic form, the lacking trenchancy of the Germanic idea. In his view this resulted in German disdain of the Germanic volunteers, whom they regarded at a par with Poles, Romas, Russians and the workshy.[102] Nonetheless, in a speech, shortly afterwards,

---

97. HLC, private archive Terje Emberland, *Oberst Kjeldstrup, dagbogsoptegnelser*, 20 September 1941.
98. From a newspaper article 'Värvade till Tyskland', *Trots Allt*, 5–11 May 1944. For more examples see Karl Holter, *Frontkjempere* (Store Bjørn Forlag, 1951), p 78; Rolf Michaelis, *Die 11. SS-freiwilligen Panzer-Grenadier Division 'Nordland'*, (Michaelis Verlag, 2001), p 31. Sentence No. 923 reprinted in C.F. Ruter, Dick de Mildt and L. Hekelaar Gombert, *Justiz und NS-Verbrechen: Sammlung deutscher Strafurteile wegen nationalsozialistischer Tötungsverbrechen, 1945–1966, bd. XLIX*, (University Press Amsterdam, 2012), p 194. Meldungen aus Norwegen Nr.46 vom 15. Oktober 1942, reprinted in Larsen (2008), p 849.
99. Evald O. Solbakken, *I fengsel og landflyktighet* (Tiden Norsk Forlag, 1945), p 133.
100. Christensen et al. (1998), p 192.
101. HLC, Sigurd Sørlie private archive, Pl-Andreas B. Nilsson, letter of 15 February 1944. See also HLC, Sigurd Sørlie private archive, Pl-Andreas B. Nilsson, letter of 22 February 1944.
102. Letter of 4 April 1944 from Gottlob Berger to Rudolf Brandt, reprinted as document 523 in 'T Veld (1976), vol. 2, p 1312.

he emphasised the great trouble during the early war years with turning the Germanic volunteers coming from pacifist and spineless countries into good soldiers. Had it not been for the 'prep-school' at Sennheim, where the men could gradually learn to accept the German demands, Berger believed they would have broken down under the harsh discipline, which came natural to German soldiers.[103]

From Germanic to European Community: French and Italians in the Waffen-SS

As, gradually, it became clear that Germany had to instrumentalise resources from all the occupied European countries to win what had then become a war of attrition, the German propaganda, within as well as without the SS, shifted its emphasis onto the so-called European Idea. Focus was now on commonalities in European culture and history, which was juxtaposed with 'the culture-destructive Asiatic Bolshevism'. This shift opened up for recruiting a number of west and south European non-Germanic groups into the Waffen-SS.

Among others, a large number of French were admitted.[104] There is some uncertainty as to the actual number, but it would have been between 10 and 20,000 for all services and the Waffen-SS put together.[105] In the summer of 1941, following the German attack on the Soviet Union, the *Legion des Volontaires Françaiscontre le Bolchevisme* (LVF) was raised. Initially, the collaboration with the Germans did not involve the SS. It emanated from radical right-wing groups, primarily in Paris, who sought a closer co-operation with the Germans than that conducted by the Vichy government. Shortly, after the launch of Operation Barbarossa, a proclamation was signed by a number of right-wing leaders, such as Jacques Doriot of the *Parti Populaire Français* (PPF) and Marcel Déat of the *Rassemblement National Populaire* (RNP), supporting Germany's struggle with Bolshevism. These groups were characterised by Pan-European ideas. They hailed Hitler as the new Charlemagne, who could unite Europe on a basis of radical

---

103. BAB, NS19/3987, 'Auf dem Weg zumgermanischen Reich'. Undated speecch by Gottlob Berger (maybe at the *'VI Tagung' auf der Plassenburg vom 28.2. bis 5.3.1944*). See also BAB, NS19/3519, letter of 9 February 1942 from Berger to Führungshauptamt, *Freiwillige aus germanischen Ländern*, p 4.
104. Only limited research has been done of the French soldiers with the Waffen-SS. One reason for that is that the surviving German sources are fragmentary. Thus, there is tantamount to nothing on the French Waffen-SS division. A survey of this kind of research can be found in Philippe Carrard, *The French Who Fought for Hitler: Memories from the Outcasts* (Cambridge University Press, 2010), p 17ff.
105. In his classical study of the Waffen-SS, Stein fix the number at 20.000. Gordon informs that 10.000 reported for service with LVF and the Waffen-SS. See Bertram M. Gordon, *Collaborationism in France during the Second World War* (Cornell University Press, 1980), p 244. In a speech by Berger the number of French volunteers in Waffen-SS is 2,480 men. BAB, NS19/3888, no date 1944. For a survey concerning numbers by research in general see J.G. Shields, 'Charlemagne's Crusaders: French Collaboration in Arms, 1941–1945', *French Cultural Studies*, 2007, 18; 83, p 103 note 4.

right-wing ideology.[106] Over the summer 1941, 3,000 French joined the LFV, which was then subordinated one of the Wehrmacht's infantry divisions. In this framework it was employed at the front until it was relieved and used in counter-insurgency operations until 1944.[107]

In the following years, the Vichy regime, headed by Pierre Laval, tried to tie closer links with the LVF in order to deprive collaborators like PPF's Doriot of the influence with the Germans engendered by their connexion with the legion. In late 1942, Himmler suggested to Hitler that a French SS regiment be raised in addition to the existing LVF. Within the SS there had so far been a certain aversion of French participation, but the increased need of personnel changed this and France joined the club of Germanic countries.[108] Unlike LVF, the French regiment, which was upgraded to 'assault brigade' in the process, should accept only men who were 'SS worthy' and of Germanic appearance.

On 22 July 1943, Laval proclaimed the formation of the regiment and, over the next six months, 30 officers, 44 NCOs and 1,614 soldiers signed up. The unit, *Französisches SS-Freiwilligen-Sturmbrigade*, was formed at Sennheim under the leadership of a Swiss former army officer, *Sturmbannführer* Heinrich Hersche who spoke French, which was the command language of the assault brigade.[109] During a new stint at the front in 1944, the LVF sustained heavy casualties fighting the Red Army. During re-organisation at Greifenburg in East Prussia, the remnants were swallowed by the assault brigade, which was now made an SS division named after Charles the Great: *33. Waffen-Grenadier-Division der SS Charlemagne*. However, despite the influx from LVF this division never reached beyond brigade strength.[110]

Although Hitler was not impressed by the French soldiers, many fought with a fervour equal to that of the North-European Germanic volunteers and, for example, personnel of *Division Charlemagne* continued to fight in Berlin during the last days of the war.[111]

Like the north Europeans, many French volunteers came from pro-Nazi and Fascist environments. A German report of November 1943 states that, while 20 per cent came from PPF and other Fascist groups like the RNP, 10 per cent had links to the Vichy militia *La MiliceFrançaise*.[112] However, not all volunteers joined because of political or ideological persuasion. Forced labourers in Germany might improve their condition markedly by signing up for military service.[113]

---

106. Jackson (2003), p 192.
107. Shields (2007), p 85ff., and Gordon (1980), p 245ff.
108. BAB, NS19/3888, Undated speech (1944) by Gottlob Berger.
109. Gordon (1980), p 265ff. Estes (2008), Chapter 4.
110. BAMA, N756/208/a, *Übername der Französischen Legion (LVF)*. Jüttner, 26 October 1944, and Gordon (1980), p 265.
111. Hans W. Neulen, *An deutscher Seite: internationale Freiwillige von Wehrmacht und Waffen-SS* (Universitas, 1992), p 110. The casualties of the 1,000 strong battalion were severe, probably more than 750.
112. Jackson (2003), p 194ff.
113. Gordon (1980), p 267ff. See also Robert Forbes, *For Europe: The French Volunteers of the Waffen-SS* (Stackpole Books, 2010), p 22ff.

As early as 1942, Berger noticed with mixed feelings that the Wallonian legion raised under the auspices of the army at about the same time as the Germanic legions, did not show the same teething troubles as did the legions of the SS.[114] In January 1943, the leader of the Fascist *Rexist* movement, Léon Degrelle, launched a campaign to persuade Berlin that the Wallonians were actually a Germanic tribe who, under the influence of Rome and France, had lost their Germanic language. On this background Degrelle suggested that the legion be made a part of the SS.[115] Initially Berger had reservations but in May 1943, at a meeting with Himmler, Degrelle got the recognition of the Wallonians as a Germanic people. Then, the legion was transformed into the *5. SS-Freiwilligen-Sturmbrigade Wallonien* with Degrelle as its political leader.[116]

In October 1944, the assault brigade was re-named *28. SS-Freiwilligen-Panzer-Grenadier-Division Wallonien*. When in April 1945, it was annihilated in tough battle with the Red Army on the Oder, Degrelle managed to escape to Spain where he lived until his death in 1995. The Wallonian, whom Himmler had elevated to the status of Germanic man, never relinquished his Nazi creed and he became a central figure in the European neo-Nazi and Fascist milieus after the war.

In the course of the Second World War, also a large group of Italians ended up in the Waffen-SS.[117] In September 1943, Italy seceded from the alliance of Axis Powers, and Mussolini subsequently founded the *Fascist Repubblica Sociale Italiana*, based in the German occupied northern parts of the country. This was the beginning of admission to the SS of those Italians who still wanted to be part of the German war effort.[118] The men in question were a mixture of diehard party members since the 1920s or youngsters, who had been brought up with the Fascist ideology of the youth organisations, and whose motives were loyalty to Mussolini and Fascism.[119] Moreover, many volunteers simply wanted to escape Italy because they feared the personal

---

114. Letter of 9 April 1942 from Berger to Rauter, reprinted as document 141 in 'T Veld (1976) vol. 1, p 687. BAB, NS19/1557, Letter of 2 April 1942 from Berger to Himmler, *Belgische Frage.*
115. Jay Howard Geller, 'The Rôle of Military Administration in German Occupied Belgium, 1940–1944', *The Journal of Military History*, Vol. 63, No. 1, 1999, p 118ff. Estes (2008), Chapter 4. *Hauptamt*'s alleged reservation was not as bad as not to mention the Wallonians on a par with French and Estonians as possible soldiers in the future Germanic armoured corps. BAB, NS19/1735, Letter of 10 February 1943 from *Germanische Leitstelle* to Himmler.
116. Geller (1999), p 121.
117. Also, a number of Spaniards, ca. 1,000, joined the Waffen-SS. About these, see Estes (2008), Chapter 3, and Wayne H. Bowen, 'The Ghost Battalion: Spaniards in the Waffen-SS, 1944–1945', *Historian*, Vol. 63, No.2, 2001, pp 373–385.
118. There has only been limited research of the Italian Waffen-SS. The most important investigation was made by Carlo Gentile, '*Zwischen Ideologie und Opportunismus: Die Italiener und die SS 1943–1945*'. Unpublished paper, *Himmler's Super-National Militia: Indigenous Participation in SS and Police Units in the Context of the Second World War*, UMK Institute of History and Archival Science in Torun, 2014. See also Thomas Casagrande, *Südtiroler in der Waffen-SS*, (Raetia, 2016), pp 140–154.
119. Gentile (2014).

consequences of defeat. The brutal German suppression of partisans, frequently involving Italians on both sides, indicated a violent post-war reckoning.[120]
Already in August 1943, when Italy was clearly on the brink of military collapse, Himmler ordered the formation of special battalions for Italian volunteers and, in the long term, he envisaged raising two Italian SS divisions.[121] On 7 September 1944, Jüttner ordered the formation of the *Waffen-Grenadier-Brigade der SS (italienische Nr. 1)* and, in October, Berger claimed that 15,000 men were on their way to the training area Münsingen in Germany, where the brigade was to be formed.[122] Towards the conclusion of the war, the units of this brigade were employed against partisans in northern Italy – an employment characterised by a steady trickle of desertions.[123]
The military value of the Italian units varied and their employment at the front was very modest. In the early autumn 1943, several lesser Italian units operated on the German side – For example, the second SS armoured corps employed an Italian battalion against partisans in Istria, though with meagre results.[124] However, other Italian SS forces actually clashed with the Allies. Thus, in the early summer 1944, an Italian battle group, probably the one which was later named *Kampfgruppe Binz*, faced the advancing Allies in Italy and, according to an internal German evaluation – performed fairly well.[125]

Who Joined – and Why

Although throughout the war, there was a steady decline in recruiting standards, also as far as the Germanic volunteer was concerned, certain physical and racial requirements remained. In Denmark, about half of those applying for service were admitted, and a similar ratio applied for Norway.[126] While the numbers concerning

120. Keith Lowe, *Savage Continent: Europe in the Aftermath of World War II* (Viking, 2012), p 150.
121. BAMA, N756/196, RFSS, 31 August 1943; Gentile (2014).
122. BAMA, N756/196, *Aufstellung der Waffen-Gren. Brigade der SS (italienische Nr. 1)*, 7 September 1944. BAMA, N756/196, Berger, 19.10.1943. Gentile (2014) gives a somewhat lower figure, viz. 13.000 men. Other sources estimate that 10,000, excluding the German speaking minority in Alto Adige/Südtirol, served with the Waffen-SS and police formations under the SS. NAKEW, WO 208/4517, Memo concerning. Karl Wolff January 1968, p 2. For same figures in another source see NAKEW, WO204/12990, Extracts from PWB Report on Conditions in Occupied Italy, No. 28, 8 October 1944.
123. BAMA, RH3-29/2, *Kampfgruppe Binz, Starke und Bewaffnung der Kampfgruppe Binz*, 14 March 1945. On desertions, see NAKEW, WO204/12990, Extracts from PWB Report on Conditions in Occupied Italy, No. 28, 8 October 1944.
124. BAMA, RS2-2/20, KTB Nr. 7, den 3.8.1943–3.12.1943, entry on 27 October and 24 November 1943.
125. BAB, NS19/3297, *Notiz über eine Besprechung beim Reichsführer SS am 29.5.1944.* See also NAKEW, WO204/12990, Extracts from PWB Report on Conditions in Occupied Italy, No. 28, 8 October 1944.
126. Christensen et al. (1998), p 365ff. Svein Blindheim, *Nordmenn under Hitlers fane: dei norske frontkjemparane* (Noreg, 1977), p 7. This must be seen in the context of the number of rejections in the start of the war.

Flanders is unknown, in the Netherlands, apparently, out of 30,000 applicants 25,000 were admitted.[127] The explanation of the modest rejection rate might be the fact that the recruitment also included the *Landstorm Nederland*, a kind of home guard under the SS with lower entry conditions.[128]

Although among the Germanic volunteers the reasons for volunteering varied a great deal, a large group was clearly ideologically motivated. Apart from the way that youngsters from Nazi households were sometimes expected by parents and friends to sign up, it is noteworthy that there were no elements of coercion attached to recruitment. Basically, the political motives seem to have been slightly more prominent among the Scandinavians compared to their counterparts in Belgium and the Netherlands – but everywhere political issues in combination with personal and family networks played a pivotal role in recruiting efforts. About half the Danish applicant were organised Nazis, and it is assumed that around 25 per cent more had some connexion with the Nazi settings.[129] The situation in Belgium and the Netherlands was probably more diverse, although many there had connexions to NSB or VNV or other Nazi groupings. A survey of 450 young Dutch, who served with the German colours has shown that many signed up during the so-called 'hunger months' in the winter 1944-1945. At that time the daily food rations in the western Netherlands contained as little as 600 kcal. Even among the young from NSB homes there was a remarkable absence of conscious political motives.[130] In comparison with Denmark and Norway, apparently, the proportion of organised Nazis was somewhat smaller. In the Netherlands, an estimated 40 per cent were members of the NSB.[131] In Belgium, too, the motives of some volunteers were characterised by the possibility of economic gain.[132] A number of Flemish volunteers were recruited under false pretensions being told that they were on their way to well-paid jobs in the eastern occupation zones.[133] To volunteers with families it might also have been part of the motivation that their family might buy food in well-supplied SS shops instead of having to haggle on the black market.[134]

---

127. Zee (1967), p 58. 'T Veld (1976), vol. 1, p 408.
128. On *Landstorm Nederland*, see ibid., p 372ff.
129. Vegard Säther, *'En av oss': Norske frontkjempere i krig og fred* (Cappelen Damm, 2010). Christensen et al. (1998), p 39ff.
130. Henry L. Mason, *The Purge of Dutch Quislings: Emergency Justice in the Netherlands* (Martinus Nijhoff, 1952), p 22ff. A Dutch SS-deserter estimated 1941, based, inter alia, on his experiences at the SS prep-school in Sennheim that the main motive among the volunteers were 50 per cent Nazi persuasion, 20 per cent wished to escape from debt, prosecution etc., and 30 per cent were adventurers. BB, E27, 1000/721, Archive No. 9928, vol. 2, D110, *Bericht über die Einvernahme eines Uof. der holländischen Armee*, 4 November 1941, p 3.
131. 'T Veld (1976), vol. 1, p 408.
132. Mason (1952), p 25, note 62. It should be noted that many joined with the prospect of serving in their own country. The risk of being involved in actual combat may have appeared remote to this specific group as opposed to those joining Waffen-SS front units.
133. Stein (1984), p 154ff.
134. Wever (1984), p 152ff.

In all North and West-European countries it was a minority of the young men who decided to join. In the summer 1943, the SS made a survey of this state of affairs, and, with only small variations, the four big Germanic countries showed a similar modest outcome of 0.1 per cent of the total male population.[135] Despite the possibility of striking the anti-Bolshevist chord, in particular immediately after Operation Barbarossa, the SS did not succeed in attracting other than the most fervent pro-Germans, radical right-wing groups, and people with socio-economical and perhaps other kinds of problems. The fact that Germany was an occupying power clearly obscured the anti-Communist reasoning. This can be seen in an SD report from Norway. The report, which was conceived shortly after the invasion of the Soviet Union, described the popular reactions to Barbarossa and the conclusion was clear: Until the attack, the public feeling in Norway had been decidedly anti-Soviet because of its onslaught on Finland, but now the SD noticed many statements to the effect that together with the United Kingdom and the United States, the USSR represented the civilised world's struggle against Nazi barbarism.[136] In Denmark, the mood was more or less as dismissive. A thorough survey of public opinion during the occupation period shows that there were mixed feelings as to which was the gravest threat to Denmark, Germany or the Soviet Union, but there was 'scant sympathy' with participation in Germany's war.[137] During *Frikorps Danmmark*'s leave in Denmark in 1942 as well as at several later occasions, this was further stressed by the clashes between the soldiers and the civilian population.[138]

Ideology with Consequences

SS philosophy changed from elitist, German nationalism in the early 1930s, to Pan-Germanism early in the war and arrived at somewhat broader European Nazi worldview towards its end. Regardless, throughout the war, the belief the Germanic tribes were superior to other races was put into practical action time and time again.

For the Germanic volunteers this meant, among other things, that they quite often received preferential treatment in the SS legal system.[139] Even pro-English Norwegian policemen, who would normally be perceived as enemies, gained from this attitude.[140] In December 1943, after a large-scale purge of unreliable elements within the Norwegian

135. NAWA, T175, r.192, s.21574712. See also 'T Veld (1976), vol. 1, p 405ff. and Wever (1984), p 34.
136. Meldungen aus Norwegen Nr. 23 vom 16. Juli 1941, reprinted in Larsen (2008), p 337.
137. Palle Roslyng-Jensen, *Danskerne og besættelsen: holdninger og meninger 1939-1945* (Gads Forlag, 2007), p 162.
138. BAB, NS19/1863, Letter of 21 July 1943 from *Abt C II /RSHA* concerning the effect of recruitment for Waffen-SS.
139. See, for instance, an investigation of the Dutch volunteers' refusal to swear allegiance undertaken by the SS in 1944. It is reprinted as documents 503, 503I, 527, 531 and 586 in 'T Veld (1976), vol. 2. See also the Chapter on SS' judiciary.
140. Emberland and Kott (2012), pp 405–416.

police, 271 policemen were deported to Germany. They ended up in concentration camp Stutthof, but they were never treated in the same way as the ordinary detainees in this very tough camp, where 85,000 out of 110,000 prisoners died during the war. Instead of prison uniforms, the policemen were issued with Italian military clothing, they were fed German military ration packs in lieu of ordinary prison food, and the working conditions and accommodation were clement compared with other inmates. Treating the Norwegians this way was an SS attempt to win over the policemen for the Germanic cause. The Danish *Unterscharführer* Peter Lodahl Petersen – nicknamed the Germanic thane – presided over an ideological indoctrination programme. More than once, the Norwegians were encouraged to sign up for police service in occupied Europe or to join the Waffen-SS.[141] Although all the prisoners rejected these proposals the treatment remained mild to the end.[142]

Similar patience was shown a small group of UK citizens, who were recruited from prisoner-of-war camps to join a British *Freikorps*. From 1942 onwards, it was contemplated if – in connexion with a propaganda campaign in Great Britain – it might be worthwhile to raise a corps of British Fascists for employment at the eastern front. In the course of 1943, this project came under Waffen-SS and, in January 1944, such a force was formally organised. Nonetheless, recruiting in the camps to this unit – initially called the Legion of Saint George – had begun as early as July the year before. As British volunteers working with the project believed that that name was too directly referring to England, not Great Britain, the unit was re-designated the British Free Corps.[143] By the end of January 1944, this corps organised only 15 members and it never went beyond 50.[144] If it had not been for the soldiers' extensive privileges it would not have made any sense wasting space on subjects of a unit from a country with which Germany was still at war.[145] The closest these men ever came to actual combat with the German colours was, in 1945, when 12 of them were detailed to *Division Nordland*. There, their union jack sleeve badges raised an eyebrow or two

141. Henrik Skov Kristensen, *Straffelejren: Faarhus* (Nyt Nordisk Forlag, 2011), p 294.
142. For an almost similar case related to Norwegian students deported to Germany due to their pro-English sentiments see Jorunn Sem Fure, 'A vekke norske akademikeres rasebevissthet' in Fure and Emberland (2009), pp 244-261 and Michael Sars and Knut Erik Tranoy (eds.), *Tysklandsstudentene* (J.W. Cappelen, 1946).
143. Adrian Weale, *Renegades: Hitler's Englishmen* (Pimlico, 2002), p 89ff. See also Adrian Weale, *The SS: A New History* (Brown, 2010), p 279ff. BAMA, N756/233/a, Himmler's formation order 20 January 1944. For evidence on recruiting in November 1943 respectively July 1943, see NAKEW, HO45/25817, *Statement of Alfred Vivian Minchin 8 June 1945* and NAKEW, HO45/25820, *Statement of Kenneth Edward Jorden Berry, 3 July 1945*.
144. BAMA, N756/233/a, Berger to Himmler, 29 January 1944, *Aufstellung der britischen Freiwilligen-Einheit im Rahmen der Waffen-SS*. See also Weale (2002), Appendix 5, for a role of members. Apart from Englishmen, this unit comprised soldiers from New Zealand, South Africa, Canada and Australia. BAMA, N756/a *Aufstellung der britischen Freiwilligen-Einheit in Rahmen der Waffen-SS*, 29 January 1944.
145. NAKEW, HO45/25817, Statement of Alfred Vivian Minchin, 8 June 1945.

among the Scandinavian and Dutch volunteers.[146] Nevertheless, the not very gung-ho Brits managed to talk themselves out of contributing to the 'final struggle against Bolshevism'. Most of them spent the last part of the war performing traffic control, driving lorries, or helping refugees.[147]

Also, the general public in the Germanic countries were much more leniently treated by the SS than were citizens in southern Europe and, in particular, those of Slavonic areas. As early as 1940, Himmler reminded his men that the populations of the Germanic countries were kindred with Germans and should be won over for the German cause.[148] Although the SS did participate in atrocities in Germanic countries the general attitude was vastly different from the other occupied territories. Thus, in December 1944, Himmler instructed the HSSPF in the Essen area, Karl Gutenberger, that 70,000 Dutch refugees being evacuated to his region from the Arnhem area were to be 'treated well, because they were of Germanic stock and destined to fuse with the Reich'.[149]

---

146. Weale (2002), p 162.
147. NAKEW, HO45/25819, Movements of the British Free Corps undated note. Ibid., p 168.
148. Gingerich (1991), p 68ff.
149. Telex of 5 December 1944 from Himmler to K. Gutenberger, reprinted as document 606 in 'T Veld (1976), vol. 2, p 1441.

Chapter Nine

'VOLKSDEUTSCHE' IN THE WAFFEN-SS

In the mid-1930s, 10 million ethnic Germans lived in countries outside the three great, totally or partially, Germanophone states, Germany, Austria and Switzerland.[1] The most important, in this respect, were Czechoslovakia, the USSR and Poland, followed by the French regions of Alsace and Lorraine. Additionally, there were Germanophones in Yugoslavia, Romania, Hungary and Italy (Alto Adige), as well as in the Baltic countries, eastern Belgium, and in southern Denmark.[2]

From a Nazi point of view, all these groups – the *Volksdeutsche* – were of 'German blood' and, ideally, ought to be united in a Greater German Reich. However, the right to speak on behalf of the German minorities was fraught with internal struggles over power and responsibilities among various Nazi institutions. The primary contenders were Alfred Rosenberg's *Außenpolitisches Amt* (APA), the party's foreign department, *Auslands-Organisation der NSDAP* (AO) and not least the foreign ministry, *Auswärtiges Amt*, under Joachim von Ribbentrop. The latter forged an alliance with Himmler and the SS in order to clip the wings of APA, Rosenberg and AO. Moreover, a number of private organisations wielded their influence. One of these the *Verein für das Deutschtum im Ausland* was an establishment that, since the days of the Weimar Republic, was co-operating with the German state.

In 1935, Rudolf Hess, Hitler's party deputy, ordered that a new party office be set up to cover this area. The SS member, Otto von Kursell, became head of this office. While he purposively implemented the *Gleichschaltung* – Nazi regimentation – of the organisations of the German minorities, he tried to keep aloof of the conflicts. To Himmler, the appointment of Kursell became a means to increase the influence of the SS and, gradually, his office managed to out-manoeuvre other players in this field. In 1936, however, a disagreement arose between Kursell and Himmler. Consequently, in 1937, Kursell was dismissed as the head of the office, which, from then onwards, was designated *Volksdeutsche Mittelstelle* (VOMI).

---

1. Apart from these countries, there were 285,000 Germanophones in Luxembourg and 10,000 in Liechtenstein.
2. Valdis O. Lumans, *Himmler's Auxiliaries. The Volksdeutsche Mittelstelle and the German National Minorities of Europe, 1933–1945* (University of North Carolina Press, 1993), pp 22 and 38. See also Robert Herzog, *Die Volksdeutschen in der Waffen-SS* (Institut für Besatzungsfragen, 1955), p 2, and Doris L. Bergen, 'The Nazi Concept of "Volksdeutsche" and the Exacerbation of Anti-Semitism in Eastern Europe, 1939–45' in *Journal of Contemporary History*, Vol. 29, No. 4, October 1994, pp 569–582.

Although VOMI was never integrated in the SS, in reality, from the mid-1930s, it functioned as a de facto SS office with Himmler as the top boss. Like his predecessor, the new head, Werner Lorenz, as well as his chief of staff, Hermann Behrends, were high-ranking SS officers. In particular after Himmler's appointment as *Reichskommissar für die Festigungdeutschen Volkstums* in 1939, VOMI became involved, under SS control, in activities concerning *Volksdeutsche* in the occupied countries – predominantly recruitment for the Waffen-SS.[3]

Recruitment of Volksdeutsche

In 1944, 150,000 Waffen-SS men – a fourth of the total strength – were from *Volksdeutsche* communities. At the end of the war, this figure had risen to 300,000, or almost a third of all the soldiers, who had passed through the ranks of the Waffen-SS.[4] Since no systematic recruitment had taken place before the war, this volume was the result of merely a few year's focused efforts. Moreover, the VOMI had been holding back anxious not to offend the home countries of the *Volksdeutsche*.[5] This attitude had worked well with the SS' priorities that, from the inter-war period up to 1942, were focused on recruiting the very best and using the military service to tie the minorities as close as possible to the Third Reich – and in particular to the SS.[6]

However, the same reserve did not apply to several hundred thousand of *Volksdeutsche* who, after Hitler's and Stalin's partition of Eastern Europe, immigrated to Germany. They came from the areas that the Soviet Union annexed in 1939–1940; viz. the Baltic States, eastern Poland, as well as the Romanian provinces Bukovina and Bessarabia. Waffen-SS recruiting officers got first choice in the transit camps for these immigrants. And such camps were run by the VOMI.[7] They enthusiastically exploited the fact that the new-comers were not eligible for German national service until such a time when they became German citizens. Therefore, recruiting among these the SS might bypass the *Wehrmacht*.[8]

As early as in 1941, the SS began to coerce *Volksdeutsche* in occupied areas into the Waffen-SS. Immediately after the conquest of Serbia, a Waffen-SS muster commission had recruited a large number and, as of August 1941, Serbian *Volksdeutsche*

3. On the relations between SS and VOMI, see Lumans (1993), p 31ff.
4. Stein (1984), p 168. In January of that year Himmler mentioned that 140,000 *Volksdeutsche* from Romania, Slovakia and Hungary had been admitted. BAB, NS19/4012, *Rede des Reichsführers-SS, Reichsinnenminister Himmler auf der Tagung der RPA-Leiter am 28. Januar 1944.* Lumans in Marble (2012), p 223.
5. Lumans (1993), p 211ff.
6. Herzog (1995), p 6.
7. Lumans (1993).
8. Only few documents concerning the SS' recruitment in the immigrant camps have survived. Some insight may be gained from the Moscow based material from the *Fürsorge und Versorgungsamt der Waffen-SS* (RGVA, 1372/3). See, for example, RGVA, 1372/3/97, *Der SS-Fürsorgeführer 'Warthe' to Fürsorge- und Versorgungsamt der Waffen-SS, Betr.: Fürsorgebericht für Monat Mai 1940,* 1 June 1940.

were conscripted to the Waffen-SS. Over the following years, 22,000 ethnic Germans were conscripted from Serbia and the so-called Banat – the plain between the Danube and Romania.[9] In August 1942, internal SS documents stated that soldiers of *Division Prinz Eugen* were no longer volunteers as they were drafted under the 'threat of sanctions'.[10]

The ambition went beyond the confines of Serbia. It was Himmler's perception that, due to their racial attachment to Germany, the German minorities everywhere in the occupied countries were under obligation to enlist for military service with the Third Reich. 'Those who do not sign up shall see their homes demolished', was Berger's candid remark referring to Serbia and Romania.[11] In other words, the attitude was that all *Volksdeutsche* males had a de facto obligation to volunteer. No legal basis and no publicity were sought. In August 1942, Himmler declared that, from then on, he would regard all men to be under obligation to serve but that, for political reasons, this had to be kept secret.[12] The leaderships of the minorities were instrumentalised in forcing the young men into service with the Waffen-SS, and the governments of the various countries were persuaded to let their *Volksdeutsche* youth do their national service with the Waffen-SS rather than with their mother countries' armies.[13] Over the following years, in parallel with adoption of more or less wide-ranging agreements with Croatia, Slovakia, Hungary and Romania; the pressure on the Germanophone minorities all-over Europe increased. This created the basis for employing hundreds of thousands of *Volksdeutsche* soldiers during the last war years.

The massive influx made almost all Waffen-SS formations end up with huge numbers of *Volksdeutsche*. Although the formations raised relatively late in the war like *Prinz Eugen, Horst Wessel, Nordland, Division Reichsführer-SS* and the 31st Division saw the largest proportions, the earlier division also had their share. Moreover, quite a few *Volksdeutsche* were employed as concentration camp guards.[14]

Romania and Hungary

Two of the largest ethnic German communities in Europe were those of Romania with 750,000 members and Hungary with 500,000. It was from these two countries that the bulk of the *Volksdeutsche* soldiers came. From Romania 63,000 filed into the Waffen-SS and an even larger arrived from Hungary.[15] Alone after the German

---

9. Lumans (1993), p 235.
10. BAB, NS7/91, Internal letter from *Hauptamt SS-Gericht, Überstellung ungarischer und volksdeutscher Freiwilligen zur Arbeitsabteilung der Waffen-SS bei Dienstverweigerung*, 18 November 1942.
11. BAB, NS7/91, *Aktenvermerk für SS-Oberführer Bender, Wehrpflicht der Volksdeutschen aus dem Südost-Raum*, 14 February 1945.
12. Nuremberg document NO-2038, Letter from *SS Richter beim Reichsführer-SS* to *SS-Standartenführer Dr. Brandt, Wehrpflicht der deutschen aus den Volksgruppen*, 19 February 1945.
13. Lumans (1993), p 215.
14. See the list of the distribution of *Volksdeutsche* recruits in BAB, NS19/4.
15. Numbers from Lumans (1993), p 22.

occupation of Hungary in 1944, 40,000 were forcibly enrolled.[16] Nevertheless, even much smaller communities of Germans abroad rendered a relativily high contribution, and in Denmark, for example, 1,500 men from the minority of about 30–40,000 joined the Waffen-SS, even though the SS authorities put significantly less pressure on the Germans here than in the Balkans.[17]

Recruitment in Romania was directed by the *Volksdeutsche* SS officer, Andreas Schmidt, who had close ties with Berger's *Hauptamt* and, in March 1941, married Berger's daughter, Krista. From October 1939 to June 1940, he successfully conducted a secret recruiting campaign of 1,000 Romanians and, subsequently, became the leader of the minority's organisation.[18]

Up to the assault on the Soviet Union, the relations between the SS and the foreign ministry deteriorated. The Germans wanted the Romanian army to play a significant role in the operation, and for this reason there was no wish to upset the allies. Nevertheless, neither Berger nor Schmidt stopped their recruiting efforts, which made Ribbentrop demand that all further admission of Romanians to the Waffen-SS was terminated. Himmler, however, carried on clandestinely and, between autumn 1941 and spring 1943, 6,000 Romanians entered the Waffen-SS.[19] Early 1943, after the defeat at Stalingrad, for the first time recruitment in Romania was undertaken legally. During the fighting in southern Russia a large number of Romanian *Volksdeutsche* had been absorbed into German formations. As Hitler as well as many others among the German leaders saw the defeat as partly due to the incompetence of their allies, he forbade re-integration of *Volksdeutsche* into the Romanian army. In early March, therefore, Ribbentrop asked the embassy in Bucharest to draft an agreement allowing Romanian *Volksdeutsche* to serve in the German ranks.[20] After its approval in April the same year, the SS launched a recruiting campaign in the country that resulted in 50,000 new recruits by the turn of the year. Together with earlier and later campaigns as well as recruitment of Romanian *Volksdeutsche* outside Romania these efforts made 63,000 Romanians serve with the German colours.[21]

Unlike the Serbians, the *Volksdeutsche* Romanians had the option of doing national service with their own army, but compared with the attitude in neighbouring Hungary the willingness during the 1943-campaign to join the Waffen-SS was immense. This had several reasons. Many of those recruited were either deserters from the Romanian army or men, who might expect to be conscripted for it, and it was known to exercise a brutal discipline.[22] Flogging was still a common method

---

16. Concerning numbers see Milata (2009), p 217. On Hungary, see Norbert Spannenberger, *Der Volksbund der Deutschen in Ungarn 1938–1944 unter Horthy und Hitler*, 2nd edition (R. Oldenbourg, 2005).
17. On their number see Christensen et al. (1998).
18. The following is based on Milata (2009).
19. Milata (2009), p 77ff and 217.
20. Ibid., pp 134ff.
21. Ibid., p 217.
22. Ibid., p 58ff.

of punishment.[23] Moreover, the pay and the support of relatives were better with the Waffen-SS – at least on paper. The huge numbers admitted in 1943, however, entailed difficulties concerning the promised payment to the soldiers' next of kin.[24] But nobody knew of this when joining. Another positive element was that, after the signature of the recruiting agreement, the soldiers might retain their Romanian citizenship.[25]

In Hungary, too, the process was characterised by the country's status as one of Germany's closest allies, and Berger and Himmler therefore had to consider the foreign ministry as well as Hungarian authorities. During the inter-war years, the Hungarian *Volksdeutsche* organisations had been Nazified just as the Romanian ones. I 1938 *Volksbund der Deutschen in Ungarn (VDU)* was the central organisation in that regard and at that time it was under Nazi control.

A year after Hungary in 1939 had joined the Anti-Comintern Pact, it annexed the north-western parts of Romania with the support of Germany and Italy. Not only were the majorities of these areas – Transylvania (Siebenbürgen) and Satu Mare (Sathmar) – Hungarian, there was also a German minority of 45,000. In return for Germany's support of the annexation, Hungary recognised VDU as the only legitimate representative of the country's *Volksdeutsche* who, from then on, was treated as one unified group.[26]

However, the relations between the Hungarian authorities and the *Volksdeutsche* remained strained, and it did not improve at the Hungarian annexation of a piece of the Yugoslav region Batschka. On that occasion, 175,000 were added to the group of *Volksdeutsche* already living in Hungary. Many of the Batschka newcomers had been looking forward to becoming German citizens and had no inclination to becoming Hungarians. The Germans saw the Hungarian army, like that of Romania, as an ally in the upcoming operations against Russia. This meant that VOMI as well as the SS had to tread carefully not to upset the uneasy balance between these two countries. SS' first recruiting happened secretly; men of the *Volksdeutsche* minority were brought to Germany under the guise of having to work in war production. However, while only 500 Hungarians volunteered, in the autumn 1941, 2,000 from the Batschka region joined the Waffen-SS.[27] The illegal recruiting, though, soon created strained relations with the German foreign ministry as well as with Hungarian authorities. It was not until January 1942, after tough negotiations with the Hungarians, that the first legal recruiting effort was begun. Facilitated by Ribbentrop the Germans were now allowed to recruit up to 20,000 – a number that the Hungarians regarded as utterly unrealistic.[28]

---

23. Mark Axworthy, 'Peasant Scapegoat to Industrial Slaughter: The Romanian Soldier at the Siege of Odessa' in Paul Addison and Angus Calder (eds.), *Time to Kill: The Soldiers' Experience in the West, 1939–1945* (Pimlico, 1997), p 229.
24. See documents in the package *Akten betreffend Rumänien Familienunterhalt. 1941–1944*, RGVA, 1372/3/450.
25. Milata (2009), p 212ff.
26. Lumans (1993), p 222.
27. Ibid., p 224; Spannenberger (2005), p 311.
28. Spannenberger (2005), p 309ff.

Moreover, there were certain constraints hampering recruitment; viz. *Volksdeutsche* who were already serving with the Hungarian army were out of bounds, economic allowances for next of kin were not to exceed the level in the Hungarian army, and those enlisted would have their Hungarian citizenship annulled right away. Nonetheless, thanks to an intensive campaign and a considerable pressure placed upon the *Volksdeutsche* men, the target number was practically reached. In the summer 1942, SS' own people noted that not only was huge 'moral pressure' applied to the young men, there were also incidents where windows were smashed if the sons failed to 'volunteer'.[29]

It was obvious that the Waffen-SS saw the Hungarians as a valuable resource. The following year, Himmler ordered a renewed effort with a view to enrolling another 30–50,000 from among the 100,000 Volksdeutsche serving with the Hungarian colours.[30] In May 1943, that kind of recruitment was agreed to. Hungary wanted to reduce her participation at the eastern front, and the *Volksdeutsche* were a useful bargaining chip vis-à-vis the Germans. Over the summer, about 18,000 soldiers were enlisted, but the renewed effort never reached its ambitious aim. A third recruitment wave was set in motion when, in March 1944, the Hungarian government probed for peace among the western Allied Powers. Subsequently, Germany occupied the country and propped up a pro-German administration. Now, the SS was let loose and all *Volksdeutsche* men between 17 and 35 were now drafted into the Waffen-SS. This meant an addition of 40,000 soldiers of whom the vast majority was involuntarily enrolled. Those who tried to avoid German military service by joining the Hungarian army were rejected by Hungarian authorities. In total, 120,000 Hungarian *Volksdeutsche* passed through the organisations of either the Waffen-SS or other SS formations making the country the biggest contributor of foreign soldiers to the German war effort. Most of those serving with the Waffen-SS went to 18th *SS-Freiwilligen-Panzer-Grenadier-Division Horst Wessel* or the 31st *SS-Freiwilligen Grenadier-Division* – both examples of late-raised formations with primarily *Volksdeutsche* personnel. The 31st division, which for no known reason never received an honorary title like most other SS divisions, was made up primarily of soldiers from the Batschka region. The division received its many new, forcibly enrolled recruits in October 1944. Much key personnel were the left-overs from the Muslim Kama Division which had been dissolved earlier the same year. Officers and NCOs were, as in most *Volksdeutsche* formations, from the Reich. Thus, in many ways, this division's characteristics were like those of the other of its kind, but different from the distinct German-Germanic Waffen-SS formations. The bulk of the personnel came from the same, fairly secluded community, speaking the same language and same dialect, shared identical local loyalties, and had the same religious background. In many cases, they knew each

---

29. RGVA, 1372/3/141, *Fürsorge- und Versorgungsamt der Waffen-SS 'Ausland', Tätigkeitsbericht der SS-Feldpostprüfstelle vom Monat Mai 1942*, 31 July 1942.
30. Spannenberger (2005), p 320.

other beforehand. Only about 15 per cent were between 20 and 30 years of age. The remainder of the personnel were either quite young or rather old.[31]

Why Join?

While a considerable number of *Volksdeutsche* did not sign up voluntarily, there were many who did despite the fact that a lot of them might have chosen to serve with their own country's armed forces. In the autumn 1942, the VOMI made a survey of the reasons why ethnic German Hungarians joined. No doubt, the primary motive was the belief that the struggle for the Third Reich was a destiny shared by Germany and the *Volksdeutsche* communities.[32] Similarly, ideological motivation seems to have been a key issue among many.[33] But in countries like Romania and Hungary, there might have been other important ground such as fear of harassment if one served in the national army and the possibility of economic benefits.[34]

To get an illustration of the importance of the treatment within the national armed forces one might take a look at the Slovak ethnic Germans. Since Hitler's annexation in 1939 of Bohemia and Moravia, Slovenskýštát (the Slovak Republic) became a German client state. The *Volksdeutsche* included ca. four per cent of the population and enjoyed extensive autonomy. In this country, the early recruitment for the Waffen-SS was disappointing. In January 1940, only 140 had joined and, by the end of 1942, 600 had signed up. A major reason was that, unlike the Hungarian and the Romanian armies, the Slovak Army treated the *Volksdeutsche* very well. The soldiers served in their own units and, frequently, under the minority's own officers. It was not until 1942, when the Slovak government accepted that the *Volksdeutsche* had to do their national service with the Waffen-SS, that the process got under way.[35] Until April 1944, this change allowed conscription of another 5,000 men.[36] A new attempt was made in the autumn 1944, when all men between 18 and 35 years of age were called up, but the outcome of this is unknown.[37]

---

31. Lumans (1993), p 226. The surviving documents are fragmentary, and the following is based on Rudolf Pencz, *For the Homeland! The History of the 31st Waffen-SS Volunteer Grenadier Division* (Helion & Company, 2002). Unfortunately, this book appears without any notes for which reason it is difficult to see on what grounds Pencz builds. However, it is obvious that the author has used various source material, primarily from the Military Archive in Freiburg. However, there is no divisional archive there.

32. Spannenberger (2005), p 322.

33. Milata (2009). See in particular p 174ff.

34. Spannenberger (2005), p 322.

35. Lumans in Marble (2012), p 204ff.

36. NAKEW, GFM 33/2256, Letter of 11 April 1944 from *Deutsche Gesandtschaft Pressburg* to *Auswärtiges Amt betr. Transport der zur Waffen-SS eingerükten Volksdeutschen aus der Slovakei.* Forbackground see ibid.: *Auswärtiges Amt, Abt. Deutschland, Vortrags-Notiz,* 17 August 1942 and telegram 1280 from *Deutsche Gesandtschaft Pressburg to Auswärtiges Amt,* 12 August 1942.

37. NAKEW, GFM 33/2256, Letter of 20 September 1944 from *Deutsche Gesandtschaft Pressburg* to *Auswärtiges Amt betr. Schreiben des Reichsarbeitsführers [...] von 4.9.44.*

Many *Volksdeutsche* recruits had economic motives. There was, for example, a striking discrepancy between a Romanian soldier's pay and that of a Waffen-SS man, and only the SS provided family support. A training report from *SS-Grenadier-Ausbildungs-Bataillon Ost* explains how, in a society of shortage, joining the Waffen-SS might lead to improved living conditions. In the late summer 1943, it was told that 900 *Volksdeutsche* had arrived. However, some of the new recruits from Ukraine, Hungary and Slovakia were not at all *Volksdeutsche*, they merely claimed so in order to obtain better circumstances.[38] On the other hand, deciding to volunteer for the Waffen-SS in Denmark – a country characterized by a comparatively high living standard and low unemployment during most of the war – was hardly motivated by monetary reasons.

The question why 300,000 *Volksdeutsche* men happened to serve with the Waffen-SS can be adequately answered only by scrutinising it in connexion with the relevant temporal and geographical situation. Over time, the enlistment method changed from voluntariness to conscription of large groups of the populations. The basis for this was the successful Nazification of almost all *Volksdeutsche* organisations, German control of the countries where these groups lived, and the extensive scope of action which the SS was given or usurped.

The Experience of the Volksdeutsche in the Waffen-SS

How did the encounter between the *Volksdeutsche* soldiers and the Waffen-SS evolve? Of course, the situation varied according to circumstances like the soldiers' national background, motivation and the time of joining. The first volunteers joining the *Verfügungstruppe* in the 1930s were convinced Nazis. They were highly motivated and thoroughly selected by the SS. Therefore, they were positive and willing to submit to many ordeals, maybe they even saw the harsh treatment as a testimony to being an élite force. However, as the war progressed and forced enrolment began the situation changed. One reason might have been the disappointing realities of attrition and shortage that met the personnel upon arrival at the fronts.[39]

Moreover, the chaotic situation of the welfare system contributed to making the SS unpopular with the troops as well as at home. It has already been touched upon that the allowances for the families were paid irregularly and, what was worse, in many cases the next of kin were not informed of the demise of their loved ones and did not receive the pensions they were entitled to, or they had to live with never getting the fallen soldier's belongings sent home.[40] With those concerned these kinds

---

38. VAP, Höhere SS- und Polizeiführer Russland Süd, folder 18, SS Gren. Ausb. Btl. Ost. Ausbildungsbericht für den Monat August 1943.
39. Milata (2009), p 235ff.
40. On Romania see documents in package *Akten betreffend Rumänien Familienunterhalt.1941–1944*, RGVA, 1372/3/450. On Hungary see BAB, NS19/2016, *Tätigkeitsbericht der SS-Feldpostprüfstelle für August 1942*. On Transnistria see RGVA, 1372/3/43, Letter of 24 June 1943 from SS-Ogruff. Prütz mannto Gottlob Berger. RGVA, 1372/3/43, *SS-Hauptamt-Nachrichtstelle*, 24 June 1943 and RGVA, 1372/3/43, *SS-Hauptamt-Nachrichtstelle*, 24 June 1943. Examples from Christensen et al. (1998), p 384ff.

of failures and deficiencies were not well received. However, this did not necessarily happen due to arrogance towards the *Volksdeutsche* on the part of the SS. Because of the immense workload, the SS often showed similar shortcomings vis-a-vis Reich German soldiers' families.[41]

To many *Volksdeutsche* German was not their native tongue, and linguistic problems were pervasive and recurring. In October 1940, the *HSSPF Ost* noted that the huge numbers of *Volksdeutsche* did not have a proper command of German and, consequently, wrote in Polish. This had caused the field post offices to complain about difficulties of a practical nature as well as concerning censorship routines.[42] The dearth of proficiency in German forced the responsible officers to offer – on their own account – language lessons to the soldiers. This happened, for example by the eighth Squadron, later to become part of the Cavalry Brigade, which at the end of 1940 received a good many Romanian *Volksdeutsche*.[43]

In a report concerning the training of *Volksdeutsche* in 1940 one gets a closer insight into the challenges produced by cultural disparities and linguistic troubles. In January, 1,000 recruits aged 17 to 40 years arrived to the SS camp in Babruisk from Romania. Generally, they were peasants and artisans from rural areas, they spoke a coarse dialect and were hardly able to express themselves in High German. The men were described as backward due to their rural upbringing and their learning ability was limited. According to this report, the mood upon arrival was good. As most of them had disappointing experiences from the Romanian army, they held positive expectations of the training and leadership levels in the Waffen-SS. In October, the enthusiasm had abated, which the instructors believed to be due to false presumptions concerning the nature of the service, but most of them adapted nevertheless. However, the underlying attitude was negative thus emphasising the obvious clash of cultures. This materialised as a lack of understanding of the way German discipline worked, not least the use of collective punishment. As to this report, apparently, they would have preferred that the culprit himself got a sound thrashing like in the Romanian army. The NCOs complained that the soldiers apologised instead of actually doing something to improve. Moreover, there was no turn for the better when several acted cowardly in their first enemy engagements and generally lacked fighting spirit and understanding of the greater cause.[44] The report concluded that the Romanian *Volksdeutsche* seemed to follow the rule that 'my stomach is my god – and additionally abundant rest'.[45]

---

41. Example in RGVA, 1372/3/98, *SS-Fürsorgeführer 'Ostsee', Wehrkreis II, Fürsorgebericht August 1941*.
42. VAP, *8. SS-Kav.Div. 'FG' 2, 1. SS Totenkopf-Reiterregiment, Warschau*, 24 October 1940.
43. VAP, *8. SS-Kav.Div. 'FG' 3, Tätigkeitsbericht der 8. Schwadron vom 1.12 40–31.1.1941*.
44. The reports from *Waldlager Bobruisk* can be found in VAP, *Nachschubkommandantur der Waffen-SS Russland-Mitte 1943*, VA Prag, Box 1, *Tätigkeitsberichte Ia, Partisanenbekämpfung SS-Waldlager. Gliederung und Besetzung der N-Kdtur, SS Jäger-Btl-Ausbildung, Probleme. 1943*.
45. VAP, *Nachschubkommandantur der Waffen-SS Russland*, box 1, *Ia. Tätigkeitsbericht*, 8 October 1943.

There were more high-ranking officers who found the *Volksdeutsche* wanting as soldier material. In September 1942, Hans Jüttner concluded about a group of Hungarian *Volksdeutsche* soldiers that they would never become 'fit for soldiering'.[46] It is not clear if this dressing-down was an expression of Jüttner's personal opinion of the recruits or rather a spill over from his strained relations with Berger, whose *Hauptamt* had recruited them. However, similar sentiments were afoot among the general-officers-commanding the divisions. In 1941, Eicke expressed the view that both physically and mentally the newly arrived *Volksdeutsche* were not up to speed, and that the best solution might be to form *Volksdeutsche* units explicitly apt for handling their specific challenges.[47] The *SS-Grenadierausbildungsbataillon Ost* stationed in Ukraine was equally worried about their *Volksdeutsche* recruits. Not only did they include men with a record, there were also several who saw themselves more as Poles and Slovaks than Germans, and their solidarity was rather with the Ukrainian civilians than with the Waffen-SS. Thus, two soldiers with Slovak background guarding reaping allowed the Ukrainians to steal grain while themselves having intercourse with Ukrainian girls. Allegedly, the two had told their mates that if they became fed up with the Waffen-SS, they would cross to the partisans.[48]

On this background, it is hardly surprising that, from time to time, disagreements occurred between, on the one hand, the Reich German officers and NCOs imbued with the SS ethos and, on the other, the more or less forcibly enrolled *Volksdeutsche*. Frequently, this led to an overbearing attitude towards the latter. That, within the officer corps, service with *Volksdeutsche* units was regarded as a loss of prestige seems a clear indication of contempt. The former general-officer-commanding the prevailingly *Volksdeutsche Division Prinz Eugen*, Otto Kumm, later claimed that when rebuking officer cadets at Bad Tölz it was common to threat them with a transfer to that division.[49] Prejudice towards the Balkans did not only include the majority population, but obviously also the German minorities. Romanian *Volksdeutsche* were called 'Gypsies', 'Swap-Germans' or 'Marsh-Germans' and were described as being 'well-suited as cannon-fodder'.[50] The fact that German and Germanic NCOs and soldiers made such condescending remarks indicates that the attitudes within the SS towards the Balkans and Eastern Europe were harmful to integration – even when it came to those 'related by blood'.

Repeatedly, Himmler sought to ameliorate the situation admonishing about the importance of respecting the *Volksdeutsche*. An order from Christmas 1942 ran that no-one was won for the Führer's cause by unfriendly and bad treatment.[51]

46. Quote from Milata (2009), p 246. *'ihrer körperlichen Mängel so offenkundig, dass ein Soldat sie niemals für wehrdiensttauglich erklärt haben würde'*. See also Hoehne (1995), p 441.
47. Milata (2009), p 247.
48. VAP, *Höhere SS- und Polizeiführer Russland Süd, folder 18, SS-Gren.Ausb.Btl.Ost* to *Führungshauptamt, Ausbildungsbericht für den Monat September 1943*, 1 October 1943.
49. Otto Kumm, *Vorwärts, Prinz Eugen! Geschichte der 7. SS-Freiwilligen-Division 'Prinz Eugen'* (Winkelried, 2007), p 39.
50. Milata (2009), pp 242 and 247. BAB, NS19/351, Copy of letter of 14 September 1942 from *Gebietsführer R. Gassner to Volksgruppenführer Franz Basch, Volksbund der Deutschen in Ungarn*.
51. VAP, *SS-Ausb. Btl.z.b.v. 1, Behandlung von volkdeutschen und germanischen Freiwilligen in der Waffen-SS, RFSS, 6.12.1942*.

Internally, Himmler had the *Hauptamt* monitoring the treatment of the *Volksdeutsche*. There the soldiers' letters were censored to find complaints about their superiors, and more than once the units were admonished to behave decently.[52] A case of late summer 1943 concerning *Division Prinz Eugen* made Himmler react sharply. Two hundred newly arrived Croats clashed with the NCOs, who were to train them. In several cases, the NCOs had used derogative expressions like 'Croatian turd', 'Gypsy' and 'Serb' as descriptions of the soldiers' mothers. In another case, nine of those, who were particularly demotivated, were forced to shake hands with Communist prisoners in front of the company, and others were awarded disciplinary drill for not understanding German.[53] Hence, the problem developed into, what the SS regarded as, mutiny. One hundred and seventy-three men refused to serve and demanded to be transferred to Croatian units. This, however, did not happen. Suggestions that the men were transferred to the concentration camp Dachau and court-martialled was not heeded, and instead the mutineers were given German lessons and education. At the same time, Himmler wrote to General Phleps, the commander of *SS-Gebirgskorps*, to teach him a lesson about how unfair the Croatian soldiers had been treated. Particularly the offending remarks concerning the soldiers' mothers saddened Himmler, and he therefore demanded of Phleps that 'on every single occasion when an NCO or a private offends the mother of a fellow-soldier [...] you have him shot immediately'. In cases when it was not possible to find out what had happened right away, a tribunal should undertake a brief investigation and interrogate witnesses. If this indicated clearly who the offender was, he was to be shot or, in particularly serious cases, hanged in front of the company.[54] But although Himmler tried to display an obliging and protecting attitude, there is nothing to suggest that the average *Volksdeutsche* soldier ever became the dedicated political soldier of the leadership's dreams.

Among the reasons, the lack of career opportunities within the Waffen-SS for those with a *Volksdeutsche* background obviously played a major role, a problem that arose from a combination of linguistic difficulties, educational level and sheer prejudices. This is particularly interesting as there was a considerable shortage of officers.[55] Relative to the large number of *Volksdeutsche*, only few rose to NCO or officer ranks. The Romanians who, in 1943, were transferred to the Germanic armoured corps, provide a fitting example.[56] Of 8,000 all told, only a minuscule proportion, 0.62 per cent, were NCOs or officers. In *Division Nordland*, which was subordinated to the corps, only 22 were NCOs, while there were 5,738 privates of the minority in Romania. However, this was partly caused by a comparatively low educational level and the fact that of those joining only few were officers. The agreements with countries like Romania included a provision that personnel who had completed officers or NCO training were not to be recruited.[57]

52. BAB, NS19/2016, *Tätigkeitsbericht der SS-Feldpostprüfstelle für August 1942*. VAP, *SS-Ausb. Btl.z.b.v. 1, SS-Führungshauptamt den 3. February 1943.*
53. Wittmann in *East European Quarterly* XXXVI, No. 3, 2002, p 261ff.
54. Ibid., p 265ff.
55. Wegner (1990), p 282ff.
56. Milata (2009), p 282ff. Numbers for the 3rd Germanic armoured corps see Wegner (1990).
57. Milata (2009), p 245.

What was the Value of the Volksdeutsche to the Waffen-SS?

On the background of the numerous problems posed by the *Volksdeutsche* with the Waffen-SS, it seems pertinent to ask whether the efforts and resources, which the SS system put into the project of recruiting training them, paid off.

Looking at this in a purely numerical fashion the answer is affirmative. It gave the SS an opportunity for expansion, allowing extension of the concentration camp system and raising numerous field formations. This process had not been possible without the *Volksdeutsche*. But it is a lot more difficult to give a precise verdict as to the military usefulness of the soldiers. Many were attached to relatively strong formations such as *Das Reich* and *Nordland*, and seem to have been fairly well-integrated or, at least, made toe the line by the divisional culture. However, looking more closely at the formations dominated by *Volksdeutsche* the image is less clear. *Division Prinz Eugen* showed considerable cohesion and managed, from time to time, to execute complicated operations buttressing the German military presence in the Balkans. Conversely, there was a trend that divisions manned by *Volksdeutsche* from the south-eastern parts of Europe, and generally staffed by forced enrolment, did not have the same value on the battlefield as formations formed at an earlier stage. Thus the SS and the *Wehrmacht* were inclined to estimate formations with a large proportion of *Volksdeutsche* as less useful than those consisting of Germans exclusively.[58]

However, though many *Volksdeutsche* did not fight wholeheartedly for the Nazi creed, they were not exempt from contributing to the crimes perpetrated by the Third Reich, be it as concentration camp guards, in counter-insurgency operations, or in the killings of civilians. They definitely did so as soldiers of formations like *Prinz Eugen* and *Reichsführer-SS*. At the end of the war, the Third Reich's exploitation of these groups had dire consequences. An extensive and bloody purge scorched Central and Eastern Europe leaving millions of *Volksdeutsche* displaced, raped, maltreated or killed.[59]

---

58. Stein (1984), p 192. The opposite point of view – that there was no difference between Reich Germans' and *Volksdeutsche*'s fighting – see Valdis O. Lumans, 'The Etnic Germans of the Waffen-SS in Combat: Dregs or Gems?' in Marble (2012), p 252.

59. Lowe (2012), pp 125ff. and 230ff. A comprehensive though not entirely flawless description can be found in Heinz Nawratil, *Schwarzbuch der Vertreibung 1945 bis 1948. Das letzte Kapitel un bewältigter Vergangenheit* (Universitas, München, 2003).

Chapter Ten

EASTERN EUROPEAN WAFFEN-SS SOLDIERS OF NON-GERMAN ETHNICITY

The research of the soldiers in the Waffen-SS has by and large been focused on those who were recruited in the North-western European Germanic countries, such as Holland and Scandinavia. As we have discussed these volunteers had strong ideological motives and to a large extent came from Fascist or Right-Wing extremist groups in their home countries. The same tendency can also be found among soldiers from other parts of Europe such as France and Italy, but in these cases, and even more so when it comes to Eastern Europeans in the Waffen-SS the reasons behind their entry was complex: coercion and material factors in many cases played a much bigger role than ideological motivation. These groups have until relatively recently remained in the periphery of research and have not attracted the same scholarly attention as, for instance, the Scandinavian volunteers. In his classic 1966 study, George Stein included a chapter about the Baltic and Muslim volunteers. He concluded that these units, except the three divisions raised in the Baltic States, were practically useless in combat, even when it came to less demanding anti-partisan tasks.[1] Published a few years later, Alexander Dallin's essay *The Kaminsky Brigade: A Case-Study of Soviet Disaffection* was an in-depth study of a single unit, whose members were recruited in Russia.[2] Apart from Stein's monograph and Dallin's essay, the Waffen-SS soldiers from Eastern Europe were a virtually untouched subject by academic scholars studying the Third Reich until a few notable studies have surfaced during the last two decades.[3] The East European soldiers in German armed service did receive some attention earlier from authors with an interest in obscure military units or from revisionist far right historians.[4] A third approach was offered by scholars from émigré groups studying the history of their nation under Soviet and Nazi domination. They often tended to neglect or downplay the fact that many (but far from all) east Europeans in German armed service fought

---

1. Stein, 193
2. Alexander Dallin, 'The Kaminsky Brigade: A Case-Study of Soviet Disaffection' in Boris I. Nicolaevsky, Janet Rabinowitch and Ladis K.D. Kristof, *Revolution and Politics in Russia; Essays in Memory of B.I. Nicolaevsky* (Indiana University Press, 1973).
3. See, for example, Franziska A. Zaugg, Albanische Muslime in der Waffen-SS (Ferdinand Schöningh Verlag, 2016).
4. See, for example, Antionio A. Munz, *Forgotten Legions. Obscure Combat Formations of the Waffen-SS* (Axis Europa Books 1991). Joachim Hoffmans main works on the subject are *Die Ostlegionen 1941–1943. Turkotartaren, Kaukasier, Wolgafinnen im deutschen Heer* (Rombach-Verlag 1976) and *Kaukasien 1942/43. Das deutsche Heer und die Orientvölker der Sowjetunion* (Rombach-Verlag 1991).

within the SS in favour of an uncritical and heroic interpretations of the soldiers as reluctant cannon fodder or misguided idealist who merely fought for their nation's survival. Thus, several books written from this perspective treated the subject of collaboration with Nazi Germany and the SS as a minor one, within a greater theme of national assertion and survival for small nations squeezed between the great powers Nazi Germany and the Soviet Union.[5] More recently, however, scholars have begun critically to address the collaboration of Eastern Europeans and their contribution to the Holocaust and other Nazi crimes, including placing the East European soldiers in the Waffen-SS in an ideological and crime-oriented context, rather than merely viewing them as agents of national aspirations of independence.[6] This said, even recent scholarship, aiming at a comprehensive understanding of the Waffen-SS, have occasionally failed fully to make the study of East Europeans a priority. In this sense, there have been only limited progress from Stein and onwards.[7]

The recruitment to the Waffen-SS of that wide and diverse group of Eastern European ethnicities whom the Nazis derogatorily termed *Fremdvölker* (i.e. foreign people) cannot be put on a simple formula. To study this subject means engaging a huge and highly diverse topic. Indeed, the very notion of collaboration may be in dispute as the proper label for these soldiers from eastern Europe. The fact that recruitment for the Waffen-SS in Estonia and Latvia over a short course of time went from being voluntary to becoming forced conscription testify to this.[8] The term becomes even more contestable if applied on groups such as former Soviet soldiers who 'volunteered' for German armed service primarily in order to escape the genocidal conditions in German POW camps. As noted by Bernhard Chiari in his study on life in occupied Belarussia, choices between collaboration and resistance were determined by the sheer desire to survive rather than by political or ideological fiat.[9] Whereas Belorussia was at the very center of the *Bloodlands*, as Timothy Snyder has termed the area between Germany and Russia where first Stalin then Hitler carried out systematic mass killings, certain other

5. Per Anders Rudling, 'Review Essay: "The Honor They So Clearly Deserve:" Legitimizing the Waffen-SS Galizien', *Journal of Slavic Military Studies*, Vol. 26, No. 2, 2013, pp 114–137.
6. The recent scholarship includes Leonid Rein, 'Untermenschen in SS Uniforms: 30th Waffen-Grenadier Division of Waffen SS', *Journal of Slavic Military Studies*, no. 20, 2007, pp 329–345; Per Anders Rudling, '"They Defended Ukraine": The 14. Waffen-Grenadier-Division der SS (Galizische Nr. 1) Revisited', *Journal of Slavic Military Studies*, 2012, Vol. 25, No. 3, pp 329–368. The most updated and thorough contribution is the three chapters on viz. Balts, Slavs and Muslims in the Waffen-SS in Böhler & Gerwarth (2017).
7. The non-Germanic Waffen-SS soldiers hardly figure at all in Leleu (2007). Neither does the most updated German-language anthology on the subject contain any chapter on Eastern Europeans in the Waffen-SS: Schulte, Lieb and Wegner (2014). While this book was in the editorial process a new study, hopefully overcoming the existing lacunae was forthcoming: Franciska Anna Zaugg, *Rekrutierungfür die Waffen-SS in Südosteuropa* (De Gruyter, 2021).
8. Harold Otto, 'How the Germans Conscripted "Volunteers" for the Latvian Legion', Latvia in World War II (Latvijas vestures instituts, 2000), pp 208–213.
9. Bernhard Chiari, *Alltag hinter der Front* (Droste Verlag, 1998), p 4.

parts of the Soviet Union were less affected.[10] Life in Estonia (and to a certain extend Latvia) resembled, at least with regard to the majority population, what the Italians or French experienced under German rule. Thus, individual leverage was bigger, but equally significant the local elites had not fully been exterminated, neither by Stalin, nor by Hitler. This created a situation where the Germans had to address, at least to a modest degree, the interests of local actors. Also, in other cases, such as the Moslems in Yugoslavia, the structural pressure was less intense but here recruitment is often interpreted purely as a collective phenomenon – explained by pointing out that joining the Waffen-SS was either: (a) an act of self-defense against other ethnic and religious groups under the civil-war like conditions which characterized Yugoslavia or, (b) simply the expression of ethnic nationalism directed towards a competing and dominant ethnic groups, like the Croats towards the Serbs in Yugoslavia, or the Ukrainians against the Russians in the Soviet Union.[11]

This chapter will primarily address the relationship between the Waffen-SS and its Eastern European soldiers. This can best be done by dividing the *Fremdvölker* into three sub-categories, Balts, Slavs and Muslims. After studying each of these groups in turn, the chapter concludes with some general observations about the problems and challenges related to the recruitment of Eastern Europeans for the Waffen-SS, irrespectively of their origin.

The Baltic Countries

During the inter-bellum period the three Baltic states, Estonia, Latvia and Lithuania, were fraught with internal tensions between the majority populations and a number of minorities; viz. Germans, Jews, Poles and Russians. Additionally, there were social conflicts and a political culture characterised by authoritarian and nationalistic movements moulding these countries into 'mild' presidential dictatorships.[12] In 1940, concurring with the Molotov-Ribbentrop agreement, Stalin annexed all three of these states to the Soviet Union and launched a social and political regimentation process leading to incarcerations, deportations and killings. The terror culminated in mass deportations a week before the start of Operation Barbarossa. The 1940-1941 experience of Stalinist rule left a deep impact on Baltic societies. On the one hand, it almost completely negated the traditional animosity against Germany in Estonia and Latvia where the majority of the population had been peasants under German landlords until independence. On the other hand, Soviet terror strained ethnic relations – especially stirring up anti-Semite sentiments - and helped create a more violent mentality.

Shortly, after the German occupation of Estonia, Latvia and Lithuania, German military and police units commenced admitting Balts into their ranks. They were

---

10. Timothy Snyder, *Bloodlands* (Basic Books, 2010).
11. John A. Armstrong, 'Collaborationism in World War II: The Integral Nationalist Variant in Eastern Europe', *The Journal of Modern History*, Vol. 40, No. 3 (Sep., 1968), pp 396–410.
12. David Kirby, *The Baltic World 1772–1993* (Longman, 1995), p 317ff.

employed in *Sicherungs-Gruppen* (security units) set up in order to perform guard and security tasks in the hinterland. In addition, a large number of police units, *Shutzmannschaften*, were established in order to catch, guard and kill Baltic Jews, as well as to carry out various guard and policing tasks.[13]

The initial relief in the Baltic states of being liberated from Soviet terror gradually gave way to more sobering sentiments as it became clear that the Germans had no plans of re-establishing the three countries independence. On the contrary, in July 1941 the region was, together with most of Belorussia, made a *Reichskommissariat* (with the name of Ostland) under a newly established Ministry for the Occupied Eastern Territories. Further south a *Reichskommisariat Ukraine* was established in a similar vein. In both cases, the area in question was divided up in smaller entities called *Generalkommissariats* (each under a German Commissioner General). In contrast to Ukraine, the German administration in the Baltic states co-opted a sizeable number of middle and high ranking civil servants. Unlike the Quisling government in Norway, they rarely represented radicalised pro-Nazi ideas, and their aspirations was to achieve independence, rather than assimilation in to the Third Reich, as were the German plans.[14] Whereas many Baltic figures cooperating with the Germans perceived armed formations as a means to restore national independence, the SS' perspective was that of gradually assimilating the Baltic states in to the future Greater Germanic Reich; thus military service in police and Waffen-SS formations could be instrumental in transforming racially 'worthy' Balts into Germanics.[15]

It is likely that it was the German Commissioner General in Latvia, Otto Heinrich Drechsler, who, after having had contact with Latvian right-wing nationalists, was the first to propose that Balts should be serving in the Waffen-SS.[16] This proposal was made in October 1941, but neither Himmler nor Hitler accepted it, fearing that the idea represented aspirations for re-establishing Baltic national armies. On a more general note, the idea also contravened Hitler's general policy for the occupied Soviet territories – that there should under no circumstances be raised regular armed units among the local population. In May 1942, another proposal for recruitment of Baltic volunteers from all three Baltic States was submitted to Himmler by SS-Sturmbannführer With. While dismissing the proposal, Himmlers' wording indicated the dilemma, he obviously faced: 'The formation of Waffen-SS

---

13. This early phase has been described in Toomas Hiio et al., 'Estonian Military Units in German Armed Forces and Police during the Second World War' in *The Museum of the Occupation of Latvia. Yearbook 2004* (2005), p 34ff. See also Toomas Hiio, 'Estonian Security Groups and Eastern Battalions in German Army in 1941–1944' in Hiio (2006).
14. Myllyniemi (1973).
15. Matthew Kott, Arunas Bubnys & Ülle Kraft, 'The Baltic States: Auxiliaries and Waffen-SS soldiers from Estonia, Latvia, and Lithuania', Jochen Böhler & Robert Gerwarth (Eds.), *The Waffen-SS. A European History* (Oxford University Press, 2017), p 123. Björn M. Feldner, *Lettland im Zweiten Weltkrieg. Zwischen sowjetischen und deutschen Besatzern 1940–1946*, Ferdinand Schöningh, 2009, p 255ff.
16. The following is based on Hiio (2006), p 823ff.

units of Estonians, Latvians or Lithuanians is certainly tempting, but inherently very dangerous', he stated.[17]

By late summer, Himmler's position had changed, probably under the influence of the continuous lack of manpower in combination with his ongoing plans for asimilating the most Germanic-like Balts as part of *Generalplan Ost*. Himmler was now willing to raise an Estonian legion – allegedly because the Estonians had a higher concentration of Germanic blood than the Latvians and Lithuanians. The timing was also caused by the fact that the contracts with those staffing the *Sicherungs-Gruppen*, co-operating with Army Group North, were about to expire. Moreover, these men were militarily experienced because, due to German losses in the winter 1941-1942, many of them had been employed at the front. On 28 August 1942 – first anniversary of the German 'liberation' of Tallinn – the formation of an Estonian legion under the Waffen-SS was officially announced.[18]

Many Estonian men had either been enrolled in the Red Army, prior to its withdrawal from the country, or they were already wearing German uniform. Hence, the potential for recruiting additional volunteers in Estonia was limited and the overwhelming majority of men entering the legion were former members of the *Sicherungs-Gruppen*. Another factor contributing to the meagre harvest of fresh recruits was popular discontent with Germany's occupation policy. Also, the legion was seen as a purely German project.[19] Soon it was realised, too, that Estonian officers were not employed according to their original rank and that, generally, the cadres were German. Moreover, knowledge of the tough conditions at the eastern front hampered the will to join, and this was further exacerbated by the total annihilation of an Estonian battalion at Stalingrad. In order to bolster recruitment the SS in spring 1943 appointed Estonian Colonel Henn-Ants Kurg as commander of what had now become an Estonian SS brigade. Prior to that, other steps had been taken: More than 500 men were transferred from the police to the legion and as of March 1943, outright conscription was introduced in Estonia.[20]

In autumn 1942, *SS- und Polizeiführer* Walther Schröder discussed the possibility of raising Latvian armed forces with the head of the Latvian local administration, General Oskars Dankers. The Latvians were perfectly willing to contribute with a regular army, which, however, the SS did not really wish as the area was predestined for Germanisation. Nonetheless, the Germans had an obvious need for soldiers and when, in January 1943, Himmler visited the second SS brigade at the front at Leningrad, he saw two Latvian police battalions which were subordinated this brigade. These battalions allegedly impressed him enough to make him decide to turn them into a Latvian SS brigade (Figure 10.1).[21] The constantly deteriorating situation at the front may have been the decisive motivation for Himmler to do so, and the disastrous circumstances

17. Rolf Michaelis, *Estonians in the Waffen-SS*, Schiffer Military History, 2009, p 20.
18. Hiio (2006), p 929ff.
19. The following is based on ibid., p 933.
20. Myllyniemi (1973), p 229. Toivo U. Raun, *Estonia and the Estonians* (Hoover Institution Press, 1991), p 158.
21. Valdis O. Lumans, *Latvia in World War II* (Fordham Univ. Press, 2006), p 272ff. See also BAB, NS19/382, *SS-Befehl, Reval 15.3.1943*.

Figure 10.1 A Latvian officer is decorated, 1944 (Frihedsmuseet)

at Stalingrad in January 1943 made Hitler approve. Thus, in March 1943, the Latvian legion was raised.[22] The Germans had great expectations. First, because Latvia had a larger population than Estonia and, secondly, because the Latvian authorities had intimated that a huge number might be attracted. On this background the aim was to form an entire Latvian division.[23] Initially, the Latvian legion seemed to honour the hopes in as much as 15,000 joined within a few months of 1943. However, as the SS was completely unprepared and was short of basic equipment it was only possible to actually draft a small group. In May, the inrush of volunteers languished and it was decided to tread the same path as in Estonia. Consequently, it was arranged that all existing units under the SS, that is police and *Schutzmannschaft* as well as the newly raised military units would now be included in the legion.[24] Furthermore, conscription was introduced, and during the course of the war no less than 150,000 Latvians were called up for service. Like with the Estonians however, it was far from all who served in the Waffen-SS. Many went to the army or to *Reichsarbeitsdienst* or *Organisation Todt*.[25]

22. BAB, NS19/382, Himmler, 24.1.1943. Stein (1984), p 176. On 11 March 1943, Jüttner gave the order. See BAB, NS.19/3523, *Aufstellung der 'Lettischen SS-Freiw.Legion'*. See also Myllyniemi (1973), p 230ff.
23. Lumans (2006), p 270.
24. Lumans (2006), p 274. See also SU, Box No. 1, *Jeckeln, 22.6.1943*.
25. Hiio et al. in *The Museum of the Occupation of Latvia. Yearbook 2004*, 2005, p 55ff., and Felder (2009), p 274. See also Andrew Ezergailis, *The Latvian Legion: Heroes, Nazis, or Victims? a Collection of Documents from OSS War-crimes Investigation Files, 1945–1950* (Historical Institute of Latvia, 1997).

As the only Baltic country, Lithuania did not contribute personnel to the Waffen-SS. Although in early 1943, the SS initiated the setting up of a legion, the plans were never implemented. Not only did the plans run into opposition from the civil servants, who were appointed by the Germans themselves; when they were carried out, nevertheless, less than 20 per cent appeared for mustering. The disappointing results convinced the occupying authorities that the Lithuanians' racial qualities were inferior to those of the Estonians and Latvians.[26]

The case of the three Baltic countries illustrates, how the notion of race was tentatively and flexibly applied by Himmler and his closest associates. It also demonstrates how Himmler based his decisions on a mixture of political considerations, Nazi ideology, and his own personal impressions. From a position of politically motivated reluctance, Himmler gradually, and based on a combination of Germany's military misfortunes and his impression from meeting Baltic soldiers in person, came to favour recruitment of Estonians and Latvians to the Waffen-SS. After the setting up of the Estonian and Latvian legions, Himmler continued to follow their battlefield performance and engaged in considering whether and on what conditions the new recruits could be worthy of carrying the SS-runes on their collars.[27] On the other hand, the Lithuanian reluctance in embracing the 'offer' of a legion, led Himmler to conclude that this ethnic groups was racially inferior.

While in Lithuania the collaboration was limited to police and *Schutzmannschaft* units assisting, over the year of 1943, the SS built up the Estonian and Latvian legions to divisions. The first step was forming the *Lettische Freiwilligen SS-Brigade* and *Estische Freiwilligen SS-Brigade*. In these the Baltic personnel was augmented by Germans from the SS infantry brigades, which, since 1941, had been busy taking part in massacres and genocide.[28] But already while these brigades were being formed, Himmler made a decision to actually raise two Latvian and one Estonian divisions.[29] They were designated *15. Waffen-Grenadier-Division der SS (lettische Nr. 1), 19. Waffen-Grenadier-Division der SS (lettische Nr. 2)* and *20. Waffen-Grenadier-Division der SS (estnische Nr. 1)*. In November 1943, the 15th division arrived at the front for the first time. By the end of March 1944, with a strength of 13,000 it was employed in Russia.[30]

---

26. BAB, NS19/3943, Himmler to Jüttner, 27 January 1943. Myllyniemi (1973), p 228ff. See also Himmler's comments concerning the Lithuanians in BAB, NS19/382, *Der Reichsführer SS*, 8 September 1943.

27. BAB, NS19/382, Jüttner to Himmler, 29 October 1942; Himmler's secretariat to Jüttner, 16 November 1942; Berger to Himmler 22.5.1943; Himmler to Jüttner, 3 August 1943; Himmler to the head of Sipo and SD, 8 September 1943.

28. BAB, NS19/382, *SS-Befehl, Reval 15.3.1943*. The second SS brigade also assumed a rôle in the 15th Latvian division, which was formed later. When, in May 1943, a filler battalion under second SS brigade was formed, 63 soldiers of 15th Latvian division and 88 from second SS brigade were detailed for the purpose. SU, Box No. 9, *Betr.,15. (lett.) SS-Freiw. Division, Riga, 4.5 1943*.

29. SU, Box No. 9, *Betr: Aufstellung der 15. Lett. SS.Freiw.Div., SS-Führungshauptamt*, 26 February 1943.

30. BAB, NS19/1475, *Stärkemeldungen*, 27 March 1944.

Later on in 1944, it was part of the German retreat through Latvia and Lithuania and it was, subsequently, to re-organise in Prussia. In May 1945, still on German soil it surrendered to British forces.[31] The other Latvian division was not formed until the end of February 1944. Numerically, it was far from being a proper division and, in March that year, it was at only 6,700 men.[32] Like the 15th division, the 19th was employed at the eastern front. Thus, it became part of the German formation that, in October 1944, the Red Army enveloped in the Courland Pocket, a peninsula in north-western Latvia. Here, the division was part of the long-lasting German defence of the area lasting until the final surrender on 8 May 1945.

The Estonian brigade was at the eastern front when, in early 1944, it was upgraded to a division. Between February and September 1944, the combat ready parts of the 20th division were employed at Narva and Tartu, but in September it was moved to Training Area Neuhammer in East Prussia, where it was brought up to the full strength of 14,000 men.[33] In early 1945, it was employed against the advancing Red Army, to whom the majority of the Estonian soldiers surrendered near Melnik in Bohemia-Moravia mid-April.

The Ukrainian Division

The Ukrainians constituted one of the largest groups of *Fremdvölker* in the Waffen-SS. In September 1939, the eastern parts of Poland – in particular the Austro-Hungarian province Galicia – was occupied by the Soviet Union and incorporated in the Soviet Socialist Republics Belarus and Ukraine. Before the war, Poland had strived to strengthen Polishness in the eastern parts of the country, where the population was predominantly Ukrainians, Jews, Lithuanians and Belarussians. This had happened through support of Polish settlers and by means of systematic employment of Poles in the administration and educational systems. The consequence was a general discontent with the Polish regime and appearance of extremist movements. The Organisation of Ukrainian Nationalists (OUN) perpetrated a number of acts of terror and defiance.[34]

The authoritarian Polish governance, however, was certainly a mild one compared with the extensive arrests, deportations and killings that followed in the wake of Stalin's annexation of eastern Poland in September 1939. In June 1941, when German tanks moved into Ukrainian territory they were received as liberators in many places. This happened in particular in the western – former Austro-Hungarian or Polish – part

31. The following is based on Hans-J.E. Stöber, *Die Sturmflut und das Ende: die Geschichte der 17. SS-Panzergrenadierdivision 'Götz von Berlichingen'*, Vol. 1, (Munin-Verlag, 1976). On the 20th division, see Rolf Michaelis, *Esten in der Waffen-SS: die 20. Waffen-Grenadier-Division der SS (estnische Nr. 1)* (Winkelried, 2006).
32. BAB, NS19/1475, *Stärkemeldungen, 27.3.1944*. In September that year, the strength was at 11,764 men. BAB, NS19/1475, *Stärkemeldungen,* 19 September 1944.
33. BAB, NS19/1475, *Stärkemeldungen,* 5 September 1944.
34. Martin Dean, 'Local Collaboration in the Holocaust in Eastern Europe' in Dan Stone, *The Historiography of the Holocaust*, (Palgrave Macmillan, 2004), p 10ff.

of the country, where people had known other forms of government. Moreover, they had a living memory of Stalin's terror – the most recent acts being the killing of thousands of political prisoners in summer 1941 before the Red Army retreated. But also, in areas that had always been Russian or Soviet the displeasure with the regime was substantial. Agriculture had been brutally collectivised leaving millions of farmers dead as a consequence of the extensive famine of 1932-1933. The Ukrainian nationalists cherished great hopes that the German invasion was a harbinger of an independent Ukraine, and the willingness to co-operate with the occupiers was extensive. However, this was by no means the German agenda.

As in other occupied Soviet territories, *Schutzmannshaft* units were formed, and they performed a crucial role in the genocide of the Jews. By the end of 1941, 26 such battalions were employed in Soviet territory and, in early 1943, no less than 300,000 East European men served with these units.[35] Moreover, local Ukrainian police forces were raised – to become known as *Militz* or *Ordnungsdienst* (OD).[36] Their tasks were manifold ranging from guard duties and actions against the black market to participation in the Holocaust.[37]

In March 1943, the German governor of Galicia, Otto Wächter, suggested to Himmler the raising of a Ukrainian SS division. After brief consideration, Himmler accepted, and it was decided that the division should enlist personnel not only from Galicia but also from parts of Ukraine located further east.[38] Initially, in order not to rouse expectations of an independent Ukraine, the division was named *14. SS-Freiwilligen-Division Galizien*.[39]

The SS' suspicion of Ukrainian nationalism also manifested itself in the choice of symbols. The badge on the volunteers' sleeves was the Galician coat of arms, and the formation staff was instructed under no circumstances to employ symbolism fit for kindling nationalist inclinations.[40] The cadres were primarily German police officers. Their job was to train the Ukrainian recruits and organise them as a horse drawn infantry division.[41] Also, the general-officer-commanding, Fritz Freitag, originated from the police.

---

35. Christopher R. Browning, *The Path to Genocide: Essays on Launching the Final Solution* (Cambridge University Press, 1993), p 105ff.

36. Dean (2004), p 27ff.

37. Ibid., p 60, and Dieter Pohl, 'Ukrainische Hilfkräfte beim Mord an den Juden' in Gerhard Paul (ed.), *Die Täter der Shoah: Fanatische Nationalsozialisten oder ganz normale Deutsche?* (Wallstein, 2002), p 209ff.

38. On Ukrainian volunteers in general see Sol Littman, *Pure Soldiers or Sinister Legion. The Ukrainian 14th Waffen-SS division* (Black Rose Books, 2003) and Michael O. Logusz, *Galicia Division. The Waffen-SS 14th Grenadier Division 1943-1945* (Schiffer Military History, 1997). See also Wolf-Dietrich Heike, *Sie wollten die Freiheit: die Geschichte der Ukrainischen Division, 1943–1945* (Podzun, 1970), Rolf Michaelis, *Ukrainer in der Waffen-SS. Die 14. Waffen-Grenadier-Division der SS (ukrainischen Nr.1)* (Winkelried, 2006).

39. Littman (2003), p 63.

40. BAB, NS19/1734, *Niederschrift. Besprechung, 12.4.1943*.

41. BAB, NS19/1785, RFSS to Wächter, March 1943. On the rôle of the police, see also BAB, NS19/1785, *Freiwilligen Division Galizien, 16.4.1943*.

He had been transferred to the SS at an earlier stage and had been responsible for the first SS brigade's mass killing of Jews in 1942.[42] Wächter and his Ukrainian associates had envisaged a huge interest for joining this formation, and they were proven right. By May 1943, two months after announcing the division, Berger reported to Himmler that 80,000 had applied and 50,000 had actually been taken on.[43] This, however, posed a challenge to the local weapons industry because, apart from Jewish forced labourers, they employed Ukrainian skilled workers. In the summer 1943, *Rüstungsskommando Lemberg* complained that a lot of working hours had been lost because of the division's enlistment; many workers had been temporarily absent on recruiting or muster activities, and those, who were taken on never returned to work. The armament command was under the impression that the motives for joining were a combination of true enthusiasm and a wish for better living conditions.[44] On top of that, the background was that for many young men the alternative would have been forced labour for the Germans.[45] The 14th SS division was a recruitment success in so far as it was possible to form it at the full establishment strength of 14,000 officers and men within only a few months.[46]

In June 1944, the first units of the 14th division left Neuhammer and shortly afterwards they were at the eastern front. Thence, the Ukrainians were moved to the Brody area in western Ukraine, where they soon faced the Red Army. On 13 July, the Soviet forces attacked across a broad front and, after a few days, the division was locked up in a pocket where, along with German units, it fought to keep the Russians at bay. The fight continued until 21-23 July, when the enveloped troops managed to break out through a narrow corridor. Over these few days, the 14th division was almost totally annihilated. The total casualty number is unknown, but it is likely that more than half the troops originally employed were lost.[47]

After the battle at Brody the survivors were brought back to Neuhammer, and there the division was re-organised and filled up with personnel coming, primarily, from Ukrainian police units. Additionally, there were replacements coming from among the guards in the extermination camps Belzec, Treblinka and Sobibor.[48] In October 1944, the division was sent to Slovakia, where riots had broken out against the Germans.[49] In Slovakia the 14th division committed several atrocities, which were often faultily attributed to the attached *SS-Sturmbrigade Dirlewanger*.[50] Subsequently, the division was transferred to Italy where it remained until Germany's eventual surrender.

---

42. Schulz and Wegmann (2003), p 344ff.
43. BAB, NS19/1785, Kruger to Berger, 11 May 1943. BAB, NS19/1785, Berger to Himmler, 3 June 1943. Concerning numbers see also Logusz (1997), p 74ff.
44. YV, O.53, F.nr. 149, *Rüstungskommando Lemberg des Reichsministers für Rüstung und Kriegsproduktion*, KTB 1 and 8 July 1943.
45. Berkhoff (2004), p 270.
46. BAB, NS19/1475 *Stärkemeldungen, 17.4.1944.*
47. Heike, *Sie wollten die Freiheit* (Podzun Pallast, 1987), p 110, Littman (2003), p 83, and Logusz (1997), p 188ff.
48. Littman (2003), p 84. Rudling (2012), p 344ff.
49. MacLean (1998), p 201.
50. Heike (1987). A critical description can be seen in Littman (2003), p 86ff.

The Russian Divisions

Although the population of areas annexed by the Soviet Union 1939–1940 were generally more anti-Communist than those living further east, there were, nevertheless, quite a few persons who were opposed to the Soviet regime or for other reasons inclined to associate with the Germans. Particularly, this was true of the resident Muslims and various other minority groups, but for religious or socio-economic reasons and due to Stalinist terror there were also willing collaborators to be found among the Russians.[51] However, the Nazi leadership did not see the Soviet peoples as potential allies, but as groups that ought to be exploited and oppressed and hence never really made full use of the anti-Soviet feelings.[52]

Nonetheless, the rapidly growing German lack of personnel resulted in the employment of Russians as unarmed local policemen in the hinterland as well as for support of the regular forces. The Russians were designated *Hilfswillige* (people willing to assist), normally abbreviated to HiWi's. They filled a number of functions like drivers or kitchen workers and their number could be quite impressive.[53] Little by little, the Russians began to solve security tasks, lightly armed, or to serve as regular soldiers. The first Russians who were armed as regular combat troops were the Cossacks. Unlike other Russian groups these were not targets for German prejudices. As early as August 1941, the first, small Cossack units were raised and, in 1943, the force had grown to 20 Cossack battalions, which were all employed at the Eastern front. The year after, they formed the 15th Cossack Cavalry Corps of about 25,000 troopers.[54] Later the anti-Stalinist liberation force, the *Russkaja Osvoboditel'naja Armija* (ROA) was founded under the command of the former Red Army Lieutenant General Andrey Vlasov.[55] In June 1944, when German formations had been pushed back to the westernmost parts of the Soviet Union, and the only territory now in German hands was what the Soviets had taken in 1939–1940, local recruitment by individual Waffen-SS divisions was given the go-ahead. The Soviet citizens, who signed up, were given a two-months trial period after which they were to be treated and fed like the rest of the formation's personnel.[56] How many the Waffen-SS enlisted this way is not known, but already before this step was taken, the SS had raised a number of units staffed, primarily, by personnel of Slavic extraction.

51. Due Enstad (2013), p 217ff. Poulsen (2007), p 182ff.
52. The following is based on Rolf-Dieter Müller, *An der Seite der Wehrmacht: Hitlers ausländische Helfer beim Kreuzzug gegen den Bolschewismus 1941–1945* (FischerTachenbuch, 2010).
53. This can be seen from contemporary rolls where the HiWi personnel were included in the overall strength. BAB, NS19/1475, *Stärkemeldungen*.
54. Müller (2010), p 207ff.
55. Ibid., p 216ff.
56. BAMA, RS2-2/29, *GnKdo II SS PzKorpsQu. Tgb. Nr. 529/44, Betr. Landeseigene Freiwillige*, 8 June 1944.

Over the war, the Waffen-SS raised two Russian divisions; viz. *29. Waffen-Grenadier-Division der SS 'RONA' (russische Nr. 1)* and *30. Waffen-Grenadier-Division der SS (russische Nr. 2)*. The 29th division was established on the foundations of the notorious Kaminski Brigade, which had been raised by the *Wehrmacht* in early 1942.[57]

Under Swastika and Crescent: Muslims in the Waffen-SS

A third important group of *Fremdvölker* were the Muslims, who were recruited in the Balkans and from the Soviet Union.[58] In the universe of the SS, this group was first and foremost defined by religion, and unlike Waffen-SS units manned by Germans and Germanics, formations of men with Moslem background were systematically assigned clerics and in other ways associated with the Muslim faith.[59]

The SS maintained a useful co-operation with the German-friendly Grand Mufti of Jerusalem, Haj Amin al-Husseini, who stayed in occupied Europe throughout the war.[60] Beginning with *13. Waffen-Gebirgs-Division der SS Handschar (kroatische Nr. 1)*, the first Muslim division to be formed a number of army imams were appointed. Each battalion received one, and the overall religious leadership was taken care of by a divisional imam. In July 1943, these were sent on a tree-weeks course in Germany, where they received instruction concerning National Socialism and the Waffen-SS. During the course, emphasis was placed on the – allegedly – many commonalities of Islam and National Socialism.[61]

This consideration for the SS soldiers' religious faith was not an exceptional *Handschar* phenomenon. In August 1943, Himmler issued a prohibition against alcohol and pork to Muslims with the Waffen-SS.[62] In April 1944, the SS even opened an imam institute headed by the grand mufti in the German town of Guben.[63]

57. Alexander Dallin, 'The Kaminsky Brigade: A Case-Study of Soviet Disaffection' in Boris I. Nicolaevsky, Janet Rabinowitch and Ladis K.D. Kristof, *Revolution and Politics in Russia; Essays in Memory of B.I. Nicolaevsky* (Indiana University Press, 1973).

58. In addition to the works referred to in the notes below, see also Bruno dee Cordier 'The Fedayeen of the Reich: Muslims, Islam and Collaborationism During World War II', *China and Eurasia Forum Quarterly*, Vol. 8, No. 1, 2010, pp 23–46. This work offers an important, albeit not fully impartial, contextualization of the Muslim contribution to armed units in the Wehrmacht and the SS.

59. However, also other types of non-Germanic units had clerics. Twelve army chaplains for example served with Division Galizia, and services in the field were tolerated. BAB, NS19/1785, Wortlaut der Platte 3 und 4. Professor Laba. See also Logusz (1997), p 88ff. For the Latvian Legion see Andrejs M. Mezmalis, *The Latvian Legion* (Riga, 2008), p 54.

60. BAB, NS19/2601, Berger den 29.4.1944.

61. BAB, NS19/2601, *13. SS-Division Abt IV, 15.3.1944* and *Der Reichführer-SS, 24.11.1943*. See also Klaus-Michael Mallmann and Martin Cüppers, *Halvmåne og hagekors. Det Tredje Rige, araberne og Palæstina* (Informations Forlag, 2009), p 222ff.

62. BAB, NS19/3285, Himmler to *SS-Hauptamt, SS-Führungshauptamt* and others, 6 August 1943.

63. On imam training at Guben, see Bernwald (2012), p 71ff.

The Croatian and Albanian Divisions

In April 1941, Yugoslavia surrendered to Germany and Croatia became an independent state governed by the Fascist *Ustaša* under Ante Pavelics. This regime launched mass murders of Jews and Serbs making large groups retreat into the mountainous areas where they joined the rapidly growing partisan movements.[64]

In February 1943, Himmler achieved Hitler's approbation to raise a Bosnian SS division for counter-insurgency operations in the Bosnian and Serb parts of Croatia. The administrative and recruiting capacity was already in place in as much as the SS had already formed the *Volksdeutsche Division Prinz Eugen*.[65] The situation characterising the formation of what was originally the *Kroatische SS-Freiwilligen-Gebirgs-Division*, later to be re-named *Division Handschar*, was similar to that of Hungary. It was an ally, whom one had to take into consideration. Pavelics and his Fascist *Ustaša* movement regarded the Muslims of the annexed Bosnia-Herzegovina as Croats who had merely lost their Catholic faith but remained perfectly suited for use by *Ustaša* and the New Croatia.[66] The enlistment efforts, therefore, caused friction between the Germans and their Croatian allies, who tried to prevent the establishment as best they could.[67] One of the stumbling blocks was that the SS refused to take on Catholics, a decision, however, that was rescinded after Croatian pressure.[68]

In mid-April 1943, only 8,000 had signed up – much below the target number. The following month, Himmler visited Zagreb and ordered that the recruitment of Catholic volunteers be intensified. However, the division was to maintain a majority of Muslims, and the ratio must not go beyond 1:10.[69] Eventually *Division Handschar* reached 15,000 troops, but the Christians remained a minority of *Division Handschar* and, on many occasions, they were at odds with the division's Muslim majority.[70]

The division was now moved to France for formation; but arriving there the soldiers mutinied on the night of 16/17 September.[71] Many of the German officers and NCOs

---

64. On *Ustaša*'s crimes see Alexander Martin Korb, *Im Schatten des Weltkriegs: Massengewalt der Ustaša gegen Serben, Juden und Roma in Kroatien 1941–1945* (Hamburger Edition, 2013).

65. On the formation of *Handschar*, see Mallmann and Cüppers (2009), p 218ff., and Lepre (1997), p 19ff., Ladislaus Hory and Martin Broszat, *Der kroatische Ustascha-Staat: 1941–1945* (Deutsche Verlags-Anstalt, 1964), p 155ff., Stefan Petke, unpublished paper, no title, from the conference 'Himmler's Super National Militia Indigenous Participation in SS and Police Units in the Context of the Second World War' at UMK Institute of History and Archival Science in Torun, 2004.

66. Lepre (1997), p 22.

67. BAB, NS19/2601, *Zwischenbericht über Werbeaktion muselmanischer Freiwilligen, den 19.4.1943*. See also ibid., p 42. After the formation of the division, the *Ustaša* frequently tried to persuade the personnel to desert by offering better pay and more lenient service conditions than those of the SS. Ibid., p 201.

68. Korb (2013), p 85. Petke (2014).

69. Lepre (1997), p 35.

70. Petke (2014) and Lepre (1997), p 48ff., p 60.

71. The following is based on ibid., p 81ff.

had addressed the Muslim soldiers in a derogatory manner, the discipline was tough and the food quality poor, and there was dissatisfaction with having been moved out of the native places in Bosnia-Herzegovina.[72] Moreover, prior to the transfer, the Yugoslav Communists partisan movement had managed to infiltrate the division, and one of the infiltrators, Ferid Dzanic, was the ringleader of the mutiny. Briefly, the mutineers managed to take control of one company and kill a few officers. However, one of the division's imams interfered and soon brought the majority of the men under control. The ringleaders were caught and a tribunal was sat down. They passed death sentences on 14 of the mutineers, who were duly shot in a field near Villefrance. Although only a few had taken part, the divisional commander used the opportunity to get rid of all personnel who were found unreliable. Eight hundred and twenty-five were detailed for 'voluntary' work in Germany. Anyone refusing would receive no food. Thus 536 accepted, and the remainder were transferred to concentration camp Neuengamme.[73]

In February 1944, after a spell in Germany, at last the division was dispatched to the Balkans to be employed in counter-insurgency operations. It numbered 21,000 all told, but still there was a dearth of officers and NCOs.[74] Upon arrival, the division was employed in Operation Wegweiser, during which it combed out partisans from forests and villages.[75] This operation was characteristic of the way *Handschar* performed throughout its existence. It was almost exclusively partisans who were targeted but, during the hunt for them, atrocities were often committed against the Serb civilian population, as well.[76]

Although the SS' experiences with Handschar were mixed, this did not prohibit intensifying ambitions for the activities in Yugoslavia. As early as 1943, Himmler had an SS corps formed under Phleps with divisions *Prinz Eugen* and *Handschar* as the assigned formations. In May 1944 then, he ordered the formation of yet another corps, the *IX. Waffen-Gebirgskorps der SS (kroatisches)*, under Sauberzweig. Consequently, a sister division of the Handschar was formed, the *23. Waffen-Gebirgs-Division der SS Kama (kroatische Nr. 2).*[77] To a large extent, the formation of Kama happened on the basis of *Handschar* key personnel. Instead, *Handschar* received 500 young German

---

72. Petke (2014). Enver Redzic, *Bosnia and Herzegovina in the Second World War* (Frank Cass, 2005), p 180ff.
73. Ibid., p 106ff.
74. BAB, NS19/1475, *Stärkemeldungen. Stand vom 27 Märtz 1943.*
75. In April 1944, at a conference in Hitler's HQ the Bosnian soldiers' brutality was mentioned. See Lepre (1997), p 150. For a detailed review of the various operations see Lepre (1997).
76. Petke (2014).
77. BAMA, N756/183b, *Die 23. Waffen-Gebirgs-Division der SS (kroatische Nr. 2 Kama)*, Wolfgang Vopersal, *Wohin der Befehl rief – aus der Geschicte der Kartsjäger der Waffen-SS*, Unpublished manuscript, 1977, and N756/183b, *Aufstellung der Waffen-Geb.Div-SS (kroatische Nr. 2)*, 17 June 1944, Lepre (1997), p 223ff. BAB, NS19/1475, *Stärkemeldungen. Stand vom 20 September 1944.*

men from the RAD (*Reichsarbeitsdienst*). According to a muster roll of September 1944 the *Kama* had at the time a mere 3,793 troops of whom 126 were officers and 374 NCOs, far from the usual full establishment strength of ca. 19,000.[78] *Kama* was never to become a fully equipped division and one of the reasons was the wave of turmoil and desertions striking both of the Croatian divisions at the time.

The spark setting this trouble ablaze was the August 1944 change of sides by Romania and Bulgaria. While this paved the way for the Red Army for crossing the Yugoslav eastern border, it also provided the partisans with much improved working conditions.[79] At the same time, Tito declared an amnesty to all who might desert before 15 September.[80] In September 1944, therefore the number of desertions by Croatian personnel rose steeply. Alone between 1 and 20 September, *Handschar* lost more than 2,000 troops, and a great deal of the divisional headquarters company deserted the following month.[81] While many wished to go back to their families to protect them, others joined the partisans. In October 1944, some 700 former *Handschar* soldiers now fought in the ranks of Tito's partisans.[82]

The desertions made the Germans consider re-organisation, and the OKW suggested disbanding the divisions to gather the German personnel in brigades, which, however, Himmler flatly refused.[83] On 17 October, in the *Kama* a mutiny flared up leading to a quick decision to dissolve the whole formation. While the reliable soldiers were transferred to *Handschar*, the German key personnel went to the 31st SS division.[84] As a consequence of the fact that *Kama* and large parts of *Handschar* had ceased to exist, the ninth mountain corps was disbanded, too. This disintegration led to increased German staffing of the *Handschar* ending at about two third. In January 1945, when the so-called *Kampfgruppe Handschar* was formed, only 1,016 men remained. The evaluation of the combat value of this battle group was that it was only to be employed alongside 'good German divisions'.[85] When the war finished, the remains of the Bosnian-Muslim SS units ended up in the frontier region between Austria and Hungary, where they had fought the Red Army as well as been involved in massacres on transports of Jewish prisoner. In May 1945, while

78. BA, NS19/1475, *Stärkemeldiungen. Stand vom 20 September 1944*.
79. BAB, NS19/1500, *Gen. Kdo. IX Waffen Geb. Korps d. SS (kroatisch), SS und Polizei Organisationsstab* to *RFSS, Betr. Monatsbericht September*, 30 September 1944.
80. Franziska Zaugg, unpublished paper, 'Albanian Muslims in the Waffen-SS' from the conference *Himmler's Super National Militia Indigenous Participation in SS and Police Units in the Context of the Second World War* at UMK Institute of History and Archival Science in Torun, (2014a), p 8.
81. Lepre (1997), p 266.
82. Lepre (1997), p 253. See also Petke (2014).
83. Ibid., p 261.
84. Ibid., p 266.
85. The muster roll is from January or February 1945. BAMA, RH, 1465, *Handschar*, without date, 1945 and BAMA, N756/183/a, *Anlage zu Obkdo. d.Hr. Gr. Süd, Nr. 7/45*.

most of the remaining personnel surrendered to the British, many Bosnians discarded the uniform and left for home.[86]

The trend of disintegration so obviously present within the Croatian formations also manifested itself in the Albanian Waffen-SS *Division Skanderbeg*, named after the Albanian national hero of the late Middle-Ages, George Kastrioti Skanderbeg. In 1939, Italy had invaded Albania, but Mussolini's overthrow in 1943, and the subsequent German occupation of the country, made large elements of the Italian occupying troops desert to the partisans. However, while the German troops never managed to take control of the entire country, they merely occupied the coast and the major towns, the partisans ruled supreme in the mountains.[87]

In April 1944, Himmler ordered an Albanian SS division to be raised. Later, this formation was named *21. Waffen-Gebirgs-Division der SS Skanderbeg (albanische Nr. 1)*, and it was planned to also raise a sister division with a view to joining the two in an Albanian mountain infantry corps. However, neither the second division nor the corps was ever formed.[88] An almost complete lack of archival material makes it impossible to examine the Albanian SS division in any kind of detail. Its task was counter-insurgency operations in Albania and Kosovo, the latter being annexed into Albania in the wake of the German Balkan campaign of 1941.[89]

The SS regarded Skanderbeg as a 'failed division' not least due to the Albanian personnel and the considerable cultural differences. From the outset, the co-operation between the SS and local clan chiefs was troublesome. For instance, the number of soldiers never came anything near what the clan chiefs had promised to provide. In September 1944, *Skanderbeg*'s strength was at 8,451 men, which was, apparently, the highest number the division ever managed to reach.[90] The Germans, on the other

---

86. Lepre (1997), p 302. On Bosnian SS-soldiers' participation in killings of Jewish forced labourers in Austria and Hungary in the last days of the war see Lappin in *Dokumentationsarchiv des österreichischen Widerstandes. Jahrbuch 2004* (Wien, 2004), pp 77–112. Contrary to Muslims in the Balkans, the Serb population got a more remote attachment to the Waffen-SS. In 1944, a connexion with the so-called *Serbische Freiwilligen-Korps* (SFK) was established. This corps had a liaison with the Serb nationalist leader Dimitrije Ljotić and his Fascist ZBOR movement, which collaborated with the Germans during the occupation. SFK was formed in 1941 and was to be, primarily, employed against Communists. Walter Manoschek, *Serbien ist judenfrei. Militärische Besatzungspolitik und Judenvernichtung in Serbien 1941/42* (Oldenburg, 1995), p 111. On SFK's participation in crimes see Ana Antić: 'Police Force Under Occupation: Serbian State Guard and Volunteers' Corps in the Holocaust' in Sara R. Horowitz (ed.): *Back to the Sources: Re-examining Perpetrators, Victims and Bystanders, Lessons and Legacies*, Bd. X. (Northwestern University Press, 2012), p 18ff.
87. Marenglen Kasmi, *Die deutsche Besatzung in Albanien 1943 bis 1944* (ZMSBw, Zentrum für Militärgeschichte und Sozialwissenschaften der Bundeswehr, 2013), p 26ff.
88. RGVA, 1372/3/437, RFSS, 4 april 1944.
89. The most thorough examination of this division is Franziska A. Zaugg, *Albanische Muslime in der Waffen-SS: Von Großalbanien zur Division 'Skanderbeg'*, (Verlag Ferdinand Schöningh, 2016) and Franziska Zaugg, 'Perfekter Krieger? Die deutsche Wahrnehmung muslimischer Albaner in der Waffen-SS zwischen 1943 und 1945' in Schulte et al. (2014b).
90. BAB, NS19/1475, *Stärkemeldungen. Stand vom 19 September 1944*.

hand, never really understood the behaviour and the culture of the Albanians and their leaders. This was particularly true of the soldiers from the northern parts of the country, where, from an SS viewpoint, the men had a markedly different perception of warfare and soldierly virtues than the Waffen-SS.[91]

Like the Croation divisions, *Skanderbeg* was employed in its local area, where it got a number of tasks that it solved with considerable brutality co-operating with local militia units. Hanging of alleged Communists was a common way of retaliation whenever sabotage or an attack had taken place.[92] Moreover, *Skanderbeg* took part in the German persecution of Jews, and an 'order of the day' issued by the plenipotentiary general in Albania states that, by 16 April 1944, this division had apprehended 300 Jews in Priština.[93]

In October, the divisional commander, *Standartenführer* August Schmidtgruber, wrote a nine pages' report on the situation in *Skanderbeg*.[94] Schmidtgruber did not think highly about the division or the Albanians generally, and the report bears witness this. The Albanian subordinates were described as primitive, barefooted peasants devoid of soldierly qualities. According to Schmidtgruber they did not care much about discipline, when raining they would leave their post, and during the dark hours they drank raki and only participated in attacks if there where prospects of looting.[95]

If one wanted to achieve any fighting gains or prevent desertions, one would have to employ extraordinarily many German officers and NCOs with the Albanian units. The fate of *Skanderbeg* was like those of all the other SS divisions staffed by Yugoslav volunteers. Romania's and Bulgaria's change of sides combined with the Red Army's advance and the partisans' promise of amnesty led to mass desertions.[96] The German reaction to the disintegration trend was to disarm large parts of the division, while reliable groups were organised in a number of minor combat teams subordinated, inter alia, to *Division Prinz Eugen*.[97]

New Turkestan

The Crimea, in the North Caucasus, and in Central Asia was home to groups of people of Turkish descent whose relationship to the central power in Moscow was rather strained. In 1916, under Czar Nikolay II, there had been riots in the Central Asian province of Turkestan and, in the 1920s, there had been widespread opposition to the Soviet regime. Therefore, recruiting opportunities seemed promising.[98] Turkmen or East Turks were common expressions for a mix of people who, in reality, at the time, were

---

91. Zaugg (2014a), p 7.
92. BAMA, RH24-21/104, *Anlage zum KTB Nr.10. Gen. Kdo. XXI. Geb.A.K. v. 1.6-30.6 1944, Gen. Kdo. XXI.Geb.A.K.*, 3 July 1944.
93. BL, B126/25553, *Heeresgruppe 7, Gen. Albanien*, 16 April 1944.
94. The following is based on BAMA, RS3-21-1, *Zusammenfassender Bericht über die Aufstellung und der Zustand der 21. Waffen-Gebirgs-Division der SS 'Skanderbeg'*, 2 October 1944.
95. Ibid.
96. Zaugg (2014a), p 8.
97. Ibid. and Munoz (1991), p 232ff.
98. Martha Brill Olcott, *The Kazahks* (Hoover Institution Press, Stanford, 1987), p 118ff.

Soviet Muslims from the areas today known as Kazakhstan, Uzbekistan, Kyrgyzstan, Tajikistan and Turkmenistan.

As early as 1941, in the occupied areas the German army started to form police units staffed by Muslims and, later, quite a few of these found their way to actual combat units. In November 1941, a more dedicated recruiting effort was undertaken in order to enlist among Turkmen and Caucasian prisoners-of-war. These were then employed by Army Group South.[99] Early the following year, formations of so-called East Legions began, and their Muslim personnel were to fill a large proportion of the posts. In the Crimean Peninsula, as much as 10 per cent of the local Tartars appear to have donned the German uniform, and 75–100,000 Turkmen did the same.[100] Moreover, there were groups of minor Caucasian peoples such as Chechens, Dagestanis and Balkars who, since the Russian conquest of their territories, had opposed the central government. Now, they were co-operative and used the situation to rise up against Soviet power.[101]

The majority of the Muslim soldiers remained under army control, and it was not until 1943 that the SS saw them as potential military recruits. In October, Berger received a suggestion to set up a Muslim SS legion.[102] The day after, Berger asked Himmler to get Hitler's approval.[103] Husseini, the grand mufti of Jerusalem, asked Berger to ascertain that the Turkmen would enjoy the same religious treatment as did the Croatians and, in return, he would encourage all Turkmen to join the Waffen-SS.[104] Berger, though, did not inform the mufti that the soon-to-be Muslim formation would be sent to Belarus right away to have its baptism of fire and to test its loyalty. As Berger put it to Himmler's ADC: 'then this lot will be tried in daily toil. If they let us down, we'll shoot them. It is very simple'.[105]

In order to supplement the Turkmen transferred by the RSHA, the 1,000 men detailed by the army and another 1,000 found among Soviet workers in Germany, recruits were also found in German prisoner-of-war camps. In January 1944, one regiment of 3,000 troops was established.[106] The regiment was designated the *1. Ostmuselmanische SS-Regiment,* and its various ethnicities – including, apart from Turkmen, also Azerbaijani and Tartars – each formed its individual subunit. Over the year, the queue of applicants dwindled, and the hope for an entire division faltered. In the autumn 1944, when the plans of a division were finally shelved, these units were re-named *Osttürkischen Waffen-Verbände der SS.*[107]

99. The following is based on Joachim Hoffmann, *Kaukasien 1942–1943: das deutsche Heer und die Orientvölker der Sowjetunion* (Rombach, 1991), p 42ff., and Mallmann & Cüppers (2009), p 215ff.
100. Numbers are from Hoffmann (1991), p 137.
101. Alex Marshall, *The Caucasus under Soviet Rule* (Routledge, 2010), p 244ff.
102. BAB, NS19/43, Letter of 14 October 1943 to Berger from *Befehlshaber der SIPO und SD.*
103. BAB, NS19/43, Letter of 15 October 1943 from Berger to Himmler.
104. Mallmann and Cüppers (2009), p 224, and BAMA, RS3-39-1, *SS-Hauptamt,* 16 December 1943.
105. BAB, NS19/43, Letter of 24 November 1943 from Berger to *SS-Sturmbannführer* Grothmann.
106. Hoffmann (1991), p 143ff.
107. Munoz (1991), p 167.

The Waffen-SS's Moslem recruits were concentrated at Camp Poniatowa ca. 40 km west of Lublin. This used to be a concentration camp, whose 14,500 Jewish inmates had been murdered in October 1943. Presumably, it was the barracks left empty by the killings that the soldiers now took over. Still there were 100 prisoners in the camp, who had been transferred from Majdanek to rid the corpses of gold and other valuables. This work was carried out in the autumn and the Turkmen soldiers, so to say, lived next door to the prisoners.[108] In Poniatowa problems arose, and reports by the German guard personnel left the impression of an undisciplined group of soldiers who drank, harassed the local women and was having frequent clashes with the German personnel.[109] Lack of equipment was another problem. In January 1944, of 1,000 rifles only 150 were received and, by the end of the year, only one of every four men was equipped with one. Not surprisingly, heavy weapons were almost completely absent. A few Dutch mortars with 250 bombs and a couple of anti-tank guns was all.[110]

In February, transfer to Belarus began.[111] The following months when the regiment was employed in counter-insurgency actions were disastrous. Shortly after arrival, *Hauptsturmführer* Heinz Billing assumed command, and he turned out to be completely unfit for the task. His inefficiency led to commotion among the men and Billing, who was drunk, immediately ordered 28 of them shot. In May, the Turkmen officer Aliev sent a report telling that Billing treated the personnel like animals constantly threatening individuals with execution. Aliev claimed that, during Billing's regime, no less than 74 had been shot.[112] What was the cause and what was effect is difficult to tell, but at the same time there were mass desertions from the unit. On 23 March 1944, an entire company deserted.[113]

Eventually, Billing was displaced, but when his successor, *Hauptsturmführer* Hermann, arrived several hundreds of the men had absconded. In the summer 1944, the regiment was attached to *Sonderkommando Dirlewanger*, and it participated, among other actions, in the suppression of the Warsaw uprising. Shortly afterwards, the Turkmen Waffen-SS personnel had a new commander, *Standartenführer* Wilhelm Hintersatz. During the First World War, being an Austro-Hungarian officer he had served on the Turk general staff. While in Turkey, he had converted to Islam and assumed the name of Harun el Raschid Bey, and it was hoped that his taking over command might strengthen the regiment's morale and community feeling.[114] As of October 1944, the unit was employed in suppression of a Slovak uprising, but despite Bey's arrival the re-organisation of the unit did not proceed too well. The connexion with *Sonderkommando Dirlewanger* had

108. Megargee (2009), Vol. I, Part B, p 890.
109. BAMA, RS3-39-1. BAB, NS19/43, Unnamed letter of 2 February 1944.
110. Bougarel (2014), p 5.
111. BAB, NS19/43, Telex from Berger to *HSSPF Russland Mitte Gottberg*, 16 February 1944.
112. BAMA, RS3-39-1, 1. ostm. SS.Regt., 20 May 1944.
113. BAB, NS19/43, *Zustandebericht* of 17 April 1944 concerning *Ostmuselmanisches SS-regiment*.
114. BAB, NS19/2839, *Osttürkisches (muselmanisches) Korps*, 14.7.1944. On Bey, see also his memoirs, Harun-el-Raschid, *Aus Orient und Occident Ein Mosaik aus buntem Erleben* (Dt. Heimat-Verl., 1954). Unfortunately, he does not write about the time with the Waffen-SS.

no positive effect on the morale. In early 1945, Bey wrote a report telling that *Dirlewanger* personnel abused and defamed the Turkmen.[115] Moreover, there was a rumour among the men that *Osttürkischen Waffen-Verbändeder SS* were to be subordinated Russian ROA formations. This ran counter to the soldiers' wishes for autonomy and contributed to the mutinous state of affairs that characterised the end of the year. In December 1944, several German officers and NCOs were murdered. Moreover, 500 soldiers led by the Turkmen officer Gulam Alkimov, commanding officer of the *Waffen-Regiment der SS Turkistan Nr. 1*, deserted to the Slovak partisans.[116]

Early 1945, again *Osttürkischen Waffen-Verbände* were re-organised and moved to Northern Italy. In spring 1945, the units located there numbered 3,800 'East Turks'.[117] However, nothing indicates involvement in combat up until the time when the remnants of the never fully formed *SS-Division Neu Turkistan* surrendered to the American first Armoured Division. This was true, also, of another unsuccessful SS division dislocated in Northern Italy – the 40,000 strong Caucasian legion, which, in October 1944, Berger had fancied raising. In the spring 1945, this effort had brought together some 2,500 man (plus almost 1,500 relatives) in what was termed the *Kaukasischen Waffen-Verband der SS.* [118] This force, too, does not appear to have had any military significance until the war ended.

115. BAB, NS31/29, *Bericht über die Entwicklung des Osttürkischen Waffen-Verbandes der SS vom Warschau bis Überlauf Alimows und über die aus dieser sich ergebenden Folgerungen.* No date and year, though written in 1945.

116. BAB, NS31/29, *Überlauf des Kommandeurs des Waffen-Regts der SS Turkistan Nr.1, Waffen-Obersturmführer Gulam Alimows, mit etwa 500 Männer seines Regimentes zu den Partisanen, 26 December 1944.*

117. BAMA, RS1/4, HSSPF Italien. Ist. Stärke von Personal und Waffen der unterstellten Einheitenund Dienststellen 9.5 und 9 April 1945.

118. BAB, NS19/759, Telex of 25 October 1944 from *SS-Standartenführer Rudolf Brandt, Persönlicher Stab Reichsführer-SS* to Berger.Ibid.: Letter of 27 October 1944 from Berger to *SS-Standartenführer Brandt, Persönlicher Stab Reichsführer-SS.* BAB, NS31/42, Daily summary 5 March 1945 North Caucasian Brigade. Another unimportant Waffen-SS unit, also with Muslim characteristics was the so-called *Indische Freiwilligen Legion der Waffen-SS,* which, in late summer 1944, was subordinated the Waffen-SS. Admission of Indians started in 1941 based on negotiations between the Germans and the Indian nationalist leader Subhas Chandra Bose. Although, at the time, Berger was interested, initially the Indians came under the army organised in their own *Infanterieregiment 950 (indische).* The personnel were, primarily, found among prisoners-of-war, who had fought for the British Empire in North Africa. By the end of 1942, there were 2,593 men. At the time, the unit was a mixture of 1.503 Hindus, 516 Sikhs and 497 Muslims. Throughout its existence, the legion was stationed in France and the Netherlands. In March 1945, at a staff meeting Hitler stated that the Indian legion was a 'joke,' and that the Indians were useless in combat. On Hitler's remarks and the numbers see Neulen (1992), p 353ff. Concerning Berger and the Indian Legion see BAB NS19/103, *Indische Legion, 21.8 1942.* A more detailed description of this unit see Rudolf Hartog, who was the legion's interpreter. In his book Hartog describes a unit fraught with disciplinary problems and internal tensions among the various groups and casts. Rudolf Hartog, *The Sign of the Tiger. Subhas Chandra Bose and his Indian Legion in Germany, 1941–1945,* (Rupa & Co, 2002).

Between Coercion and Opportunism

There were about 250,000 soldiers in the Waffen-SS categorised as *Fremdvölker* and their motivation did, of course, vary over time as well as with respect to nationality.[119] As mentioned in the introduction to this chapter, their motives and experiences are difficult to examine. Not only is the archival material scarce as to the late-raised Waffen-SS units, there are also relatively few contemporary personal accounts and other alternative sources. Moreover, many later memoir writers (published in the Baltic countries after the collapse of the Soviet Union in 1991) wanted to create distance to the Nazis. A third group of sources are the Soviet intelligence and interrogation reports. Among the varied motives for enlisting were material needs and security, as well as reasons of a more political or ideological nature concerning Anti-Semitism, nationalism and Anti-Communism.

The degree of voluntariness varied considerably and, while some had possibly joined the German forces anyway, many signed up under more or less coercive circumstances. Hence, the number of true volunteers – which can never be gauged with any precision – was low, especially east of the 1939 Soviet border. Here Stalinism had effectively eradicated the pre-revolutionary elites and apart from certain minority groups, no coherent desire to collaborate with the Germans, other than expediency can be identified. Especially among groups of urbanites, the better educated and the younger generations, Soviet rule, despite its waves of mass repression, had left an impression of a modernist, egalitarian and future oriented project worth supporting.[120] Another feature of Soviet rule, also hampered the German recruitment drive, not least among the Muslim minorities. That was the process of *korenizatsiia*– the creation of Sovietised nationalities within well-defined ethnic territories. Thus, by World War Two regional and religious identities with such as Muslim Turkoman had to a large extend been replaced by ethno-territorial ones, such as Kazakh and Kirgiz. The ensuing ethnic particularism made it more difficult for the Nazi propaganda to appeal to supranational identities, such as religion.[121]

---

119. Smith and Peterson (1974), p 207.
120. The literature on Stalinist society before and during the war is vast. For main works supportive of the thesis that significant layers of the Soviet population had internalised Stalinist norms and supported the system, see Robert W. Thurston, *Life and Terror in Stalins Russia 1934–1941*, Yale University Press, 1996; Thurston, 'Cauldrons of Loyalty and Betrayal: Soviet Soldier's Behavior, 1941 and 1945', Robert W. Thurston and Bernd Bonwetch (eds.), *The People's War. Responses to World War II in the Soviet Union*, (University of Illonois Press, 2000), pp 235–257. Jochen Hellbeck, *Revolution on My Mind. Writing a Diary Under Stalin*, (Harvard University Press, 2009); Jochen Hellbeck, *Die Stalingrad-Protokolle: Sowjetische Augenzeugen berichten aus der Schlacht*, (Fischer, 2014); Roger Reese, *Why Stalin's Soldiers Fought. The Red Army's Military Effectiveness in World War II*, (University Press of Kansas, 2011).
121. Yuri Slezkine, 'The USSR as a Communal Apartment, or How a Socialist State Promoted Ethnic Particularism', *Slavic Review*, Vol. 53, No. 2, 1994, pp 414–452. See also Terry D. Martin, *The Affirmative Action Empire: Nations and Nationalism in the Soviet Union, 1923–1939* (Cornell University Press, 2001).

This stood in contrast with the impression left by the Germans, who first and foremost gave no promises of independent statehood to the Soviet nationalities they 'liberated'. As the first – and often positive impression of the new rulers – gave way for a more detailed picture, the Nazi programme for the occupied Soviet territories was (correctly) understood by many Soviet citizens as tantamount to future subjugation, if not extermination.[122] This impression was neatly condensed in a popular song whose verse was recorded by the SD in Kiev in 1942: The Germans have come – *gut*; for the Jews – *kaput*; for the Gypsies – *tozhe* [as well]; for the Ukrainians – *pozhe* [later].[123]

Thus, among many Soviet citizens signing up for German armed service should first and foremost be seen as a survival and welfare strategy. For example, recruitment might arise from a desire to avoid the unpopular forced labour, which the Germans practised by capturing all able-bodied men who were not already engaged in other kinds of activities and send them off to Germany. Moreover, service with the Germans provided protection against German injustices to the servicemen's families. To many of those joining as early as 1941 there was also an opportunity to ameliorate one's condition by transferring to the Waffen-SS. In February 1944, it was noticed that many Latvian men applied for transfer from police battalions to Waffen-SS units. A letter concerning this conundrum stated that the motives were tri-fold, viz. a wish to be led by Latvian officers, economic reasons, and better clothing with the Waffen-SS.[124]

Much of the recruiting for units composed by Slavs and Muslims happened among prisoners-of-war. In 1941–1942, the living conditions experienced by Soviet POWs in the German camps were outright genocidal making it tempting to sign up for German police or military service in order to get out.[125] Hardly surprising, most Soviet soldiers in German service, who were later interrogated by the Soviet authorities, claimed that they had joined exclusively to get out of the prisoner-of-war camps.[126] In the words of a former Soviet army major Gill-Rodionov: 'I betrayed my country not from political motives, but to save my skin'.[127] Gill-Rodionov was, however, also representative in another way. In August 1943, after secret negotiations with Belorussian partisans he and his 1,200 strong first Russian SS National Regiment defected to the Soviet side.[128] As shown above such incidents were many during the last two years of the war,

122. Berkhoff (2004).
123. M.I. Kowal, 'The Nazi Genocide of the Jews and the Ukrainian Population', Zvi Gitelman (ed.), *Bitter Legacy, Confronting the Holocaust in the Soviet Union*, (Indiana University Press, 1997), p 53. See also 'Political and Economic Problems of the Military and Civil Administration of the Occupied Eastern Territories, December 1942' Nuremberg document 1381-PS, in *Nazi Conspiracy and Aggression*, Vol. III, United States Printing Office, 1946, p 956.
124. SU, Box no. 5, Betr: *Übertritt lett. Polizeiangehörigen zur Lett. SS-Freiw.-Legion*, 10 February 1944.
125. Karel C. Berkhoff, 'The "Russian" Prisoners of War in Nazi-Ruled Ukraine as Victims of Genocidal Massacre,' in *Holocaust and Genocide Studies*, Vol. 15, No. 1, 2001, pp 1–32.
126. See the prisoners' testimonies in G.N. Vsvarovoy, 'Turkestanskiye legionary', *Voenno-istoricheskii zhurnal*, No 2, , 1995, p 39–46.
127. John Erickson, *The Road to Berlin* (Cassell, 1993), p 95.
128. Ibid, p 96.

thus revealing how weakly the units manned by East Europeans were integrated into the Waffen-SS. Some even joined the Waffen-SS in order to contribute to the resistance against the Germans. A large number of men serving with the 14th division had joined with the purpose of stealing weapons and have military training to support the struggle of the Ukrainian and Polish resistance movements.[129]

The Fremdvölker, the SS and Racial Ideology

Small wonder that, in SS' racial environment where not even the *Volksdeutsche* were thoroughly integrated, the *Fremdvölker* remained on the side-line of the community. The SS stuck to the notion of the Nordic-Germanic race's superiority. In the last war years, this perception was supplemented by an emphasis on European values – coined the 'Europe Concept'. Here, the propaganda focused on the opposition between an allegedly tidy and sound Europe and a culturally destructive Asia, whose non-European races menaced the Europeans.

At the same time, as previously explained, the SS began to nuance and revise the rigid classification of various nationalities as being inferior. This meant that not only German and other thoroughbred Germanics might be of Germanic stock. When, for instance, Ukrainians displayed courage, spirit of self-sacrifice and leadership qualities it allegedly showed that they were bearers of Germanic blood received by miscegenation. Such positive 'racial fragments' (*Rassensplitten*) allowed integration of the bearers.[130] In the summer 1942, thus Himmler declared in front of his assembled SS leaders that wherever in the east they met 'valuable blood, they should endeavour 'winning it (for Germany) or killing it'.[131]

In other words, this did not mean an end to racial theory, it was rather a gradual development of SS-ideology. In the autumn 1944, the SS was faced with a tricky case emphasising that delineations continued to exist. A soldier of the *1. Ostmuselmanischen SS-Regiment* asked permission to marry a German girl whom he had made pregnant. The reasoning with the SS was that it would have been difficult for the young woman to realise that a man wearing the SS uniform might be a racial alien, with whom she should have no intercourse. Although it was found unreasonable to punish the soldier, the attitude was crystal clear; this had to be stopped. Following a survey of the SS units employing *Fremdvölker* it became obvious that similar cases were not unheard of, and that they had been solved by telling the parties involved that no sound issue was to be expected from mixing races, and abortion had consequently been performed.[132]

129. YV, M36, 19.2, *SS Ausbildungs-Batallion z.b.v. Betr. Eindringen der polnischen Wiederstandsbewegung in die SS-Freiw.-Div. 'Galizien', Heidelager,* 22 August 1943, YV, M36, 19.2, *SS-Führungshauptamt,* Berlin, 19 August 1943.
130. Birn in Schulte (2009). Kott, Bubnys & Kraft (2017), p 120ff.
131. BAB, NS19/4009, *Der Reichsführer-SS vor den Oberabschnittsführern und Hauptamtchefs im Haus der Flieger in Berlin am 9. Juni 1942,* p 6.
132. BAB, NS31/28, *Hauptamt, betr: Verbindungen zwischen deutschen Mädchen und fremdstämningen SS-Angehörigen,* 22 November 1944. Moreover, it is hinted the *Fremdvöker* soldiers were punished for having had intercourse with German women.

While Muslin soldiers (and those of 'Asian appearance') were still treated as *Fremdvölker*, the Estonians and Latvians were increasingly being promoted to Germanics.[133] From the very beginning of the war, the Balts had been seen as possible candidates for Germanisation and, when the SS' notion of forming national Waffen-SS legions were positively received by the Estonians and Latvians but rejected by the Lithuanians, the SS found an explanation in too much Polish blood in the Lithuanians' veins as opposed to the two other peoples' higher proportion of German genes.[134]

In several ways, the distinction between Germanic soldiers and *Fremdvölker* was emphasised. The badges worn on the uniforms distinguished between fully Germanic Waffen-SS personnel and soldiers originating among the *Fremdvölker*. The Balts, too, were subject to that distinction, and in the first years of the Baltic legions' existence the SS went out of their way to ensure that only Balts of clear Germanic appearance might wear the SS runes on their uniform collars.[135] This privilege was a recurring issue and, as late as February 1945, Himmler reacted when seeing photos of Turkmen personnel with runes on their uniforms. This made Berger insist that the runes were for German and Germanic soldiers only, and he stressed that the responsible would be punished if unauthorised use of runes be detected.[136]

Also, the divisional designations distinguished between groups of soldiers and signalled the unit composition. The early SS divisions, such as the *Wiking*, were normally known by their names alone, but in 1942 a number system was introduced. Thence onwards, while the earliest formations would carry the lowest numbers, the place of the letters 'SS' would signify their composition. A formation made up of German personnel would be called an '*SS-Division*'; one of Germanic volunteers would be a '*SS-Freiwilligen-Division*', and formations consisting of forcibly drafted soldiers would be entitled '*Division der SS*'.[137]

The Balts were *the* group of *Fremdvölker* which became most closely integrated into the Waffen-SS. This was because the SS' positive view on their racial qualities as well as due to the soldiers' relatively high motivation in combination with a relatively high percentage of native officers. The Estonian and Latvian officers served as important go-betweens mediating between the SS and the men. On the other hand, the officers were also often seen by the SS as insufficiently imbued with Nazi norms or lacking faith in the final German victory.[138] In addition, the Baltic officers and their soldiers'

133. Here after Stein (1984), p 176, and Lumans (2006), p 273. Katrin Reichelt, 'Latvia and Latvians in the Nazi Race and Settlement Policy: Theoretical Conception and Practical Implementation' in Caune (2000). Aly and Heim (2003), p 253ff.
134. Reichelt (2000), p 266ff.
135. BAB, NS19/382, Jüttner May 1942. The prohibition was not applicable to officers while training at Bad Tölz. They might also use the German rank without the prefix 'legion'. Hiio (2006), p 947. See also BAB, NS19/3676, *Beförderung lett. Freiw.-Unterführer zu SS-Führern. Reichsführer-SS*, 1 November 1943.
136. BAB, NS31/43, Berger 26 February 1945
137. Stein (1984), p 181, note 9.
138. BAB, NS19/3759,HSSPF Ostland to pers. Stab RFSS, betr. estischer Oberst Kurg, 8 February 1943.

obvious thirst for national autonomy was a stumbling block.[139] In September 1941, there was a clash between filler personnel of the Estonian 20th division and German soldiers, because the former had hoisted the Estonian Flag – an episode which was far from singular.[140] Relations between the Baltic and the German personnel was, of course, also determined by the German officers' attitude to their subordinates and many would not discard their racist prejudices.[141] In November 1944, Berger sent a report to Jüttner describing how the personnel in the *Fremdvölker* units felt that they were treated as inferior persons, and this was particularly true of the Slavs and the Muslims.[142] Often, such problems arose when German units were ordered to detail personnel to foreign formations and they chose to send those they would rather be rid of.[143] Moreover, such personnel were prone to regard their new posts as leisurely sine cure or as a punishment, which made them behave badly giving the Germans *per se* a bad reputation.[144] It was, for instance, a frequent occurrence that the Belarus personnel of the 30th division were given nicknames, and now and then they were subjected to violence and, as described earlier, many Muslims had similar experiences.[145]

Naturally, another reason for Germans not wishing to serve with *Fremdvölker* units might be the mutinies and other commotion which characterised these. The Waffen-SS was small enough to allow that rumours of problems occurring in a division would be quickly spread outside its precincts. A British tapping of a prisoner-of-war conversation gives an impression. *Standartenführer* Linge, who had served with *Division Götz von Berlichingen*, had a chat with a Wehrmacht captain. He was well-informed about the situation outside his own formation and told the captain about 'the wildest occurrences' in *Division Handschar*. According to Linge, a training instructor had his throat cut because he had called a Muslim a pig. There had also been a large-scale mutiny during which all German officers had been killed, and the soldiers had deserted to Switzerland. However, Linge held the opinion that the officers were themselves to blame for the mutiny, because they drank and beat the soldiers.[146]

As demonstrated above, there was an obvious difference between Himmler's address on a festive occasion and the realities in the barracks or in the field. A large proportion of *Fremdvölker* remained patronised, if not ostracised. In the best case, the situation resembled what an Estonian legionnaire described in his memoirs after the war. He stated that in his unit the relations with the German key personnel had been 'correct but rarely cordial'.[147] Thus, the massive influx of Eastern Europeans into the Waffen-SS

139. For an example see BAB, SSO 234A, Kvalsberg, Peteris.
140. Hiio (2006), p 61.
141. Lumans (2006), p 290; Michaelis (2006).
142. BAB, NS31/43, *Fremdvölkischen Freiwilligen-Verbänden*, 7 November 1944.
143. Heike (1970), p 40ff.
144. Lepre (1997), p 64.
145. Rein (2007), p 337.
146. NAKEW, WO208/4140, SRM 1212. The tapping happened in 1944.
147. Michaelis (2006), p 31.

never became the significant force multiplier Himmler and others had hope for. Rather it demonstrated that the peculiar mix of ideological flexibility and dogmatism that Himmler practiced could not effectively be transmitted to his own officer corps and translated in to an effective program for the integration of the non-Germanic soldiers. The Waffen-SS' extension and increased ethnic differentiation was not only an ideological challenge; it also represented a problem of integration, motivation and control that the SS never managed to deal with effectively.

Part IV

SOLDIERS AND WAR CRIMINALS

Chapter Eleven

WAFFEN-SS AND NAZI CRIMES

In the summer of 1941, a German journalist was attached to *Division Das Reich* as a *Kriegsbericter* (war correspondent). On 29 June 1941, he wrote in his diary about the advance into the Soviet Union,

> There are no longer other troops around. We are alone. [...] The villagers are apprehensive and reserved. Another village – suddenly shots are heard from up front. At the village entrance our advance guard has been shot at. All vehicles [...] turn into farms and side roads. [...] I rush forward. A few Russians are fleeing their positions [...] behind the village. Prisoners who have surrendered are brought back. Among them an eighteen-year-old, who looks like fifteen, and an elderly NCO who willingly acts as interpreter. I make a recording of the interrogation of the prisoners. We take the first red banners and red Soviet stars from their uniforms as souvenirs. On the commander's order and according to a divisional directive the prisoners are then shot. This is an occurrence, which makes me very sad.[1]

Almost simultaneously, the 4th Army Corps noted in its war diary that not only did *Division Wiking* make a severe disturbance of the traffic around Lviv due to the troop' bad road discipline, but civilians and prisoners-of-war were also shot out of hand on the roadside.[2] Shortly afterwards, in other sectors at the eastern front Waffen-SS units like the cavalry brigade and 1st SS brigade started systematically murdering the local Jewish population.[3] Subsequently, all Waffen-SS units employed at the eastern front were to play their role in the dramatic escalation of the Third Reich's atrocities that followed. For the Nazi system as a whole, as well as more specifically for the SS, the massive crimes committed at the eastern front (and its hinterland) originated in the culture of violence and crime that began during the so-called *Kampfzeit* (time of struggle) prior to 1933 and were institutionalized during the early years of Nazi rule and the campaign in Poland 1939.

The Waffen-SS became a major contributor to the regime's crimes. Regardless of where and when fighting was going on, its soldiers typically fulfilled their

---

1. IfZG, ED 373/1, *Tagebuchaufz.n 25.9.-20.10.38, 24.6.-24.10.41*, here from 29 June 1941.
2. Christensen et al. (1998), p. 94ff. Wiking's crimes at the eastern front are extensively covered in Lars Westerlund, *The Finish SS-volunteers and atrocities, 1941–1943* (SKS, 2019).
3. 1st and 2nd SS infantry brigade and the SS cavalry brigade. On this see Cüppers (2011).

Figure 11.1 Waffen-SS volunteers from Division Wiking was involved in war crimes and genocide at the Eastern front. In the sidecar we see C. F. von Schalburg who later became commander of Frikorps Danmark. (Frihedsmuseet)

role as the race warriors that Himmler wanted them to be. Previous chapters have mentioned these crimes in passing, but in the subsequent two this topic will be scrutinised which includes looking at the context, reasons and dynamics of the Waffen-SS atrocities. Paradoxically, much earlier research has dealt only scantily with the crimes of the Waffen-SS and without a broad basis in archive material. The topic is covered sporadically by Stein in his classic work and more recently by Leleu, while more comprehensive examinations are found in studies by Terry Goldsworthy and James Pontolillo. Both the latter are, however, primarily compilations of facts known from existing literature, while new archival sources are only very scarcely examined and the dynamics and causes of the crimes seldom discussed.[4]

---

4. Terry Goldsworthy, *Valhalla's Warriors. A History of the Waffen-SS on the Eastern Front 1941–1945* (Indianapolis: Dog Ear Publishing, 2007); James Pontolillo, *Murderous Elite – The Waffen-SS and Its Record of Atrocities* (Leandoer&Eckholm, 2009). While Goldsworthy's book is based almost exclusively on works in English, Pontolillo's has an extraordinarily broad literary base. Its almost encyclopaedic character spells a lasting value as a handbook.

Today, thanks to meticulous research, we know much about the crimes committed by the Third Reich. Whereas, to a large extent, the German archives have been accessible since about 10 years after the war ended, more source material has appeared, over later decades, partly because of the de-classification of western documents, partly due to the opening of archives in, what used to be, the Warsaw Pact countries. The post-war judicial reckoning with perpetrators has also created public insight.[5] Nevertheless, this does not mean that we can draw up an exhaustive list of Waffen-SS soldiers' crimes. It is far from possible to review the entire catalogue of Nazi misdeeds. While there is reliable information available concerning the perpetrators of virtually all major Nazi crimes in western Europe – units as well as persons – this is less so in the case of most Mediterranean countries, and quite different in the Balkans and the East where atrocities were committed on a massive scale.

Roughly speaking, the greater the scope, the farther east we go, and the later in time – the less we know about the crimes committed. Particularly the Soviet Union constitutes a blind spot in this respect.[6] Because of fear of punishment after the war the Germans did what they could to hide or camouflage their crimes. Moreover, much official German wartime archival material has been lost and there is generally less documentation of crimes committed late in the war compared to the early atrocities. The crimes committed in the very last phase of the war, however, constitute an important exception, because these could be investigated while the trail was still hot.

---

5. Background material and rulings from the International Military Tribunal at Nuremberg of 1945–1946 as well as a number of previous and subsequent British and American court cases were published immediately after the war. Se, inter alia, International Military Tribunal, *Trial of the Major War Criminals Before the International Military Tribunal, 14 November 1945–1 October 1946, Bd. 1-42*, International Military Tribunal, 1947. The sentences have been published in *Justiz und NS-Verbrechen: Sammlung deutscherStrafurteile wegen nationalsozialistischer Tötungsverbrechen* (Amsterdam, University Press Amsterdam, 1968–2012), Bd. 1-49. See also the series of GDR sentences published as *DDR-Justiz und NS-Verbrechen* (Amsterdam, University Press Amsterdam, 2002–2010), Vol. 1–14.

6. For more about Soviet research into Nazi atrocities see Marian R. Sanders, *Extraordinary Crimes in Ukraine: An Examination of Evidence Collection by the Extraordinary State Commission of the U.S.S.R., 1942–1946*, Ph.D. dissertation (Ohio University, 1995); Alexander E. Epifanow, *Die Außerordentliche Staatliche Kommission* (Stocker, 1997); Niels Bo Poulsen, *The Soviet Extraordinary State Commission on War Crimes: An Analysis of the Commission's Investigate Work in War and Post War Stalinist Society*, Ph.D. dissertation, (Faculty of Humanities, Copenhagen University, 2004); Marina Sorokina, "People and Procedures. Towards a History of the Investigation of Nazi Crimes in the USSR", *Kritika*, nr. 4, 2005, pp. 797–831.

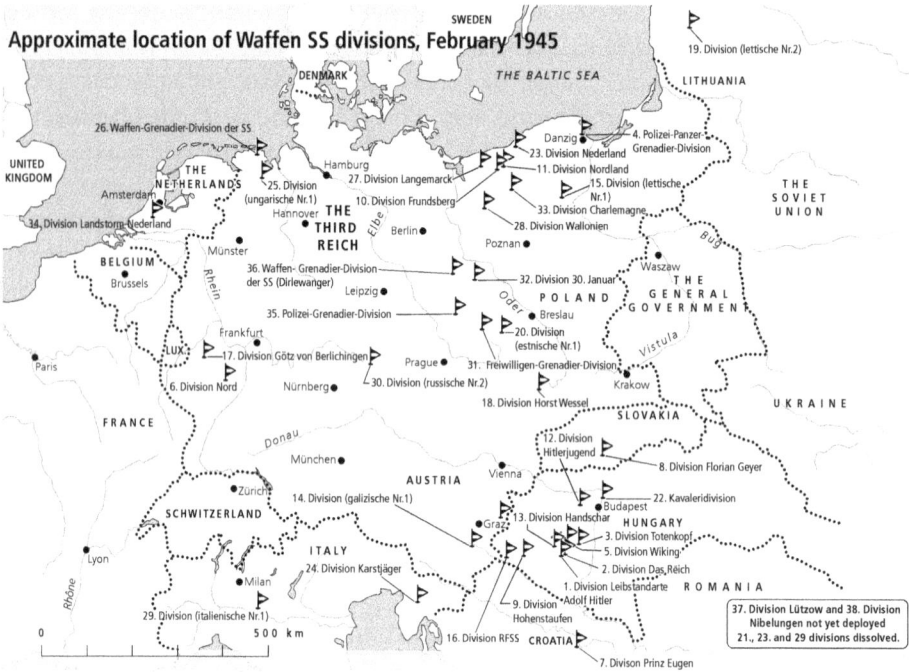

Approximate location of Waffen SS divisions, February 1945

The Waffen-SS and the Concentration Camp System

In 1934, Himmler assumed responsibility for the concentration camps which were systematised under Theodor Eicke. Until then, their operation had been decentralised and differed in many respects. The guards had come from various institutions and, for example, men from the *Leibstandarte* were assigned to the *Columbia Haus* camp.[7] Eicke regimented the use of violence in the camps and organized the guards in units called *Totenkopfverbände*.[8]

In August 1939, Hitler decided that, in case of war, parts of the *Totenkopfverbände* should be attached to the police and, therefore, not be drafted for military service. The men thus detailed were to be replaced by members of the *Allgemeine SS* of the age of 45 or more.[9] This gave Himmler a sizeable force to deploy in the field for "security" purposes.[10] When Germany attacked Poland, the *Totenkopfverbände* were committed in the field as parts of the *Einsatzgruppen*. Thus, they became core contributors to the killing actions perpetrated by the SS during and after the campaign.

---

7. Megargee (2009), p. 60.
8. On Eicke and the camps see: Buchheim et al. (1994), in particular p. 349ff.; Sydnor (1990), p. 17ff.; Koehl (1983), pp. 69ff and 107ff.
9. BAMA, RS1/1, *Betr. Führererlass über die bewaffneten Teile der SS, 17.8.1938.*
10. Stein (1984), pp. 23 and 32f. Miroslav Karny, "Waffen-SS und Konzentrationslager", Christoph Dieckmann (ed.), *Die Nationalsozialistischen Konzentrationslager. Entwicklung und Struktur* (Wallstein Verlag, 1998), pp. 787–99, here p. 788ff.

In February 1940, the *Totenkopfverbände* and the *Verfügungstruppe* were amalgamated under the designation Waffen-SS, which created a flexible mechanism through which personnel could be moved back and forth between the camp system and the field formations. Moreover, during this and the following years, a number of field units were formed with Totenkopf men as their core personnel. Thus, former concentration camp guards were dispersed across the Waffen-SS. As late as 1944, Himmler arranged that 1,000 elderly Waffen-SS soldiers were transferred to the camps from the field units. As they were replacing 1,000 younger guards, Himmler boasted that for once it had been possible to provide 'a good old fashioned SS replacement' for front line service.[11] However, it was, primarily, in *Division Totenkopf* that the heritage from the camps would survive relatively undiluted. At the time of formation, 7,000 out of 15,000 soldiers came from the camps and, more importantly, with one exception the whole staff came from Eicke's *Inspektion der Konzentrationslager*.[12]

The transfer went both ways, and those injured or in any other way unfit for combat duties were routinely used as guards in the camp system. A survey of the Auschwitz guard personnel shows that throughout the operation of the camps 523 out of 1,292 guards came from Waffen-SS units or authorities.[13] Almost as many came from the personnel replacement system, and among the remainder ca. 500 came from other camps. In the opposite direction 214 guards out of 1,897, whose service records are known, were transferred to the Waffen-SS or other authorities. The main recipient was *Division Wiking* that, between 1940 and 1945, received 52 men from Auschwitz.[14] Almost all other transfers from Auschwitz went to other concentration camps.[15]

During the almost total mobilisation of the male population of German minorities outside Germany, for reasons of age, physical fitness, or health many were drafted who were not fit for service at the front. It was not least these men who were employed

---

11. BAB, NS19/1542, Letter of 2 August 1944 from Himmler to Jüttner.
12. Karny (1998), p. 791. Sydnor (1990), p. 47. In spring 1943, during interrogation in Switzerland, a deserter from this division claimed that the former concentration camp guards displayed a particular degree of recklessness and brutality. BB, E27, 1000/721, Archive No. 9928, Bd. 4, D110, Deserteurbericht 11.5.1943, s.12.
13. Aleksander Lasik, Wacław Długoborski, Franciszek Piper and William Brand, *Auschwitz 1940–1945: Central Issues in the History of the Camp, Bd. 1* (Auschwitz-Birkenau State Museum, 2000), table 7, p. 375ff. See also Aleksander Lasik," Historical-Sociological Profile of the Auschwitz SS" in Israel Gutman and Michael Berenbaum, *Anatomy of the Auschwitz Death Camp* (Indiana university press, 1998), p. 271ff.
14. Lasik et al. (2000), table 8, p. 376ff. Approximately at the same time, *Untersturmführer* Luitpold Dertler and *Untersturmführer* Walter Renner were gazetted to Legion Norge from *Inspektion der Konzentrationslager Oranienburg*. Both were part of a major move to provide SS officers outside the field units with frontline experience. YV, O.68, 539, personnel case Wilhelm Burbock, s.21.
15. It should be noticed that in the cases of Debica and Beneschau the man in question may have been a guard there as well, because these training areas accommodated work teams of concentration camp inmates.

as guard personnel in the concentration camps. Of about 1,500 men of the German minority in Denmark enrolled in the Waffen-SS, between 50 and 100 served as camp personnel.[16] Similarly, between 800 and 3,500 Romanian *Volksdeutsche* were fed into the concentration camp system via the Waffen-SS.[17] In most cases, the recruits seem to have had no influence on whether or not they would go to the camp system, nor have they had any notion of what this might involve. However, it was made brutally clear to a number of Romanian raw recruits when Berger made a speech on their arrival in Vienna,

> Most of you will be employed as guards in the concentration camps. I am sure you will know how to tidy up amongst these bastards. It will be safer to shoot ten too many of these criminals than one too few.[18]

The transfer of officers is especially noteworthy since they acted as decision makers and conveyors of norms. A survey of the personnel files of 950 former camp officers shows that either before or after, 50 per cent were active in the field units and a number of these became commanders up to divisional levels at, for example, division *Totenkopf*, *Wiking*, *Götz von Berlichingen*, *Reichsführer-SS* and *Horst Wessel*.[19]

Waffen-SS Facilities With Affiliated Prisoner Compounds

A large number of Waffen-SS facilities had affiliated work team compounds for concentration camp prisoners. In some cases, these were sub-units under the permanent concentration camps. In other cases, they were under the control of the local German authorities. This was part of a vast heterogeneous system of incarceration and forced labour utilised by the SS and the *Wehrmacht* as well as numerous other authorities.[20]

The SS barracks in Treskau near Posen in the Warthegau was one of the places where Jewish prisoners carried out forced labour under brutal conditions.[21] A soldier of *Frikorps Danmark* stationed in Treskau noted the following in his diary,

---

16. Dennis Larsen, *Fortrængt grusomhed. Danske SS-vagter 1941–1945* (Gyldendal, 2010), pp. 210 and 215. However, this number may be as high as 200.
17. Milata (2009), p. 263.
18. Ibid., p. 236.
19. French L. MacLean, *The Camp Men: The SS Officers Who Ran the Nazi Concentration Camp System* (Schiffer Military History, 1999), pp. 10 and 281ff.
20. In her study of the concentration camp system Gudrun Schwarz counted sixteen different types of camps. Gudrun Schwarz, *Die nationalsozialistischen Lager* (Campus Verlag, 1990), p. 70.
21. Wolfgang Benz, Barbara Distel and Angelika Königseder, *Der Ort des Terrors. Geschichte der nationalsozialistischen Konzentrationslager*, Vol. 6 (C.H. Beck, 2007), p. 447.

Figure 11.2 Jewish prisoners engaged in forced labor at the Treskau compounds. The photo was taken by a Danish Waffen-SS volunteer (Frihedsmuseet)

28 November: Lately, about ten Jews – star of David on their backs – worked in the garden of the commandant's house overseen by a Sturmmann. They are suitably beaten with a stick and are working with bare legs – the temperature is 10 degrees C below zero [...] 29 November: Last night one of those wearing the star of David died; another walked past the barracks this morning with a bloody and beaten face. The Sturmmann says that he is confident that he will be rid of them all before New Year.[22]

As the war dragged on, a shortage of workforces manifested itself all over Europe and the use of such concentration camp prisoners became the order of the day.[23] Some

---

22. Claus Bundgård Christensen, Niels Bo Poulsen and Peter Scharff Smith, *Dagbog fra Østfronten: en dansker i Waffen-SS, 1941–1944* (Aschehoug, 2005), p. 51. Mario Wenzel, "Zwangsarbeitslager für Juden in den besetzten polnischen und sowjetischen Gebieten" in Wolfgang Benz, Barbara Distel and Angelika Königseder, *Der Ort des Terrors. Geschichte der nationalsozialistischen Konzentrationslager*, Vol. 9, (C.H.Beck, 2009), pp. 125–54, here p. 126.
23. While no exhaustive account of the numerous Waffen-SS facilities using prisoners can be found, a substantial overview can be gained from combining in-depth studies of the concentration camps: Megargee (2009), Vol.1, part B, p. 580ff., p. 1121. Wolfgang Benz et al., *Der Ort des Terrors. Geschichte der nationalsozialistischen Konzentrationslager*, Bd. 2 (C.H. Beck, 2005), p. 455;Bd. 4, (C.H. Beck, 2006) (b), p. 95. Robert Steegmann, *Das KZ Natzweiler-Struthof und seine Aussenkommandos an Rhein und Neckar 1941–1945*, (Metropol, 2010), p. 278ff. Peter Engelbrecht, "Die Massaker der Pottensteiner SS-Karstwehr 1943–1944 in Slowenien" in Gerhard Jochem and Georg Seiderer,eds., *Entrechtung, Vertreibung, Mord: NS-Unrecht in Slowenien und seine Spuren in Bayern 1941–1945*, (Metropol, 2005), pp. 223–36, here p. 223ff.

prisoner detachments were small or merely employed for a brief spell, others, like in Treskau, were more or less permanent. Sometimes, they might number hundreds or even thousands. For example, in the summer of 1940, a Dachau sub-camp with 180 prisoners was set up at the *Junkerschule* at Bad Tölz.[24] The prisoners were accommodated in the basement of the school and performed a number of tasks on the premises.[25] How the prisoners' presence in the school was utilised pedagogically is fittingly illustrated by the testimony of a Dutch officer cadet. Shortly after the war, he told about another Dutch cadet who had reported ill. As a disciplinary sanction, he was ordered to clean the toilets alongside the prisoners.[26]

Figure 11.3 Danish Waffen-SS soldiers at the Treskau facilities in occupied Poland. Jewish prisoners were engaged in forced labor in and around the camp (Frihedsmuseet)

In the Waffen-SS' training areas, prisoners were employed more intensively than in the schools and barracks. The sheer size of these grounds meant that a large number of manual workers were required – not least in the build-up phase when roads, firing ranges and accommodation were to be constructed. In 1943, a large tank training

---

24. BL, B162/26467, Note of 3 May 1962 concerning Dr Bohlen. On the use of slave labourers in the two other SS cadet schools see (Klagenfurt) BL, B162/9844 and Benz et al. (2006b), p. 384ff., and Megargee (2009), Vol.1, part B, p. 922ff. and (Braunschweig) Benz et al. (2006a), pp. 404 and 450, and Megargee (2009), p. 321.
25. See testimonies in DA: A 144, A 3034, A3622, ZstL.
26. NIOD, 249-0761A. *SS Junkerschule Tölz, 29.10.1948.*

area – *SS-Truppenübungslager Seelager* – was established near Dundaga (Dondangen) in western Latvia, were between 3 and 5.000 Jewish and other prisoners passed through during its existence.[27] In order to support the establishment, two sub-camps of the Riga area concentration camp Kaiserwald were pitched. In the initial phase, when the work was hurried on, the fatality rate was immense.[28] Since, during the winter 1943–1944, the prisoners were forced to sleep in open air or in tents, this is hardly surprising.[29] Due to the high mortality and two consecutive commandants' brutality the prisoners nicknamed the place the 'annihilation camp'.[30]

While little is known about this camp, researchers have found lots of evidence concerning the *SS-Truppenübungsplatz Debica* in south-eastern Poland.[31] During its existence from late 1939 to the summer of 1944, no less than four camps accommodating civilian Jews and Poles, as well as Soviet prisoners-of-war, were to be found in this training area.[32] The Jews were the largest and most permanent single group in the area numbering 1–2,000.[33] The camp for about 5,000 Russian PWs had only a brief existence after which those, who had not already died from hunger or exhaustion, were shot by soldiers of the permanent garrison, *SS-Bataillon SS-Truppenübungsplatz Debica*.[34] The Waffen-SS troops stationed in Debica participated in a number of guard, deportation and killing actions against the prisoners as well as against Jews in the local villages and the somewhat more distant cities Tarnów and Kraków. In September 1942, an *Aussiedlung* (re-settlement) of 1,300 Jews from the town Pustków, who were sent to

---

27. This estimate is based on NAWA, 263, ZZ-20, box 5, Report on interrogation of *SS-Oberführer* Eduard Bachl, 22.1.1946. There are no precise numbers concerning the prisoners in the camps Dondangen I and Dondangen II, that were situated in Seelager, in Wolfgang Benz, Barbara Distel and Angelika Königseder, *Der Ort des Terrors. Geschichte der nationalsozialistischen Konzentrationslager, Bd. 8* (C.H. Beck, 2008), p. 65ff.
28. Andrej Angrick and Peter Klein, *Die "Endlösung" in Riga: Ausbeutung und Vernichtung, 1941– 1944* (WissenschaftlicheBuchgesellschaft, 2006), p. 399. MargersVestermanis, "Die nationalsozialistischen Haftstätten und Todeslager im okkupiertenLettland 1941–1945" in *Der Ort des Terrors.Geschichte der nationalsozialistischen Konzentrationslager, Bd. 4.* (C.H. Beck, 2006) (b), p. 23, Ulrich Herbert et al. (eds.), *Die Nationalsozialistischen Konzentrationslager, Bd. II* (Wallstein Verlag, Gottingen, 1998), p. 488.
29. Benz et al. (2008), p. 65.
30. Megargee (2009), Vol. 1, part B, p. 1236ff.
31. For a detailed account of this camp and its history see BL, B162/5284, *Zentrale Stelle der Landesjustizverwaltungen Ludwigsburg, Bericht, 18.1.1963*. For a general analysis of Holocaust and the Waffen-SS units in the camp see Cüppers (2011), p. 288ff.
32. BL, B162/5283, *Allgemeines*: Historical account of the camp at Pustkow. BL, B162/5283, 6 AR-Z 280/59, note of 31 May 1961 concernning *Zwangsarbeitslager Pustkow*. Ibid.: B162/18266, Note of 4 January 1971.
33. Court case No 802, reprinted in C.F. Rüter and L. Hekelaar Gombert, *Justiz und NS-Verbrechen: Sammlung deutscher Strafurteile wegen nationalsozialistischer Tötungsverbrechen, 1945–1966, bd.XXXIX* (University Press Amsterdam, 2008), p. 333.
34. BL, B162/5283, 6 AR-Z 280/59, note concerning *Zwangsarbeitslager Pustkow*, 31 May 1961.

the death camps Belzec. During this kind of actions, the deportation process included shooting on the spot of the old, the weak and the children.[35]

A Danish volunteer, who began his service as a recruit with *Division Wiking*'s filler battalion in Debica, described in his memoirs how he, frequently, had to guard Jewish or Soviet work teams, and he made no secret of the high mortality rate and the extremely brutal treatment,

> In the autumn and winter 1941, while I was in Debica, it had turned rather cold. Sometimes, the Russians fell ill, and we were not allowed to let them into the barracks because of fear that the others might catch the illness off them. Then, when, after work, we returned home with the sick, they were locked up in an enclosure of barbed wire stretched over cheveaux-de-frise. To be true: they were actually hurled over the fence into the enclosure. The next morning, as we came out, they were frozen to death and were completely stiff. Then they were placed in a row on top of a bonfire we had made from big logs. We lit and sent them to Das ewige Feur (perpetual fire). Then they would get warm![36]

Another SS camp in the field, whose function as a concentration camp – or rather extermination camp – is well-researched, is the *Nachschubkommandantur der Waffen-SS und Polizei Russland-Mitte* in Babruysk, Belarus.[37]

Death Marches and Shooting of Prisoners

As Germans forces were required to withdraw, evacuation became necessary of concentration camps and detachments close to the front. Frequently, emptying these places led to killing off prisoners who were too sick or exhausted to come along. Many were ordered out on strenuous foot marches and guards would unhesitatingly kill anyone who could not keep up, hence the term death marches (*Todesmärsche*).[38]

For example, soldiers of *Division Kama* together with members of the divisions *Handschar* and *Prinz Eugen* guarded several death marches and also took part in large scale killings of Hungarian Jewish forced labourers in February 1945.[39] Soon after, in March–April 1945, soldiers of *Division Wiking* (together with other Waffen-SS formations) became instrumental in further massacres of Jewish prisoners who had

---

35. BL, B162/5283, Survey of the case 18 January 1963. Ibid: B162/5284, Résumé concerning SS-Btl. 'SS-Truppenübungsplatz Debica' and participation in other actions. On the Debica battalion's participation in deportations from the Kraków ghetto, see Court Case No 619, reprinted in ibid., p. 68ff., here p. 78ff.
36. Pedersen and Rasmussen (2012), p. 40. In an interview in October 2005, Georg Rasmussen told basically the same story to these authors.
37. There is a large material on the use of Jewish slave labourers in this camp can be seen in BL, B126/ 6723; BL, B126/6722; B126/6732 og B126-6728. See also Larsen and Stræde (2014).
38. Bridgman and Jones (1990) and Blatman (2011).
39. Lappin in *Dokumentationsarchiv des österreichischen Widerstandes. Jahrbuch 2004* (Wien, 2004), pp. 77–112.

been constructing fortifications along the Austrian-Hungarian border.[40] While, to a large extent, local *Hitlerjugend* and *Volkssturm* units were employed in guarding the prisoners when in transit, close-by SS units, such as Wiking, were alerted when the task was killing of sick and weak prisoners, large scale massacres or ferreting out the hideouts of escaped Jews.[41]

As late as 2–3 May 1945, the largest massacre in Austria happened were the soldiers of an unidentified Waffen-SS unit murdered 233 prisoners from concentration camp Mauthausen though temporarily placed in an interim camp at Hofamt-Priehl.[42] The prisoners at the *Junkerschule* at Bad Tölz, too, were close to becoming victims of a similar massacre. In late April, the 200 persons were to be moved in a huge column of ca. 2,500 coming from concentration camp Dachau. From the outset, there was an ominous atmosphere. Several of the officer cadets shouted that the prisoners carried the responsibility that Germany had lost the war, and they threatened to get back at them.[43] About the 24th of April, commanded by a young officer – probably from *Division Götz von Berlichingen* – a column of staggering prisoners left Bad Tölz. While marching, several prisoners were shot because they could not keep up and, having walked five kilometres, the guards halted, probably in order to arrange an all-out execution. Luckily for the prisoners, an army general appeared. Having discussed with the guards, he ordered the column back to Bad Tölz, where, on 1 May, the men were freed by American troops.[44]

Holocaust in the Field

Already before the war, the Waffen-SS contributed to the Nazi anti-Jewish policies, for example when soldiers of the *Standarte der Führer* took part in the murder and terror of the Crystal Night (*Kristallnacht*).[45] In 1939, SS soldiers in occupied Poland were involved in massacres on local Jews but it was not until the second half of 1941 that a systematic policy of extermination materialised. The attack on the Soviet Union was the moment where a number of Waffen-SS units became radically involved in the Holocaust.

---

40. Elenore Lappin, *The Death Marches of Hungarian Jews Through Austria in the Spring of 1945* (Yad Vashem Studies, vol. XXVIII, 2000), pp. 12, 19 and 25ff. Emberland and Kott (2012), p. 455.
41. Lappin (2000), p. 21. That the shootings were ordered from top level and represented a general policy of leaving no Jews alive in the frontline area is confirmed by the killing of two small groups of Jews by a maintenance company of Das Reich in late April 1945. It appears from police interrogations in the 1960s that soldiers guarding roads were under orders to apprehend Jewish 'stragglers.' BL, B162/ 5010 and B126/ 5011.
42. Lappin (2000), p. 19.
43. DA, *Dokumentation zur Geschichte des Kasernengeländes in Bad Tölz*. No year nor place, testimony by ZK.
44. DA, Kopien der ZstL Aussenlager A-E, witness interrogation by the Polish war crimes commission of WZ, born 1913; Witness interrogation by the Polish war crimes commission in Posen of TG, born 1916; Witness interrogation on 19 December 1969 of AW, born 1901.
45. Höhne (1995), p. 418ff.

On 21 May 1941, Himmler ordered that all SS units in the hinterland of the coming war in Russia would be detailed for special tasks of political-security nature, which facilitated the killing actions organised by the *Einsatzgruppen* and the *HSSPF*s.[46] The *Einsatzgruppen* were few and small and depended on external support for their killing actions.

The Waffen-SS provided such external support. Furthermore, it has been estimated that 1,500 of the *Einsatzgruppen* men were of the Waffen-SS, and at least 30 officers or 8 per cent were either former or later Waffen-SS members.[47] The Waffen-SS also received personnel familiar with such extermination duties from other sources. Men of the East European *Schutzmannschaft* and other units providing personnel for shooting Jews and guarding ghettos were later admitted into the Waffen-SS – *Schutzmannschaft-Bataillon 57*, comprising Ukrainians and Belarussians among them.[48] In the summer of 1944, having been re-organised as the *Schutzmannschafts-Brigade* 'Siegling', the unit was subordinated the Ukrainian SS division.[49] Moreover, personnel of the notorious *Arajs Kommando*, which had murdered tens of thousands of Jews in Latvia, were transferred to the Waffen-SS' Latvian units.[50]

On several occasions, the Waffen-SS field units made personnel available to the *Einsatzgruppen*.[51] In September and October 1941, soldiers of *Das Reich* took part in two murder actions. On 9 September, near the village Lagoisk 30 km north-east of Minsk a volunteer detachment of *Das Reich* together with *Einsatzkommando 8* killed 920 Jews and, a month later, another detachment of the division participated in *Einsatzkommando 9*'s liquidation of the ghetto in Vitebsk, thereby participating in killing between 4,000 and 8,000 Jews.[52] In the autumn of 1941, when the front came near the coast of the Sea of Azov a particularly close co-operation developed between the divisions *Wiking* and *Leibstandarte* and *Einsatzgruppe D*. In the previous

46. Emberland and Kott (2012), p. 219. This does not mean that, at the time, a plan existed for the systematic killing of all Soviet Jews. As demonstrated by research this was a gradual development.

47. Stein (1984), p. 264. Krausnick (1998) and Peter Klein, *Die Einsatzgruppen in der besetzen Sowjetunion 1941–1942: die Tätigkeits- und Lageberichte des Chefs der Sicherheitspolizei und des SD* (Hentrich, 1997).

48. Gerlach (1999), pp. 901ff., 907ff. and 944ff.

49. Leonid Rein, *The Kings and the Pawns: Collaboration in Byelorussia during World War II* (Berghahn Books, 2011), p. 367.

50. Andrew Ezergailis, *The Holocaust in Latvia, 1941–1944: The Missing Center* (Historical Institute of Latvia; United States Holocaust Memorial Museum, 1996), p. 173ff.

51. Among the Waffen-SS divisions of the Barbarossa campaign it was apparently only the Totenkopf and the police divisions that did not take part in major massacres. Possibly, this is due to the fact that their axis of advance passed through areas with relatively few Jews. However, for some time Division Totenkopf had the Einsatzgruppe A attached. See Ereignismeldung UdSSR Nr. 24, 16.7.1941, reprinted in Mallmann et al. (2011), p. 129.

52. Wolfgang Curilla, *Die deutsche Ordnungspolizei und der Holocaust im Baltikum und in Weißrussland, 1941–1944*, 2. durchges. Aufl. (Ferdinand Schöningh, 2006), p. 905. See also Gerlach (1999), p. 586, note 505.Gerlach (1999), p. 597.

months, either spontaneously or ordered by their officers the soldiers had perpetrated a number of atrocities and killings of Jews. However, when the ports Mariupol and Taganrog were taken the violence escalated and a significant amount of the personnel took part in large scale killings. On 8 October, the *Leibstandarte* took Mariupol almost without a fight and along with the division, *Einsatzkommando 10a* moved in.[53] The available evidence suggest that personnel of both *Wiking* and *Leibstandarte* participated when the *Einsatzkommando* subsequently initiated a 2 days' massacre against the city's Jewish population killing 8,000.[54] Soon after, on 26 October, near Taganrog an additional 1,800 Jews were murdered in a gorge sealed off by the *Leibstandarte*.[55]

A number of Waffen-SS units organized in the *Kommandostab Reichsführer-SS* worked completely detached from the *Einsatzgruppen*, but with equally fatal consequences to the local Jewish population. This staff co-ordinated the employment of several minor groups as well as three brigade-size units, namely, 1st and 2nd SS and the cavalry brigades. These men have been labelled 'Holocaust Pathfinders' by Martin Cüppers due to their activities in the late summer and autumn of 1941 where particularly 1st SS and the cavalry brigades committed systematic massacres until they were transferred to the frontline in December. Until that time, their victims numbered an estimated 57,000 men, women and children.[56]

Given such undertakings it is hardly surprising that, as early as 1941, many SS men had a fairly good insight into the systematic killings perpetrated by the *Einsatzgruppen*. Very early during the campaign in the east, a soldier wrote home, '[...] all Jews are being annihilated. We shoot them everywhere we find them regardless of age or sex. The *Führer* has ordered us to do so. I know that, in the hinterland, there are

---

53. Angrick (2003), p. 311.
54. YV, M.40.MAP, 116, Letter of 12 December 1941 from the 46th Army's *Politotdel*'s 7th battalion's commissar Oskarov to the leader of Glavpura Mekhlis. Ilya Altman, *Kholokost na territorii SSSR. Entsiklopediya* (Tsentr Kholokost, 2009), p. 567ff. On the *Leibstandarte*'s participation see ibid., p. 312ff. On *Wiking*'s participation see RK, 1353 *Rigspolitichefen, Politiets Efterretningstjeneste, 1945–1950*, Copy of Nordentoft's diary, entry on 6 February 1942. Here the massacre, which a Danish soldier witnessed or participated in, is confused with the subsequent one in Taganrog. See also the description of the massacre in the diary of a Dutch volunteer of *Regiment Westland*, NIOD, 244/1254, diary W., P.A.G., where the number of victims is set to 13.000. It may be this action that is confused with one in Nikolayev further west by a prisoner-of-war. In 1943, he told to Soviet interrogators that he had spoken with a soldier of Regiment Germania who had shot 3,000 Jews in Nikolayev and contributed to chasing 4–5,000 into a mined ditch which was subsequently filled up with earth. GARF, 2021/148/39, LL.19-20: Interrogation protocol concerning prisoner of the 79th German infantry division, no date [1943].
55. Ibid., s.315ff. See also testimony by a soldier of 73rd infantry division, who points out soldiers of Wiking and Leibstandarte as participants. GARF, 7021/148/28, L.104-105. For more on the massacres in Mariupol and Taganrog, see Stephen Tyas, "Allied Intelligence Agencies and the Holocaust: Information Acquired from German Prisoners of War", Holocaust and Genocide Studies, vol. 22, No.1, 2008, p. 8.
56. Cuppers (2011), p. 212ff.

detachments tasked with killing Jews, because while we move forward many of them escape'.[57] In October 1941, a *Wiking* soldier on leave told the Swedish military attaché in Berlin that, 'in the occupied areas, the locals kindly informed the *Sonderkommandos* who in their midst were Jews. Thereafter, these were killed including women and children'.[58]

It was in Belarus, in particular, that the Waffen-SS got involved in the eastern front Holocaust. Both in 1942 and in 1943, 1st SS brigade combined their hunting of partisans with killing Jews who had fled the ghettos.[59] From 22 August to 21 September 1942, the brigade, along with *Schutzmannschaft* and police units, also took part in Operation Nuremberg. Officially this was a major counter-insurgency operation to ferret out partisans from their hiding places in the big woods and marshes, but it was in essence a large-scale killing of innocent civilian villagers. To maximise the number of 'partisan supporters' killed, the controlling officer, HSSPF Jeckeln, included the Jewish ghetto in the town Baranowitschi whose inhabitants he had murdered.[60] Also in Poland, the Waffen-SS played a significant role in the killing process itself.[61]

The Waffen-SS was also involved in the Holocaust in other parts of Europe, for example by rounding up Jews and deporting them to concentration camps. In April 1944, *Division Skanderbeg* caught 300 Jews in Priština.[62] In Denmark, the Netherlands and Norway, too, Waffen-SS soldiers were used for rounding up, guarding and deporting these countries' Jewish groups.[63]

Looting the Victims

On a December day in 1944, two German officers in British custody happened to chat about the concentration camps. One of them, *Sturmbannführer* Werner Zorn, was the commanding officer of one of the *Division Götz von Berlichingen*'s battalions when taken prisoner in Normandy.[64] In his earlier career Zorn had been an officer in the concentration camp Buchenwald and, later, for a brief period in Auschwitz.[65] He did not disclose the atrocities being perpetrated in the camps, but he told enthusiastically about how they were run as huge business enterprises where the prisoners' toil had made the SS 'a rich club'. He emphasised that the values thus accumulated did not benefit individuals but were used for building and expanding the organisation, including the Waffen-SS.

---

57. F.D, Sverdlov, *Dokumenty obviniaiut: Kholokost: svidetel'stva Krasnoi Armii* (Nauchno-prosvetitel'nyi tsentr "Kholokost", 1996), p. 3.
58. Gyllenhaal and Westberg (2008), p. 292ff.
59. See the survey of the participation in 1942–1944 in large scale counter-insurgency and killing actions in Belarus by the units mentioned in Gerlach (1999), p. 899ff. See also Cüppers (2011).
60. Gerlach (1999), p. 931ff.
61. Andrzej (1979); Cüppers (2011),
62. BL, B126/25553, Order of the day, 16 April 1944, by the plenipotential General in Albania.
63. As to Denmark see Christensen et al. (2005).
64. NAKEW, WO208/4140, SRM 1112, 10.12.1944.
65. Dixon (2005), p. 212ff.

In the beginning the Waffen-SS had no funding at all, but what was coming from the concentration camps. Pay, clothing, the whole Leibstandarte, everything from top to bottom was not – but for one single penny – funded by the state. Everything was accumulated thanks to the concentration camp prisoners.[66]

Zorn's statement was an exaggeration, but it illustrated an important fact. The Waffen-SS as well as the rest of the SS systematically exploited, not only the prisoners' work but also their valuables. Apart from having forced labour attached to barracks and other facilities, the SS built a huge, partially prisoner driven, complex of enterprises in order to support SS activities. Uniforms and food were, to a large extent, produced by concentration camp inmates, as were the furniture in the barracks.[67] However, the Waffen-SS did not exploit the prisoners' labour only. Many of the prisoners' personal belongings, confiscated before killing them, went directly to the soldiers. Unlike most army divisions on the eastern front, *Division Totenkopf* could meet winter 1942 well equipped with mittens, caps, fur coats, warm boots and many other warm garments. At this time, Friedrich Jeckeln, who was briefly a member of *Totenkopf*, was HSSPF in *Reich Commissariat Ostland* where he was so well stocked in murdered German and Baltic Jews' possessions that he was able to equip the whole division with enough goods to allow them to hand some of it on to adjacent formations.[68] Similarly, in December that year, the *Leibstandarte* received a large consignment of winter clothing from the SS stores in the Gouvernement Générale – very likely of Polish or Jewish provenance.[69] In a letter to Himmler's secretariat the year after, regarding a shipment of fur coats from the victims in the extermination camp Kulmhof to *Bekleidungsamt* (clothing office) *der Waffen-SS* in Ravensbrück, the HSSPF Wartheland, *Wilhelm Koppe*, informed that 'further deliveries of fur might be expected in the autumn'.[70]

The huge *Operation Reinhard*, designed to annihilate the Jews of the Gouvernement Générale, resulted in an avalanche of everyday articles. In August 1942, for example, the cavalry brigade in Debica received 1,000 blankets from the action.[71]

The expansion of the Waffen-SS was costly also due to the obligatory family support, and when this was paid in other currencies than *Reichsmark* finances could be hard to come by. In the late summer of 1943, in connection with large scale recruiting of Romanian *Volksdeutsche* a need arose for Romanian *lei*. For this reason, the SS leadership considered, in co-operation with the German legation in Bucharest, to sell transit visa to

---

66. NAKEW, WO208/4140, SRM 1112, 10.12.1944.
67. Schulte (2001), pp. 125ff., and 131ff.
68. Merkl (2010), p. 202.
69. Weingartner (1974), p. 70. Also, the families of SS men got a share of the possessions of the killed Jews. Thus, the HSSPF Bach-Zelewski dispatched for distribution among the children of SS men 1,000 children's socks and 2,000 children's mittens from the actions in Belarus. Gerlach (1999), p. 680.
70. BAB, NS19/1612, Letter of 28 August 1942 from *SS-Obergruppenführer* Koppe (HSSPF of the Warthegau) to RFSS pers. staff.
71. YV, Record Gr. O.53 File Nr. 68, *Abt.IVa. Betr. 1000 Stück Schlafendecken, 19.8.42.*

Romanian Jews wishing to travel to Spain via German-occupied Europe. This concept had surfaced the previous year, and its implementation was expected to procure 50 million Romanian *lei*.[72] For reasons unknown – maybe partly because the *Auswärtiges Amt* (German foreign office) was against it, partly because in the light of a monthly need of about 200 million *lei* this was a modest sum – this idea was shelved.[73] This, however, was not the last time the SS tried to extort Jews to benefit the Waffen-SS. End of April 1944, the leader of Jew deportation, Adolf Eichmann, negotiated with the Jewish Aid and Rescue Committee's representatives in Hungary in order to exempt a large group of Jews from the upcoming deportation and killing process. During these negotiations, an ambitious and completely unrealistic proposal materialised to let one million Jews emigrate against a compensation of 400 tonnes of tea and coffee, 2 million cases of soap, 10,000 trucks and various other important sinews of war – all of it to be delivered through Turkey. Allegedly, the lorries were to be used for the motorisation of divisions *Florian Geyer* and 22nd SS voluntary cavalry.[74] In the late autumn of 1944, the SS eventually managed to carry out the scheme, albeit at a much smaller scale than anticipated. For money, 1,600 Jews were sent abroad, primarily across the border with Switzerland. The funds thus acquired were to be spent on the procurement of weapons and other important military necessities for the Waffen-SS.[75]

One of the *Leibstandarte* battalions seems to have had a more direct link to the fiscal outcome of the Nazi Jew persecution. In mid-September 1943, during the apprehension of Jews in northern Italy, the officers extorted 1½ million *Lire* from a local Jewish-Turkish businessman. This money seems to have disappeared into thin air, but half a million lire were kindly donated to the battalion's fund by the officers involved.[76]

---

72. RGVA, 1372/3/450, *Zusammenfassender Aktenvermerk. Berlin 3.8.1943* concerning *Standartenführer* Schmidt. On the problem with procuring *lei* for the support of Romanian SS volunteers see Milata (2009), p. 156ff., which, however, does not include the above document.
73. Milata (2009), p. 159.
74. Raul Hilberg, *The Destruction of the European Jews*, Vol. II, 3. ed. (Yale University Press, 2003), p. 903ff., and Raul Hilberg, *The Destruction of the European Jews*, Vol. III, 3. ed. (Yale University Press, 2003), p. 1219ff. For a discussion of the German motives behind this proposal see Bauer (1994), p. 163ff.
75. NIOD, 270c, copy of A.A. Vortragenotits of 11 November 1944 by *Gruppenleiter Inland II* Wagner. Wagner, was a key employee heading the *Inland II*, with responsibility for the ministry's occupation with the 'Jewish Issue.' Moreover, he was foreign secretary Ribbentrop's liaison officer to Himmler. As of March, he was also a secret collaborator of the SD. Doscher (1987), p. 264ff. Hilberg (2003), *Bd. II*, p. 903. For other paid releases – though without relation to the Waffen-SS – se Raul Hilberg, *The Destruction of the European Jews, Vol. I, 3.* ed. (Yale University Press, 2003), p. 101ff., Hilberg (2003), *Vol. II*, p. 608ff. Breitman and Aronson in *Central European History,Vol.* 25, No 2, 1992, p. 196, seem to believe that the claim that the money was for the procurement of equipment for the Waffen-SS, was merely a smokescreen. The real reason was rather that the Jews might be a pawn used for obtaining a separate peace with the west.
76. SentenceNo 685 reprinted in C.F Rüter and Karl Dietrich Bracher, *Justiz und NS-Verbrechen: Sammlung deutscher Strafurteile wegen nationalsozialistischer Tötungsverbrechen, 1945–1966. Bd. XXX* (University Press Amsterdam, 2004), pp. 27ff. and 43.

This example shows that it was not only the SS institutions and units that benefitted collectively from looting – but also individuals profited, too. In Norway, the German policy secured that SS volunteers in need of homes got preferential treatment when flats were left unoccupied after the deportation of 800 Jewish tenants to Auschwitz.[77] In other cases, high-ranking Waffen-SS officers furnished their flats with Jewish possessions. In 1942, the, later divisional and corps commander, Wilhelm Bittrich possessed Jewish furniture, silver and household appliances in his flat for close to 5,000 *Reichsmark*.[78] In December 1944, from the SS stores in Oranienburg close to concentration camp Sachsenhausen 27,000 watches were distributed among the Waffen-SS divisions. These were given, primarily, to snipers and men who had excelled in destroying tanks.[79] This kind of re-cycling items from the concentration camp prisoners had happened before. In May 1943, each of the divisions *Leibstandarte, Das Reich* and *Totenkopf* had received 500 watches from Auschwitz, and late in the year wounded soldiers in the field hospitals received Christmas presents in the form of watches, fountain pens etc. that had belonged to deceased victims.[80] Particularly valuable watches were used as present to soldiers for outstanding gallantry on the battlefield.[81]

Partisans and Counter-Insurgency

Especially at the eastern front, but in the Balkans and occupied Eastern Europe as well, the German authorities made the civilian population collectively responsible for acts of insurgency, sabotage and subversive activities and the scope of the massacres on civilians swelled due to the fact that, often, the Holocaust was fused with of counter-insurgency actions. Actions of retaliation were systematically carried out completely out of proportion with the insurgency – real or imagined – a policy that began in Poland. There, *Verfügungstruppe* units, and *Totenkopf* components, later to be transferred to the Waffen-SS, committed atrocities.[82] Retaliations against civilians were also committed during the campaign in the west. Between 20 and 28 May, *Division Totenkopf* murdered 250 civilians in the Franco-Belgian frontier region on the Canal coast.[83]

When German forces invaded the Soviet Union, they were directed to punish civilians for real or alleged opposition. Thus, before the onslaught, *Division Wiking* trained such measures. On 11 June, briefly before the launch of Operation

77. *Meldungen aus Norwegen Nr. 49 vom 15. Dezember 1943* reprinted in Larsen (2008), p. 942.
78. NAWA, 362, ZZ-16, Box 6, Letter of 10 July 1942 from Bittrich to Karl Wolff; Letter of 13 August 1942 from Karl Wolff to *SS-Oberführer* Huber, leader of the *Gestapostelle Wien*; Letter of 15 August 1941 from *SS-Oberführer* Huber, to Karl Wolff.
79. Christensen et al. (1998), p. 266. See also NAWA, T175-sp.74, *Betr. Uhren Verteilung an Angehörige der Waffen-SS, 29.11.1944.*
80. Sydnor (1990), p. 332, note 36. Hilberg (2003), Vol. III, p. 1022ff.
81. Hilberg (2003),Vol. III, p. 1023.
82. See chapter on 1939. See also VAP, *8.SS-Kav.Div "FG" 3, Florian Geyer, Gefechtsbericht der 1. SS-Totenkopf Reiterstandarten, 10.4.1940* concerning their shooting of 250 Polish civilians.
83. Lieb (2007), pp. 15ff. and 518. See also Merkl (2010), p. 171.

Barbarossa the division issued an instruction entitled *Kampf gegen feindliche Hinterlist und Heimtücke* (combat against hostile ruses and callousness). The instruction gave examples of the Soviet modus operandi including acts such as sniping from villages. In case of this activity, the unit that was attacked was to encircle the village, torch it on all sides, and call for artillery support.

Shortly after the launch of the campaign, *Division Wiking* experienced an incident almost identical to this textbook example. On 2 July 1941, during the passage of a village, the commanding officer of *Regiment Westland*, Hilmar Wäckerle, was killed by what the troops believed to be a sniper. Unable to identify the origin of the shot, various, all ideologically based, interpretations of the incident materialized. In one version the culprit was a Tatar soldier, in another a Jew, and some believed him merely to be a partisan.[84] As a reaction, *Westland*'s 2nd battalion was committed in retaliation against the village suspected of housing the shooter.[85] In October 2013, the Norwegian SS soldier Olav Tuff, who had arrived at the division about a month after the episode, explained that this had not been a singular event. A sentry, he witnessed how his unit herded people of an unnamed village into a church, soaked the edifice with petrol and lit it. Tuff estimated that there had been 2–300 victims.[86] Although no other village massacres are mentioned, other sources convey information on *Wiking*'s hunts for and executions of partisans, too.[87]

From the years 1941–1942, there are accounts of similar deeds committed by divisions *Das Reich, Leibstandarte* and *Totenkopf*.[88] A British prisoner-of-war, a former *Leibstandarte* soldier, for example, described how, in early 1943, in the retaliation of

---

84. BAB, SSO Wäckerle's personal file. Letter of 2 July 1941 from Steiner to Himmler. Steiner informs that Wäckerle had been killed 'in an ambush by a stray Tatar.' *SS-Division Wiking's Tagesmeldung* (daily report) of 2 July 1941 gives another explanation in BAB, NS19/2854, Letter of 6 July 1941 to Himmler from *Führungshauptamt betr.: Tagesmeldungen der SS-Divisionen*. This claims that Wäckerle was killed when he peeped into a seized Soviet tank. After the war, a soldier of Westland's 7th company told that the shot was fired from a field and not, as believed by others, from a church tower. However, there was a firm belief that Wäckerle had been killed by partisans and, for this reason, soldiers had been employed to searching the area to find the culprit. HLC, PA Terje Emberland, Box 1, *Zeugen-Vernehmung, Bayerisches Landeskriminalamt, 28.5.1987.* To see a survey of interpretations concerning the death of Wäckerles, consult also Terwisscha van Scheltinga (2008), p. 346ff.
85. BAMA, RS4/1297/4: *KTB II/Westland, 2.7.1941.* See also ibid., p. 349ff.
86. http://www.nrk.no/fordypning/--nordmenn-deltok-i-drap-pa-sivile-1.11262316.   Accessed on 22 October 2013. In the interview atrocities against Ukrainian Jews were also mentioned.
87. NAWA, 362, ZZ-16, Box 43, Letter of 2 September 1941 from Riedweg to Berger. Joannes Benedictus van Heutsz, *Wiking door Rusland*, Uitgeverij "Storm", 1942, p. 29ff. Olaf Nielsen, *Slettet af rullen: en frikorpsmands opgør med fortiden* (Aros, 1977), p. 70. Det Kongelige Bibliotek, HS 1979/126, Brøndums erindringer, p. 51.
88. Merkl (2010), p. 208; Sydnor (1990), p. 201. BB, E27, 1000/721, *Archiv nr. 9928, Bd.3, Bericht 98, 18.11.1942; BB, E27, 1000/721, Archiv nr. 9928, Bd.4, SS 103, Deserteurbericht 3.2.1943. VAP, N SS DR ks. 8:* file9: *D-R Ia: Besondere Anordnungen für das Gebiet hinter der Front,* 20 December 1941.Ibid: *D-R Abt.Ic, 7 June 1943: Divisions-Sonderbefehl Ic, nr. 14. betr. Listenmäßige Erfassung samtlicher russischer Zivilisten durch den Starosten.* Roes (2005), p. 85.

a partisan ambush against his battalion, under Jochen Peiper, had burnt a village and shot the inhabitants.[89] This act of terror paled in comparison to the deeds of the police division, the largest SS formation in the Leningrad sector. In late September 1943, a battalion of this division participated in a major partisan suppression operation in the Gatchina area during which 54 villages were burnt down, cattle were stolen, and the civilians were either forcibly moved or shot.[90]

In Belorussia and northwestern Ukraine especially, the 1st SS brigade and Dirlewanger's unit were at work. Centred on Babruysk and Hegewald, Waffen-SS battalion-size training units were employed in the suppression of partisans and civilians in the area.[91] These actions were linked with the extermination of Jews but, increasingly, they were also becoming a means for procuring workforces for Germany. Thus, in November 1942, Himmler ordered that all civilians fit for work, captured in partisan hunts, were to be shipped off to Germany for forced labour.[92]

It was not only in the Soviet Union that the hunt for partisans entailed suffering by civilians. The divisions *Prinz Eugen, Nordland* and *Skanderbeg* committed atrocities in the countries that are known today as Albania, Bosnia, Croatia, Montenegro and Serbia. But also in Slovenia, which was partially annexed by Germany, shooting of hostages, burning of villages, massacres and deportations were used for suppression of the local opposition and partisan movement.[93]

In Greece, too, the Waffen-SS took part in the suppression of partisans and, as in Yugoslavia, it happened with outrageous brutality. January to September 1944, the police division was stationed in the country and committed one of the most horrendous massacres. On 10 July, the division's *SS-Panzer-Grenadier-Regiment 7*'s 2nd company massacred the village Distomo, which was under suspicion of harbouring partisans. In an orgy of murder, rape, looting and torching 297 civilians were killed.[94]

While at the eastern front and in the Balkans, army units often committed atrocities that were comparable to what was perpetrated by the *SS*, the situation was different further west. In the countries of Western Europe, the German counter-insurgency

89. NAWA, 263, ZZ-20, box. 7, Interrogation of SS *Rottenführer* Otto Sierkofthe SS *Leibstandarte*. 17 November 1944. Sml. Weingartner (1974), p. 126. For another example see Westemeier (2014), p. 246.

90. GARF, 7021/151/14, L.218.

91. On partisan hunts and executions of suspects by the Hegewald-based *SS-Gren.Ausb.Btl.Ost*, see *VAP, Höhere SS- und Polizeiführer Russland Süd*, file 18: Letter of 11 June 1943 to SS FHA by an *SS-Hauptsturmführer* om *SS-Gren.Ausb. Btl.Ost* employment in *Unternehmen Lenz*. Ibid: Letter from *SS-Gren.Ausb.Btl.Ost* to SS FHA, 1 August 1943. *Ausbildungsbericht für den Monat Juli 1943*.

92. BAB, NS19/1671, Order by Himmler of 3 November 1942.

93. Yugoslav War Crimes Commission, *Report on the Crimes of Austria and the Austrians against Yugoslavia and her Peoples* (Belgrade, 1947), p. 142. Tamara Griesser-Pečar, *Das zerrissene Volk Slowenien 1941–1946: Okkupation, Kollaboration, Bürgerkrieg, Revolution* (Böhlau, 2003), p. 31ff. Tim Kirk, "Limits of Germandom. Resistance to the Nazi Annexation of Slovenia", *The Slavonic and East European Review*, Vol. 69, No. 4, 1991, pp. 646–67.

94. Mark Mazower, *Inside Hitler's Greece: The Experience of Occupation, 1941–1944* (Yale University Press, 1993), p. 212; Pontolillo (2009), p. 41.

activity was less brutal and more selective than in the Balkans and in the eastern front. However, the viciousness increased over the war years, and in France and Italy, the SS employed measures from the stock they had created at the eastern front to a much larger extent than Wehrmacht units. Both Waffen-SS divisions deployed to Italy, the *Leibstandarte* and the *Reichsführer-SS* had shares in the German war crimes.[95] The latter was particularly ruthless in this field as, out of the 10,000 civilians killed by the Germans, this division was responsible for 2,000.[96]

In Western Europe, it was *Das Reich* which made itself particularly notorious when perpetrating, in June 1944, the massacre of more than 600 civilians in Oradour-sur-Glane.[97] But *Division Hitlerjugend*'s misdeeds predated this. On 2 April 1944, its reconnaissance unit had been sabotaged while under rail transport, and though there had been no casualties on the German side, two punitive units were immediately detailed to the town Ascq, which lay near the railway. According to eyewitnesses, these units shot randomly into crowds of civilians in the streets as well as in houses, which were also looted of valuables. Moreover, 30–40 Frenchmen were taken to the derailed train where they were interrogated by the officer in charge, *Obersturmführer* Walter Hauck, and some of his colleagues. Having been forced to repair the rails, on Hauck's orders, they were shot. The aggregate number of killed civilians was 86.[98] Most likely, this was not the last of the division's atrocities on French soil. On 13 August 1944, soldiers of an unknown unit – though probably *Hitlerjugend* – executed 18 men and torched the high street of the town Tourouvre on the Orne.[99] Also other Waffen-SS units shot civilians indiscriminately during the fighting in Western Europe from 1944 to 1945.[100]

SS troops were also employed in connection with strikes and riots in the occupied areas. In October 1940, the *Leibstandarte* was sent to Prague in the wake of anti-Nazi

---

95. On Leibstandarte's atrocities during its short service in Italy in August-September 1943 see: Robert M.W. Kempner, *SS im Kreuzverhör: die Elite, die Europa in Scherben schlug*, Erw. Neuaufl. (Delphi Politik, F. Greno, 1987), pp. 213–23. Gentile (2012), p. 88; NAKEW, WO209/2244, PWIS(H)/LDC/299, Report on interrogation of PW KP 49359 Sturmbannfue. Jacob Hanreich, 29 August 1944, s.4. BAMA, RS2-2/20, KTB nr. 7, 3 August 1943–1943 December 1943, reference 11 September and 13 September.

96. Gentile (2012), p. 201.

97. See earlier in this book.

98. NAKEW, WO 311/691, Report on the Interrogation of Members of *Aufkl. Batl. 12*, 12 *SS-Pz.Div. "HJ"* on Murders at Ascq, France. NAKEW, WO208/4450, Interrogation of Colonel Wachsmuth 4 October 1944, who tells about the Hitlerjugend division's killing of 90 civilians at Arcuqes after a railroad ambush. Wachsmuth declared that, while General Falkenhausen wished for the prosecution of the perpetrators, Dietrich declined. Even von Rundstedt could not repeal Dietrich's decision. Cf. Lieb (2007), p. 574.

99. Beevor (2012), s.446. The suspicion that the guilty were of the *Division Hitlerjugend*, can be corroborated by the testimony of a Dutch SS soldier serving with the division's 26th SS armoured infantry regiment. He confessed that in Mid-August 1944 a village had been burnt (he called it Martin on the Seine) and all men were shot. NAKEW, WO208/3627: Points from the interrogation of various PW Kempton Park Camp 5 Nov 44,. 7 November 1944. Cf. Lieb, p. 462ff.

100. See Lieb (2007), p. 220; Weingartner (1979), pp. 47, 87, 103 and 113.

demonstrations.[101] In January 1941, the SS units were part of the forces committed by Reinhard Heydrich to quell the Czech opposition.[102] Leibstandarte provided marksmen for the atrocities following the Czech resistance movements assassination of Heydrich, and a soldier later recalled his participation in the execution of several hundred civilians due to the extra pay associated with 'working' overtime.[103] Similarly, SS reserve forces in Amsterdam and Bergen were committed as riots broke out in these cities.[104] The year after, the same happened during the Slovak rising. Both the crushing, in the spring of 1943, of the uprising in the Warsaw ghetto and the extremely bloody suppression of the Polish Home Army, the year after during the Warsaw rebellion comprised the reserve unit of the cavalry division.[105]Additionally, the propaganda unit of *Division Wiking* as well as brigades *Dirlewanger* and *Kaminski*, some of the unruliest SS units, were involved. These two contributed to making the suppression not only bloody but also an orgy of looting, murdering and raping – rather than combatting the rioters. Over 4–5 August 1944, the worst days of the rebellion, these two units contributed considerably to boosting the fatalities to 30–40,000. Subsequently, the Germans changed policy and decided to show mercy on women and children.[106] Apparently, further moderation took place as, on 12 August, the 9th army noted in its war diary that the SS no longer murdered all civilian whom they met in the city.[107] However, when, on 2 October, the Polish Home Army surrendered the death toll had swollen to almost 200,000 civilians.[108]

The role of the Waffen-SS in the suppression of uprisings in Germanic countries was less apparent and more indirect. This mostly took place by the employment of small groups of veterans who would combat sabotage and resistance activities more generally. Thus, in Belgium, the Netherlands, Denmark and Norway a number of death squads were organised. With national variations, the philosophy behind this measure was that through murders in areas where, for instance, liquidations of informants had taken place, the resistance movements might be discredited. Another tactic, often employed in Denmark, was to stage bomb attacks appearing very much like the resistance movement's sabotage actions, thus demolishing popular edifices or killing random passers-by.[109] In June 1944, Himmler sanctioned the implementation

---

101. Weingartner (1974), p. 37. See BB, E27 1000/721, 2185 for an account by one of the participating SS men.

102. BAB, NS19/2574, Letter of 30 January 1941 from Heydrich to Himmler.

103. Felix Römer, *Kameraden: Die Wehrmacht von innen* (Piper, 2012), p.47.

104. Stein (1984), p. 47.

105. Włodzimierz Borodziej, *The Warsaw Uprising of 1944* (University of Wisconsin Press, 2005), p. 81. Cüppers (2011), p. 308. According to Davies (2005), p. 666, however, the soldiers at hand were from Wiking's Anti-Aircraft battalion.

106. Borodziej (2005), p. 80ff.

107. Sentence No 860 reprinted in Rüter and Hekelaar Gombert (2010), p. 500.

108. Cüppers (2011), p. 309. See also the obviously sanitised account of the fights in BAB, R20/45b, *Tagebuch Erich von Bach*, pp. 106–16.

109. See Lauridsen (2012), Vol. 10, p. 76 ff. for examples of actual actions.

of counter-terror in Belgium in the form of killings. The killers were – at least in Flanders – mostly Waffen-SS veterans whom the SD had engaged as auxiliary police.[110] At the turn of year 1943–1944, Berlin ordered similar procedures to be applied in Denmark. Here too, the killers were to a large extent former Waffen-SS personnel. Five out of seven members of the notorious 'Peter-Group' were ex-Waffen-SS and their murders and bomb assaults cost at least 160 Danes their lives.[111] Fifty per cent of the 'Schiøler Group' were former Waffen-SS soldiers. This gang perpetrated a two-digit number of killings, torture, explosive assaults and arrests.[112] From the autumn of 1943 to the end of the war, the Germans in the Netherlands committed at least 54 murders, nicknamed *Silbertanne* (silver spruce) killings. Most, possibly all, Dutch perpetrators were Waffen-SS veterans organised in *Kommando Feldmaijer* and selected for the job precisely because of their past as front soldiers.[113] In Norway the counter-terror was nicknamed *Blumenpflücken* (flower picking). Unlike what happened in the three other countries, the counter-terror in Norway was on a more limited scale and it was generally carried out by German SIPOs (security police men).[114] Nevertheless, the *SS-Skijegerbataljon Norge* (SS ski hunter battalion Norway) was manned by Norwegians and employed in counter-terror actions in the volunteers' homeland. In several places, sub-units of these battalions were committed to hunting down resistance groups which – here and there – led to bloody clashes and casualties on both sides.[115]

Prisoners-Of-War

In the autumn of 1943, a *Division Totenkopf* soldier defected to Switzerland. Shortly afterwards, the deserter characterised his former unit's treatment of prisoners as 'little food and ample beating'. Shooting and maltreatment of prisoners-of-war by the Waffen-SS were among the accusations that led to its condemnation, after the war, by the International Military Tribunal at Nuremberg as a criminal organisation.[116]

110. Werner Warmbrunn, *The German Occupation of Belgium 1940–1944* (Peter Lang, 1993), p. 146.
111. Pedersen (2000), Henrik Lundtofte, *Gestapo. Tyskpoliti og terror i Danmark 1940–1945* (Gads Forlag, 2003), p. 157, Frank Bogh, *Petergruppen: tysk terror i Danmark* (Documentas, 2004), p. 17ff.
112. Lasse Bruun Jonassen and Jonas Lind, *Schiøler-gruppen: danske terrorister i tysk tjeneste 1944–1945* (Informations Forlag, 2012), p. 15.
113. Sentence No 923 reprinted in Rüter et al. (2012), p. 192ff. See also http://www.waffen-ss.nl/silbertanne-e.php, accessed on 12 October 2012.
114. Berit Noekleby, *Gestapo: tyskpolitii Norge 1940–1945* (Aschehoug, 2003), p. 151ff.
115. Emberland and Kott (2012), p. 474ff. Johannes Andenas, Olav Riste, and Magne Skodvin, *Norway and the Second World War*, 3rd ed., (Tanum-Norli, 1983), p. 75.
116. In the sentence, it was stated that "There is evidence that the shooting of unarmed prisoners of war was the general practice in some Waffen-SS divisions." Judgement, 30 September-1 October, 1946 from Trial of the Major War Criminals before the International Military Tribunal, Nuremberg, 1945–1946, vol.1, p. 255ff.

It appears that, as early as the campaign in Poland, some units ordered all surrendering enemies shot. When the fighting was over, the two cavalry regiments formed in Poland became involved in comprehensive killings of prisoners-of-war.[117] However, the first well-documented examples of Waffen-SS' atrocities against prisoners-of-war appear during the campaign in the west the following spring, with Wormhoudt and Le Paradis representing the most well-investigated cases.[118] After the Le Paradis massacre, the Totenkopf division perpetrated more crimes. Most noticeably, black African soldiers from the French colonies were murdered. Between 17 and 20 June 1940, the unit seems to have been involved in between two and five separate massacres, in which 200 French colonials were killed.[119] A *Totenkopf* deserter explained how the officer commanding his company had declared that 'the men are not worthy of living, why should we feed them in Germany; shoot them!'[120]

Four years later, France was again on the stage for bloody atrocities against prisoners-of-war. Now, primarily, *Division Hitlerjugend* made itself notorious. Over the first few days of the fights in Normandy, the division murdered at least 187 Allied soldiers. Later, the *Leibstandarte* perpetrated the massacre at Malmedy. Another series of atrocities against prisoners-of-war took place when, in September 1943, after Italy's surrender to the western Allies, Italian forces were disarmed by German troops. Hitler had ordered that Italians resisting disarmament should not be regarded as prisoners-of-war, and this order was meticulously carried into practice.[121]

While atrocities against prisoners-of-war at the western front were largely a battlefield phenomenon happening during or in the hours immediately after capture, Soviet soldiers were not only in dire danger of being shot on capture, but they were also very much at risk of dying in German custody. Although all prisoner-of-war camps were guarded by the army, the SS could handle prisoners until such time when they were brought to larger camps in the hinterland. This turned out to be fatal to many a Red Army prisoner. The SS soldiers marched into the Soviet Union with a strongly negative and demonised view of their opponents. In the weeks prior to the attack, Eicke, for example, spoke more than once to his officers emphasising that commissars were to be shot. He gave as a ground for this measure that the Soviet Union had not signed the Geneva Conventions.[122] *Division Wiking* internal communications also stressed that the Soviet Union could not be expected to fight according to the laws of war.[123]

117. BB, E27, 1000/721, *Archiv Nr. 9928, Bd.4, SS 103, Deserteurbericht 3.2.1943*. BB, E27 1000/721, 2185. Account by an SS man of *Das Reich*. Interrogation of February 1943. Michaelis (2010), p. 9.
118. For other examples of SS units killing captured British soldiers, see NAKEW, WO208/4647.
119. Sydnor (1990), p. 116ff. See also Merkl (2010), p. 170ff. Lieb (2007), p. 18ff.; Scheck (2006).
120. BB, E27, 1000/721, *Archiv nr. 9928, Bd. 4, D110, Deserteurbericht 11.5.1943*, p. 16.
121. See *II SS Panzerkorps'* war diary, BAMA, RS2-2/20, KTB Nr. 7, 3 August 1943– 1943 December 1943, reference 12.9.
122. Sydnor (1990), p. 153ff.
123. Christensen et al. (1998), p. 92f.

Right from the beginning of fighting in the Soviet Union, the employed SS divisions shot prisoners.[124] While in *Totenkopf* ordinary prisoners were murdered occasionally, Jews and commissars were killed more systematically.[125] The general officer commanding the division, Eicke himself declared that it was 'the Führer's will' that such prisoners should be shot as the retaliation of the alleged Soviet murder of German prisoners-of-war.[126]

There are numerous examples of *Division Wiking* soldiers shooting prisoners – occasionally in groups of up to 200.[127] Late in the war, two Norwegian deserters from the division, living in separate Swedish internment camps, explained that prior to the attack on the Soviet Union orders had been given not to take any prisoners.[128] To a large extent, this order was put into practice. This became obvious through episodes along *Wiking*'s axis of advance on Soviet territory where unarmed civilians, as well as prisoners-of-war, were shot. If the two Norwegians are to be trusted, General Felix Steiner visited *Regiment Germania* after its first major attack. Out of 300 prisoners, he pointed out 200 with 'the least Germanic looks' and ordered them shot.[129] In the autumn of 1941, the Swedish defence attaché in Berlin had a conversation with a fellow Swede serving with *Division Wiking* who told that 'taking prisoners rarely happened in the SS unless the Russians surrender in groups larger than company. If not, they were shot out of hand. Prisoners were treated ruthlessly and herded forward with spades and beatings'.[130] At Christmas 1943, another Swedish Wiking volunteer told the Swedish security police about his two years at the eastern front. He claimed that, for extended periods, the SS had taken no prisoners but killed 'all and sundry'.[131]

Initially, the Germans unhesitatingly let hundred-thousands of prisoners die from starvation, exposure and exhaustion. However, later in the war, the need for workers led to a slightly more humane treatment of Soviet prisoners.[132] From 1942, the prisoners were increasingly used as a workforce in occupied Europe and for that reason it became advantageous to secure their survival beyond the time of capture. The ensuing moderation influenced the Waffen-SS. Thus, in 1943, prior to the launch of the Kursk offensive

124. For *Leibstandarte* examples, see Krausnick (1998), p. 200, and Westemeier (2014), p. 208ff. For Das Reich, see IfZG, ED 373/1,Tagebuch Aufz.n 25.9.-20.10.38, 24.6.-24.10.41, her 29.6.1941. For Totenkopf, seeBB, E27, 1000/721, Archiv nr. 9928, Bd.5, SS118, *Deserteurbericht* 6.11.1943. For Wiking, see earlier in this book. For the police division see Rass (2003), p. 336.
125. Sydnor (1990), pp. 160ff., 186, note 58, and p. 316ff.
126. Weise (2013), p. 298f.
127. So far, the most meticulous examination can be seen in Emberland and Kott (2012), p. 234ff. An early investigation into this matter can be seen in Christensen et al. (1998), *passim*. Apart from these places and in the body text below, see also Pedersen and Rasmussen (2012), p. 72. Helweg-Larsen (2008), p. 131ff. GARF, 7021/148/14, L.18.
128. Solbakken (1945), p. 129.
129. Ibid., p. 130.
130. Gyllenhaal and Westberg (2008), p. 290.
131. Ibid.
132. This development is described by Streit (1978), in particular is Chapters VIII, X and XI.

General Hausser, commanding 2nd SS armoured corps, ordered that in the upcoming offensive it would be of the essence to take prisoners, because they would constitute a valuable workforce in the Third Reich. The soldiers might have been expected to draw a sigh of relief that, now, they could take prisoners with no bad conscience, but it appears that the SS authorities believed they would rather react with surprise and ill will. Thus, the general had to emphasise that there were financial gains to be made by the arms industry, and he stressed that 'we SS men do not display any false humanity, but we do know what is important for the conduct of the war'.[133] This order was a break away from the established practise, and, later that year, a deserter from the *Leibstandarte* found it relevant mentioning that this order was running counter to the methods so far used when handling prisoners.[134] However, even after this order had been issued, SS soldiers to some extent continued to shoot prisoners at the eastern front.[135]

Waffen-SS and the Exploitation of Civilians in Occupied Areas

In October 1943, in his notorious speech in Posen, referring to the comprehensive forced labour in the east, Himmler expressed that 'if 10,000 Russian women dies of exhaustion when digging a tank pit or they do not is of no other concern to me than whether or not the pit gets finished'.[136] The conditions under which Soviet civilians and other *Fremdvölker* were forced to work is a relatively under-researched part of the German war in the east. On 31 January 1942, a Norwegian *Sturmbannführer* serving with *Division Wiking*'s *Regiment Germania* noted in his diary that civilians were working in severe cold and high wind to keep the roads of the staging area free of snow. This episode represents a brief insight into what undoubtedly was a common phenomenon.[137]

---

133. BAMA, RS2-2/14, Sonderbefehl von 2.5.1943. Shortly before, there had been a similar change of policy in Sonderkommando 4a. Mid-March, its sub-units were ordered to minimise the killings as much as possible. This was explicated with reference to the enormous need for workers in Germany. Therefore, from now on partisan suppression should aim at providing human resources for forced labour. *Anweisung des Sonderkommandos 4a vom 19. März an alle Kommandoführer zur Unterdrückung der sowjetischen Partisanen.* Reprinted as document No 86 in Heinz Kühnrich, *Der Partisanenkrieg in Europa 1939–1945* (Dietz,1968), p. 623ff.
134. BB, E27, 1000/721, *Archiv nr. 9928, Bd.5, SS 111, Deserteurbericht 28.9.1943.*
135. On Leibstandarte's shooting of two Russian soldiers after the fight in Hungary in February and March 1945 see GARF, 7021/148/14, L.209. On a Totenkopf order, not to take any prisoners, see GARF, 7021/148/37, L.15, Telegram from 3. Ukrainian front to Glavpurkka, 5.2.1945. On the shooting of Soviet prisoners-of-war during *Division Nordland*'s fights in Courland in the winter of 1944–1945 see GARF, 7021/151/14, L.219. On a *Division Nordland* order of March 1945 not to take prisoners see Christensen et.al. (1998), p. 234ff.
136. BAB, NS19/4010, *Rede des Reichsführers-SS bei der SS-Gruppenführertagung in Posen am 4. Oktober 1943.*
137. HLC, Private archive Terje Emberland, boks 4, Account of 27 February 1942 on the *I. SS regiment Germania*'s activities from 8 January to 22 February 1942 by SS-Sturmbannführer Bakke.

On several occasions, Waffen-SS units detailed personnel for guarding forced labourers at the eastern front.[138] For example, in the spring of 1944, soldiers – possibly from the SS camp at Babruysk – guarded a large group of forced labourers employed in fortification works in the three lines named Panther-, Bären- and Biber-Stellung (panther, bear and beaver positions). This was a huge piece of construction work going on for six months. Ca. 1,000 civilians and as many prisoners dug 82 km trenches and cut down trees, etc. on the glacis so as to allow free arcs.[139]

In April 1943, Himmler spoke with leading officers of divisions *Leibstandarte, Das Reich* and *Totenkopf.* The conversation took place at the University of Kharkiv and was about the possibilities of defeating the Soviet Union. Himmler opined that Russia had to be bled white, thus being robbed of its manpower. A precondition to make this happen was that 'every tract of land that we yield to the enemy must be left barren and empty of human beings. Either they must be transported and used as a labour force in Germany, for Germany, or they must perish in battle'.[140] It is hard not to interpret this as the encouragement of the officers either to forcibly move all civilians west or to kill them.

However, this was no new missive. To some extent, such an approach had been practised in the near front areas since the winter 1941–1942 when, for the first time, German forces had had to go on the defensive. Thus, *Leibstandarte* and *Wiking* had burnt villages in their sectors at Mius.[141] Also in central Russia the civilians were driven out of the frontline areas. In *Division Das Reich*'s position on the Istra this happened in a belt of 10 kilometres. Later that winter, the division was ordered to patrol the hinterland and apprehend all men of ages 16 to 50 years.[142] Of the remaining civilians, as many

---

138. BB, E27, 1000/721, *Archiv nr. 9928, Bd.7, Deserteurbericht 16.2.1945*, 466, p. 4: Thirteen men of *Division Wiking* valuable blood, they should endeavour 'winning it (for Germany) or killing its filler unit were employed with guarding Polish fortification workers at Tarnow in August 1944. See also Himmler's order on drafting civilians for the construction of positions for three SS divisions in the Kharkiv (*Totenkopf, Das Reich* and the cavalry division). VAP, *Höhere SS- und Polizeiführer Russland Süd, Ks. 19, Aktenvermerk af 6.9.1943.* The formations were taken out of the area shortly after, and it is unknown if the draft was actually put into effect. See also a letter of 21 December 1943 from Himmler's ADC to *SS-Oberführer* Rohde, Hochwald asking for 1,000 forced labourers via the chief counter-insurgency officer for the Latvian brigade, needed for construction of positions. BAB, NS19/382. See also BAMA, RS3/36 1a, letter of 14 January 1944.

139. BAB, NS19/2823, Letter of 24 May 1944 from *SS-Wirtschafts-Verwaltungshauptamt to RFSS, betr. Baugruppe Russland-Mitte – Einsatz Stellungsbau.*

140. *Nazi Conspiracy and Aggression*, Vol. IV (United States Government Printing Office, Washington, 1946), p. 573.

141. GARF, 7021/148/22, L.24ff., "Nationalkomitee Freies Deutschland, obvinitel'niy material nemetskikh soldat protiv soldat" in *Ofitserov nemetskoy armii* (here, p. 5). A Wiking soldier's testimony of having taken part in a burning and killing action 1942–1944, see GARF, 7021/148/28, L.L.19-22 and LL.27-28, Interrogation of the SS NCO Adam Noll, 17 February 1944 and 20 February 1944, as well as testimony by V.V. Kalugin on 17 February 1944.

142. VAP, N *SS Das Reich*, box. 7, Annex to KTB autumn 1941. Ia., Order of 8 December 1941 from 46th armoured corps concerning the defence of the Istra position. On the division's possible later razing in the Rzhev area, see GARF, 7021/148/28, LL.86-87, Undated testimony by a soldier of 86th Infantry division [1944].

as possible should be set to work.[143] At the beginning of the German retreat after the Kursk battle, at least one of the regiments of the *Leibstandarte* was under orders to burn – if possible – the villages they might have to leave. In particular, the battalion commanded, at the time, by Jochen Peiper was so efficient in solving this task that its soldiers nicknamed themselves the 'soldier-lamp-battalion', as they used to torch villages by throwing hurricane lanterns into houses.[144] Later that year, when *HSSPF* Hans-Adolf Prützmann rallied his subordinates to prepare for a possible German withdrawal across the Dnepr, this concept had not changed. He demanded that wherever the Red Army might go, they would find only properties razed to the ground and that not one kilogram of crops nor one single horse must fall into enemy hands. The only civilians, who might be left, were the old and infirm who could not work and who would only burden the hard-pressed Soviet food supplies.[145]

In March 1942, Gauleiter (leader of a Nazi district) Fritz Sauckel was appointed *Generalbevollmächtigter für den Arbeitseinsatz* (plenipotentiary for work). Following his selection, and in particular after the defeat at Stalingrad, the use in Germany of forced labourers from occupied Europe increased. A large number of workers were gathered through raids on occupied territories in Poland and the Soviet Union. Mostly, these actions were conducted by local police units, but close to the front where troops were present these, too, might be committed. During 2nd armoured corps' long sojourn in the Kharkiv area prior to the Kursk battle, *Division Das Reich* took part in such activities. A case of May 1943, confirms how *Das Reich* diligently carried out this task. Here soldiers of that division had an altercation with *Wehrmacht* personnel as it became clear that the latter actively sabotaged the rounding up of civilians warning them that the Waffen-SS was on its way.[146] At the same time, *Das Reich* personnel bound for home leave was detailed for guarding trains transporting these civilians to Germany.[147] A few months later, soldiers of *Division Wiking* were committed to a similar task capturing 400 Ukrainians.[148] End of February 1944, from their area of operations in northern Russia *Sturmbrigade Langemarck* arranged a transportation of 500 persons for work in Germany.[149]

In addition to the officially sanctioned violence, individually initiated atrocities also took place. For example, in the summer of 1943, the German army's *Feldgendarmerie* (military police) investigated a number of complaints by German agricultural civil

143. VAP, N *SS Das Reich*, box. 7, Annex to KTB autumn 1941. Ia., Order of 20 January 1942.
144. NAKEW, WO209/2244, PWIS(H)/LDC/299, Report of 29 August 1944 on interrogation of PW KP 49359 Sturmbannfue. Jacob Hanreich, p. 43.
145. VAP, *Höhere SS- und Polizeiführer Russland Sud, Aktenvermerk* of 8 September 1943 concerning "*Räumung des Ost-Dnepr-Raumes.*"
146. VAP, SS D-2 "*DR K.11, Meldung über einen Vorfall mit Wehrmachtsangehörigen, 25.5.1943.* Subsequent document *Stellungsnahme zur meldung des SS-Ustuf. Grime, 6/SS*" DF "*uber Zwischenfälle mit Wehrmacht angehörigen im Kolchos "kommuna Litwinowa" am 22. 5 43.*
147. BAMA, RS2-2/24, KTB No 5 with annexes. 27.3.-31.5.1943, p. 176, see back. For more references on forced labourers see ibid., pp. 164, 168 and 176.
148. Esper (1981), p. 29. The episode is described as an action aiming at interning all susceptible civilian men and, at the same time, make sure that no able-bodied man was forgotten.
149. GARF, 7021/148/28, L.10.

servants in Ukraine. The complaints concerned German soldiers' atrocities against civilians – in particular looting, violence and rape. Quite a few were about Waffen-SS personnel of the divisions forming up before the Kursk offensive. The rapes committed by SS soldiers were so common that a whole village had been deserted by its inhabitants because of the overwhelming frequency of sexual assaults by members of the *Leibstandarte* then forming up in the area.[150]

Another example concerns the 2nd SS armoured corps which in 1943 was sent to Italy to stiffen Italian resolve. There was pervasive anger among the Waffen-SS personnel, when Mussolini was toppled and Italy seceded from the alliance with Germany. In the corps' war diary, the shift led to a harangue about the treacherous and cowardly Italians.[151] At the same time, the division received orders from *Führer* HQ that if the Italians opposed being disarmed, the officers were to have a drumhead court-martial and be shot. The soldiers, then, were to be sent to concentration camps. The *Leibstandarte* personnel were told that 'Russian procedures' would apply. Among other things, in case of armed clashes, women and children were to be used as human shields on the decks of the tanks.[152] Apparently, the soldiers perceived the staffs' infuriated attitudes and the information from superiors as carte blanche for going berserk. A contemporary observer sent a complaint to SS' HQ:

> The men's understandable fury (concerning the Italian treason) was not to be assuaged easily. In spite of the Italians' numerical superiority, they were much too spineless to oppose letting themselves be disarmed with no further ado. However, the way the men let out steam had nothing in common with soldierly conduct – let alone with the Waffen-SS. Dozens of people were held up in the streets, threatened with pistols and forced to cede their watches and jewellery. Shops selling photo equipment, ladies' garments and bags were looted, women raped etc., etc.[153]

The year after, rapes were routinely committed by *Division Hitlerjugend* in Normandy – at least if the veterans' tales are to be trusted as they boasted about it to newcomers.[154]

End Phase Crimes

The Waffen-SS' contributions to crimes committed during the Second World War's end phase were not limited to the killings and atrocities on the roads walked by concentration camp prisoners on their 'death marches' as described earlier in this chapter. Forced

---

150. BAB, NS19/3717, Letter of 2 August 1943 from OKW to Wolff.
151. BAMA, RS2-2/20, KTB 8 and 11 September 1943.
152. BB, E27, 1000/721, *Archiv Nr. 9928, Bd.5, SS 111, Deserteurbericht 28.9.1943.*
153. BAB, NS19/2220, Letter of 1 October 1943 from *Oberführer* Kranefuss to Brandt. See also NAKEW, WO209/2244, PWIS(H)/LDC/299, Report on interrogation of PW KP 49359 Sturmbannfue. Jacob Hanreich, 29.8.1944, p. 4.
154. NAKEW, WO209/2244, Court of Inquiry, 10 March 1945, Exhibit No.7, Record of the Evidence of Grenadier Bernhard Herholz, pp. 7–8.

labourers and German civilians and soldiers also fell victims. In the final months, many Waffen-SS units showed higher combat morale than the *Wehrmacht*. This might be part of the reason why – when it came to harassing war-weary soldiers and civilians wishing to surrender their villages to avoid unnecessary havoc – most perpetrators were found in the ranks of the Waffen-SS. Because of the chaos of the last days, it is difficult to gauge the precise number of shootings or hangings perpetrated by Waffen-SS soldiers.[155] Although many of these cruelties concerned ordinary civilians or mayors wishing to open their towns to the advancing Allies, most were against concentration camp prisoners or prisoners-of-war as well as foreign civil workers and forced labourers.[156] In March 1945, a company commander of the *Leibstandarte*, for example, ordered his soldiers to kill on apprehension a number of escapees from a prisoner-of-war camp.[157] At the end of March 1945, even more radically, an officer of the *Waffen-SS Division zur Vergeltung* ordered 208 foreign workers shot, which duly happened on three separate occasions.[158]

An especially detailed insight into the dynamics of end phase crimes is offered from a court case against *Unterscharführer* (sergeant) Dieter of *Division Hitlerjugend'* straining battalion. In spring 1945, retreating with his section Dieter encountered a cyclist. He asked the man to stop, but he cycled on shouting that they prolonged the war and that it was a disgrace that they fought on. According to Dieter's testimony in court, an SS officer ordered them to 'lay down the man' – a colloquial term for shooting a prisoner.[159] With two to three rounds of his pistol Dieter personally shot the cyclist – a local farmer – and another SS man assaulted the wounded man crushing his skull with a heavy wine bottle. Then, taking the bike with them as booty, the soldiers marched on leaving the man to die. At the end of April 1945, Dieter was ordered to Quickborn north of Hamburg to guard some of the division's APCs that were undergoing repair at a local garage. He lodged with other soldiers in the inn where, on the 29th, a farmer's wife

---

155. For two examples see Sentence No 62 reprinted in Rüter-Ehlermann et al. (1969), p. 571ff and Sentence No 1156a in Laurenz Demps, C.F. Rüter, and L. Hekelaar Gombert. *DDR-Justiz und NS-Verbrechen: Sammlung ostdeutscher Strafurteile wegen nationalsozialistischer Tötungsverbrechen. Bd. IV* (Amsterdam University Press (AUP); K.G. Saur Verlag, 2004), p. 377ff.

156. For a characteristic example. see H.I. Sagel-Grande, H.H. Fuchs, C.F. Rüter and Fritz Bauer, *Justiz und NS-Verbrechen: Sammlung deutscher Strafurteile wegen nationalsozialistischer Tötungsverbrechen, 1945–1966. Bd. XV* (University Press Amsterdam, 1976), p. 465ff. Civilians suspected of opposition against the regime also risked execution. On 28. April 1945, five suspected members of the Bavarian resistance movement were executed in Alttotting by a Waffen-SS detachment commanded by *SS-Sturmbannführer* K. Mühldorf. Sentence No 241 reprinted in Rüter-Ehlermann et al. (1971), *Bd. VII*, p. 455ff. Sentence No 111, reprinted in Adelheid L. Rüter-Ehlermann, C.F. Rüter and Fritz Bauer, *Justiz und NS-Verbrechen: Sammlung deutscher Strafurteile wegen nationalsozialistischer Tötungsverbrechen, 1945–1966. Bd. III* (University Press Amsterdam, 1969), p. 725ff.

157. Sentence No 491 reprinted in H.I. Sagel-Grande, H.H. Fuchs, C.F. Rüter and Fritz Bauer, *Justiz und NS-Verbrechen: Sammlung deutscher Strafurteile wegen nationalsozialistischer Tötungsverbrechen, 1945–1966. Bd. XVI* (University Press Amsterdam, 1976), p. 379ff.

158. Sentence No 458 reprinted in H.I. Sagel-Grande et al. (1976), *Bd. XIV*, p. 561ff.

159. Sentence No 428 reprinted in H.I. Sagel-Grande et al. (1975), pp. 584–614, here p. 598.

came to see him. Having been away for a couple of days, she had returned to her farm where she had had an altercation with two Soviet forced labourers. This culminated – so she claimed – in their threatening her with slashing her throat. Together with a police officer and his assistant an SS man went to the farm to tell the Russians that their behaviour might have dire consequences. To stress his seriousness, the policeman tapped the butt of his pistol. Leaving the place, the SS soldier rebuked the policeman that he had been too appeasing – 'many more should be killed'.[160] New disagreements between the farmers' wife and the workers – now supported by their friends – occurred. She complained anew to the SS detachment. On 30 April, Dieter and six of his men went to the farm. Here, he shot one forced labourer, but realising that the other one was a woman, he found he needed new instructions and went away having locked her up. In the night, Dieter came back with two SS men and had the woman executed in the farmyard.[161]

---

160. Ibid., p. 604.
161. Ibid.

Chapter Twelve

EXPLAINING THE ATROCITIES: CONTEXT AND MOTIVES

The winter of 1941–1942 was tough on the German troops employed in the Demyansk Pocket, but it was still worse for the Soviet civilians who suffered from the extremes of hunger, cold and lack of shelter. This, however, made no impression on Theodor Eicke, the general-officer-commanding *Division Totenkopf.* In January 1942, in one of the division's journals, he encouraged his soldiers to see the locals the way Heinrich Heine's forlorn grenadier did in a poem: 'What do I care for the woman, what do I care for the child. I have higher aspirations. Let them go begging if they are hungry.'[1] Being a Nazi *Altkämpfer*, Eicke undoubtedly represented the most ideologically committed segment of the Waffen-SS but there is no doubt that Nazi ideology played a central role in the justification and rationalization of the crimes committed by many an SS soldier. However, other factors were also at play, including, for example, career ambitions, peer pressure, dispersal of responsibility and the general brutalization of war.[2] The present chapter offers an analysis of how these various components may help us understand how the monstrous atrocities described in the Chapter 11 could take place.

The early research of Nazi crimes tended to demonize the perpetrators, and portray them as deviants, psychopaths and sadists with a particular proclivity for authoritarianism.[3] Later research tended to emphasize structural explanations such as, for example, Bauman's famous interpretation of the Holocaust being a product primarily

---

1. Heinrich Heine *Die Grenadiere*. A romanza that appeared first in 1822 as a kind of Napoleon apotheosis. Weise (2013) p. 302.
2. For a usefull overview of how the perpetrators have been represented in scholarly studies and collective memory see Thomas Kühne, 'Dämonisierung, Viktimisierung, Diverzifizierung. Bilder von nationalsozialistischen Gewalttätern in Gesellschaft und Forschung seit 1945', Oliver von Wrochen (ed.) *Nationalsocialistische Täterschaften. Nachwirkungen in Gesellschaft und Familie,* (Metropol, 2016), pp. 32–55.
3. See forexample Kogon (1991). Inspired by the German philosopher Theodor Adorno, several psycho-social investigations have also endeavoured to pin-point certain authoritarian commonalities with the SS perpetrators of crimes. Henry Victor Dicks, *Licensed Mass Murder: A Socio-Psychological Study of Some SS Killers* (Heinemann for Sussex University Press, 1972). John Steiner and Jochen Fahrenberg, "Die Ausprägung autoritärer Einstellung beiehemaligen Angehörigen der SS und derWehrmacht (Eine empirische Studie)", *Kölner Zeitschrift fur Soziologie und Sozialpsychologi,* Vol. 22, No. 3, 1970, pp. 551–66. John M. Steiner, "The SS Yesterday and Today – a socio-psychological view", Joel E. Dimsdale (red.), *Survivors, Victims, and Perpetrators: Essays on the Nazi Holocaust* (Hemisphere, 1980).

of bureaucratic and dehumanizing decision-making in a modern rational state.[4] Detailed empirical historical accounts have since clearly demonstrated how face-to-face killings and executions committed by soldiers and guards in German uniforms remained a central genocidal practice throughout the war and throughout the Nazi territories, something which cannot be explained solely by looking at bureaucratic procedures and mechanisms. Furthermore, a number of sociological, psychological and historical studies have demonstrated how all the perpetrators of mass violence and killings during the Second World War were generally quite ordinary people and not deviants in any particular way.[5] Their deeds were not a product of pathological personalities, but were rather the results of the extreme environment and culture within which they operated. Important factors were conformism and loyalty to their co-killers, the role of authority figures and careerism as well as – not least – acceptance and internalisation of Nazi ideology and the consequent dehumanisation of the victims.[6]

The Chain of Command: Crimes Ordered Directly by Higher Authorities

Treue und Gehorsam (loyalty and obedience) were SS' key values. These notions embodied the expectation of unconditional loyalty to the SS' norms and values and equally manifest obedience when it came to orders given by superiors.[7] In many cases, it is hard to follow the flow of orders through the SS chain of command. Orders were later destroyed, or they were oral and, frequently, delivered in the organisation's cryptic colloquialisms such as 'take the Jews for a walk', which meant that the officer – in this case, the officer commanding *Das Reich*'s maintenance company – wanted to see them killed. Similarly, a *Hitlerjugend* company commander's expressions 'do it radically' and 'act ruthlessly' gave a young soldier the impression that no prisoners should be taken.[8] Thus, direct, written and explicit instructions by Himmler to violate contemporary international law were rare but they were also not necessary given the training the men had received,

4. Zygmunt Baumann, *Modernity and the Holocaust* (Cornell University Press, 1989).
5. See for example Christopher R. Browning, *Ordinary Men: Reserve Police Battalion 101 and the Final Solution in Poland* (Harper Perennial, 1998).
6. Browning 1998; Harald Welzer and Michaela Christ, *Täter: wie aus ganz normalen Menschen Massenmörder warden* (Fischer Taschenbuch, 2005); James Waller, *Becoming Evil: How Ordinary People Commit Genocide and Mass Killing*, 2nd ed. (Oxford University Press, 2007). For a comprehensive survey see Gehard Paul, 'Von Psychopathen, Technokraten des Terrors und "ganz gewöhnlichen Deutschen"' in Paul (2002), p. 13ff. Jürgen Matthäus, Historiography and the Perpetrators of the Holocaust, in Stone (2004), p. 197ff. Peter Scharff Smith "Dehumanization, social contact and techniques of Othering. Combining the lessons from Holocaust studies and prison research" in Anna Eriksson (ed.) *Punishing the Other. The social production of immorality revisited*, Routledge 2015.
7. See "Befehl und Gehorsam" in Buchheim et al. (1994), pp. 215–320. See also Herbert Jäger, *Verbrechen unter totalitärer Herrschaft; Studien zur nationalsozialistischen Gewaltkriminalität* (Walter Verlag, 1967).
8. NAKEW, WO209/2244, Exhibit No. 6, Record of the Evidence of Grenadier George Mertens, 10 March 1945, p. 9ff.

the ideological universe they operated within and the oral orders they received. Himmler himself is known for orally sanctioning even the most draconian actions in various fora, as long as the purpose served the *Führer*'s will and the ideological raison d'être of the Third Reich.

Large killing actions were normally ordered by central authorities and occasionally delivered in writing. Thus, Himmler's signature is found on the brutal order, frequently quoted in research, committing the cavalry division in the Pripyat Marshes in the late summer of 1941. On that occasion, the division's personnel murdered tens of thousands.[9] In August 1941, another compilation of guidelines was issued to units under the *Kommandostab Reichsführer-SS* explicitly sanctioning mass-murder. At the slightest suspicion that local Jews might be in contact with partisans, the troops were to ruthlessly annihilate all Jews.[10] Even late in the war such orders have been issued. On 1 August 1944, briefly after the outbreak of the Warsaw rising by the Polish Home Army, a telex was received by SS HQ in Warsaw. In this Himmler instructed that the insurgents, as well as the civilian population, should be 'wiped out by the tens of thousands'.[11]

Many of the guidelines and policies providing the framework for the Waffen-SS criminal activities actually originated with the *Wehrmacht*. This was true for the previously described criminal orders that formed the basis for the war of extermination in the east.[12] The killings in the autumn of 1943, of Italians by *Division Prinz Eugen* was ordered directly by the *Führer* HQ. These were a means of retaliation against 'Italy's treason' and applied to both Waffen-SS and the *Wehrmacht*. Similar orders conveyed via the army are to be found among the archival material of the 2nd SS armoured corps.[13]

From comprehensive German court records, it appears that the final decisions on committing crimes, even very serious ones, were often made at a low level. This is hardly surprising given that the authority to order mass murder in reality had been delegated to the lower cadres through the aforementioned criminal orders and as a result of the ideological culture which in itself proscribed murder of 'subhumans' and other enemies of the Nazi state. In March 1945, a *Rottenführer* who had deserted to Switzerland explained that it was easy to get permission to kill Russians. 'Any man in the company might obtain the *Feldwebel*'s (company sergeant major's) permission to put a person to death, who was suspicious or had been disobedient.'[14]

---

9. VAP, N *SS-T-ST/RGT 3, Kommandosonderbefehl betr. Richtlinien für die Durchkämmerung und Durchstreifung von Sumpfgebieten durch Reitereinheiten, 28.7.1941.*

10. BAMA, RS1/16, *Richtlinien für den Einsatz der Kommandostab RF/SS unterstellten Verbände. 8.folge. Auswertung bisheriger Kampferfahrungen.* No date, but later than 18 August 1941.

11. Sentence No 860, reprinted in Rüter and Hekelaar Gombert (2010), p. 498.

12. Concerning these, see the 1941 chapter.

13. BAMA, RH19IX/16 fra 2012, Letter of 23 September 1943 from *Oberbefehlshaber der Heeresgruppe.*

14. BB, E27, 1000/721, Archiv Nr. 9928, Bd.7, Deserteur-Sammel-Bericht, 27.3.1945, 490, p. 2. Normally, the rank Feldwebel was not used in the Waffen-SS, he was called *Oberscharführer*. The use here may have happened because of the Swiss authorities' lack of insight into the Waffen-SS rank system.

Ideology and the War of Extermination

Nazi ideology played a key role in the crimes committed by the Waffen-SS, partly by dehumanising and demonising the victims, partly by rationalising the exterminations as being necessary for the survival of the Germanic race.[15] In July 1941, Himmler explained to the filler personnel bound for *Division Nord* at the eastern front that the Soviets were 'a racial mix of people whose names could hardly be pronounced, and whose appearances are so vile that one can kill them without mercy.'[16] The year after, Himmler spoke to the officers of *Division Das Reich* describing the war was a matter of extinction of either Russia or the German Reich. He declared that many a German soldier had entered the war in the east with an 'overly delicate, civilised and decadent attitude'. As a result, some had even perceived 'the Jews as human beings'. However, Himmler stressed that 'we, the SS men, are less prone than others to that kind of nonsense.'[17] In the autumn of 1943, Himmler made his notorious speech in Posen where he spoke openly about the projected extermination of the European Jews, a matter which he had already enlightened the officer cadets of the *SS Junkerschule* Bad Tölz about a year earlier.[18]

The intention behind such speeches, along with the intensive ideological tuition previously described, was that the soldiers should internalise Nazi ideology and act in its spirit. And according to Nazi ideology as it developed during the war and especially within the SS, killing Jews and subhumans were good deeds.[19] As explained by a German historian, in the SS, the ideological training had murder of Jews, as its purpose (*'Ausbildungsziel Judenmord'*).[20]

In several diaries and other contemporary documents, there are clear indications that the Nazi ideology was, indeed, internalised by many an SS man and in a way that rationalized heinous crimes. In March 1942, in his diary an officer of the police division lamented that his men did not understand that the Nordic race's struggle was about life or death: 'In this, even the slightest compassion is a setback.' Having watched a film on the deportation of Jews from the ghetto at Lublin, he concluded that this clearly demonstrated why it was necessary to treat them as sub-humans.[21] In the winter of 1941–1942, during a dinner conversation in Nazi-friendly circles

---

15. Peter Scharff Smith "Dehumanization, social contact and techniques of Othering – combining the lessons from Holocaust studies and prison research" in: Anna Eriksson (ed.) Punishing the Other: The social production of immorality revisited Routledge 2016.
16. BAB, NS19/4008, *Der Reichsführer-SS zu den Ersatzmannschaften für die Kampfgruppe Nord am Sonntag, den 13. Juli 1941, in Stettin.*
17. BAB, NS19/4008, *Rede des Reichsführers-SS am 19.6.1942 vor dem Führerkorps der Division [Das Reich].*
18. BAB, NS19/4008, *Rede des Reichsführers-SS am 23.11.1942 – SS-Junkerschule Tölz.*
19. Welzer 2006; Smith 2016.
20. Jürgen Matthäus et al. (2003).
21. Quoted from Captain Hoffman's diary entries of 10 and 21 March 1942, reprinted in *True to Type* (1945), p. 63. For more examples see the entries of 1 and 7 April 1942 on Poland and Poles.

in Copenhagen, a Danish *Division Wiking* volunteer talked openly about the shooting of 9,000 Jews in Taganrog and explained that 'the Jews were not human beings'. He offered as proof that Jews 'like horses do not dare to look into the eyes of a human being'.[22]

Brutalisation and Exchange of Experience

Unterscharführer Dieter, who was the primary perpetrator in the killings of forced labourers at Quickborn in the spring of 1945, had been involved in violence since the 'time of struggle' in the early 1930s, culminating in the killing of a communist in a violent assault. In 1942, Dieter came to Waffen-SS *Regiment Germania* and over the following years, he served with a number of units, took part in counter-insurgency operations in Yugoslavia, and ended up, in 1945, as a contributor to the end phase crimes killing Russian workers. Dieter's career is illustrative of the fact that some SS men had a long record of violence. He proceeded from scuffles and fatal violence in his early life to the perpetration of end phase crimes 10 years later. And in between he took part in partisan suppression at the eastern front and in the Balkans.[23]

A recent study of the German warfare and counter-insurgency operations in France 1943–1944 indicated that experiences from the eastern front were conducive to atrocities against captured partisans, civilians and Allied prisoners-of-war.[24] The validity of this view is underpinned by a number of Waffen-SS examples that show that the soldiery had difficulties adapting to rules quite different from those characterising the war in the east. In the autumn of 1942, after three months of sustaining heavy casualties in the Demyansk Pocket *Frikorps Danmark* was granted home leave. On that occasion, the SS leadership found it pertinent to remind the soldiers that since 'their compatriots were of high cultural standard' they had better adjust their general behaviour. This admonition, however, was not of much help and the home leave was ridden with conflicts. Even though the *Frikorps* soldiers were frequently provoked by other Danes, their reactions to real or imagined hassles were out of all proportion: a citizen of Caucasian-black origin was assaulted, Copenhagen Jews were harassed, jazz-loving swingers were assaulted and their hair cut, and in a number of episodes bayonets and firearms were used against civilians.[25]

There were several aspects to the brutalisation process. Most importantly, probably, at the first killing one stepped over a threshold. This eased repetition because such crimes became normalised and part of the corporate culture in the Waffen-SS. Officers and NCOs who had participated in killing actions carried the experience with them in their subsequent careers. They accumulated expertise of killing. For instance, when

---

22. RK, 1353 Rigspolitichefen, Politiets Efterretningstjeneste, 1945–1950, reprint of the diary of Knud Nordentoft, entry of 6 February 1942. Large parts of this diary had been published. See Hardis og Nordentoft (2005).

23. Rüter-Ehlermann et al. (1969), p. 598.

24. Lieb (2007), p. 70. See for a modification of his views on p. 95ff.

25. Christensen et al. (1998), p. 353ff.

the maintenance company of *Das Reich* murdered Jews in Austria in spring of 1945, they knew how the victims were most conveniently placed in a mass grave. They used, what was called *Sardinenpackung* (sardine tin packing), forcing the victims to lay down in the graves on top of those already killed.[26] One of the Leibstandarte soldiers accused of participation in the massacre at Malmédy explained that he had shot an American soldier in the back of his head, because 'I know from my service with the *Totenkopf* units that this is the usual way to do it.'[27]

Brutalisation was not only a matter of front service. The raw recruits learned from their more experienced comrades. The familiarisation with committing crimes against civilians and prisoners-of-war comprised an expectation that the men were capable of displaying the necessary harshness. Those who tried to avoid were shamed. A soldier trying to avoid becoming an accomplice of *Division Das Reich*'s hanging of 100 French in Tulle was told by an NCO that he was a *Franzenkopf* (frog head) and humbled him for lack of courage.[28] Similarly a soldier with no front experience who refused to shoot a prisoner during forced digging at Litoměřice (Leitmeritz) was derided for being a paper pusher by an officer and his fellow soldiers. Thus, pressured, the soldier shot at the victim though without killing him, and another more experienced man then killed him off.[29]

These examples indicate a 'corporate culture' very different from the one described by the American researcher Christopher Browning, which he has revealed in his famous study of the 101st police battalion. In 1942–1943, this unit committed extensive killings of Polish Jews. In contravention of the SS culture, the commanding officer, Police Major Wilhelm Trapp, made the participation optional and for those wishing to abstain, there were no immediate consequences. The battalion's first major criminal task was the shooting of 1,500 women, children and elderly at the village Józefów. In the early morning of 13 July 1942, Trapp rallied his men in a semi-circle around himself explaining what was to happen. There were tears in his eyes and, obviously, he struggled not to cry. In the speech, he informed the soldiers that he had received a disagreeable mission of execution, but that the elderly men, who did not want to participate, would be free to abstain. While 12 or 13 men stepped forward and were relieved. Subsequently, they were set to other tasks. Briefly, before the action, a doctor instructed the soldiers on how best to go about the job thus inspiring further requests to be let off the hook. Both of Trapp's two closest subordinates were from the SS, and they both despised him as being weak and characterised by a less than military attitude – a view they would repeat many years hence, when they were interrogated about the crimes. Obviously, the two officers did not like Trapp's offer to the soldiers, and one of them declined to allow the last abstainers to leave. The other abused the first man who accepted Trapp's offer.[30]

---

26. See the chapter on 1945.
27. William C.C. Cavanagh, *A Tour of the Bulge Battlefield* (Pen & Sword, Barnsley, 2001), p. 87.
28. Hastings (2009), p. 136.
29. BL, B162/6400, Letter of 5 October 1960 from *Justitzgebäude Appelhofplatz* in Cologne to *Zentrale Stelle der Landesjustizverwaltungen* in Ludwigsburg, Ibid.: Letter of 19 November 1962, concerning interrogation of E.R.
30. See *One Day in* Józefów in Browning (1993), p. 169ff.

For some, the willingness to kill innocent people simply became the epitome of SS membership. In March 1942, *Hauptsturmführer* and *Verfügungstruppe* veteran Karl Dietrich commanded a battlegroup of German police and Ukrainian *Schutzmannschaft* soldiers employed in Belarus. During a counter-insurgency operation, the battle group was informed by a police officer in charge of a sub-unit that in a village there were 92 Jews unfit for work. As Dietrich received the message, he ordered an officer on his staff to convey his order that this group was to be executed and to oversee that it was done. Excusing himself in various ways, this police officer tried to avoid complicity in murder. Dietric blamed him with the words, 'what kind of an officer are you, sir?' and 'you, police officers, have not improved very much.' The latter remark, of course, was to be understood that, unlike the SS, the police was not willing to execute murders of civilians. Hence, Dietrich found someone else to convey and execute the order. On 4 March, personnel of the Ukrainian *Schutzmannschaft* battalion shot between 30 and 40 Jews, the majority of whom were women, children and elderly persons.[31]

Violence as a Conversational Topic

During their service, the SS soldiers got insight into Nazi crimes and, when they shared their impressions, they contributed to sustaining the 'corporate culture' and helped rationalize and legitimize the misdeeds. Although participants in killing actions – and in particular those systematically involved in the Holocaust – were *Geheimnisträger* (persons with insight in a classified matter), there were lively discussions on the violence committed within the Waffen-SS. In the Allied prisoner-of-war and internment camps such stories were a hot topic among the German soldiers.[32] But despite *Wehrmacht* officers' sometimes distancing themselves from such brutal recollections, it was clearly a different matter for some of the SS prisoners. A Dane interned in Camp Hälsingmo in Sweden co-habited with a number of Waffen-SS deserters. In a letter he wrote that 'There is hardly one evening that you don't fall asleep to the accompaniment of German SS stories and Nazi war songs.' The soldiers bragged about 'having participated in tormenting the Russian and Croat populations'.[33] Similarly, a commanding officer of a *Division Nordland* battalion entertained his fellow prisoners in Internment Camp

---

31. Sentence No 604 reprinted in H.I. Sagel-Grande and Fritz Bauer, *Justiz und NS-Verbrechen: Sammlung deutscher Strafurteile wegen nationalsozialistischer Tötungsverbrechen, 1945–1966*. Bd. XXII (University Press Amsterdam, 1981), p. 445ff., here p. 462.

32. In his comparative study based on the American bugging of paras and SS soldiers, the German historian Frederik Müllers realises a markedly greater disinclination among the SS soldiers than among the paras to talk about the war crimes. He attributes this to the fact that the latter had more extensive participation in the crimes and, therefore, might have feared punishment. Müllers (2012), 77ff.

33. SAMA, RS, F 8 EA: 22, Excerpt from letter of 24 August 1944 by Jørn Hagensborg, Hälsingmo [internment camp for, inter alios, Danish SS men] to Anna Hagensborg, Tjörnarp.

Faarhus about his participation in murdering civilians and burning down villages in Croatia and described these atrocities as 'rather amusing occurrences'.[34] Similarly, a German officer of *Das Reich* told an army lieutenant colonel about the massacre in Oradour and explained laughingly that 'it was the wrong town. Just too bad for them. Subsequently, it turned out that there were no partisans there'.[35]

It was not only the boredom of the prisoner-of-war camp that led to conversations on killings and atrocity. Sources indicate that the chat was lively throughout the war. A *Hauptsturmführer,* under interrogation about his contribution to the killings of 1,500 Jews in the Waffen-SS camp in Babruysk, denied his participation, though he admitted that the Jewish issue including the physical extermination of the Jews had been freely discussed by the officers' messes as well as among the private soldiers.[36] In April 1943, following executions in the same camp, over dinner, several of the perpetrators told fellow SS men about the killings. Apart from scoffing at the victims, they produced a large bunch of bloody złoty notes, which they then shared among themselves.[37]

Even fresh recruits had several sources of possible knowledge of the SS' crimes. As described previously, many barracks had sub-concentration camps attached. In the case of training institutions and transit camps, such places might have had a large volume of soldiers passing through. Young soldiers, who were undergoing training at the SS interpreter school in Berlin were for example billeted in Sachsenhausen and shared rooms with the camp guards.[38] A Waffen-SS deserter stressed that the physical closeness contributed to providing insight into the brutality applied in the camps. Following the campaign in France, he was posted to his division's filler unit based at concentration camp Dachau where he witnessed the abuse of the prisoners.[39]

Not only were the atrocities no secret, they were an object of boasting. Within the bounds of the violent militaristic culture of the SS and the Waffen-SS participation in atrocities could boost one's status. Thus, it was with shameless self-assertion that, in autumn 1941, a German Sturmmann told Danish Frikorps soldiers that, before New Year, he would certainly manage to kill off all Jewish forced labourers.[40] A half-British-half-German Waffen-SS soldier, who came from the Leibstandarte to

34. Kristensen (2011), p. 264ff.
35. NAKEW, WO208/4140, SRM 1150: Lieutenant Colonel von der Heydte in conversation with a lieutenant on 30 December 1944. On the issue of whether Das Reich had confused two towns of the same name, see Hastings (2009), p. 184ff.
36. BL, B62, 6723, *Sonderkommission Hamburg, Vernehmungsprotokoll, 23.11.1970.* For another example concerning internal dissemination of knowledge of the SS' mass murders in Poland 1939–1940, see Cüppers (2011).
37. BL, B62, 6723, *Hessisches Landeskriminalamt, Zeugenvernehmung, 6.12.1966.*
38. Bernwald (2012), p. 44.
39. BB, E27, 1000/721, *Archiv Nr. 9928, Bd. 4, D110, Deserteurbericht 11.5.1943,* p. 17.
40. Christensen et al. (2005), p. 51. In the same diary, it is told how a prisoner-of-war working for the *Frikorps* was shot for having been accused of stealing cigarettes, p. 85.

the tiny British Free Corps, regaled his comrades with stories of ghetto obliterations in Krakow and Warsaw, over defenestration of Jewish women from tall buildings, to his participation in the execution of 200 Poles.[41]

It is characteristic of the 'relaxed' attitude of many Waffen-SS soldiers to the crimes they had obviously committed that they spoke freely about them to people outside the SS.[42] The diary of Knud Nordentoft, briefly the leader of the SS welfare office in Copenhagen, illustrates this. Thanks to his office and to his position as one of the leading cultural personalities of the Danish Nazi party, he communicated with several Danish volunteers. From autumn 1941 onwards, his diary comprises frequent entries on Nazi crimes, the sources of which are, mostly, conversations with SS volunteers. One of these had told him that, 'The Germans shoot these Jews [...]; all of them. They annihilate 20,000, 30,000 or 40,000 in the small towns.'[43]

While the above examples related to outsiders who came from circles affiliated with the Waffen-SS, in other cases their audience were total strangers. In March 1945 an episode occurred when two German NCOs of the remnants of Division Handschar had finished shooting at least 40 Jews in Austria. It is a proof of the matter-of-fact way they went about killing innocent people that, after the action, they asked one of the unit's nurses to clean their uniforms that had become soiled with blood and cerebral matter. Having heard how the uniforms had become stained, she declined. Her reaction, though, did not dismay the two. They spent the following days bragging about their deed to friends and local women.[44]

---

41. NAKEW, KV2/254, Thomas Heller Cooper. That this was not merely loose talk can be corroborated by the fact that, for some time, this man served with an SS battalion in Debica. The personnel helped out in deportations to extermination camp Belzec. A witness accused the man of having shot, during transportation to Tarnow, between 10 and 20 Jews. Se BL, 162/18266, *Staatsanwaltschaft bei Landgericht Hannover, Verfg., 9.4.1971*, p. 17.

42. Apart from the below examples, see also Dirk Heinrichs, "Hauptmann d. R. Wilm Hosenfeld. Retter in Warschau" in Wette (2002), p. 77, Sentence No 1619, reprinted in Laurenz Demps, C.F. Rüter, and L. Hekelaar Gombert, *DDR-Justiz und NS-Verbrechen: Sammlung ostdeutscher Strafurteile wegen nationalsozialistischer Tötungsverbrechen. Bd. XI* (Amsterdam University Press (AUP), K.G. Saur Verlag, 2008), p. 77ff., Sentence No 1452, reprinted in Ibid. Bd VIII, p. 715 ff; Sentence No 1531, reprinted in Ibid. Bd X p. 55ff. Cüppers (2011), p. 276. Court case No 1531, reprinted in Demps et al. (2007), p. 55ff. Testimony of a letter by a soldier of the Totenkopf Division, quoted after Kristensen (2011), p. 266ff. YV, M.40 MAP, 114: Letter to the leader of Glavpurkka Mekhlis from the leader of the 18th Army's politotdel's (political platoon's) 7th unit, Colonel Commissar Mamonov, undated, probably late November 1941, copy of letter of 29 November 1941 from an SS-man field post No 20361-D. GARF, 7021/148/36, L.28, *Vypiska is protokola polititjeskogo oprosa v/plennogo unterofitsera Asmusa Sjtammer is sjtaba 3 tankovoj armii* [Transcript of the protocol of political questioning by prisoner NCO Asmus Shtammer on the staff of 3rd armoured army], no date [1943–1944].

43. RK, 1353, Politiets Efterretningstjeneste 1945–1950, Copy of Knud Nordentoft's diary 10 January, 6 February 1942, 18 January and 25 June 1943.

44. Elenore Lappin, *Die Rolle der Waffen-SS beim Zwangsarbeitseinsatz ungarischer Juden im Gau Steiermark und bei den Todesmärschen ins KZ Mauthausen (1944/45)*. Christine Schindler, 2004, p. 90.

The Importance of Battlefield Conditions

To get a comprehensive impression of the circumstances of the crimes, it is necessary to look at the context. A reasonable partial explanation of the atrocities committed by the German army and the Waffen-SS during the campaign in Poland is that the units were inexperienced and the soldiers were prone to seeing an enemy behind every lamppost. This was also what happened during the First World War in Belgium during the summer and autumn of 1914, where German atrocities befell the civilian population. The soldiers were not accustomed to the chaotic battlefield and perceived fire by regular troops in well-camouflaged position as being ambushes by civilian snipers. Moreover, the unexpectedly high casualty rates increased the soldiers' aggressiveness inspiring atrocities against civilians and captured enemy combatants.[45]

The Waffen-SS formations in France in 1940 and, to some extent, those of the Russian campaign of 1941 were largely inexperienced, and their baptism of fire must have been very stressing indeed.[46] When combined with Nazi ideology, this became a deadly cocktail. Written accounts reaching Berlin from the Eastern demonstrate how the opponents' racial traits were thought to be important.[47] A little into July 1941, Division Totenkopf reported that, in a number of tough fights over some concrete bunkers on the border between Latvia and Russia, one shelter was defended by twenty Jews.[48] Shortly after, Leibstandarte reported that a certain sector of the front was defended exclusively by 'Asians' who, having spent all their ammunition, were annihilated in their tranches – thus the post-action report.[49] Similar Totenkopf men who encountered African colonial soldiers in France would not give the Moroccans quarter, but killed them all.[50]

In other cases, like that of the Le Paradis massacre, we cannot see similar ideological motives and, apparently, huge casualties combined with determined resistance from the enemy triggered the slaughter. As late as August 1944, a Swedish officer of Division Nordland's *Aufklärungs Abteilung 11* (reconnaissance battalion 11) took it out on the prisoners after his unit had sustained serious losses. In a frenzy, he personally killed three and had his men shooting the remainder.[51]

This could also be influenced by the Waffen-SS soldiers' experiences of Soviet atrocities against German prisoners-of-war and wounded as well as their desecration of German corpses. On 9 July 1941, a company from Das Reich was completely ripped up by a violent attack from a wood believed to be free of enemies. When the area had

---

45. On the atrocities in Belgium, 1914, see Horne and Kramer (2001).
46. To most of the Totenkopf Division's men, the campaign in France was their first active service as was Barbarossa for the Wiking soldiers.
47. BAB,NS19/2854: *Zusammenfassender Bericht der Tagesmeldungen der SS-Divisionen, 6.7.1941; Zusammenfassender Bericht der Tagesmeldungen der SS-Divisionen, 10.7.1941; Zusammenfassender Bericht der Tagesmeldungen der SS-Divisionen, 17.7.1941.* Merkl (2010), p. 192.
48. BAB, NS19/2854, *Zusammenfassender Bericht der Tagesmeldungen der SS-Divisionen, 10.7.1941.*
49. BAB, NS19/2854, *Zusammenfassender Bericht der Tagesmeldungen der SS-Divisionen, 17.7.1941.*
50. Sydnor (1990), p. 116ff.
51. Gyllenhaal and Westberg (2008), p. 291.

been retaken, it appeared that all prisoners and wounded had been shot and their bodies pillaged. Das Reich's aggregate losses were 83 killed in the fight and the subsequent murders – among them the officer commanding and all platoon commanders.[52] In another incident, Soviet troops ambushed a field ambulance of the same division and killed 40 patients. This produced an order to Das Reich soldiers not to take prisoners for eight days.[53] Also in 1942 and 1943 were such orders apparently issued by Waffen-SS divisions.[54]

At the western front, similar dynamics were seen. Ten days after the Normandy landings, Götz von Berlichingen's *SS-Panzer-Grenadier-Regiment 37* detailed two men for a nocturnal reconnaissance task. The next morning, allegedly their comrades found them strangled. According to an eyewitness, the commanding officer, Obersturmbannführer Erwin Horstmann, inferred that the regiment was facing a Sing-Sing division. Using this expression Horstmann referred to the American prison, thus exploiting the widespread Nazi belief that criminals were the mainstay of many American units. Subsequently, Horstmann selected two Americans, allegedly Jewish, out of 15 prisoners. He had them shot the following night, and sent one of the remaining Americans back to Allied lines to tell the tale.[55] As we can see, the traditional 'an eye for an eye' concept went hand in hand with an ideologically tainted perception of the opponent's origin and ethnicity.

The loss of commanders and other highly profiled persons was a frequent motive for revenge. The loss of Standartenführer Hans-Friedemann Goetze, who was highly respected by the troops, probably played a role in the Le Paradis massacre.[56] Other massacres, too, were triggered by beloved commanders' or fellow soldiers' death. Jürgen Stroop's reaction at seeing his good acquaintance Untersturmführer Otto Dehmke killed, during the suppression of the uprising in the Warsaw ghetto, was – according to his adjutant – to have hundreds of Jewish prisoners shot out of hand.[57] Also, in France revenge motives were extant – in Oradour as well as in the less well-known massacre of Maille. On 25 August 1944, following an ambush by the Résistance outside Maille

---

52. BAB, NS19/2854, *Zusammenfassender Bericht der Tagesmeldungen der SS-Divisionen, 19.7.1941.*

53. Hastings (2009), s.10. For a third account – perhaps overlapping with these two – concerning a retaliatory action by *Das Reich* against 100 Soviet prisoners-of-war see BB, E27, 1000/721, Archiv Nr. 9928, Bd.9, 8722/d4493, *SS Bericht nr. 101, 15.5.1942.*

54. Well-known, but not documented, is also that, after the discovery in early 1942 of murdered SS-soldiers, Sepp Dietrich ordered that for three days no prisoners be taken. Allegedly, this order cost 4,000 soldiers their lives. See Stein (1966), s.273. That the *Leibstandarte* issued orders of this kind is substantiated in the memoirs of a soldier who, during the re-conquest of Kharkiv saw his officer shooting a prisoner giving the reason that 'orders from higher up was not to take prisoners.' Roes (2005), p. 72. Concerning an episode from Wiking in 1942, see Westerlund (2019), p. 48. Concerning an order from Wiking in 1943, see Christensen et al. (1998), p. 398.

55. Interrogation of Erich Schienkiewitz, 16 October 1944, here after Müllers (2012), p. 106ff. After the war, the American military tribunal in Dachau sentenced Schienkiewitz to prison for life for his part in this crime. http://www1.jur.uva.nl/junsv/JUNSVEng/DTRR/files/us018.htm. Accessed on 23 August 2013.

56. Weise (2013), p. 290.

57. Cuppers (2011), p. 299ff.

on the important route of retreat from southern France towards Paris, the village was razed to the ground, 124 civilians, of whom 42 were women and 44 children, were killed. The unit, which was probably the one responsible for the atrocity, was Götz von Berlichingen's filler battalion. This unit had a record of clashes with the Résistance, and 10 days previously the commanding officer Hauptsturmführer Walter Siems had been wounded in a partisan ambush.[58] In this context, it is worth mentioning that often it was the perpetrators who claimed that their acts had been triggered by the enemy's actions. Thus, for example, Jochen Peiper vindicated his shooting of civilians during the Battle of the Bulge with an assertion that a number of Leibstandarte wounded soldiers had been maltreated by Belgian partisans.[59]

The crimes per se, might have been a means for the SS leadership to bind members even closer together. The SS soldiers' involvement in the Nazi crimes contributed to a comprehensive understanding of the 'tasks' that the SS thought fit to execute on the regime's behest and, as an additional benefit, it strengthened the cohesion within the units involved.[60] The knowledge of the crimes committed by the Waffen-SS and the SS generally also diminished the inclination to surrender. Thus, the Waffen-SS benefited from the crimes in the sense that they created a community of perpetrators who were united by joint guilt and by the fear that they and their loved ones might be subject to a similar treatment if the Third Reich lost the war.

Waffen-SS crimes – No Different From The Wehrmacht?

In the autumn of 1944, a Swedish soldier told his country's defence attaché in Berlin about *Division Wiking*'s killing of female prisoners-of-war. He added though that 'the Waffen-SS was not alone in so doing – the *Wehrmacht* did similarly.'[61] The comprehensive research over the latest decades of the German army's numerous crimes committed in occupied Europe justifies the question whether, after all, the Waffen-SS was not *Soldaten wie andere auch* (soldiers like all others) when it came to the extent and the character of the crimes. In the mid-1990s, the exhibition *Vernichtungskrieg* (extermination war) came to the conclusion – may be for the sake of controversy – that so they were indeed. It was claimed that, from 1941 onwards, the *Wehrmacht's* mentality was the same as that of the 'Himmler troops'.[62]

---

58. Lieb (2007), p. 464ff. Apart from these incidents, there was also killings of prisoner following the death in Demyansk, on 2 June 1942, of the *Frikorps Danmark* commander Christian von Schalburgs. Christensen et al. (1998), p. 155ff.
59. Weingartner (1979), p. 54ff.
60. For the welding effect of sexual violence, see Regina Mühlhäuser, 'Between "Racial Awareness" and Fantasies of Potency. Nazi Sexual Politics in the Occupied Territories of the Soviet Union, 1942–1943' in Dagmar Herzog, *Brutality and Desire: War and Sexuality in Europe's Twentieth Century* (Palgrave Macmillan, 2009), p. 201.
61. Gyllenhaal and Westberg (2008), p. 290.
62. Hannes Heer and Klaus Nauman, "Einleitung" in *Hannes Heer and Klaus Naumann* (1995), p. 30.

Thanks to relatively new case studies on the Waffen-SS units produced since the 1990s and the increased curiosity concerning the crimes committed by the *Wehrmacht*, it is now possible to compare the two organisations. The complicity of atrocities against prisoners-of-war and civilians was no distinctive feature with the Waffen-SS alone. Such deeds were an integral part of all German military activity and occupation policy on the eastern front. There and in the Balkans, army divisions participated in several cases of mass murder, and by and large German generals obeyed Hitler's orders to kill captured commissars and they co-operated smoothly with the *Einsatzgruppen*.[63] Moreover, there were certain *Wehrmacht* formations – the paras among others – whose mentality was very close to that of the Waffen-SS, and in Greece as well as in Italy they committed extensive massacres.[64]

Conversely, among the Waffen-SS formations, there were considerable variations in their known perpetration of Nazi crimes. To a large extent, this can be explained by external factors. The divisions fighting in the Soviet Union in 1941, were deployed in areas with a large number of Jews, and the crimes committed by these troops frequently happened out of euphoria of a war almost won. In 1944, the situation was very different. Late-formed formations rarely clashed with potentially victimised groups, as these had already been murdered or deported. Moreover, the fear of punishment had changed.

Even with these reservations kept in mind, there is no doubt that the rate of crimes with Waffen-SS units was higher than that of the *Wehrmacht*. Of 600 known killings of civilians during the 1940 campaign in France *Division Totenkopf* counted 250 and, together with the *Leibstandarte*, it was responsible for the two largest massacres of British prisoners-of-war. One hundred divisions were part of the campaign. The aggregate number of victims during the fights in 1943–1945 in Western Europe and Italy are known in much greater detail than those of the eastern front and this is where the difference between the Waffen-SS and the *Wehrmacht* can be clearly distinguished. Although a number of army and paratroops committed terrible village massacres during the counter-insurgency operations in Italy, in 1943–1944, it is remarkable that 2,000 of 10,000 persons were the victims of one division, namely, *Reichsführer-SS*.[65]

The only big massacres in France, where women and children made up a significant proportion of the victims, were also perpetrated by the Waffen-SS. In Oradour *Das Reich* was responsible, in Maille probably *Götz von Berlichingen*. In April 1944, long before the Allied landings, the aforementioned massacre at Ascq was carried out. Again, it was an SS division that perpetrated the crime, namely, *Division Hitlerjugend*. In the days immediately after the landings in Normandy, the very same formation became notorious for its numerous killings of Allied prisoners-of-war.

Although the image of what happened at the eastern front is less clear, it strikes the eye that, right from the beginning of the campaign and frequently without being

---

63. Hürter (2007).
64. Müllers (2012). Gentile (2012).
65. Gentile (2012), p. 201.

ordered, SS soldiers were very officious killing suspicious civilians, Jews and prisoners-of-war.[66] However, it is difficult to draw an unambiguous picture of the incidents in this theatre of war. The *Wehrmacht* was often equally brutal in its counter-insurgency and dealings with Jews and prisoners.[67]

Still, while researching for this book, no sources indicating a somewhat lower degree of brutality in the Waffen-SS compared to the *Wehrmacht* appeared, whereas the opposite often was the case. In June 1943, for example, *Ausbildungsbataillon Ost* (training battalion east) was committed to a major counter-insurgency operation in the Zhytomyr area, during which it would co-operate with *Wehrmacht* units, Hungarian soldiers and the troops from the SD. In his post-action report the commanding officer, a *Sturmbannführer*, complained about the slackness and lack of commitment of the army soldiers. Referring to the 72 executions and burnings of villages undertaken en-route, he criticized that officers and men of the *Wehrmacht* 'had been dismissive of these necessary measures'. In December 1943, a similar clash occurred in the Leningrad sector. The local army commandant in Batetskiy forbade the *2. Lettische SS-Freiwilligen-Brigade* to shoot eight civilians, whom the brigade suspected of collaborating with the partisans. The brigade, which had already shot without permission seven other civilians, complained about this order. Thus, they managed to have the commandant removed from his post and, later, court-martialled.[68] In the spring of 1943, the military police investigated a number of violence and robbery cases in Ukraine and, again, it appeared that the SS assumed a super-representation in the statistics. In 72 cases where the perpetrating unit was identified, 53 were due to SS personnel but only 19 army soldiers.[69]

Several more incidents point to Waffen-SS soldiers as even greater perpetrators than those of the *Wehrmacht*. There were more than a few occurrences during the ultimate phase of the war, and there were many officers, NCOs and men who busily exploited their latitude of action to initiate or commit crimes instead of trying to prevent them. Moreover, the crimes' role in the collective identity is remarkable. The sources indicate pride in being harsh, despising and rejecting those who failed in case of murder actions.[70]

As can be seen from the above, the Nuremberg sentence that the Waffen-SS was a part of a criminal organisation certainly makes as much sense today as it did in 1946. As a tool in the Nazis' genocidal ethnic re-organisation of Europe, the Waffen-SS was willing and efficient. Not all the soldiers got the 'opportunity' to show their commitment in this respect, but many did, and almost all obeyed when ordered to commit atrocities. Moreover, many crimes were initiated from below, because the men had internalised the Nazi norms and ways of action. The SS soldiers, therefore, took part in the misdeeds actively and independently and in disproportionately large numbers.

---

66. Merkl (2010), p. 195.
67. This is the conclusion Christian Gerlach draws from his comparison of the SS', the police's and the Wehrmacht's counter-insurgency operations in Belarus 1942–1944. Gerlach (1999), p. 906.
68. Jürgen Kilian, *Wehrmacht und Besatzungsherrschaft im Russischen Nordwesten 1941–1944: Praxis und Alltag in der Militärverwaltungszone der Heeresgruppe Nord* (Schöningh, 2012), p. 581.
69. BAB, NS19/3717.
70. However, similar attitudes were seen outside the SS, for example, in the 101st police battalion examined by Christopher Browning. During interrogation after the war, several explained their dissent to participating in the unit's killing actions by having been 'weak.'

Part V

WAFFEN-SS AFTER 1945

Lost in the Post-war World?

With the demise of Nazi Germany, a historian faces difficulties tracing the approximately 600,000 SS soldiers who survived the war.[1] Apart from the general chaos arising from the collapse of the Third Reich, there are several reasons for that. During the war, the Waffen-SS provided the basic framework for the soldiers' lives, and it is, relatively speaking, easier to identify individual soldiers or groups of soldiers in this period. However, as the SS was disbanded this way of tracing SS-men ceased to exist. However, to some extent, the Allies kept tabs on the former Waffen-SS soldiers, whom they separated from other groups of prisoners, and it was not until their release from the prisoner-of-war camps, from the late 1940s onwards, that most tracks of them went cold. From then on, the Waffen-SS no longer appears as a collective phenomenon. Because of the transnational and multi-ethnical character of the Waffen-SS, upon their release the soldiers dispersed in various directions; many of them adopting fairly successfully to the new circumstances, but a certain number nevertheless clung to the norms and beliefs they had been socialised into during their service in the Waffen-SS.

The trendsetting SS veterans' association, the *Hilfsgemeinschaft auf Gegenseitigkeit der Angehörigen der ehemaligen Waffen-SS* (HIAG), was practically a continuation of the Waffen-SS. Nevertheless, HIAG never managed to organise more than a minor part of the veterans settling in Germany. The same goes for the relatively small Waffen-SS ex-soldiers' organisations outside Germany. Among the challenges was also the fact that quite a few had emigrated to the USA, Latin America, the Middle East, Australia and South Africa. In the Soviet Union and the Soviet dominated parts of Eastern Europe, until the collapse of the Iron Curtain in 1989, SS-veterans had to tread especially carefully.

A significant part of the veterans, though, were deeply marked by their experiences and the Waffen-SS mentality and carried an ideological SS-heritage with them into the post-war life – orally as well as in their deeds. Politically, they busied themselves on the extreme right wing. However, the Nazi underground resistance that some Germans had hoped for, and the Allies had feared, never materialised, and the SS-veterans never represented any serious threat to the new Europe rising from the rubble after 1945.

---

1 Georg Meyer, "Soldaten wie andere auch? Zur Einstellung ehemalige Angehörige der Waffen-SS in die Bundeswehr" in Harald Dickerhof (ed.), *Festgabe Heinz Hürten zum 60. Geburtstag* (P. Lang, 1988), pp. 545–94, here p. 550.

272   WAR, GENOCIDE AND CULTURAL MEMORY

Nonetheless, there is much to commend a continuation of the Waffen-SS history beyond May 1945. First, the soldiers' patterns of behaviour in captivity and as veterans allow us an insight into the internalisation of SS norms. Secondly, Waffen-SS veterans formed the probably most comprehensive, international network of post–Second World War ex-soldiers; and it is undoubtedly the only large, transnational, cohesive group of former collaborators and dedicated Nazis. Although only a small part of the former Waffen-SS members organised nationally and internationally, they were after all tens of thousands. Thirdly, it was not until after the end of war that the Nazis' crimes could be thoroughly investigated and prosecuted.

One more important point is that, although, in 1945, the SS ceased to exist, it still held a sway of fascination as well as disgust. It is of interest, therefore, to investigate and analyse how notions and myths about the Waffen-SS and the veterans as a group became important elements in the Europeans' interpretation and understanding of the Second World War – an undertaking which undoubtedly helped form the identity of individuals as well as of the various European nation states.

To a minority, the SS had a decidedly mesmerising effect, which was mirrored in an extensive amateurish historical interest. This fascination also made Waffen-SS militaria expensive collectors' items, and it has inspired re-enactment rallies where adults dress up as Waffen-SS soldiers and role-play wartime events. While SS veterans have remained outcasts in Western European countries, since the demise of Communism, there has been a remarkable change of attitude in the former Eastern Bloc. After the fall of the Berlin Wall, in countries like Estonia, Latvia and Ukraine the SS soldiers have changed from being pariahs to assuming a more or less heroic status in the bygone struggle against Communism. For this reason, too, it is most interesting – and sometimes very disquieting – to see how the SS' legacy has been cultivated, conveyed and used from 1945 till today.

Chapter Thirteen

SURRENDER AND IMPRISONMENT

It was far from all SS soldiers who were prepared to die for Hitler and Nazism. In March 1945, the western Allies crossed the Rhine, and the following month the Soviet offensive against Berlin was launched. No one doubted any longer that the downfall of the Third Reich was imminent. Thus, as a soldier of the Reich one might choose to go down with the regime or try to survive either by surrendering oneself to the Allies or by deserting.

During the last days of the war, the German SS men fought primarily in their own country and might hope to return to civilian life when the war was over. The foreign Waffen-SS soldiers' situation was different; many of them would be facing trial in their home countries. Nonetheless, many perceived prosecution at home as preferable compared to falling into the hands of the Red Army, for example by seeking refuge in the remaining embassies in Berlin, such as the Danish and Swedish.[1] These endeavours were not particularly successful, but many succeeded in avoiding capture in various other ways. From the eastern shores of the Baltic Sea, Baltic Waffen-SS soldiers got across to the Swedish coast or to Denmark and mixed with refugees. At the moment of surrender, other non-German SS men hurried into civvies pretending to be forced labourers, or they hid with friends, family, or girlfriends.

The extent to which the former SS soldiers managed to hide may be illustrated by the case of the 1st SS brigade. During post-war legal processes in West Germany, almost 1,000 former members of the unit were asked about their spell as prisoners-of-war, and it turned out that 10 per cent had completely avoided incarceration.[2] Considering their war record as continuous participants in genocide it comes as no surprise that former members of the 1st SS brigade would do whatever it took to evade captivity. Those who, like the 1st SS brigade, belonged among the very worst henchmen of the Holocaust, were of course especially tempted to try to assume new identities during their imprisonment or simply lie low vis-à-vis the victors. Through listening to radio, Allied broadcasts, or the Nazis' own propaganda, there was an awareness that the Allies had an ambitious agenda of bringing Nazi culprits to justice and that SS men were very much in the allied spotlight. Hence, some SS veterans attempted to enter post-war times with a false identity. All in all, about 100,000 Germans are estimated to have gone underground at the war's termination.[3]

---

1. Jacob Kronika, *Berlins Undergang* (H. Hagerup, 1945), pp. 143, 152f and 176ff. Wiking Jerk, *Ragnarok : en frivillig svensk Waffen-SS-soldat berattar om slutstriden i Europa 1945* (Nordland, 1996), p. 127ff. Gyllenhaal and Westberg (2008), p. 287.
2. Cüppers (2011), p. 314.
3. Heiner Wember *Umerziehung im Lager: Internierung und Bestrafung von Nationalsozialisten in der britischen Besatzungszone.* (Deutschlands, Klartext-Verl., 1991), p. 27.

Schleswig and Holstein are particularly well-researched areas. Together with the southern parts of Germany, these parts attracted lots of party apparatchiki as well as police and SS institutional cadres. Moreover, it was to this 'fortress North' that, in May 1945, Himmler arrived with his entourage. His aim was to secure for himself a prominent place in the new government of Grand Admiral Karl Dönitz – the new incumbent of the office of head-of-state. Although the *Reichsführer*'s castles in the air came to nothing as, on 6 May, Dönitz formed a government without his participation, the men who had followed him to northern Germany were assisted by the new government in changing identities.[4] When Himmler realised that he would not get a post in Dönitz's government he travelled south towards the Alps like so many other Nazis. Clad in an army NCO's uniform he went under the identity of Heinrich Hitzinger and, on 21 May, he was apprehended by British troops near Bremervörde a short distance south of the Elbe. Two days later, after his correct identity had been disclosed, he committed suicide by biting through a poisonous capsule he had hidden in the corner of his mouth.[5]

While a number of high-ranking SS officers took their own lives, the commanders of the Waffen-SS' field formations mostly surrendered collectively together with their subordinates. This happened particularly where units facing the western Allies were concerned. Conversely, upon the German capitulation, divisions like

Figure 13.1 Volunteers from Latvia in May 1945 (Frihedsmuseet)

---

4. "Festung Nord' and 'Alpenfestung': das Ende des NS-Sicherheitsapparates" in GerhardPaul and Klaus-Michael Mallmann, *Die Gestapo im Zweiten Weltkrieg: 'Heimatfront' und besetztes Europa* (Primus, 2000), p. 583ff. See also Longerich (2008), p. 754ff.
5. Longerich (2008), p. 756ff.

Leibstandarte, Das Reich, Totenkopf and *Wiking* fighting the Soviet army in Austria tried desperately to make their way into territory occupied by the western powers.[6] In other cases, where units found it difficult to avoid capture by the Red Army there was seldom an organised surrender; rather the men attempted as individuals and in small groups to move westwards in order to reach the lines of American and British troops, as happened in the cases of the SS units fighting along the Oder river in Germany.

The Early Days of Captivity

It is difficult to gauge how many Waffen-SS men actually ended up in prisoner-of-war camps. In Allied statistics and studies of German POWs, it is far from always possible to identify SS soldiers – or SS personnel in general.[7] This problem is aggravated by the fact that far from all SS men went into captivity with a formal identity as Waffen-SS service members or were detained in prisoner-of-war camps. SS personnel of the occupied nations staying in their homelands at the German surrender, generally were prosecuted by national judiciaries. Moreover, many SS prisoners' status soon changed to one of the war crime suspects.[8]

It was a herculean task for the Allies to find and separate the SS men among several million prisoners-of-war. Check of service records, other documents and uniform insignia were some of the methods employed for their identification.[9] The difficulty was increased by the fact that, following the surrender, like Himmler, many SS men were still at large and had changed their identities. In order to locate these and other possible war criminals as well as to assume control of the enormous masses on the German roads, a system of patrols, checkpoints and raids was organised. Alone during the first fortnight after the cease-fire, the British caught at the Danish border 2,500 persons not belonging to the *Wehrmacht* out of the 95,000 German troops that had so far crossed heading south. Undoubtedly, a considerable number of these were SS men of various types.[10]

After the German capitulation, a Waffen-SS soldier from Alto Adige (South Tyrol) walked all the way from north to south through Germany pretending to be a Polish worker. On 18 May, he passed a checkpoint and noted in his diary, 'many are standing in the sun arms above their heads; the blood type [tattoo] becomes their fate – I have been lucky with my pass.'[11] As this quote illustrates, the blood-type tattoos on the arms of

---

6. For the Leibstandarte, see Westemeier (2014), p. 367ff.
7. Neither in German majorworks such as Erich Maschke (ed.), *Zur Geschichte der deutschen Kriegsgefangenen des Zweiten Weltkrieges, 15 Bd.* (E. und W. Gieseking, 1962), nor in *Das Deutsche Reich und der Zweite Weltkrieg can* such statistical information be found.
8. Kurt W. Böhme, *Die deutschen Kriegsgefangenen in amerikanischer Hand. Beiheft 2* (Verlag Ernst und Werner Gieseking, 1973), p. 72ff.
9. See examples in Wember (1991), p. 38.
10. Stephan Linck, "'Festung Nord" und "Alpenfestung":das Ende des NS-Sicherheitsapparates' in Paul and Mallmann, *Die Gestapo im Zweiten Weltkrieg*, p. 592.
11. BAMA, N756/398a: Copy of diary by an anonymous soldier of the SS police division's reserve company.

SS personnel became important in the identification process.[12] And the hunt for former SS members was not limited to the roads. In the camps, too, the authorities sought persons who had changed their identities.[13] For that reason, many an SS man tried to get rid of his blood type tattoo and the really desperate tried by burning cigarettes, razor blades, acid, or silver nitrate.[14] Others were helped by medical doctors even in some cases in the camps, where the health staff assisted.[15] Thus, Gustav Lombard, a former regimental commanding officer of the SS cavalry brigade, persuaded the doctor of a Soviet prisoner-of-war camp to remove his tattoo allowing him to change identity to Major Gustav Müller.[16]

Merely a few years hence, SS men who had managed to stay put could start feeling a little more secure. In July 1947, the authorities in the American occupation zone decided that new policy initiatives aimed at apprehending members of organisations that had been declared criminal by the Nuremberg Military Tribunal should not be taken concerning personnel below the rank of *Scharführer* (colour sergeant/staff sergeant).[17]

In other cases, former SS soldiers benefitted from not being identified as such upon capture. In the immediate aftermath of the war, the Soviet authorities released more than one million prisoners, who were unfit for work. This happened from the camps close to the front as well as from hospitals and camps in the hinterland. In the spring of 1945, initial registering of prisoners had been undertaken in a somewhat haphazard way, which led to the release of many individuals who rightly belonged in prison because of crimes committed in the Soviet Union and others who possessed a knowledge of interest in the Soviet intelligence services.[18]

---

12. SANDFDOC, Box 221: Div. Intelligence summaries, No.152: 8.10.1944. NAKEW, WO208/3626, Report on the tattooing of blood group on SS personnel Kempton Park camp 28.10.1944. IfZG, OMGUS, 7/41-2/9-10, CI Monitor no. 7, 3.3.1945, anneks III: 'Tattooing of the SS'.
13. Andreas Hilger, *Deutsche Kriegsgefangene in der Sowjetunion, 1941–1956: Kriegsgefangenenpolitik, Lageralltag und Erinnerung* (Klartext, 2000), p. 260.
14. IfZG, OMGUS, 7/41-2/9-10, CI Monitor No. 16, 5.5.1945, item 5.
15. NAKEW, WO208/3627, Nazi terrorism in PW camps. 3.11.1944. Verton (2007), p. 212. Wember (1991), p. 53. In some late cases, the forcibly drafted Waffen-SS recruits dodged tattooing fearing post-war consequences. Hans von Vultejus, *Forpligtet: en dansk/tysk skæbne, som tysk soldat 1943–1945* (Forlaget Underskoven, 2011), Diary entry on 17 August 1944, p. 178.
16. Orientirovka of 22.4.1948 from GUPVI MVD, reprinted p. 313ff. in V.A. Zolotarev (ed.). *Velikaya Otechestvennaya: Nemetskie Voennoplennye v SSSR 1941–1955 gg. Russkii Arkhiv*, T. 24 (13–3). Terra, 2002.
17. Nonetheless, this a curfew might apply to this group and, like higher-ranking personnel they were bound to undergo de-Nazification. IfZG, OMGUS, 3/153-3/17, Circular letter from OMGUS to the military governments of the five areas under American occupation (Bavaria, Baden-Württemberg, Hessen, Bremen and the American sector in Berlin) concerning Arrest by German police of members of organisations found criminal by the international military tribunal, 9.7.1947.
18. RGVA, 1/23/14: *Repatriatsiya voennoplennykh*, p. 2. Christensen et al. (1998), p. 392. Hilger (2000), p. 317.

In the west, too, some Waffen-SS soldiers obtained a quick release from the prisoner-of-war camps. The first to go were the non-German SS men. In late 1945, the British started releasing all non-German prisoners or transferring them to their home countries. Former Waffen-SS soldiers from the areas which the Soviet Union had annexed in 1939–1940, were the luckiest. At the Yalta Conference, the western Allied had promised to repatriate all Soviet citizens after the war, but the Baltic and Polish territories were not included. Already before the German surrender, the Latvian generalissimo, Bangerskis advised Latvian SS soldiers to get behind the American and British lines, and on 23 May 1945, he wrote to Field Marshal Harold Alexander, whom he knew from the Latvian War of Independence 1919–1920. In the letter, Bangerskis asked the western Allies to recognise the Latvians as political refugees rather than prisoners-of-war from an SS formation.[19] Other Latvian dignitaries, who had held high office under German rule, joined in the choir and their endeavours were soon crowned with success.[20] At the end of July, the British separated the Latvian SS legionnaires in the Neuengamme prisoner-of-war camp from the other Waffen-SS prisoners and, after a brief interview to establish whether they had been drafted or were volunteers they were transferred to a camp for 'displaced persons'.[21] Thus, the majority of the Latvians had been whisked out of the prisoner-of-war system without anybody asking about their possible involvement in the Nazi crimes.[22]

Much the same happened to Estonian SS soldiers and members of the Ukrainian *Division Galizien,* albeit it took men from the latter unit a little longer to go through this process. In May 1945, the 11,000-strong division surrendered to the British in Austria and was transferred to a prisoner-of-war camp near Rimini, Italy. Concurring with the Yalta treaty, the British initiated forced repatriation of the soldiers to the Soviet Union. They managed to ship 3,000 along before they met opposition from an unexpected quarter. The Ukrainian men were predominantly RC and, in summer 1945, Ukrainian Archbishop Ivan Buchko persuaded Pope Pius XII to intervene.[23] Moreover, the British had great compassion for the Ukrainians, who behaved well-disciplined and had a sizeable diaspora coming to their rescue.[24] As in the case of the Balts, the fact that they belonged to an SS formation was played down. When, over the following years, these soldiers were admitted into Canada, Australia and the UK no in-depth scrutiny of their possible complicity in Nazi crimes was undertaken.[25]

---

19. SU, Hoover Institution Archives, Stanford University, 15. Waffen-SS Grenadier Division, box 7, President of the Latvian National Committee, Order no. 3, 29.4.1945. Schulz and Wegmann (2003), p. 55.
20. David Cesarani, *Justice Delayed: How Britain Became a Refuge for Nazi War Criminals* (Phoenix Press, 2001), p. 46ff.
21. Blosfelds (2008), p. 205. See also Wember (1991), p. 61, note 161.
22. Cesarani (2001), pp. 50 and 45ff.
23. Howard Margolian, *Unauthorized entry: The Truth about Nazi War Criminals in Canada, 1946–1956* (University of Toronto Press, 2000), p. 135.
24. See report from the Rimini camp: http://lib.galiciadivision.com/veryha-eng/d02.html, accessed on 22 November 2012.
25. Cesarani (2001), p. 102ff.

However, not all Waffen-SS soldiers from the territories taken by the Red Army were reluctant to go home.[26] Already in 1944, when the Germans withdrew from Yugoslavia, lots of *Division Handschar*'s locally recruited soldiers began trickling back to their loved ones. Quite a few – and in particular those who had changed sides timely – avoided prosecution in their native country.[27] Probably, the Romanian *Volksdeutsche* were the largest group coming home to a country then dominated by the Communists. Unlike most Germans in eastern and central Europe, these were not banished from their native soil. Thus, out of the 63,000 Romanian *Volksdeutsche* in the Waffen-SS a very large number returned to Transylvania after the war.[28]

While the Balts and the Western Ukrainians were released from the camps, other Soviet citizens were deported to the Soviet Union. Neither were Western European Waffen-SS soldiers freed; soon after the war had ended they were transferred for prosecution in their home countries.[29] The last to get out of the western allies' camps were SS soldiers of German decent. Their release began in earnest in the fall of 1947, when the British decided to let go Waffen-SS men and officers born in 1919 or later, and continued through 1948.[30] After that point, the remaining SS soldiers were all men charged with war crimes.

Ideological Soldiers in Captivity

After the war, many SS soldiers tried to construct a myth of their experiences in captivity as a martyrdom.[31] Allegedly, their incarceration was characterised by 'unspeakable visitations, lies, condemnation, unwarranted accusations, arbitrariness, physical violence and hatred'.[32] Several captive veterans claimed that the treatment they experienced was 'a crime at a par with the Holocaust'.[33] When considering the SS men's accounts of their experiences in captivity and internment, one should bear in mind that they had an obvious interest in changing black to white, denying their own crimes and blowing up the Allies' real or imagined injustices.[34]

---

26. One year after the war ended, a person of the Division Hitlerjugend accepted repatriation to Poland from captivity by the western Allies. Margolian (2000), p. 185ff.
27. Bernwald (2012), p. 324ff. Lappin (2004), p. 85. See also Franziska Zaugg (2014). Here we are informed that a considerable number of Muslim SS volunteers were prosecuted in Yugoslavia and Albania. See note 52.
28. Milata (2009), p. 296ff.
29. NAKEW, WO309/1424: 21. Army Group, letter of 30 July 1945: Disposal of non-German nationals.
30. Westemeier (2016), p. 194.
31. See the analysis of the graphic overview of captivity in the SS veterans' publications and in Karsten Wilke, *Die 'Hilfsgemeinschaft auf Gegenseitigkeit'* (HIAG) *1950–1990 – Veteranen der Waffen-SS in der Bundesrepublik* (Ferdinand Schöningh, 2011), p. 129ff.
32. *Twelve Years with Hitler* (Schiffer Military History, 1999), p. 239. Another example is Oluf Krabbe, *Danske Soldater i Kamp paa Østfronten 1941–1945*, Bogan, 1998.
33. Cüppers (2011), p. 331.
34. There are a number of examples – primarily newspaper scraps and other secondary material – compiled by the veterans themselves. See the package BAMA, N756/398a.

Undoubtedly, the Waffen-SS men were in a category of their own with a reputation for being incurable Nazis, and for this reason, they risked harsh treatment especially immediately after the war.[35] In the summer of 1945, there was also a shortage of shelter, clothes, food, water, hygiene and other basic necessities in several western prisoner-of-war camps.[36] In March 1946, a Danish NCO wrote a letter. He described the conditions in his camp on the Moselle.

> We live in tents, or something of that designation, constructed by a wire body with roofing felt wound around, in the middle there is a tinplate stove for wich we get fuel twice a week – burning time two hours. Every morning 250 grams of bread, for lunch a watery vegetable soup, for supper a watery milk soup. Last time we got any fat was for Christmas, when we had one spoonful per person. Every man has two blankets and a handful of straw. Temperatures have reached 20½ degrees (C) below zero.[37]

Conditions were no better in the Soviet Union. Out of the estimated 3 million German prisoners interned there during the war a third of them died before it ended, but then survival chances improved considerably.[38] Out of 136 Norwegian SS soldiers, 42 died while the mortality figure among the 175 captured Danish soldiers was 50.[39] In both categories the demises mostly happened during the war when the food was extremely scarce – not only for the prisoners but also for the Soviet civilians as well.[40] Another important reason for the high number of fatalities during the war was that the prisoners were taken during, or in the wake of, the big encirclement battles arrived in a very poor condition and in numbers that entailed overcrowding of the camps. From camp No 62 near Kyiv, where many SS prisoners were herded together after the war, it was reported that those prisoners coming from the Cherkassy Pocket – where, for example, *Divisions Wiking* had been enclosed – were physically weak, filthy, infested with lice and ill.[41]

However, neither in the east nor in the west did the Waffen-SS have any excess mortality compared to other German armed forces. Seen in relation to their number of prisoners the Waffen-SS and the *Wehrmacht* had almost identical mortality rates; at nine and eight per cent, respectively.[42] Thus, we may conclude that the discrimination against SS prisoners upon arrival was not as bad as to cause higher mortality.

---

35. Hans Werner Neulen, *Eurofaschismus und der Zweite Weltkrieg: Europas verratene Söhne* (Universitas, 1980), p. 159. See also Weingartner (1979).

36. Lowe (2012), p. 116.

37. RK, Letter of 19 March 1946 to the Foreign Ministry, j.nr. 6.U.41/a/298. See also the description of the daily food ration in a camp in Austria in BAMA, N756/398a, typewritten pages by anonymous member of Resk-SS-Pol.Div, 26 May 1946.

38. Andreas Hilger, *Deutsche Kriegsgefangene in der Sowjetunion. Kriegsgefangenenpolitik, Lageralltag und Errinnerung*, (Klartext,2000).

39. Ringheim (2003), p. 137ff. Christensen et al. (1998), p. 388ff.

40. Lowe (2012), p. 117.

41. RGVA, 1/15/102: *Doklad o deyatel'nosti lagerya no. 62 1943–1950*, p. 15. It appears from the same material that as of 1 January 1950, there were among the ca. 800 prisoners 244 Dutch, 105 Yugoslavs, 45 Danes, 43 French, 11 Fins and 10 Norwegians, of whom the majority were probably former Waffen-SS soldiers.

42. Overmans (2000), p. 290.

Normally, SS soldiers taken prisoners in their own country or transferred thereto were not granted prisoner-of-war status. They were instead considered as detainees accused of treason, and for that reason, they risked poor conditions as well as rough treatment. A social-medicinal survey of former Norwegian soldiers showed that many had been subjected to mock executions during their stint in captivity.[43] The treatment appears to have been equally harsh elsewhere in the former occupied countries.[44] Alone in the Dutch internment camp Harskamp, 11 former SS soldiers died of unnatural causes, mostly by 'being shot trying to escape'.[45]

In the prisoner-of-war camps as well as in those of internment, there seems to have been a high degree of cohesion among the former Waffen-SS men. This could facilitate an almost complete takeover of life inside the fence.

In Great Britain where it was desired to divide the prisoners along political lines, there were some camps where the 'blacks', that is, the Nazi sympathisers, upheld regular dictatorships.[46] In January 1945, there were a number of altercations in the British prisoner-of-war camp Beckton Marshes, where strong prisoners – many with an affiliation with the Waffen-SS – bullied the others. In one case an anti-Nazi prisoner was forced to salute by a *heil* in front of an SS rune made from pebbles and spread out on the ground. A former *Unterscharführer* was knocked unconscious because he was regarded as a traitor. When he was brought before the doctor – an erstwhile troop physician with *Division Hitlerjugend* – the latter expressed the attitude that the beating was justified. In lieu of treating him, he ordered him to keep his mouth shut. Such incidents were allowed to happen without the British interfering. The trendsetting prisoners had organised camp life 'along Nazi totalitarian lines' including Nazi tutorials, Sunday meetings and a 'camp Gestapo' with a *Rollkommando* (in this context: flying bully squads) at its disposal for beating some 'order' into stray individuals. The terror regime was so violent that a British report stated that the declared anti-Nazis did not fare better than the inmates in a German concentration camp.[47]

---

43. Inger Cecilie Stridsklev, "Norske frontkjempere 1941–1945 50 aar senere" in *Tidsskrift for Den norske lægeforening*, nr. 11, 1995, pp. 1379–1384. For some more examples of 'creative investigation' see the chapter 'Tvilsomme etterforskningsmetoder?' in Johannes Andenas, *Det vanskelige oppgjoret: rettsoppgjoret etter okkupasjonen* (Tanum-Norli, 1980), p. 171ff.

44. Søren Billeschou Christiansen and Rasmus Hyllested, *Paa den forkerte side: de danske landssvigere efter befrielsen* (Aarhus Universitetsforlag, 2011). Kristensen (2011). István Deák, Jan Tomasz Gross and Tony Judt, *The Politics of Retribution in Europe: World War II and Its Aftermath* (Princeton University Press, 2000).

45. Evertjan van Roekel Meinsma, *Nederlanders in de Waffen-SS* (Rijksuniversiteit Groningen, 2000), s.66. See also http://www.waffenss.nl/wssna.php.

46. NAKEW, FO939/13, Screening rapport 6.1.1948. See also material on Cultybraggan Camp near Comrie in Perthshire, UK, to be found in NAKEW, WO208/4633.

47. NAKEW, WO208/3628, Report on incidents at 183 PW base camp Beckton between 5 and 15 January 1945. 19 January 1945. For a description of life in American camp Ruston in Louisiana, see the report reprinted in Müllers (2012), p. 159ff.

Things did not necessarily change with Germany's surrender. From Neuengamme – transformed into the British Civil Internment Camp No 6 – it was heard that a 'well-organised SS regime' was extant in the camp. And there were more camps where the inmates ran the intramural business.[48] In June 1945, an SS officer sentenced an NCO to death and had him executed because he did not salute by *Heil Hitler*. Later, the officer was sentenced by a West German court to four years' imprisonment.[49]

As the examples above documents, for a considerable group, the camp conditions and the prisoner-of-war identity fostered a sense of victimhood while Nazi values were upheld. This was, of course, not conducive to fostering change and consciousness of belonging to a nation of perpetrators.[50] The increasing tensions between east and west and rumours of an imminent war between them also contributed to the notion that the western Allies would soon be needing the Waffen-SS.[51] The self-consciousness and the perception of being special were boosted by the fact that, generally, the Waffen-SS men were released later than *Wehrmacht* soldiers and in many cases kept isolated from other prisoners. In some camps SS personnel thus developed into a numerically dominating group.[52] The consequence was, presumably, that it was made even more unlikely that a change in world view would materialise.[53] The SS men did not only perceive themselves unjustly penalised but they also remained amongst people completely sharing their views. A psychiatrist even claimed that traitors, who had not been Nazis before their sentence, were influenced during their prison term by hardcore prisoners convinced of the Nazi gospel.[54] In September 1946, a Danish Waffen-SS soldier, serving his sentence in Camp Faarhus, tellingly wrote 'they locked us up to de-Nazify us, but the longer they keep us, the stronger our faith'.[55]

---

48. Wember (1991), pp. 53 and 70ff. See also IfZG, POLAD, 752/31, Letter from the American consulate general in Hamburg to the American ambassador of 10 July 1946. Here was conveyed a tale by the Communist *Hamburger Volkszeitung* that in camp there was extensive use of Nazi titles and Heil Hitler salute as well as better nourishment than in Hamburg's working class quarters. Hartmann Lauterbacher, *Erlebt und mitgestaltet: Kronzeuge einer Epoche 1923–1945 : zu neuen Ufern nach Kriegsende* (K.W. Schütz, 1984), p. 337.
49. Verfahren Lfd.Nr. 342, URL http://www1.jur.uva.nl/junsv/brd/Dienstdeufr.htm. See also Vultejus (2011), p. 284. Such cases are known from outside the SS, too. Mid-May 1945, a *Wehrmacht* court martial was convened in a Canadian prisoner-of-war camp in the Netherlands in order to sentence seamen for having deserted and joined the Dutch resistance movement. The two were sentenced to death and executed by means of rifles made available by the Canadian guard personnel. Knippschild in Haase and Paul (1995), p. 137.
50. Ibid., p. 57.
51. If the former HJ leader and Gauleiter of Südhannover-Braunschweig Hartmann Lauterbacher's memoirs are to be trusted, as late as spring 1947, both army General Guderian and Waffen-SS Generalen Steiner believed that they might soon again preside over re-established German military forces and that '*nicht [...] alleszu Ende sei mit dem nationalsozialistischen deutschen Reich.*' Lauterbacher (1984), p. 342.
52. IfZG, OMGUS, 15/123-3/16, Statistical survey of the number of interned persons in Greater Hesse, Baden-Württemberg and Bavaria, 1.2.1947.
53. Westemeier (2016), p. 200
54. Gudmund Magnussen, *Report on the Eight Congress of Scandinavian Psychiatrists in Copenhagen, Denmark, 1946* (Munksgaard, 1947), p. 567.
55. Kristensen (2011), p. 163.

Chapter Fourteen

PROSECUTION AND FLIGHT

In March 1945, an American interrogation officer asked *Unterscharführer* Kurt Kretschmer of *Division Das Reich* about his division's massacres and other atrocities in Southern France. He replied, 'I do not know what happened, I was not there.'[1] The scope of the Nazi crimes made the investigation and prosecution gigantic tasks. In many cases 'a perfect crime' was at hand. Apart from the perpetrators, there were hardly any surviving witnesses. But even if evidence was extant it was uncertain that this would fall into the hands of the prosecutors and the judges. In the early processes, the war and the chaos of the times were still so close that the prosecution lacked a proper survey and the knowledge that later historical research based on archival material has been able to provide. Under these conditions, the perpetrators had an opportunity of lying their way out of their complicity in a way that would not be possible today.[2]

Apart from being faced with an enormous burden of investigation, the Allies were hampered by big politics and the economic and military interests. In many cases, political-pragmatic considerations took precedence over the judicial processes. Therefore, the prosecution of the Nazi henchmen was imperfect in more than one way. First, because some sentences were passed on the basis of limited investigation and documentation. Secondly, because of limited resources or political consideration, many perpetrators were either not prosecuted at all, had very mild sentences or were granted amnesties.[3]

The Sentence at Nuremberg

In November 1945, in the South-German city of Nuremberg, the Allies started the legal reckoning with the Nazi top tier. Over the following year, not only 22 surviving top Nazis but also the entire administrative and political system constructed by the Nazis, were being prosecuted. The tribunal had the authority to sentence whole institutions and

---

1. Interrogation of Kurt Kretschmer on 30 March 1945, reprinted in Müllers (2012), p. 142.
2. Leon Goldensohn and Robert Gellately, *The Nuremberg Interviews* (Vintage Books, 2005), pp. 268 and 272. A good example is Bach-Zelewski's testimony before the Nuremberg court. On the one hand, he told candidly about the atrocities during counter-insurgency operations and the war of extermination in the occupied territories in the east. On the other, he described himself as innocent and even insubordinate having tried to save the Jews wherever possible.
3. See, inter alia, Hilary Camille Earl, *The Nuremberg SS-Einsatzgruppen Trial, 1945–1958: Atrocity, Law, and History* (Cambridge University Press, 2009), p. 9.

284 WAR, GENOCIDE AND CULTURAL MEMORY

organisations as criminals. The reason for this was to ease later prosecution of individual persons; hence the membership of such bodies would in itself become a criminal act.[4] From 1 September to 1 October 1946, the sentences were passed: 12 death sentences, seven imprisonments and three acquittals, the NSDAP, the Gestapo, the SD and the SS were declared criminal organisations.[5]

Along with other SS organisations, the Waffen-SS was dealt with in this sentence. In their testimonies, General Hausser and others tried to convince the court that the Waffen-SS was the fourth service of the *Wehrmacht*, completely separate from the SS. However, to no avail.[6] Apart from having been a tool in the Nazis' foreign policy, it was also mentioned that the Waffen-SS had provided personnel for the *Einsatzgruppen*, and bore responsibility for 'numerous massacres and atrocities in occupied territories such as the massacres of Oradour and Lidice'. Additionally, the judges found that the Waffen-SS had been directly involved in shooting prisoners-of-war, and it was an extra burden on the Waffen-SS that the concentration camp guards had made up a proportion of its personnel.[7]

After the end of the international trials in Nuremberg, the American occupying authorities in Germany launched another 12 court procedures – also in Nuremberg. These targeted various parts of the power apparatus of the Third Reich, against individual perpetrators and the weapons industry. During the trials, 185 were prosecuted.[8] A number of SS men, many of whom had served with the Waffen-SS, were in the dock in the subsequent trials. These court cases comprised one against the notorious *SS-Einsatzgruppen*, one concerning the SS' *Rasse- und Siedlungshauptamt*, and one dealing with the administration of the concentration camps. In several cases, the result was death sentences.[9] Among the convicted was Gottlob Berger. In 1949, in the case named the Wilhelmstraße Process conducted against a number of German top civil servants he was sentenced to 25 years' imprisonment.[10] In the light of the enormity of the Nazi crimes, the big international Nuremberg process, as well as the subsequent American ones, were but drops in the ocean. However, this did not mean that all guilty parties at lower levels were off the hook, and the Nuremberg processes were not the only ones, in which the culprits of the SS and the Waffen-SS were accused, although most perpetrators never faced justice in a courtroom.

---

4. See, inter alia, Hilary Camille Earl, *The Nuremberg SS-Einsatzgruppen Trial, 1945–1958: Atrocity, Law, and History* (Cambridge University Press, 2009), p. 9.
5. Judgement, 30 September-1 October 1946 from Trial of the Major War Criminals Before the International Military Tribunal, Nuremberg, 1946, vol.1, p. 307.
6. See quotations by Hausser and others. From the witness interviews in Nuremberg in Goldsworthy (2007), pp. 29ff., 99, 128ff., 131 and 151ff.
7. Trial of the Major War Criminals Before the International Military Tribunal, Nuremberg, 1946, Vol. 22, p. 514.
8. Earl (2009), p. 2.
9. Ibid., pp. 3 and 11.
10. Rempel in Smelser and Syring (2003), p. 56.

The Soviet Investigation and Conviction

Being one of the central organisations perpetrating the Nazi acts of violence, the SS became the focus of Soviet attention at an early stage. Already during the war, the reckoning started with those who had participated in the Nazi crimes in the Soviet Union. As early as the first war year, Soviet military tribunals executed suspected war criminals, but it was particularly after the Allied Moscow declaration of October 1943 stating that war criminals should be punished in the country for their misdeeds, that public cases were conducted against German war criminals.[11]

In December 1943, the prosecutor in the east Ukrainian city Kharkiv stressed that the divisions *Leibstandarte* and *Totenkopf* were the formations that had made themselves particularly guilty of extensive crimes in the city.[12] Shortly afterwards, in January 1944, an order was issued by the security service NKVD to its sub-divisions to speed up the search for war criminals in the prisoner-of-war camps.[13] In August the same year, camps were established specifically for war criminals and active fascists and with a particularly harsh regime. Members of the SS, the *Sonderkommandos*, the *Geheime Feldpolizei*, the *Feldgendarmerie* and the Gestapo as well as a number of other groups were selected as inhabitants of these.[14]

Finding proof supporting the suspicions was difficult, and the Soviet investigation was hampered by a number of issues.[15] Among other things, in the investigation endeavours there were rarely made any distinctions among the various parts of the German occupation agencies. Frequently, Waffen-SS, the *Sonderkommandos*, and the Gestapo were mentioned as almost synonymous quantities.[16] It was not uncommon that the material was so faulty that it referred to non-existent SS units.[17]

The Soviet authorities kept tabs on individuals as well as units accused of war crimes, and in some cases, Waffen-SS men were among them. In September 1946, the prisoner-of-war camps were told to be on the look-out for members of the *Totenkopf*, because its personnel had 'been especially active committing atrocities' with remarkable cruelty. In April 1948, this formation was again pinpointed together with other German units as collectively responsible for war crimes.[18] Apart from the *Totenkopf*, from which 137

---

11. On the early sentences see Andrea Hilger, Ute Schmidt, and Gunther Wagenlehner, *Sowjetische Militärtribunale, Vol.1* (Bohlau, 2001), p. 1ff. The Moscow declaration is reprinted in BeateRuhm von Oppen, *Documents on Germany under Occupation, 1945–1954* (Oxford University Press, 1955), p. 1.

12. Ignatik Fedorovich Kladov, *The People's Verdict; a Full Report of the Proceedings at the Krasnodar and Kharkov German Atrocity Trials* (Hutchinson & Co. Ltd., 1944), p. 48.

13. *Rasporyazhenie* of 11 January 1944 from UPVI NKVD, reprinted p. 289f. in Zolotarev (2002).

14. *Rasporyazhenie* of 30 August 1944 from UPVI NKVD, reprinted p. 295f. in Zolotarev (2002).

15. Poulsen (2004).

16. GARF, 7021/16/13, L.1-2: Interrogation protocol Wilhelm Freusch, 4.7.1943; GARF, 7021/16/13, L.6-8: Interrogation protocol Günter Azobeck, 4.7.1943.

17. GARF, 7021/148/38, LL.6-7: Interrogation protocol, 15.4.1943.

18. Hilger (2000), p. 264.

prisoners-of-war had been identified, other SS units were mentioned, too. *Florian Geyer* with 128 prisoners and the *Leibstandarte* with 28.[19]

In 1949, the Soviet Union launched a process aiming at having all the remaining prisoners-of-war convicted as war criminals.[20] Among these a very high proportion were Waffen-SS. In September 1949, the minister for the interior, Boris Kruglov, sent the Soviet leadership a list of 37,000 prisoners against whom, allegedly, there existed incriminating evidence. Of these 13,000 were SS men.[21] A few months later, it became obvious that the regime intended to convict all remaining Waffen-SS members as war criminals whether or not there was 'sufficient evidence sustaining accusations of actual criminal activity'.[22] Around the turn of the year 1949–1950, 19,000 prisoners were convicted – a large number of them being Waffen-SS.

The former Waffen-SS soldiers, who had most reason to fear Soviet captivity, were those of Soviet citizenship. It is, however, difficult to tell how many of the 320,000 collaborators apprehended and convicted in the Soviet Union, who had actually served with the Waffen-SS.[23] In May 1945, 5,000 Estonian SS soldiers surrendered to the Red Army in western Czechoslovakia. Their fate in captivity is the best-researched. While 40 of them – the officers presumably – faced a tribunal shortly after capture, the rest were sent to filtration camps. In these camps, Soviet security forces screened all citizens who, for whatever reason, had been present on German territory during the war. From there the way led to either NKVD's construction battalions, to Gulag's labour camps or into exile in Siberia. While in the late 1940s, the youngest were released, the bulk was not pardoned until, in 1955, special amnesties were granted to German collaborators. A minor group remained incarcerated until the 1960s and 70s.[24] In the camps, fatalities were rampant, especially during the war and the early post-war years. Although it seems that very few Soviet citizens have been executed only for having served with the German forces, many perished. According to statistics of 1949 on Balts categorised as prisoners-of-war – typically due to their service with the SS – almost 1,300 out of 6,400 Estonians and ca. 500 of 3,450 Latvians died in Soviet captivity.[25]

19. *Orientirovka*, of 22 April 1948 from GUPVI MVD, reprinted p. 313ff. in Zolotarev (2002).
20. Hilger et al. (2001), p. 14.
21. Additionally, there were 10,000 persons with an affiliation with tainted *Wehrmacht* units, 4,500 members of SA, 4,000 officers and soldiers from 'penal units' and 1,700 persons with a background in intelligence agencies as well as 1,300 who had served in prisoner-of-war or concentration camps. Hilger (2000), p. 270.
22. Friedrich-Christian Schroeder, 'Das Sowjetrecht als Grundlage der Prozesse gegen deutsche Kriegsgefangene' in Hilger et al.(2001), p. 78.
23. Martin Dean, 'Where Did All the Collaborators Go?' in *Slavic Review*, Vol. 64, No. 4, 2005, pp. 791–798, here p. 791.
24. Hiio and Kaasik in Hiio (2006), p. 967. For an account in greater detail illustrating the huge disparity of fate of Estonian soldiers in the Soviet Union see Kaasik in Hiio et al. (2009), pp. 345–58.
25. Hiio et al. (2009), p. 352.

The Tribunals of the Western Allies

The Americans, the British and the French conducted a large number of smaller court cases in their occupation zones and, in many of these, Waffen-SS personnel were in the dock. In the summer of 1946, the Malmédy case, which was the most comprehensive of these, was conducted in the former SS barracks near concentration camp Dachau. Seventy-three former Waffen-SS members of all ranks were being prosecuted including General Sepp Dietrich, commander of the 6th armoured army, the commanding officer of the *Leibstandarte*'s 1st SS armoured regiment, Jochen Peiper, and private soldiers of that regiment who had actually perpetrated the crime. The indictment concerned responsibility for and execution of the massacre at Malmédy, where 82 captured American soldiers had been murdered.

The court case attracted huge attention from the media. There was no doubt that, prior to the Battle of the Bulge, Peiper and his deputy commander, Poetschke, had declared that prisoners-of-war would hamper the advance and were to be shot. The evidence was overwhelming, and 40 victims bore traces of having been shot through the head. Nor could a number of cases of Belgian women, children and elderly being shot at close quarters be explained away.[26] The sentences were severe: While 43 were sentenced to death, 22 to lifelong imprisonment, all the remaining accused got shorter terms in jail. While Peiper was among those sentenced to death, Dietrich got a life sentence.[27]

In 1940 as well as in 1944, Waffen-SS soldiers had murdered British servicemen. Thus, Britain, too, ran court cases against former SS men. The most spectacular case was the one against Kurt Meyer, former commander of *Division Hitlerjugend* and one of the main characters responsible for the formation's murder of British and Canadian prisoners-of-war in Normandy in the summer of 1944. Almost since the time of perpetration, this misdeed had been known to British authorities. Thus, in July 1944, SHAEF (Supreme Headquarters Allied Expeditionary Forces) organised an investigating commission which, thanks to local witnesses and autopsy of the bodies of the killed prisoners-of-war, was able to conclude that, in a number of incidents after the Normandy landings, *Division Hitlerjugend* had murdered a large number of Allied captured personnel. Over the summer of 1945, British authorities identified no less than 99 members of the relevant parts of the division. These were interrogated and, on 31 October, Meyer was formally accused of having ordered that no prisoners be taken, of, in a number of cases, having ordered prisoners to be shot, and of, in five cases, having been directly involved in killings of prisoners-of-war.[28] In December, Meyer faced a British military tribunal and, after a two weeks' trial, he was found guilty and sentenced to death.[29]

---

26. Westemeier (2014), pp. 330, 337–45 and 383–403.
27. Ibid, p. 397.
28. The above was based on Margolian (2000), pp. 125–56.
29. Ibid., p. 167ff.

Another wanted man was *Standartenführer* Wilhelm Mohnke, one of the main suspects of *Division Hitlerjugend*'s killings. In spite of several requests for extradition, the British never succeeded in having him extradited from Soviet custody.[30] In 1955, Mohnke quietly arrived in Western Germany and in the 1970s the British again tried to have him tried – though now by German authorities. However, this foundered because the German prosecution believed that 'there was not sufficient evidence'. After his release from Soviet custody, Mohnke ran a successful lorry business outside Hamburg. In 2001, he died 90 years old.[31] Nonetheless, one more British trial was conducted of *Hitlerjugend* personnel, namely, the commanding officer of the 26th *SS-Panzer-Grenadier* regiment's 2nd battalion, Bernhard Siebken, and three of his subordinates for having killed three prisoners-of-war outside their battalion HQ.[32] Siebken and his adjutant, Dietrich Schnabel, were found guilty and sentenced to death. On 20 January 1949, they were both hanged in the prison in Hameln.[33]

A week later, another Waffen-SS officer, Fritz Knöchlein, followed them to the gallows. He was the main felon of the Le Paradis massacre, where, in May 1940, *Division Totenkopf* had murdered 100 British prisoners. After the war ended, Knöchlein had successfully hidden, and it was not until the end of 1946 that his true identity was revealed.[34] In the autumn of 1948, a British court in Altona sentenced him to death for having led the massacre, and he was duly executed a few months later.[35] Knöchlein had, in vain, tried to have the sentence repealed on account of having allegedly been maltreated during interrogation.[36]

Maybe, his self-defence was inspired by the development in the USA. There, the Malmédy massacre was keenly discussed having been raised by, the later much renowned, Senator Joseph McCarthy. Since one of the leading interrogators was of Jewish faith, the defence for Peiper and others, Burton Ellis, managed to persuade McCarthy that torture had been applied and that the interrogations, therefore, were merely an example of Jewish desire for revenge over innocent men.[37] Moreover, McCarthy and many others argued that, in the light of the emerging Cold War, it would be unwise to execute an unnecessary number of Germans, thus endangering the re-armament of Germany. This led, among other things, to a hearing in the US Senate, and the sentences passed in 1946 were alleviated, little by little. None were executed and, as the last, in 1956, Peiper was released. Dietrich had been released the previous year.[38]

---

30. NAKEW, WO311/689, Interim Report Haut du Bosq, 6 August 1947. See also ibid., p. 176ff.
31. Margolian (2000), p. 184ff.
32. Ibid., p. 179.
33. Pontolillo (2009), pp. 332 and 335.
34. Pontolillo (2009), p. 74. Merkl (2010), p. 432.
35. NAKEW, WO309/734, 200 War Crimes trial Centre, Hamburg, British Army of the Rhine, Paradis War Crimes Trial, 25 August 1948.
36. See the material on the matter in NAKEW, WO208/4685.
37. Westemeier (2014), pp. 398 and 448ff.
38. Ibid., pp. 500 and 508ff.

Meyer, too, who had been sentenced by the British, was luckier than his two subordinates. While they had been found directly guilty of murder, Meyer's responsibility was indirect and, already in 1946, his death sentence was commuted to lifelong imprisonment.[39] In September 1954, he was released from the prison in Werl, north-western Germany. The Waffen-SS organisation HIAG arranged a hero's welcome for the released war criminal. A torchlight procession and welcoming addresses were supplemented by a coming home present: a sponsored car from a manufacturer in Düsseldorf – one of HIAG's strongholds.[40] A few years hence, Meyer himself was to lead the HIAG.

Another Waffen-SS master criminal escaping alive from British judicial scrutiny was General Max Simon. In 1947, a British military tribunal in Italy had sentenced Simon to death on the grounds that, as commander of *Division Reichsführer-SS*, in the late summer and autumn of 1944, he had ordered a number of massacres of Italian civilians.[41] The most notorious of these happened in the town Sant'Anna di Stazzema where 560 individuals were killed.[42] In January 1948, nonetheless Simon was reprieved and the sentence commuted to life in prison.[43] On 30 November 1954, he walked out of the war criminals' prison in Werl.[44]

Reckoning in the Occupied and Neutral Countries

Around Europe, the former Waffen-SS soldiers were dealt with based on each country's specific war time experiences and other national peculiarities, as the examples below will demonstrate.

In France, there was a great many prosecutions of German war criminals and in many of these, the Waffen-SS appeared centre stage.[45] The centre of attention was on *Division Das Reich*'s massacre in Oradour sur Glane. Shortly after this crime, it became known in France and the world beyond, but it was not until nine years hence that, in January–February 1953, a law court in Bordeaux indicted and launched a process against the perpetrators. This process was characterised by two facts. First, it had not been possible to bring into the dock anyone of officer rank. Secondly, 14 out of 21 accused were French citizens of Alsace, most of them having been drafted into the Waffen-SS against their will. These elements entailed national controversy and anger in Alsace about the – rather mild – sentences passed on these men. Shortly after these sentences were passed, therefore, the French parliament had to read a bill granting amnesty. The law was adopted and, by 1958, all the accused – even those of German origin – had been released.[46]

---

39. Margolian (2000), p. 168ff.
40. Ibid., p. 183.
41. Merkl (2010), p. 415.
42. Ibid., p. 403ff.
43. Ibid., p. 420. See the considerations on a possible reprieve Simon in NAKEW, WO311/605, in particular Lieutenant General Max Simon Sentence, 30.12.1947 and S. of S, 8.1.1948.l.
44. Ibid., p. 454.
45. Ibid., p. 739, footnote 1.
46. Farmer (1999), p. 169. The case is thoroughly described in ibid., pp. 135–70.

In smaller countries that had been occupied by Germany, the reckoning with the Waffen-SS was mostly focused on local collaborators. Like in the Soviet Union, the general accusation against the SS veterans was that they had committed national treason by joining the armed forces of a hostile country. Conversely, little or no investigation was made into the possible complicity in crimes committed beyond the national borders. Initially, Belgium introduced the death penalty for joining the German forces but, later, the scope of punishment for membership of the Waffen-SS was commuted to15–20 years' imprisonment. For those who had served merely with the Flemish and Wallonian legions it was much less, five years' imprisonment at the maximum.[47] Léon Degrelle, commander of the Wallonian legion, was among those foreseen to be executed. In early May 1945, he was in Oslo where he managed to get on a plane to Spain. In 1945, Degrelle was sentenced to death in absentia by a Belgian court, but he lived on in Spain unharmed until his death in 1994.[48]

In Denmark, the judicial reckoning was characterised by the conundrum that the wartime national government had approved of Danish officers and NCOs stepping outside number with the Danish Defence Forces to join the German war effort.[49] Shortly after the liberation, however, the Danish parliament adopted a criminal surcharge that made service with German armed forces punishable. Nonetheless, in July 1945, the Copenhagen magistrate's court acquitted three former members of the *Frikorps Danmark* for the reason that they might have perceived the government's policy as an encouragement to join. The sentence raised huge controversy in the press, and the prosecution immediately appealed to the higher court. One of the accused was tried by the supreme court and was sentenced to two years' imprisonment. This created a precedent and was subsequently used as a legal rule of thumb in the roughly 3,300 cases of service with the German colours.[50]

In the Netherlands, 6,800 were convicted for having fought for Germany, the majority of whom had been with the Waffen-SS. Initially, the typical sentence was 15 years' imprisonment but, as time went by, eight years became the norm. Due to the subsequent introduction of amnesty, only a few served that long sentences.[51] Dutch officers, who had joined German service, as well as many informers and the top NSB people were sentenced to death. However, far from all were actually executed. Out of 138 death sentences, 36 were executed. Moreover, other punishment methods were applied such as loss of citizenship and confiscation of private means.[52] In 1965, though,

---

47. Luc Huyse, 'The Criminal Justice System as a Political Actor in Regime Transitions: The Case of Belgium, 1944-50' in István Deák, Jan Tomasz Gross and Tony Judt, *The Politics of Retribution in Europe: World War II and Its Aftermath* (Princeton University Press, 2000), pp. 157–72, here p. 166.

48. Anne Kristin Furuseth, *Norske nazister paa flukt: jakten paaet nytt hjemland i Argentina*, (Unpublished manuscript, 2013), p. 48ff.

49. Christensen et al. (1998), pp. 48 and 397.

50. Christensen et al. (1998), p. 397ff.

51. Meinsma (2000), p. 67.1

52. Mason (1952), p. 64ff.

a rule was introduced according to which the 60,000 people who had forfeited their citizenship due to treason might redeem it, and former Waffen-SS soldiers were sought re-integrated into society.[53]

Of ca. 200 Swedish volunteers, the surviving 170 were interrogated by security police upon their return. They were prosecuted only to the extent that they had dodged Swedish military service, spied against Sweden or left the country illegally. In all other cases, the judiciary left them in peace, and information about German war crimes, volunteered during the interview, was not followed up.[54] Nor were the many Baltic refugees, who arrived in Sweden during the last war years, scrutinised about their past. Among these were quite a few former Waffen-SS soldiers, who might have been involved in the Holocaust.[55] However, Sweden displayed no particular inclination to examine the backgrounds of the refugees, which, from the 1980s onwards, led to accusations by the Simon Wiesenthal Centre claiming that Sweden was a sanctuary for fugitive war criminals.[56] Aleksandrs Plesners, the former commander of the Latvian Legion of the Waffen-SS, was among the persons whom the Centre wished the Swedes to prosecute.[57]

Like Sweden, a number of European countries were disinclined to conduct any legal prosecution of former SS volunteers, namely, Ireland, Iceland, Finland and Spain.[58] Conversely, during and after the war, Switzerland prosecuted persons who had signed up for service with the German colours. According to Swiss law, it was illegal to volunteer for military service in another country. Between 1940 and 1943, the most prominent Swiss SS man, Franz Riedweg had led the *Germanische Leitstelle*. In December 1947, he was sentenced in absentia to 16 years' imprisonment for encouragement to join foreign military service and for conspiring against the state of Switzerland.[59]

The Federal Republic

Towards the end of the 1950s, the Federal Republic slowly began to investigate perpetrators of Nazi crimes. Kurt Meyer, the chairman of HIAG stated on that occasion that 'where crime begins, fellowship ends'.[60] Meyers, himself, had been convicted for crimes committed in Normandy and, on this background, his statement appears somewhat hollow. A broad survey of the Nazi crimes would expose the HIAG members' extensive complicity and, Meyer's declaration should be seen in the light of a statement

53. Ibid., p. 68.
54. Gyllenhaal and Westberg (2008), p. 301.
55. Mats Deland, *Purgatorium: Sverige och andra världskrigets förbrytare* (Atlas, 2010).
56. Helene Lööw, 'Swedish Policy Towards Suspected War Criminals, 1945-87', *Scandinavian Journal of History, 1988*, pp. 135–53.
57. Efraim Zuroff, 'Sweden's refusal to prosecute Nazi war criminals – 1986-2002', *Jewish Political Studies Review 14:3-4*, Fall 2002, p. 88.
58. Gyllenhaal and Westberg (2008), p. 301.
59. *Bericht des Bundesrates an die Bundesversammlung über die Verfahren gegen nationalsozialistische Schweitzer wegen Angriffs auf die Unabhängigkeit der Eidgenossenschaft, 7. November 1948, BB, BE2001 (E), 1967/113 A.44.10.1.Uch., Bd.75, Prozess gegen Max Leo Keller.*
60. Wilke (2011), p. 91.

by the minister of justice, Wolfgang Haussmann. He argued that the tasks of the newly established war crimes unit *Zentrale Stelle der Landesjustizverwaltung* (Central for Justice in the *Länder*) were not to conduct 'a misapprehended and perfectionist hunt for minor wearers of the uniform who, without knowledge of the background for and the aim of the extermination process, executed the superior level's orders to kill'.[61]

A marked disinclination to follow-up on crimes committed by others than the most high-profile and obvious culprits was a noticeable characteristic of the West German reckoning with the past. Lack of resources and low priority hampered the collection of evidence and led to rather cursory interviews of the possible perpetrators. The investigations were additionally disadvantaged by the fact that, occasionally, the investigators had a past with the SS and that, behind the stage, the witnesses were allowed to co-ordinate their testimonies.[62] On top of these shortcomings, came the weaknesses of the West German legislation. When the statute of limitations for a number of National Socialist crimes was extended in the autumn of 1968, it was required that, in the moment of his misdeed, the accused must have made a special contribution such as particular cruelty or an explicated hate of Jews.[63]

In several court cases in the Federal Republic, the spotlight nevertheless was on the Waffen-SS. In January 1957, in Arnsberg in North Rhine-Westphalia three Waffen-SS soldiers were accused of having shot, in 1945, 208 Russian forced labourers.[64] A total of more than 60 cases against former Waffen-SS soldiers were tried in East and West Germany.[65] Even as research for this book started, the prosecution of Waffen-SS veterans still was not finished. Thus, in March 2010, the court in Aachen sentenced the 88-year-old Heinrich Boere to imprisonment for life. He was found guilty of the *Silbertanne* murders that he had committed in the Netherlands in the company of fellow Waffen-SS men.[66] And indeed, as we finish this book the prosecution of former members of the SS is still ongoing. In the summer of 2021, the German public prosecutor announced that charges would be brought against 16 men and 1 woman who had served in concentration camps.[67] The men were former SS guards, the oldest of whom in August 2021 was 100 years old, a man who between 1942 and 1945 had been on duty in Sachsenhausen. These cases went to trial despite the high age of the accused, they were all over 95 years old, which presented a number of challenges. The Sachsenhausen guard has since turned 101 years old and the case is still ongoing in 2022.[68]

---

61. Ibid.
62. Cüppers (2011), pp. 334ff. Westemeier (2014), pp. 378ff., 589ff.
63. Cüppers (2011), p. 324.
64. Bert Oliver Manig, *Die Politik der Ehre. Die Rehabilitierung der Berufssoldaten in der frühen Bundesrepublik*, (Wallstein Verlag, 2004), p. 577.
65. Survey done by the authors based on the sentences that can be seen in a survey of Nazi crimes at URL http://www1.jur.uva.nl.
66. http://www.washingtontimes.com/news/2010/jul/6/nazi-suspect-dies/, accessed on 18 September 2013.
67. *Flensborg Avis* 12 August, 2021, Ritzaus Bureau (International) 7 October, 2021, *Jydske Vestkysten* 18 October, 2021.
68. https://www.evangelisch.de/inhalte/197199/16-02-2022/sachsenhausen-prozess-vertagt, assessed 25 February 2022.

The Flight from Liberated Europe

From 1945 and until the end of the decade, thousands of SS men and other Nazis disappeared from liberated Europe in a combination of flight and emigration. They fled partly to General Franco's Spain, partly to South America – primarily to Juan Perón's Argentina – and to various Middle East countries, inter alia, Syria and Egypt. As a number of Allies eased migration or merely lessened their immigration control, a significant number of former Waffen-SS soldiers from Eastern Europe, ended up in the United Kingdom, Australia, Canada and the United States.

The scope of this 'brown emigration' is hard to fix exactly because quite a few left illegally and under a false identity. However, there are other factors hampering the creation of a reasonable overview. Simultaneously with the exodus of Nazi collaborators and war criminals from Europe the period was characterised by the movements of displaced persons without connection with the Nazis' terror regime.[69] It even happened that victims and henchmen travelled on the same boat or used the same intermediaries – hence it was difficult to distinguish between the two when looking merely at immigration figures. It is also important to stress that the group, which is frequently designated war criminals and collaborators, covers a very broad and heterogenous group of people. At one end of the continuum, we find characters like Adolf Eichmann, Josef Mengele, Erich Priebke and Walter Rauff. They were all persons who either – as Eichmann and Rauff – were principal organisers of SS's mass murder of Europe's Jews, or had bloody hands themselves – as had Mengele and Priebke – the latter being personally responsible for the murder, in March 1944, of 335 Italian civilians at Fosse Ardeatine near Rome. Such men had all the reason to go underground and try to vanish from European soil in their quest for sanctuary from Allied persecution. Elsewhere on this continuum, we find 'political' refugees, who were not necessarily among the worst henchmen but wished to find a place where they might continue their political toil for the benefit of Nazism. A third group were 'economic' refugees, who believed their job probabilities might be more promising elsewhere. Examples of the latter were collaborators who had little chance of making a career in their home countries or technicians from the German arms industry. All these groups might bring wives and children along thus increasing considerably the size- of the 'brown emigration'.

Detailed research concerning this migration is moreover hampered by myths. If the early, speculative literature is to be trusted, the flight from Europe was diligently co-ordinated by the organisations *Die Spinne* (the spider) and *Odessa* (*Organisation der ehemaligen SS Angehörigen* (organisation of former SS personnel)). And, if this was not enough, the planning was so effective that not only the No 2 party official after Hitler,

---

69. This topic is dealt with in a number of works many of which have a speculative and sensationalist streak. Central among recent research based on archival material are Uki Goni, *The Real Odessa: How Perón Brought the Nazi War Criminals to Argentina*, Rev. ed. (Granta Books, 2003); Gerald Steinacher, *Nazis on the Run: How Hitler's Henchmen Fled Justice* (Oxford University Press, 2011); Margolian (2000).

Martin Bormann, but also the Führer himself succeeded in getting themselves to South America. At least that was what transpired through the bush telegraph.[70]

There were, indeed, several very efficient organisers helping former SS members to escape, but, despite rumours at the time, there was no such thing as a single omnipotent SS flight organisation.[71] However, in the early post-war years, many Waffen-SS members managed to slip silently out of Europe. There were many reasons for that, one being the fact that, for various reasons, quite a few individuals were ready to help the Nazi refugees on the way. One of the several principal escape routes went through Scandinavia where, over the years 1946–1947, the Argentine consulate general in Copenhagen arranged extensive issues of false passports and immigration permissions.[72] Another route went to Genoa and other Italian ports via Alto Adige, where the generally Germanophone population were very helpful, as was the RC church in the cases of Catholic 'repentant' Nazis.[73]

South America – and in particular Argentina – was a favourite destination, and Norway offers an especially well-researched example. From Norway ca. 350–400 collaborators, including families, fled to Argentina.[74] Among them were a number of former Waffen-SS volunteers. One was Sophus Kahrs, formerly company commander in Legion Norge who fled, together with a small group of fellow prisoners, from a Norwegian prison leaving the country on board the boat 'Solbris'. After a year of adventurous voyage, they arrived in Argentina.[75]

If we dare to generalise from the Norwegian emigration, it appears likely that the European exodus of Nazis to South America culminated by the end of the 1940s. There are different reasons for this lapse of time. First, the extensive flight required the existence of a large network that took some time to set up. Secondly, the decision to emigrate would sometimes need some time before maturing, and those imprisoned had to get out. Thirdly, the general pattern was that the men would go first, and the families would follow, when they had settled down. Moreover, the process was influenced by economic trends and about 1949 an economic crisis hit Argentina making the country less attractive as an immigration terminus.[76]

Australia, Canada, the UK and the USA, too, were also the destination for a large number of former Nazi collaborators and Waffen-SS soldiers. These came mainly

70. Holger M. Meding, *Flucht vor Nürnberg? Deutsche und österreichische Einwanderung in Argentinien, 1945–1955* (Böhlau, 1992), p. 123ff.
71. Oliver Schröm, *Stille Hilfe für braune Kameraden: das geheime Netzwerk der Alt und Neonazis* (Links, 2001). See also Furuseth (2013).
72. NAWA, 263, ZZ-17, box 6, Undated report (ca. 1948), *Illegal Emmigration of Nazis from Germany to Argentina. RK, Udenrigsministeriet, Den diplomatiske repræsentation i Buenos Aires, gruppeordnede sager 1945–1958*, journal number 36.S.65, letter No. 669 from the Ministry for Foreign Affairs to the legation in Buenos Aires, 8 December 1947.
73. Steinacher (2011), p. 32ff. See also Furuseth (2013), p. 24ff.
74. Anne Kristin Furuseth, *Da freden brot los. Norsk NS-migration til Argentina etter 1945* (Unpublished Master Thesis from the University of Oslo; Oslo, 2011), p. 50. See also Furuseth (2013).
75. Furuseth (2011), p. 49.
76. Furuseth (2011), p. 49ff.

from the Baltic countries and Ukraine. As far as a large group of Balts, Ukrainians and *Volksdeutsche* were concerned, their exit out of Europe happened via the Displaced Persons System. From the beginning of 1947, when the emptying of the DP camps started in earnest and into the early 1950s, more than one million people were resettled in 113 countries. The biggest recipient was the United States with 400,000 immigrants, of whom 10,000 are assumed to have been Waffen-SS veterans.[77] About 12,000 from the Waffen-SS *Division Galizien* came to Australia, Canada and the UK.[78]

77. Mark Wyman, *DP: Europe's Displaced Persons, 1945–1951* (Balch Institute Press, 1989), p. 202. Pontillo (2009), p. 411.
78. Wyman (1989), p. 191ff.

Chapter Fifteen

THE VETERANS UNIONISE

Considerable parts of the post-First World War veterans' movement helped pave the way for the Nazi *Machtergreifung*.[1] Knowing this, it is hardly surprising that, in September 1945, the Allies forbade veterans' associations and groups wishing to glorify the German military heritage.[2] In December 1949, the ban was lifted in the western occupation zones, and a number of veterans' societies sprang up. They comprised a wide variety of associations spanning from large communities of interests to small loosely organised bands of comrades sharing a common past in the same unit or arm. While some were based on common interests in material or nostalgic issues, others were founded by individuals who had obvious political agendas and ambitions of bringing back the soldier and militarism into German politics.[3]

Many of these had existed secretly before and striven to ascertain the former regular soldiers' right to receive a pension.[4] During the early life of the Federal Republic, it was primarily the provision for war veterans and their bereaved as well as the re-establishment of German defence forces that characterised the relationship between the young state and the veterans it had inherited from the Third Reich. The existing pension schemes and provision for invalids had broken down when the victorious powers cancelled all pensions and social rights for public servants.[5] In December 1950, the West German government passed legislation re-introducing pensions to disabled ex-servicemen, war widows and their children as well as returned prisoners-of-war. This law benefitted – directly or indirectly – a total of four million West Germans.[6] Veterans of the *Wehrmacht* and the SS who were not disabled were not covered by this arrangement, and now a dispute began over what the Federal Republic owed to those who had fought for Hitler, including those of the Waffen-SS. In April 1951, this conundrum was partially solved as the pensions were restored to officers and NCOs of the *Wehrmacht*. Personnel of the Waffen-SS were not accepted as soldiers employed by the state and were, therefore, not comprised by the law.

---

1. James M. Diehl, *The Thanks of the Fatherland: German Veterans after the Second World War* (University of North Carolina Press, 1993), pp. 18–27.
2. Kraft Frhr. Schenck zu Schweinsberg, "Die Soldatenverbände in der Bundesrepublik" in Georg Picht, *Studien zur politischen undgesellschaftlichen Situation der Bundeswehr, Bd. 1* (Eckart, 1965), p. 98.
3. Diehl (1993), p. 182.
4. Schweinsberg (1965), p. 98ff.
5. Diehl (1993), p. 65.
6. Ibid., p. 109ff.

Thus, over the following years, a change in the legislation to also include the Waffen-SS personnel became a key activity for the HIAG – the main SS veterans' organisation. Soon after, when the contours of a West German defence force emerged, the veterans' struggle was extended to advocating for admission on par with former *Wehrmacht* servicemen.

HIAG

The trendsetting post-war veterans' organisation for the SS, the HIAG (*Hilfsgemeinschaft auf Gegenseitigkeit der Angehörigen der ehemaligen Waffen-SS*) originated in Northwestern Germany. About 1948, the seeds were sown by a loose grouping in the greater Hamburg area and, in the following years, many local groups sprang up; all of them using the designation HIAG.[7] The name was chosen because of its innocent and non-politicising ring; alluding to the support of destitute or disabled former SS soldiers. However, HIAG was also to perpetuate the attitudes and values of the SS and to fight aggressively for equality of the Waffen-SS vis-a-vis the *Wehrmacht*. In 1952–1953, the first *Landesverbände* (federal state associations) was set up in the *Länder* (federal states) Schleswig-Holstein and Baden-Württemberg, and, in August 1953, the *Bundesverbindungsstelle* (nationwide liaison office) was established in Cassel. By the end of the 1950s, HIAG matured as a countrywide organisation with HQ in Bonn.[8]

In its early years, HIAG faced internal disagreement, and there were numerous clashes between local associations, the leadership and individual members.[9] When, at the end of the 1950s, the former general-officer-commanding *Division Hitlerjugend*, Meyer (Panzermeyer) took over the presidency the problems were – if not solved – at least swept under the carpet. Meyer's policy was that HIAG – at least publicly – should profess allegiance to the democratic values of the Federal Republic and seek influence via contact with mainstream political parties like the SPD (Germany's Social Democrats Party) and the CDU (Christian Democratic Union). Thus, the HIAG began navigating a course set out by a leader with flair for the politically presentable and a good network of political contacts.[10]

---

7. Schweinsberg (1965), p. 105. British authorities took a more relaxed stance on soldiers' associations than their southern neighbours, the Americans. Even before December 1949, when the ban against such groups was lifted, a number of such semi-official clubs were extant within the British occupation zone. Diehl (1993), p. 65.

8. BAMA, B438/396, *Arbeits- und Lagebericht des Bundesvorstandes*. Bundesprecher Hubert Meyer at *38. Ordentlichen Bundesversammlung*; Willy Schafer, "10 Jahre Kampf um das Recht', *Der Freiwillige*, October 1962, p. 20. BAMA, B438/1, *Protokol über die landessprecher-Tagung der HIAG am 1. und 2. August 1953 in Marburg/Lahn*. BAMA, B438/213, *Satzung des "Bundesverbandes der Soldaten der ehemaligen Waffen-SS e.V."* carried at a members' meeting on 18–19 April 1959.

9. See Wilke (2011). See also BAMA, N756/413a, *Gesellschafft zum Studium von Zeitfragen*. *Vertrauliche Information 8.3.1958*: "*Die HIAG in der Krise? Zur Situation der Hilfsgemeinschaften der ehemaligen Waffen-SS.*"

10. BAK, B145/3544, Note of unknown origin stamped as having been received on 27 November 1959.

During the 1950s, HIAG appeared to succeed in attracting positive publicity, and it was met with certain goodwill by the big mainstream political parties. The latter was possibly due to exaggerated notions of the number of potential voters organised in HIAG based on the leaderships' claim to representing all former Waffen-SS soldiers. Not least in the early years of the organisation's existence, this led to grossly overstated claims concerning the number of SS veterans in the Federal Republic as well as the size of HIAG. Even taking stateless veterans into account, there were hardly ever more than 250–300,000 former Waffen-SS men in the Federal Republic. Nonetheless, HIAG claimed to represent the interests of more than a million ex-servicemen.[11] The same trend showed in the organisation's table of members. In 1954, in a letter to the Federal Chancellor Konrad Adenauer, former General Felix Steiner claimed that HIAG had 45,000 members.[12] It was later claimed that, at one point, the number of members was as high as 70,000.[13] Research has however demonstrated that the number hardly was ever more than 20,000, which equivalates eight per cent of the Waffen-SS veterans living in the Germany.[14]

From the late 1950s onwards, the conditions for HIAG's work changed. As politicians realised that HIAG's modest size hardly allowed them to significantly influence the outcome of general elections, their interest in the process of the veterans' re-integration into society declined. At the same time, a flurry of Anti-Semite and Nazi graffiti went over the Federal Republic between Christmas 1959 and the end of January 1960. The authorities tried to explain the ca. 700 incidents away as a remote-controlled campaign by the GDR in order to discredit Western Germany. Nevertheless, in combination with the trials of the henchmen of the Third Reich these incidents contributed to stir up emotions and put HIAG on the defensive.[15] Yet, the increasing number of court cases against Nazi criminals simultaneously helped keep the HIAG members united. Many cases involved former Waffen-SS personnel and this helped strengthen the SS veterans' internal cohesiveness and the backing of their leaders.[16]

Moreover, the members grew older and no longer had the need to fight for issues like their right to seek jobs in the newly established *Bundeswehr*. Therefore, HIAG's activities shifted focus and increasingly dealt with history and the Waffen-SS's reputation. However, this is not to say that HIAG's history of the 1960s and beyond was simply

---

11. "Eine glatte Rechnung", *Der Freiwillige*, June 1956, pp. 3, s.13 and78.
12. BAK, B136/5147, Letter of 3 March 1954 from Steiner to Bundeskanzler Adenauer.
13. Hermann Weiss, "Alte Kameraden von der Waffen-SS" in Wolfgang Benz (ed.), *Rechtsextremismus in der Bundesrepublik: Voraussetzungen, Zusammenhänge, Wirkungen* (Fischer Taschenbuch Verlag, 1984), p. 161.
14. Wilke (2011), p. 13. In 1956, a note in Wiking-Ruf, told that 6.8 per cent of the former Waffen-SS soldiers were members of HIAG. Hans Peter Kuhnen, *Die Vergangenheitsbewältigung der HIAG – Hilfsgemeinschaft ehemaliger Angehöriger der Waffen-SS* (unpublished manuscript in Yad Vashem's library), 1973, p. 3.
15. "Antisemitismus ohne Hintermänner", *Der Spiegel*, Nr. 9, 1960, p. 18ff. Manig (2004), pp. 581f. and 83ff.
16. Wilke (2011), p. 421ff.

one of decline. Parts of the German public reacted adversively to the youth rebellion of the late 1960s and some supported HIAG which experienced a certain influx of new members. It was not until the 1980s, that the organisation really began to crumble.[17] During that decade certain institutions from whom the HIAG sought support instead chose to create distance between themselves and the SS veterans. In 1982, the German Social Democratic Party, SPD, decided that membership in HIAG should be a reason for expulsion. A few years later, the Christian Democratic Union, CDU, made a similar decision likely influenced by the fact that the West German National Intelligence Service in its annual reports 1979–1985 had mentioned HIAG as a right-wing extremist organisation.[18]

In May 1991, after years of discussions, HIAG decided that the organisation was to be dissolved at the turn of year 1992/3.[19] However, while the nationwide organisation ceased to exist, to some extent local, lower level, branches continued their activities.

HIAG's members and activities

It is remarkable that most of HIAG's trendsetting members were officers, and that, not least, Generals Hausser, Steiner, Gille and Meyer played prominent roles. In this and other fields, HIAG continued the military hierarchy and the social norms that had been established in the Waffen-SS. Over time, for demographic reasons, the member populace changed as the older generation, including many officers at the levels of colonel and general, died or became inactive. However, this never made HIAG an organisation controlled by NCOs or private soldiers born in the 1920s – at least not publicly – but increasingly younger men and men of lower ranks came to the fore.[20]

Over the years, the overall number of HIAG members declined. From a culmination point in the 1950s of ca. 20,000 members, the number fell to about 3,000 in 1991.[21] It is important to keep in mind that, over time, there was a large turnover of members. Thus, the aggregate number of persons, who had been members at some point in time, was larger than what meets the eye at first sight. Old age, illness, demise and dissatisfaction with the leadership led to withdrawals from the organisation. But, still,

---

17. Ibid., p. 415ff.
18. BAMA, B438/396, Arbeits- und Lageberichtdes Bundesvorstandes. Bundessprecher Hubert Meyer at *38. Ordentlichen Bundesversammlung;* BAMA, B438/230, Letter from General Müller Vorsitzende VdS to the Minister for Defence 20 April 1983, ibid.: HIAG Oberallgäu-Information Nr. 4/82 (pp. 3–4).
19. BAMA, B438/396, *Ergebnisniederschrift der am 11. Mai 1991 in Soltau stattgefundenen 37. Ordentlichen Bundesversammlung, 8.7.1991.*
20. In BAMA, N756/405c there are copies of a number of letters of the 1970s that warned the German trade unions of the former private SS volunteer H.R., the class of 1926. Wolfgang Vopersal, *Der Freiwilliges* mainstay *Referent für Kriegsgeschichte* was born in October 1927 and served with Division Totenkopf during the war http://startext.net-build.de:8080/barch/MidosaSEARCH/N756-37281/index.htm, accessed on 24 January 2013.
21. BAMA, B438/396, Survey of the voting associations at the 37th meeting in Soltau on 10–11 June 1991.

there was also a steady trickle of new members joining, who, for various reasons, found the time and the will to busy themselves with veteran affairs. Many abstained from joining while still working, or did not realise until later that they had a need to speak with likeminded persons.[22]

Peering into one of the associations of the HIAG, the *Truppenkameradschaft der Handschar*, provide us with examples of this trend. This association was formed as late as 1982, though it did not become a part of HIAG until 1984.[23] Its activities up to 1992 show that, on several occasions, new members joined. The number of participants at the annual veteran rallies differed considerably. In 1988, only 13 turned up at the rally, 15 the year after, but 48 in 1990, 35 in 1991 and 80 in 1992.[24]

In the 1950s, when HIAG saw the light of day through various local initiatives, the most prominent members emphasised that its aim was, primarily, social work. Although, to some extent, there was a wish to blur the true political ambitions, there is no reason to doubt that an important part of HIAG's efforts aimed at supporting disadvantaged former fellow soldiers. Alone the years 1950–1959, saw HIAG spend 1.25 million Deutsch Marks, so their own claim, to such purposes.[25] In 1951, the aid consisted of 425 packets and 2,500 Deutsch Marks to the relatives of former Waffen-SS soldiers. Another huge post was 1,500 Deutsch Marks for travel costs for those who wished to visit their loved ones in the war criminals' prisons in Werl and Landsberg.[26] The organisation also launched a search for missing Waffen-SS soldiers, which contributed to providing a humanitarian touch. This was useful for linking up with political parties, institutions like the Red Cross and churches, and the locals in the towns where HIAG convened high-profile 'search rallies'.[27] At these rallies, the veterans met in order to ascertain where the missing persons had last been seen, or find possible witnesses to their death. They were also social gatherings where fellow soldiers met – often with their wives accompanying them.

Although HIAG's rallies boasted local representatives, not all were pleased with seeing the SS veterans' behaviour when getting together. When, in 1957, HIAG planned a big search rally in Bavaria, the Minister of the Interior felt obliged to send a letter referring

---

22. An undated letter from a member of the Danish freikorps written sometime after 21 June 1971 provides an example of a person taking up contact with fellow soldiers of the Waffen-SS in the 1970s. A copy is held by the authors.

23. BAMA, B438/377, An invitation to join Truppenkameradschaft der Handschar in Altensteig 21–22 September 1985; Ibid.: Information from HIAG to Kurt Schwer/ Truppenkameradschaft der Handschar, 11 April 1984.

24. BAMA, B438/377, *Truppenkameradschaft der Handschar. Rundschreiben 30.10.1988*; Ibid.: *Truppenkameradschaft der Handschar. Rundschreiben 4/89, den 7.7.1989*; *Truppenkameradschaft der Handschar. Rundschreiben 4/90., 25.9.1990*; Ibid: *Truppenkameradschaft der Handschar. Rundschreiben 4/91. 9.9. 1991*; Ibid.: *Truppenkameradschaft der Handschar. Rundschreiben 3/92., 4. September 1992.*

25. Schenck zu Schweinsberg, "Die Soldatenverbändein der Bundesrepublik" in Picht (1965), p. 108ff.

26. NAKEW, FO1014/622, Political Report No.13, 16.1.1952.

27. Wilke (2011), p. 235ff.

to HIAG's rally in the North-west German town Minden the previous year, when 10,000 Waffen-SS veterans had met. Based on the experiences from that assembly, the Minister admonished that the upcoming meeting should not transgress its purpose as a search rally. He stressed how certain activities might rekindle memories of the Waffen-SS such as marches.[28] Staging military marches through towns was a practice used several times before by HIAG, and they had been very similar to those arranged by the Nazis 20 years before.[29] And there were other provocative elements of HIAG's ceremonial manifestations. On the wreaths being laid down on graves the divisional badges were attached as was the SS motto *Meine Ehre heißt Treue*. The wreath-laying ceremonies were accompanied by singing the SS' official anthem: *Wenn alle untreu werden* ('If all become unfaithful, we remain loyal,' a German patriotic song written in 1814 by Max von Schenkendorf). Already in 1955, Paul Hausser, at the time the central character of the veteran milieu, had to caution veterans not to use expressions and imagery 'that might be perceived the wrong way'.[30] Apparently, this went unnoticed in Austria where, in October 1956, the first public Waffen-SS rally took place as part of a major soldiers' gathering at the town Haag near Linz. The veterans formed up below a board carrying the SS runes and displayed them on the façade of one of the inns. Thereafter, there was a torchlight procession and march to a new war memorial where a wreath laying-ceremony took place.[31] On 4–5 May 1960, *Division Nord* rallied to the Bavarian town Windheim, and local authorities noticed that still there were episodes ranging from sporting of Nazi symbols to singing the SS tune *Wir sind die schwarze Garde, die Adolf Hitler liebt.*[32]

The veterans and right-wing extremism

As these examples demonstrate, many SS veterans clung to the past – but did they also attempt to bring it back? During the war and in the immediate aftermath, there was widespread fear amongst the Allies that a Nazi resistance movement – so-called *Werwölfe* – might materialise. The SS in particular was expected to be willing to continue the fight after German defeat.[33] Some of the SS men who were still at large did actually participate in various resistance against the Allies or joined forces with the criminal underworld, which existed in the larger cities after the defeat, but real resistance movement was never seen.[34]

---

28. BAK, B136/6827, Letter of 28 June 1957 from Bundesminister des Innern to HIAG/ Helmuth Thöle.
29. Wilke (2011), p. 259ff.
30. Schenck zu Schweinsberg, "Die Soldatenverbände in der Bundesrepublik" in Picht (1965), p. 110.
31. *Der Freiwillige*, December 1956, p. 16.
32. BAK, B136/6828, Cover letter from Verfassungsschutz to Bundeskanzleramt,14.7.1960.
33. SANDFDOC, Box 221, Divisional Intelligence Summary No. 91.
34. John Biddiscombe, "'The Enemy of our Enemy": A View of the Edelweiss Piraten from the British and American Archives", *Journal of Contemporary History, Vol. 30, No.1*, 1995, pp. 37–63.

In 1949, the Federal Republic was founded creating a new battlefield for political power and influence. Here, democratic parties and movements competed with persons, groups and parties that, in various ways, wanted their past back. There were, among others, the *Nationaldemokratische Partei* (national democratic party) and the *Deutsche Reichspartei*, (German Reich party) that both grew up to a point.[35] Thus in the early 1950s, only a few, scarcely veiled, Nazi parties existed alongside the established democratic parties CDU and SPD. The HIAG leadership had the choice between leaning on the extreme right-wing parties or rather liaise with the centric parties of the fledgling Federal Republic. This choice was not only a political one but also a question of how much leeway there was before the Allies, following HIAG at a distance and with considerable scepticism, would demand measures be taken against the organisation.

British Foreign Office documents show that, in the early 1950s, there was some apprehension concerning the newly founded soldiers' organisations. From the outset, HIAG was in the crosshairs as a possible breeding ground for neo-Nazi tendencies.[36] Thus, in November 1951, shortly after the foundation of HIAG it was discussed if it should be banned.[37] Asked by General McCloy about a possible German reaction to a ban of the organisation and arrest of its leading character, Gille, the Federal Chancellor Konrad Adenauer replied that, apart from a small extremist minority, reactions would probably be positive.[38] From other quarters, too, German authorities were met with demands for outlawing HIAG.[39] While HIAG as such was never banned, the authorities repeatedly adopted measures against planned HIAG events.[40] On their part, HIAG's leadership tried to portray Waffen-SS as idealistic and politically naive soldiers, now democratically minded, who did not wish to return to the past.[41] As a part of this strategy, HIAG's regulations stated that the organisation was loyal to the Federal Republic and its democratic parliamentarian system.[42]

---

35. The German, post-war, extreme right is described in-depth in Tauber (1967). On NDP and DR, see pp. 68ff., 85ff., 98ff.
36. NAKEW, FO371/97949, Note of 19 June 1952. NAKEW, FO371/97949, Despatch No.140 of 9 June 1952 from the British High Commissioner in Germany to the Foreign Secretary.
37. NAKEW, FO1014/622, Telegram of 8 November 1951 from the representative at the Allied Control Council to FO. See also NAKEW, FO371/97949, Letter of 28 October 1952 from the British High Commissioner in Germany to FO concerning General Ramcke's speech. Tauber (1967), p. 296.
38. NAKEW, FO1014/622, Telegram 8 November 1951 from the representative at the Allied Control Council to FO.
39. BAK, B136/6828, Letter of 4 June 1963 from *Bundesminister des Innern* to the permanent undersecretary at the Chancellor's Office; The letter was eventually sent on 15 June 1963.
40. Kurt Hirsch, "SS gestern, heute und ..." (Verlag Schaffende Jugend, 1957), p. 80.
41. Kurt Meyer and Michael Mende, *Grenadiers*, translated by Robert J. Edwards, J.J. Fedorowicz (Publishing, Inc., 2001), pp. 392, and 395.
42. David Clay Large, "Reckoning without the Past: The HIAG of the Waffen-SS and the Politics of Rehabilitation in the Bonn Republic, 1950–1961" in The Journal of Modern History, Vol. 59, No. 1 Mar., 1987, p. 83. BAMA, B438/213, *Satzung des "Bundesverbandes der Soldaten der ehemaligen Waffen-SS e.V."* approved at the meeting of members 18–19 April 1959.

Prior to the general election in 1953, HIAG passed a public resolution declaring allegiance to the Federal Republic and democracy and encouraged that one's vote is cast for the benefit of the state supporting, that is, democratically minded, parties.[43] However, at the same time, there was an admonition to take HIAG's demand of full rehabilitation seriously. This was conveyed in a manner that led to the impression that only if democracy acknowledged the SS veterans would they acknowledge democracy.[44] The civil service in Bonn, therefore, wondered if the masks would not fall, if, one day, a chance might appear in German politics to make a sharp turn to the right.[45] Deliberations of this kind were appropriate, at least if one looks at the lower rungs of HIAG's hierarchy or simply makes an analysis of the organisation's actions.

It is obvious, looking at the discussion whether or not to recommend to the members to vote for specific parties at the general election of 1953, that HIAG did not muster unconditional support for democracy. The extreme right-wing parties, for which Waffen-SS veterans ran for election in several constituencies, were described by HIAG in its internal minutes as 'the *so-called* radical parties'. The voices criticising the nomination of far-right Waffen-SS candidates were troubled mostly because these parties would hardly be big enough to effect any changes, and the candidates might be used for fuelling the slander about the Waffen-SS.[46]

Reports from HIAG's meetings provide examples that members often had a hard time exchanging their Nazi heritage with a liberal democratic worldview.[47] When, in October 1952, the former German para general and long-time French prisoner-of-war, General Hermann-Bernard Ramcke, addressed a HIAG rally in Bremen he – according to contemporary records – worked himself up into a fury over the Allies. He declared that the true war criminals were those 'who without any tactical reason destroyed whole cities, bombed Hiroshima and produced yet more nuclear weapons'.[48] On this background, he claimed that the Allies' lists of German war criminals should be seen as 'honours lists'.[49] His words were received with enthusiasm by the ca. 2,000 attendants, but caused consternation among the HIAG top-level leaders. They tried more than once to drag Ramcke from the podium and eventually evicted him from the meeting.[50]

43. BAMA, B438/1, Protokol über die Landessprecher-Tagung der HIAG am 1. und 2. August 1953 in Marburg/Lahn.
44. "Eine glatte Rechnung", *Der Freiwillige*, June 1956, p. 3.
45. BAK, B145/3544, Note without provenience, stamped as incoming on 27 November 1959.
46. BAMA, B438/1, *Protokol über die Landessprecher-Tagung der HIAG am 1. und 2. August 1953 in Marburg/Lahn.*
47. NAKEW, FO1014/622, Political report No. 13, 16 January 1952.
48. Wilke (2011), p. 266.
49. NAKEW, FO371/97949, Letter of 28 October 1952 from the British High Commission in Germany to FO informing about General Ramcke's address. For slightly differing minutes, see Tauber (1967), p. 351ff. See also Wilke (2011), p. 265.
50. NAKEW, FO371/97949, Letter of 29 October 1952 from the British High Commission in Germany to FO containing further information about Ramcke's speech. Ibid.: Note of 28 October 1952 concerning General Ramcke's speech from the British resident in Verden an der Aller.

Radical views and parties on the right of the political continuum were no rare sights. They attracted SS veterans and former SS soldiers at the forefront of a wild undergrowth of right-wing extremist groups and parties blossoming in the political landscape of the 1950s. At the general election in 1953, Police and SS General Karl Brenner ran, though in vain, for the extreme right-wing party *Nationale Sammlung* (national unity) in Baden-Württemberg – one of the few federal states where this party had a candidate. During Nazism, he had held various posts in the police and the Waffen-SS and had, for example, managed counter-insurgency activity in the Balkans and in Belarus.[51] While the election was a disaster and led to the crumbling of the party, *Deutsche Reichspartei* was larger and more successful having placed yet another Waffen-SS man, General Lothar Debes, at the front. During his career, he had filled the posts of commandant of the *Junkerschulen* at Brunswick and Bad Tölz and, in 1957, the party leadership made him a candidate for the Federal Parliament.[52]

HIAG stayed aloof from party politics, cultivating no explicit attachment to the extreme right-wing, and served its own interests through the mainstream parties. This happened primarily via the two conservative Christian parties the CDU and the CSU (Christian Social Union), but relations with the SPD were for some time excellent, too.[53] Like Hans Wissebach, CDU, some parliamentarians had a past with the Waffen-SS and did not hide their sympathies with HIAG.[54] Moreover, politicians of the mainstream parties were frequently seen at HIAG's meetings and rallies.[55] On several occasions, according to the organisation's own records, the later Social Democrat Federal Chancellor Helmuth Schmidt spoke at such events.[56] Also, cultural celebrities and publicly known experts spoke occasionally at HIAG's arrangements. Dr. Hans Buchheim, of the Munich based *Institut für Zeitgeschichte* (Institute for Contemporary History), one of the Germany's most renowned experts on Nazism and the SS, addressed on one occasion a branch of HIAG to the theme of 'political and unpolitical thoughts'.[57] However, it seems that, in the 1970s, the public keenness for participating in HIAG events was abating. The explanation for this may be the cumulative effect of more and more SS crimes being revealed, the increasing public consciousness about it, and the general political turn to the left experienced in Germany throughout this period. This hit HIAG in the form of demonstrations against its events, increased

51. On Brenner, see Schulz and Wegmann (2003), p. 163ff. On *Nationale Sammlung*, see Tauber, *Beyond Eagle and Swastika*, pp. 616f. and 803.
52. On Debes, see Schulz and Wegmann (2003), p. 206ff.
53. NAKEW, FO1014/622, Political Report No.53, 27 March 1952. Schweinsberg in Picht (1965). Hermann Weiss, "Alte Kameraden von der Waffen-SS", in Benz (1984), p. 162.
54. Weiss in ibid., p. 165.
55. BAK, B136/6827, Draft note concerning the HIAG rally in Hameln. BAMA, B438/233, *Bundesgeschäftführung v. Hans Lierk, 22.10.1982; ibid.: Bundesgeschäftführung v. Hans Lierk, 3.9.1982.*
56. BAMA, B438/233, *Aktennotitz 25.9.1982.* BAMA, B438/233, Invitation from HIAG *Kreisgemeinschaft Stuttgart 16.4.1957.*
57. BAMA, B438/233, *Bundesgeschäftführung v. Hans Lierk, 3.9.1982.*

surveillance and documentary activity by leftist groups as well as associations of victim and opponents.[58] In March 1976, for instance, after public protests HIAG Hamburg had to give up hosting a lecture by Skorzeny.[59]

Over the 1980s, HIAG was further ostracised. In 1985, due to public demonstrations HIAG Hamburg had to cancel a planned 35-year anniversary celebration.[60] Apparently, the rising level of conflict with the public and the general left-turn drove HIAG members in the opposite direction. Anyway, in the 1980s, HIAG was challenged by a small, but militant, circle of Waffen-SS veterans calling themselves *Kameradenkreis der ehemaligen Waffen-SS* (fellowship circle of the late Waffen-SS). This was a Nazi group publishing the magazine *Leithefte* (guidance booklets). The name was a rehash of the eponymous SS magazine, and its content was extreme.[61] Since several of the men in the *Kameradenkreis* had been either members of or sympathisers with HIAG, they had contacts within the organisation who provided them with names and addresses of Waffen-SS veterans to whom they then sent their pamphlets uninvitedly. The badly printed and amateurish magazine caused the leaders of HIAG considerable trouble, and it fortified the opponents in their opinion of the veterans as incurable right-extremists.[62]

It is revealing of the members' latent Nazism that the leadership, because of the challenge by those behind the *Leithefte*, wondered if not *Der Freiwillige* ought to move in a similar direction.[63] In 1988, in a letter to the editor of *Der Freiwillige*, Helmuth Thöle, HIAG's chairman, Hubert Meyer, suggested if not the two of them ought to meet the *Leithefte* circle and discuss the integration of many of the *Leithefte*'s ideas in *Der Freiwillige*.[64] Although, over the following months, Meyer had a lengthy correspondence with one of the men behind *Leithefte*, Friedhelm Kalhagen, no reconciliation took place. After all, the positions were too far apart. While Meyer claimed to have always felt a soldier not perceiving himself as one serving a party guard, his opponent declared that it was ridiculous denying that the Waffen-SS personnel had been political soldiers, and that, right from the 1950s, he had worked to bring Nazism into HIAG.[65] Meyers' version of German democracy that he – in spite of its shortcomings – preferred as the best

---

58. Karl Sauer, *Die Verbrechen der Waffen-SS. Eine Dokumentation* (Röderberg Verlag,1977). Wilke (2011), pp. 269–85.
59. Sauer (1977), p. 85.
60. Wilke (2011), p. 276.
61. A number of these *Leithefte*, at least 31 issues were published from 1985 to 1990 can be found at BAMA, B438/228. See also B438/396, Letter of 28 February 1990 from *Truppenkammeradschaft der Kavellerie-Division* to HIAG's *Geschäftführer*.
62. BAMA, B438/228, Letter of 8 November 1985 from Kurt Portugall to Hans Lierk.
63. Ibid.
64. BAMA, B438/228, Letter of 30 January 1988 from Hubert Meyer to Helmut Thöle.
65. BAMA, B438/228, Letter of 17 February 1988 from Hubert Meyer to Friedhelm Kalhagen; Letter of 12 February 1988 from Friedhelm Kalhagen to Hubert Meyer, Letter of 20 February 1988 from Friedhelm Kalhagen to Hubert Meyer.

possible governance system, was juxtaposed with Kalhagen's notion that it was nothing but a manifestation of a Jewish divide and rule strategy.[66]

In March 1988, this correspondence had ceased and, in the autumn, the leadership cautioned members not to engage further in the *Leithefte* circle.[67] The warnings, unequivocally implored the members not to have any dealings with the *Leithefte* group, but, nonetheless, there is certain duplicity in the leadership's confession to democracy. A message to the members 'encouraged them to stick together not follow the pied pipers. Let us nurture the old bond and, not least considering our children and grandchildren's interests, vow to freedom and democracy.'[68]

The SS veterans' international network

In most countries which housed a significant number of SS veterans, organisations similar to the HIAG sprung up after the war. Quite a few veterans stayed in contact with fellow soldiers living outside their own country and a complex network of formal and informal contacts between former Waffen-SS soldiers existed during most of the Cold War era.

During the early 1950s, there were some indications that Gille, a leading figure in the German veterans' milieu, actively worked towards creating an international SS veterans' organisation. Probably, his motive was that, at a time when a European army was on the agenda, it might be attractive for him and other SS generals to provide a fully fledged movement of former Waffen-SS soldiers. For many reasons, this came to nothing. A large scale international Waffen-SS gathering was planned to take place in Germany, but the government, who had got wind of it, refused to grant visa to participants.[69] In spring 1952, the same attitude led to the cancellation of an international meeting for veterans of *Wiking*.[70]

Generally, foreign veterans were welcomed at HIAG rallies, and in their publications, the international perspective took up quite a lot of space. In September 1956, at the big search rally at Minden, allegedly, there were 10,000 veterans present of whom many were foreigners – among others, Flemings, French, Dutch and Swiss.[71] According to contemporary media, alone the Belgians were there with 400 participants.[72] In 1977,

---

66. BAMA, B438/228. Letter of 8.3.1988 from Hubert Meyer to Friedhelm Kalhagen in Witten. Letter of 5 March 1988 from Friedhelm Kalhagen to Hubert Meyer.
67. BAMA, B438/228, Circularletterfrom Hubert Meyer to TKT's members 1 September 1988; *Rundschrieben des HIAG-Bundesvorstandes 4/88 vom 6.10.1988.*
68. BAMA, B438/228, Circular letter of 1 September 1988 from Hubert Meyer to TKT's members.
69. NAKEW, FO1014/622, Political Report No.29, 5.2.1952.
70. NAKEW, FO371/97949, Despatch no.140 of 9 June 1952 from the British high commissioner in Germany to the foreign secretary.
71. *Der Freiwillige, September 1956*, p. 3.
72. BAK, B136/6827, Letter from Auswärtiges Amt to Bundeskanzleramt, 26.9.1956 with annex. *Der Freiwillige, September 1956*, p. 9.

too, the span of international participation was considerable when former officer cadets from the *Junkerschule* at Bad Tölz gathered in town. Six hundred participants from 12 countries were there.[73]

It was in HIAG's best interest that the foreigners were visible at the veterans' rallies. Precisely these groups' war participation was of post-war importance to the Waffen-SS self-image as a European movement facing the Bolshevik menace – not as a German, national army of occupation. A key element of the veterans' perception of Waffen-SS' history was its pan-European character.[74]

At the same time, it was obvious that HIAG took its task seriously in supporting volunteers in need – regardless of their nationality. Over the 1950s, *Der Freiwillige* concurrently encouraged members to spend their holidays abroad helping out in hotels run by wives of imprisoned fellow soldiers. Members were also stimulated to help find jobs for former Norwegian, Flemish and Croatian volunteers. Active support of veterans from abroad was seriously meant, which one might realise by the fact that letters to HIAG might be written in the veteran's mother tongue – rather than in German.[75]

Also, rallies outside Germany saw participants from various nations. In September 1955, there was a Scandinavian Waffen-SS rally at Malmö where, among others, the head of the Danish SS veterans' association Erik Lærum addressed the audience. It was hardly coincidental that this meeting was held in Sweden. This was 'neutral ground' where it was possible to meet without any protests. Moreover, the city was the home base of Per Engdahl's *Nysvenska Rörelsen* (new Swedish movement) and, thus, one of Europe's few remaining bastions of Nazism.[76] It was remarkable, also, that several internationally renowned neo-Nazis took part in the rally.[77]

Veterans without uniformity

Between 1958 and 1978, German-American sociologist John Steiner followed a group of 300 mainly senior SS veterans He concluded that there was a significantly higher degree of explicit authoritarian and anti-democratic attitudes among these men compared to the control group from the *Wehrmacht*. While the veterans also harboured strong anti-Soviet sentiments, open Anti-Semitism was more rarely noticed.[78] Steiner's investigation was limited to German veterans and seems especially to have focused on

---

73. BAMA, N438/149, *Protokoll der Landessprechertagung am 4. und 5. Dezember im Hotel "Holländischer Hof" in Lich/Hessen, 19.1.1977*, p. 5.
74. See for instance "Brief eines französischenKameraden", *Der Ausweg, Nr. 7*, December 1951.
75. Der Freiwillige: Nr. 9, 1956, p. 15; Nr. 5, 1958,p. 23; Nr. 9, 1958, p. 29; Nr. 11, 1958, p. 24; Nr. 12, 1958, p. 25. Nr. 6, 1959, p. 29; Nr. 7, 1959, p. 24, Nr.7, 1959, p. 26.
76. Helene Lööw, *Nazismen i Sverige: 1924–1979 :pionjärerna, partierna, propagandan* (Ordfront Förl., 2004), p. 51ff.
77. BAMA, N756/405c, Newsletter from*CrP Informationsdienst (Club republikanischer Publizisten im Grünwalder Kreis), Dezember 1958* on HIAG. http://www.annefrank.org/nl/Wereldwijd/Monitor-Racisme-Homepage/Onderzoeksonderwerpen/Kroniek-extreemrechts/Oude-Kameraden/Portretten/, accessed on 7 November 2012.
78. Steiner in Dimsdale (1980), p. 441.

men who on the one hand had done fairly well after the war, yet had maintained a high degree of identification with the Waffen-SS. There were, however, also many former SS soldiers who did not join veterans' organisations or who in some cases became active participants in the leftist German peace movement or ended up as left wing icons like the German author Günther Grass.[79]

Although the organized Waffen-SS veterans undoubtedly reflected attitudes and beliefs that were shared among many other former SS soldiers, it is important to stress, that there was considerable variation among the surviving soldiers – a diversity conditioned not only by societal, national and generational factors but also by the fact that the Waffen-SS was stratified both by rank and by nationality. If we nevertheless try to characterise the Waffen-SS veterans, we might divide them into several groups.

A significant number joined veterans associations, which tried to make themselves palatable in a world, where the political return of Nazism appeared, over time, increasingly unlikely. This was not tantamount to reckoning with the past or to challenge the norms that had characterised the SS. Rather, this was an endeavour to redefine the Waffen-SS as a purely military phenomenon without relinquishing the ethos and the values that had characterised the organisation.

In the immediate aftermath of the Second World War as well as later, there were opposite currents of minor groups that would not necessarily discard Nazism as their political ideology. Therefore, HIAG and other veteran organisations were constantly challenged by forces from their own ranks. However, the openly right-wing extremist organisation of veterans remained a fringe phenomenon.

Apart from all these, there were – in Germany as well as abroad – a third group that did not want any affiliation with HIAG, because they felt no affinity to Waffen-SS as an organisation or because they feared becoming ostracized. In this group, one could undoubtedly place many of the *volksdeutsche* who were gang-pressed in to the Waffen-SS, but of course also many of those who the SS had labelled *fremdvölker*. This did not mean that veterans from the former Soviet Union, such as Estonians, Latvians and Ukrainians, fully failed to organize. Until the demise of the Soviet Union, their organisation, however, existed exclusively outside the eastern bloc, and they had little to gain from HIAG or the other Western European veterans' associations. Nor did they seek approval from the populations of their host countries, but were engaged in obtaining acknowledgement from their various diasporas. As we shall see below, the end of the Cold War created new possibilities for some of these veterans.

---

79. Duscheleit (2006).

Chapter Sixteen

THE WAFFEN-SS IN POST-WAR REMEMBRANCE CULTURE

The year is 1944, a section of Waffen-SS soldiers of *SS-Panzer-Grenadier Regiment 24 'Danmark'* are on patrol in the Oranienbaum Pocket. All of them are clad in SS uniforms and armed with rifles or machine guns. It is twilight and everything is calm. Prepared for action, the SS men steal forward searching for partisans. But wait a minute – there is something entirely amiss in chronology and geography. In fact, these are young men in a forest in Northern Zealand, and the year is 2013. They are re-enactors, members of *Fronthistorisk Forening Danmark* (the Society for Front History, Denmark) claiming to be re-enacting history.[1]

Today, most SS veterans have passed away, but the Waffen-SS survives in the cultural practices through which we commemorate and understand the past, such as the above-described re-enactment episode. In the contemporary world, Himmler's black corps simultaneously serves as an important signifier among extremist right-wing groups, as a rallying point in the nation-building processes in certain east European countries, as an ingredient in pop-culture and as a symbol of the darkest sides of twentieth-century history. In mainstream political culture Nazism and its symbols, especially the swastika and the SS runes, have come to represent the antithesis of democratic values. The story of the Third Reich and the SS in the words of Alec Ryrie thus serves an important role in contemporary western society:

> It was the struggle against Nazism which crystallised that great modern act of faith, 'human rights', which we all believe in even if we struggle to justify it philosophically. So when we retell that struggle, we reinforce and defend the sacred story on which our collective values depend.[2]

While this observation is valid regarding the overall political culture of western societies, there are important undercurrents where wholly different perspectives on the Waffen-SS live on. This chapter offers an introduction to the diverse ways in which the history of the Waffen-SS is used today.

---

1. Camilla Stockmann"Danske mænd klæder sig ud i nazi-uniformer og genopforer krigenved Østfronten, www.politiken.dk,12 January 2013.
2. Professor Alec Ryrie quoted in 'Why is the Public so Obsessed with Nazis?', *History Today*, vol. 70, no. 3, 2020.

Notions of the Waffen-SS

During the war, in the occupied countries, there was a general impression of Nazi collaborators as pathological deviants. The early post-war literature reinforced this notion by demonising the SS as the hub of Nazi crime. At the same time, there were many who attempted to delimit the SS, and by implication, the Waffen-SS, from the German population per se, in order to save the latter from accusations of complicity in war crimes. Characteristic of this trend was the book by the German professor Friedrich Meineckes, *Die deutsche Katastrophe: Betrachtungen und Erinnerungen*. Appearing in 1946, the book portrayed the Waffen-SS as an instrument that the Nazis had exploited for keeping the army in check and dominating Germany.[3] In this period, SS was seen as an omnipotent organisation and the personnel was frequently described as sadists or otherwise pathologically maladjusted individuals. This was a widespread understanding. In the summer of 1945, referring to the Italian criminologist and geneticist Lombroso, the Norwegian professor of psychiatry, Dr Gabriel Langfeldt, stated,

> Recently, I inspected a large group of [Norwegian Waffen-SS] front soldiers interned in the Ila prison. It was as if staring into the eyes of primeval human beings. Their sombre gaze, their often-disfigured faces and their dysplastic bodies; all reminded me of Lombroso's 'criminal man'.[4]

Conversely, post-war scientific research on the traitors' mentality and social background happening in many European countries showed that they were young men whose most important deviation from their peers was their political inclination. Modest intellectual capabilities, deviant character traits, previous sentences or dysfunctional upbringing seem to have had scant relevance.[5] Thus, having served their term in prison, most SS veterans managed to get a decent life and very few got into further contact with the criminal justice system.[6] These findings have been corroborated by later international research into perpetrators of Nazi war crimes.[7]

---

3. Friedrich Meinecke, *Die deutsche Katastrophe, Betrachtungen und Erinnerungen* (E. Brockhaus, 1946), p. 78.
4. Lindstad (2010), p. 5. Lombroso, whose theories are not recognised by modern science, opined that criminals possessed specific physical and mental characteristics that were inherited. For a similar description of Danish SS soldiers shortly after 1945 see Christiansen and Hyllested (2011), p. 38.
5. On Denmark see Karl O. Christiansen, "Recidivet blandt danske landssvigere", *Kriminalvidenskab, aarg. 58*, 1970, and Thomas Sigsgaard, *Psykologisk undersøgelse af mandlige landssvigere i Danmark under besættelsen* (Direktoratet for Fængselsvæsenet,1954. On the Netherlands see Mason (1952). On Norway see Fröshaug in Magnussen (1947), pp. 556–67. Same Author "A Social-Psychiatric Examination of Young Front-Combatants", in Nils Antoni et al. (eds.), *Acta Psychiatrica et Neurologica Scandinavica, Vol. XXIX*, 1954, pp. 443–65.
6. Fröshaug, in *Acta Psychiatrica et Neurologica Scandinavica, Vol. XXIX*, 1954, pp. 443–65, here 463.
7. Browning (1998), Welzer and Christ (2005).

However, it was not so much research as the political changes that helped redefine the image of the SS soldiers. In the late 1940s, in large segments of the western public, the start of the Cold War became very important for the impression of the German soldiers' performance on the eastern front. To a large extent, the Communist threat overshadowed the memory of Nazi misdeeds and the German war against the Soviet Union assumed a shine of justified self-defence. This re-interpretation was most distinct in Germany and the United States.[8] It merits mentioning, however, that this process had many layers and nuances and that it differed amongst countries. This narrative was fuelled by the massive Soviet atrocities under Stalin. The fact that no independent scholars had access to Soviet archives also contributed. Thus, the war in the east could not be adequately covered, and the research of the German war effort was almost exclusively limited to dedicated military historians who in many cases failed to fully integrate the crimes of the Nazi system in their analysis of military events.

In the early post-war years, the popular literature was not always negative in its assessment of the Waffen-SS, and several of the best-selling works of the time contained positive descriptions of SS men.[9] During the same period, a number of SS men published memoirs, novels and semi-documentary works on the war. These covered a continuum from Erich Kern's best-selling novels, over Skorzeny's and Meyer's memoirs, to Hauser's and Steiner's claims of writing the history of the Waffen-SS. In their different ways, all these books endeavoured to present the Waffen-SS men as anti-Communist élite fighters.[10]

Doing an online search on 'Waffen-SS' in the database of *Worldcat* in the summer of 2021, around 4,500 hits appeared and a similar number of items can be purchased in one of the major on-line stores.[11] A large proportion of these are books like the ones mentioned above. They are representative of the attitudes found at websites like the *Feldgrau.com*, existing since 1995. In that literature and on such websites and within similar social media groups, the Waffen-SS is regarded as an insulated military phenomenon and the organisations' relation to the overall SS is mostly reduced to an issue of minor significance. This way, the Waffen-SS is being distanced from the SS, the police, the concentration camps, Holocaust and the brutal European occupation policy in stark contrast to the reality of events as described in this book.[12]

---

8. See Ronald M. Smelser and Edward J. Davies, *The Myth of the Eastern Front: The Nazi-Soviet War in American Popular Culture* (Cambridge University Press, 2008).

9. George L. Mosse, *Fallen Soldiers: Reshaping the Memory of the World Wars* (Oxford University Press, 1990), p. 210. Heinz G. Konsalik, *Der Arzt von Stalingrad* (Kindler, 1956), p. 319. On this novel and Konsalik's work see Maggie Sargeant, "Memory, distortion and the war in German popular culture: the case of Konsalik" in William Kidd and Brian Murdoch (eds.), *Memory and Memorials: The Commemorative Century* (Ashgate, 2004), pp. 195–206.

10. Jerk Wiking, *Endkampf um Berlin* (Durer, 1947), Holter (1951); Willem Sluyse, *Die Jünger und die Dirnen*, (Dürer-Verlag, 1954).

11. 4.410 books registered at worldcat.com found on 4 June 2021. 4.697 hits at Amazon.com found on 30 June 2015.

12. Williamson (1995), p. 8.

Often, the 'fascination' literature is created around accounts by veterans, who describe their experiences, as well as personal letters and diaries and the occasional official document – fragments of war diaries, muster rolls, etc. The enthusiasm for personal and technical details is enormous.[13] This approach is often explained as a wish to let the veterans speak for themselves, as they have never before had the opportunity.[14] Normally, authors of this kind of literature claim that they will not judge but leave the verdict to the reader. The reality is, however, that this literature is characterised by a flagrant lack of critical approach to the veterans' stories, and an obvious fascination and heroization is easily detected in language, use of imagery and choices of themes.

The enormous amount of publications on the Waffen-SS and the fact that even rather ambiguous works are to be had from big, well-established websites indicate that there is a huge commercial audience – presumably primarily consisting of males. A vast unified fascination landscape hardly exists, rather the audience consists of overlapping societies and groupings like amateur historians, collectors and re-enactors, speculators and right-wing extremists.

The commercial aspects of the Waffen-SS fascination may be illustrated by a Danish court case. In 2012, a storm arose in Danish media as two men were discovered having stolen, over quite some time, volumes of material on the Waffen-SS from the regional and the national archives. The subsequent sentences of 24 and 19 months' imprisonment, respectively – relatively severe from a Danish point of view – were handed down because the theft had gone on systematically for several years. According to official accounts, the thieves had stolen what amounted to two seven feet of shelf space or more than 1,000 documents. A large part of the documents was about Danish SS members and had been filed with their court cases from the post-war judicial reckoning. The accused declared that they were writing a book about a Danish Waffen-SS volunteer. However, the case also disclosed that, in a number of cases, the material had been sold. Thus, one of the thieves told that on one occasion he had sold a Waffen-SS Salary Book for 17,000 kroner (ca. £ 1,500).[15] Later discoveries in the case indicate that much more had been stolen than that which the thieves had actually been sentenced for.[16]

---

13. See for example the French four volumes encyclopaedia on Waffen-SS: Charles Trang, *Dictionnaire de la Waffen-SS, 4 vol.* (Heimdal, 2012). This, almost 2,000 pages A4, briefly mentions the most notorious crimes, but is primarily characterised by a huge number of photos, technical and biographical details on various Waffen-SS units and personnel.

14. See for an example Williamson (1995), p. 9.

15. The case was extensively covered by the Danish press. As to the sentence see http://jyllands-posten.dk/indland/politiretsvaesen/article5492162.ece assesed 24 February 2022. See also the report *Sikringstiltag I Statens Arkivers læsesale*, Statens Arkiver, Copenhagen, June 2013, p. 3 at http://www.sa.dk/media(4894,1030)/Sikringstiltag_i_Statens_Arkivers_l%C3%A6sesale.pdf, accesssed 1 November 2013.

16. Martin Q. Magnussen, *De forsvundne nazidokumenter, Den ufortalte historie om tyveriet fra Rigsarkivet*, (Grønningen 1, 2019). There is nothing new in SS artefacts being stolen. For example, in 1979, when the highly-decorated Waffen-SS general Wilhelm Bittrich died, unknown burglars thoroughly searched his home in their quest for militaria. Schulz and Wegmann (2003), p. 116.

Figure 16.1 Soldiers from Frikorps Danmark during training in occupied Poland (Frihedsmuseet)

This also stresses the SS' commercial and emotional attraction. Thus, collectors must constantly watch out for fakes. These might be artefacts like uniforms and medals, but also false veterans. Much memoir literature is characterised by accounts that have either been written under pen names, or are not easily verified with respect to the authors' claims of being former Waffen-SS soldiers. This snag is known also from other kinds of memoirs linked to extreme situations. Examples are false biographies concerning the Holocaust, and the veracity of whole or half-documentary novels like those of Sven Hassel (pen name of the Danish-born Børge Willy Redsted Pedersen) and Guy Sajers have been doubted.[17] Similar examples of either dubious or outright bogus accounts about service with the Waffen-SS are known, too.[18]

Roleplaying in Waffen-SS Uniforms

The re-enactment milieu is one of the sub-cultures where intensive dedication to Waffen-SS is found. This so-called revival of the past – which, of course, is no revival at all but production and communication of certain interpretations of history – have

---

17. Carrard (2010), pp. 26ff and 35ff.
18. Peter Neumann, *Other Men's Graves* (Weidenfeld and Nicolson, 1958).

early modern roots and embraces a broad thematic and chronological spectrum.[19] Military re-enactment is particularly popular, and the Second World War seems to be a very attractive period. Moreover, there is a lot that indicates that, among the popular, conspicuous re-enactment groups, German troops are predominantly prevalent – not least the Waffen-SS.[20] Large, well-organised Waffen-SS re-enactment groups are found mainly in the Anglo-Saxon world. Not only do they have original uniforms and authentic weapons at their disposal, some also possess extensive parks of vehicles and other equipment. On certain occasions, Waffen-SS re-enactments are presented to a larger audience such as at public shows at museums and historical festivals, etc.[21]

As in all re-enactment, visual authenticity and precision are of paramount importance. Thus, uniforms must be correct, and the equipment must be original or precise replicas. Therefore, the military expertise that such shows offer to the public is mainly of a purely military-technical nature. What is shown is, generally, the use of military equipment, application of battle procedures and daily life in the field. The interpretation of history, which is thus offered to the audiences, is typically devoid of anything but the most superficial references to Nazism. Moreover, Waffen-SS'extensive catalogue of war crimes and their significant role in the war of extermination is not addressed. Several re-enactment group websites comprise general declarations distancing themselves from political extremism, and they profess not to be Nazis, while a number of websites also give shorter or longer descriptions of the Nazi regime's wrongdoings. However, this is rarely reflected in the actual shows, where the Nazi context is not integrated. This leads to ahistorical and unrealistic communication about the élite Waffen-SS soldiers, which lack information on killings and atrocities against civilians and prisoners-of-war.[22]

In many cases, a considerable apologetic relativism towards Waffen-SS' crimes can be found on re-enactor websites. For instance, the British re-enactment group *Kameraden bis zum Ende, 4.1.Pz.Gr.Rgt.4 'Der Führer'*, re-enacts actions of the *Regiment der Führer*, the unit perpetrating the massacre in Oradour. On its website, this group writes; 'Although the "DF" Rgt. like many other Armed Forces were implicated in atrocities which happened throughout the war, we believe in taking an un-biased view, all nations carried out atrocities even the ones who won. To say that the Germans alone committed

19. For a broad definition of re-enactment as an analytical instrument see Jerome De Groot, "Review Essay. Affect and empathy: re-enactment and performance as/in history", *Rethinking History 15, No. 4*, 2011, pp. 587–99.
20. See the thread about re-enactment at Axis History Forum http://forum.axishistory.com/viewtopic.php?f=40&t=173714, accessed 24 February 2022.
21. On several occasions, thus, the Danish museum village 'Andelslandsbyen' at Holbæk has used Waffen-SS re-enactors at their arrangements. Similarly, at the *Jydske Dragonregiments Veteranpanserforenings* (Jutland Dragoon Armoured Veterans' Association) annual Classic Military Show.
22. If the state-owned Russian TV Russia Today is to be trusted, Latvian Waffen-SS re-enactors have performed patriotic tuition in kindergardens clad in Latvian SS soldiers' uniforms http://rt.com/news/nazi-patriotic-lesson-kindergarten-latvia-012/

them, worse still solely the Waffen-SS, is a historically inaccurate and an uneducated view (sic!).'[23] At an earlier website of another British re-enactor group, dressing up as *Division Totenkof* soldiers, these were described as being 'like all other young men caught in a web of ideology, politics and total war, which is incomprehensible to the average man in the street of the year 2000'.[24]

Waffen-SS Mythology in Contemporary Armed Forces

Military professionals from various nations have long been fascinated by an alleged German 'Genious for War' – studying and imitating it in order to prevail in war.[25] This probably explains why Waffen-SS symbols and other references to the organisation occasionally appear in contemporary western armed forces.

The roots of the matter may be traced back to the early post-war years, when former German officers, including a number of Waffen-SS generals, were employed by the US Army Historical Service to write accounts of combat at the eastern front.[26] During the late forties and early fifties a number of leading SS generals, such as Hausser, Gille and Steiner attempted to promote the Waffen-SS as a model force from which much could be learned about contemporary warfare. In 1952, Steiner was among the driving forces in founding in Munich the *Gesellschaft für Wehrkunde* (society for defence knowledge) a lobbying organisation working for the re-armament of West Germany. This organisation quickly grew to having local groups all over the Federal Republic.[27] As a member of the HIAG leadership, this way too Steiner had opportunities for corresponding with the federal government.[28] However, this and the membership of the *Gesellschaft für Wehrkunde* were far from Steiner's only leverage. In 1951, he published the book *Die Wehridee des Abendlandes* (Defence Notion of the Occident) in which he argued that the European Waffen-SS troops under his command were the forerunners of NATO, since they – just like the European resistance movements – had fought for European ideals and freedom.[29] More books

23. http://www.panzergrenadier.net/df/about.php, accessed 24 February 2022.
24. http://www.totenkopf.co.uk, accessed 1 February 2012.
25. Samuel J. Newland, *Victories are not Enough. Limitations of the German Way of War*, (US Army War College, 2005), pp. 1f. Smelser and Davies (2008).
26. Kevin Soutor, "To Stem the Red Tide. The German Report Series and its Effect on American Defense Doctrine, 1948–1954", The Journal of Military History, No. 57, October 1993, p. 653-688. For a full list of reports thus written see *Guide to Foreign Military Studies, 1945-1954* [catalogue & Index] (Historical Division, Headquarters, United States Army, Europe, 1954).
27. Meyer in Dickerhof, p. 559.
28. BAK, B136/5147, Letter of 3 March 1954 from Steiner to Bundeskanzler Adenauer.
29. Felix M. Steiner, *Die Wehridee des Abendlandes* (Parma-Edition, 1951). A draft for this book was made in the early autumn 1949. At that time, Steiner had a work in two volumes in mind entitled "Der Zusammenbruch des totalen Krieges" to be published under the nom de plume of Felix Y. Ryk. See NAWA, 263, ZZ-16, Box 50, Lag Steiner, Felix, Note inGerman of 17 September 1949 concerning *SS-Obergruppenführer* Steiner.

followed in which he expanded his assertions and further styled himself as a military innovator.[30] This self-staging, however, did not persuade every one of his military qualities nor of the degree of his loyalty to western, democratic values.[31]

In general, the attempts by Waffen-SS veterans in the German Federal Republic to gain themselves a military role in the post-war Bundeswehr came to nothing, save the admission of a few dozen officers up to the rank of lieutenant colonel.[32] Also in other parts of Europe, such as Sweden and Denmark, one may find cases where SS veterans were employed as military advisors or tutored military cadets.[33] This, however, seems to have remained a fringe phenomenon, and the official policy was clearly to keep those who had fought in the rank of the Germans at an arm's length. However, there were to some extent interactions between the veterans and the armed forces. As part of its outreach to German veterans, the Bundeswehr participated in various HIAG gatherings, and alone in 1975–1976, *Bundeswehr* representatives were present at 27 HIAG events.[34]

This complex and uneasy relationship continued after the veterans no longer could be regarded a military asset and it increasingly took the form of outright fascination with SS-symbols among certain groups in the armed forces. In the 1990s, in the Danish army, a battalion created a nationality badge looking like the one worn by the Danes of the Waffen-SS. This, however, was promptly stopped by the Chief Army Operational Command, even before it reached the production line. This was a particularly sensitive matter as the battalion was bound for Bosnia where *Division Nordland* containing many Danish SS soldiers had been stationed in the autumn of 1943.[35] In 2002, another Danish example occurred as a wooden signpost *Forsynerpassagen* (suppliers' passage) put up centrally in the Danish Camp Viking in Afghanistan sported three SS runes in lieu of the three letters s.[36] In Afghanistan, contingents of other countries have made similar

---

30. Felix Steiner, *Von Clausewitz bis Bulganin; Erkenntnisse und Lehren einer Wehrepoche* (Deutscher Heimat-Verlag, 1956); Felix Steiner, *Die Freiwilligen; Idee und Opfergang* (Plesse Verlag, 1958); Felix M. Steiner, *Die Armee der Geächteten* (Plesse Verlag, 1963). Steiner's post-war life is merely cursorily dealt with in the only scholarly based work on him, Gingerich in Smelser and Syring (2003), pp. 431–40.

31. See for example the review by R.V. *Hume in International Affairs, Vol. 34, No. 1,* 1958, p. 85.

32. MacKenzie (1997), p. 137.

33. Sten Krarup, "Lærum-sagen 1954", *Krigshistorisk Tidsskrift*, april 2006, pp. 3–26. Gyllenhaal and Westberg (2008), p. 288.

34. Wilke (2011), p. 268. Sauer (1977), p. 84ff.

35. Interview on 5 June 2011 of former Chief Army Operational Command, Lieutenant General Kjeld Hillinsø.

36. Erik Thomle, "Dansk lejr med tragisk klang", *Jyllandsposten,*27 March 2002. Anders Lange, "Fortsat uro om skilt med SS-runer", *Jyllandsposten*, 3 April 2002. See also the debate on the case in *Folketinget* (Danish Parliament) on 10 April 2002 as well as Minister for Defence Svend Aage Jensby's written reply of 10 April 2002 to queries Nos 1531–32 and 1546–49 by MPs Villy Søvndal and Søren Søndergaard. The signpost was skilfully made and the explanation that it had been too difficult to cut rounded s in the wood is hardly believable – r and p had been nicely rounded.

uncouth impressions using SS symbols. In 2010, two Czech NCOs were dismissed for having worn, a year previously, helmets with the divisional badges of *Hohenstaufen* and *Dirlewanger* engraved. A third Czech soldier was repatriated later as it appeared that he had acquired a tattoo with the SS motto *Meine Ehre Heißt Treue*.[37] In 2010, a section of US Marine Corps snipers in Afghanistan had themselves photographed posing in front of a Stars-and-Stripes banner and a blue colour with SS runes.[38]

It is notable, that whenever such transgressions have happened they have been widely condemned by the authorities, as the political culture of most western democracies is founded on the notion of Nazism as an absolute evil. Indeed, all the examples of Waffen-SS fascination quoted above are unlikely to be representative of general culture. If one, however, looks east of the former iron curtain, the memory culture related to the Waffen-SS looks slightly different.

East European Waffen-SS Comemoration

While the SS volunteers, collaborators and other supporters of Nazism increasingly have been marginalised in the commemoration culture of Western Europe and the United States, the fall of the Berlin Wall and the collapse of the Soviet Union opened a new politico-historical front, which had so far been relatively under-researched. The emergence of independent states on the soil of the late Soviet Union, and the re-creation of existing states, once one-party dictatorships, into post-Communist communities challenged the ideological and historical-cultural foundations of these societies. Strife developed between old and new élites, and the former East Bloc countries came under considerable stress in the transformation to democracies with market economies. In its wake came redundancy and differentiation of salaries as well as new consumption patterns and lifestyles into the once monolithic and authoritarian communities. The shifts of power entailed renewed discussion of, among other things, the Soviet war crimes and the collaboration with the Nazis.

The result was a complex clash of understandings concerning national histories. In the 1990s and 2000s obvious divisions appeared between, on the one side Russia and, on the other, a number of other countries – primarily the Baltic states, Ukraine and Poland. In Russia, the victory over Fascism in the Great Patriotic War was the one most uniting feat of them all and it became a significant source of positive identification with the state and, thus, a key to the legitimacy of the state.[39] Another important aspect of the war's legacy was Russia's insistence on being seen as a leading great power.

---

37. "Czech troops in Nazi symbols row", *BBC News*, 10 November 2009; "Analyst: Ignorance, crisis of values explains Czech soldiers with SS symbols", *Radio Praha*, 4 March 2010.
38. Adam Weinstein, "Marines Sport Nazi SS Flag in Afghanistan", www.motherjones.com, 9 February 2012. "US Marine sniper unit photographed with 'Nazi SS' flag", *BBC News* 9 February 2012.
39. Tatiana Zhurzhenko, "The geopolitics of memory", *Eurozine* 10 May 2007 at www.eurozine. com.

This notion embraced the 1939 Molotov-Ribbentrop agreement's territorial gains, controversial still as late as the 2000s, as well as those of 1945 after the Allied attack on Japan. It also had a lot to do with the Soviet Union being the largest continental power of the joint Allied effort to eradicate Nazism and liberate Europe, for which reason it claimed a moral right to control the central and eastern parts of the continent and expected a permanent seat in the United Nations' Security Council. In the 1990s and 2000s, this alleged right was instrumentalised by Russian foreign policy to have a say in external issues concerning the Baltic countries and Ukraine. Apart from the unsolved border and minority problems – Russian claims concerned these countries' alleged attempts to revive Fascism.[40]

Not least in Estonia and Latvia would the Waffen-SS soldiers play a role. Every year on the 16th of March, the anniversary of the Latvian Legion's first employment has been commemorated by a parade in the Riga city centre. Until, at the end of the 1990s, the activity became too contentious, a number of key persons participated; the president, the minister for defence and the chief of defence.[41] For a while, 1998–2002, the day was a national holiday because the legionnaires were regarded as the protagonists of Latvian independence.[42] A frequent argument used by the legionnaires for donning another country's uniform was that 'we wore German uniforms, but at heart, we were Latvians'.[43] Throughout the first decades of the twenty-first century a virtual diplomatic war was waged by Russian and Latvian authorities over the legion's characteristics, its role and its participation in the Nazi misdeeds.

In Estonia, too, the Waffen-SS veterans and others who had fought for the Germans made their strong impress on national commemoration. After the independence, on the initiative of Estonian as well as foreign Waffen-SS veterans and sympathisers, memorial plagues were put up in public locations. The Narva area was the geographical centre of this Waffen-SS centred commemorative culture. In 1944, for more than six months, SS units consisting of many Estonians kept superior Soviet forces at bay in this frontier area with Russia. From the perspective of many Estonians, in this way the Waffen-SS troops protected Estonia against the return of the Communists. It was glossed over, though, that the very same forces prohibited the liberation of

---

40. In the spring of 2014, inter alia, in the run up to Russia's annexation of Ukrainian Crimea, it was repeatedly claimed by Moscow authorities that the Kiev government replacing the absconded former pro-Russian President Viktor Fedorovych Yanukovych, was characterised by Fascist elements from Western Ukraine. For another example see A. Dyukov and V.Simidel, "The Latvian SS Legion and the Nuremberg Tribunal's Decisions", *International Affairs* Vol. 57 [published by the Russian ministry of foreign affairs], 2011, pp. 232–38.

41. Eva-Clarita Onken, *Revisionismus schon vor der Geschichte: aktuelle Kontroversen in Lettland um die Judenvernichtung und die lettische Kollaboration während der nationalsozialistischen Besatzung* (Wissenschaft und Politik, 1998), pp. 10ff. and97ff.

42. Formally, the holyday had been consecrated the memory of all, who fought in the Second World War, whether with German or with Soviet forces.

43. Onken (1998), p. 96.

prisoners-of-war and Jewish prisoners from the local concentration camps. Moreover, Estonian troops' participation in the Klooga massacre immediately prior to the Red Army's seizure of the country was either ignored or vehemently doubted. Perhaps even more telling was the re-burial of the highly decorated Baltic SS officer Alfons Rebane, who, after the war, had stayed in the UK and, later, in Germany. In 1999, his earthly remains, until then, since 1976, buried in Germany, were transferred to Estonia. The transfer and re-burial had all the characteristics of an official military ceremony. While the urn with his ashes was carried to the grave by Estonian officer cadets, other troops formed a lane.[44] Another noticeable contribution to Estonian commemoration was the issue, in 2008, of a calendar with photos of original recruiting posters for Estonian Waffen-SS. According to international media, the calendar was sold out in 12 days.[45]

The Myth of the Waffen-SS Will Live On

The difference in how official and semi-official circles interact with the Waffen-SS' history in the 'west' and the 'east' is not a simple question of right and wrong but relates to different societal experiences and political cultures during the twentieth century. Interpretations of the past change depending on the point in time of society's looking back, and at the same time history use is always a matter of power relations and the configuration of society. The use of the Waffen-SS is an obvious example. There is no everlasting historical narrative, and in liberal societies, everyone should be given the opportunity of interpreting, researching and communicating history. Therefore, it is not likely that the undercurrents of Waffen-SS history use described in this chapter are likely to die away with the passing of time. However, accepting a pluralistic use of history is not the same as accepting that the context should be forgotten – the context in which the Waffen-SS soldiers served, their misdeeds and the character of the system they fought for. Thus, serious, research-based history concerning the Waffen-SS and its communication should always focus on Nazism and Hitler's war of extermination – that is one of the main contexts you need to keep track of if you want to understand the role of the Waffen-SS and its soldiers. Such an approach may well go hand in hand with acknowledging that far from all Waffen-SS soldiers fought zealously and voluntarily for the Third Reich. Most east European SS soldiers are a case in point here.

However, when SS' ideology and SS crimes are forgotten, played down or explained away there is very good reason to be on guard. More often than not such use of history may be linked to political projects in opposition to the values and norms associated with pluralistic, democratic societies.

---

44. For a detailed coverage of the re-burial with photos see "Endlich in der Heimaterde, die Umbettung des Standartenführers Alfons Rabane [sic!]", *Der Freiwillige Nr. 2*, 2000, pp. 17–20.
45. http://www.telegraph.co.uk/news/worldnews/europe/estonia/3965268/Russiansprotest-at-Estonia-SS-calendar.html, accessed on 4 July 2012.

EPILOGUE

THE NAZI'S EUROPEAN SOLDIERS

On 24 April 1945, a scarce and poorly equipped jumble of SS fanatics, young boys and middle-aged reservists arrived in Bavaria as reinforcements for the 13th SS corps. There, under the impressive designation 38. SS-Panzer-Grenadier-Division 'Nibelungen' they were now facing American troops. The name was a reference to the German composer Richard Wagner's famous four-opera cycle, *The Ring of the Nibelung*, based on his interpretation of Norse Sagas and the German Medieval heroic poem *Nibelungenlied*. The complete work, 15 hours, ends in the *Götterdämmerung* (the twilight of the gods), the end of the world. It is fair to guess that the reason why the SS leadership, in March 1945, decided on this name was their premonition of the imminent end fight on German soil. Initially, it had been considered to call the division *Junkerschule Tölz* after the institution providing the officers.

The division's designation bears witness to the fact that, as in all cases where the central SS authorities were involved, ideology was in focus. From what we know about the Nazis' view of the military situation in spring 1945 it seems reasonable to assume that the name Nibelungen was meant to symbolise that, now, the last fanatical warriors plunged themselves into battle. Now, it was neck or nothing, and if the enemy was not stopped, Armageddon waited – a downfall that, according to Hitler, the Germans deserved were they not strong enough to win the war.

But Himmler's last array of warriors did not fight to death, and although millions of soldiers and civilians fell victim to the Third Reich's struggle, the day of doom envisaged by the top Nazis did not materialize for everyone – not even within the Waffen-SS. Here and there along the front, Waffen-SS soldiers fought to the last round, committed suicide or went underground to fight on for Nazism as 'werewolves', but, in May 1945, the vast majority surrendered alongside the army. Moreover, it was a minority of the Waffen-SS veterans who continued fighting for the re-birth of Nazism after the war had ended.

In that sense, the experiment of training an army of political soldiers never fully succeeded. In the end, the combination of ideological tuition, cultivation of an élite identity, and the creation of a judicial system identifying, segregating and punishing those who failed had to yield to realities. This is hardly surprising. History offers plenty of examples of self-styled élites, who in the end, when faced with obliteration, displayed limited courage and devotion to the cause that they claimed to possess. Whether the Jacobins during the French revolution, the Bolshevik Cheka or the SS, they did not live up to their own élitist self-perception, but were, nevertheless, merciless and inhumane towards those segregated from the community, they had defined. Thus, one of the provinces of Waffen-SS' expertise was, precisely, participation in Nazi crimes.

Seen from Himmler's and the Nazi leadership's perspective, therefore, the Waffen-SS was not a failure. Although in the last phases of the war, most soldiers had been forcibly drafted and did not intend to die for the cause of the Third Reich, they were commanded by officers and NCOs, the majority of whom were strong believers in Nazi ideology. The mixture of either lukewarm, sceptical or ideologically dedicated SS men varied over time and with the various formations. In divisions populated by what the Nazi derogatively called *Fremdvölker*, many soldiers had been forcibly drafted, they were poorly equipped and the military value was modest. But, for extended periods, many formations possessed excellent fighting power, and a number of divisions were among the most effective German formations of this war. For these SS men, the will to fight fitted hand-in-glove with their readiness to kill not only hostile troops, but also civilian men, women and children if this fitted into the Nazi scheme of things.

As demonstrated throughout this book, there are, for most SS-units, examples of how they committed serious atrocities and, compared with the *Wehrmacht*, the Waffen-SS' complicity in such endeavours was disproportionately high. From the formations, where much source material can be found, a continuous pattern is seen of war crimes, atrocities against civilians and participation in the Holocaust. This is true of divisions like *Wiking, Das Reich, Prinz Eugen* and *Reichsführer-SS* as well as the SS brigades. The crimes committed by these units are relatively well-documented, but among the other divisions the level of atrocities was high as well, though it is not possible, today, to create a comprehensive picture as the sources are few and fragmentary.

One important explanation of the Waffen-SS' higher frequency of crimes is that a core of convinced Nazis and early recruited soldiers carried on as trendsetters of many Waffen-SS units throughout the war. When private soldiers of Division Wiking took part in the Holocaust during the onslaught on the Soviet Union it can be explained, for example, by ideological motives. However, atrocities took place also in units whose personnel were not necessarily voluntary or fervent Nazis. Here, the officer corps played a key role. The members were representatives of a culture where crimes against civilians and prisoners-of-war were accepted as solutions to military problems as for instance in the case of suppression of partisans or when there was a shortage of personnel for guarding prisoners. Waffen-SS' crimes were not primarily a product of individual actions nor merely the circumstances of war – although both might have been parts of the equation – it was the corporate ideological culture itself that was the main reason.

When studying the universe of Nazi ideology and horrendous crimes within which the Waffen-SS worked, an alien and brutal world appears. This does not mean that the soldiers were psychopaths or deviants. This book confirms, what other investigations have already demonstrated: the Nazi henchmen were normal human beings and not mentally ill. The historical, social and geographical context within which they operated – the Nazi racial state – created a framework radically different from what most of us know today, and, for that reason, to the participants in this war, their deeds often made sense. In particular, among the German and Northern European soldiers there was a strong belief in racial distinction and society's right, or even obligation, to regulate human reproduction on the basis of eugenics. It was a time of many a political and ideological dream of grand solutions and utopian societal schemes. In this spirit the notion of totalitarianism was coined by the Italian Fascists as a positive expression of the resolve to subordinate the whole of society to one single will.

The SS order and the Waffen-SS were extreme and radical expressions of such political, ideological and cultural currents – organisations that went further than any other important institution in the late modern era to create – what Erving Goffman coined – the 'total institution'. This means an institution that endeavours *Gleichschaltung* and all-encompassing control of all involved individuals. This terminology is mostly used in the study of prisons and mental hospitals, where those present are deprived of their liberty and where the authorities conduct surveillance of the inmates around the clock. In the SS order, this direct physical form of control was replaced by a multidirectional regimentation and processes of social control which included ideological indoctrination and the system of SS-laws and punishments, as well as the creation of a violent and Nazified culture. These factors combined to create norms, rules and sanctions that heavily influenced the SS men's conduct. The entire private sphere of these men was regimented, and ideology a constant presence. The SS men had to have the leadership's approval of their spouses as well as their possible socialising with 'other races'. Furthermore, the use of symbols such as runes, skulls, Nazi Christmas candles, celebrations of holidays and solstice and other rituals helped foster the experience of SS as an order. In other words, being an SS man was to be a way of living encompassing every corner of life – leisure, upbringing, sexual activity and war.

The overwhelming majority of the early recruited SS men were willing members of this universe and, since throughout the war, the Waffen-SS recruited its officers and NCOs primarily among Nazi veterans and the ideologically most fervent soldiers. Thus, by and large, they became exactly the soldiers Himmler craved for. But as the war dragged on and began in earnest to take its toll of the Nazi society's economic, political and demographic capital, the Waffen-SS developed in a more pragmatic direction; SS' military branch began moving away from the original order notion in its purest form. This was to some extent a conscious choice, partly because of the chaos of war which entailed lack of central control and caused improvisations and a certain modification of ideology. In light of the ever-increasing need of soldiers men were also procured outside the ranks of Germans and those deemed of Germanic origin and they were often drafted involuntarily.

In this way, one might describe the Waffen-SS as it changed over the war years, as a sort of colonial army. The officer corps and the soldiery of a number of core units were from the mother country, but surrounded by indigenous units that were required to mobilise sufficient personnel. These had 'white' officers and were less exquisitely equipped and trained than the core troops, and they were not regarded as equals. But they were indispensable, and to keep them motivated it was necessary that the colonial power showed them some respect and granted the individual groups certain prerogatives such as local home rule or vague promises of autonomy and the use of symbols and rites associated with their homeland.

The colonial army metaphor makes it probably easier to understand the relation between the core SS and its periphery and it explains why many of the *Fremdvölker* soldiers did not fight wholeheartedly and, in many cases, deserted. While, in April 1945, the mainly German soldiers of *Division Nibelungen* put up some resistance to the Americans, a number of units staffed by *Fremdvölker* such as *Division Neu Türkistan* or *Handschar* had long ago lost their fighting enthusiasm. In these formations, the personnel neither believed in the German cause nor did they experience any serious attempts at integration, which might otherwise have been conducive to their willingness to fight.

But with formations with many Germanic, *Volksdeutsche* and Reich German volunteers, though a few being not genuinely voluntary, the case was different. In such formations, a significant part of the Waffen-SS soldier's pattern of behaviour was in accordance with the SS top tier's wishes. As a rule, the SS believers among the soldiers together with the officers constituted a critical mass securing conformity and action along the lines of the leadership's wishes. Thus, the Waffen-SS might be held together by a combination of ideological persuasion and career ambitions with the addition of fear and passive following. This worked as long as the SS continued to be a strong organisation in a relatively well-functioning society, but as the war drew to its end, signs of dissolution showed. Towards the end, the Waffen-SS' inner cohesion was weak. This is confirmed by the fact that, to a large extent, the veterans did not organise after the war, and if they did it was primarily on the basis of nationality with none or little co-operation across the borders.

Veteran organisations like HIAG, with obvious right-wing extreme characteristics, were never to become powerful organisations or any kind of threat against the established democratic order in spite of many members' continued Nazi mentality. What might give rise to some apprehension today, is not the presence of the very last veterans who cultivate a whitewashed version of their own past and the history of the Third Reich. It is much more disquieting to watch the continued disinclination by many – mainly men – to see the Waffen-SS as the organisation it was, namely a willing and effective tool for the Nazis' perpetration of their crimes. It was an institution to whom war was boundless and the creation of a Nazified Europe was their raison d'être. Nevertheless, fascination of the Waffen-SS is often displayed with a view only to their supposed military qualities and without any interest in the immoral and criminal nature of their efforts. As it appears in this book, this is indeed a misunderstanding and a distortion of history. In the military SS, ideology, norms and values were fused with military action creating the arguably most brutal and criminal military organisation of our time.

APPENDIX

Waffen-SS Rank – British Rank

Reichsführer-SS – None
SS-Oberst-Gruppenführer – General
SS-Obergruppenführer – Lieutenant General
SS-Gruppenführer – Major General
SS-Brigadeführer – Brigadier
SS-Oberführer – None
SS-Standartenführer – Colonel
SS-Obersturmbannführer – Lieutenant Colonel
SS-Sturmbannführe – Major
SS-Hauptsturmführer – Captain
SS-Obersturmführer – Lieutenant
SS-Untersturmführer – Second Lieutenant

Non-commissioned Officer Ranks

SS-Sturmscharführer – Warrant Officer Class 1
SS-Hauptscharführer – Warrant Officer Class 2
SS-Oberscharführer – Staff Sergeant
SS-Scharführer – Sergeant
SS-Unterscharführer – Coporal/Bombardier

Soldiers

SS-Rottenführer – Lance Corporal
SS-Sturmmann – Senior Private
SS-Oberschüze – None
SS-Schüze – Private

LIST OF ABBREVIATIONS

AO – Auslands Organisation der NSDAP
APA – Aussenpolitisches Amt
DNSAP – Danmarks Nationalsocialistiske Arbejderparti
DP – Displaced Persons
HIAG – Hilfsgemeinschaft auf Gegenseitigkeit der Angehörigen der ehemaligen Waffen-SS.
HSSPF – Höherer SS- und Polizeiführer
LAH – Leibstandarte
LVF – Légion des volontaires français contre le bolchévisme
NS – Nasjonal Samling
NSB – Nationaal-Socialistische Beweging
NSDAP – Nationalsozialistische Deutsche Arbeiterpartei
NSDAP – Nationalsozialistische Deutsche Arbeiterpartei – Nordschleswig
NSKK – Nationalsozialistisches Kraftfahrkorps
NVA – Nationale Volksarmee
OD – Ordnungsdienst
OKH – Oberkommando des Heeres
OKW – Oberkommando der Wehrmacht
OT – Organisation Todt
RAD – Reichsarbeitsdienst
RFSS – Reichsführer-SS
ROA – Russkaja Osvoboditel'naja Armija
RONA – Russkaja Osvoboditelnaya Narod'naya Armija
RSHA – Reichssicherheitshauptamt
RuSHA – SS-Rasse- und Siedlungshauptamt
SA – Sturmabteilung
SD – Sicherheitsdienst
SFK – Serbische Freiwilligen-Korps
SFK – Sudetendeutsches Freikorps
SHAEF – Supreme Headquarters Allied Expeditionary Force
VNV – Vlaamsch Nationaal Verbond
VOMI – Volksdeutsche Mittelstelle

BIBLIOGRAPHY

Addison, Paul and Angus Calder. *Time to Kill: The Soldiers Experience in the West, 1939–1945.* Pimlico, 1997.

Allen Michael. 'Oswald Pohl – Chef der SS-Wirtschaftsunternehmen'. In *Die SS: Elite unter dem Totenkopf. 30 Lebensläufe,* edited by Ronald Smelser and Enrico Syring. Schöningh, 2003.

Altman, Ilja. *Kholokost na territorii SSSR. Entsiklopedija.* Tsentr Kholokost, 2009.

Andrzej, Wirth. *The Stroop Report: The Jewish Quarter of Warsaw Is No More!* Pantheon Books, 1979.

Angrick, Andrej. *Besatzungspolitik und Massenmord: die Einsatzgruppe D in der südlichen Sowjetunion 1941–1943.* Hamburger Edition, 2003.

Angrick, Andrej and Peter Klein. *Die 'Endlösung' in Riga: Ausbeutung und Vernichtung, 1941–1944.* Wissenschaftliche Buchgesellschaft, 2006.

Antoni, Nils. *Acta Psychiatrica et Neurologica Scandinavica.* Vol. XXIX, 1954.

Arneberg, Sven T. *Legionærerne. Normenn i skyttegravskrig ved Leningrad 1942–43.* Thorsud, 2004.

Arvidsson, Stefan. 'Germania'. In *Jakten på Germania: fra nordensvermeri til SS- arkeologi.* Edited by Jorunn Sem Fure and Terje Emberland. Humanist forlag, 2009.

Axworthy, Mark, 'Peasant Scapegoat to Industrial Slaughter: The Romanian Soldier at the Siege of Odessa'. In *Time to Kill: The Soldiers Experience in the West, 1939–1945,* edited by Paul Addison and Angus Calder, Pimlico, 1997.

Bahro, Berno. *Der SS-Sport: Organisation, Funktion, Bedeutung,* Schöningh Paderborn, 2013.

Bartov, Omer. *Hitler's Army: Soldiers, Nazis, and War in the Third Reich.* Oxford University Press, 1992.

Bauer, Fritz and Adelheid L. Rüter-Ehlermann. *Justiz und NS-Verbrechen: Sammlung deutscher Strafurteile wegen nationalsozialistischer Tötungsverbrechen 1945–1966.* Vol. VI. University Press Amsterdam, 1971.

Baumann, Zygmunt. *Modernity and the Holocaust.* Cornell University Press, 1989.

Beevor, Antony. *Berlin: The Downfall 1945.* Penguin Books, 2002.

Beevor. Antony, *D-Day: D-Day and the Battle for Normandy.* Penguin, 2012.

Benz, Wolfgang. *Rechtsextremismus in der Bundesrepublik: Voraussetzungen, Zusammenhänge, Wirkungen.* Fischer Taschenbuch Verlag, 1984.

Benz, Wolfgang, Barbara Distel and Angelika Königseder. *Der Ort des Terrors. Geschichte der Konzentrationslager: Frühe Lager, Dachau, Emslandlager.* C.H. Beck, 2005.

Benz, Wolfgang, Barbara Distel and Angelika Königseder. *Der Ort des Terrors. Geschichte der Konzentrationslager: Sachsenhausen, Buchenwald, mit Nebenlagern,* C.H. Beck, 2006 (a).

Benz, Wolfgang, Barbara Distel and Angelika Königseder. *Der Ort des Terrors. Geschichte der Konzentrationslager: Flossenbürg, Mauthausen, Ravensbrück.* C.H. Beck, 2006 (b).

Benz, Wolfgang, Barbara Distel and Angelika Königseder. *Der Ort des Terrors. Geschichte der Konzentrationslager: Stutthof, Groß-Rosen, Natzweiler.* C.H. Beck, 2007.

Benz, Wolfgang, Barbara Distel and Angelika Königseder. *Der Ort des Terrors. Geschichte der nationalsozialistischen Konzentrationslager: Riga, Warschau, Kaunas, Vaivara, Plaszów, Klooga, Chelmno, Belzec, Treblinka, Sobibor.* C.H. Beck, 2008.

Benz, Wolfgang, Barbara Distel and Angelika Königseder. *Der Ort des Terrors. Geschichte der nationalsozialistischen Konzentrationslager: Arbeitserziehungslager, Durchgangslager, Ghettos, Polizeihaftlager, Sonderlager, Zigeunerlager, Zwangsarbeitslager.* C.H. Beck, 2009.

Beorn, Waitman Wade. *Marching into Darkness: The Wehrmacht and the Holocaust in Belarus.* Oxford University Press, 2014.

Bergen, Doris L. 'The Nazi Concept of "Volksdeutsche" and the Exacerbation of Anti-Semitism in Eastern Europe, 1939–45'. *Journal of Contemporary History.* Vol. 29, No. 4, Oct. 1994.

Berkhoff, Karel C. *Harvest of Despair: Life and Death in Ukraine under Nazi Rule.* Belknap Press of Harvard University Press, 2004.

Berkhoff, Karel C. 'The "Russian" Prisoners of War in Nazi-Ruled Ukraine as Victims of Genocidal Massacre'. *Holocaust and Genocide Studies.* Vol. 15, no. 1, 2001.

Besjanov, Vladimir. *Desjat Stalinskikh udarov.* Ast, 2005.

Biddiscombe, Alexander Perry. *Werwolf!: The History of the National Socialist Guerrilla Movement, 1944–1946.* University of Toronto Press, 1998.

Biddiscombe, Alexander Perry. 'The Problem with Glasshouses: The Soviet Recruitment and Deployment of SS Men as Spies and Saboteurs'. *Intelligence and National Security.* Vol. 15, No. 3, 2000.

Biddiscombe, Alexander Perry. 'The Enemy of Our Enemy: A View of the Edelweiss Piraten from the British and American Archives'. *Journal of Contemporary History.* Vol. 30, No. 1, 1995.

Birn, Ruth Bettina. *Die höheren SS- und Polizeiführer:Himmlers Vertreter im Reich und in den besetzten Gebieten.* Droste Verlag, 1986.

Birn, Ruth Bettina. 'Die SS - Ideologie und Herrschaftsausübung: zur Frage der Inkorporierung von "Fremdvölkischen"'. *Die SS, Himmler und die Wewelsbur,* edited by Jan Erik Schulte. *Schriftenreihe des Kreismuseums Wewelsburg 7.* Schöningh, 2009.

Birstein, Vadim J. *Smersh. Stalin's Secret Weapon.* Biteback Publishing, 2013.

Blatman, Daniel. *The Death Marches: The Final Phase of Nazi Genocide.* Belknap Press of Harvard University Press, 2011.

Blindheim, Svein. *Nordmenn under Hitlers fane: dei norske frontkjemparane.* Noreg, 1977.

Blood, Philip W. *Hitler's Bandit Hunters: The SS and the Nazi Occupation of Europe.* Potomac Books, 2006.

Blosfelds, Mintauts. *Stormtrooper on the Eastern Front: Fighting with Hitler's Latvian SS.* Pen & Sword Military, 2008.

Boll, Bernd and Hans Safrian. 'Auf dem Weg nach Stalingrad. Die 6. Armee'. In *Vernichtungskrieg: Verbrechen der Wehrmacht 1941–1944.* Edited by Hannes Heer and Klaus Naumann, Zweitausendeins, 1995.

Boog, Horst, Werner Rahn, Reinhard Stumpf and Bernd Wegner. *Der Globale Krieg. Die Ausweitung zum Weltkrieg und der Wechsel der Initiative. Das Deutsche Reich und der Zweite Weltkrieg.* Vol. 6. Deutsche Verlags-Anstalt, 1990.

Boog, Horst. *Das deutsche Reich in der Defensive. Das Deutsche Reich und der Zweite Weltkrieg.* Vol. 7. Deutsche Verlags- Anstalt, 2001.

Boog, Horst, Jürgen Förster and Joachim Hoffmann. *Der Angriff auf die Sowjetunion.* Fischer, 1991.

Boog, Horst and Rolf-Dieter Müller. *Der Zusammenbruch des Deutschen Reiches. Das Deutsche Reich und der Zweite Weltkrieg.* Vol. 10/1. Deutsche Verlags-Anstalt, 2008.

Borodziej, Włodzimierz. *The Warsaw Uprising of 1944.* University of Wisconsin Press, 2005.

Bowen, W. H. 'The Ghost Battalion: Spaniards in The Waffen-SS, 1944–1945'. *Historian,* 63, 2001.

Bracher, Karl Dietrich and C. F. Rüter. *Justiz und NS-Verbrechen. Sammlung deutscher Strafurteile wegen national- sozialistischer Totungsverbrechen.* University Press Amsterdam, 1976.

Breitman, Richard. 'Friedrich Jeckeln'. *Die SS: Elite unter dem Totenkopf; 30 Lebensläufe,* edited by Ronald Smelser and Enrico Syring. Schöningh, 2003.

Breitman, Richard and Shlomo Aronson. 'The End of the 'Final Solution? Nazi Plans to Ransom Jews in 1944'. *Central European History.* Vol. 25, No. 2, 1992.

Bremm, Klaus-Jürgen. Die Waffen-SS. Hitlers überschätzte Prätorianer. Wbg Theiss, 2018.

Bridgman, Jon and Richard H. Jones. *The End of the Holocaust: The Liberation of the Camps.* Areopagitica Press, 1990.

Broszat, Martin. *Nationalsozialistische Polenpolitik 1939–1945.* Fischer-Bücherei, 1965.

Browning, Christopher R. *Nazi Policy, Jewish Labor, German Killers.* Cambridge University Press, 2000.

Browning, Christopher R. *Ordinary Men: Reserve Police Battalion 101 and the Final Solution in Poland.* Harper Perennial, 1998.

Buchheim, Hans, Martin Broszat, Hans-Adolf Jacobsen and Helmut Krausnick. *Anatomie des SS-Staates.* DTV Deutscher Taschenbuch, 1994.

Burleigh, Michael and Wolfgang Wippermann. *The Racial State: Germany 1933–1945.* Cambridge Univ. Press, 1994.

Buttar, Prit. *Between Giants: The Battle for the Baltics in World War II.* Osprey Publishing, 2013.

Böhler, Jochen. *Auftakt zum Vernichtungskrieg: die Wehrmacht in Polen 1939.* Fischer Taschenbuch Verlag, 2006.

Böhler, Jochen and Robert Gerwarth. *Waffen-SS-A European History,* Oxford University Press, 2017.

Böhme, Kurt W. *Die deutschen Kriegsgefangenen in amerikanischer Hand.* Gieseking, 1973.

Böhme, K. W. *Die deutschen Kriegsgefangenen in sowjetischer Hand: eine Bilanz.* Gieseking, 1973.

Baade, Fritz. *Unsere Ehre heisst Treue; Kriegstagebuch des Kommandostabes Reichsführer SS, Tätigkeitsberichte der 1. und 2. SS-Inf.-Brigade, der 1. SS-Kav.-Brigade und von Sonderkommandos der SS.* Europa Verlag, 1965.

Carlsen, Cecilie Damgaard and Henry Lias Büchmann Nielsen. *Waffen-SS på Vestfronten. Et studium af massakrerne på allierede krigsfanger 1940 og 1944.* MA-Thesis, Roskilde University, 2012.

Carrard, Philippe. *The French Who Fought for Hitler: Memories from the Outcasts.* Cambridge University Press, 2010.

Casagrande, Thomas. *Die volksdeutsche SS-Division 'Prinz Eugen': Die Banater Schwaben und die nationalsozialistischen Kriegsverbrechen.* Campus-Verl., 2003.

Casagrande, Thomas. *Südtiroler in der Waffen-SS. Vorbildliche Haltung, Fanatische Überzeugung.* Edition Raetia, 2016.

Cavanagh, William C. C. *A Tour of the Bulge Battlefield.* Pen & Sword, 2001.

Caune, Andris. *Latvia in World War II: materials of an International Conference 14–15 June 1999, Riga.* Latvijas vēstures institūta apgāds, 2000.

Cesarani, David. *Justice Delayed: How Britain Became a Refuge for Nazi War Criminals.* Phoenix Press, 2001.

Chiari, Bernhard. *Alltag hinter der Front: Besatzung, Kollaboration und Widerstand in Weissrussland 1941–1944.* Droste Verlag, 1998.

Christensen, Claus Bundgård. 'Kvinderne fra Lublin. Bevogtningspersonalet i Majdanek'. *Historisk Tidsskrift.* Vol. 106, No. 2, 2013.

Christensen, Claus Bundgård, Niels Bo Poulsen and Peter Scharff Smith. 'Germanic volunteers from northern Europe'. In *Waffen-SS-A European History,* Oxford University Press. Edited by Böhler, Jochen and Robert Gerwarth, 2017.

Christensen, Claus Bundgård, Niels Bo Poulsen and Peter Scharff Smith. 'Per Sørensen: Officer og gerningsmand'. In *Danskere i krig, 1936–48.* Edited by Rasmus Mariager. Gyldendal, 2009.

Christensen, Claus Bundgård, Niels Bo Poulsen and Peter Scharff Smith. *Dagbog fra Østfronten: en dansker i Waffen-SS,* 1941–44. Aschehoug, 2005.

Christensen, Claus Bundgård, Niels Bo Poulsen and Peter Scharff Smith. 'The Danish Volunteers in the Waffen SS and their Contribution to the Holocaust and the Nazi War of Extermination'. In *Denmark and the Holocaust.* Edited by Mette Bastholm Jensen and Steven L. B. Jensen. Institute for International Studies, Department for Holocaust and Genocide Studies, 2003.

Christensen, Claus Bundgård, Niels Bo Poulsen and Peter Scharff Smith. 'Legion Norge. Forskelle og ligheder med de øvrige "germanske" legioner i Waffen SS'. *Historisk Tidsskrift.* Vol. 100, No. 2, 2000.

Christensen, Claus Bundgård, Niels Bo Poulsen and Peter Scharff Smith. 'The Danish volunteers in the Waffen SS and German warfare at the east front'. *Contemporary European History.* Vol. 8, No. 1, 1999.

Christensen, Claus Bundgård, Niels Bo Poulsen and Peter Scharff Smith. *Under hagekors og Dannebrog: Danskere i Waffen SS*. Aschehoug, 1998.

Christensen, Claus Bundgård, Niels Bo Poulsen and Peter Scharff Smith. 'Kryssing og de østfrontsfrivillige'. *Siden Saxo*, nr. 1, 1995.

Christiansen, Karl O. 'Recidivet blandt danske landssvigere'. *Kriminalvidenskab*, årg. 58, 1970.

Christiansen, Søren and Rasmus Hyllested. *På den forkerte side: de danske landssvigere efter befrielsen*. Aarhus Universitetsforlag, 2011.

Citino, Robert M. *Death of the Wehrmacht. The German Campaigns of 1942*. University Press of Kansas, 2007.

Clark, Christopher. 'Josef "Sepp" Dietrich'. *Die SS: Elite unter dem Totenkopf; 30 Lebensläufe*, Edited by Ronald Smelser and Enrico Syring. Schöningh, 2003.

Clark, Lloyd. *Arnhem: Jumping the Rhine, 1944 and 1945 : The Greatest Airborne Battle in History*. Headline Review, 2008.

Conze, Eckart. 'Adel unter dem Totenkopf. Die Idee eines Neuadels in den Gesellschaftvorstellungen der SS'. In *Adel und Moderne. Deutschland im europäischen Vergleich im 19. und 20. Jahrhundert*, Edited by Eckart Conze og Monika Wienfort. Böhlau Verlag, 2004.

Conze, Eckart, Norbert Frei, Peter Hayes and Mosche Zimmermann. *Das Amt und die Vergangenheit: deutsche Diplomaten im Dritten Reich und in der Bundesrepublik*. Karl Blessing Verlag, 2010.

Curilla, Wolfgang. *Die deutsche Ordnungspolizei und der Holocaust im Baltikum und in Weissrussland, 1941–1944*. Ferdinand Schöningh, 2006.

Cüppers, Martin. '... auf eine so saubere und anständige SS-mäßige Art': die Waffen-SS in Polen 1939–1941. In *Die Gestapo im Zweiten Weltkrieg: 'Heimatfront' und besetztes Europa*. Edited by Gerhard Paul and Klaus-Michael Mallmann. Primus, 2000.

Cüppers Martin. *Halvmåne og hagekors. Det Tredje Rige, araberne og Palæstina*. Informations Forlag, 2009.

Cüppers, Martin. *Wegbereiter der Shoa. Die Waffen-SS, der Kommandostab Reichsführer-SS und die Judenvernichtung 1939–1945*. Primus, 2011.

Dallin, Alexander. *German Rule in Russia, 1941–1945, a Study of Occupation Policies*. MacMillan, 1957.

Dallin, Alexander. *Odessa, 1941–1944: A Case Study of Soviet Territory under Foreign Rule*. Center for Romanian Studies, 1998.

Dallin, Alexander. 'The Kaminsky Brigade: A Case-Study of Soviet Disaffection'. In *Revolution and Politics in Russia*. Edited by Boris I. Nicolaevsky. Indiana University Press, 1973.

Danielsen, Rolf and Stein Ugelvik Larsen. *Fra idé til dom: noen trekk fra utviklingen av Nasjonal samling*. Bergen: Universitetsforlaget, 1976.

Deák, István, Jan Tomasz Gross, and Tony Judt. *The Politics of Retribution in Europe: World War II and Its Aftermath*. Princeton University Press, 2000.

Dean, Martin. *Collaboration in the Holocaust: Crimes of the Local Police in Belorussia and Ukraine, 1941–44*. St. Martin's Press, 2000.

Dean, Martin. 'Local Collaboration in the Holocaust in Eastern Europe'. In *The Historiography of the Holocaust*. Edited by Dan Stone. Palgrave Macmillan, 2004.

Dean, Martin. 'Where did All the Collaborators Go?'. *Slavic Review*. Vol. 64, No. 4, 2005.

Deist, Wilhelm and Manfred Messerschmidt. *Ursachen und Voraussetzungen der deutschen Kriegspolitik*. *Das Deutsche Reich und der Zweite Weltkrieg*. Vol. 1. Deutsche Verlags-Anstalt, 1979.

Deist, Wilhelm. *The German Military in the Age of Total War*. Berg Publishers, 1985.

Deland, Mats. *Purgatorium: Sverige och andra världskrigets förbrytare*. Atlas, 2010.

Demps, Laurenz, C. F. Rüter and L. Hekelaar Gombert. *DDR-Justiz und NS-Verbrechen: Sammlung ostdeutscher Strafurteile wegen nationalsozialistischer Tötungsverbrechen*. Vol. III. Amsterdam University Press (AUP); K.G. Saur Verlag, 2003.

Demps, Laurenz, C. F. Rüter and L. Hekelaar Gombert. *DDR-Justiz und NS-Verbrechen: Sammlung ostdeutscher Strafurteile wegen nationalsozialistischer Tötungsverbrechen*. Vol. IV. Amsterdam University Press (AUP); K.G. Saur Verlag, 2004.

Demps, Laurenz, C. F. Rüter and L. Hekelaar Gombert. *DDR-Justiz und NS-Verbrechen: Sammlung ostdeutscher Strafurteile wegen nationalsozialistischer Tötungsverbrechen*. Vol. VIII. Amsterdam University Press (AUP); K.G. Saur Verlag, 2006.

Demps, Laurenz, C. F. Rüter and L. Hekelaar Gombert. *DDR-Justiz und NS-Verbrechen: Sammlung ostdeutscher Strafurteile wegen nationalsozialistischer Tötungsverbrechen*. Vol. X. Amsterdam University Press (AUP); K.G. Saur Verlag, 2007.

Demps, Laurenz, C. F. Rüter and L. Hekelaar Gombert. *DDR-Justiz und NS-Verbrechen: Sammlung ostdeutscher Strafurteile wegen nationalsozialistischer Tötungsverbrechen*. Vol. XI. Amsterdam University Press (AUP); K.G. Saur Verlag, 2008.

De Groot, Jerome. 'Review Essay. Affect and empathy: re-enactment and performance as/ in history'. *Rethinking History*, 15, no. 4, 2011.

De Zayas, Alfred M. *The Wehrmacht War Crimes Bureau, 1939–1945*. University of Nebraska Press, 1989.

Dicks, Henry Victor. *Licensed Mass Murder: A Socio-Psychological Study of Some SS Killers*. Chatto: Heinemann for Sussex University Press, 1972.

Diehl, James M. *The Thanks of the Fatherland: German Veterans after the Second World War*. University of North Carolina Press, 1993.

Dimsdale, Joel E. *Survivors, Victims, and Perpetrators: Essays on the Nazi Holocaust*. Hemisphere, 1980.

Dixon, Jeremy. *Commanders of Auschwitz: The SS Officers Who Ran the Largest Nazi Concentration Camp, 1940–1945*. Schiffer Military History, 2005.

Duscheleit, Otto-Ernst. *Von der Waffen-SS zum Friedensdienst: mein Weg aus Schweigen und Vergessen*. Brandes & Apsel, 2006.

Dyukov, A. and V. Simidel. *The Latvian SS Legion and the Nuremberg Tribunal's Decisions*. International Affairs [Published by the Russian Ministry of Foreign Affairs]. Vol. 57, 2011.

Döscher, Hans-Jürgen. *Das Auswärtige Amt im Dritten Reich: Diplomatie im Schatten der 'Endlösung'*. Siedler, 1987.

Earl, Hilary Camille. *The Nuremberg SS-Einsatzgruppen Trial, 1945–1958: Atrocity, Law, and History*. Cambridge University Press, 2009.

Echternkamp, Jörg and Rolf-Dieter Müller. *Der Zusammenbruch des deutschen Reiches 1945*. Das Deutsche Reich und der Zweite Weltkrieg, Vol. 10/2. Deutsche Verlags-Anstalt, 2008.

Eisenhower, John S. D. *The Bitter Woods: The Dramatic Story, Told at All Echelons; from Supreme Command to Squad Leader; of the Crisis That Shook the Western Coalition: Hitler's Surprise Ardennes Offensive*. Putnam, 1969.

Emberland, Terje. 'Viking og odelsbonde'. Edited by Jorunn Sem Fure and Terje Emberland. *Jakten på Germania: fra nordensvermeri til SS-arkeologi*, Humanist forlag, 2009.

Emberland, Terje and Matthew Kott. *Himmlers Norge: nordmenn i det storgermanske prosjekt*. Aschehoug., 2012.

Engelbrecht, Peter. 'Die Massaker der Pottensteiner SS-Karstwehr 1943–1944 in Slowenien'. In *Entrechtung, Vertreibung, Mord: NS-Unrecht in Slowenien und seine Spuren in Bayern 1941–1945*. Edited by Gerhard Jochem and Georg Seiderer. Metropol, 2005.

English, John A. *Surrender Invites Death. Fighting the SS in Normandy*. Stackpole Books, 2011.

Enstad, Johannes Due. *Soviet Citizens under German Occupation. Life Death and Power in Northwest Russia 1941–1944*. Phd- thesis, University of Oslo, 2013.

Epifanow, Alexander E. *Die Außerordentliche Staatliche Kommission*. Stöcker, 1997.

Erickson, John. *The Road to Berlin*. Phoenix Giants, 1996.

Erickson, John. *The Road to Stalingrad*. Weidenfeld, 1993.

Estes, Kenneth W. *A European Anabasis Western European Volunteers in the German Army and SS, 1940–1945*. Columbia University Press, 2008.

Evans, Richard J. *The Third Reich at War: How the Nazis Led Germany from Conquest to Disaster*. Penguin, 2009.

Ezergailis, Andrew. *The Holocaust in Latvia, 1941–1944: The Missing Center.* Historical Institute of Latvia; United States Holocaust Memorial Museum, 1996.

Ezergailis, Andrew. *The Latvian Legion: heroes, Nazis, or victims?: A collection of documents from OSS war-crimes* investigation files 1945–1950. Historical Institute of Latvia, 1997.

Farmer, Sarah Bennett. *Martyred Village: Commemorating the 1944 Massacre at Oradour-Sur-Glane.* University of California Press, 1999.

Fey, Will. *Armor Battles of the Waffen-SS.* Stackpole Books, 2003.

Figueiredo, Ivo de. 'De norske frontkjemperne – hva litteraturen sier og veien videre'. *Historisk Tidsskrift.* No. 4, 2001.

Forbes, Robert. *For Europe: The French Volunteers of the Waffen-SS.* Stackpole Books, 2010.

Frankson, Anders and Niklas Zetterling. *Slaget om Kursk: historiens største panserslag.* Aschehoug, 2003.

Fritz, Stephen G. *Ostkrieg: Hitler's War of Extermination in the East.* University Press of Kentucky, 2011.

Fröshaug, Harald. 'A Social-Psychiatric Examination'. In *Acta Psychiatrica et Neurologica Scandinavica.* Edited by Nils Antoni. Vol. XXIX, 1954.

Fröshaug, Harald. 'The Young "Patriots"'. In *Report on the Eight Congress of Scandinavian Psychiatrists in Copenhagen, Denmark, 1946.* Edited by Gudmund Magnussen. Munksgaard, 1947.

Fure, Jorunn Sem and Terje Emberland. *Jakten på Germania: fra nordensvermeri til SS-arkeologi.* Humanist forlag, 2009.

Furuseth, Anne Kristin. *Da freden brøt løs. Norsk NS-migration til Argentina etter 1945.* Master thesis Oslo University, 2011.

Furuseth, Anne Kristin. *Norske nazister på flukt: jakten på et nytt hjemland i Argentina.* Upublisched manuscript, 2013.

Förster, Jürgen. 'Die Sicherung des 'Lebensraumes'. In *Der Angriff auf die Sowjetunion.* Edited by Horst Boog, Jürgen Förster and Joachim Hoffmann. Fischer, 1991.

Förster, Jürgen. 'Die weltanschauliche Erziehung in der Waffen-SS'. In *Ausbildungsziel Judenmord? 'Weltanschauliche Erziehung' von SS, Polizei und Waffen-SS im Rahmen der 'Endlösung'.* Edited by Matthäus, Jürgen, Konrad Kwiet, Jürgen Förster, Richard Breitman and Udo Rennert. Fischer Taschenbuch Verlag, 2003.

Förster, Jürgen. *Die Wehrmacht im NS-Staat: eine strukturgeschichtliche Analyse. Durchgesehene Auflage.* Oldenbourg, 2009.

Förster, Jürgen. 'Freiwillige für den Kreuzzug Europas gegen den Bolschewismus'. In *Der Angriff auf die Sowjetunion.* Edited by Horst Boog, Jürgen Förster and Joachim Hoffmann. Fischer, 1991.

Geller, Jay Howard. 'The Role of Military Administration in German Occupied Belgium, 1940–1944'. *The Journal of Military History.* Vol. 63, No. 1, 1999.

Gentile, Carlo. 'Politische Soldaten; Die 16. SS-Panzer-Grenadier-Division, Reichsführer-SS' in Italien 1944'. *Quellen und Forschungen aus italienischen Archiven und Bibliotheken.* Vol. 81, 2001.

Gentile, Carlo. *Wehrmacht und Waffen-SS im Partisanenkrieg: Italien 1943–1945,* Schöninghn 2012.

Gentile, Carlo. 'Zwischen Ideologie und Opportunismus: Die Italiener und die SS 1943–1945'. *Himmlers Supernational Militia Indigenous Participation in SS and Police Units in the Context of the Second World War,* UMK Institute of History and Archival Science in Torun, Unpublished paper, 2014. Gerlach, Christian. *Kalkulierte Morde: die deutsche Wirtschafts- und Vernichtungspolitik in Weißrußland 1941 bis 1944.* Hamburger Edition, 1999.

Gerwarth, Robert. *Hitler's Hangman: The Life of Heydrich.* Yale University Press, 2011.

Gerwarth, Robert and John Horne. 'Vectors of Violence: Paramilitarism in Europe after the Great War, 1917–1923'. *The Journal of Modern History.* Vol. 83, No. 3, 2011.

Gingerich, Mark Philip. *Toward a Brotherhood of Arms: Waffen-SS Recruitment of Germanic Volunteers, 1940–1945.* Thesis (Ph. D.), University of Wisconsin-Madison, 1991.

Glantz, David M and Jonathan M House. *The Battle of Kursk.* University Press of Kansas, 1999.

Goeschel, Christian. *Selbstmord im dritten Reich.* Suhrkamp, 2011.

Goldensohn, Leon and Robert Gellately. *The Nuremberg Interviews.* Vintage Books, 2005.

Goldsworthy, Terry. *Valhalla's Warriors. A History of the Waffen-SS on the Eastern Front 1941–1945.* Dog Ear Publishing, 2007.

Gordon, Bertram M. *Collaborationism in France during the Second World War.* Cornell University Press, 1980.

Griesser-Pečar, Tamara. *Das zerrissene Volk Slowenien 1941–1946: Okkupation, Kollaboration, Bürgerkrieg, Revolution.* Böhlau, 2003.

Groscurth, Helmuth. *Tagebücher eines Abwehroffiziers: 1938–1940.* Deutsche Verlagsanstalt, 1970.

Gross, Jan. *Revolution from Abroad.* Princetown University Press, 2002.

Guide to Foreign Military Studies, 1945–1954. Historical Division, Headquarters, United States Army, Europe, 1954.

Gutman, Israel and Michael Berenbaum. *Anatomy of the Auschwitz Death Camp.* Indiana University Press, 1998.

Gutmann, Martin R. *Building a Nazi Europe. The SS's Germanic Volunteers.* Cambridge University Press, 2017.

Gyllenhaal, Lars and Lennart Westberg. *Svenskar i krig, 1914–1945.* Historiska Media, 2008.

Günther, Hans F. K. *Rassenkunde des deutschen Volkes.* J. F. Lehmanns Verlag, 1926.

Günther, Helmut. *Hot Motors, Cold Feet. A Memoir of Service with the Motorcycle Battailon of SS-Division "Reich" 1940–1941.* J.J. Fedorowicz Publishing, 2004.

Hahl, Fritz. *Mit 'Westland' im Osten. Ein Leben zwischen 1922 und 1945.* Munin Verlag, 2000.

Handbook on German Military Forces. Louisiana State University Press, 1990.

Harder, Thomas. *Kryssing. Manden, der valgte forkert.* Lindhardt og Ringhof, 2014.

Hardis, Arne and Knud Nordentoft. *Forræderens dagbog: en dansk nazist 1941–45.* Lindhardt & Ringhof, 2005.

Harun-el-Raschid. *Aus Orient und Occident Ein Mosaik aus buntem Erleben.* Bielefeld: Dt. Heimat-Verl., 1954.

Hastings, Max. *Das Reich. The March of the 2nd Panzer Division through France, June 1944.* Pan, 2009.

Hatheway, Jay. *In Perfect Formation: SS Ideology and the SS-Junkerschule-Tölz.* Schiffer Pub., 1999.

Hausser, Paul. *Soldaten wie andere auch: Der Weg der Waffen-SS.* Munin Verlag, 1966.

Haygood, William Converse. 'A GI's Wartime Letters'. *The Wisconsin Magazine of History.* Vol. 59, No. 2, Winter, 1975–1976.

Hellbeck, Jochen. *Revolution on My Mind. Writing a Diary Under Stalin.* Harvard University Press, 2000.

Hellbeck, Jochen. *Die Stalingrad-Protokolle: Sowjetische Augenzeugen berichten aus der Schlacht.* Fischer, 2014.

Herbert, Ulrich. *Die Nationalsozialistischen Konzentrationslage.* Vol. II. Wallstein Verlag, Gottingen, 1998.

Heer, Hannes. *Stets zu Erschiessen sind Frauen, die in der Roten Armee dienen. Geständnisse deutscher Kriegsgefangener über ihren Einsatz an der Ostfront.* Hamburger Edition, 1995.

Heer, Hannes and Klaus Naumann. *Vernichtungskrieg: Verbrechen der Wehrmacht 1941–1944.* Zweitausendeins, 1995.

Heer, Hannes and Klaus Nauman. *Vernichtungskrieg: Verbrechen der Wehrmacht 1941–1944.* Zweitausendeins, 1995.

Heike, Wolf-Dietrich. *Sie wollten die Freiheit: die Geschichte der Ukrainischen Division, 1943–1945.* Podzun, 1970.

Heinrichs, Dirk. 'Hauptmann d. r. Wilm Hosenfeld. Retter in Warschau'. In *Die Wehrmacht: Feindbilder, Vernichtungskrieg.* Edited by Wolfram Wette. S. Fischer, 2002.

Helweg-Larsen, Flemming. *Dødsdømt: Flemming Helweg-Larsens beretning.* Edited by Henrik Skov Kristensen and Ditlev Tamm. Gyldendal, 2008.

Herzog, Dagmar. *Brutality and Desire: War and Sexuality in Europe's Twentieth Century.* Palgrave Macmillan, 2009.

Herzog, Robert. *Die Volksdeutschen in der Waffen-SS.* Tübingen: Institut für Besatzungsfragen, 1955.

Heutsz, Joannes Benedictus van. *Wiking door Rusland.* Storm, 1942.

Hiio, Toomas. *Estonia, 1940–1945: Reports of the Estonian International Commission for the Investigation of Crimes Against Humanity.* Estonian Foundation for the Investigation of Crimes against Humanity, 2006.

Hiio, Toomas. *Estonian Military Units in German Armed Forces and Police during the Second World War.* The Museum of the Occupation of Latvia, Yearbook 2004.

Hiio, Toomas and Peeter Kaasik. 'Estonian Units in the Waffen-SS'. In *Estonia, 1940–1945: Reports of the Estonian International Commission for the Investigation of Crimes Against Humanity.* Edited by Toomas Hiio. Estonian Foundation for the Investigation of Crimes Against Humanity, 2006.

Hiio, Toomas, Meelis Maripuu and Indrek Paavle. *Estonia since 1944: Reports of the Estonian International Commission for the Investigation of Crimes Against Humanity.* Estonian Foundation for the Investigation of Crimes Against Humanity, 2006.

Hilberg, Raul. *The Destruction of the European Jews.* Vol. I. New Haven (Conn.); Yale University Press, 2003.

Hilberg, Raul. *The Destruction of the European Jews.* Vol. II. New Haven (Conn.); Yale University Press, 2003.

Hilberg, Raul. *The Destruction of the European Jews.* Vol. III. 3. New Haven (Conn.); Yale University Press, 2003.

Hilger, Andreas. *Deutsche Kriegsgefangene in der Sowjetunion, 1941–1956: Kriegsgefangenenpolitik, Lageralltag und Erinnerung.* Klartext, 2000.

Hilger, Andreas, Ute Schmidt and Günther Wagenlehner. *Sowjetische Militärtribunale.* Vol. 1. Böhlau, 2001.

Hirsch, Kurt. *SS gestern, heute und ...* Verlag Schaffende Jugend, 1957.

Hoffmann, Joachim. *Kaukasien 1942–43: das deutsche Heer und die Orientvölker der Sowjetunion.* Rombach, 1991.

Holter, Karl. *Frontkjempere.* Store Bjørn, 1951.

Husemann, Friedrich. *Die guten Glaubens waren: Geschichte der SS-Polizei-Division (4. SS-Polizei-Panzer-Grenadier-Division) 1939–1942.* Vol. 1. Munin Verlag, 1971.

Husemann, Friedrich. *Die guten Glaubens waren: Geschichte der SS-Polizei-Division (4. SS-Polizei-Panzer-Grenadier-Division) 1943–1945.* Vol. 2. Munin Verlag, 1973.

Huyse, Luc. 'The Criminal Justice System As a Political Actor in Regime Transitions: The Case of Belgium, 1944–50'. In *The Politics of Retribution in Europe: World War II and Its Aftermath.* Edited by István Deák, Jan Tomasz Gross and Tony Judt. Princeton University Press, 2000.

Hoehne, Heinz. *Der Orden unter dem Totenkopf: die Geschichte der SS.* Weltbild-Verlag, 1995.

Ingrao, Christian. *The SS Dirlewanger Brigade: The History of the Black Hunters.* Skyhorse Pub., 2011.

International Military Tribunal. Trial of the Major War Criminals before the International Military Tribunal, 14 November 1945–1 October 1946. Vol. 1–42. International Military Tribunal, 1946–1947.

Jackson, Julian. France: *The Dark Years, 1940–1944.* Oxford University Press, 2003.

Janzer, Alois. *Als in Deutschland die Blutfahnen wehten: unfreiwillig bei der Waffen-SS; Erinnerungen 1943–1948.* Lauber, 2010.

Jäger, Herbert. *Verbrechen unter totalitärer Herrschaft; Studie zur nationalsozialistischen Gewaltkriminalität.* Walter Verlag, 1967.

Jensen, Mette Bastholm and Steven L. B. Jensen. *Denmark and the Holocaust.* Institute for International Studies, Department for Holocaust and Genocide Studies, 2003.

Jerk, Wiking. *Endkampf um Berlin.* Dürer, 1947.

Jerk, Wiking. *Ragnarök: en frivillig svensk Waffen-SS-soldat berättar om slutstriden i Europa 1945.* Nordland, 1996.

Jochem, Gerhard and Georg Seiderer. *Entrechtung, Vertreibung, Mord: NS-Unrecht in Slowenien und seine Spuren in Bayern 1941–1945.* Metropol, 2005.

Jonassen, Lasse Bruun and Jonas Lind. *Schiøler-gruppen: danske terrorister i tysk tjeneste 1944–45.* Informations Forlag, 2012.

Jones, Michael K. *Tilbagetoget: Hitlers første nederlag.* Gyldendal, 2011.

Judt, Tony. *Postwar: A History of Europe since 1945.* Random House, 2005.

Kalmbach, Peter. *Wehrmachtjustiz*. Metropol-Verlag, 2012.

Karny, Miroslav. 'Waffen-SS und Konzentrationslager'. *Die Nationalsozialistischen Konzentrationslager. Entwicklung und Struktur*. Edited by Christoph Dieckmann Wallstein Verlag, 1998.

Kasmi, Marenglen. *Die deutsche Besatzung in Albanien 1943 bis 1944*. Zentrum für Militärgeschichte und Sozialwissenschaften der Bundeswehr, 2013.

Kaasik, Peeter. 'Prisoners of War of Estonian Origin as Soviet Prisoners of War'. In *Estonia since 1944. Reports of the Estonian International Commission for the Investigation of Crimes Against Humanity*. Edited by Toomas Hiio, Meelis Maripuu and Indrek Paavle. Estonian Foundation for the Investigation of Crimes Against Humanity, 2009.

Keegan, John. *Six Armies in Normandy. From D-Day to the Liberation of Paris*. Penguin Books, 1994.

Keller, Sven. 'Elite am Ende. Die Waffen-SS in der letzten Phase des Krieges 1945'. In *Die Waffen-SS. Neue Forschungen*. Edited by Jan Erik Schulte, Peter Lieb and Bernd Wegner. Ferdinand Schöningh, 2014.

Kempner, Robert M. W. *SS im Kreuzverhör: die Elite, die Europa in Scherben schlug*. F. Greno, 1987.

Kershaw, Ian. *The End: Hitler's Germany, 1944–1945*. Allen Lane, 2011.

Kershaw, Robert J. *It Never Snows in September: The German View of Market-Garden and the Battle of Arnhem, September 1944*. Ian Allan Pub., 2008.

Kidd, William and Brian Murdoch. *Memory and Memorials: The Commemorative Century*. Ashgate, 2004.

Kiekenap, Bernhard. *SS-Junkerschule: SA und SS in Braunschweig*. Appelhans, 2008.

Kilian, Jürgen. *Wehrmacht und Besatzungsherrschaft im Russischen Nordwesten 1941–1944: Praxis und Alltag in der Militärverwaltungszone der Heeresgruppe Nord*. Schöningh, 2012.

Kirk, Tim. 'Limits of Germandom. Resistance to the Nazi Annexation of Slovenia'. *The Slavonic and East European Review*. Vol. 69, No. 4, 1991.

Kirkebæk, Mikkel. *Beredt for Danmark: Nationalsocialistisk ungdom 1932–1945*. Høst & Søn, 2004.

Kirkebæk, Mikkel. *Schalburg: en patriotisk landsforræder*. Gyldendal, 2008.

Kladov, Ignatik Fedorovich. *The People's Verdict; a Full Report of the Proceedings at the Krasnodar and Kharkov German Atrocity Trials*. Hutchinson & Co. Ltd., 1944.

Klausch, Hans-Peter. *Antifaschisten in SS-Uniform: Schicksal und Widerstand der deutschen politischen KZ-Häftlinge, Zuchthaus- und Wehrmachtstrafgefangenen in der SS-Sonderformation Dirlewanger*. Edition Temmen, 1993.

Klein, Peter. *Die Einsatzgruppen in der besetzen Sowjetunion 1941–42: die Tätigkeits- und Lageberichte des Chefs der Sicherheitspolizei und des SD*. Hentrich, 1997.

Klietmann, Kurt-Gerhard. *Die Waffen-SS: Eine Dokumentation*. Der Freiwillige, 1965.

Klink, Ernst. 'Die Operationsführung'. In *Der Angriff auf die Sowjetunion*. Edited by Horst Boog, Jürgen Förster and Joachim Hoffmann. Fischer, 1991.

Klint, Helge, *Krigsdagbog 7. maj - 11. august 1942*. Richard Levin, 1978.

Knippschild, Dieter. ' "Für mich ist der Krieg aus", Deserteure in der Deutschen Wehrmacht'. In *Die anderen Soldaten: Wehrkraftzersetzung, Gehorsamsverweigerung und Fahnenflucht im Zweiten Weltkrieg*. Edited by Norbert Haase and Gerhard Paul. Fischer, 1995.

Koehl, Robert Lewis. *The Black Corps: The Structure and Power Struggles of the Nazi SS*. University of Wisconsin Press, 1983.

Kogon Eugen. *SS Hitlers Terrorkorps*. Roth, 1991.

Kokurin, Alexander. 'Evacuation of the Convicts from the Prisons of the Latvian SSR People's Commissariat of the Interior 1941'. In *Latvia in World War II*. Edited by Andris Caune. Latvijas vestures instituta apgads, 2000.

Konsalik, Heinz G. *Der Arzt von Stalingrad*. Kindler, 1956.

Koonz, Claudia. *Mothers in the Fatherland: Women, the Family, and Nazi Politics*. St. Martin's P., 1986.

Koop, Volker. *'Dem Führer ein Kind schenken': die SS-Organisation Lebensborn*. Böhlau, 2007.

Korb, Alexander Martin. *Im Schatten des Weltkriegs: Massengewalt der Ustaša gegen Serben, Juden und Roma in Kroatien 1941–1945*. Hamburger Edition, 2013.

Krabbe, Oluf. *Danske soldater i kamp på Østfronten 1941–1945*. Bogan, 1998.

Kraft Frhr. Schenck zu Schweinsberg, 'Die Soldatenverbände in der Bundesrepublik'. In *Studien zur politischen und gesellschaftlichen Situation der Bundeswehr*. Edited by Georg Picht. Vol. 1. Eckart, 1965.

Krausnick, Helmut. *Hitlers Einsatzgruppen: die Truppe des Weltanschauungskrieges 1938–1942*. Fischer-Taschenbuch-Verl., 1998.

Kristensen, Henrik Skov. *Straffelejren: Fårhus, landssvigerne og retsopgøret*. Nyt Nordisk Forlag Arnold Busck, 2011.

Kronika, Jacob. *Berlins Undergang*. H. Hagerup, 1945.

Kumm, Otto. Vorwärts. *Prinz Eugen! Geschichte der 7. SS-Freiwilligen-Division "Prinz Eugen"*. Winkelried, 2007.

Kunz, Andreas. 'Die Wehrmacht 1944/45'. In *Der Zusammenbruch des deutschen Reiches 1945. Das Deutsche Reich und der Zweite Weltkrieg*. Edited by Jörg Echternkamp and Rolf-Dieter Müller. Vol. 10/2, Deutsche Verlags-Anstalt, 2008.

Kunz, Andreas. *Wehrmacht und Niederlage: die bewaffnete Macht in der Endphase der nationalsozialistischen Herrschaft 1944 bis 1945*. Oldenbourg Wissenschaftsverlag, 2007.

Kuhnen, Hans Peter. *Die Vergangenheitsbewältigung der HIAG – Hilfsgemeinschaf ehemaliger Angehöriger der Waffen-SS*. Unpublished manuscript, Yad Vashems, Jerusalem, 1973.

Lankenau, Bernhard Heinrich. *Polizei im Einsatz während des Krieges 1939–1945 in Rheinland-Westfalen*. Hauschild, 1957.

Lappin, Eleonore. *Die Rolle der Waffen-SS beim Zwangsarbeitseinsatz ungarischer Juden im Gau Steiermark und bei den Todesmärschen ins KZ Mauthausen (1944/45)*. Christine Schindler, 2004.

Lappin, Elenore. 'The Death Marches of Hungarian Jews through Austria in the Spring of 1945'. *Yad Vashem Studies*, Vol. XXVIII, 2000.

Large, David Clay. 'Reckoning without the Past: The HIAG of the Waffen-SS and the Politics of Rehabilitation in the Bonn Republic, 1950–1961'. *The Journal of Modern History*, Vol. 59, No. 1, March 1987.

Larsen, Dennis. *Fortrængt grusomhed: danske SS-vagter 1941–45*. Gyldendal, 2010.

Larsen, Dennis and Therkel Stræde. *En skole i vold. Bobuisk 1941–44*. Gyldendal 2014.

Larsen, Stein Ugelvik. *Meldungen aus Norwegen 1940–1945: die geheimen Lageberichte des Befehlshabers der Sicherheitspolizei und des SD in Norwegen*. Vol. 1. Oldenburg, 2008.

Larsen, Stein Ugelvik. *Meldungen aus Norwegen 1940–1945: die geheimen Lageberichte des Befehlshabers der Sicherheitspolizei und des SD in Norwegen*. Vol. 2. Oldenburg, 2008.

Lasik, Aleksander. 'Historical-Sociological Profile of the Auschwitz SS'. In *Anatomy of the Auschwitz Death Camp*, Indiana University Press, 1998.

Lasik, Aleksander, Wacław Długoborski, Franciszek Piper and William Brand. *Auschwitz 1940–1945: Central Issues in the History of the Camp*. Vol. 1. Auschwitz-Birkenau State Museum, 2000.

Lauridsen, John T. *Werner Bests korrespondance med Auswärtiges Amt og andre tyske akter vedrørende besættelsen af Danmark 1942–1945*. Vol. 1–10, Museum Tusculanum, 2012.

Lauterbacher, Hartmann. *Erlebt und mitgestaltet: Kronzeuge einer Epoche 1923–1945: zu neuen Ufern nach Kriegsende*. Preussisch K. W. Schütz, 1984.

Lehmann, Rudolf and Ralf Tiemann. *Die Leibstandarte*. Vol. VI/1. Munin Verlag, 1986.

Lehnstaedt, Stephan. *Okkupation im Osten: Besatzeralltag in Warschau und Minsk 1939–1944*. Oldenbourg Wissenschaftsverlag, 2010.

Leleu, Jean-Luc. *La Waffen-SS: Soldats politiques en guerre*. Librairie Académique Perrin, 2007.

Lehnhardt, Jochen. 'Die Inszenierung des nationalsozialistischen Soldaten: Die Waffen-SS in der NS-Propaganda'. In *Die Waffen-SS. Neue Forschungen*. Edited by Jan Erik Schulte, Peter Lieb and Bernd Wegner (red.), Ferdinand Schöningh, 2014.

Lehnhardt, Jochen. *Die Waffen-SS: Geburt einer Legende: Himmlers Krieger in der NS-Propaganda*. Ferdinand Schöningh, 2017.

Lepre, George. *Himmler's Bosnian Division: The Waffen-SS Handschar Division, 1943–1945*. Schiffer Military History, 1997.

Lieb, Peter. *Konventioneller Krieg oder NS-Weltanschauungskrieg?: Kriegführung und Partisanenbekämpfung in Frankreich 1943/44*. Oldenbourg, 2007.

Linck, Stephan. 'Festung Nord' und 'Alpenfestung': das Ende des NS-Sicherheitsapparates'. In *Die Gestapo im Zweiten Weltkrieg: "Heimatfront" und besetztes Europa*. Edited by Gerhard Paul, and Klaus-Michael Mallmann. Primus, 2000.

Lingen, Kerstin von. 'Gardesoldat, Ordensritter, Kriegsverbrecher? Karl Wolffs Selbstbild zwischen SS und Waffen-SS'. In *Die Waffen-SS. Neue Forschungen*. Edited by Jan Erik Schulte, Peter Lieb and Bernd Wegner. Schöningh, 2014.

Littman, Sol. *Pure Soldiers or Sinister Legion. The Ukrainian 14th Waffen-SS division*. Black Rose Books, 2003.

Lindstad, Bjørn. *Den frivillige. En frontkjemper forteller sin historie*. Kagge Forlag, 2010.

Logusz, Michael O. *Galicia Division. The Waffen-SS 14th Grenadier Division 1943–1945*. Schiffer Military History, 1997.

Longerich, Peter. *Geschichte der SA*. Verlag C.H. Beck, 2003.

Longerich, Peter. *Heinrich Himmler*. Siedler, 2008.

Lowe, Keith. *Savage Continent: Europe in the Aftermath of World War II*. Viking, 2012.

Lower, Wendy. 'A New Ordering of Space and Race: Nazi Colonial Dreams in Zhytomyr, Ukraine, 1941–1944'. *German Studies Review*. Vol. 25, No. 2, May 2002.

Lower, Wendy. *Nazi Empire-Building and the Holocaust in Ukraine*, University of North Carolina Press, Chapel Hill, 2005.

Lucas, James. *Das Reich: The Military Role of the 2nd SS Division*. Cassell, 2006.

Lucks, Günter. *Ich war Hitlers letztes Aufgebot: meine Erlebnisse als SS-Kindersoldat*. Rowohlt Taschenbuch, 2010.

Lumans, Valdis O. *Himmler's Auxiliaries. The Volksdeutsche Mittelstelle and the German National Minorities of Europe, 1933–1945*. University of North Carolina Press, 1993.

Lumans, Valdis O. 'Recruiting Volksdeutsche for the Waffen-SS: From Skimming the Cream to Scraping the Dregs'. In *Scraping the Barrel. The Military Use of Substandard Manpower, 1860–1960*. Edited by Sanders Marble. Fordham University Press, 2012.

Lumans, Valdis O. 'The Etnic Germans of the Waffen-SS in Combat: Dregs or Gems?'. In *Scraping the Barrel. The Military Use of Substandard Manpower, 1860–1960*. Edited by Sanders Marble. Fordham University Press, 2012.

Lund, Allan A. *Hitlers håndlangere: Heinrich Himmler og den nazistiske raceideologi*. Samleren, 2001.

Lundtofte, Henrik. *Gestapo. Tysk politi og terror i Danmark 1940–1945*. Gads Forlag, 2003.

Luther, Craig W. H. *Blood and Honor: The History of the 12th SS Panzer Division 'Hitler Youth', 1943–1945*. R. J. Bender Pub., 1987.

Lærum, Erik. *Dansk soldat i krig og fred*. Kultur og Politik, 1955.

Lööw, Heléne. *Nazismen i Sverige: 1924–1979: pionjärerna, partierna, propagandan*. Ordfront Förl, 2004.

Lööw, Heléne. 'Swedish Policy Towards Suspected War Criminals, 1945–87'. *Scandinavian Journal of History*, 1988.

MacLean, French L. *The Camp Men: The SS Officers Who Ran the Nazi Concentration Camp System*. Schiffer Military History, 1999.

Maclean, French L. *The Cruel Hunters: SS-Sonderkommando Dirlewanger, Hitler's Most Notorious Anti-Partisan Unit*. Schiffer Pub., 1998.

Maclean, French L. *The Field Men: The SS Officers Who Led the Einsatzkommandos-the Nazi Mobile Killing Units*. Schiffer Pub., 1999.

Magnussen, Gudmund. *Report on the Eight Congress of Scandinavian Psychiatrists in Copenhagen, Denmark, 1946*. Munksgaard, 1947.

Magnussen, Martin Q. *De forsvundne nazidokumenter, Den ufortalte historie om tyveriet fra Rigsarkivet*, Grønningen 1, 2019.

Maier, Klaus A. and Horst Rohde, *Das Deutsche Reich und der Zweite Weltkrieg*. Vol. 2. Deutsche Verlags-Anstalt,

Mallmann, Klaus-Michael. '... Mißgeburten, die nicht auf diese Welt gehören' : die deutsche Ordnungspolizei in Polen 1939–1941'. *In Genesis des Genozids: Polen 1939–1941*. Edited by Mallmann, Klaus-Michael and Bogdan Musial. Wissenschaftliche Buchgesellschaft, 2004.

Mallmann, Klaus-Michael, Andrej Angrick, Jürgen Matthäus and Martin Cüppers. *Die 'Ereignismeldungen UdSSR' 1941*. WBG-Wissenschaftliche Buchgesellschaft, 2011.

Mallmann, Klaus-Michael and Martin Cüppers. *Halvmåne og hagekors det Tredje Rige, Araberne og Palaestina*. Informations Forl., 2009.

Mallmann, Klaus-Michael and Martin Cüppers. *Nazi Palestine: The Plans for the Extermination of the Jews in Palestine*. Enigma Books, 2010.

Mallmann, Klaus-Michael and Bogdan Musial. *Genesis des Genozids: Polen 1939–1941*. Wissenschaftliche Buchgesellschaft, 2004.

Mallmann, Klaus-Michael and Gerhard Paul. *Karrieren der Gewalt: nationalsozialistische Täterbiographien*. Primus, 2011.

Manig, Bert Oliver. *Die Politik der Ehre. Die Rehabilitierung der Berufssoldaten in der frühen Bundesrepublik*. Wallstein Verlag, 2004.

Manoschek, Walter. *'Serbien ist judenfrei': militärische Besatzungspolitik und Judenvernichtung in Serbien 1941/42*. Oldenbourg, 1995.

Manoschek, Walter. '"Gehst mit Juden erschiessen?". Die Vernichtung der Juden in Serbien'. In *Vernichtungskrieg: Verbrechen der Wehrmacht 1941–1944*. Edited by Hannes Heer and Klaus Naumann. Zweitausendeins, 1995.

Marble, Sanders. *Scraping the Barrel: The Military Use of Substandard Manpower, 1860–1960*. Fordham University Press, 2012.

Margolian, Howard. *Conduct Unbecoming: The Story of the Murder of Canadian Prisoners of War in Normandy*. University of Toronto Press, 2000.

Margolian, Howard. *Unauthorized Entry: The Truth about Nazi War Criminals in Canada, 1946–1956*. University of Toronto Press, 2000.

Mariager, Rasmus. *Danskere i krig, 1936–48*. Gyldendal, 2009.

Martin, Dean. 'Local Collaboration in the Holocaust in Eastern Europe'. In *The Historiography of the Holocaust,* Edited by Dan Stone. Palgrave Macmillan, 2004.

Martin, Terry D. *The Affirmative Action Empire: Nations and Nationalism in the Soviet Union, 1923–1939*. Cornell University Press, 2001.

Marshall, Alex. *The Caucasus under Soviet Rule,* Routledge, 2010.

Maschke, Erich. *Zur Geschichte der deutschen Kriegsgefangenen des Zweiten Weltkrieges*. Vol. 15. E. und W. Gieseking, 1962.

Mason, Henry L. *The Purge of Dutch Quislings: Emergency Justice in the Netherlands*. Martinus Nijhoff, 1952.

Matthäus, Jürgen, Konrad Kwiet, Jürgen Förster, Richard Breitman and Udo Rennert. *Ausbildungsziel Judenmord? 'Weltanschauliche Erziehung' von SS, Polizei und Waffen-SS im Rahmen der 'Endlösung'*. Fischer Taschenbuch Verlag, 2003.

Mazower, Mark. *Inside Hitler's Greece: The Experience of Occupation, 1941–44*. Yale University Press, 1993.

Meding, Holger M. *Flucht vor Nürnberg?: deutsche und österreichische Einwanderung in Argentinien, 1945–1955*. Böhlau, 1992.

Megargee, Geoffrey P. *Encyclopedia of Camps and Ghettos, 1933–1945*. Vol. 1. Indiana University Press, 2009.

Meinecke, Friedrich. Die deutsche Katastrophe, Betrachtungen und Erinnerungen. E. Brockhaus, 1946.

Meinsma, Evertjan van Roekel. *Nederlanders in de Waffen-SS*. Doctoral Skriptie Rijksuniversiteit Groningen, 2000.

Melson, Charles D. 'German Counterinsurgency in the Balkans: The Prinz Eugen Division Example, 1942–1944'. *The Journal of Slavic Military Studies*, 20, No. 4, 2007.

Merkl, Franz Josef. *General Simon: Lebensgeschichten eines SS-Führers; Erkundungen zu Gewalt und Karriere, Kriminalität und Justiz, Legenden und öffentlichen Auseinandersetzungen.* Wissner, 2010.

Messenger, Charles. *Hitler's Gladiator: The Life and Times of Oberstgruppenführer and Panzergeneral-Oberst Der Waffen- SS Sepp Dietrich.* Brassey's Defence Publishers, 1988.

Messerschmidt, Manfred. *Die Wehrmachtjustiz 1933–1945.* Schöningh, 2008.

Meyer, Georg. 'Soldaten wir andere auch? Zur Einstellung ehemalige Angehörige der Waffen-SS in die Bundeswehr'. In *Festgabe Heinz Hürten zum 60. Geburtstag.* Edited by Harald Dickerhof. P. Lang, 1988.

Meyer, Hubert. *The 12.th SS. The History of the Hitler Youth Panzer Division.* Vol. 1. Stackpole Books, 2005.

Michaelis, Rolf. *Cavalry Divisions of the Waffen-SS.* Schiffer Publishing Ltd., 2010.

Michaelis, Rolf. *Die 10. SS-Panzer-Division 'Frundsberg'.* Michaelis-Verlag, 2004.

Michaelis, Rolf. *Die 11. SS-freiwilligen panzer-Grenadier Division 'Nordland'.* Michaelis Verlag, 2001.

Michaelis, Rolf. *Esten in der Waffen-SS: die 20. Waffen-Grenadier-Division der SS (estnische Nr. 1).* Winkelried, 2006.

Michaelis, Rolf. *SS-Heimwehr Danzig in Poland, 1939.* Schiffer Military History, 2008.

Michaelis, Rolf. *Ukrainer in der Waffen-SS. Die 14. Waffen-Grenadier-Division der SS (ukrainischen Nr.1),* Winkelried, 2006.

Michels, Eckard. *Deutsche in der Fremdenlegion 1870–1965: Mythen und Realitäten.* Schöningh, 1999.

Milata, Paul. *Zwischen Hitler, Stalin und Antonescu: Rumäniendeutsche in der Waffen-SS.* Böhlau Verlag, 2009.

Mosse, George L. *Fallen Soldiers: Reshaping the Memory of the World Wars.* Oxford University Press, 1990.

Munoz, Antonio J. *Forgotten Legions: Obscure Combat Formations of the Waffen-SS.* Paladin Press, 1991.

Musial, Bogdan. *Konterrevolutionäre Elemente sind zu erschiessen. Die Brutalisierung des deutsch-sowjetischen Krieges im Sommer 1941.* Propyläen, 2000.

Mühlenberg, Jutta. *Das SS-Helferinnenkorps: Ausbildung, Einsatz und Entnazifizierung der weiblichen Angehörigen der Waffen-SS 1942–1949.* Hamburger Edition, 2010.

Müller, Klaus-Jürgen. *Armee und Drittes Reich 1933–1939.* Ferdinand Schöningh, 1987.

Müller, Rolf-Dieter. *An der Seite der Wehrmacht: Hitlers ausländische Helfer beim 'Kreuzzug gegen den Bolschewismus' 1941–1945.* Fischer Tachenbuch, 2010.

Müller, Rolf-Dieter. *Hitlers Ostkrieg und die deutsche Siedlungspolitik: die Zusammenarbeit von Wehrmacht, Wirtschaft und SS.* Fischer Taschenbuch Verl., 1991.

Myllyniemi, Seppo. *Die Neuordnung der Baltischen Länder, 1941–1944: nationalsozialistischen Inhalt der deutschen Beatzungspolitik.* Suomen Historiallinen Seura, 1973.

Nawratil, Heinz. *Schwarzbuch der Vertreibung 1945 bis 1948. Das letze Kapitel unbewältigter Vergangenheit.* Universitas, 2003.

Nazi Conspiracy and Agression. Vol. IV. United States Government Printing Office, Washington, 1946.

Neulen, Hans W. *An deutscher Seite: internationale Freiwillige von Wehrmacht und Waffen-SS.* Universitas, 1992.

Neulen, Hans W. *Eurofaschismus und der Zweite Weltkrieg: Europas verratene Söhne.* Universitas, 1980.

Neumann, Peter. *Other Men's Graves.* Weidenfeld and Nicolson, 1958.

Nicolaevsky, Boris I., Janet Rabinowitch and Ladis K. D. Kristof. *Revolution and Politics in Russia: Essays in Memory of B.I. Nicolaevsky.* Indiana University Press, 1973.

Nielsen, Olaf. *Slettet af rullen: en frikorpsmands opgør med fortiden.* Aros, 1977.

Noekleby, Berit. *Gestapo: tyskpolitii Norge 1940–1945.* Aschehoug, 2003.

Olcott, Martha Brill. *The Kazakhs.* Hoover Institution Press, 1987.

Otto, Harold. 'How the Germans Conscripted 'Volunteers' for the Latvian Legion', Latvia in World War II. Latvijas vestures instituts, 2000.

Overmans, Rüdiger. *Deutsche militärische Verluste im Zweiten Weltkrieg.* R. Oldenbourg, 2000.

Paul, Gerhard. *Die Täter der Shoah: Fanatische Nationalsozialisten oder ganz normale Deutsche?*. Wallstein, 2002.

Paul, Gerhard. 'Von Psychopathen, Technokraten des Terrors und 'ganz gewöhnlichen Deutschen'. In *Die Täter der Shoah: Fanatische Nationalsozialisten oder ganz normale Deutsche?* Edited by Gerhard Paul. Wallstein, 2002.

Paul, Gerhard and Klaus-Michael Mallmann. *Die Gestapo im Zweiten Weltkrieg: 'Heimatfront' und besetztes Europa*. Primus, 2000.

Pedersen, Andreas Monrad. *Schalburgkorpset: historien om korpset og dets medlemmer 1943–45*. Odense universitetsforlag, 2000.

Pedersen, Bjarne Salling and Georg Rasmussen. *I krig for fjenden - SS-frivillig Georg Rasmussens erindringer*. Informations Forlag, 2012.

Pencz, Rudolf. *For the Homeland! The History of the 31st Waffen-SS Volunteer Grenadier Division: Danubian-Swabian Grenadiers on the Danube and in Silesia*. Helion, 2002.

Picht, Georg. *Studien zur politischen und gesellschaftlichen Situation der Bundeswehr*. Vol. 1. Eckart, 1965.

Pierik, Perry. *From Leningrad to Berlin: Dutch Volunteers in the Service of the German Waffen-SS 1941–1945: The Political and Military History of the Legion, Brigade and Division Known as "Nederland"*. Aspekt, 2001.

Pohl, Dieter. 'Ukrainische Hilfkräfte beim Mord an den Juden'. In *Die Täter der Shoah: Fanatische Nationalsozialisten oder ganz normale Deutsche?* Edited by Gerhard Paul. Wallstein, 2002.

Pohl, Oswald. *Credo. Mein Weg zu Gott*. A. Girnth, 1950.

Pois, Robert A. *National Socialism and the Religion of Nature*. Croom Helm, 1986.

Pontolillo, James. *Murderous Elite - The Waffen-SS and Its Record of Atrocities*. Leandoer & Eckholm, 2009.

Poulsen, Henning. *Besættelsesmagten og de danske nazister: Det politiske forhold mellem tyske myndigheder og nazistiske kredse i Danmark 1940–43*. Gyldendal, 1970.

Poulsen, Niels Bo. *Den store fædrelandskrig: statsmagt og mennesker i Sovjetunionen 1939–1955*. Høst & søn, 2007.

Poulsen, Niels Bo. *The Soviet Extraordinary State Commission on War Crimes: An Analysis of the Commission's Investigate Work in War and Post War Stalinist Society*. Thesis (Ph.D.). Københavns Universitet, 2004.

Poulsen, Niels Bo. *Germanic SS-Soldiers and Nazi Counterinsurgency Warfare 1941–1945. Insurgency and Counterinsurgency: Irregular Warfare from 1800 to the Present*. Den Haag, 2001.

Pringle, Heather Anne. *The Master Plan: Himmler's Scholars and the Holocaust*. Hyperion, 2006.

Pringle, Heather. 'Fra forfedrenes rom til 'Ahnenerbe'. In *Jakten på Germania: fra nordensvermeri til SS-arkeologi*. Edited by Jorunn Sem Fure andTerje Emberland. Humanist forlag, 2009.

Rass, Christoph, *'Menschenmaterial'. Deutsche Soldaten an der Ostfront. Innenansichten einer Infanteriedivision 1939–1945*, Schöningh, 2003.

Redzic, Enver, *Bosnia and Herzegovina in the Second World War*. Frank Cass, 2005.

Reichelt, Katrin. 'Latvia and Latvians in the Nazi Race and Settlement Policy: Theoretical Conception and Practical Implementation'. In *Latvia in World War II: materials of an International Conference 14–15 June 1999*. Edited by Andris Caune. Latvijas vēstures institūta apgāds, 2000.

Rein, Leonid. *The Kings and the Pawns: Collaboration in Byelorussia during World War II*. Berghahn Books, 2011.

Rein, Leonid. 'Untermenschen in SS Uniforms: 30th Waffen-Grenadier Division of Waffen SS'. *The Journal of Slavic Military Studies*, 20, 2, 2007.

Rempel, Gerhard. 'Gottlob Berger. Ein Schwabengeneral der Tat'. In *Die SS: Elite unter dem Totenkopf. 30 Lebensläufe*, Edited by Ronald Smelser and Enrico Syring. Ferdinand Schöningh, 2000.

Reese, Roger. *Why Stalin's Soldiers Fought. The Red Army's Military Effectiveness in World War II*. University Press of Kansas, 2011.

Reynolds, Michael Frank. *Men of Steel: I SS Panzer Corps: The Ardennes and Eastern Front 1944–45*. Spellmount, 1999.

Ringheim, Ane Dalen. *Bak piggtråd i øst: nordmenn i sovjetisk fangenskap, 1940–55.* Institutt for forsvarsstudier, 2003.

Roes, Jörn. *Freiwillig in den Krieg. Auf den Spuren einer verlohrenen Jugend.* Edition q, 2005.

Rohrkamp, René. *Weltanschaulich gefestigte Kämpfer' die Soldaten der Waffen-SS 1933–1945; Organisation - Personal - Sozialstrukturen.* Schöningh, 2010.

Römer, Felix. *Kameraden: Die Wehrmacht von innen.* Piper, 2012.

Roslyng-Jensen, Palle. *Danskerne og besættelsen: holdninger og meninger 1939–1945.* Gads Forlag, 2007.

Rossino, Alexander B. *Hitler Strikes Poland. Blitzkrieg, Ideology, and Atrocity.* University Press of Kansas, 2003.

Rudling, Per Anders. 'They Defended Ukraine': The 14. Waffen-Grenadier-Division der SS (Galizische Nr. 1) Revisited'. *Journal of Slavic Military Studies.* Vol. 25, No. 3, 2012.

Rudling, Per Anders. 'Review Essay: "The Honor They So Clearly Deserve": Legitimizing the Waffen-SS Galizien'. *Journal of Slavic Military Studies.* Vol. 26, No. 2, 2013.

Ruhm von Oppen, Beate. *Documents on Germany under Occupation, 1945–1954.* Oxford University Press, 1955.

Rüter, C. F. and L. Hekelaar Gombert. *Justiz und NS-Verbrechen: Sammlung deutscher Strafurteile wegen nationalsozialistischer Tötungsverbrechen, 1945–1966.* Vol. XL. University Press Amsterdam, 2009.

Rüter, C. F. and L. Hekelaar Gombert. *Justiz und NS-Verbrechen: Sammlung deutscher Strafurteile wegen nationalsozialistischer Tötungsverbrechen, 1945–1966.* Vol. XXXIX. University Press Amsterdam, 2008.

Rüter, C. F. and L. Hekelaar Gombert. *Justiz und NS-Verbrechen: Sammlung deutscher Strafurteile wegen nationalsozialistischer Tötungsverbrechen, 1945–1966.* Vol. XLIII. University Press Amsterdam, 2010.

Rüter, C. F. and Dick de, Hekelaar Gombert, L. Mildt. *Justiz und NS-Verbrechen: Sammlung deutscher Strafurteile wegen nationalsozialistischer Tötungsverbrechen, 1945–1966.* Vol. XLIX. University Press Amsterdam, 2012.

Rüter, C. F. and L. Hekelaar Gombert. *Justiz und NS-Verbrechen: Sammlung deutscher Strafurteile wegen nationalsozialistischer Tötungsverbrechen, 1945–1966.* Vol. XLVIII. University Press Amsterdam, 2012.

Rüter-Ehlermann, Adelheid L., H. H. Fuchs, C. F. Rüter and Fritz Bauer. *Justiz und NS-Verbrechen: Sammlung deutscher Strafurteile wegen nationalsozialistischer Tötungsverbrechen, 1945–1966.* Vol. VII. University Press Amsterdam, 1971.

Rüter-Ehlermann, Adelheid L., H. H. Fuchs, C. F. Rüter and Fritz Bauer. *Justiz und NS-Verbrechen: Sammlung deutscher Strafurteile wegen nationalsozialistischer Tötungsverbrechen, 1945–1966.* Vol. VIII. University Press Amsterdam, 1972.

Rüter-Ehlermann, Adelheid L., C. F. Rüter and Fritz Bauer. *Justiz und NS-Verbrechen: Sammlung deutscher Strafurteile wegen nationalsozialistischer Tötungsverbrechen, 1945–1966.* Vol. II. University Press Amsterdam, 1969.

Rüter-Ehlermann, Adelheid L., C. F. Rüter and Fritz Bauer. *Justiz und NS-Verbrechen: Sammlung deutscher Strafurteile wegen nationalsozialistischer Tötungsverbrechen, 1945–1966.* Vol. III. University Press Amsterdam, 1969.

Sagel-Grande, H. I. and Fritz Bauer. *Justiz und NS-Verbrechen: Sammlung deutscher Strafurteile wegen nationalsozialistischer Tötungsverbrechen, 1945–1966.* Vol. XXII. University Press Amsterdam, 1981.

Sagel-Grande, H. I., H. H. Fuchs, C. F. Rüter and Fritz Bauer. *Justiz und NS-Verbrechen: Sammlung deutscher Strafurteile wegen nationalsozialistischer Tötungsverbrechen, 1945–1966.* Vol. XIII. University Press Amsterdam, 1975.

Sagel-Grande, H. I., H. H. Fuchs, C. F. Rüter and Fritz Bauer. *Justiz und NS-Verbrechen: Sammlung deutscher Strafurteile wegen nationalsozialistischer Tötungsverbrechen, 1945–1966.* Vol. XIV. University Press Amsterdam, 1976.

Sagel-Grande, H. I., H. H. Fuchs, C. F. Rüter and Fritz Bauer. *Justiz und NS-Verbrechen: Sammlung deutscher Strafurteile wegen nationalsozialistischer Tötungsverbrechen, 1945–1966.* Vol. XV. University Press Amsterdam, 1976.

Sagel-Grande, H. I., H. H. Fuchs, C. F. Rüter and Fritz Bauer. *Justiz und NS-Verbrechen: Sammlung deutscher Strafurteile wegen nationalsozialistischer Tötungsverbrechen, 1945–1966.* Vol. XVI. University Press Amsterdam, 1976.

Sagel-Grande, H. I., H. H. Fuchs, C. F. Rüter and Fritz Bauer. *Justiz und NS-Verbrechen: Sammlung deutscher Strafurteile wegen nationalsozialistischer Tötungsverbrechen, 1945–1966.* Vol. XX. University Press Amsterdam, 1979.

Sanders, Marian R. *Extraordinary Crimes in Ukraine: An Examination of Evidence Collection by the Extraordinary State Commission of the U.S.S.R., 1942–1946.* Thesis (Ph.D.). Ohio University, 1995.

Sars, Michael and Knut Erik Tranøy. Tysklandsstudentene, J.W. Cappelen, 1946.

Sargeant, Maggie. 'Memory, distortion and the war in German popular culture: the case of Konsalik'. In *Memory and Memorials: The Commemorative Century.* Edited by William Kidd and Brian Murdoch. Ashgate, 2004.

Sauer, Karl. *Die Verbrechen der Waffen-SS. Eine Dokumentation.* Röderberg Verlag, 1977.

Sayer, Ian and Douglas Botting. *Hitler's last General. The case against Wilhelm Mohnke.* Bantam Press, 1989.

She, Manachem. 'Die Ermordung italienischer Kriegsgefangener, September–November 1943'. In *Vernichtungskrieg: Verbrechen der Wehrmacht 1941–1944.* Edited by Hannes Heer and Klaus Naumann. Zweitausendeins, 1995.

Scheck, Raffael. *Hitler's African Victims: The German Army Massacres of Black French Soldiers in 1940.* Cambridge University Press, 2006.

Scheck, Raffael. '"They Are Just Savages": German Massacres of Black Soldiers from the French Army in 1940'. *The Journal of Modern History,* 77, No. 2, Juni 2005.

Schenk, Dieter. *Die Post von Danzig: Geschichte eines deutschen Justizmords.* Rohwolt, 1995.

Schilde, Kurt. *Vom Columbia-Haus zum Schulenburgring: Dokumentation mit Lebensgeschichten von Opfern des Widerstandes und der Verfolgung von 1933 bis 1945 aus dem Bezirk Tempelhof.* Hentrich, 1987.

Schindler, Christine. *Schwerpunkt Mauthausen: Jahrbuch des Dokumentationsarchivs des österreichischen.* Widerstandes 2004.

Dokumentationsarchiv des österreichischen Widerstandes. LIT, 2004.

Schneider, Klaus. *Spuren der Nibelungen 1945: die Kämpfe bei Bad Abbach und die Rettung von Regensburg: eine Dokumentation über Soldaten der 38. Grenadier-Division "Nibelungen" der Waffen-SS.* K. Vowinckel-Verlag, 1999.

Schreiber, Franz. *Kampf unter dem Nordlicht: deutsch-finnische Waffenbruderschaft am Polarkreis: die Geschichte der 6. SS- Gebirgs-Division Nord.* Munin Verlag, 1969.

Schreiber, Gerhard, Bernd Stegemann and Detlef Vogel. *Das Deutsche Reich und der Zweite Weltkrieg.* Vol. 3. Dt. Verl.-Anst, 1984.

Schroeder, Friedrich-Christian. 'Das Sowjetrecht als Grundlage der Prozesse gegen deutsche Kriegsgefangene'. In *Sowjetische Militärtribunale.* Vol. 1. Edited by Andreas Hilger, Ute Schmidt and Günther Wagenlehner. Böhlau, 2001.

Schulte, Jan Theo. *Zwangsarbeit und Vernichtung: Das Wirtschaftsimperium der SS.* Schöningh, 2001.

Schulte, Jan Erik. *Die SS, Himmler und die Wewelsburg. Schriftenreihe des Kreismuseums Wewelsburg 7,* Schöningh, 2009.

Schulte, Jan Erik. 'Hans Jüttner. Der Mann im Hintergrund der Waffen-SS'. In *Die SS: Elite unter dem Totenkopf; 30 Lebensläufe.* Edited by Ronald Smelser and Enrico Syring, Schöningh, 2003.

Schulte, Jan Erik, Peter Lieb and Bernd Wegner. *Die Waffen-SS. Neue Forschungen.* Ferdinand Schöningh, 2014.

Schulz, Andreas and Günter Wegmann. *Die Generale der Waffen-SS und der Polizei: (1933–1945): die militärischen Werdegänge der Generale, sowie der Ärzte, Veterinäre, Intendanten, Richter und Ministerialbeamten im Generalsrang.* Vol. 1. Biblio-Verlag, 2003.

Schulz, Andreas and Günter Wegmann. *Die Generale der Waffen-SS und der Polizei: (1933–1945): die militärischen Werdegänge der Generale, sowie der Ärzte, Veterinäre, Intendanten, Richter und Ministerialbeamten im Generalsrang,* Vol. 2. Biblio-Verlag, 2005.

Schulz, Andreas and Günter Wegmann. *Die Generale der Waffen-SS und der Polizei: (1933–1945): die militärischen Werdegänge der Generale, sowie der Ärzte, Veterinäre, Intendanten, Richter und Ministerialbeamten im Generalsrang*, Vol. 3. Biblio-Verlag, 2008.

Schulz, Andreas, Dermot Bradley, Ernest Henriot and Dieter Zinke. *Die Generale der Waffen-SS und der Polizei: (1933–1945) : die militärischen Werdegänge der Generale, sowie der Ärzte, Veterinäre, Intendanten, Richter und Ministerialbeamten im Generalsrang*. Vol. 4. Biblio-Verlag, 2009.

Schulz, Andreas and Günter Wegmann. *Die Generale der Waffen-SS und der Polizei: (1933–1945): die militärischen Werdegänge der Generale, sowie der Ärzte, Veterinäre, Intendanten, Richter und Ministerialbeamten im Generalsrang*, Vol. 5. Biblio-Verlag, 2011.

Schulz, Andreas and Günter Wegmann. *Die Generale der Waffen-SS und der Polizei: (1933–1945): die militärischen Werdegänge der Generale, sowie der Ärzte, Veterinäre, Intendanten, Richter und Ministerialbeamten im Generalsrang*, Vol. 6. Biblio-Verlag, 2011.

Schulze, Hagen. *Freikorps und Republik, 1918–1920. Wehrwissenschaftliche Forschungen. Abteilung militärgeschichtliche Studien*, Harald Boldt Verlag - Boppard am Rhein, 1969.

Schulze-Kossens, R. *Militärischer Führernachwuchs der Waffen-SS. Die Junkerschulen*. Munin Verlag, 1982.

Schwarz, Gudrun. *Die nationalsozialistischen Lager*. Campus Verlag, 1990.

Schwarz, Gudrun. *Eine Frau an seiner Seite: Ehefrauen in der 'SS-Sippengemeinschaft'*. Baufbau Taschenbuch Verlag, 2000.

Seidler, Franz W. *Die Organisation Todt: Bauen für Staat u. Wehrmacht 1938–1945*. Bernard & Graefe, 1987.

Shields, J. G. 'Charlemagnes Crufersaders: French Collaboration in Arms, 1941–1945'. *French Cultural Studies*. Vol. 18, No. 83, 2007.

Sigmund, Anna Maria. *'Das Geschlechtsleben bestimmen wir': Sexualität im Dritten Reich*. Heyne, 2009.

Sigsgaard, Thomas. *Psykologisk undersøgelse af mandlige landssvigere i Danmark under besættelsen*. Direktoratet for Fængselsvæsenet, 1954.

Sluyse, Willem. *Die Jünger und die Dirnen*. Dürer-Verlag, 1954.

Smelser, Ronald M. and Edward J. Davies. *The Myth of the Eastern Front: The Nazi-Soviet War in American Popular Culture*. Cambridge University Press, 2008.

Smelser, Ronald and Enrico Syring. *Die SS: Elite unter dem Totenkopf: 30 Lebensläufe*. Schöningh, 2003.

Smith, Peter Scharff. 'Dehumanization, Social Contact and Techniques of Othering. Combining the Lessons from Holocaust Studies and Prison Research'. In *Punishing the Other. The Social Production of Immorality Revisited*. Editing by Anna Eriksson. Routledge 2015.

Snyder, Timothy. *Bloodlands*. Basic Books, 2011.

Solbakken, Evald O. *I fengsel og landflyktighet*. Tiden Norsk Forlag, 1945.

Sorokina, Marina. 'People and Procedures. Towards a History of the investigation of Nazi Crimes in the USSR'. *Kritika*, No. 4, 2005.

Kevin Soutor. 'To Stem the Red Tide. The German Report Series and Its Effect on American Defense Doctrine, 1948–1954'. *The Journal of Military History.*Vol. 57, oktober 1993.

Spannenberger, Norbert. *Der Volksbund der Deutschen in Ungarn 1938–1944 unter Horthy und Hitler*. R. Oldenbourg, 2005.

Speer, Albert. *Erinnerungen*. Propyläen-Verlag; Ullstein, 1969.

Stang, Knut. 'Dr. Oskar Dirlewanger'. In *Karrieren der Gewalt: nationalsozialistische Täterbiographien*. Edited by Klaus-Michael Mallmann and Gerhard Paul. Sonderausg. Primus, 2011.

Steegmann, Robert. *Das KZ Natzweiler-Struthof und seine Aussenkommandos an Rhein und Neckar 1941–1945*. Metropol, 2010.

Steele, Dennis. 'Reliving and Memorializing World War II History'. *Army*. Vol. 49, No. 5, 1999.

Stegemann, Bernd. 'Die italienisch-deutsche Kriegsführung im Mittelmeer und in Afrika'. In *Der Mittelmeerraum und Südosteuropa. Das Deutsche Reich und der Zweite Weltkrieg*. Vol. 3. Edited by Gerhard Schreiber, Bernd Stegemann, and Detlef Vogel. Dt. Verl.-Anst., 1984.

Stein, George H. *The Waffen SS: Hitler's Elite Guard at War, 1939–1945*. Cornell University Press, 1984.

Stein, George H. and H. Peter Krosby. 'Das finnische Freiwilligen-Bataillon der Waffen-SS'. *Vierteljahrshefte für Zeitgeschichte*. Vol. 14, No. 4, 1966.

Steinacher, Gerald. *Nazis on the Run: How Hitler's Henchmen Fled Justice*. Oxford University Press, 2011.

Steiner, Felix. *Die Freiwilligen der Waffen-SS: Idee und Opfergang*. Verlagsgesellschaft, 1992.

Steiner, Felix. *Die Freiwilligen; Idee und Opfergang*. Plesse Verlag, 1958.

Steiner, Felix. *Von Clausewitz bis Bulganin; Erkenntnisse und Lehren einer Wehrepoche*. Deutscher Heimat-Verlag, 1956.

Steiner, Felix. *Die Armee der Geächteten*. Plesse Verlag, 1963.

Steiner, Felix. *Die Wehridee des Abendlandes*. Parma-Edition, 1951.

Steiner, John M. 'The SS Yesterday and Today – A Sociopsychological View'. In *Survivors, Victims, and Perpetrators: Essays on the Nazi Holocaust*. Edited by Joel E Dimsdale, Hemisphere, 1980.

Steiner, John and Jochen Fahrenberg. 'Die Ausprägung autoritärer Einstellung bei ehemaligen Angehörigen der SS und der Wehrmacht (Eine empirische Studie)'. *Kölner Zeitschrift für Soziologi and Sozialpsychologi*. Vol. 22, No. 3, 1970.

Stone, Dan. *The Historiography of the Holocaust*. Palgrave Macmillan, 2004.

Strassner, Peter. *Europäische Freiwillige: die Geschichte der 5. SS-Panzer-division Wiking*. Munin Verlag, 1968.

Streim, Alfred. *Die Behandlung sowjetischer Kriegsgefangener im 'Fall Barbarossa': eine Dokumentation unter Berücksichtigung der Unterlagen deutscher Strafverfolgungsbehörden und der Materialien der Zentralen Stelle der Landesjustizverwaltungen zur Aufklärung von NS-Verbrechen*. Müller, Juristischer Verlag, 1981.

Streit, Christian. *Keine Kameraden: die Wehrmacht und die sowjetischen Kriegsgefangenen 1941–1945*. Dt. Verlagsanst., 1978.

Stridsklev, Inger Cecilie. 'Norske frontkjempere 1941–45 50 år senere'. *Tidsskrift for Den norske lægeforening*, No. 11, 1995.

Sverdlov, F. D. *Dokumenty obviniaiut: Kholokost: svidetel'stva Krasnoĭ Armii. Moskva: Nauchno-prosvetitel'nyĭ tsentr. Kholokost*, 1996.

Sydnor, Charles W. *Soldiers of Destruction: The SS Death's Head Division, 1933–1945*. Princeton University Press, 1990.

Sørlie, Sigurd. *Solkors eller hakekors. Nordmenn i Waffen-SS 1941–1945*. Dreyer, 2015.

Tames, I. *Besmette jeugd: de kinderen van NSB'ers na de oorlog*. Balans, 2009.

Tauber, Kurt P. *Beyond Eagle and Swastika: German Nationalism since 1945*. Wesleyan University Press, 1967.

Terwisscha van Scheltinga, Gerard. *Trouw zonder eer: het gewelddadige leven van een SS-officier*. Aspekt, 2008.

Theel, Christopher. '"Parzifal unter den Gangstern?" Die SS- und Polizeigerichtsbarkeit in Polen 1939–1945'. In *Die Waffen-SS. Neue Forschungen*. Edited by Jan Erik Schulte, Peter Lieb and Bernd Wegner, Ferdinand Schöningh, 2014.

Thurston, Robert W. *Life and Terror in Stalins Russia 1934–1941*. Yale University Press, 1996.

Thurston, Robert W. 'Cauldrons of Loyalty and Betrayal: Soviet Soldier's Behavior, 1941 and 1945', Robert W. Thurston and Bernd Bonwetch (eds.), *The People's War. Responses to World War II in the Soviet Union*. University of Illonois Press, 2000.

Tieke, Wilhelm. *Das Ende zwischen Oder und Elbe: der Kampf um Berlin 1945*. Motorbuch, 1994.

Tieke, Wilhelm. *Im Feuersturm letzter Kriegsjahre: II. SS-Panzerkorps mit 9. und 10. SS-Division 'Hohenstaufen' und 'Frundsberg'*. Munin-Verlag, 1975.

Tieke, Wilhelm. *Tragödie um die Treue*. Munin-Verlag, 1971.

Trang, Charles. *Waffen-SS: dictionnaire*. Vol. 4. Heimdal, 2012.

Tuchel, Johannes. 'Die Kommandanten des Konzentrationslagers Flossenbürg. Eine Studie zur Personalpolitik in der SS'. In *Die Normalität des Verbrechens: Bilanz und Perspektiven der Forschung zu den nationalsozialistischen Gewaltverbrechen: Festschrift für Wolfgang Scheffler zum 65. Geburtstag*. Edited by Helge Grabitz. Edition Hentrich, 1994.

Tyas, Stephen. 'Allied Intelligence Agencies and the Holocaust: Information Acquired from German Prisoners of War'. *Holocaust and Genocide Studies*. Vol. 22, No. 1, 2008.

Ulateig, Egil. *Dagbok frå ein rotnorsk nazist.* Oslo, 1987.

Umbreit, Hans. *Deutsche Militärverwaltungen 1938/39: d. militär. Besetzung d. Tschechoslowakei u. Polens.* Deutsche Verlags-Anstalt, 1977.

Ungváry, Krisztián. *Battle for Budapest: One Hundred Days in World War II.* I.B.Tauris, 2003.

'T Veld, N. K. C. A. *De SS en Nederland. Documenten uit SS-Archieven 1935–1945.* Vol. 1. Martinus Nijhoff, 1976.

'T Veld, N. K. C. A. *De SS en Nederland. Documenten uit SS-Archieven 1935–1945.* Vol. 2. Martinus Nijhoff, 1976.

Verton, Hendrik C. *In the Fire of the Eastern Front: The Experiences of a Dutch Waffen-SS Volunteer on the Eastern Front 1941–45.* Helion & Co., 2007.

Vestermanis, Margers. 'Die nationalsozialistischen Häftstätten und Todeslager im okkupierten Lettland 1941–1945'. In *Die Nationalsozialistischen Konzentrationslager.* Vol. 1. Edited by Ulrich Herbert. Wallstein Verlag, 1998.

Vestermanis, Margers. 'Das SS-Seelager Dondagen – ein Modell für die geplante nazistische "Neuordnung Europas"'. *Militärgeschichte* 2/1986.

Vieregge, Bianca. *Die Gerichtsbarkeit einer 'Elite': Nationalsozialistische Rechtsprechung am Beispiel der SS- und Polizei- Gerichtsbarkeit.* Nomos, 2002.

Vogel, Detlef. 'Der deutsche Überfall auf Jugoslawien und Griechenland'. In *Der Mittelmeerraum und Südosteuropa. Das Deutsche Reich und der Zweite Weltkrieg.* Vol. 3. Edited by Gerhard Schreiber, Bernd Stegemann and Detlef Vogel. Deutsche Verlags- Anstalt, 1984.

Vopersal, Wolfgang. *Wohin der Befehl rief-aus der Geschichte der Kartsjäger der Waffen-SS.* Unpublished manuscript, 1975.

Vultejus, Hans von. *Forpligtet: en dansk/tysk skæbne, som tysk soldat 1943–45.* Forlaget Underskoven, 2011.

Vormann, Nikolaus. *Tscherkassy.* Scharnhorst Buchkameradschaft, 1954.

Wachsmann, Nikolaus. *Hitler's Prisons: Legal Terror in Nazi Germany.* Yale University Press, 2004.

Wagenlehner, Günther. *Die russischen Bemühungen um die Rehabilitierung der 1941–1956 verfolgten deutschen Staatsbürger: Dokumentation und Wegweiser.* Friedrich Ebert Stiftung, 1999.

Warlimont, Walter. *Im Hauptquartier der deutschen Wehrmacht 39–45.* Bernard & Graefe Verlag, 1978.

Waller, James. *Becoming Evil: How Ordinary People Commit Genocide and Mass Killing.* Oxford University Press, 2007.

Warmbrunn, Werner. *The German Occupation of Belgium 1940–1944.* Peter Lang, 1993.

Weale, Adrian. *Renegades: Hitler's Englishmen.* Pimlico, 2002.

Weale, Adrian. *The SS: A New History,* Brown, 2010.

Wegner, Bernd. *Hitlers politische Soldaten: Die Waffen-SS 1933–1945: Leitbild, Struktur und Funktion einer nationalsozialistischen Elite.* Ferdinand Schöningh, 1990.

Wegner, Bernd. '"Hitlers, zweiter Feldzug". Militärische Konzeption und strategische Grundlagen'. In *Der Globale Krieg. Die Ausweitung zum Weltkrieg und der Wechsel der Initiative. Das Deutsche Reich und der Zweite Weltkrieg.* Edited by Horst Boog, Werner Rahn, Reinhard Stumpf and Bernd Wegner. Vol. 6. Deutsche Verlags-Anstalt, 1990.

Wegner, Bernd. '"My Honour Is Loyalty". The SS as a Military Factor in Hitler's Germany'. In *The Germany Military in the Age of Total War.* Edited by Wilhelm Deist. Leamington, 1985.

Wegner, Bernd. 'Auf dem Wege zur pangermanischen Armee. Dokumente zur Entstehungsgeschichte des IIII. ("germanischen") SS-Panzerkorps'. *Militärgeschichtliche Mitteilungen.* No. 2, 1980.

Weidinger, Otto. Das Reich I, 1934–1939. J.J. Fedorowicz Publishing, 1990.

Weidinger, Otto. Das Reich II, 1940–1941. J.J. Fedorowicz Publishing, 1995.

Weidinger, Otto. Division Das Reich: der Weg der 2. SS-Panzer-Division "Das Reich": die Geschichte der Stammdivision der Waffen-SS. 1943–1945. bd. 5. Munin, 1982.

Weidinger, Otto. *Kameraden bis zum Ende: der Weg des SS-Panzergrenadier-Regiments 4 'DF' 1939–1945 : die Geschichte einer deutsch-österreichischen Kampfgemeinschaft.* Plesse-Verlag, 1962.

Weidinger, Otto. *Tulle und Oradour die Wahrheit über zwei 'Vergeltungsaktionen' der Waffen-SS.* Nation-Europa-Verl., 1999.

Weigley, Russell F. *Normandy to Falaise. A Critique of Allied Planning in 1944. Historical Perspectives of the Operational Art.* Center of Military History. United States Army, 2005.

Weinberg, Gerhard L. *A World at Arms: A Global History of World War II.* Cambridge University Press, 1994.

Weingartner, James J. *Crossroads of Death: The Story of the Malmédy Massacre and Trial.* University of California Press, 1979.

Weingartner, James J. *Hitler's Guard: The Story of the Leibstandarte SS Adolf Hitler, 1933–1945.* Southern Illinois University Press, 1974.

Weingartner, James J. 'Sepp Dietrich, Heinrich Himmler, and the Leibstandarte SS Adolf Hitler, 1933–1938'. *Central European History.* Vol. 1. No. 3, 1968.

Weise, Niels. *Eicke: Eine SS-Karriere zwischen Nervenklinik, KZ-System und Waffen-SS.* Ferdinand Schöningh, 2013.

Weiss, Hermann. 'Alte Kameraden von der Waffen-SS'. In *Rechtsextremismus in der Bundesrepublik: Voraussetzungen, Zusammenhänge, Wirkungen.* Edited by Wolfgang Benz. Fischer Taschenbuch Verlag, 1984.

Weitbrecht, Dorothee. 'Ermächtigung zur Vernichtung. Die Einsatzgruppen in Polen im Herbst 1939'. In *Genesis des Genozids : Polen 1939–1941.* Edited by Klaus-Michael Mallmann og Bogdan Musial. Wissenschaftliche Buchgesellschaft, 2004.

Westemeier, Jens. *Hans Robert Jauss. Jugend, Krieg und Internierung.* Konstanz University Press, 2016.

Welzer, Harald and Michaela Christ. *Täter: wie aus ganz normalen Menschen Massenmörder werden.* Fischer Taschenbuch, 2005.

Welzer, Harald, Michaela Christ and Svenja Hums. *Gärningsmän: hur helt vanliga människor blir massmördare.* Daidalos, 2007.

Welzer, Harald, Sabine Moller and Karoline Tschuggnall. *Opa war kein Nazi: Nationalsozialismus und Holocaust im Familiengedächtnis.* Fischer Taschenbuch, 2002.

Wember, Heiner. *Umerziehung im Lager: Internierung und Bestrafung von Nationalsozialisten in der britischen Besatzungszone Deutschlands.* Klartext-Verl., 1991.

Wenzel, Mario. 'Zwangsarbeitslager für Juden in den besetzten polnischen und sowjetischen Gebieten'. In *Der Ort des Terrors der nationalsozialistischen Konzentrationslager.* Edited by Wolfgang Benz, Barbara Distel and Angelika, C.H. Beck, 2009.

Westemeier, Jens. *Himmlers Krieger. Joachim Peiper und die Waffen-SS in Krieg und Nachkriegszeit.* Ferdinand Schöningh, 2014.

Westemeier, Jens. *Joachim Peiper: (1915–1976): SS-Standartenführer: eine biographie.* Biblio Verlag, 1996.

Westemeier, Jens. *Joachim Peiper: A Biography of Himmler's SS Commander.* Schiffer Military History, 2007.

Westerlund, Lars. *The Finish SS-volunteers and atrocities, 1941–1943.* SKS, 2019.

Wette, Wolfram. *Die Wehrmacht: Feindbilder, Vernichtungskrieg, Legenden.* S. Fischer, 2002.

Wette, Wolfram. *Militarismus in Deutschland: Geschichte einer kriegerischen Kultur.* Primus, 2008.

Wever, de Bruno. 'Belgium'. In *The Oxford Handbook of Fascism.* Edited by Richard James Boon Bosworth, Oxford Univ. Press, 2009.

Wever, Bruno de. *Oostfronters: Vlamingen in het Vlaams Legioen en de Waffen SS.* Lannoo, 1984.

Wever, Bruno de. 'Rebellen an der Ostfront. Die flämischen Freiwilligen der Legion "Flandern" und der Waffen-SS'. *Vierteljahrshefte für Zeitgeschichte,* 39, No. 4, 1991.

Wiedner, Hartmut. 'Soldatenmisshandlungen im Wilhelminischen Kaiserreich (1890–1914)'. *Archiv für Sozialgeschichte.* Vol. 22, 1982.

Wildt, Michael. *Generation des Unbedingten: das Führungskorps des Reichssicherheitshauptamtes.* Hamburger Edition, 2002.

Wildt, Michael and Tom Lampert. *An Uncompromising Generation: The Nazi Leadership of the Reich Security Main Office*. University of Wisconsin Press, 2009.

Wilke, Karsten. *Die 'Hilfsgemeinschaft auf Gegenseitigkeit' (HIAG) 1950–1990 Veteranen der Waffen-SS in der Bundesrepublik*. Ferdinand Schöningh, 2011.

Williamson, Gordon. *Loyalty Is My Honour: Personal Accounts from the Waffen-SS*. Brown Books, 1995.

Wilson, Paul J. *Himmler's Cavalry: The Equestrian SS, 1930–1945*. Schiffer Publishing, Limited, 2000.

Winter, Bettina. 'Die Geschichte der NS-Éuthanasie-Anstalt Hadamari', In *'Verlegt nach Hadamar': die Geschichte einer NS-'Euthanasie'-Anstalt ; eine Ausstellung des Landeswohlfahrtsverbandes Hessen*. Edited by Bettina Winter, Gerhard Baader and Johannes Cramer. Eigenverl. d. LWV Hessen, 1991.

Winter, Bettina, Gerhard Baader and Johannes Cramer. *'Verlegt nach Hadamar': die Geschichte einer NS-'Euthanasie'- Anstalt ; eine Ausstellung des Landeswohlfahrtsverbandes Hessen*. Eigenverl. d. LWV Hessen, 1991.

Wistrich, Robert and Hermann Weiss. *Wer war wer im Dritten Reich: ein biographisches Lexikon; Anhänger, Mitläufer, Gegner aus Politik, Wirtschaft, Militär, Kunst und Wissenschaft*. Fischer-Taschenbuch-Verl., 1993.

Witte, Peter, Uwe Lohalm and Wolfgang Scheffler. *Der Dienstkalender Heinrich Himmlers 1941/42*. Christians, 1999.

Wittmann, Anna M. 'Mutinity in the Balkans: Croat Volksdeutsche, the Waffen-SS and Motherhood'. *East European Quarterly* XXXVI. No. 3, 2002.

Wiwjorra, Ingo. 'Arkaisme og krisen i det moderne. Ideen 'Ahnenerbe'. In *Jakten på Germania: fra nordensvermeri til SS-arkeologi*. Edited by Jorunn Sem Fure and Terje Emberland. Humanist forlag, 2009.

Wood, James A. 'Captive Historians, Captivated Audience: The German Military History Program, 1945–1961'. *The Journal of Military History*. Vol. 69, No. 1, 2005.

Wodak, Ruth and John E. Richardson. *Analyzing Fascist Discourse: European Fascism in Talk and Text*. Routledge, 2013.

Wolf-Roskosch, Florian. *Ideologie der Waffen-SS. Ideologische Mobilmachung der Waffen-SS 1942–45*. Diserta Verlag, 2014.

Wolfe, Robert. *Americans as Proconsuls: United States Military Government in Germany and Japan, 1944–1952*. Southern Illinois University Press, 1984.

Wyman, Mark. *DP: Europe's Displaced Persons, 1945–1951*. Balch Institute Press, 1989.

Yakolev, Alexander N. *A Century of Violence in Soviet Russia*. Yale University Press, 2002.

Yugoslav War Crimes Commission. Report on the Crimes of Austria and the Austrians against Yugoslavia and Her Peoples. Belgrade, 1947.

Zaugg, Franziska A. *Albanische Muslime in der Waffen-SS*. Ferdinand Schöningh Verlag, 2016.

Zaugg, Franziska, *Albanian Muslims in the Waffen-SS*, Unpublished paper, Supernational Militia Indigenous Participation in SS and Police Units in the Context of the Second World War. UMK Institute of History and Archival Science in Torun, 2014.

Zaugg, Franziska. 'Perfekter Krieger? Die deutschen Wahrnehmung muslimischer Albaner in der Waffen-SS zwischen 1943 und 1945'. In *Die Waffen-SS. Neue Forschungen*. Edited by Jan Erik Schulte, Peter Lieb and Bernd Wegner. Ferdinand Schöningh, 2014.

Zee, Sytze van der. *25,000 landverraders. De SS in Nederland. Nederland in de SS*. Den Haag: Kruseman, 1967.

Zentner, Christian and Friedemann Bedürftig. *Das Grosse Lexikon des Zweiten Weltkriegs*. Südwest Verlag, 1993.

Zetterling, Niklas. *Blitzkrig!: 1939–1941*. Spartacus, 2011.

Zetterling, Niklas. *Normandy 1944: German Military Organization, Combat Power and Organizational Effectiveness*. J.J. Fedorowicz Publishing, 2000.

Zetterling, Niklas and Anders Frankson. *Tjerkassy 44: inringningen på östfronten.* Norstedt, 2006.

Ziemke, Earl F. *Stalingrad to Berlin. The German defeat in the east.* Barnes & Noble, 1996.

Ziemke, Earl F. and Magna E. Bauer. *Moscow to Stalingrad: Decision in the East.* Military Heritage Press, 1988.

Zimmermann, John. 'Die deutsche militärische Kriegführung im Westen 1944/45'. In *Das Deutsche Reich und der Zweite Weltkrieg.* Edited by Horst Boog and Rolf-Dieter Müller. Vol. 10/1. Deutsche Verlags-Anstalt, 2008.

Zolotarev, V. A. *Velikaja Otetjestvennaja: Nemetskie Voennoplennye v SSSR 1941–1955 gg. Russkiï Arkhiv,* T. 24. Terra, 2002.

Zuroff, Efraim. 'Sweden's refusal to prosecute Nazi war criminals – 1986–2002'. *Jewish Political Studies Review,* 14:3–4, Fall 2002.

ARCHIVES

Only the most important groups are mentioned under the individual archives. In cases where the archive group is labelled by name, the original title is offered; otherwise, a short description is provided in English.

Austria:

Simon Wiesenthal Center, Wien: SWC
Material about Waffen-SS and HIAG

Czech Republic:

Vojenský ústřední archiv, Prag: VAP
Materials about Waffen-SS: Divisions, regiments and schools.

Denmark:

Det Kongelige Bibliotek, København: KB
HS 1979/126: Brøndums erindringer
Rigsarkivet København: RK
RA 1353: Knud Nordentoft collection
RA 101-1-30-2, 06292: Poul Ranzow Engelhardt collection

France:

Memorial Museum, Caen: MMC
TE331: Eugène Finance

Germany:

Insititut für Zeitgeschichte, München: IfZG
ED 373/1: Nachlass Huge Landgraf
MA: Auswärtiges Amt
NO: Nürnberg files
OMGUS: Office of Military Government for Germany, USA

Bundesarchiv, Berlin: BAB
A9: SS-Listen
A20: SS-Listen

DP: Generalstaatsanwalt der DDR 1949-1990
NS3: SS-Wirtschafts- und Verwaltungshauptamt
NS7: SS- und Polizeigerichtsbarkeit
NS19: Persönlicher Stab Reichsführer-SS
NS31: SS-Hauptamt
NS33: SS-Führungshauptamt
NS34: SS-Personalhauptamt
NS48: Lebensborn
R70 : Besetzte Gebiete
SSO: SS-personalakter (tidl. Berlin Document Center).

Bundesarchiv, Freiburg: **BAMA**
B438: HIAG
RH: German army
RS1: Waffen-SS higher headquarters
RS2: Waffen-SS corps and armies
RS3: Waffen-SS divisions
RS4: Various Waffen-SS units (below divisional level)
RS8: Waffen-SS personell administration
N756: Wolfgang Vopersal collection

Bundesarchiv, Koblenz: **BAK**
B: Bundeskanzleramt

Bundesarchiv, Ludwigsburg: **BL**
Assorted court material

Kz-Gedenkstaette-Dachau: **DA**
Assorted court material

Israel:

Yad Vashem, Jerusalem: **YV**
M 36: Voinsky Arkhiv Prag
M.40.MAP: Archives in Russia: Podolsk
M.55: Central Government Archive of Ukraine
O.53: File Nr. 68, Ludwigsburg, USSR Collection
O.68: SS Personel Files

Netherlands:

NIOD, Amsterdam: NIOD
NIOD.Coll.Doc. II, 750a: SS-Vrijwilligers
NIOD.Coll.Doc. II, 758a : SS-Vrijwilligers
NIOD.Coll.Doc. II, 892 : SS-Vrijwilligers
205: Militair-Historisch Archiev Praag
206: Speciaal Archief Moskou Osobyi

Norway:

Riksarkivet, Oslo: RO
RA PA-1193: Institutt for Norsk Okkupasjonshistorie
RAFA-3182: SS- und Polizeigericht Nord (IX)
Senter for Holocaust og Livssynsminoriteter: HLC
Sigurd Sørlies privatarkiv
Terje Emberlands privatarkiv

Russia:

Gosudarstvennyi arkhiv Rossiiskoy Federatsyi, Moscow: GARF
Fond 7021: The Extraordinary State Commission
Rossiiskii gosudarstvennyi arkhiv sotsyalno-politicheskoy istorii, Moscow: RGASPI:
Fond 269: A.N. Tolstoj
Rossiiskii gosudarstvennyi voennyi arkhiv, Moscow: RGVA
Fond 1372: SS

Switzerland:

Bundesarchiv, Bern: BB
BE2001 (E), 1967/113, A.44.10.1.Uch., Bd.75, Prozess gegen Max Leo Keller
E27, 06.B.2.e.3.a.2: Landesverteidigung /Nachrichtenbeschaffung und Auswertung /
    Deserteur-Einvernahmen
E2001 (E) 1967/113 A.44.10.1.Uch. Bd.75: Prozess Riedweg Franz

Serbia:

Vojni arhiv, Beograd: VAB
MNO.FNRD: Documents related to the German occupation 1941–1944.

Slovenia:

Arhiv Republike Slovenije, Ljubjana: ARB
SI AS 1641: SS- und Waffen Unterführerschule Laibach (1943–1945)

Sweden:

Riksarkivet, Stockholm: RS
Allmänna Säkerhetstjänesten (1938–46)
Säkerherspolisens SÄPO med föregängeres arkiv (1886–1982)
Stadsarkivet i Malmø: SAMA
F-7: 1–9: Kriminalpolisen i Malmø. Handlingar angående flyktningar, 1943–44.

South Africa:

South African National Defence Force Documentation Centre, Pretoria: SANDFDOC
Divisional documents Group 1. 6th. Armoured Division.

UK:

National Archives, Kew: NAKEW
FO: Foreign Office
GFM: Copies of captured records of the German, Italian and Japanese Governments
HO: Home Office
HW: Government Communications Headquarters
KV: The Security Service
PREM: Prime Minister's Office
TS 26: Treasury Solicitor and HM Procurator General: War Crimes Papers
WO: War Office

USA:

Stanford University: SU
15. Waffen-SS Grenadier Division Box 1-18
Waffen-SS 7. Panzer Division Adolf Hitler Vol. 1
Daniel Lerner Collection Box 1-7
United States Holocaust Memorial Museum, Washington DC: USHMM
RG-50.593, Dr. John Steiner collection
National Archives, Washington DC: NAWA
Group 263: CIA

INDEX

www.ingramcontent.com/pod-product-compliance
Lightning Source LLC
Chambersburg PA
CBHW030636270326
41929CB00007B/97